CW01359895

PERSONAL INJURY PRACTICE IN THE SHERIFF COURT

THIRD EDITION

PERSONAL INJURY PRACTICE IN THE SHERIFF COURT

THIRD EDITION

By

RONALD E. CONWAY
Solicitor Advocate, Partner, Bonnar & Co

W. GREEN

THOMSON REUTERS

First edition 1999 by Ronald E. Conway
Second edition 2003 by Ronald E. Conway

Published in 2011 by W. Green, 21 Alva Street,
Edinburgh EH2 4PS
Part of Thomson Reuters (Professional) UK Limited
(Registered in England & Wales, Company No 1679046.
Registered Office and address for service: Aldgate House,
33 Aldgate High Street, London EC3N 1DL)

http://www.wgreen.thomson.com

Typeset by YHT Ltd, London
Printed and bound in Great Britain by CPI Antony Rowe,
Chippenham, Wiltshire

ISBN 978-0-414-01837-2

A catalogue record for this title is available
from the British Library

All rights reserved. UK statutory material used in this publication is acknowledged as Crown Copyright. No part of this publication may be reproduced or transmitted, in any form or by any means, electronic, mechanical, photocopying, recording or otherwise, or stored in any retrieval system of any nature, without prior written permission of the copyright holder and the publisher, application for which should be made to the publisher, except for permitted fair dealing under the Copyright, Designs and Patents Act 1988, or in accordance with the terms of a licence issued by the Copyright Licensing Agency in respect of photocopying and/or reprographic reproduction. Full acknowledgement of publisher and source must be given. Material is contained in this publication for which publishing permission has been sought, and for which copyright is acknowledged. Permission to reproduce such material cannot be granted by the publishers and application must be made to the copyright holders.

No natural forests were destroyed to make this product; only farmed timber was used and replanted.

© 2011 Thomson Reuters (Professional) UK Limited

Thomson Reuters and the Thomson Reuters Logo
are trademarks of Thomson Reuters.

DEDICATION

To my wife Anne

FOREWORD

By the Right Honourable Lord Carloway

In the preface to the second edition of this work, published in 2003, Mr Conway referred to the uncertainty which continued to exist in relation to the privative jurisdiction of the Court of Session. Almost a decade later, the position remains essentially the same. However, the Report of the Lord Justice Clerk's Civil Courts Review in 2009 recommended that the limit be raised from £5,000 to £150,000. However, because of the advantages of the bulk of trade union sponsored, and insurance company defended, litigation being dealt with by specialist practitioners in the Court of Session, there ought, the Review urges, to be a specialist all-Scotland sheriff court for personal injuries work based in Edinburgh.

The Scottish Government's response has been to welcome the proposals, expressing the view that it is "minded to accept" the increase in the privative jurisdiction and the concept of the specialist sheriff court. Should the proposals be implemented, the fourth edition of this book will see the sheriff court covering the conduct of almost all personal injuries litigation other than that with particular high value and complexity or those low value actions raised in the new District Courts. Put shortly, personal injury work will largely become the preserve of the sheriff court.

The preface also expressed the hope that the second edition would be the last which would have to deal with the "arcana" of written pleadings, in light of their effective abolition in Court of Session personal injury cases, in the wake of Lord Coulsfield's Report, and in the Summary Cause Rules. The new Personal Injuries Actions Rules of 2009 have introduced the Court of Session's simplified style of pleadings for personal injury cases into the Sheriff Court. Mr Conway's treatment of this subject, however, rightly cautions against complacency on the part of the careless pleader. The requirement of fair notice remains. All parties ought to set out their positions candidly, if not in the formulaic and loquacious manner adopted in recent years. Even the most seasoned practitioner will benefit from a read of Mr Conway's chapter in this crucial area of practice.

All those engaged in this area of work will also be given a practical view of the new system of timetabling, which has operated so successfully in the Court of Session, and which is now also transferred to the Sheriff Court. It ought to allow defended cases to proceed according to a prescribed series of procedural steps set out in a clear programme. This, it is no doubt hoped, will bring an end to repeated continuations and hasten cases, away from legal debate, towards proof of fact.

The third edition, like its predecessors, provides model guidance to the practitioner on how to conduct personal injuries litigation. It will prove to be an important tool for the practitioner in daily practice and an equally invaluable starting point for the trainee or diploma student trying to grasp the realities of personal injury work. All of those who read it will find something which will improve their skills, especially in relation to dealings with the client, preparation for proof and, generally, in the written and oral advocacy skills necessary to persuade the court of the merits of their cases.

Colin JM Sutherland
October 2011

PREFACE

The constant white water of change for personal injury practitioners continues unabated. There has been dramatic procedural change via Ch.36 of the Ordinary Cause Rules, ending—at a stroke—the malign spell of written pleadings.

There is proposed and imminent reform of the Summary Cause Rules for personal injury cases.

Recent major statutory changes include the Work at Height Regulations 2005, the Construction (Design and Management) Regulations 2007 and the Damages (Scotland) Act 2011. There is the weekly deluge of case law from both north and south of the border.

And, of course, in the background there is the processing of the Gill Review proposals which, if implemented, will place the sheriff court firmly at the centre of personal injury practice.

Against this background, the aims of this book are necessarily modest. It is written by and for a lawyer who acts for pursuers. It seeks to provide a snapshot of current practice and procedure, an overview of recent case law, and a guide to further reading and study.

The choice of subject matter reflects the daily concerns of a busy personal injury practice like Bonnar and Company, and any virtues the book may possess are a result of the daily grind of casework, discussion and front line litigation. So it is with considerably more than the customary nod to colleagues that I offer my thanks to solicitors Veronica McManus, Peter Crooks, Julian Hanrahan, Simone Sichi, April Meechan and Jacqueline Lewis, and to all Bonnar paralegals.

Thanks are also due to Fraser Simpson, Solicitor, who kindly read and revised the Summary Cause chapter in draft.

Ciara Daly at W. Green provided exemplary case management skills, with polite but timely reminders of deadlines, and has produced what to my eyes is a very handsome publication.

In legal terms however, the *sine qua non* of this edition is my colleague Mary MacFarlane who collected scattered bits and pieces, endured endless rewrites and rethinks, and managed to collate and present to the publishers something resembling a finished text. She has my heartfelt thanks.

The law is as stated at October 27, 2011, with the exception of Ch.16 which anticipates new Summary Cause Rules. Should there be any changes made after publication to the legislation mentioned, they will be listed on the W. Green webpage: *http://www.sweetandmaxwell.co.uk/wgreen/*.

October 26, 2011

CONTENTS

Foreword vii
Preface ix
Table of Cases xiii
Table of Statutes xxix
Table of Scottish Statutes xxxi
Table of Statutory Instruments xxxiii
Table of Ordinary Cause Rules and Summary Cause Rules xxxvii

Part I—Personal injury claims
1. Taking instructions 1
2. Funding the file 9
3. Constructing the claim on liability 19
4. Evidence on damages 27
5. Deduction of benefits 43
6. Limitation and time bar 47
7. Negotiation and settlement before action 55
8. Ordinary cause procedure in personal injury cases 60
9. Pleadings in personal injury actions 72
10. After the action is raised 86
11. Expert evidence 120
12. Preparation for proof 128
13. Proof 142
14. Procedure after proof 156
15. Appeals 162
16. Summary causes 170

Part II—Common causes of action
17. Road traffic accidents 181
18. Slips and falls 199
19. Occupiers' liability cases 220
20. Accidents at work 227
21. Occupational illness and disease 251
22. Damages for stress at work, bullying and harassment 289
23. Accidents to children 300
24. Holiday claims 308
25. Construction accidents 317

Appendices
1. Damages Information sheet 327
2. Accidents at Work Checklist 330
3. Pre-Action Protocols in Scotland for disease and
   for ordinary cases 336

4. Police Reports... 345
5. Ordinary Cause Forms... 347
   Form P11—initial writ
   Form P12—specification of documents
   Form P16—statement of valuation of claim
   Form P17—minute of pre-proof conference
6. Summary Cause Forms:.. 359
   Form 10—statement of claim
   Form 10a—form of response
   Form 10b—specification of documents
   Form 10e—statement of valuation
   Form 10f—minute of pre-proof conference

Index.. 373

TABLE OF CASES

A v Glasgow City Council [2010] CSIH 9; 2010 S.C. 411; 2010 S.L.T. 358.... 6–03, 21–21
AC Billings & Sons v Riden [1958] A.C. 240; [1957] 3 W.L.R. 496 HL....... 18–17, 19–07
AS v Sister Bernard Mary Murray [2005] CSOH 70... 6–10
AXA General Insurance Ltd, Petitioners [2010] CSOH 2; 2010 S.L.T. 179; 2010 G.W.D. 7-118.. 21–32
AXA General Insurance Ltd, Petitioners [2011] CSIH 31; 2011 S.L.T. 439; 2011 S.C.L.R. 305.. 21–32
Adamson v Roberts, 1951 S.C. 681; 1951 S.L.T. 355 Court of Session (Inner House). 17–16
Agnew v Scott Lithgow Ltd (No.1), 2001 S.C. 516; 2001 S.L.T. 876 Court of Session (Outer House).. 10–15, 21–25
Agnew v Scott Lithgow Ltd (No.2), 2003 S.C. 448; 2003 S.C.L.R. 426 Court of Session (Inner House)... 21–22, 21–23
Ahmed v Glasgow City Council, 2000 S.L.T. (Sh Ct) 153; 2000 Rep. L.R. 130 Sh Pr... 23–06
Airns v Chief Constable of Strathclyde Police, 1998 S.L.T. 15........................ 13–08
Aitchison v Glasgow City Council. See A v Glasgow City Council
Aktieselskabet de Danske Sukkerfabrikker v Bajamar Compania Naviera SA (The Torenia) [1983] 2 Lloyd's Rep. 210 QBD.. 11–03
Alcock v Chief Constable of South Yorkshire [1992] 1 A.C. 310; [1991] 3 W.L.R. 1057 HL.. 4–18
Alexander v Midland Bank Plc [2000] I.C.R. 464; [1999] I.R.L.R. 723 CA (Civ Div)... 21–52
Ali v Courtaulds Textiles Ltd [1999] Lloyd's Rep. Med. 301; (2000) 52 B.M.L.R. 129 CA (Civ Div)... 21–23
Allan v Scott, 1972 S.C. 59; 1972 S.L.T. 45 Court of Session (Inner House)......... 13–20
Allen v British Rail Engineering Ltd (BREL) [2001] EWCA Civ 242; [2001] I.C.R. 942; [2001] P.I.Q.R. Q10... 21–25
Allison v Chief Constable of Strathclyde, 2004 S.C. 453; 2004 S.L.T. 340 Court of Session (Inner House)... 14–03
Allison v London Underground Ltd [2008] EWCA Civ 71; [2008] I.C.R. 719; [2008] I.R.L.R. 440... 20–13, 20–14
Allison v Orr. See Allison v Chief Constable of Strathclyde
Amy Whitehead's Legal Representative v Graham Douglas. See W's Parent and Guardian v Douglas
Anderson v Lothian Health Board, 1996 S.C.L.R. 1068; 1996 Rep. L.R. 88 Court of Session (Inner House)... 20–37
Anderson v Newham College of Further Education [2002] EWCA Civ 505; [2003] I.C.R. 212... 18–22
Angus v Glasgow Corp, 1977 S.L.T. 206 Court of Session (Inner House)............ 15–04
Armagas Ltd v Mundogas SA (The Ocean Frost) [1986] A.C. 717; [1986] 2 W.L.R. 1063 HL.. 3–03
Armstrong v Armstrong, 1970 S.C. 161; 1970 S.L.T. 247 Court of Session (Inner House)... 14–07
Armstrong v British Coal Corp [1998] C.L.Y. 2842 CA (Civ Div).... 21–17, 21–47, 21–51
Ashcroft's Curator Bonis v Stewart, 1988 S.L.T. 163 Court of Session (Outer House).. 17–24, 17–32
Assicurazioni Generali SpA v Arab Insurance Group (BSC) [2002] EWCA Civ 1642; [2003] 1 W.L.R. 577; [2003] 1 All E.R. (Comm) 140............................... 15–04
Association of British Travel Agents ("ABTA") v Civil Aviation Authority ("CAA"). See R. (on the application of Association of British Travel Agents Ltd (ABTA)) v Civil Aviation Authority

Bailey v Ministry of Defence [2008] EWCA Civ 883; [2009] 1 W.L.R. 1052; [2008] LS
  Law Medical 481 21–04
Baker v Quantum Clothing Group Ltd [2011] UKSC 17; [2011] 1 W.L.R. 1003; [2011]
  I.C.R. 523 .... 1–03, 21–40
Baker v Willoughby [1970] A.C. 467; [1970] 2 W.L.R. 50; [1969] 3 All E.R. 1528
  HL 15–06, 17–08
Balfour v William Beardmore & Co Ltd, 1956 S.L.T. 205 Court of Session (Outer
  House) 21–17
Ball v Street [2005] EWCA Civ 76; [2005] P.I.Q.R. P22 20–27
Ballantyne v John Young & Co (Kelvinhaugh) Ltd, 1996 S.L.T. 358 Court of Session
  (Outer House) 10–11
Barber v Somerset CC [2004] UKHL 13; [2004] 1 W.L.R. 1089; [2004] 2 All E.R.
  385 .... 22–04, 22–05, 22–06, 22–07
Barclay v British Airways Plc [2008] EWCA Civ 1419; [2010] Q.B. 187; [2009] 3 W.L.R.
  369 24–06
Bark v Scott, 1954 S.C. 72; 1954 S.L.T. 210 Court of Session (Inner House) 17–18
Barker v Corus UK Ltd [2006] UKHL 20; [2006] 2 A.C. 572; [2006] 2 W.L.R. 1027 21–04
Barker v Murdoch, 1979 S.L.T. 145 Court of Session (Inner House) 15–07, 17–07
Barrie v Caledonian Railway (1902) 5 F.30 .... 12–06, 12–08
Barrow v Bryce, 1986 S.L.T. 691 Court of Session (Outer House) 17–16
Baxter v Harland & Wolff [1990] I.R.L.R. 516 CA (NI) 21–40
Beaton v Strathclyde Buses, 1993 S.L.T. 931 Court of Session (Outer House) .. 6–09, 6–10
Beaumont v Surrey CC, 66 L.G.R. 580; (1968) 112 S.J. 704 23–06
Becfar [1982] E.C.R. 52, ECJ 20–05
Beck v United Closures & Plastics Plc, 2001 S.L.T. 1299; 2002 S.C.L.R. 154 Court of
  Session (Outer House) 4–21, 20–18
Bell v Glasgow Corp, 1965 S.L.T. 57 Court of Session (Inner House) 17–05
Bhatia v Tribax Ltd, 1994 S.L.T. 1201 Court of Session (Outer House) 10–35, 16–04
Bhatt v Fontain Motors Ltd [2010] EWCA Civ 863; [2010] P.I.Q.R. P17 20–42
Bilton v Fastnet Highlands Ltd, 1998 S.L.T. 1323; 1997 G.W.D. 28–1443 Court of
  Session (Outer House) 21–29
Binnie v Rederij Theodoro BV, 1993 S.C. 71; 1992 G.W.D. 34–2013 Court of Session
  (Inner House) 12–02, 13–19
Bishop v Bryce, 1910 S.C. 426; 1910 1 S.L.T. 196 Court of Session (Inner House).. 13–05
Black v British Railways Board, 1983 S.L.T. 146 Court of Session (Outer House).. 21–26
Black v Wrangler (UK) Ltd Unreported March 14, 2000 Court of Session 21–15
Blair Bryden Partnership v Adair, 1995 S.L.T. (Sh Ct) 98; 1995 S.C.L.R. 358 Sh Pr 10–27
Blair v FJC Lilley (Marine) Ltd, 1981 S.L.T. 90 Court of Session (Inner House) 15–07
Blake v Lothian Health Board, 1993 S.L.T. 1248 Court of Session (Outer House)... 6–03
Bonar v Trafalgar House Offshore Fabrication Ltd, 1996 S.L.T. 548; 1996 Rep. L.R.
  19 Court of Session (Outer House) 4–12, 4–25, 21–14
Bonnington Castings Ltd v Wardlaw [1956] A.C. 613; [1956] 2 W.L.R. 707 HL 21–02
Bonnor v Balfour Kilpatrick Ltd, 1974 S.L.T. 187 Court of Session (Outer House). 10–12
Bowen v Airtours Plc [1999] C.L.Y. 3945 24–02
Bowman v Harland & Wolff [1991] N.I. 300; [1992] I.R.L.R. 349 21–47
Boyd v Lanarkshire Health Board, 2000 G.W.D. 9-341 Court of Session (Outer
  House) 20–39
British Telecommunications Plc v Reid [2003] EWCA Civ 1675; [2004] I.R.L.R. 327;
  (2003) 100(41) L.S.G. 33 18–18
Britton v Maple & Co Ltd, 1986 S.L.T. 70 Court of Session (Outer House) 21–08
Broadfoot's CB v Forth Valley Acute Hospital NHS Trust, 2003 G.W.D. 26-279 8–20
Brogan's Tutors v Glasgow DC, 1978 S.L.T. (Notes) 47 Court of Session (Outer
  House) 23–09
Brookes v JP Coates (UK) Ltd [1984] 1 All E.R. 702; [1984] I.C.R. 158 QBD 21–12
Brookes v South Yorkshire Passenger Transport Executive [2005] EWCA Civ 452.. 21–47
Brown v City of Edinburgh DC, 1998 G.W.D. 32-1675 18–24
Brown v Corus (UK) Ltd [2004] EWCA Civ 374; [2004] P.I.Q.R. P30; (2004) 148
  S.J.L.B. 418 .... 21–04, 21–49
Brown v North Lanarkshire Council [2010] CSOH 156; 2011 S.L.T. 150; 2011 Rep.
  L.R. 4 23–07

Table of Cases

Bryce v Allied Ironfounders Ltd, 1969 S.L.T. (Notes) 29 Court of Session (Outer House) 9–24, 10–12
Buchan v Thomson, 1976 S.L.T. 42 Court of Session (Inner House) 9–10, 17–15
Buhus-Orwin v Costa Smeralda Holidays Ltd [2001] C.L.Y. 4279 24–07
Burgess v Plymouth City Council [2005] EWCA Civ 1659; [2006] I.C.R. 579 18–22
Burns v Harper Collins Ltd, 1997 S.L.T. 607; 1996 S.C.L.R. 1135 Court of Session (Outer House) 4–19
Butler v Grampian University Hospitals NHS Trust, 2002 S.L.T. 985; 2002 Rep. L.R. 83 Court of Session (Outer House) 20–18, 20–20
Cameron v Lanarkshire Health Board, 1997 S.L.T. 1040 Court of Session (Outer House) 13–05
Campbell v Elliot Group Ltd [2009] CSOH 63; 2009 G.W.D. 16-255 18–22
Campbell v Golding, 1992 S.L.T. 889 Court of Session (Outer House) 10–30
Campbell v Lothian Health Board, 1987 S.L.T. 665 Court of Session (Outer House) 20–34
Canning v Kings & Co Ltd, 1986 S.L.T. 107 Court of Session (Outer House) 21–16
Cantwell v Criminal Injuries Compensation Board [2001] UKHL 36; 2002 S.C. (H.L.) 1; 2001 S.L.T. 966 4–14
Carnegie v Lord Advocate (No.3) 2001 S.C. 802; 2001 G.W.D. 13-512 Court of Session (Inner House) 6–03
Carragher v Singer Manufacturing Co, 1974 S.L.T. (Notes) 28 Court of Session (Outer House) 21–16, 21–41
Carson v McDonald, 1987 S.C.L.R. 415 Sh Ct 17–12
Cartledge v E Jopling & Sons Ltd [1963] A.C. 758; [1963] 2 W.L.R. 210 HL 21–20
Catleugh v Caradon Everest Ltd, 1999 G.W.D. 32-1554 Court of Session (Outer House) 22–04
Causton v Mann Egerton (Johnsons) Ltd [1974] 1 W.L.R. 162; [1974] 1 All E.R. 453CA (Civ Div) 12–08
Cavin v Kinnaird, 1994 S.L.T. 111; 1993 S.C.L.R. 618 Court of Session (Outer House) 11–08, 17–08, 17–33
Ceva Logistics Ltd v Lynch (t/a SW Lynch Electrical Contractors) [2011] EWCA Civ 188; [2011] I.C.R. 746 20–16
Chaudhari v British Airways Plc, *The Times*, May 7, 1997 CA (Civ Div) 24–06
Cheesman v International Travel Service Ltd, 2008 Rep. L.R. 66; 2008 G.W.D. 11-206 Court of Session (Outer House) 24–05
Cherry Steven v Lanarkshire Housing Association Ltd Unreported April 10, 2007 Hamilton Sh Ct 19–06
Chinn v Cyclacel Ltd [2010] CSOH 33; 2010 G.W.D. 14-268 21–23
Chittock v Woodbridge School [2002] EWCA Civ 915; [2002] E.L.R. 735; [2003] P.I.Q.R. P6 23–07
City of Glasgow Council, Petitioners, 1998 G.W.D. 29-1459 12–16
Clark v City of Edinburgh Council [2010] CSOH 144; 2011 Rep. L.R. 11; 2010 G.W.D. 39-789 17–13
Clark v McLean, 1994 S.C. 410; 1995 S.L.T. 235 Court of Session (Inner House) ... 10–19
Clark v Scott Lithgow Ltd, 2006 Rep. L.R. 16 Court of Session (Outer House) 21–23
Clarke v Edinburgh & District Tramways Co Ltd, (1919) 1 S.L.T. 24 9–21
Clegg v McKirdy & MacMillan, 1932 S.C. 442; 1932 S.L.T. 250 Court of Session (Inner House) 14–10
Clegg v North Ayrshire Council Unreported May 7, 2002 Court of Session 20–18
Cleisham v British Transport Commission, 1964 S.C. (H.L.) 8; 1964 S.L.T. 41 HL .. 13–20
Cleland v Campbell, 1998 S.L.T. 642; 1998 Rep. L.R. 30 Court of Session (Outer House) 10–29, 10–32
Cleland v Quinn Direct Unreported October 22, 2010 Arbroarth Sh Ct 17–13
Clifton v Hayes, 2004 G.W.D. 2-23 8–33
Comber v Greater Glasgow Health Board, 1989 S.L.T. 639; 1989 S.C.L.R. 515 Court of Session (Outer House) 6–10
Comer v James Scott & Co (Electrical Engineers) Ltd, 1976 S.L.T. (Notes) 72 Court of Session (Outer House) 10–47
Comer v James Scott & Co (Electrical Engineers) Ltd, 1978 S.L.T. 235 Court of Session (Outer House) 6–04

Common Services Agency v Scottish Information Commissioner [2006] CSIH 58; 2007 S.C. 231; 2007 S.L.T. 7 3–09
Comrie v National Coal Board, 1974 S.C. 237 Court of Session (Inner House) 21–22
Conner v Bradman & Co Ltd [2007] EWHC 2789 (QB) 4–11
Conway v Hitec Hydraulic Engineering Ltd Unreported March 25, 2007 Sh Ct 21–49, 21–51
Cook v UIE Shipbuilding Scotland, 1989 S.C.L.R. 156 10–04
Cordiner v British Railways Board, 1986 S.L.T. 209 Court of Session (Outer House) 13–18, 19–01
Coughlan v Thomson Holidays [2001] C.L.Y. 4276 24–08
Countess of Lindsay v Fife Scottish Omnibuses Ltd Unreported May 30, 2002 Court of Session 17–05
Cowan v Toffolo Jackson & Co Ltd, 1998 S.L.T. 1000; 1997 Rep. L.R. 40 Court of Session (Outer House) 6–08, 21–25
Cowie v Atlantic Drilling Co Ltd, 1995 S.C. 288; 1995 S.L.T. 1151 Court of Session (Inner House) 10–32
Cox v Rolls Royce Industrial Power (India) Ltd [2007] EWCA Civ 1189 21–37
Coyle v William Fairey Installations Ltd, 1991 S.C. 16; 1991 S.L.T. 638 Court of Session (Inner House) 16–03
Crane v Premier Prison Service [2001] C.L.Y. 3298 QBD 20–27
Craner v Dorset CC [2008] EWCA Civ 1323; [2009] I.C.R. 563; [2009] P.I.Q.R. P10 18–22
Cross v Highlands & Islands Enterprise, 2001 S.L.T. 1060; 2001 S.C.L.R. 547 Court of Session (Outer House) 22–02, 22–03, 22–07
Cullen v North Lanarkshire Council, 1998 S.C. 451; 1998 S.L.T. 847 Court of Session (Inner House) 20–03, 20–37, 20–38
Cuthbertson v Merchison Castle School, 2001 S.L.T. 13 Sh Ct 23–06
D's Parent and Guardian v Argyll and Clyde Acute Hospitals NHS Trust, 2003 S.L.T. 511; 2003 S.C.L.R. 485 Court of Session (Outer House) 10–32
Daks Simpson Group Plc v Kuiper, 1994 S.L.T. 689; 1994 S.C.L.R. 373 Court of Session (Outer House) 7–05
Datec Electronic Holdings Ltd v United Parcels Service Ltd [2007] UKHL 23; [2007] Bus. L.R. 1291; [2007] 1 W.L.R. 1325 .... 13–04, 15–04
Davidson v Lothian and Borders Fire Board, 2003 S.L.T. 939; 2003 S.C.L.R. 750 Court of Session (Inner House) 20–36
Davie (Alexander) v Edinburgh Corp (No.1), 1977 S.L.T. (Notes) 5 Court of Session (Outer House) 19–06
Davie (Alexander) v Edinburgh Corp (No.2), 1978 S.L.T. (Notes) 37 Court of Session (Outer House) 11–16
Davie v Edinburgh Corp (No.2), 1953 S.C. 34; 1953 S.L.T. 54 Court of Session (Inner House) 11–01, 13–10
Davies v Taylor [1974] A.C. 207; [1972] 3 W.L.R. 801 HL 4–07, 13–13, 15–07
Dawn Jacobs v Tesco Stores Plc Unreported November 19, 1998 CA 18–19
Dawson v Scottish Power Plc, 1999 S.L.T. 672; 1998 G.W.D. 38-1975 Court of Session (Outer House) 23–02, 23–09
Deans v George Newbury Coachbuilder Unreported September 13, 2003 Sh Ct 21–47, 21–51
Deep Vein Thrombosis and Air Travel Group Litigation, Re [2005] UKHL 72; [2006] 1 A.C. 495; [2005] 3 W.L.R. 1320 24–06
Delaney v McGregor Construction (Highlands) Ltd, 2003 Rep. L.R. 56; 2003 G.W.D. 10-290 Court of Session (Outer House) 20–41
Desouza v Waterlow [1999] R.T.R. 71; [1998] P.I.Q.R. P87 CA (Civ Div) 17–31
Devaney v Yarrow Shipbuilders Ltd, 1999 S.L.T. 561; 1999 G.W.D. 1-49 Court of Session (Outer House) 9–22
Devenney v Greater Glasgow Health Board, 1989 S.L.T. 578; 1989 S.C.L.R. 349 Court of Session (Outer House) 14–03
Devlin v Strathclyde RC, 1993 S.L.T. 699 Court of Session (Outer House) 23–02
Dickins v O2 Plc [2008] EWCA Civ 1144; [2009] I.R.L.R. 58; (2008) 105(41) L.S.G. 19 .... 22–07, 22–08
Dimond v Lovell [2002] 1 A.C. 384; [2000] 2 W.L.R. 1121 HL 17–13

Table of Cases

Dineley v Lothian Health Board [2007] CSOH 154.. 15–05
Dingley v Chief Constable of Strathclyde (No.1), 1998 S.C. 548; 1998 G.W.D. 13-677
    Court of Session (Inner House).. 11–01, 13–13, 21–05
Divit v British Telecommunications Plc, 1997 G.W.D. 12-530............................ 20–36
Dominion Technology Ltd v Gardner Cryogenics Ltd (No.1) Court of Session (Outer
    House).. 1–10
Donald v Rutherford, 1984 S.L.T. 70 Court of Session (Inner House).................. 6–08
Donaldson v Hayes Distribution Services Ltd, 2005 S.C. 523............................ 20–17
Donnachie v Happit Unreported December 5, 2001 Court of Session................. 10–43
Doughty v Rolls Royce Plc [1992] 1 C.M.L.R. 1045; [1992] I.C.R. 538 CA (Civ Div). 20–05
Duff v East Dunbartonshire Council, 2002 Rep. L.R. 98; 2002 G.W.D. 26-921...... 19–02
Dugmore v Swansea NHS Trust [2002] EWCA Civ 1689; [2003] 1 All E.R. 333; [2003]
    I.C.R. 574... 21–29
Duncan v Lord Advocate (No.1), 1987 S.L.T. 349 Court of Session (Outer House). 10–60
Duncanson v South Ayrshire Council, 1999 S.L.T. 519; 1998 S.C.L.R. 1015 Court of
    Session (Outer House).. 20–20
Eagle v Chambers (No.1) [2003] EWCA Civ 1107; [2004] R.T.R. 9; (2003) 100(36)
    L.S.G. 43... 17–08
Easdon v A Clark Co (Smithwick) Ltd [2006] CSOH 12.................... 8–33, 8–34, 8–38
Ehrari (A Child) v Curry [2007] EWCA Civ 120; [2007] R.T.R. 42; (2007) 151 S.J.L.B.
    299.. 17–08, 23–04
Elliot v J&C Finney (No.1), 1989 S.L.T. 605 Court of Session (Inner House)......... 6–09
Ellis v Bristol City Council [2007] EWCA Civ 685; [2007] I.C.R. 1614; [2007] P.I.Q.R.
    P26... 18–22
Ellison v Inspirations East Ltd, 2003 S.L.T. 291; 2002 G.W.D. 35-1172 Court of
    Session (Outer House).. 3–11, 24–01
Ellon Castle Estates Co Ltd v MacDonald, 1975 S.L.T. (Notes) 66 Court of Session
    (Outer House).. 10–04
English v Emery Reimbold & Strick Ltd [2002] EWCA Civ 605; [2002] 1 W.L.R. 2409;
    [2002] 3 All E.R. 385... 15–05
English v North Lanarkshire Council, 1999 S.C.L.R. 310; [1999] Eu. L.R. 701Court of
    Session (Outer House)................................. 10–11, 12–23, 20–03, 20–05, 20–28
Esdale v Dover DC [2010] EWCA Civ 409... 18–09
Factortame Ltd v Secretary of State for the Environment, Transport and the Regions
    (Costs) (No.2) [2002] EWCA Civ 932; [2003] Q.B. 381; [2002] 3 W.L.R. 1104. 11–17
Fairchild v Glenhaven Funeral Services Ltd (t/a GH Dovener & Son) [2002] UKHL
    22; [2003] 1 A.C. 32; [2002] 3 W.L.R. 89 HL...................... 21–04, 21–17, 21–37
Fairfield Shipbuilding & Engineering Co Ltd v Hall [1964] 1 Lloyd's Rep. 73; 1964 S.C.
    (H.L.) 72 HL... 18–23
Ferla v Secretary of State for Scotland, 1995 S.L.T. 662 Court of Session (Outer
    House).. 6–03, 6–10
Fidge v Governing Body of St. Mary's School See National Union of Teachers v St
    Mary's Church of England (Aided) Junior School Governing Body
Findlay v National Coal Board, 1965 S.L.T. 328 Court of Session (Outer House).. 10–09
Flood v University Court of the University of Glasgow [2010] CSIH 3; 2010 S.L.T.
    167; 2010 G.W.D. 3-47... 22–04
Fox v Glasgow City Council, 2001 Rep. L.R. 59; 2001 G.W.D. 3-131 Sh Ct........ 18–14
Francovich v Italy (C–6/90) [1991] E.C.R. I–5357; [1993] 2 C.M.L.R. 66 ECJ....... 20–05
Franklin v British Railways Board [1993] S.T.C. 487; [1993] I.R.L.R. 441 CA (Civ
    Div).. 4–10
Fraser v State Hospitals Board for Scotland, 2001 S.L.T. 1051; 2001 S.C.L.R. 357
    Court of Session (Outer House)... 22–04
Fratelli Costanzo SpA v Comune di Milano (103/88) [1989] E.C.R. 1839; [1990] 3
    C.M.L.R. 239, ECJ.. 20–05
Frew v Field Packaging Scotland Ltd, 1994 S.L.T. 1193 Court of Session (Outer
    House).. 10–29, 10–31
Froom v Butcher [1976] Q.B. 286; [1975] 3 W.L.R. 379 CA (Civ Div)................ 17–07
Frost v Chief Constable of Yorkshire Police. See White v Chief Constable of South
    Yorkshire
Futter v Bryceland, 2000 G.W.D. 9–339 Court of Session (Outer House)............. 17–08

Fytche v Wincanton Logistics Plc [2004] UKHL 31; [2004] 4 All E.R. 221; [2004] I.C.R.
  975.. 20–33
G v Glasgow City Council [2010] CSIH 69; 2011 S.C. 1; 2011 S.C.L.R. 116............ 6–03
G v S [2006] CSOH 88; 2006 S.L.T. 795; 2007 S.C.L.R. 137 Court of Session (Outer
  House)... 8–04
Galbraith's Curator ad Litem v Stewart (No.2), 1998 S.L.T. 1305; 1998 Rep. L.R. 64
  Court of Session (Outer House).. 23–03, 23–09
Gallagher v Kleinwort Benson Trustees Ltd Unreported March 12, 2003 Court of
  Session... 19–03
Ganley v Scottish Boat Owners' Mutual Insurance Association, 1967 S.L.T. (Notes)
  46... 10–24
Gardiner v Motherwell Machinery & Scrap Co Ltd [1961] 1 W.L.R. 1424; [1961] 3 All
  E.R. 831 HL.. 21–03
Gemmell v Macfarlane, 1991 S.L.T. (Notes) 36.. 17–17
Ghan, Herrick and Gerard v Mattessons Walls Ltd [1997] C.L.Y. 5807............... 21–52
Gibson v British Insulated Callender Construction Co Ltd, 1973 S.C. (H.L.) 15; 1973
  S.L.T. 2 HL.. 10–11
Gibson v Strathclyde RC, 1993 S.L.T. 1243; 1992 S.C.L.R. 902 Court of Session (Inner
  House)... 18–05, 18–09
Gibson v West Lothian Council [2011] CSOH 110; 2011 G.W.D. 23-524............ 18–12
Gibson v Whyte [2007] CSOH 17.. 3–01
Gillanders v Arthur Bell (Scotch Tweed) Ltd Unreported April 26, 2005 Court of
  Session... 11–02
Gillies v Glynwed Foundries Ltd, 1977 S.L.T. 97 Court of Session (Inner House)... 18–23
Gilmour v East Renfrewshire Council (No.2), 2004 Rep. L.R. 40; 2003 G.W.D. 39-
  1062 Court of Session (Outer House).. 18–22
Gilmour v East Renfrewshire Council Unreported May 29, 2002 Court of Session... 20–18
Gilmour's Tutor v Renfew CC, 1970 S.L.T. (Notes) 47 Court of Session (Outer
  House)... 14–13
Glasgow City Council v Scottish Information Commissioner [2009] CSIH 73; 2010
  S.C. 125; 2010 S.L.T. 9... 3–09
Glasgow Corp v Muir [1943] A.C. 448; [1943] 2 All E.R. 44 HL....................... 22–07
Gordon v Glasgow Corp Unreported June 26, 1923 Court of Session (Inner House). 18–06
Gordon v Inverness Town Council, 1957 S.L.T. (Notes) 48 Court of Session (Outer
  House)... 18–12
Gorrie v Marist Bros, 2002 S.C.L.R. 436; 2001 G.W.D. 39-1484 Sh Pr............... 22–12
Govan v National Coal Board, 1987 S.L.T. 511; 1987 S.C.L.R. 337 Court of Session
  (Outer House)... 10–47
Gracey v Sykes, 1994 S.C.L.R. 909 Sh Pr.. 10–27
Graham v East of Scotland Water Authority, 2002 S.C.L.R. 340; 2002 Rep. L.R. 58
  Court of Session (Outer House)... 19–02
Grant v Eastern Scottish Omnibuses Ltd, 1998 G.W.D. 32-1676....................... 17–05
Grant v Lothian RC, 1988 S.L.T. 533 Court of Session (Outer House).............. 18–12
Gray v Boyd, 1996 S.L.T. 60; 1995 S.C.L.R. 1075 Court of Session (Inner House).. 10–24
Green v Argyll & Bute Council Unreported February 28, 2002 Court of Session.... 22–08
Grieves v FT Everard & Sons Ltd [2007] UKHL 39; [2008] 1 A.C. 281; [2007] 3 W.L.R.
  876... 21–32
Griffin v South West Water Services Ltd [1995] I.R.L.R. 15 Ch D..................... 20–05
Gunn v Wallsend Slipway and Engineering Co, *The Times,* January 23, 1989 QBD. 21–38
Guy v Strathkelvin DC, 1997 S.C.L.R. 405; 1997 Hous. L.R. 14 Court of Session
  (Outer House)... 19–05
HMA v Wilson Unreported June 15, 2001 Aberdeen High Court....................... 11–15
Haggarty v Glasgow Corp (No.2), 1964 S.L.T. (Notes) 95 Court of Session (Outer
  House)... 19–04
Haigh & Ringrose Ltd v Barrhead Builders Ltd (No.2), 1981 S.L.T. 157 Court of
  Session (Outer House)... 9–21
Hamilton v Seamark Systems Ltd, 2004 S.C. 543; 2004 G.W.D. 8-167 Court of Session
  (Outer House)... 8–20, 8–37, 8–39, 10–17
Harrhy v Thames Trains Ltd [2003] EWHC 2286 (QB)..................................... 4–18

Table of Cases

Harris v BRB (Residuary) Ltd [2005] EWCA Civ 900; [2005] I.C.R. 1680; [2006] P.I.Q.R. P10 21–40
Harrison v Derby City Council [2008] EWCA Civ 583 18–06
Harrison v RB Tennent Ltd, 1992 S.L.T. 1060 Court of Session (Outer House) 13–25
Hartley v Burnley BC [1996] C.L.Y. 5670 County Court 18–06
Hayward v Edinburgh Royal Infirmary, 1954 S.C. 453; 1954 S.L.T. 226 Court of Session (Inner House) 10–21
Healy v A Massey & Son Ltd, 1961 S.C. 198; 1961 S.L.T. 235 Court of Session (Outer House) 2–11
Henderson v 3052775 Nova Scotia Ltd [2006] UKHL 21; 2006 S.C. (H.L.) 85; 2006 S.L.T. 489 10–29
Henderson v Occidental Petroleum (Caledonia) Ltd, 1990 S.L.T. 314; 1989 S.C.L.R. 737 Court of Session (Outer House) 9–11
Henderson v Patrick Thomson Ltd, 1911 1 S.L.T. 284 Court of Session (Outer House) 12–06, 12–07
Henderson v Redpath Dorman Long, 1975 S.L.T. (Sh. Ct.) 27 Sh Pr 15–05
Hendry v Alexander Taylor & Sons, 2008 Rep. L.R. 38; 2007 G.W.D. 36-624 Court of Session (Outer House) 10–50
Henser-Leather v Securicor Cash Services Ltd [2002] EWCA Civ 816 .... 20–32, 20–35
Hepburn v Scottish Power Plc, 1997 S.C. 80; 1997 S.L.T. 859 Court of Session (Inner House) 10–45
Herring v Ministry of Defence [2003] EWCA Civ 528; [2004] 1 All E.R. 44; (2003) 100(24) L.S.G. 36 4–07
Hewat v Edinburgh City Council, 1944 S.C. 30; 1944 S.L.T. 193 Court of Session (Inner House) 11–03
Higgins v DHL Unreported October 31, 2003 Court of Session 8–35
Highland Venison Marketing Ltd v Allwild GmbH, 1992 S.L.T. 1127; 1992 S.C.L.R. 415 Court of Session (Outer House) 3–11
Hislop v Lynx Express Parcels, 2003 S.L.T. 785; 2003 S.C.L.R. 441 Court of Session (Inner House) 20–27
Holtby v Brigham & Cowan (Hull) Ltd [2000] 3 All E.R. 421; [2000] I.C.R. 1086 CA (Civ Div) 21–17, 21–37
Holtes v Aberdeenshire Council [2006] CSOH 134; 2006 S.L.T. 871; 2006 G.W.D. 29-647 18–22
Hone v Going Places Leisure Travel Ltd [2001] EWCA Civ 947 24–02
Horkulak v Cantor Fitzgerald International [2004] EWCA Civ 1287; [2005] I.C.R. 402; [2004] I.R.L.R. 942 22–12
Howitt v W Alexander & Sons Ltd, 1948 S.C. 154; 1948 S.L.T. 334 Court of Session (Inner House) 14–02
Hughes v Grampian Country Food Group Ltd [2007] CSIH 32; 2007 S.L.T. 635; 2008 S.C.L.R. 157 20–36
Hughes v Lord Advocate [1963] A.C. 837; [1963] 2 W.L.R. 779 HL 23–02
Hughes' Tutrix v Glasgow DC, 1982 S.L.T. (Sh. Ct.) 70 19–05
Humphries v Elmegirab, 1998 S.C.L.R. 783 Sh Ct 17–12
Hunter v Hanley, 1955 S.C. 200; 1955 S.L.T. 213 Court of Session (Inner House) .. 23–07
Hunter (Margaret) v Murray (William) Unreported April 11, 2002 Court of Session. 20–25
Hunter v Perth and Kinross Council 2001 S.C.L.R. 856; 2001 Rep. L.R. 95 (Note) Court of Session (Outer House) 23–06
Hutchison v Henderson, 1987 S.L.T. 388 Court of Session (Outer House) 9–26, 17–20
Inglis v London Midland & Scottish Railway Co, 1941 S.C. 551; 1941 S.L.T. 408 Court of Session (Inner House) 19–01
Innes v Glasgow Corp Unreported 18–06
Iqbal v Dean Manson Solicitors [2011] EWCA Civ 123; [2011] C.P. Rep. 26; [2011] I.R.L.R. 428 22–13
Islip Pedigree Breeding Centre v Abercromby, 1959 S.L.T. 161 HL 15–04
Jackson v Horizon Holidays Ltd [1975] 1 W.L.R. 1468; [1975] 3 All E.R. 92 CA (Civ Div) 24–07
James Sim Ltd v Haynes, 1968 S.L.T. (Sh. Ct.) 76 2–13
James v Fairley [2002] EWCA Civ 162; [2002] R.T.R. 19 .... 17–08, 23–04
James v Preseli Pembrokeshire DC [1993] P.I.Q.R. P114 CA (Civ Div) 18–06

Jamieson v Jamieson [1952] A.C. 525; [1952] 1 All E.R. 875 HL........................ 10–21
Jenkins v Allied Ironfounders Ltd [1970] 1 W.L.R. 304; [1969] 3 All E.R. 1609
    HL.. 10–11, 13–04
Jennings v Forestry Commission [2008] EWCA Civ 581; [2008] I.C.R. 988........... 25–02
John Ramsey v Alexander Souter, 1864 2 M. 891.. 10–34
John Summers & Sons Ltd v Frost [1955] A.C. 740; [1955] 2 W.L.R. 825 HL....... 20–29
John Young & Co (Kelvinhaugh) Ltd v O'Donnell, 1958 S.L.T. (Notes) 46 HL..... 25–13
Johnson v Sweeney, 1985 S.L.T. (Sh. Ct.) 2.. 19–02
Johnston v Chief Constable of the Royal Ulster Constabulary (222/84) [1987] Q.B.
    129; [1986] 3 W.L.R. 1038, ECJ.. 20–05
Johnston v Lithgows Ltd, 1964 S.L.T. (Notes) 96 Court of Session (Outer House).. 14–08
Johnston v Perth and Kinross Council, 2002 S.C.L.R. 558 Sh Pr...................... 13–05
Johnstone v Glasgow DC, 1986 S.L.T. 50 Court of Session (Inner House)... 13–18, 19–06
Jolley v Sutton LBC [2000] 1 W.L.R. 1082; [2000] 3 All E.R. 409 HL................. 23–02
Karanakaran v Secretary of State for the Home Department [2000] 3 All E.R. 449;
    [2000] Imm. A.R. 271 CA (Civ Div)... 3–01
Kay's Tutor v Ayrshire and Arran Health Board, 1986 S.L.T. 435 Court of Session
    (Inner House)... 15–05
Kearn-Price v Kent CC [2002] EWCA Civ 1539; [2003] E.L.R. 17; [2003] P.I.Q.R. P11 23–07
Keating v Elvin Reinforced Concrete Co [1962] 2 All E.R. 139....................... 18–18
Keefe v Isle of Man Steam Packet Co Ltd [2010] EWCA Civ 683..................... 21–46
Keen v Tayside Contracts, 2003 S.L.T. 500; 2003 Rep. L.R. 22 Court of Session (Outer
    House)... 4–18, 22–01
Kelly v First Engineering Ltd, 1999 S.C.L.R. 1025; 1999 Rep. L.R. 106 Court of
    Session (Outer House).. 20–27
Kendal v Davies, 2001 S.C.L.R. 140; 2000 Rep. L.R. 126 Court of Session (Outer
    House)... 4–23, 9–03, 9–30, 16–06
Kennedy v Lees of Scotland Ltd, 1997 S.L.T. 510; 1996 S.C.L.R. 978 Court of Session
    (Outer House).. 4–22
Kennedy v Norwich Union Fire Insurance Society, 1993 S.C. 578; 1994 S.L.T. 617
    Court of Session (Inner House)... 9–22, 10–22
Keppie v Marshall Food Group Ltd, 1997 S.L.T. 305; 1996 Rep. L.R. 101 Court of
    Session (Outer House).. 10–33
Kerr v East Ayrshire Council, 2005 S.L.T. (Sh Ct) 67; 2005 Hous. L.R. 35.......... 19–04
Kerr (John) v HM Advocate, 1958 J.C. 14; 1958 S.L.T. 82 HCJ...................... 1–04
Kerr v Hailes (Plant) Ltd, 1974 S.L.T. (Notes) 31 Court of Session (Outer House). 25–13
Kevin Taylor v George Smith, 2003 S.C.L.R. 926....................................... 18–12
Kidd v Grampian Health Board, 1994 S.L.T. 267 Court of Session (Outer House)... 6–10
King v Fife Council, 2004 Rep. L.R. 33; 2003 G.W.D. 39-1063 Court of Session (Outer
    House).. 25–13
King v RCO Support Services Ltd [2001] I.C.R. 608; [2001] P.I.Q.R. P15 CA (Civ
    Div).. 20–16
Kirkham v Link Housing Group Ltd [2010] CSOH 31; 2010 S.L.T. 321; 2010 Rep.
    L.R. 44... 19–06
Kmiecic v Isaacs [2011] EWCA Civ 451; [2011] P.I.Q.R. P13......................... 25–11
Kozokowska v Kozokowski, 1997 G.W.D. 17-802...................................... 18–12
Kyle v P&J Stormonth Darling WS, 1993 S.C. 57; 1992 S.C. 533 Court of Session
    Inner House... 6–09
Lagden v O'Connor [2003] UKHL 64; [2004] 1 A.C. 1067; [2003] 3 W.L.R. 1571 HL 17–13
Laing v Aberdeen Magistrates, 1912 S.C. 196; 1911 2 S.L.T. 437 Court of Session
    (Inner House).. 18–05
Laing v Scottish Grain Distillers Ltd, 1992 S.C. (H.L.) 65; 1992 S.L.T. 435 HL..... 9–01,
    13–20
Lambie v Toffolo Jackson Ltd (In Liquidation), 2003 S.L.T. 1415; 2004 Rep. L.R. 8
    Court of Session (Inner House)... 21–23
Lamont v Monklands DC, 1992 S.L.T. 428 Court of Session (Outer House)........ 10–11,
    18–14
Lane v Shire Roofing Co (Oxford) Ltd [1995] I.R.L.R. 493; [1995] P.I.Q.R. P417 CA
    (Civ Div)... 25–02
Lappin v Britannia Airways Ltd, 1989 S.L.T. 181 Court of Session (Outer House)... 4–25

Laroche v Spirit of Adventure (UK) Ltd [2009] EWCA Civ 12; [2009] Q.B. 778; [2009] 3 W.L.R. 351.. 24–06
Laverton v Kiapasha (t/a Takeaway Supreme) Unreported November 19, 2002 CA 18–19
Lee v National Coal Board, 1955 S.C. 151; 1955 S.L.T. 202 Court of Session (Inner House)... 12–02
Lenaghan v Ayrshire and Arran Health Board, 1994 S.C. 365; 1994 S.L.T. 765 Court of Session (Inner House)... 12–21
Letford v Glasgow City Council Unreported June 26, 2002............................ 18–09
Lever v Greenock Motor Services Co Ltd, 1949 S.C. 88; 1949 S.L.T. 94 Court of Session (Inner House)... 14–03
Liddell v Middleton [1996] P.I.Q.R. P36 CA (Civ Div)........................... 17–08, 17–33
Lister v Hesley Hall Ltd [2001] UKHL 22; [2002] 1 A.C. 215; [2001] 2 W.L.R. 1311 22–12
Litster v Forth Dry Dock & Engineering Co Ltd [1990] 1 A.C. 546; [1989] 2 W.L.R. 634 HL... 15–05, 20–03
Little v East Ayrshire Council, 1998 S.C.L.R. 520; 1998 G.W.D. 18–885 Court of Session (Outer House)... 21–22, 21–23
Littlejohn v Wood & Davidson Ltd, 1997 S.L.T. 1353 Court of Session (Outer House) 9–20
Lochgorm Warehouses v Roy, 1981 S.L.T. (Sh. Ct.) 45................................. 16–06
Logan v Strathclyde Fire Board Unreported January 12, 1999.................. 20–12, 20–38
Lord Advocate v Gillespie, 1969 S.L.T. (Sh. Ct.) 10.................................... 12–02
Lothian Hotels v Ferer, 1981 S.L.T. (Sh. Ct.) 52.. 16–05
Love v Motherwell DC, 1994 S.C.L.R. 761 Sh Pr.. 19–01
Loveday v Renton (No.1) [1989] 1 Med. L.R. 117 QBD................................ 15–05
Lowrie v Colvilles Ltd, 1961 S.L.T. (Notes) 73 Court of Session (Outer House)..... 10–55
McArthur v Raynesway Plant Ltd (preliminary procedure), 1980 S.L.T. 74 Court of Session (Outer House).. 10–21
McArthur v Strathclyde RC, 1995 S.L.T. 1129; 1994 S.C.L.R. 752 Court of Session (Outer House)... 10–13, 18–17
McAvoy v Glasgow DC, 1993 S.L.T. 859; 1993 S.C.L.R. 393 Court of Session (Outer House).. 3–11
McCaffery v Greater Glasgow Health Board Unreported March 28, 2003 Court of Session... 6–09
McCallum v British Railways Board, 1991 S.L.T. 5 Court of Session (Inner House) 13–08
McClafferty v British Telecommunications Plc, 1987 S.L.T. 327; 1987 S.C.L.R. 473 Court of Session (Outer House)... 18–06, 18–24
McCluskey v Wallace, 1998 S.C. 711; 1998 S.L.T. 1357 Court of Session (Inner House)... 17–08
McColl v Barnes, 1992 S.L.T. 1188; 1991 S.C.L.R. 907 Court of Session (Outer House)... 4–25
McCook v Lobo [2002] EWCA Civ 1760; [2003] I.C.R. 89............................. 25–10
McCrae v Bryson (Expenses), 1923 S.C. 896; 1923 S.L.T. 672 Court of Session (Inner House)... 14–10
McCrindle v Sandilands, 1980 S.L.T. (Notes) 12 Court of Session (Outer House).... 9–20
McCusker v Saveheat Cavity Wall Insulation Ltd, 1987 S.L.T. 24 Court of Session (Inner House).. 13–20, 15–06, 18–12
Macdonald v Glasgow Western Hospitals. See Hayward v Edinburgh Royal Infirmary
McDougall v Gordon Speirs (t/a John Duncan Removal) Unreported February 25, 2003 Court of Session... 20–38
McDougall v Strathclyde RC, 1996 S.L.T. 1124; 1996 Rep. L.R. 27 Court of Session (Inner House)... 23–06
McDyer v Celtic Football & Athletic Co Ltd (No.1), 2000 S.C. 379; 2000 S.L.T. 736 Court of Session (Inner House)................................. 6–06, 13–19, 19–01
McEwan v Lothian Buses Plc, 2006 S.C.L.R. 592; 2006 Rep. L.R. 134 Court of Session (Outer House).. 18–22
MacFarlane v Falkirk Council, 2000 S.L.T. (Sh Ct) 29; 1999 G.W.D. 37-1788 Sh Pr.. 10–18, 10–19, 10–27
McFarlane v Thain [2009] CSIH 64; 2010 S.C. 7; 2010 S.C.L.R. 55 Court of Session (Inner House)... 8–33
McFarlane v Wilkinson [1997] 2 Lloyd's Rep. 259; [1997] P.N.L.R. 578 CA (Civ Div) 4–17
McGarvie v NG Bailey & Co Ltd Unreported February 26, 2002 CA................ 25–10

McGhee v British Telecom Unreported December 20, 1995 Court of Session........ 10–19
McGhee v National Coal Board [1973] 1 W.L.R. 1; [1972] 3 All E.R. 1008 HL..... 21–03
McGhee v Strathclyde Fire Brigade Unreported January 18, 2002 S.C........ 18–22, 20–03
McGlone v British Railways Board, 1966 S.C. (H.L.) 1; 1966 S.L.T. 2 HL.......... 13–06,
23–02
McGowan v W&JR Watson Ltd [2006] CSIH 62; 2007 S.C. 272; 2007 S.L.T. 169... 8–37,
10–06, 20–29
McGuffie v Forth Valley Health Board, 1991 S.L.T. 231 Court of Session (Inner
House).. 19–01
McInally v John Wyeth & Brother Ltd, 1992 S.L.T. 344 Court of Session (Outer
House).. 10–51
McInnes v Alginate Industries Ltd, 1980 S.L.T. (Sh. Ct.) 114 Sh Pr................... 16–06
McIntosh v Edinburgh City Council, 2003 S.L.T. 827; 2003 G.W.D. 22-664 Court of
Session (Outer House).. 20–36
McKenna (James) v British Railways Board and First Engineering Ltd Unreported
August 15, 2003 Court of Session.. 21–49
Mackenzie v Digby Brown & Co, 1992 S.L.T. 891; 1992 S.C.L.R. 339 Court of Session
(Outer House)... 6–09
MacKenzie v Lothian and Borders Police, 1995 S.L.T. 1332; 1995 S.C.L.R. 737 Court
of Session (Outer House).. 14–07
MacKenzie v Mackay, 1989 S.L.T. 810; 1989 S.C.L.R. 341 Court of Session (Outer
House).. 9–23
McKenzie v McKenzie, 1943 S.C. 108; 1943 S.L.T. 169 Court of Session (Inner
House)... 13–05, 13–06
Mackie v Dundee City Council, 2001 Rep. L.R. 62; 2001 G.W.D. 11-398 Sh Ct.... 20–27
Mackie's Executrix v AB 2000 Ltd, 2004 S.C. 334; 2004 S.L.T. 141 Court of Session
(Inner House).. 6–07
McKillen v Barclay Curle & Co Ltd, 1967 S.L.T. 41 Court of Session (Inner
House).. 22–08
Mackintosh v Galbraith (1900) 3 F. 66; (1900) 8 S.L.T. 241 Court of Session (Inner
House).. 14–09
McLaren v Harland and Wolff Ltd, 1991 S.L.T. 85; 1990 S.C.L.R. 658 Court of
Session (Outer House)... 6–10, 21–26
McLaughlin v East and Midlothian NHS Trust, 2001 S.L.T. 387; 2000 S.C.L.R. 1108
Court of Session (Outer House).. 20–18, 20–27
McLaughlin v Strathclyde RC, 1992 S.L.T. 959 Court of Session (Outer House).... 18–06
McLaughlin v Strathclyde RC, 1996 Rep. L.R. 179 Sh Ct................................. 18–09
McLellan v Dundee City Council [2009] CSOH 9; 2009 Rep. L.R. 61; 2009 G.W.D. 5-
86.. 20–12
McManus v British Railways Board, 1993 S.C. 557; 1994 S.L.T. 496 Court of Session
(Inner House).. 15–07
McMenemy v Argyll Stores Ltd, 1992 S.L.T. 971; 1992 S.C.L.R. 576 Court of Session
(Outer House)... 4–25
McMillan (Maurice) v Lord Advocate, 1991 S.L.T. 150 Court of Session (Outer
House)... 18–24, 19–01
McMurray (Patricia) v Safeway Stores Plc Unreported July 4, 2000 Court of
Session... 10–60
McNeill v Roche Products Ltd (No.2), 1989 S.L.T. 498; 1988 S.C.L.R. 629 Court of
Session (Outer House).. 1–09
McPhee v Glasgow Corp, 1910 1 S.L.T. 380 Court of Session (Outer House)....... 12–06,
12–08
McQueen v Glasgow Garden Festival (1988) Ltd, 1995 S.L.T. 211 Court of Session
(Outer House)... 13–19
McTear v Imperial Tobacco Ltd [2005] CSOH 69; 2005 2 S.C. 1; 2005 G.W.D.
20-365.. 11–02, 13–10, 21–05
McVinnie (Laraine) v McVinnie (William), 1995 S.L.T. (Sh. Ct.) 81; 1995 S.C.L.R.
480.. 12–19
McWilliams v Sir William Arrol & Co Ltd [1962] 1 W.L.R. 295; [1962] 1 All E.R. 623
HL.. 20–35
Macdonald v County Council of Argyll, 1953 Sh. Ct. Rep. 345...................... 18–06

Magee & Co (Belfast) Ltd v Bracewell Harrison & Coton, 1981 S.L.T. 107; 1980 S.L.T.
  (Notes) 102 Court of Session (Outer House).. 9–20
Maguire v Harland & Wolff Plc [2005] EWCA Civ 1; [2005] P.I.Q.R. P21; (2005)
  102(12) L.S.G. 26... 21–38
Main v McAndrew Wormald Ltd, 1988 S.L.T. 141 Court of Session (Inner
  House)... 11–13, 12–13, 13–10
Mains v Uniroyal Englebert Tyres Ltd (No.1), 1995 S.C. 518; 1995 S.L.T. 1115 Court
  of Session (Inner House)... 1–03
Majrowski v Guy's and St Thomas's NHS Trust [2006] UKHL 34; [2007] 1 A.C. 224;
  [2006] 3 W.L.R. 125.. 22–13
Makepeace v Evans Bros (Reading) [2000] B.L.R. 287; [2001] I.C.R. 241 CA (Civ
  Div).. 25–10
Malcolm v Fair, 1993 S.L.T. 342 Court of Session (Outer House)..................... 17–08
Mallon v Spook Erections Ltd, 1993 S.C.L.R. 845 Sh Ct.................................... 19–03
Malpas v Fife Council, 1999 S.L.T. 499; 1999 S.C.L.R. 550 Court of Session (Outer
  House)... 14–13
Manson v Skinner, 2002 S.L.T. 448; 2002 G.W.D. 10–315 Court of Session (Inner
  House)... 14–05
Margereson v JW Roberts Ltd [1996] Env. L.R. 304; [1997] 6 Re. L.R. 74 CA (Civ
  Div).. 21–38
Marinello v Edinburgh City Council [2011] CSIH 33; 2011 S.L.T. 615; 2011 S.C.L.R.
  473... 22–13
Marshall v Southampton and South West Hampshire AHA (152/84) [1986] Q.B. 401;
  [1986] 2 W.L.R. 780 ECJ... 20–05
Matheson v Press Offshore Ltd, 1992 S.L.T. 288 Court of Session (Inner House)... 12–04
Matthews v Glasgow City Council [2006] CSIH 1; 2006 S.C. 349; 2006 S.L.T. 88... 25–06
Mattocks v Mann [1993] R.T.R. 13 CA (Civ Div)... 17–14
Mearns v Smedvig Ltd, 1999 S.C. 243; 1999 S.L.T. 585 Court of Session (Outer
  House)... 10–60
Merrick Homes Ltd v Duff (No.2), 1997 S.L.T. 53 Court of Session (Outer
  House)... 14–03
Miller v Perth and Kinross Council, 2002 Rep. L.R. 22; 2001 G.W.D. 40–1530 Court
  of Session (Outer House).. 20–19
Miller v South of Scotland Electricity Board, 1958 S.C. (H.L.) 20; 1958 S.L.T. 229
  HL.. 10–21, 23–02
Milne v Rank City Wall Ltd, 1987 G.W.D. 14-525... 18–19
Milner v Carnival Plc (t/a Cunard) [2010] EWCA Civ 389; [2010] 3 All E.R. 701; [2010]
  2 All E.R. (Comm) 397... 24–07
Mitchell v Atco [1995] C.L.Y. 3722 County Court.. 21–52
Mitchell v Glenrothes Development Corp, 1991 S.L.T. 284 Court of Session (Outer
  House)... 4–14
Mitchell v HAT Contracting Services Ltd (No.2), 1993 S.L.T. 734 Court of Session
  (Outer House)... 10–32
Mitchell v Inverclyde DC, 1998 S.L.T. 1157; 1998 S.C.L.R. 191 Court of Session
  (Outer House)... 20–36
Mitchell v Laing, 1998 S.C. 342; 1998 S.L.T. 203 Court of Session (Inner House)... 5–01,
  5–06
Moffat v Marconi Space and Defence Systems Ltd, 1975 S.L.T. (Notes) 60 Court of
  Session (Outer House)... 10–11, 18–23
Moon v Garrett [2006] EWCA Civ 1121; [2006] C.P. Rep. 46; [2006] B.L.R. 402.... 25–11
Mooney (Grace) v Glasgow DC (Process: Order for Disclosure of Information), 1989
  S.L.T. 863 Court of Session (Outer House)... 10–57, 12–16
Mooney v Lanarkshire CC, 1954 S.C. 245; 1954 S.L.T. 137 Court of Session (Inner
  House)... 19–07
Moore v Greater Glasgow Health Board, 1978 S.C. 123; 1979 S.L.T. 42 Court of
  Session (Inner House)... 10–51
Moore v Hotelplan Ltd (t/a Inghams Travel) [2010] EWHC 276 (QB)................ 24–05
Morgan v Liverpool Corp [1927] 2 K.B. 131... 19–04
Morris v Breaveglen Ltd (t/a Anzac Construction Co) [1993] I.C.R. 766; [1993]
  I.R.L.R. 350 CA (Civ Div)... 25–12

Morrison v J Kelly & Sons Ltd, 1970 S.C. 65; 1970 S.L.T. 198 Court of Session (Inner House) 15–04
Morrison v Waters & Co (1906) 8 F. 867; (1906) 14 S.L.T. 127 Court of Session (Inner House) 14–08
Morton v Glasgow City Council, 2007 S.L.T. (Sh Ct) 81; 2007 Rep. L.R. 66 Sh Ct 23–03, 23–09
Morton v West Lothian Council [2005] CSOH 142; 2006 Rep. L.R. 7; 2005 G.W.D. 35-667 3–01
Morton v West Lothian Council [2008] CSIH 18 .... 18–11, 18–12
Mughal v Reuters Ltd [1993] I.R.L.R. 571; [1995] 6 Med. L.R. 43 QBD 21–52, 21–54
Muir v Glasgow Corp. *See* Glasgow Corp v Muir
Muir v National Coal Board, 1952 S.L.T. (Notes) 21 Court of Session (Outer House) 9–25
Mullen v Quinnsworth [1990] 1 I.R. 59 .... 18–19, 18–24
Mulligan v Midland Bank Unreported June 30, 1997 21–52
Munro v Aberdeen City Council [2009] CSOH 129; 2009 S.L.T. 964; 2009 Rep. L.R. 116 20–18
Murdoch v Moray Council Unreported April 27, 2005 18–13
Murphy v Lord Advocate (Negligence), 1981 S.L.T. 213 Court of Session (Outer House) 21–47
Murray v Edinburgh DC, 1981 S.L.T. 253 19–03
Murray v National Association of Round Tables of Great Britain and Ireland, 2002 S.L.T. 204; 2002 S.C.L.R. 295 Court of Session (Inner House) 6–06
Murray v Nicholls, 1983 S.L.T. 194 Court of Session (Outer House) 9–24
National Union of Teachers v St Mary's Church of England (Aided) Junior School Governing Body [1997] 3 C.M.L.R. 630; [1997] Eu. L.R. 221 CA (Civ Div) ... 20–05
Neilson v Household Coal and Iron Co (1842) 4 D. 1193 9–02
Neilson v Motion, 1992 S.L.T. 124 Court of Session (Outer House) 7–10
Nelhams v Sandells Maintenance Ltd, 46 Con. L.R. 40; [1996] P.I.Q.R. P52 CA (Civ Div) 25–12
Nicholls v Rushton, *The Times*, June 19, 1992 CA (Civ Div) 4–17, 17–09
Nicol v British Steel Corp (General Steels) Ltd, 1992 S.L.T. 141 Court of Session (Outer House) 6–05, 21–22
Nimmo v Alexander Cowan & Sons Ltd [1968] A.C. 107; [1967] 3 W.L.R. 1169 HL 1–03, 10–11, 18–23
Nisbet v Chief Constable of Strathclyde, 2003 S.C. 324; 2003 S.L.T. 634 Court of Session (Inner House) 20–16
Nugent v Glasgow City Council [2009] CSOH 88; 2009 G.W.D. 24-392 18–09
O'Carroll v Ryanair, 2009 S.C.L.R. 125; 2008 Rep. L.R. 149 Sh Ct 24–08
Ocean Frost, The. *See* Armagas Ltd v Mundogas SA
O'Donnell v Murdoch McKenzie & Co Ltd, 1967 S.C. (H.L.) 63; 1967 S.L.T. 229 HL 13–18
O'Neill v DSG Retail Ltd [2002] EWCA Civ 1139; [2003] I.C.R. 222; (2002) 99(40) L.S.G. 32 20–38
O'Neill v University of the West of Scotland [2011] CSOH 52; 2011 Rep. L.R. 58; 2011 G.W.D. 13-313 18–22
Orme v Ferguson, 1996 S.L.T. (Sh Ct) 2; 1995 S.C.C.R. 752 Sh Pr 17–31
Ormsby v Chief Constable of Strathclyde [2008] CSOH 143; 2008 S.C.L.R. 783; 2009 Rep. L.R. 2 4–19
Orr v Metcalfe, 1973 S.C. 57; 1973 S.L.T. 133 Court of Session (Inner House) 13–22
Overseas Tankship (UK) Ltd v Miller Steamship Co Pty Ltd (The Wagon Mound) [1967] 1 A.C. 617; [1966] 3 W.L.R. 498 PC 15–04
Pace v Cully, 1992 S.L.T. 1073 Court of Session (Outer House) 17–07
Page v Smith [1996] A.C. 155; [1995] 2 W.L.R. 644 HL 4–17, 21–54
Palmer v Marks and Spencer Plc [2001] EWCA Civ 1528 18–22
Parker v Lanarkshire Health Board, 1996 S.C.L.R. 57 Court of Session (Inner House) 13–06
Paterson v Costain Mining Ltd, 1988 S.L.T. 413; 1988 S.C.L.R. 70 Court of Session (Outer House) 21–14
Paterson v Kelvin Central Buses Ltd, 1997 S.L.T. 685; 1996 S.C.L.R. 358 Court of Session (Outer House) 13–25

Phillips v Air New Zealand Ltd [2002] EWHC 800 (Comm); [2002] 1 All E.R. (Comm) 801; [2002] 2 Lloyd's Rep. 408 24–06
Pickford v ICI Plc [1998] 1 W.L.R. 1189; [1998] 3 All E.R. 462 HL........... 21–52, 21–54
Pilmar v Balkan Holidays Ltd Unreported February 16, 2007 Sh Ct 24–04
Popi M, The. *See* Rhesa Shipping Co SA v Edmunds (The Popi M)
Porter v Strathclyde RC, 1991 S.L.T. 446 Court of Session (Inner House)........... 18–23
Poterala v Uniroyal Tyres Ltd, 1993 S.L.T. 1072; 1993 S.C.L.R. 403 Court of Session (Outer House)... 10–57
Prentice v William Thyne Ltd, 1989 S.L.T. 336 Court of Session (Outer House)...... 4–25
Prescott v Bulldog Tools [1981] 3 All E.R. 869 QBD.................................... 10–60
Preston v Grampian Health Board, 1988 S.L.T. 435 Court of Session (Outer House)... 13–23
Purryag v Greater Glasgow Health Board, 1996 S.L.T. 794; 1996 Rep. L.R. 48 Court of Session (Outer House) 4–27
Qualcast (Wolverhampton) v Haynes [1959] A.C. 743; [1959] 2 W.L.R. 510 HL..... 20–34
Quantum Claims Compensation Specialists Ltd v Powell, 1997 S.C.L.R. 242, Sh Pr . 2–19
Quigley v Hart Builders (Edinburgh) Ltd [2006] CSOH 118............................. 12–04
Quinn v McGinty, 1999 S.L.T. (Sh Ct) 27; 1998 Rep. L.R. 107 Sh Pr 21–09
R (A Child) v Iberotravel Ltd (t/a Sunworld Ltd) [2001] C.L.Y. 4453 QBD......... 24–02
R. (on the application of Association of British Travel Agents Ltd (ABTA)) v Civil Aviation Authority [2006] EWCA Civ 1356; [2007] 2 All E.R. (Comm) 898; [2007] 2 Lloyd's Rep. 249.. 24–03
R. (on the application of Factortame Ltd) v Secretary of State for Transport, Local Government and the Regions. *See* Factortame Ltd v Secretary of State for the Environment, Transport and the Regions (Costs) (No.2)
Rae v Glasgow City Council, 1998 S.L.T. 292; 1997 Rep. L.R. 79 Court of Session (Outer House).. 21–15
Rae v Scottish Power Plc Unreported November 8, 2001 Court of Session........... 25–04
Rawlinson v Initial Property Maintenance Ltd, 1998 S.L.T. (Sh Ct) 54; 1998 Rep. L.R. 17... 10–60
Reid v Galbraith's Stores, 1970 S.L.T. (Notes) 83 Court of Session (Outer House). 18–19
Reid v Planet Welding Equipment Ltd, 1980 S.L.T. (Notes) 7 Court of Session (Outer House)... 10–32
Reid v Ski Independence, 1999 S.L.T. (Sh Ct) 62; 1998 G.W.D. 31-1576............. 24–08
Rennie v Scott Lithgow Unreported January 27, 2005.................................... 21–23
Rennie v Upper Clyde Shipbuilders, 1989 G.W.D. 20–1258.............................. 21–37
Rhesa Shipping Co SA v Edmunds (The Popi M) [1985] 1 W.L.R. 948; [1985] 2 All E.R. 712 HL.. 13–04
Richardson v Butcher [2010] EWHC 214 (QB)... 17–33
Richardson v Pitt-Stanley [1995] Q.B. 123; [1995] 2 W.L.R. 26 CA (Civ Div)........ 21–09
Riches v Edinburgh Corp, 1976 S.L.T. (Notes) 9 Court of Session (Inner House)... 13–18
Robb v Salamis (M&I) Ltd [2006] UKHL 56; [2007] 2 All E.R. 97; 2007 S.C. (H.L.) 71.. 20–13, 20–14
Roberts v British Railways Board, 1998 S.C.L.R. 577; 1998 Rep. L.R. 84 Court of Session (Outer House)... 12–13
Robertson v British Bakeries Ltd, 1991 S.L.T. 434 Court of Session (Outer House)... 4–12, 4–25
Robertson v Forth Road Bridge Joint Board (No.2), 1995 S.C. 364; 1996 S.L.T. 263 Court of Session (Inner House).. 4–18
Robertson v The Scottish Ministers [2007] CSOH 186................................... 22–13
Robinson v Midlothian Council [2009] CSOH 109; 2009 G.W.D. 27-443..... 21–39, 21–45
Rolls Royce Industrial Power (India) Ltd v Cox. *See* Cox v Rolls Royce Industrial Power (India) Ltd
Roofcare Ltd v Gillies, 1984 S.L.T. (Sh. Ct.) 8 Sh Pr..................................... 16–06
Ross v British Coal Corp, 1990 S.L.T. 854 Court of Session (Outer House)......... 10–29
Rothwell v Chemical and Insulating Co Ltd. *See* Grieves v FT Everard & Sons Ltd
Rush v Glasgow City Council, 1947 S.C. 580; 1948 S.L.T. 37 Court of Session (Inner House).. 18–05
Salter v UB Frozen & Chilled Foods Ltd, 2004 S.C. 233; 2003 S.L.T. 1011 Court of Session (Outer House)... 4–17

Scaife v Falcon Leisure Group (Overseas) Ltd [2007] IESC 57.......................... 24–04
Scott v Chief Constable of Strathclyde, 1999 S.L.T. (Sh Ct) 66; 1999 G.W.D. 5-232 Sh
    Pr.. 16–06
Scott v Cormack Heating Engineers Ltd, 1942 S.C. 159; 1942 S.L.T. 126 Court of
    Session (Inner House).. 10–24
Scott v Glasgow DC, 1994 G.W.D. 28–1715... 19–01
Scott v Lothian RC, 1999 Rep. L.R. 15; 1998 G.W.D. 33–1719 Court of Session (Outer
    House).. 23–07
Scout Association v Barnes [2010] EWCA Civ 1476...................................... 23–08
Shanks v Gray, 1977 S.L.T. (Notes) 26 Court of Session (Inner House)................ 9–31
Sharif v Singh (t/a India Gate Tandoori Restaurant), 2000 S.L.T. (Sh Ct) 188; 2000
    G.W.D. 28-1070 Sh Pr... 10–27
Shell Tankers UK Ltd v Jeromson [2001] EWCA Civ 101; [2001] I.C.R. 1223; [2001]
    P.I.Q.R. P19.. 21–37
Sheriff v Klyne Tugs (Lowestoft) Ltd [1999] I.C.R. 1170; [1999] I.R.L.R. 481 CA (Civ
    Div)... 22–14
Shuttleton v Duncan Stewart & Co Ltd, 1996 S.L.T. 517; 1995 S.C.L.R. 1137 Court of
    Session (Outer House)... 6–03, 21–21
Sienkiewicz v Greif (UK) Ltd [2011] UKSC 10; [2011] 2 W.L.R. 523; [2011] 2 All E.R.
    857.. 21–05, 21–34, 21–37
Simmons v British Steel Plc [2004] UKHL 20; 2004 S.C. (H.L.) 94; 2004 S.L.T. 595. 4–19
Simpson v ICI Ltd, 1983 S.L.T. 601 Court of Session (Inner House)..................... 4–17
Skinner v Aberdeen City Council, 2001 Rep. L.R. 118; 2001 G.W.D. 16-657 Court of
    Session (Outer House)... 20–38
Smith v Hastie Unreported March 19, 2002 Court of Session........................ 13–06
Smith v Manchester Corp (1974) 17 K.I.R. 1; (1974) 118 S.J. 597 CA (Civ Div)... 4–12
Smith v Northamptonshire CC [2009] UKHL 27; [2009] 4 All E.R. 557; [2009] I.C.R.
    734... 20–04, 20–25
Smith v Shaw & McInnes Ltd Unreported April 24, 2001 Court of Session.......... 21–21
Smith v Strathclyde RC, 1979 S.L.T. (Notes) 79 Court of Session (Outer House)... 10–11
Smith v Wright & Beyer Ltd [2001] EWCA Civ 1069...................................... 21–51
Smoldon v Whitworth [1997] E.L.R. 249; [1997] P.I.Q.R. P133 CA (Civ Div)....... 23–07
Sneddon v Deulag Services Ltd... 8–34, 8–38
Somervell v Somervell (1900) 8 S.L.T. 84 Court of Session (Outer House).......... 10–54
Spence v Wilson (No.2), 1998 S.L.T. 959; 1998 Rep. L.R. 50 Court of Session (Outer
    House).. 10–35
Spencer-Franks v Kellogg Brown & Root Ltd [2008] UKHL 46; [2009] 1 All E.R. 269;
    2008 S.C. (H.L.) 159... 20–18, 20–24
Stainsby v Fallon [2010] CSIH 64; 2010 S.C. 773; 2010 Rep. L.R. 127......... 17–05, 23–04
Stark v Ford, 1996 S.L.T. 1329; 1996 Rep. L.R. 127 Court of Session (Inner House) 9–30
Stevenson v East Dunbartonshire Council, 2003 S.L.T. 97; 2002 G.W.D. 39-1312
    Court of Session (Outer House)... 22–05
Stewar v Cooper Oil Tools (GB) Ltd, 1997 G.W.D. 35-1787............................ 21–40
Stewart v Speed Unreported March 28, 2006 Kirkcaldy Sh Ct............................ 7–11
Stone v Mountford, 1995 S.L.T. 1279 Court of Session (Outer House)................ 10–32
Stout v United Kingdom Atomic Energy Authority, 1979 S.L.T. 54 Court of Session
    (Inner House).. 9–21
Strachan v Caledonian Fish-selling & Marine Stores Co Ltd, 1963 S.C. 157; 1963
    S.L.T. (Notes) 21 Court of Session (Inner House)................................... 12–29
Strathmore Group v Credit Lyonnais, 1994 S.L.T. 1023 Court of Session (Outer
    House).. 9–20
Sunderland v North British Steel Group Plc, 1992 S.L.T. 1146 Court of Session (Outer
    House).. 16–03
Sutherland v Hatton. See Barber v Somerset CC
Syme v Scottish Borders Council, 2003 S.L.T. 601; 2002 S.C.L.R. 1066 Court of
    Session (Outer House)... 18–04, 18–12, 18–13
TSB Scotland Plc v James Mills (Montrose) Ltd (in receivership), 1992 S.L.T. 519
    Court of Session (Outer House)... 12–19
Taplin v Fife Council, 2003 S.L.T. 653; 2003 Rep. L.R. 9 Court of Session (Outer
    House).. 22–05

Taylor v Glasgow City Council, 2002 S.C. 364; 2002 S.L.T. 689 Court of Session (Inner House).. 20–03, 20–36, 20–38
Taylor v Serviceteam Ltd [1998] P.I.Q.R. P201 County Court......................... 21–08
Taylor v Smith, 2003 S.C.L.R. 926... 18–11, 18–12
Taylor v Wincanton Group Ltd [2009] EWCA Civ 1581................................. 18–22
Telfer v Glasgow Corp, 1974 S.L.T. (Notes) 51 Court of Session (Outer House).... 23–02
Thomas v Thomas [1947] A.C. 484; [1947] 1 All E.R. 582 HL........................ 15–03
Thompson v Smiths Shiprepairers (North Shields) Ltd [1984] Q.B. 405; [1984] 2 W.L.R. 522 QBD... 21–12, 21–17, 21–40
Thomson v Cremin [1956] 1 W.L.R. 103 (Note); [1953] 2 All E.R. 1185 HL......... 19–07
Thomson v Glasgow Corp, 1961 S.L.T. 237 Court of Session (Inner House)......... 13–08
Thomson v Kvaerner Govan Ltd [2003] UKHL 45; 2004 S.C. (H.L.) 1; 2004 S.L.T. 24... 13–16, 15–03
Thorne v Strathclyde RC, 1984 S.L.T. 161 Court of Session (Outer House)............ 1–10
Threlfall v Hull City Council [2010] EWCA Civ 1147; [2011] I.C.R. 209; [2011] P.I.Q.R. P3... 20–13, 20–32
Tiffney v Flynn [2007] CSOH 149; 2007 S.L.T. 929; 2007 G.W.D. 28–496............ 17–25
Titchener v British Railways Board [1983] 1 W.L.R. 1427; [1983] 3 All E.R. 770 HL 19–02
Todd v Clapperton [2009] CSOH 112; 2009 S.L.T. 837; 2009 Rep. L.R. 90............ 19–04
Todd v Roman Catholic Diocese of Dunkeld and Dundee City Council Unreported May 10, 2004 Tayside Central and Fife Sh Ct................................. 14–03
Todd v Thomson Tour Operators Ltd Unreported July 2, 2000 CA..................... 24–02
Tomlinson v Congleton BC [2003] UKHL 47; [2004] 1 A.C. 46; [2003] 3 W.L.R. 705... 19–02
Tonner v FT Everard & Sons Ltd, 1994 S.C. 593; 1994 S.L.T. 1033 Court of Session (Inner House).. 10–58
Toole v Bolton MBC [2002] EWCA Civ 588.. 20–33
Torenia, The. *See* Aktieselskabet de Danske Sukkerfabrikker v Bajamar Compania Naviera SA
Towers v Jack, 2004 Rep. L.R. 100... 8–34
Tudhope v Finlay Park (t/a Park Hutchison Solicitors), 2004 S.L.T. 783; 2005 S.C.L.R. 125 Court of Session (Outer House)... 8–04
Turner v Mansfield Corp (1975) 119 S.J. 629 CA (Civ Div)............................. 13–19
Unilever Plc v Procter & Gamble Co [2000] 1 W.L.R. 2436; [2001] 1 All E.R. 783 CA (Civ Div).. 7–05
United Wholesale Grocers Ltd v Sher, 1993 S.L.T. 284 Court of Session (Outer House)... 25–02
Van Klaveren v Servisair (UK) Ltd, [2009] CSIH 37; 2009 S.L.T. 576; 2009 G.W.D. 18–280 Court of Session (Inner House).. 7–06
Vernon v Bosley (No.2) [1999] Q.B. 18; [1997] 3 W.L.R. 683 CA (Civ Div)............ 11–10
W's Parent and Guardian v Douglas [2006] CSOH 178; (2007) 93 B.M.L.R. 42; 2006 G.W.D. 37–737.. 11–14
Wagon Mound, The. *See* Overseas Tankship (UK) Ltd v Miller Steamship Co Pty Ltd
Walker v Northumberland CC [1995] 1 All E.R. 737; [1995] I.C.R. 702 QBd........ 22–04, 22–11
Wall v Silver Wing Surface Arrangements Unreported November 16, 1981 QBD... 24–01
Wallace v City of Glasgow DC, 1995 S.L.T. 23... 19–01
Walsh v TNT UK Ltd [2006] CSOH 149; 2006 S.L.T. 1100; 2006 G.W.D. 30–660.. 20–38
Ward v Coltness Iron Co Ltd, 1944 S.C. 318; 1944 S.L.T. 405 Court of Session (Inner House)... 9–03
Ward v Scotrail Railways Ltd, 1999 S.C. 255; 1999 G.W.D. 1–53 Court of Session (Outer House)... 22–12
Ward v Tesco Stores Ltd [1976] 1 W.L.R. 810; [1976] 1 All E.R. 219 CA (Civ Div)... 18–19, 18–24
Wardle v Scottish Borders Council, 2011 Rep. L.R. 74; 2011 G.W.D. 10–243 Sh Ct... 23–07, 23–09
Weir v Robertson Group (Construction) Ltd [2006] CSOH 107; 2006 Rep. L.R. 114; 2006 G.W.D. 25–575.. 8–37
Wells v Wells [1999] 1 A.C. 345; [1998] 3 W.L.R. 329 HL............................... 4–14
Wenham v Bexley [1999] C.L.Y. 287 County Court.. 18–22

Wharf v Bildwell Insulations Ltd [1999] C.L.Y. 2047 QBD............................. 20–27
Wheat v E Lacon & Co Ltd [1966] A.C. 552; [1966] 2 W.L.R. 581 HL....... 19–03, 19–07
White v Chief Constable of South Yorkshire [1999] 2 A.C. 455; [1998] 3 W.L.R. 1509
 HL.. 4–16, 4–18
White v Inveresk Paper Co Ltd (No.2), 1987 S.C. 143; 1988 S.L.T. 2 Court of Session
 (Outer House).. 4–25
White (Brian) v White [2001] UKHL 9; [2001] 1 W.L.R. 481; [2001] 2 All E.R. 43.. 17–25
William Nimmo & Co Ltd v Russell Construction Co Ltd (No.2), 1997 S.L.T. 122;
 1995 S.C.L.R. 1148 Court of Session (Inner House)............................... 15–08
Williams v Farne Salmon & Trout Ltd, 1998 S.L.T. 1329; 1998 Rep. L.R. 32 Court of
 Session (Outer House)... 21–29
Williamson v GB Papers Plc, 1994 S.L.T. 173 Court of Session (Outer House)....... 8–37,
 13–25, 18–23
Williamson v McPherson, 1951 S.C. 438; 1951 S.L.T. 283 Court of Session (Inner
 House)... 10–41
Wilsher v Essex AHA [1987] Q.B. 730; [1987] 2 W.L.R. 425 CA (Civ Div)........... 21–04
Wilson v Best Travel [1993] 1 All E.R. 353 QBD... 24–04
Wilson v Debenhams Retail Plc Unreported September 20, 2010 Stirling Sh Ct..... 18–19
Wilson v Dunbar Bank Plc [2008] CSIH 27; 2008 S.C. 457; 2008 S.L.T. 301......... 15–04
Wilson v Exel UK Ltd (t/a Exel) [2010] CSIH 35; 2010 S.L.T. 671; 2010 S.C.L.R.
 486.. 22–12
Wilson v Morinton Quarries Ltd, 1979 S.L.T. 83... 21–21
Winterhalder v Leith CC Unreported July 18, 2000 CA................................. 18–06
Wisely v John Fulton (Plumbers) Ltd, 1998 S.C. 910; 1998 S.L.T. 1026 Court of
 Session (Inner House).. 5–01, 13–26
Wolfson v Forrester, 1910 S.C. 675; 1910 1 S.L.T. 318 Court of Session (Inner
 House).. 19–04
Wong Mee Wan v Kwan Kin Travel Services Ltd [1996] 1 W.L.R. 38; [1995] 4 All E.R.
 745.. 24–05
Wood v Philips TMC Ltd, 1994 S.L.T. 142 Court of Session (Outer House)......... 12–29
Wright v Greenwich LBC [1996] C.L.Y. 4474 County Court........................... 18–06
Wright v Stoddard International Plc [2007] CSOH 138; 2008 Rep. L.R. 37; 2007
 G.W.D. 33-565... 21–17
Young v Kent CC [2005 EWHC 1342 (QB).. 23–02
Young v Post Office [2002] EWCA Civ 661; [2002] I.R.L.R. 660; [2002] Emp. L.R.
 1136... 22–07
Zubair v Younis [1995] C.L.Y. 1629 County Court....................................... 17–14

TABLE OF STATUTES

1930	Third Party (Rights Against Insurers) Act (20 & 21 Geo. 5 c.25)........................ 9–14
	s.2(2)........................... 21–09
1940	Law Reform (Miscellaneous Provisions) (Scotland) Act (3 &46 Geo. 6 c.42)....... 10–09
1958	Interest on Damages (Scotland) Act (6 & 7 Eliz. 2 c.61)... 13–22
1960	Occupiers' Liability (Scotland) Act (8 & 9 Eliz. 2 c.30)... 18–14, 19–01—19–07, 20–17
	s.1(3)........................... 19–01
	s.2(1)........................... 19–01
	s.3(1)........................... 19–05
1961	Factories Act (9 & 10 Eliz. 2 c.34)................. 20–04, 20–18
	s.4............................. 21–16
	s.14............................ 10–31
	s.28............................ 18–21
	s.29............................ 10–11
	(1).................... 21–16, 21–41
	s.63................... 21–16, 21–37
	s.176(1)........................ 20–18
1963	Office, Shops and Railway Premises Act (c.41)............ 20–04
	s.63............................ 18–21
1968	Law Reform (Miscellaneous Provisions) (Scotland) Act (c.70)
	s.10............................ 3–08
	(1)............................ 9–23
	(2)(a)......................... 9–23
	(4)................... 9–23, 17–35
1969	Employers' Liability (Compulsory Insurance) Act (c.57) 7–03, 21–09
1971	Sheriff Courts (Scotland) Act (c.58)
	s.31A.......................... 16–24
1972	Administration of Justice (Scotland) Act (c.59)...... 1–10, 3–05, 6–06, 10–54, 16–22, 21–46
1973	Prescription and Limitation (Scotland) Act (c.52) 6–02—6–10
	s.17.............. 6–02, 10–15, 21–23
	(2)..... 6–02, 6–10, 10–15, 21–20
	(a)......................... 21–21
	(b)................ 6–03—6–06, 10–15, 21–22
	(3)............................ 6–02

	s.18........................ 6–02, 6–07
	(4).............................. 6–07
	s.19A..... 6–02, 6–03, 6–08—6–10, 10–08, 10–14, 10–15, 10–19, 21–23, 21–25, 21–26
	s.22............................. 6–02
	(3)............................ 6–05
1974	Health and Safety at Work Act (c.37).......... 3–05, 9–23, 10–32
	s.1(2)........................... 20–04
	s.16..................... 3–06, 20–12
	s.47(2)......................... 20–02
	Sch.1........................... 20–04
1976	Damages (Scotland) Act (c.13) . 6–07
1979	Pneumoconiosis etc. (Workers Compensation) Act (c.41) 21–09
1980	Solicitors (Scotland) Act (c.46)
	s.61A(1)................. 2–18, 2–19
	Limitation Act (c.58).............
	s.33............................ 6–10
1982	Civil Jurisdiction and Judgments Act (c.27)..................... 9–08
	s.41(3)......................... 9–07
	(6)............................ 9–07
	s.42(5)......................... 9–07
	Sch.1 art.6..................... 9–08
	Sch.8 r.3....................... 9–08
	Administration of Justice (Scotland) Act (c.53)...... 4–20—4–24
	s.8............... 4–20—4–23, 4–25, 5–06, 9–30
	s.9................. 4–24, 4–25, 9–30
	s.12............................ 4–25
1984	Roads (Scotland) Act (c.54)... 18–04, 18–17
	s.1(1).......................... 18–04
	s.5............................ 18–04
	s.60(1)......................... 18–17
	s.151(1)........................ 18–04
1985	Companies Act (c.6)
	s.652........................... 9–14
1986	Insolvency Act (c.45)
	s.87............................ 9–13
	s.113........................... 9–13
	s.130(2)........................ 9–13
	Sch.B1 para.43(6).............. 9–13
	Legal Aid (Scotland) Act (c.47)
	s.18(2)......................... 14–07
1987	Housing (Scotland) Act (c.26) 19–04, 19–05
	Sch.10.3(1)(a)................. 19–04

	(b).................... 19–04		s.104........................ 5–03	
	Sch.10.4.................... 19–04		s.105........................ 5–03	
	Sch.10.5.................... 19–04	1995	Children (Scotland) Act (c.36). 23–01	
1988	Civil Evidence (Scotland) Act (c.32)............... 3–08, 3–11, 12–19, 13–08	1997	Social Security (Recovery of Benefits) Act (c.27)......... 1–09, 5–01—5–07	
	Road Traffic Act (c.52)......... 9–23, 10–30, 17–30, 17–31		s.15.... 10–02, 10–32, 13–26, 15–10	
	s.30........................ 17–05		(2)............................ 5–01	
	s.143(1)...................... 17–23		Protection from Harassment Act (c.40)........... 22–01, 22–13	
	s.151......... 7–03, 10–32, 17–23		s.8.......................... 22–13	
	(2)(b)...................... 17–23		s.18B........................ 22–13	
	s.152........................ 17–31	1998	Data Protection Act (c.29)...... 3–09	
	(2)........................ 17–31	2006	Compensation Act (c.29)....... 21–17	
	s.154........................ 17–23		s.3.................. 21–04, 21–37	
1991	New Roads and Street Works Act (c.22).................. 18–17		(1)(d)...................... 21–34	
	s.140(4)...................... 18–17		Companies Act (c.46)	
	Age of Legal Capacity (Scotland) Act (c.50).............. 6–02		s.1000........................ 9–14	
	s.1(i)(a)...................... 23–01		s.1001........................ 9–14	
1992	Social Security Contributions and Benefits Act (c.4)		s.1030(2)..................... 21–10	
	s.103.................. 5–02, 5–07	2010	s.1031........................ 21–10 Third Party (Rights Against Insurers) Act (c.10)....... 21–10	

TABLE OF SCOTTISH STATUTES

2001	Housing (Scotland) Act (asp 10)		2004	Vulnerable Witnesses (Scotland)
	Sch.4............................. 19–04			Act (asp 3).................... 8–21
	(1)............................. 19–04			s.12............................ 12–12
	(2)............................. 19–04	2009	Damages (Asbestos-related
2002	Freedom of Information (Scot-			Conditions) (Scotland) Act
	land) Act (asp 13).......... 3–09,			(asp 4)...................... 21–32
	17–02, 18–11,	2011	Damages (Scotland) Act
	18–13, 18–15			(asp 7)................. 8–29, 9–11
	Sch.1............................ 3–09			

TABLE OF STATUTORY INSTRUMENTS

1931	Asbestos Industry Regulations (SI 1931/1140)............. 21–37
1960	Shipbuilding and Ship-Repairing Regulations (SI 1960/1932)......................... 21–37
	reg.70........................... 21–37
1961	Construction (General Provisions) Regulations (SI 1961/1580).................. 25–12
1966	Construction (Working Places) Regulations (SI 1966/94). 25–12
1969	Asbestos Regulations (SI 1969/690).................. 21–16, 21–37
1974	Woodworking Machines Regulations (SI 1974/903).... 21–16
	Agricultural (Tractor Cabs) Regulations (SI 1974/2034)......................... 21–16
1981	Transfer of Undertakings Regulations (SI 1981/1794)... 21–08
1987	Civil Legal Aid (Scotland) Regulations (SI 1987/381)
	reg.21............................. 2–15
	Control of Asbestos at Work Regulations (SI 1987/2115)................. 21–16, 21–37
1988	Control of Substances Hazardous to Health Regulations (SI 1988/1657)..... 20–02, 21–16
1989	Civil Legal Aid (Scotland) (Fees) Regulations 1989 (SI 1989/1490)
	reg. 5............................. 2–17
	reg.11............................ 2–20
	Noise at Work Regulations (SI 1989/1790).......... 8–07, 10–48, 20–02, 21–16, 21–40, 21–42, 21–46
	reg.4............................ 21–18
	reg.5............................ 21–18
	reg.6............................ 21–42
	reg.11.................. 21–18, 21–42
1992	Management of Health and Safety at Work Regulations (SI 1992/2051)............. 20–02, 20–32, 22–07
	Health and Safety (Display Screen Equipment) Regulations (SI 1992/2792)........ 1–03, 20–02, 20–40, 21–54
	reg.4........................... 20–40

reg.5........................... 20–40
reg.7........................... 20–40
Manual Handling (Operations) Regulations (SI 1992/2793) 1–03, 1–04, 9–04, 20–02, 20–03, 20–36—20–39, 21–16, 21–54, 25–03, 25–04
reg.2........................... 20–36
reg.4................... 20–37, 21–18
  (1)(a)........................ 20–37
  (b)........................ 20–37
Sch.1........................... 20–38
Provision and Use of Work Equipment Regulations (SI 1992/2932).................. 21–54
Personal Protective Equipment at Work Regulations (SI 1992/2966).......... 1–03, 20–02, 20–31—20–35, 21–16, 25–03, 25–04
reg.2........................... 20–32
reg.4........................... 20–32
reg.6........................... 20–33
reg.7................... 20–33, 21–18
reg.9................... 20–34, 21–18
reg.10.......................... 20–35
Workplace (Health, Safety and Welfare) Regulations (SI 1992/3004).......... 1–03, 10–04, 10–11, 18–21, 19–03, 20–02, 20–15—20–23, 21–16
reg.3(1)(b)..................... 25–03
reg.4........................... 20–16
  (1)............................ 20–16
  (2)............................ 20–16
reg.5........................... 20–18
  (1)............................ 20–18
  (3)(a)........................ 20–18
reg.7........................... 20–18
reg.8........................... 20–19
reg.11.......................... 20–20
reg.12.......... 18–21, 20–18, 20–21
  (1)..................... 18–22, 18–23
  (2)..................... 18–22, 18–23
  (3).......... 18–21, 18–22, 18–23, 20–16, 20–18
reg.13.......................... 20–22
  (1)—(4)..................... 20–15
reg.14.......................... 20–18
reg.17................... 20–16, 20–17

reg.18	20–18	
reg.19	20–18	
reg.20	20–18	
reg.21	20–18	

Package Travel, Package Holidays and Package Tours Regulations (SI 1992/3288)............ 24–01—24–02
- reg.2............ 24–02
- reg.4............ 24–02
- reg.5............ 24–02
- reg.6............ 24–02
- reg.13........... 24–02
- reg.14........... 24–02
- reg.15........... 24–02
- (a)............. 24–02

1994 Control of Substances Hazardous to Health Regulations (SI 1994/3246)............ 21–16

1995 Reporting of Injuries, Diseases and Dangerous Occurrences Regulations (SI 1995/3163)................ 3–05

1996 Construction (Health, Safety and Welfare) Regulations (SI 1996/1592)...... 1–03, 20–15, 21–16, 25–03—25–06
- reg.2(1)................ 25–03
- reg.3(1)................ 25–03
- reg.4(1)................ 25–04
- (2)............... 25–04, 25–10
- reg.5............ 25–05
- reg.6............ 25–05
- reg.8............ 25–05
- reg.9............ 25–05
- reg.15........... 25–03
- reg.19........... 25–03
- reg.20........... 25–03
- reg.21........... 25–03
- reg.22........... 25–03
- reg.25........... 25–05
- reg.26(1)................ 25–03
- (2)............... 25–03
- reg.27........... 25–05
- reg.28........... 25–05

Act of Sederunt (Civil Legal Aid Rules) (SI 1996/2148)
- reg.7............ 2–17

1997 Advice and Assistance (Scotland) Regulations (SI 1997/382)
- reg.16(3)............ 2–07

1998 Provision and Use of Work Equipment Regulations (SI 1998/2306)............ 1–03, 9–04, 10–48, 20–02, 20–24—20–30, 21–49, 25–02, 25–03, 25–05
- reg.2............ 20–18
- (1)............ 20–24
- reg.3............ 20–25
- (3)............ 20–25
- reg.4............ 20–13, 20–26
- (3)............ 20–27
- reg.5............ 20–27
- reg.7............ 20–28
- reg.8............ 20–12, 20–28
- reg.9............ 20–12, 20–13, 20–28
- reg.11........... 20–29
- regs 11—24....... 20–29
- regs 25—30....... 20–30

Lifting Operations and Lifting Equipment Regulations (SI 1998/2307)......... 1–03, 20–02, 20–41—20–41
- reg.3............ 20–41
- reg.4............ 20–41
- (1)—(2)............ 20–41
- reg.5............ 20–41
- reg.6............ 20–41
- reg.8............ 20–41
- reg.9............ 20–41
- reg.10........... 20–41
- reg.11........... 20–41

Act of Sederunt (Fees of Solicitors in the Sheriff Court) (SI 1998/2675)
- reg.5............ 14–04

1999 Control of Substances Hazardous to Health Regulations (SI 1999/437)....... 10–48, 21–16

Management of Health and Safety at Work Regulations (SI 1999/3242)....... 1–03, 3–06, 10–48, 10–57, 11–06, 16–10, 20–02, 20–06—20–14, 22–01, 22–07
- reg.3............ 10–48, 11–06, 20–07, 20–12, 20–14, 20–17
- reg.4............ 20–08, 20–14
- reg.5............ 20–09, 20–14
- reg.6............ 20–37
- reg.7............ 20–10, 20–14
- reg.10........... 20–11, 20–14
- reg.13........... 20–12, 20–14
- reg.22........... 20–06
- Sch.1............ 20–08, 20–14

2002 Control of Substances Hazardous to Health Regulations (SI 2002/2677)............ 11–07, 21–16, 21–29
- reg.6............ 21–18, 21–29
- reg.7............ 21–29
- reg.9............ 21–18
- reg.11........... 21–18
- reg.12........... 21–18

European Community (Rights Against Insurers) Regulations (SI 2002/3061)....... 17–03, 17–30

2005	Work at Height Regulations (SI 2005/735)............. 1–03, 9–04, 20–02, 20–15, 20–42	2007	Construction (Design and Management) Regulations (SI 2007/320)..... 1–03, 9–04, 20–02, 21–16, 25–06—25–12

2005 Work at Height Regulations (SI 2005/735)............. 1–03, 9–04, 20–02, 20–15, 20–42
- reg.4............................ 20–42
- reg.5............................ 20–42
- reg.6............................ 20–42
  - (2)........................... 20–42
  - (3)........................... 20–42
  - (5)(a)....................... 20–42
- reg.7(2)....................... 20–42
- reg.8............................ 20–42
- reg.9............................ 20–42
- reg.10.......................... 20–42
- reg.12.......................... 20–42
- Sch.6........................... 20–42

Control of Vibration at Work Regulations (SI 2005/1093)................ 21–16, 21–18, 21–43, 21–50—21–51
- reg.4............................ 21–43
- reg.5..................... 21–43, 21–50
- reg.6..................... 21–43, 21–50
- reg.7............................ 21–43
- reg.7............................ 16–10

Control of Noise at Work Regulations (SI 2005/1643)... 21–16
- reg.5............................ 21–18
- reg.6............................ 21–18
- reg.7............................ 21–18
- reg.10.......................... 21–18

2007 Construction (Design and Management) Regulations (SI 2007/320)..... 1–03, 9–04, 20–02, 21–16, 25–06—25–12
- Pt 1............................. 25–07
- Pt 2............................. 25–07
- Pt 3............................. 25–07
- Pt 4............................. 25–07
- Pt 5............................. 25–07
- reg.9(1)(b)..................... 25–07
- reg.13(6)....................... 25–07
  - (7)........................... 25–07
- reg.16.......................... 25–07
- reg.22(1)(c).................... 25–07
- reg.25.......................... 25–07
  - (1)........................... 25–07
  - (2)........................... 25–07
  - (4)........................... 25–07
- regs 25—45..................... 25–07
- reg.26.......................... 25–08
- regs 26—44..................... 25–07
- reg.27.......................... 25–08
- reg.28.......................... 25–08
- reg.29.......................... 25–08
- reg.31.......................... 25–08
- reg.34.......................... 25–08
- reg.35.......................... 25–08
- reg.36.......................... 25–08
- reg.37.......................... 25–08
- reg.38.......................... 25–08
- reg.44.......................... 25–08
- reg.45.......................... 25–07
- Sch.2........................... 25–07

TABLE OF ORDINARY CAUSE RULES AND SUMMARY CAUSE RULES

1993 Ordinary Cause Rules (SI 1993/1956)
- Ch.9 10–24
- Ch.10 10–26
- r.3.1 8–02
- r.9.1 8–08
- r.9.3 .... 2–13, 8–08
- r.9.5 8–08
- r.9.6 .... 8–08, 8–43
- r.9.7 .... 8–08, 8–37, 10–04
- r.9.12 10–27
    - (3)(c) 10–27
- r.9A 8–21
- r.10.5 10–26
- r.13.1 8–03
    - (4) 8–03
- r.15 8–15
- r.16.2(a) 10–03
- r.17.2(i) 10–28
    - (4) 10–30
- r.18 8–10
- r.18.3(2) 10–22
- r.22 .... 8–13, 10–20
- r.22.1 10–24
- r.22.2(b) 10–57
- r.28.2 .... 8–07, 10–55, 10–56
    - (3) 10–51
- r.28.3 .... 8–07, 10–51
- r.28.4 10–53
- r.28.6 10–55
- r.28.10 10–58
    - (1)(b) 10–59
    - (c) 10–58
    - (5) 10–559
- r.28.12 10–59
- r.28.13(3) 10–59
- r.28A 8–13
- r.29.3 12–19
- r.29.14(1)(a) 12–03
    - (b) 12–18
- r.29.20 13–12
- r.31.1 15–02
- r.31.3 15–11
- r.31.4(1) 15–09
    - (5) 15–09
    - (a) 15–09
- r.32A(1) 12–12
- r.36 .... 8–01, 8–04, 9–11
- r.36.4 9–11
- r.36.6 9–11
- r.36.9(1) 10–32
    - (3) 10–32
    - (5) 10–32
    - (d) 10–32
- r.36.12 9–34
- r.36.19 8–29
    - (2) 8–29
- r.36.A1 8–04
- r.36.B1 8–05
    - (b) 9–27
- r.36.C1 8–06
- r.36.D1 8–07
- r.36.E1 8–08
    - (6) 8–08, 10–08
    - (7) 8–09, 10–08
    - (8) 8–10
    - (9) 8–11
    - (11) 8–12
    - (12) 8–12
    - (13) 8–13
    - (14) 8–14
- r.36.F1 .... 8–15, 10–23
- r.36.G1 .... 8–09, 8–10, 8–12, 8–16, 8–23, 8–42, 8–43, 10–03, 10–08, 11–14
    - (1A)(g) 12–09
    - (1B)(9) 12–09
    - (2) 8–17
    - (3) 8–18, 8–28
    - (4) 8–19
    - (5) 8–19
    - (b) 10–17
    - (6) 8–19, 10–17
    - (7) 8–20, 10–18
    - (8) 8–28
    - (8A) 8–21
    - (8B) 8–21
    - (9) 8–21
    - (10) 8–22
- r.36.G1(A)(g) 12–04
- r.36.H1 8–24
- r.36.J1 .... 8–25, 10–16
    - (3)(a) 10–16
    - (b) 10–16
    - (5) 8–18, 8–25
- r.36.K1 .... 8–26, 8–41, 12–11
    - (4) 8–27
- r.36.L1 .... 8–28, 10–17

2002 Summary Cause Rules (SSI 2002/132)
 Ch.34.................... 16–06, 16–13
 r.8.5............................. 16–21
 r.8.6............................. 16–21
 r.8.8............................. 16–21
 r.8.13(1)........................ 16–21
 r.11.............................. 16–12
 r.11.1............................ 16-11
 r.12.1............................ 16–22
 r.13.1............................ 16–22
 r.14.1............................ 16–22
 r.18.1............................ 16–22
 r.18.3............................ 16–22
 r.23.3............................ 16–23
  (7)............................ 16–23
  (8)............................ 16–23
 r.25.1............................ 16–24
  (3)............................ 16–25
  (4).................... 16–25, 16–26
  (5)............................ 16–25
  (6)............................ 16–25
 r.25.3............................ 16–26
  (2)............................ 16–26
 r.34.1(2)........................ 16–06
 r.34.2........................... 16–06
  (1)............................ 16–06
  (4)............................ 16–06
 r.34.3........................... 16–08
  (1)............................ 16–08
  (2)............................ 16–08
 r.34.4.................... 16–10, 16–11
 r.34.5........................... 16–21
  (3)............................ 16–12
 r.34.6........................... 16–11
  (2)............................ 16–11
   (a)......................... 16–12
   (c)......................... 16–15
   (h)......................... 16–19
  (5)............................ 16–21
  (7)............................ 16–16
 r.34.7........................... 16–16
 r.34.8.................... 16–17, 16–18
 r.34.9........................... 16–20
  (3)............................ 16–21
 r.34.11.......................... 16–22
 r.34.12.......................... 16–22
2010 Summary Cause Rules Amendment (Personal Injury Actions).................... 16–06
2011 Summary Cause Rules Amendment (Recovery of Evidence in Personal Injuries Actions).................... 16–01
 reg.2........................... 16–02

PART I—PERSONAL INJURY CLAIMS

CHAPTER 1

TAKING INSTRUCTIONS

Good enough seldom is.[1] By the time your client sits down across your desk, he has already made his most important decision. He has instructed you. The amount of compensation he will receive (if any), and when he will receive it, will depend almost entirely on your skill and determination. Formidable opponents are already mobilised and lie in wait to deny or diminish payment. Not all lawyers are the same. The keys to successful litigation are early preparation, and a willingness to travel the extra mile in your client's interests.   1–01

Lord McCluskey once wrote that the judge "makes such decisions as are necessary *in the light of the matters presented to him* to declare which litigant wins and which loses" [emphasis added].[2] The litigator should have this phrase at the forefront of his mind at all times. Personal injury cases routinely turn on facts not law. You cannot win cases without evidence, and nothing is going to turn up unless you bring it. From the day you open the file, you should focus on the collecting and marshalling of your proof of the facts.

THE INITIAL INTERVIEW

Many people are still reluctant to see solicitors at all. You should be friendly and relaxed, but businesslike. You can save a lot of time if you contact the client in advance of the first meeting and ask him to write out a general statement outlining the facts of the accident. You will always require personal details such as full name, date of birth, address, telephone contact numbers (both mobile and residential), email address and national insurance number. At the meeting begin by asking the client to describe the accident in his own words, and listen without interruption. You will then have a general impression of the accident's circumstances. You will tend also to have a lot of irrelevant material, such as a history of previous but wholly unconnected accidents. More importantly, you will have to elicit from your client crucial matters of legal relevance which he is likely to omit. You should refer to the standard checklists included for the common causes of action. These are not a substitute for thought, but will assist you in finding a ground of liability. You need to focus the   1–02

---

[1] Malcolm Forbes in *Fortune* Magazine.
[2] Lord McCluskey, the Reith Lectures 1987, published as *Law Justice and Democracy* (London: Sweet & Maxwell, 1987).

statement, using your knowledge of relevant and admissible evidence. From the first meeting, you should develop a working case theory and liability analysis, and you should be constantly on the lookout for evidence to support this.

FIND A STATUTORY CASE

1–03 Your first priority must be the search for facts which might support a statutory case. Life is a lot easier if you find one. You generally will not have to worry about reasonable foreseeability.[3] Some statutes and regulations impose strict liability and many require to be implemented in so far as is reasonably practicable, transferring a very heavy burden of proof to the defenders.[4] The contents of the duty of care are fixed by statute and not by shrieval vagary.[5]

The main workplace health and safety statutes are as follows:

- Workplace (Health, Safety and Welfare) Regulations 1992.
- Personal Protective Equipment at Work Regulations 1992.
- Manual Handling (Operations) Regulations 1992.
- Health and Safety (Display Screen Equipment) Regulations 1992.
- Construction (Health, Safety and Welfare) Regulations 1996.
- Provision and Use of Work Equipment Regulations 1998.
- Lifting Operations and Lifting Equipment Regulations 1998.
- Management of Health and Safety at Work Regulations 1999.
- Work at Height Regulations 2005.
- Construction (Design and Management) Regulations 2007.

All of these Regulations are made under the Health and Safety at Work Act 1974. They are supplemented by detailed Codes of Practice or Guidance Notes published by the Health and Safety Executive ("the HSE") and available from them. The Regulations or Guidance provide a detailed and prescriptive framework for almost all workplace accidents. The HSE now makes all of its principal publications freely available on its website, and capable of PDF download. You should search under "HSE Free Publications" and make this a well used shortcut.

As a bare minimum you must have access to the legislation and guidance, and know your way around them. Do the premises constitute a workplace, and who had effective control? Was the pursuer carrying out work which might be defined as "construction"? Was the work activity a manual handling operation?

---

[3] *Mains v Uniroyal Englebert Tyres Ltd*, 1995 S.L.T. 1115, but see what was said in *Baker v Quantum Clothing Group* [2011] UK SC 17.
[4] *Nimmo v Alexander Cowan*, 1967 S.L.T. 277.
[5] A phenomenon frequently observed by the author.

"Equipment" can now conceivably be subject to no less than four statutory regimes, and you will require to make detailed enquiries as to what the equipment was and when it was first provided.[6]

Anticipate an allegation of sole fault or contributory negligence by establishing the nature of any training and instruction your client has received, and what if anything he could have done to prevent the accident. All of these matters will be of critical importance in the claim, and are unlikely to be volunteered.

The truth is always in the details. Many accidents involve difficult facts and complicated processes. You must make a determined effort to comprehend these from the outset. This can be extremely time-consuming, particularly where technical matters are concerned. You must slow the client down until you understand what he is saying. Google will give you immediate access to a wealth of information about the technical processes involved. Many proprietary manufacturers of plant and equipment have their own websites carrying pictures and descriptions of their products. A specialist site such as "howstuffworks"[7] gives good general explanations of workings of almost all power tool equipment. Pictures of all kinds of equipment can be obtained from the Google "Images" site. By the end of the first interview, you should have sufficient material to enable you to form a provisional view on the basis of claim at statute and common law.

The client's statement

A good reliable statement from the client is the foundation stone of the whole case, whether at negotiation or litigation. Get it right the first time by taking full details from the client, understanding what he tells you and setting it out in a typewritten statement which you will send to the client for his approval, amendment, signature and return. The statement should be in the first person and past tense, all in his own words and expressions. There is always a temptation to avoid or omit "bad facts" or to put a gloss on what the client says in an effort to improve the litigation prospects. "Precognoscers as a whole appear to be gifted with a measure of optimism which no amount of disillusionment appears to damp."[8] Resist the temptation to embellish, and always include facts which appear adverse.

1–04

The format of the statement should be along the following lines:

    1. *Personal details*. Full name, and maiden surname (if applicable), of client, family details, date of birth, national insurance number (for Compensation Recovery Unit, hereafter referred to as

---

[6] See Provision and Use of Work Equipment Regulations 1998 (SI 1998/2306); Personal Protective Equipment at Work Regulations 1992 (SI 1992/2966); Workplace (Health, Safety and Welfare) Regulations 1992 (SI 1992/3004); Employers' Liability (Defective Equipment) Act 1969.
[7] *http://www.howstuffworks.com/* [Accessed September 8, 2011].
[8] *Kerr v HM Advocate*, 1958 S.L.T. 82, [84].

"CRU", purposes), address including postcode, telephone numbers, email address, current employment status, educational or trade qualifications.
2. *The accident context.* Set out the background to the accident.

   In workplace accidents this will mean describing the nature of the employer's business, your client's job description and his role in the process of the undertaking.

   In construction accidents you would describe the building under construction or renovation, advise when works began, what trades were on site, who was the main contractor, who was your client's employer, and your client's role in the construction process.

   In pavement tripping accidents you would describe the locus, confirm that it was maintained by the local authority, and establish where your client had been earlier and where he was going.

   In accidents involving machinery you would describe the kind of machine (including the proprietary name), describe how it worked, what it produced, who operated it, and what training was required.
3. *The accident circumstances.* There should be a chronological description of what happened and details of persons present. Note the names, addresses and telephone numbers of all potential witnesses. In workplace accidents always establish who your client's superior was, what instructions were given to the client, or what instructions should have been given. Note exactly what was said after the accident, particularly if it might be characterised as an admission.
4. *Surrounding circumstances.* Under this heading you will be looking for the kind of facts which might help to show that the accident was reasonably foreseeable, or that it was caused by some failure of instruction or training. You should take note of any previous complaint which relates to the accident circumstances, and note when and to whom these complaints were made. There may be a complaints book. Check whether there is a health and safety committee and find out if the accident was discussed at a health and safety meeting. Find out if there were any previous accidents or near misses which were similar in kind. Check what information about the preventive and protective measures has been provided to the client in terms of the employers' obligation under the Management of Health and Safety at Work Regulations 1999 r.10.
5. *Details of the injury.* You should have completed a damages pro forma at the first meeting. Extend this in the written statement, and note to cover all the heads of claim which are outlined in the quantum of damages section.

Your client has consulted you to obtain a legal remedy. So where, for example, the accident involves an injury caused by lifting, you should instinctively focus the statement on a possible breach of the Manual Handling Operations Regulations 1992. You would elicit from the client the weight of the items, and the frequency with which they were lifted, and take from him whether manual lifting could be eliminated completely or the dangers reduced by mechanical aids. It is a truism that unless you know the answers you are looking for, you will not know the questions to ask.

Above all the statement should not simply tell a story but should be directed towards a cause of action.

Relationship with the client

Research[9] has indicated that your client will place absolute trust in your ability to control the claims process, will seldom question your advice on quantum or liability, and will rarely change solicitors after initial instructions have been given. The following points should be explained at the first meeting:

- Liability will generally depend on negligence or breach of duty. Your office is not a cash dispenser machine. It can be helpful to explain matters by the use of a simple phrase such as "no claim without blame".
- Although the claim is directed against an organisation or individual, it will be settled by an insurance company who will control the defence from the outset. You should advise your client that you will attempt to negotiate a settlement with the insurers as soon as possible.
- Assure the client that you will proceed with all possible speed. Discuss a timetable, and tell the client that you will keep him advised of all significant developments. A reasonable framework might be the timetable contained in the Scottish Voluntary Pre-Action Protocol. The corollary of this is that you should not be expected to deal with frequent telephone calls and status enquiries, or to have impromptu meetings which are little more than hand-holding sessions.
- Make sure that the client realises that you expect his full co-operation and assistance. He will require to attend at all case meetings, and medical examinations. He will provide all documentary evidence and witness details as requested.

Anyone can open a file. There is no point in doing so unless you believe there is a realistic prospect of obtaining damages. If you decline to act either initially or at any stage thereafter it is important that you send a letter to the client explaining the position and advising him of the date of the expiry of the triennium.

---

[9] Hazel Genn, *Hard Bargaining, Out of Court Settlement in Personal Injury Actions* (Oxford: Oxford University Press, 1987).

AFTER THE MEETING

1–06 You should have a clear idea as to whether you intend to act. You may have already agreed this. It will save a lot of time in answering telephone enquiries if your standard Law Society engagement letter contains information as to the likely progress of the claim. You should extend your client's statement on liability and damages, know the names and addresses of potential witnesses, and consider other avenues for investigation. It is always worthwhile to send the statement on liability and damages to your client for revision, approval and signature. The statement should show the date it was taken, the date it was typed, and the client should add the date on which he signs it. It should also identify the person who took the statement. This ensures that all matters are properly addressed from the outset, and the case can proceed on a sound footing.

INITIAL ADVICE ON QUANTUM

1–07 In all but the most minor injuries, it is unwise to give any detailed quantification of the claim at the first interview. If you do set a figure, you can rest assured that your client will remember it when any caveats are forgotten. Explain that you will need to obtain evidence of loss before you can discuss the range of expected damages. Chapter 4 describes in detail the evidence which you will require to collect. At the first meeting you should obtain from your client, GP and hospital details and medical mandates for access to the medical records. You should obtain a general outline of wage loss, recent wage slips and a mandate to the client's employer for further wage details if required. Ask your client to keep receipts for property losses, and to note any extra travel or medical expenses which he might incur. In most orthopaedic injuries there will be some kind of services claim on behalf of a relative who provides assistance, such as dressing, cutting up food, washing and housekeeping. Take a file note of the helper's identity and a general picture of the level of care provided. In serious cases where this is likely to be significant, the advice should be that a carer's diary is kept noting the amount of time spent on the client by a named carer on a daily basis. It is helpful for the office to have a pro forma checklist on which all these matters are addressed from the outset.

Compensation Recovery Unit ("CRU")

1–08 It is never too early to introduce this subject. The client must be made aware of the effects of the Social Security Recoupment Regulations. Broach the subject at the first interview, to avoid having to spring a very rude surprise on your client at a later date. If in doubt check the position on the CRU page of the Department for Works and Pensions ("DWP") website.

BENEFITS ADVICE

If your client was working as an employed earner (including a company 1-09
director) and was injured in the course of his employment, he may be
eligible for industrial injuries disablement benefit. He must have suffered
an "industrial accident", or an industrial disease which arises from a
prescribed occupation. An industrial accident means simply an accident
that arose in the course of his employment, and benefit is not limited to
industrial workers. Prescribed diseases are referred to in a later chapter.
There is no need to prove fault, and cases where liability would be
extremely difficult to establish at common law are covered by the scheme,
e.g. accidents caused by skylarking or horseplay of another employee.

You will have to prove that the accident has caused a loss of faculty
and a percentage disablement which must be assessed at least 14 per cent.
The percentage assessment will be carried out by the DWP in accordance
with their own guidelines. The award may be final or provisional,
depending on the nature of the injury. Provisional assessments will be
reviewed at the end of the period. Where final assessments are made,
payment is for life, and very significant sums can be involved. Claims will
be accepted from nine weeks after the date of the accident, and there is a
90-day waiting period after which benefit can be paid.[10] Claims can be
made at any time and may be backdated, but only three months' arrears
will be paid. The information from the DWP forms can be very useful in
your claim at common law. The date and fact of the accident will be
established, and you can obtain access to medical information in the form
of the DWP medical reports. The courts may also look to the DWP
assessment in the evaluation of quantum.[11] An application form is
available from the local benefits office. Separate legal advice and assistance under legal aid is available to assist the client in completing the
form. Industrial injuries disablement benefit is a recoupable benefit in
terms of the Social Security (Recovery of Benefits) Act 1997, but only
against wage loss.

URGENT ACTION

In an ideal world you would receive your instructions shortly after the 1-10
accident from a client who brings photographs of the accident locus. In
fact there will be occasions when you are instructed so late that proceedings must be raised immediately to avoid the expiry of the triennium.
More frequently you will recognise situations where critical evidence is in
danger of disappearing unless urgent steps are taken to preserve it. All
you may need to do is direct the client to take photographs or to take

---

[10] A claimant for occupational deafness benefit must apply not later than five years after he last worked in a prescribed occupation, and he must have worked in that occupation for 10 years. Claims for occupational asthma must be made within 10 years of working in a prescribed occupation.

[11] See, e.g. *McNeill v Roche Products Ltd*, 1989 S.L.T. 498—DSS assessment noted at 35%.

photographs yourself. Occasionally you will require to take immediate court action using the provisions of the Administration of Justice (Scotland) Act 1972 to obtain inspection facilities.[12]

In appropriate cases, a summary application should be drafted immediately seeking the inspection, photographing or preservation of the documents or property. You will have to show that there is a prima facie case to answer, and that proceedings are likely to be brought. Where you are seeking the preservation of evidence you should say so in the petition. You must be able to state that proceedings are likely, even without the inspection, preservation, etc. of the property or documents in question.[13] This section can also be used where there is no particular urgency for inspection, etc. but you wish to see the item in question prior to the action being raised. A good example of this principle in action is the case of *Thorne v Strathclyde RC*,[14] where the pursuer was allowed pre-action inspection facilities of a machine to enable him to consider particular features of the machine. In that case the pursuer had formulated general allegations of fault, which he wished to make more specific following inspection.

---

[12] The text of the Act is set out in full at para.10–54.
[13] See the case of *Dominion Technology Ltd v Gardner Cryogenics Ltd (No.1)*, 1993 S.L.T. 828.
[14] *Thorne v Strathclyde RC*, 1984 S.L.T. 161.

CHAPTER 2

FUNDING THE FILE

The purpose of the initial meeting is to come to a preliminary assessment of the client and the claim, and to decide whether you will act. You should make clear at the outset the basis on which this meeting proceeds (e.g. legal advice and assistance, free first interview, fixed fee interview), but there is no need to launch into a detailed discussion about costs at this stage. Your approach will depend to a large extent on the client's story and the strength of the case. After you have decided to act, it is a professional obligation to send out a written engagement letter containing at least the information prescribed by the Law Society. This chapter considers some of the options. **2–01**

THE LEGAL AID SCHEME

The Scottish Legal Aid Board ("SLAB") currently estimates that 75 per cent of all adults in Scotland are now eligible for legal aid. Practitioner experience suggests the figure is considerably lower. On any view the legal aid scheme is a significant aspect of the personal injury landscape. You may well be advising persons at a particularly vulnerable life stage, where injury has left them out of work, in receipt of benefits and eligible for legal aid. The details of the scheme, including the governing legislation, and practical guidelines on the Board's policies are contained in the SLAB's online guide *Civil Legal Assistance Handbook* ("The Guide").[1] The following is not in any way meant to replace the official Guide, but highlights some practice points. The Board has gone completely online and digital as from March 2011. Please note that the following paragraph references relate to the Guide. **2–02**

The Legal Advice and Assistance Scheme

This covers preliminary investigation and preparation of the claim, negotiation with the insurers, and preparation of a civil legal aid application if negotiations fail. Form AA/APP/CIV can quite properly be used and submitted for the initial interview, even where the subsequent advice is not to proceed with the claim. Where an initial home visit is required for a housebound client, reasonable travelling time to the client's home can be charged. The Board advises at Pt III para.2.5 that the solicitor **2–03**

---

[1] See *http://www.slab.org.uk/profession/handbook/Civilhandbookmastercopy* [Accessed September 9, 2011].

requires to see documentary evidence of income and capital, including wages statement, benefit statement and bank or savings statement. Whilst it is possible to commence advice and assistance without sight of this information, it can cause difficulties further down the line if it is not provided, so it is prudent to address the matter before significant work is carried out.

Increases

2–04 The initial limit of expenditure is £95. The solicitor can self certify an immediate increase to £180, but only where civil legal aid is available for court proceedings, and the matter is likely to be resolved only by preparing for court. In particular self certification is not appropriate for prescribed Industrial Injuries Benefit applications.

Requests for an increase—the Template Increase Scheme

2–05 Since the last edition of this book, the Board have made significant improvements to the Scheme with regard to increases for further necessary work. Part III para.5.1 describes areas where the Template Increase Scheme applies. Paragraphs 52 and 53 set out the Template Increase Scheme for personal injury claims.

- For claims between £3,000—£10,000 you can apply for an immediate template increase to £750.00.
- For claims in excess of £10,000 you can apply for an immediate template increase to £1,200.00.

The purpose is to cover the following further work:

1. Intimating the claim.
2. Obtaining medical records.
3. Instructing, obtaining and reading a medical report.
4. Entering negotiation with opponent.
5. Corresponding and meeting with client as necessary.
6. Obtaining statements from witnesses (two statements allowed).
7. Assisting the applicant in applying for civil legal aid if negotiations prove unsuccessful.

Non-template increases

2–06 These should only be necessary in cases where damages are below £3,000. Before obtaining an increase, the Board will expect to know:

- What happened.
- Why it should not have happened.
- Whether the injuries are a direct result.
- What the loss is.
- Whether a claim has been intimated.

(See Pt III para.5.97.)

With this level of damages, the Board are seeking your assurances that negotiations are meaningful, and that the Scheme is not being used as a blank cheque to fund work where there is no realistic prospect of recovery. Very many solatium-only claims fall within this bracket, and increases for further necessary work will be granted provided you address the necessary criteria. You will have to state the further work which you intend to carry out, but reference to the work described in the template increase will usually suffice.

Recovery of fees from principal sum

One of the most difficult concepts for the client to understand is that he is legally aided only if he loses. If there is any recovery, then, subject to a Hardship Application, fees and expenses must be recovered from the principal sum. The test for hardship is now extremely stringent.[2] In the nature of things this is not going to cause a problem until the case is completed and the client sees his damages reduced. You must always be conscious of this when negotiating any extra-judicial settlement, particularly where small sums are involved. Many insurers want to pay no costs at all on settlements of under £750, and your fees will have to come out of the sum recovered. The Board's advice is that an explanation should be given to the client at the start of the case. Most clients will ignore or misunderstand any explanation. The reality is that the advice *must* be given before any settlement is agreed.

Civil legal aid—section one certificate

Application for a legal aid certificate

The application must now be made online, and has three essential elements:

    (a) Completed application form.
    (b) Signed Statutory Statement (formerly the Legal Aid memo) as to the nature of the case and the client's interest in it.
    (c) Evidential statements and documents.

2–07

2–08

The Guide contains detailed advice on the kind of information which is required. In particular an applicant will require to show:

    1. Probable cause.
    2. Reasonableness.

Probable cause

The Board will require to see evidence that the claim is soundly based in law. Part IV para.4.65 provides a detailed checklist of the Board's requirements in this area. It is worth repeating in full.

2–09

---

[2] Advice and Assistance (Scotland) Regulations 1996 (SI 1996/382) reg.16(3).

"Evidential requirements—pursuer applications
This section gives information about the general evidential requirements for an application to raise reparation proceedings. You should also refer to the individual guidelines covering specific types of reparation claims applications should include:

- A statement by the applicant detailing the circumstances that resulted in the injury or loss. This should:
    - give a clear, unambiguous and adequately detailed picture of what happened, where and when;
    - include details of the applicant's title to sue and describe any duties of care owed by the opponent whether in common law or by statute;
    - give full details of any prior complaints about the practices or hazards that led to the injury;
    - give details of the loss or injury suffered, with an estimation of the amount of damages sought;
    - in cases involving injury or losses sustained because of prolonged acts or omissions by the opponent, give information about when the applicant became aware that these losses or injuries justified raising the action;
    - contain information about any earnings before and after the accident, with details of time spent off work, with vouching to support this, if available; and
    - supply any information about the applicant's future employability, restrictions on their domestic or social life and details of dependency on, or services received from, others.

- Any photographs and sketches of the hazard that are available.
- Supporting information if it is available. If supporting information is not available, an explanation should be given.
- A medical report in case involving personal injuries, particularly if the injuries are of a more modest nature where careful consideration needs to be given to the level of damages being sought.
- Any expert reports that have been obtained showing liability or causation.
- All relevant ancillary documents such as wages certificates, contracts, police reports or receipts where appropriate to vouch any alleged losses or breach of duties.
- Information about the steps taken to negotiate the claim and to settle without raising court proceedings. Details of any response received from the opponent should be provided with information about any offers of settlement made and the reasons these are not acceptable.
- Details about the prospects of recovery in the case."

There are also particular requirements for the following types of case:

4.66 Road traffic accidents.
4.68 Accidents at work.
4.69 Industrial disease claims.
4.70 Tripping cases.
4.72 Condensation or dampness claims.
13.74 MRSA claims.

Reasonableness

In assessing reasonableness a number of factors will be taken into account including: **2–10**

- the value of the claim;
- the prospects of recovery; and
- attempts made to negotiate settlement of the claim without referral to court.

There is detailed advice at Pt IV para.3.3 of the Guide. Pay particular attention to the section marked "Prospects of Success". The Board have observed that in almost all solicitor applications the prospects are marked "excellent" or "good". They have made it clear that they will not take this assessment at face value. You must give particulars to enable the Board to place the case in a numerical category which they employ. You should have a standard format for legal aid applications where all of these matters are addressed before the application is decided, rather than dealing with matters behind hand at the review stage.

Legal aid statements

The legal aid statutory statement is perhaps better known to practitioners as the "legal aid memo". Each application must be accompanied by an outline memo containing a brief indication of the facts and law relied upon, which must be signed both by the applicant and the solicitor. You must ensure that any statement in the memo is absolutely accurate. Your opponent can found on the memo, as evidence on credibility,[3] and also as evidence of its contents in terms of the Civil Evidence (Scotland) Act 1988 s.2(1)(b). **2–11**

Review of refusal

The review must normally be lodged within 15 days of refusal, although you can ask for extra time if there is a special reason. The applicant must sign the application for review. You should include a statement of any matters which you wish the Board to consider, including any further statements or documents, and then re-submit all papers which accompanied the original application. **2–12**

---

[3] *Healy v A. Massey and Son Ltd*, 1961 S.L.T. 235.

Effect of Legal Aid Certificate

2–13 The client must again be advised that the Legal Aid Board will only pay his expenses if he loses. A standard letter should be sent explaining this, adding that if he is unsuccessful the client may be found liable in the defender's expenses, but that this is frequently modified to the extent of his legal aid contribution. He should be advised that his legal costs will constitute a first charge against any damages recovered, and that he should contact the Board if there is a significant change in his financial circumstances. The client should be designed in the instance on all steps of process as an assisted person. In practice this means adding the abbreviation "A.P." on each part of the instance where the pursuer's name appears. Failure to do so might well result in the court's refusal to modify expenses[4] (and a claim for professional negligence). The certificate must be lodged in process, and intimation made to the defender.[5] It is usually convenient to lodge the legal aid certificate at the same time as the initial writ is returned to court, when the action is defended.[6] If at any time the certificate is terminated or suspended, the opponent must be advised. Where legal aid has been in place for 24 months and no final account has been submitted a Stage Report using the form Civ/Rep must be sent.

Fee exemptions

2–14 Where legal aid has been granted, assisted persons have the benefit of a fee exemption order. This proceeds on an application form signed by the solicitor at the outset of the case or entitlement. Thereafter for subsequent events in the proceedings an abbreviated docquet confirming entitlement should be submitted by the solicitor. These forms are available on the Scottish Courts website.[7]

Sanction for experts

2–15 An expert witness is entitled to give opinion evidence on scientific matters which are outwith the ordinary experience of the judge or jury. He generally has no unique factual information about the case and cannot be obliged to testify on that basis. In an ordinary action the Board will normally grant sanction on request for at least one medical expert and one specialist expert, e.g. ergonomist, health and safety expert. The Board have set up a template system for expert witnesses. Application is made on form CIV/SANCTION. There are two categories. The first is a template increase where there is no need to send substantial information such as pleadings, as long as the expert's fee is within the template limit. You should note that this sanction will not cover a supplementary report of any kind, even where there is funding left over from the original grant. Where the fee is in excess of the template limit, or there are other com-

---

[4] *James Sims Ltd v Haynes*, 1968 S.L.T. (Sh. Ct.) 76.
[5] Civil Legal Aid Rules 1987 r.3(1)–(4).
[6] OCR 9.3.
[7] *http://www.scotcourts.gov.uk/* [Accessed September 9, 2011].

plexities, you require to go to section E of the form and make a detailed application sending pleadings and fee funding justification. Where a template sanction has been granted you do not require to make a further request to cover an expert's attendance at court, provided the costs of the attendance are within the limits shown in the CIV/SANCTION form. General practitioners and treating consultants are not "experts" as such. Neither is the photographer whom you instruct to photograph the accident locus. They are factual witnesses. Theoretically you do not require prior sanction from the Board. The reality is that these persons will charge like expert witnesses, and the Board should be notified in advance. You must clear any significant item of expenditure in advance with the Board.[8]

Settlement in legal aid cases

Where advice and assistance has been granted, the principal sum and any expenses recovered must be forwarded to the Board with the legal advice and assistance account. If you are accepting expenses recovered from the defender with no claims against the Legal Aid Fund, there is no need to forward any monies. The principal sum can be sent to the client, and expenses taken to fees. Where the expenses recovered are less than the amount claimed in fees, the fee will be deducted from the principal sum. Where a civil legal aid certificate has been issued, you should ask your opponent to make the principal sum payable to the client, or to yourself. If you are accepting judicial expenses in full of your claim against the Board, you can pay the principal sum immediately to the client. In personal injury actions the Board will expect you to take steps to recover the judicial expenses from your opponent by way of agreement or taxation. Alternatively, you can charge an agent and client account under the legal aid certificate. Currently legal aid rates are less than one half of judicial rates. In straightforward cases where the pursuer has been successful, it is generally more profitable to accept judicial expenses, provided there are no significant contra-findings in the course of the action. Any shortfall between the amount claimed under the civil legal aid certificate and the judicial expenses recovered from your opponent will be deducted from the principal sum, and there is no discretion or hardship application available. What this means in practice is that you must never settle or compromise actions on a "no expenses due to or by" basis, but must always seek to recover the judicial expenses from your opponent. All of this may take some time to resolve, and you should ask the Board to make an interim payment to account of the principal sum, ensuring that they retain any possible shortfall. Acceptance of judicial expenses in full of your claim against the fund extinguishes any right to claim for work carried out under Legal Advice and Assistance.

2–16

---

[8] Civil Legal Aid (Scotland) Regulations 1987 (SI 1987/381) reg.21.

Increases against the fund

2–17 In cases of special difficulty you can seek to charge an increase on your agent and client account against the fund. The grounds are[9]:

(a) the complexity of the proceedings and the number, difficulty or novelty of the questions involved;
(b) the skill, specialised knowledge and responsibility required of and the time and labour expended by the solicitor;
(c) the number and importance of the documents prepared or perused;
(d) the place and circumstances of the proceedings in which the solicitor's work of preparation for and conduct of it has been carried out;
(e) the importance of the proceedings or the subject matter thereof to the client;
(f) the amount or value of money or property involved;
(g) the steps taken with a view to settling the proceedings, limiting the matters in dispute or limiting the scope of any hearing; and
(h) any other fees and allowances payable to the solicitor in respect of other items in the same proceedings and otherwise charged for in the account.

You may apply for an increase whether the case is won or lost, and the increase against the legal aid fund is independent and separate from any motion against your opponent for an increase in judicial expenses, although it is submitted that much the same considerations should apply. The application is made to the sheriff by motion,[10] and either an account of expenses, or an estimate of the probable amount of expenses (separating fees and outlays), should be attached. The motion should specify the grounds relied upon. On receipt of the motion the court may thereafter dismiss the application. Where it does not do so, it will fix a hearing. The solicitor must intimate to the Board, giving 14 days' notice. The Board is entitled to appear or be represented at any hearing on the motion. The Board can also cite any party to the cause (including your client). The rationale for the last provision is that where the solicitor is awarded an increase as against the legal aid fund, there might be a reduction of any principal sum payable to the client by way of damages. The Board will not cite your client in unsuccessful cases where there is no award of damages to be reduced. In successful actions, it is generally more profitable for the solicitor to accept judicial expenses in full and final settlement of the claim against the fund. In that situation there is usually no advantage in seeking an increase under the legal aid certificate, although you may wish to take the advice of your law accountants in this regard. Where the action has been unsuccessful and no damages have been recovered, application should be made if appropriate.

---

[9] The Civil Legal (Scotland) (Fees) Regulations 1989 (SI 1989/1490) reg.5(4).
[10] See Civil Legal Aid Rules 1987 (SI 1987/492) reg.7.

PRIVATE FUNDING

2–18 The days when clients would ask the cost of legal services and be fobbed off with well worn platitudes like "how long is a piece of string?" are long gone, even for the litigation department. If you are acting privately, it should be possible to give a written estimate of the cost to the client of investigating the claim, obtaining reports, and attempting to negotiate a settlement. If negotiations are successful, the insurers will normally meet your extra-judicial settlement fee, based on the pre-action protocol agreement. You are not restricted to this amount if you have completed a written fee agreement with your client in advance under s.61A(1) of the Solicitors (Scotland) Act 1980. In those circumstances you are not obliged to concur in any remit to the auditor for taxation, which is the general rule where a solicitor sues for fees.

CONDITIONAL FEE AGREEMENTS

2–19 The Solicitors (Scotland) Act 1980 s.61A(3) now makes it competent for solicitors to enter into a speculative fee agreement with the client for litigation work only. This enables you to charge a success fee to clients on the understanding that no fee will be charged if the client is unsuccessful. The success element is calculated as an agreed percentage uplift on the judicial expenses recovered, excluding the elements for post, incidents and outlays. Separately an agreement under the Solicitors (Scotland) Act 1980 s.61A(1) enables the solicitor to charge a percentage uplift on an agent and client basis. These arrangements are not contingency fee agreements, whereby the solicitor agrees in advance to accept a percentage slice of any damages awarded. Such an arrangement is a *pactum de quota litis*. It is prohibited to solicitors, and unenforceable by them.[11] The utility of the speculative agreement was previously extremely limited. The expenses payable to the other side if the action was lost meant that for middle value cases the speculative action was attractive only to the most determined litigant or the man of straw. The client can now take out an "after the event" insurance policy against losing the action, for payment of a single premium.

CASH FLOW

2–20 Cash flow presents a particular problem for all litigation practices. Work in progress and outlays have to be funded out of this year's profits for files which will be paid some years hence at previous years' rates. Every opportunity should be examined to minimise and recover outlays. In legal aid cases where a civil legal aid certificate has been issued, outlays which have been paid under advice and assistance, and also under the s.1 certificate, can be recovered in certain circumstances. The civil legal aid

---

[11] *Quantum Claims Compensation Specialists Ltd v Powell*, 1997 S.C.L.R. 242.

certificate must be in existence at the date of claim, the action must not be concluded, and the outlays must actually have been incurred. They don't have to be paid, i.e. there must be an invoice but not necessarily a receipt. The outlays must total at least £150. Subject to these conditions, reimbursement will be made by SLAB using form SLA/ROL/1. Where outlays of £100 or over have been made under advice and assistance, or where the sum of combined outlays under advice and assistance and the civil legal aid certificate amounts to at least £150, there is a civil legal aid certificate in existence, and the action has not been concluded, application can be made for reimbursement using form SLA/ROL/2. SLAB will also make an interim payment to account of fees in accordance with reg.11 of the Civil Legal Aid (Scotland) Fees Regulations 1989. At least two years must have elapsed since the effective date of the certificate, or there must have been 20 days of proof. The Board will pay 75 per cent of your estimate of fees at the date of the application. You should complete SLAB form SLA/POA/3 in all appropriate cases.

No win, no fee

2–21 One observer has stated that "no win, no fee" has "kicked open the doors of court for middle income clients".[12] However it has to be said that its introduction has also heralded a particularly turbulent period for practitioners. There is no doubt about the public appetite for this kind of arrangement as shown by the initial success of claims management companies such as Claims Direct. The challenge for the legal profession in Scotland is to establish itself as a client friendly first port of call for all accident victims. It is probably the duty of the solicitor to advise a client of the existence of alternative funding such as legal aid, trade union backing or legal expenses insurance. But there is no obligation on a solicitor to act on a legal aid basis, as long as the client is able to make an informed choice. Solicitors will now have to conduct their own risk assessment of cases and clients, or face up to hours of wasted time and work. The overwhelming majority of court actions are now conducted on a speculative basis. "No win, no fee" has changed the litigation landscape irrevocably.

---

[12] Michael Napier, writing in *The Times*, July 11, 1995.

CHAPTER 3

CONSTRUCTING THE CLAIM ON LIABILITY

HOW JUDGES DECIDE

In the case of *Karanakaran*,[1] Lord Justice Sedley stated: **3–01**

> "The civil standard of proof, which treats anything which probably happened as having definitely happened, is part of a pragmatic legal fiction. It has no logical bearing on the assessment of the likelihood of future events or (by parity of reasoning) the quality of past ones. It is true that in general legal process partitions its material so as to segregate past events and apply the civil standard of proof to them: so that liability for negligence will depend on a probabilistic conclusion as to what happened. But this is by no means the whole process of reasoning. In a negligence case, for example, the question will arise whether what happened was reasonably foreseeable. There is no rational means of determining this on a balance of probabilities: the court will consider the evidence, including its findings as to past facts, and answer the question as posed. More importantly, and more relevantly, a civil judge will not make a discrete assessment of the probable veracity of each item of the evidence: he or she will reach a conclusion on the probable factuality of an alleged event by evaluating *all* the evidence about it *for what it is worth*. Some will be so unreliable as to be worthless; some will amount to no more than straws in the wind; some will be indicative but not, by itself, probative; some may be compelling but contra-indicated by other evidence. It is only at the end-point that, for want of a better yardstick, a probabilistic test is applied. Similarly a jury trying a criminal case may be told by the trial judge that in deciding whether they are sure of the defendant's guilt they do not have to discard every piece of evidence which they are not individually sure is true: they should of course discard anything they think suspect and anything which in law must be disregarded, but for the rest each element of the evidence should be given the weight and prominence they think right and the final question answered in the light of all of it. So it is fallacious to think of probability (or certainty) as a uniform criterion

---

[1] *Karanakaran v Secretary of State for the Home Department* [2000] 3 All E.R. 449.

of fact-finding in our courts: it is no more than the final touchstone, appropriate to the nature of the issue, for testing a body of evidence of often diverse cogency."[2]

In litigation, as in all dramatic art, a persuasive story:

- accounts for or explains all of the known or undisputed or undeniable facts in a way which is preferable to the defenders' counter story;
- has persons acting in character and provides reasons for their actions;
- accords with common sense and the known rules of plausibility, and is supported by details; and
- is told by credible witnesses.

It is even better if the story concerns a pursuer whose evidence, demeanour and moderation causes the judge to want to find for him.

3–02 Think inside the box from the moment the file is opened. The lawyer's art consists in the identification of evidence, the preservation of evidence and the presentation of evidence. Identification of evidence means using your knowledge both of the rules of evidence, and also of the substantive law to know what to look for, to be aware of the hierarchy of evidence and to find and keep what is likely to weigh most heavily.

All of this may seem to be stating the obvious, but in practice many solicitors view the collection of evidence as something to be addressed only after negotiations have broken down. The nature of the evidence will vary from case to case, but determined efforts to obtain it at an early stage will pay rich dividends throughout the negotiation and litigation process.

DOCUMENTARY EVIDENCE

3–03 Although it may seem counter-intuitive, contemporaneous written evidence where available is generally much more compelling than oral testimony. A frequently cited passage is the dicta of Lord Justice Goff in *The Ocean Frost*[3] where he said:

> "Speaking from my own experience I have found it essential in cases of fraud when considering the credibility of witnesses always to test their veracity by reference to the objective facts proved independently of their testimony, in particular by reference to the documents in the cases and also to pay particular regards to their motives and to the overall probabilities."

---

[2] This formulation has been specifically approved in Scotland. See Lord Glennie in *Morton v West Lothian Council* [2005] CSOH 142 and Lord Brodie in *Gibson v Whyte* [2007] CSOH 17.

[3] *The Ocean Frost* [1985] 1 Lloyd's Rep. 1.

Frequently documentary evidence has been drawn at a time where there is no immediate thought of litigation and parties have not made their dispositions. Critical sources are:

1. The initial medical attendance.
2. The accident report.
3. The record of any contemporary accident investigation.

You should be aware that if the case proceeds to litigation, these records will feature prominently in any subsequent proof. Additionally, the written records should be a critical part of your ongoing case assessment. There will be times when it will be clear from these initial records that the client's case cannot survive the scrutiny described by Lord Justice Sedley. In that case withdraw sooner rather than later.

Medical records

In serious cases the likelihood is that your client will have attended the Accident and Emergency Department of the hospital nearest the accident locus. The admission record will show the time of arrival and the initial incident narrative. Medical staff are quite properly more concerned with treatment than obtaining a reliable history, and the records at this stage are notoriously inaccurate. Moreoever what is noted on the first attendance sheet tends to be repeated on the subsequent hospital notes. So discrepancies are to be expected. General Practitioner notes are in a different category. Usually there have been a few days before an appointment can be obtained. Whilst GPs might not be concerned with the difference between a slip and a trip anything which constitutes a major inconsistency should give you considerable pause. There may be an explanation, but your client's GP as an adverse witness is a difficult hurdle to overcome.

3–04

The accident report

Under the Reporting of Injuries, Diseases and Dangerous Occurrences Regulations 1995 ("RIDDOR"), various reporting requirements are placed on employers. Any accidents connected with work where an employee is killed or suffers a major injury; a member of the public is killed or taken to hospital; an employee is away from work following an accident for more than three days; an employee suffers from a reportable disease; a dangerous occurrence or near miss; or a reportable gas incident where someone has died or suffered a major injury in connection with gas supply must be reported to the Health and Safety Executive ("HSE") or the Environmental Health Department of a Local Authority. There are four HSE offices in Scotland, located in Edinburgh, Glasgow, Aberdeen and Inverness. A small number of these incidents will be investigated by the HSE, and an even smaller number will result in a prosecution under the Health and Safety at Work Act 1974. If your client is seriously injured and there appears to have been no HSE involvement, you should not hesitate to report the matter directly and ask them to investigate. Where

3–05

there is a successful prosecution, the copy complaint and extract conviction should be obtained as previously described. In other cases you can see the HSE report and photographs on payment of a fee. The HSE officials are generally anxious to emphasise that these are simply factual reports, i.e. they do not constitute expert or opinion evidence on best practice. Very frequently the information which the factual statement contains is extremely limited. Where there has been a serious accident, the HSE will have investigated, taken statements including handwritten statements and perhaps produced a technical report. These will generally be made available on request, albeit in redacted format after any criminal proceedings have been concluded. There may well be letters to the defender company advising on a change of system of working following the accident. The full and unredacted file can only be recovered by way of specification of documents once proceedings are raised, or by a pre-action summary application in terms of the Administration of Justice (Scotland) Act 1972. The safety responsibility for shops and offices lies not with the HSE, but with the Environmental Health Services of the local authority.

Health and safety online

3–06 The internet has added a new dimension to investigation work. The HSE website is by far the most useful. The topic index gives access to HSE leaflets and free publications which can be downloaded and printed out. The "Bookfinder" section enables a search to be made for all HSE publications, which can be ordered direct or frequently downloaded for free. These official guidelines and literature prepared by organisations such as the HSE, the British Standards Institution or the Royal Society for the Prevention of Accidents are very useful shortcuts on liability. They are frequently accepted by the courts as authoritative statements of good practice. Approved Codes of Practice are issued by the HSE under s.16 of the Health and Safety at Work Act 1974. The objective is to provide practical guidance to statutory provisions, or regulations. They enjoy a special status in criminal proceedings, in that where the provisions of the Code are relevant to an alleged contravention, a failure to observe those provisions is enough for conviction, unless the court is satisfied that there have been other measures which have secured compliance. Failure to observe the terms of a Code does not of itself establish civil liability. The cause of the action is not the breach of the Code, but the common law failure to take reasonable care, with the Code indicating the contents of that duty. It is significant that the "competent person" who now has to assist in the health and safety arrangements under the Management of Health and Safety at Work Regulations 1999 ("MHSWR"), is expected to be conversant with best practice and recent literature, including presumably the HSE publication list.[4] Papers which are out of print can generally be supplied by the British Library.

The most useful practitioner resource is the HSE gateway publication, *Essentials of Health and Safety at Work*, 4th edn, available free online.[5]

---

[4] MHSWR, *Approved Code of Practice*, paras 46–47.
[5] *http://www.hse.gov.uk/pubns/books/essentials.htm* [Accessed September 9, 2011].

This contains guidance on a diverse variety of topics, including risk assessment, personal protective equipment, stress at work and the safe use of machinery, and has an in-depth reading list on each subject. The great advantage for the practitioner is that he has immediate access to invaluable practical and technical information without incurring the expense of an expert report at this stage. The specialist publications, which are obtained on a case-by-case basis, should be filed together to form a practitioner health and safety library.

OFFICIAL EVIDENCE

The importance of independent evidence has already been stressed. Evidence which is both independent and official carries even more weight. The main sources are considered below.

Police evidence

Police involvement may arise in any number of situations, but the most common is the road traffic accident. A preliminary enquiry and payment will obtain a police abstract of the accident, containing witness details and the identity of the reporting officer. Where criminal proceedings are pending, no precognition facility of police witnesses will be granted. There is nothing to stop you contacting the civilian witnesses. Where proceedings are pending, your client will generally be involved. If the case proceeds to trial, it is advisable to keep a watching brief, noting all the evidence. You might wish to extend a typewritten transcript, but you should in any event keep your own handwritten notes, which can be produced in evidence if necessary. Where there is a plea of guilty or a conviction which is relevant to the cause of action, you should write to the sheriff clerk with details and ask for an extract conviction and a copy of the original complaint, with the relevant fee. Such a conviction is admissible in terms of the Law Reform (Miscellaneous Provisions) (Scotland) Act 1968 s.10, and the effect is to transfer the onus of proof to the defender. Where no proceedings are being taken, or where the prosecution is unsuccessful, steps should be taken to interview the reporting officer as quickly as possible. Payment will require to be made to the chief constable before a meeting can be arranged. At the meeting you should establish the level of road traffic knowledge and expertise of the officers involved. In serious accidents the local police officers will generally be first to the scene, but will thereafter contact the traffic police. The traffic police will take measurements, note vehicle and impact positions, and obtain witness statements, which are kept in a police notebook. They will frequently take photographs and prepare a sketch plan. Copies of the sketch plan and photographs will normally be provided on payment of a fee. At the interview, ask the officer to read from the police notebook, and find out what his evidence is based on. The traffic police by reason of their experience, training and qualifications are expert witnesses. Whilst the ultimate issue of what constitutes reasonable care is always for the court, the views of these police witnesses will be very influential. Ordinary police officers who attend accidents will usually be witnesses only to facts. One aspect which should always be investigated is what the various participants said to the police. This might be in response to a formal caution and charge, but might simply be hearsay admissible under the Civil Evidence (Scotland) Act 1988.

Freedom of Information (Scotland) Act 2002

3–09 This came into force on January 1, 2005. In the nature of things Scottish public authorities are major employers, occupiers and organisations with general duties to members of the public. They are routine defenders in personal injury actions, and are subject to the terms of the above Act ("FOISA"). The full list of Scottish public authorities is contained in Sch.1 of the Act but includes local authorities, the Scottish Executive, universities and further education colleges. Each authority should set up a publication scheme to ensure that information which they hold can be accessed by members of the public. A Code of Guidance has been issued. For practitioners the first stopping point should be the Freedom of Information Commissioner's website "*itspublicknowledge*"[6] where there is a full library of all recent decisions by the Information Commissioner, helpfully catalogued by statutory reference. Some information may be treated as exempt under either "absolute exemption", or "qualified exemption". The authority should provide the information within 20 days of the request. Where the request is refused or otherwise not implemented, the applicant should then request an internal review. If still dissatisfied, the applicant has the right of appeal to the Information Commissioner. In the main the courts have interpreted the legislation widely. In *Common Services Agency v Scottish Information Commissioner*[7] the applicant sought details of recorded instances of childhood leukemia. The authority originally refused on the basis that there might be indirect identification of living individuals, and consequently a breach of the Data Protection Act 1998. The Inner House upheld the Information Commissioner's decision that the information should be sent to the applicant in a "barnardised" format, where individuals were not identified. Lord Marnoch stated:

> "I am of the opinion that the statute, whose whole purpose is to secure the release of information, should be construed in as liberal a manner as possible and, so long as individual and other private rights are respected, and the cost limits are not exceeded, I do not myself see any reason why the Commissioner should not be awarded the widest discretion in deciding the form and type of information which should be released in furtherance of its objectives, including that of giving advice and assistance under Section 15 of the Act."

---

[6] *http://www.itspublicknowledge.info/home/ScottishInformationCommissioner.asp* [Accessed September 9, 2011].
[7] *Common Services Agency v Scottish Information Commissioner* [2006] CSIH 58.

Note that the obligation is to provide "information". There is no right to insist on the production of a particular document, only the information contained in it.[8]

ORAL EVIDENCE

Witnesses to the facts should be contacted as quickly as possible. The client will have supplied some addresses, and you should impress on him the need to obtain and provide further names wherever possible. The ideal way of obtaining statements is to have the witness attend at your office, where a detailed statement can be taken. The reality is that most witnesses do not wish to become involved in legal process. The only persons likely to accept your invitation are friends and relatives of the pursuer. Whilst it is helpful to know what they will say, you must remember that the sheriff will not treat their evidence as wholly disinterested. It is the independent witnesses who will hold the key. No one is legally obliged to assist you in any way at this stage. A comparatively painless way of obtaining information is by the use of witness questionnaires. This method is routinely used by insurance companies. These can be in a standard form, e.g. road traffic accidents, or specially adapted by you to the circumstances of the accident. The accompanying letter should be courteous and polite, and should emphasise that completion of the questionnaire might prevent the need for court proceedings. It must be sent out with a stamped addressed envelope. You should always acknowledge with thanks the return of the questionnaire, even when its contents are adverse to your client's case. The returned questionnaire will give you an opportunity to make contact by a follow-up telephone call, and to clarify or expand on any information. If the questionnaire is not returned, or you are dissatisfied with the information, you should consider using an enquiry agent. Your instructions to the agent should contain an outline of the facts of the case, with specific questions for the witnesses. It is also helpful to ask the enquiry agent for an informal assessment of witness credibility. In important cases, there is no substitute for speaking to the witness yourself, and you should arrange to call at the witness's convenience. **3–10**

EVIDENTIAL STATUS OF STATEMENTS

It is good practice to have full statements extended and then sent to the witness to be signed, dated and acknowledged as correct. There may be circumstances where the court will accept this kind of statement on its own as evidence of its contents, e.g. the witness might disappear or die. As long as the court is satisfied that it is truly a statement, and not simply a precognition (i.e. a version of events which is filtered through the mind of the solicitor), then it is admissible under the Civil Evidence (Scotland) **3–11**

---

[8] *Glasgow City Council v Scottish Information Commissioner*, 2010 S.C. 125.

Act 1988. In *Ellison v Inspirations East Limited*,[9] it was accepted that handwritten notes taken by a solicitor did not constitute a precognition and were admissible for what they were worth. In the case of *Highland Venison Marketing Ltd v Allwild GmbH*[10] Lord Cullen indicated that where a solicitor drew a precognition in the presence of a witness, sent the precognition to the witness for revisals, made alterations in terms of the revisals and then had the document retyped and signed, it was an admissible statement and not a precognition. Effectively the witness had adopted the statement as his own.[11] These situations occur relatively infrequently, and there will always be doubts about the weight of such evidence. Much greater scope arises for the use of statements or questionnaires in cross-examination. You can always attack witness credibility on the grounds that he said something different on a previous occasion. Handwritten material can be used with devastating effect.

LIABILITY QUICK FIX: THE SOLICITOR AS INVESTIGATOR

Locus inspection

3–12 It can be very difficult to understand what has happened from verbal descriptions. Develop the habit of examining the locus wherever possible. Obvious examples are road traffic, pavement tripper, or occupiers' liability accidents. It can be difficult to obtain access to factories, in which case the client should be asked to obtain photographs. A locus inspection by the solicitor can put all the witness statements in an entirely different light.

Photographs

3–13 Seeing is believing, and nothing has quite the evidential impact of good photographic evidence. Every office should have a camera. The photographs do not have to be state of the art, and certainly at the preliminary stage there is usually no need to hire a professional photographer. You should use the camera to photograph accident sites, damaged vehicles, damaged property and of course the victim's injuries. This can be particularly important where there are painful but transient injuries, such as extensive bruising. Use the camera's date facility, and don't print anything smaller than 5" x 7".

---

[9] *Ellison v Inspirations East Limited*, 2003 S.L.T. 291.
[10] *Highland Venison Marketing Ltd v Allwild GmbH*, 1982 S.L.T. 1127.
[11] Cf. *McAvoy v City of Glasgow District Council*, 1993 S.L.T. at [859] where a statement taken and revised by a solicitor remained a precognition and was inadmissible. Note that what was said to the solicitor by the deceased witness in that case was admissible *quantum valeat*.

CHAPTER 4

EVIDENCE ON DAMAGES

This chapter does not consider in any detail the substantive law on quantification of damages, but rather addresses the evidence which the practitioner should collect at the same time as constructing the case on liability. This will be presented either to the insurers or solicitors during negotiations, or thereafter to the court. **4–01**

MEDICAL EVIDENCE

Your concern is to have a report which is comprehensive and authoritative. In all but very minor injuries, you should instruct a consultant. Insurers do not instruct general practitioners, and are unlikely to be impressed by the contents of a GP report. Typically, your client will have been seen at the accident and emergency department of a hospital near the accident locus. He might have further hospital treatment there as an inpatient, or be transferred to his local hospital, or be discharged to the care of his GP. In these circumstances, you should obtain a consultant's report, making sure that you instruct the speciality to the injury. Should the treating consultant be instructed? The treating consultant knows your client and the case notes, and the court will sometimes take this into account. However, there is a natural tendency for the treating doctor to believe in the success of his own handiwork, and to minimise future problems. This is harmless enough in simple cases where there is full recovery. In serious cases the insurers will instruct one of a relatively small number of consultants on their list. These persons tend to be not only eminent medical practitioners, but tried and tested court performers accustomed to justifying their opinions under cross-examination. On balance, where you think there are likely to be continuing problems, it is prudent to instruct an independent consultant with experience in medico-legal work. Expert lists are available online as described in the later chapter on experts. Another advantage is that an independent consultant, who takes an interest in medico-legal work, is less likely to view the occasional witness citation as an intolerable interruption of his clinical routine. Some clients will ask you if they should visit their GP for the sole purpose of having their complaints noted to support a later personal injury claim. The Department of Work and Pensions ("DWP") formerly issued guidance. In particular: **4–02**

1. Solicitors should not automatically advise all accident victims to visit their GP following the accident unless they need diagnosis or treatment.

2. It is not appropriate to advise accident victims to see their GP for no other reason than to have minor injuries recorded.
3. Where no diagnosis or treatment is sought, but a record of injuries is thought to be advisable for evidential purposes, the solicitor should consider:
    (a) taking photos where injuries are visible;
    (b) making a detailed note of the apparent injuries;
    (c) referral to a specific forensic medical examiner or other trained doctor who has indicated they are willing to provide this specialist service

When to instruct the report

4–03 You should instruct the expert after your client has regained full mobility, and returned to work following any absence. Any lingering aches and pains may be resolved by the time the consultant arranges the appointment. In any event, the expert can take a view as to how serious these are.

In serious cases where there are likely to be continuing impairments and restrictions, it is prudent to obtain an initial report about three months after the accident. This should alert you to other experts' reports which may be required, e.g. neurologist, neuropsychologist, nursing care reports. You will not be attempting to settle the claim on the basis of this report, but this will enable you to take a general view and instruct any further particular lines of enquiry.

Instructions to consultant

4–04 You should ensure that the consultant has sight of all relevant medical records. If he practises in the hospital where your client was treated, he can obtain sight of the case notes. In other cases you will require to obtain copy records under mandate. Your client is entitled to these under the Data Protection Act 1998. The British Medical Association ("BMA") website has a very useful guide to the provisions entitled *Access to Health Records by Patients*.[1] There is a standard £10 administration fee, and you will be liable for reasonable photocopying charges up to an inclusive maximum of £50. You should send the records to the consultant together with your client's statement and any photographs or papers which clarify either the accident locus, or the immediate after-effects of the injury.

Contents of the report[2]

4–05   1. *Personal details*. The report should contain the name, address and date of birth of the client, together with the date of the accident and the date of examination.

---

[1] http://www.bma.org.uk/ethics/health_records/AccessHealthRecords.jsp [Accessed September 10, 2011].

[2] This section is based on a format agreed between the BMA and the Law Society of England.

2. *History*. There should be a précis of the facts of the accident, with a full medical history of all treatment thereafter. Any relevant past medical history should be included.
3. *Examination*. Details of the examination should be provided in terms which are comprehensible to an informed layman. X-rays should only be taken if necessary. If earlier X-rays or MRI scans were taken, they should be recovered and sent to the consultant.
4. *Opinion and prognosis*. A precise opinion and prognosis should be given in each case. If either is provisional pending sight of relevant medical records or X-rays, this should be stated in the report. This part of the report should summarise the nature of the injury, the current position, and the likely prognosis. It is particularly important that the consultant identifies any potential future complications, such as osteo-arthritis, giving percentage figures for the likelihood of the event occurring. Where possible, a timescale should also be predicted. The report should address the effect which the injury has had now and may have in the future on any or all of the following:
    (a) Life expectancy.
    (b) Overall quality of life.
    (c) Ability to return to current employment.
    (d) Future employment prospects.
    (e) Ability to live independently.
    (f) Any anticipated current or future needs (e.g. help in attending to the garden).
    (g) Any anticipated special needs with regard to housing.
    (h) Any anticipated future needs in relation to transportation.
    (i) Any restrictions or limitations upon recreational, social or sporting activities.
5. *Other reports*. Where the client appears to be suffering from other symptoms outwith the consultant's area of expertise, these symptoms should be noted, with advice as to the identity of the relevant specialist whose further opinion should be sought.

After report received

Check with your client that the factual details of the report are accurate, and make sure that you understand what it means, using a basic medical dictionary as an aid if necessary. If there are any factual errors, or you do not fully understand the report, contact the consultant either by letter or telephone. Whilst you should never seek to influence the consultant's clinical judgment, it is perfectly proper to ask him to amend the report to clear up any factual inaccuracies or ambiguities. You should always send the report to your client and ask him to confirm its accuracy, before disclosing it to the other side. If it contains any unexpected diagnosis or conclusions, these should be addressed at a meeting with the client.

4–06

Make prompt payment of the report fee. A supportive expert is an invaluable asset. Don't jeopardise the relationship by failing to make timeous payment.

Past losses and future losses

4–07 The court's forensic approach to past events is simple. Anything it considers more likely than not to have happened is treated as a certainty on the balance of probabilities rule, i.e. the 51 per cent test. The approach to future losses is different. The court will not decide between possibilities on an either/or basis but instead will adopt a nuanced approach on a loss of chance, excluding losses which are merely speculative, but otherwise awarding damages for lost opportunitites, even although the likelihood would not pass the balance of probabilities test.[3] The task for the practitioner is to enable the court to make predictions which are evidence based. So if you are acting for a young person who has suffered an injury which prevents a career, e.g. in the police or armed forces, you should concentrate efforts on obtaining evidence from school teachers, youth leaders or other mentors that this would have been the chosen career model. A useful example is the case of *Herring v Ministry of Defence*[4] where the claimant proved loss of a career in the police.

Property losses

4–08 It is unlikely that your client will be able to produce purchase receipts for damaged items. You should certainly have him retain all replacement estimates, invoices, and papers such as dry cleaning receipts. Note the age and condition of any damaged items, but be prepared to argue that replacement costs are the appropriate measure where there is no second-hand market for items such as clothing.

Miscellaneous charges

4–09 Your client should prepare a list of all prescription payments made by him, and should also include the purchase cost for over-the-counter medicines such as painkillers. You can also include the cost of any special treatment outwith the NHS, e.g. osteopaths' fees, where this has been reasonably incurred. Where there have been frequent visits to the hospital or to the GP, it is worthwhile to make up a travelling expenses schedule based on your client's actual transport costs, e.g. taxi or bus fares, or a petrol allowance for a private car. Your client doesn't need to keep every receipt. It will generally be sufficient to have one or two receipts as illustrations of the general transport costs, together with a schedule based perhaps on his NHS appointment card. A moderate and well-prepared schedule can also be useful in persuading the court to adopt a more generous attitude to your client's general pain and suffering.

---

[3] *Davies v Taylor* [1974] A.C. 207.
[4] *Herring v Ministry of Defence* [2003] EWCA Civ 528.

WAGE LOSS

4–10 You should ask your client for a recent wage slip at the first interview. Wage loss is based on his expected net earnings.[5] Ask the insurers to produce a 13-week pre-accident wage schedule. If there are any special circumstances about this period, e.g. low wages due to holidays, sickness, or where your client might have obtained overtime payments during his period of absence, be prepared to argue that your client's weekly loss is not simply the pre-accident average. It is generally straightforward to work out the total wage loss. Check what sick payments have been made. Many companies and local authorities have service contracts whereby sick pay is repayable by your client, in the event of a successful damages claim against a third party. It is vitally important to check on this before settlement and to obtain a copy of the contractual terms. A difficulty which frequently arises is that the employer will seek to recover gross payments from your client. The better view is that they are only entitled to the net amounts which your client can recover from the defender, leaving the employer to recover tax and national insurance from the Inland Revenue and DWP respectively.[6] It is important to clarify this, or your client will have a shortfall.

Future wage loss[7]

4–11 Where the court is satisfied that there will be continuing absence from work, and loss of future earnings, the general rule is that your client will be compensated on a multiplier and multiplicand approach. The multiplicand is the net wage which he would have received, calculated as at the date of proof. The multiplier is the figure used to calculate the future number of years over which damages should be payable. Vigorous efforts should be made to obtain evidence to support this approach. Frequently there will be an industrial injuries disablement award, either for life or for a significant period, and details should be obtained from your client. Your client may have seen a Jobcentre Disability Employment Adviser, in which case you should know what was said to him, and keep any correspondence. Check on the normal retirement age in your client's job. Identify a comparator employee on the same level and status as your client and whose career path and earnings might mirror his own. An argument that is frequently deployed by defenders is that your client would have been made redundant in any event and that with the depressed state of the employment market, would be unlikely to obtain other employment. A variation of this argument arises when your client becomes unfit for his previous employment, but may be fit for a number of less demanding occupations, e.g. sedentary and light work, or may

---

[5] See generally The Hon Lady Paton QC, *McEwan and Paton on Damages for Personal Injuries in Scotland*, 2nd edn (London: Sweet & Maxwell), p.24/1.

[6] This was the view of the Court of Appeal in England in the case of *Franklin v British Rail Board* [1993] I.R.L.R. 441; [1994] C.L.Y. 1993.

[7] See the article by R. Milligan, "Approaching Future Wage Loss", 1995 S.L.T. 173 which is still a useful guide to the key cases.

actually be in such work at lower wages at the date of the proof. In these situations it is prudent to instruct an employment expert. Such an expert will be able to advise on the state of the employment market in general, your client's prospects of re-employment, and any continuing wage loss which he is likely to suffer. Encourage your client to seek employment, and to keep copies of job advertisements, application letters, replies and details of any interviews. Apart from any other considerations, this approach is likely to evoke an element of judicial sympathy. Never advise your client simply to sit back and await his award of damages.

The current Actuarial Tables in use are Ogden 6, and these should be the starting point for all calculations. These tables are much more sophisticated than previous versions, and take into account the client's pre-accident educational status, as being a good indicator of future employability The tables enable a comparison to be drawn between anticipated future earnings if fit for pre-accident employment, and actual future employment post-accident. Where a person meets the Ogden definition of disablement post-accident, the court should apply different discounts to future earnings, depending on educational status and qualifications. This should lead to persons who meet the disability definition, and with low educational attainments receiving increased damages. The approach should also remove the need to consider a separate head for loss of employability. Practitioners should be aware, however, that the United Kingdom courts seem reluctant fully to embrace the philosophy behind the new tables, and cross-checks on damages calculations using the traditional methods should be carried out.[8]

LOSS OF EMPLOYABILITY OR DISADVANTAGE ON THE LABOUR MARKET

4–12 This is known to the insurers as *Smith v Manchester*[9] damages, after the leading English case in which it was established. Whilst it can be awarded in addition to a sum placed on a multiplier approach, it is frequently used as an alternative basis of award, and is generally much less advantageous. The award is made to reflect the possibility that your client will be thrown onto the labour market, where he is at a disadvantage as a result of his injury. You will need to know the likelihood of redundancy or dismissal. How long has your client worked for a particular employer, and is there a written redundancy policy (e.g. last in, first out)? What are the general economic prospects for the company? Where your claim is against a third party, your client's personnel manager might supply this information by letter. Ascertain the work activities which are now curtailed, and be able to argue that this makes your client a less attractive employment prospect at interview. The amount which a court might award is very difficult to predict. Relevant factors are the severity of injury, the pursuer's age and work history, the eligibility for other kinds of employment, and wage

---

[8] See, e.g. *Conner v Bradman Ltd* [2007] EWHC 2789 QBD.
[9] *Smith v Manchester Corporation* (1974) 17 K.I.R. 1; [1974] C.L.Y. 843.

earning capacity. The courts have occasionally cross-checked any award by comparing it against multiples of the annual net salary. For example, in the case of *Robertson v British Bakeries Ltd*,[10] Lord Osborne would have awarded twice the pursuer's net salary for loss of employability. Lord Gill in *Bonar v Trafalgar House Offshore Fabrications Ltd*[11] awarded the sum of £20,000, or just less than one year's net earnings. In any negotiation you should take the client's annual net salary as at least a starting point and be prepared to argue for a figure based on two or three times the annual net salary where there is a genuine likelihood of future loss of employment. Where the disadvantage is highly speculative, you will have to settle for a lesser sum.

LEISURE PURSUITS

Where there is any restriction on hobbies or sports, obtain club membership cards, merit certificates or details of awards, which illustrate the diminution in your client's enjoyment of life. **4–13**

PENSION LOSS

Where your client is dismissed from pensionable employment by reason of his injury, there will be a loss under this head. You will require full details of the pension scheme from his employers, and thereafter the proper expert is an actuary. The current approach taken by the Scottish courts is based on what was said in the cases of *Mitchell v Glenrothes*[12] and *Cantwell v CICA*.[13] In particular, where the pursuer was in receipt of an ill health pension, the period of absence before retirement age represented a claim for loss of earnings, and ill health pension benefits received could not be set off against the loss of earnings claim, but the period after retirement age represented a claim for loss of pension, and pension benefits received after that date must be deducted. Following the decision of the House of Lords in the case of *Wells v Wells*,[14] the discount rate to be applied is now 2.5 per cent. Make sure that you instruct an actuary who is familiar with the case law, and in particular the current approach taken by the courts in respect of multipliers, investments rates and the Ogden tables. **4–14**

PSYCHIATRIC INJURY

There are two practical areas of concern for practitioners. The first is how to approach the true nervous shock type cases where exposure or parti- **4–15**

---

[10] *Robertson v British Bakeries Ltd*, 1991 S.L.T. 971.
[11] *Bonar v Trafalgar House Offshore Fabrications Ltd*, 1996 S.L.T. 54.
[12] *Mitchell v Glenrothes*, 1991 S.L.T. 284.
[13] *Cantwell v CICA*, 2001 S.L.T. 966.
[14] *Wells v Wells* [1998] 3 W.L.R. 329.

cipation in a single event, e.g. an explosion has caused psychiatric symptoms. The second is the much more common situation where the client develops what is sometimes described as "psychological overlay" which maintains or exacerbates symptoms in the absence of clear organic cause.[15] You will frequently be consulted by clients who narrate a variety of symptoms, ranging from shock to clinical disorder, which they relate to the accident circumstances. Typical symptoms might be loss of confidence, sleep disturbance, flashback experiences, avoidance behaviour, loss of libido. It is now recognised that psychological injury arises very frequently, and the practitioner should be alert for it. Frequently the client will deny any relevant symptoms on direct questioning, but an interview with the spouse or a close friend will reveal a change in behaviour.

NERVOUS SHOCK

4–16 This is not a medical term of art, but an expression used by lawyers to describe various psychiatric illnesses. In this section the term is used to describe the consequences of a single event trauma, e.g. a road traffic accident. The whole area of recovery of damage for nervous shock is the subject of constant criticism and review.[16] The current position for practitioners is summed up in the House of Lords decision of *Frost v Chief Constable of Yorkshire Police*, and is settled for the time being.[17] The following rules of thumb are suggested for screening cases at this time.

Primary victims

4–17 These are persons who are directly involved in the accident circumstances, e.g. the passenger in the car which collides with the lorry. This definition will generally exclude bystanders. In the case of *Salter v UB Frozen and Chilled Foods Ltd*,[18] it was held that a work colleague who averred that he had suffered psychiatric illness after blamelessly causing the death of a colleague whilst using a forklift truck, was entitled to an enquiry on these averments as a primary victim. A person on the support ship *Tharos* during the *Piper Alpha* disaster who suffered psychiatric injury was not a primary victim. (Although he was in fear for his own life, the Court of Appeal found as a matter of fact that this fear was "unreasonable").[19] Broadly, the prospects of recovery for primary victims are as follows:

---

[15] The other area of psychiatric disorder caused by occupational stress is dealt with in Ch.22.
[16] See Scottish Law Commmission, *Damages for psychiatric injury* (The Stationery Office, 2002), Discussion Paper No.120.
[17] *Frost v Chief Constable of Yorkshire Police* [1998] 3 W.L.R. 1059.
[18] *Salter v UB Frozen and Chilled Foods Ltd*, 2004 S.C. 233.
[19] *Macfarlane v Wilkinson, The Times*, February 13, 1997.

(i) *Nervous reaction amounting to distinct psychiatric disorder or clinical condition.* The court should award damages even where there are no accompanying physical injuries, as long as personal injury was reasonably foreseeable. This follows the decision by the House of Lords in *Page v Smith*,[20] where a plaintiff, who was involved in a car accident and who suffered no physical injury, successfully recovered for exacerbation of pre-existing myalgic encephalitis ("ME").

(ii) *Shock and distress not amounting to a clinical disorder or condition.* It is likely that a Scottish court will follow the approach of the Court of Appeal in England, as set out in the case of *Nicholls v Rushton*,[21] which was approved by the House of Lords in *Page v Smith*. In that case the plaintiff had been involved in a car accident. There was no physical injury. His county court award of damages for "severe shock and shaking up" was overturned by the Court of Appeal. There will be no recovery in damages for a nervous reaction alone, which falls short of an identifiable psychological illness. So that where you are instructed by a client whose only complaints are of shock and distress, it is unlikely that you can recover damages under this head unless you have a report from a psychiatrist confirming that the symptoms amount to clinical psychiatric disorder.[22]

(iii) *Shock and distress not amounting to clinical disorder or condition, in addition to physical injuries.* Where there is any physical trauma or injury, a victim can recover for a nervous reaction which falls short of a recognised psychiatric condition (see *Nicholls v Rushton*, as above). This means that if you are instructed by a road traffic accident victim who has suffered bruising and distress, you can recover for the latter even although a psychiatrist will not classify the symptoms as a distinct psychiatric disorder.

Secondary victims

These are persons who, although not directly involved, have witnessed **4–18** distressing accidents. They are known as "secondary victims", and recovery is much more problematic by reason of public policy controls. As the authorities stand, you must be able to show a "proximity relationship" between your client and the injured person. This category is normally restricted to persons who directly perceived the accident events, and have close ties of love and affection with the victim.[23] These are sometimes referred to as the "hearness, nearness and dearness tests".

---

[20] *Page v Smith* [1995] 2 W.L.R. 644.
[21] *The Times*, June 19, 1997.
[22] *Simpson v ICI*, 1983 S.L.T. 601.
[23] *Alcock v Chief Constable of South Yorkshire Police* [1992] 1 A.C. 310.

There is a useful review of all authorities in *Keen v Tayside Contracts*.[24] The claims of ordinary bystanders are denied on the basis that they are presumed to be of sufficient fortitude or "phlegm" to endure the sight of such calamities unscathed. Persons who have witnessed a particularly horrific incident may be able to claim.[25] Rescuers who objectively expose themselves to danger or reasonably believed that they were in danger should be entitled to recover.[26] The control mechanisms set up by the courts mean that the rights of recovery for psychiatric injury for secondary victims are now extremely restrictive. In most cases this will involve your telling the client from the outset that there is no claim.

Psychological overlay

4-19 Once liability for injury has been established, the victim must be taken as found, whether they have eggshell skull or eggshell personality. There must be a causative link between the condition and the accident. But this need not be the exclusive or even predominant cause. It must simply be a material cause, i.e. it cannot be excluded on the de minimis rule (*Simmons v British Steel Corporation*, 2004 S.C. (H.L.) 94). This should be kept in mind as there are likely to be a number of factors at work in any clinical presentation. You will need a psychiatrist to diagnose a psychiatric disorder. He will require full access to all medical records, and not merely those relating to the accident. Generally he will come to a diagnosis based on the American *Diagnostic Manual of Psychiatry*. An associated condition is where the pursuer has suffered a physical injury, which is accompanied by a psychological component which prevents full recovery. A specific indicator is a referral to a hospital pain clinic. The condition is sometimes referred to as chronic pain disorder.[27] This is one situation where the solicitor should *always* instruct the treating psychiatrist. You will also require witness statements from family members or friends, which highlight the client's post-accident attitude with regard to restriction of social activities, and his general malaise. There is always an unspoken suspicion in this situation of malingering. Psychiatrists will tend to take what is said to them at face value. In *Ormsby v The Chief Constable of Strathclyde Police*[28] a leading psychiatric expert witness Dr Alan Carson put matters as follows:

> " ... [B]ut I think the key issue is the factual basis of a number of reported events. It must be understood that when one is dealing with depressive disorder and/or post traumatic stress disorder, one is entirely reliant on the patient's description of their symptoms and in believing these symptoms to be true in making a diagnosis."

---

[24] *Keen v Tayside Contracts*, 2003 S.L.T. 500. Lady Paton's approach to the particular facts of that case was doubted in *Harrhy v Thames Trains Ltd* [2003] EWHC 2286 (QB).

[25] *Robertson v Forth Road Bridge Joint Board*, 1996 S.L.T. 263 (employees who witnessed the death of a colleague who was blown off the Forth Road Bridge did not have the requisite proximity relationship with the deceased, and were denied recovery).

[26] *Frost v Chief Constable of Yorkshire Police* [1998] 3 W.L.R. 1059.

[27] For example, *Burns v Harper Collins*, 1997 S.L.T. 607.

[28] *Ormsby v The Chief Constable of Strathclyde Police* [2008] CSOH 43.

In serious cases the best advice for the practitioner is to confront the unspoken allegation, and to be prepared to ask the court to deal with this on either/or basis, i.e. the claimant is genuine, or he is a malingerer. This means making strenuous efforts to build up a clear before and after picture. Reference has already been made to statements from work colleagues and other disinterested parties. The attitude of the client's GP will be pivotal here. Whilst the GP will be reluctant to enter into any expert psychiatric dispute, he can be a critical supportive witness with reference to the general medical history and the attitude to illness and work related absence.

SERVICES CLAIMS UNDER THE ADMINISTRATION OF JUSTICE (SCOTLAND) ACT 1982

Section 8

4–20 This enables the injured person to claim for services provided by relatives down to the date of proof, and thereafter if it appears that the services will continue to be necessary. Services typically will mean hospital visits, assistance with washing or dressing, or time spent cooking or shopping.[29] In practice it may be helpful to distinguish three possible situations, as follows.

1. Minor orthopaedic injuries

4–21 Typically there will be a full recovery within a six-month period. During that time the injured person might receive assistance with washing, dressing, cooking or other household chores. The courts will generally make a modest lump sum award with reference to decided cases, without the need for any detailed computation. In *Beck v United Closures and Plastics Plc*,[30] a lump sum of £500 was awarded for services provided over a few weeks.

2. More serious injuries with ongoing assistance

4–22 In this situation there is permanent injury and a continuing requirement for help on an occasional basis. In the case of *Kennedy v Lees of Scotland Ltd*[31] Lord Gill stated that expert evidence on the cost of care was not appropriate in this kind of case. The court should take a broad approach and in that case he calculated the need for services at 10 hours weekly overall, with the appropriate rate being £2 an hour, which was about one half of the agency rate quoted at the proof. No doubt a similar calculation could be made placing reliance on the national minimum wage.

---

[29] See R. Milligan, "Services" (2001) 39 Rep. Bull.
[30] *Beck v United Closures and Plastics Plc*, 2001 S.L.T. 1299.
[31] *Kennedy v Lees of Scotland Ltd*, 1997 S.L.T. 510.

3. Serious cases involving substantial elements of continuing care

4–23 In these circumstances you require a cost of care report from a nursing and disability expert who has visited your client. They will then assess the need for care, comment on the amount of care required and cost this out at commercial rates. The courts generally then make a discount if the care is supplied by a relative. The case of *Kendal v Davies*[32] is a useful example of the approach to be taken.

Where the relative has given up employment to care for an injured person, a useful starting point might be details of their previous wage. You should have a statement of the carer's full daily timetable. You should ask the carer to keep a diary for a period of say three months. In catastrophic injury cases you should take a "Day in the Life" video.

Section 9

4–24 This enables the injured party to claim value for services which he would have supplied to a relative free of charge but for the accident. Typical examples relate to gardening, DIY, home decoration and maintenance. Where possible, estimates from local tradesmen should be obtained, remembering that the claim can only properly relate to the labour element, and not materials, which would have been used up in any event.

PROVISIONAL DAMAGES

4–25 You will have to deal with many clients where the medical prognosis is unclear on important matters. If the uncertainty is likely to be resolved within the triennium, you should delay settling until a definite medical opinion is available. Where such an opinion cannot be given, you should consider whether there is scope for a claim for provisional damages. The normal rule is that damages are assessed on a once and for all basis. This accords with the public policy aim of finality of litigation: insurers are entitled to meet claims and close their files. When applying a once and for all assessment, the court does not require to be satisfied that future damage is likely to occur on the balance of probabilities. Instead the court must do its best to put a value on the risk of future loss, on the evidence before it. Clearly there will be occasions when this "crystal ball" approach might cause substantial injustice. The Administration of Justice (Scotland) Act 1982 s.12 provides that where the defender (the "responsible person") was at the time of the act or omission a public authority, a public corporation or insured or otherwise indemnified in respect of the claim and:

---

[32] *Kendal v Davies* [2000] Rep. L.R. 126.

"(a) There is proved or admitted to be a risk that at some definite or indefinite time in the future the injured person will, as a result of the act or omission which gave rise to the cause of the action, develop some serious disease or suffer some serious deterioration in his physical or mental condition,"

the court may make an award of provisional damages.

These damages are to be assessed on the assumption that the injured person will *not* develop the disease or suffer a deterioration, and reserves that person's right to return to the court for further damages if he later develops the disease or suffers a deterioration.

The courts interpret this rule restrictively. You will have to show that the deterioration comprises a recognisable medical threshold, and is not simply a continuation or exacerbation of an existing problem.[33] The deterioration should also have significant practical effects on everyday life, e.g. on employment.[34] There may be problems where there are a number of supervening and undifferentiated factors which might precipitate the deterioration.[35] Whilst the risk need not be substantial, a very minor risk may influence a judge to refuse to exercise his discretion to grant provisional damages where there are other doubtful factors.

The common category of cases which might be suitable relate to asbestos exposure cases where there is, e.g. pleural thickening and a risk (which is normally assessed at between 5–10 per cent) of developing mesothelioma, and head injury cases where there is a risk of epilepsy.[36] Certain orthopaedic injuries where there is a strong risk of osteo-arthritis may be appropriate, but only where the deterioration will have a particularly significant impact on day-to-day life and employment.[37]

Where you consider that a claim for provisional damages might be appropriate, you will need a specific medical report which addresses the following matters:

4–26

1. What is the anticipated deterioration? Is it a new and separate medical development, or merely an exacerbation of an existing problem?

---

[33] See *Prentice v Thynne*, 1989 S.L.T. 336: provisional damages refused where there was evidence that there was already osteoarthritis in a fractured femur. The development of osteoarthritis was not a risk but a certainty.

[34] See *Robertson v British Bakeries*, 1991 S.L.T. 971: provisional damages awarded for ankle injury with greater than 50% chance of osteoarthritis. In the circumstances a serious deterioration with particular impact on employment position.

[35] See *Bonar v Trafalgar House*, 1996 S.L.T. 54: occupational asthma. Provisional damages refused because the future event which might trigger a serious deterioration could not be defined with any particularity.

[36] See *Lappin v Britannia Airways*, 1989 S.L.T. 181: parties agreed provisional damages appropriate. See also *McColl v Barnes*, 1992 S.L.T. 1188: provisional damages awarded with right to return to court within seven years of date of decree for risk of post-accident epilepsy.

[37] *White v Inveresk Paper (No.2)*, 1988 S.L.T. 2: 10% chance of development of osteoarthritis. Provisional damages refused. *McMenemy v Argyll Stores*, 1992 S.L.T. 971: fractured elbow. Risk of osteoarthritis and further operation held not to be a serious deterioration. Provisional damages refused.

2. What will the results of this deterioration be for the client in his day-to-day life?
3. What is the risk of the deterioration, expressed as a percentage if possible?
4. Where the risk is a diminishing risk, e.g. epilepsy, what are the reducing percentages?
5. What is the timescale for the development of the condition?

Even where provisional damages might be appropriate, the court will wish to impose a time limit on the right to make a further application.

Where a claim for provisional damages applies, the claim is valued on the basis that the deterioration will *not* develop, and the client is given the opportunity to return to the court in the event that it does. The first practical point is that evaluation on this basis is likely to be less than a once and for all valuation where the risk is taken into the final assessment.

You will find that insurers have a strong antipathy towards provisional damages claims. They will naturally wish their files to be closed, and not left open for a potentially much larger claim at some time in the future. In serious cases where you have a strong supporting medical report, you should raise proceedings concluding for provisional damages. The drafting implications are considered later. Even in doubtful cases you should certainly raise the issue both with the insurer and the client. In so far as the client is concerned, you must protect yourself against any future accusation that you have under-settled by ignoring any serious medical complication in the future. You should always discuss any once and for all settlement with the client against the background of:

(a) the opportunity of going back to the court for more damages at some time in the future; and
(b) a reduced initial award for general damages which will be valued on the basis that the serious deterioration will not occur.

You should make a practical distinction between the asbestos cases, where the serious deterioration will be catastrophic, and other situations. In the asbestos cases you should rarely settle except on a provisional damages basis. In other situations the possibility of provisional damage should be considered with the client and either insisted upon, or alternatively used as a bargaining counter with the insurers, depending on the particular circumstances and your instruction. As a matter of prudence you should explain matters fully to your client in writing and obtain written instructions on settlement.

Drafting the schedule

4–27 Even in pre-litigation cases, it is a useful discipline to draft a Schedule using form PI6 as the template. This forces the practitoner to address the main heads of damage, and in particular to think about the application of interest. A properly drawn schedule should set insurer expectations, and

Evidence on Damages 41

should both inform and persuade. From the template the heads of claim are as follows:

Solatium

This is a total figure, but may be subdivided into past and future. It is **4–28** helpful to include case law reference, as well as an indication of value on the *Judicial Studies Board Guidelines* (10th edn). The normal rule on interest is that where there has been a full recovery interest will run at 4 per cent to the date of recovery, and at 8 per cent thereafter. In that situation there is no division of solatium into past and future. Most sheriff court cases will come under this head. Where there are continuing symptoms, interest will run at 4 per cent on that part of solatium which is attributable to the past, usually around two-thirds to a quarter. Note that interest also runs in disease cases where the calculation can be substantial.[38] Again the likelihood is that around 50 per cent to two-thirds will be attributable to the past.

Past wage loss

Check whether there might have been any wage increases during the **4–29** client's absence and be prepared to argue for different losses over different periods. Where wage loss is continuing, the normal approach is to calculate interest on past wage loss at 4 per cent. Where there has been a return to work, interest should be calculated at 4 per cent down to the return, and then 8 per cent thereafter as the loss has crystallised.

Future wage loss

Where there is a multiplier/multiplicand approach an Ogden Tables **4–30** calculation should be carried out and put in the schedule.

Past services

These will relate to s.8 services rendered by a relative. Details should be **4–31** given of the identity of the relative, the overall duration as well as the daily time involved and the nature of the assistance. The current rate is generally taken to be around £5-£6 per hour, or the minimum wage. Where services are ongoing there should be a calculation of interest at 4 per cent. Where they have ceased, interest should be calculated at 4 per cent to the date of cessation, and thereafter at 8 per cent. A s.9 claim for services which could have been rendered by the injured person who was unable to do so should be included under this heading in general terms, and is frequently expressed as an annual figure. Interest will normally run at 4 per cent on the figure.

Future services

There can be no s.8 future services, but there may be a s.9 claim again **4–32** stated as an annual figure. An Ogden Tables multiplier should be

---

[38] *Purryag v Greater Glasgow Health Board*, 1996 S.L.T. 794.

attached, bearing mind that the person, absent injury, would have stopped providing services long before his expected date of death.

Past expenses

4–33 This is a general heading under which all other expenses such as damaged clothing, dry cleaning costs, road traffic insurance excess and any miscellaneous expense should be stated. Receipts should be enclosed wherever possible. Interest should run at 8 per cent from the date of loss.

CHAPTER 5

DEDUCTION OF BENEFITS

SOCIAL SECURITY (RECOVERY OF BENEFITS ACT) 1997

The main provisions are as follows: 5–01

1. Recoupment of benefit will take effect only on damages for loss of earnings, care costs, and loss of mobility. Damages for pain and suffering are effectively ring-fenced from clawback.
2. There is no exempt small claims threshold. If a claim is settled, or a decree granted, the insurer is obliged to repay the whole amount of the benefits to the Department for Work and Pensions ("DWP"), even if this exceeds the amount awarded.
3. After trial the judge is obliged to separate the heads of claim in any judgment to enable the benefits deduction calculation to be carried out. Only like for like deductions will be allowed, e.g. disability living allowance cannot be deducted from wage loss, but only from a cost of care award. There is to be no adjustment to the benefits position to reflect any finding of contributory negligence. Where the action is settled the same principles apply.
4. The cut-off date is the date of payment by the compensator, or a date five years from the date on which the accident occurred. In the case of a disease, it is five years from the first date of a claim for a listed benefit. Following the decision of the Inner House in *Mitchell v Laing*,[1] the court will require to specify the amounts awarded for the "relevant period" as stated. There will be no problem in cases which go to proof after the expiry of five years. The relevant period will be the five-year period from the date of the accident. Where the proof takes place within that five-year period, the court will require to deal with the relevant period by stating separate past and future amounts under the relevant heads of claim for five years from the date of the accident. For example, where there is a continuing wage loss at the date of proof, the court is obliged to specify the past wage loss, and the continuing wage loss up to a date five years from the date of the accident. Whilst the compensator can only deduct the actual amount of "like for like" compensation at the time of payment, this can be deducted from the wage loss head of claim for the whole five-year period.

---

[1] *Mitchell v Laing*, 1998 S.L.T. 203.

5. Under s.15(2) of the Social Security (Recovery of Benefits) Act 1997, any decree issued by the court will have to allocate damages under the heads of:

    (a) loss of earnings;
    (b) costs of care;
    (c) loss of mobility costs.

This applies to decrees in absence, provisional damages, summary decree, interim damages as well as final awards. It does not apply if the action settles by agreement. Otherwise the pursuer will have to furnish the court with a schedule prior to decree. A draft schedule is produced in Appendix C.

6. Interest on wage loss has now to be calculated *before* any deduction of like for like benefits.[2]

"Like for like" deductions

1. Compensation for earnings lost during the relevant period

5–02 Compensation in respect of loss of earnings during the relevant period may be reduced where the following benefits have been paid to meet the same need:

- Disability working allowance.
- Disablement pension payable under s.103 of the Social Security Contributions and Benefits Act 1992 ("the 1992 Act") (better known as industrial injuries disablement benefit).
- Incapacity benefit down to January 31, 2011.
- Employment and support allowance replaces incapacity benefit from January 31, 2011.
- Income support.
- Invalidity pension and allowance.
- Jobseeker's allowance.
- Reduced earnings allowance.
- Severe disablement allowance.
- Sickness benefit.
- Statutory sick pay.
- Unemployability supplement.
- Unemployment benefit.

2. Compensation for cost of care incurred during the relevant period

5–03
- Attendance allowance.
- Care component of disability living allowance.
- Disablement pension increase for Constant Attendance Allowance payable under ss.104 or 105 of the 1992 Act.
- Exceptionally Severe Disablement Allowance.

---

[2] *Wiseley v John Fulton (Plumbers) Ltd*, 1998 S.L.T. 1026.

3. Compensation for loss of mobility during the relevant period

- Mobility Allowance.
- Mobility component of Disability Living Allowance ("DLA Mobility").

5–04

4. Damages payments which do not require to be offset

These include pain and suffering, loss of future earnings, cost of future care, loss of future mobility, disadvantage on the labour market.

5–05

Detailed guidance is available at the Compensation Recovery Unit's ("CRU") website[3] (see in particular "Z1—*Recovery of benefits and or lump sum payments and NHS charges*).[4]

Practical effects

The practical effects of the legislation can be illustrated as follows.

5–06

The pursuer is awarded damages which consist of £10,000 for solatium and £12,000 for wage loss, a total of £22,000. He had received incapacity benefit of £15,000, and the care component of disability living allowance of £5,000 a total benefits bill of £20,000.

In that situation:

(i) There is no deduction from the £10,000 solatium award which is ring-fenced.
(ii) The wage loss of £12,000 is reduced to nil by deduction of the like-for-like incapacity benefit of £15,000. The balance of the incapacity benefit of £3,000 must be paid by the compensator to the DWP.
(iii) The full amount of the disability living allowance of £5,000 must be paid by the compensator to the DWP. There is no relevant head of claim against which it can be deducted.

In this example the pursuer will receive from the compensator the sum of £10,000, who will also have to foot the whole benefits bill of £20,000. The cost of the claim to the compensator is £30,000. Any deduction for contributory negligence does not affect the benefits bill. If in the above example the pursuer was held 50 per cent to blame, the sum due to him would be reduced from £10,000 to £5,000. The compensator will still have to meet the total benefits bill of £20,000, and the cost of the claim to the compensator will be £25,000.

In settlement discussions, solicitors will now have to insist on a breakdown of each head of claim from the insurer, so that there is agreement on the allocation of the benefits statement. "Care" does not necessarily mean services in every case, and s.8 claims under the Administration of Justice (Scotland) Act 1982 will only be affected where

---

[3] *http://www.dwp.gov.uk/other-specialists/compensation-recovery-unit/forms-and-guidance/* [Accessed September 10, 2011].
[4] Department of Work and Pensions, *Recovery of benefits and or lump sum payments and NHS charges* (June, 2011).

a "like for like" benefit, e.g. attendance allowance, has been paid. The courts are to interpret loss of mobility restrictively:

> "The head is referring to damages for patrimonial loss suffered by a person as a result of loss of mobility due to the accident. An example of such loss would be the cost of fares for journeys by bus or taxi which the victim would not have required to take but for the loss of mobility."[5]

5–07 In all dealings concerning recoupment of benefit, forewarned is forearmed. Whilst the burden of payment is on the insurer as compensator, the burden of communication and explanation remains firmly with the pursuer's agent. It is small consolation for the client to be told after the event that the majority of his award has been repaid to the DWP in accordance with the legislation. The practical effects of the legislation should be explained to the client at the first meeting. Although only the insurers can obtain a certificate of recoverable benefit, the pursuer's agent can obtain an early warning by writing direct to the CRU using form CR4. A particular trap for the unwary relates to continuing payments of industrial injuries benefit (disablement pension payable under s.103 of the 1992 Act). For example, your client may have suffered an accident which resulted in the amputation of an index finger. He may have returned to work after a period of six months' absence. He will be continuing to receive industrial injuries benefit on the basis of his disablement, even after his return to work. This is a like for like benefit against wage loss, and it will continue to erode the amount of wage loss claim until settlement.

Any settlement at all means that the insurers will foot the benefits bill in full. If the pursuer's case seems weak on liability, they may opt for repudiation and defence to the end. It does set up a community of interest for speedy resolution of strong claims where a relevant benefit is running. In the meantime the lessons for the pursuer's agent are:

1. Communicate and explain from day one.
2. Progress the claim as quickly as possible.

---

[5] *Mitchell v Laing*, 1998 S.L.T. 203 (1st Div) at [210].

CHAPTER 6

LIMITATION AND TIME BAR

At the time of publication, the Scottish Law Commission has produced both Discussion and Report consultation papers on the operation of the rules of limitation and prescription. Legislative reform is proposed. The Discussion paper contains a helpful resume of the current law and can be downloaded from the Scottish Law Commission website.[1] **6–01**

The rules for personal injury practitioners are contained in the Prescription and Limitation (Scotland) Act 1973 ("the 1973 Act"), as amended, and in particular ss.17, 18, 19A and the definitions in s.22. Section 18 applies to fatal cases. Section 17(2) provides: **6–02**

> "Subject to sub-section (3) below and section 19A of this Act, no action to which this section applies shall be brought unless it is commenced within a period of 3 years after:
>
> (a) the date on which the injuries were sustained or, where the act or omission to which the injuries were attributable was a continuing one, that date or the date on which the act or omission ceased, whichever is the later; or
>
> (b) the date (if later than any date mentioned in paragraph (a) above) on which the pursuer in the action became, or on which, in the opinion of the court, it would have been reasonably practicable for him in all the circumstances to become, aware of all the following facts—
>
> > (i) that the injuries in question were sufficiently serious to justify his bringing an action of damages on the assumption that the person against whom the action was brought did not dispute liability and was able to satisfy a decree;
> >
> > (ii) that the injuries were attributable in whole or in part to an act or omission; and
> >
> > (iii) that the defender was a person to whose act or omission the injuries were attributable in whole or in part or the employer or principal of such a person."

---

[1] Scottish Law Commission, *Report Paper 207 on personal injury actions; limitation and prescribed claims* (The Stationery Office, 2007) available at *http://www.scotlawcom.gov.uk* [Accessed September 10, 2011].

The general rule is that an action must be raised within three years of the accident where there is legal capacity. Where the injury has been caused by a continuing act or omission, time does not start to run until the act or omission ceases. In the case of a child, time does not begin to run until he reaches 16 years.[2] In the case of an incapax, time does not run during the period of incapacity.[3] Possible grounds for extending the starting point for the triennium are contained in s.17(2)(b)(i), (ii) and (iii). These are considered in turn.

Section 17(2)(b)(i)—knowledge of sufficiently serious injury

6–03 The test was considered by the Inner House in the case of *Carnegie v Lord Advocate (No.3)*.[4] In this case the allegations were that the pursuer, who was a soldier in the army, had suffered injury and distress as a result of a campaign of bullying. Reasons given for failing to take legal action within three years of injury included concern over his future in the army. The court discussed at length whether the approach to this test was subjective or objective. The court held that whilst it might be relevant to have regard to the severity of an injury to a particular individual, it was not appropriate to take in wholly subjective considerations such as fear of losing one's job. An assessment must be carried out of the benefit, in the form of damages to be obtained from the bringing of the action, in comparison with the time, trouble and expense required in the conduct of such an action. These considerations might differ in significance between one claim and another. Although *Carnegie* has been overturned by *Aitchison*,[5] it is still good law on this issue.

The typical situation where this section may be helpful is where the client has suffered an injury which is not initially disabling, but later turns out to be much more serious.

In *Blake v Lothian Health Board*,[6] Lord Caplan stated:

> "The proper question in this case seems to me to be whether a reasonable claimant would in all the circumstances consider that the facts about the injury which were known (or could have been ascertained) rendered it worthwhile to raise an action (always of course assuming liability was not in dispute)."[7]

The judgment contains further dicta to the effect that a litigation would have involved expenditure of time, possible wage loss and would generate a degree of worry. Where it required to be raised as a small claim, there would also be a degree of irrecoverable expenses. A pursuer might reasonably conclude that an action of damages which would have generated £200 in 1986 was not worthwhile. In those circumstances the court held

---

[2] Age of Legal Capacity Act 1991.
[3] Prescription and Limitation (Scotland) Act 1973 s.17(3).
[4] *Carnegie v Lord Advocate (No.3)*, 2001 S.C. 802.
[5] *Aitchison v Glasgow City Council*, 2010 S.C. 411.
[6] *Blake v Lothian Health Board*, 1993 S.L.T. 1248 at [1251].
[7] See also *Ferla v Secretary of State for Scotland*, 1995 S.L.T. 662.

that the injuries were not sufficiently serious to start time running. More recently it has been confirmed that a broad approach should be taken to the section, and that there may be circumstances where a claim which is above the "de minimis" level, might still not be sufficiently serious to set time running.[8] On the other hand if the injury is sufficiently serious, the emergence of a later distinct set of symptoms does not avail to set up a new commencement date (see the case of *Aitchison*). There may still be prospects, but it will need to be under s.19A of the 1973 Act (see, e.g. *C.G. v Glasgow City Council* [2010] CSIH 69).

Section 17(2)(b)(ii)—attributability of injury

In *Comer v James Scott & Co (Electrical Engineers) Ltd*,[9] Lord Maxwell described knowledge as follows: **6–04**

> "On the other hand, whether a person 'knows' a fact seems to me to involve a question of degree. I do not consider it advisable to attempt to define it, but at least I think it involves something approximating more to certainty than mere suspicion or guess. Moreover, in my opinion, and I think this important for the present case, some information, suspicion or belief falling short of knowledge is not transformed into knowledge if it happens to be correct. I accept that a person cannot be said to 'know' a fact if the thing which he believes with whatever conviction is not in accordance with the truth. But I do not think that the converse is correct. I do not think that any information or belief, however uncertain, necessarily amounts to knowledge within the meaning of para.(a) merely because it happens to coincide with the truth."

The client must have knowledge both of the injury, and that the injury **6–05** was capable of being caused by a particular defender. The date when both these conditions are satisfied can pose difficult questions, particularly in occupational disease cases which are considered in detail elsewhere.[10] Even in single event accidents there may be a number of potential defenders. As Lord Coulsfield stated in *Nicol v British Steel Corporation*[11]:

> "It seems to me however that the defenders' argument goes too far in suggesting that it is enough if the pursuer is aware that the injury may be attributable to an act or omission, or an act or omission of one of a particular group of persons. If that possibility is only one of a number of possibilities and there is no reason to choose between them, I doubt if it can be said that the pursuer is, in any meaningful sense, aware that the injuries attributable to the act or omission in question so as to start time running against him. Beyond that, it does

---

[8] *Shuttleton v Duncan Stewart & Co. Ltd*, 1996 S.L.T. 517.
[9] *Comer v James Scott & Co (Electrical Engineers) Ltd*, 1978 S.L.T. 235.
[10] See Ch.21 on Occupational Illness and Disease at paras 21–20 to 21–26.
[11] *Nicol v British Steel Corporation*, 1992 S.L.T. 141.

not seem to me to be possible to generalise and the question whether the pursuer was aware, or whether it was reasonably practicable for him to become aware, of sufficient facts and circumstances to start the triennium running must depend on the particular facts and circumstances."

Knowledge of the cause of injury is not the same as knowledge that a right of legal action has accrued, i.e. that the client has a good claim in law. The latter does not stop time running. It will not do as a s.17 argument that your client did not know he had a good claim in law.[12]

Section 17(2)(b)(iii)—identity of defender

6–06 This might be applicable where there is difficulty in establishing the precise legal identity of the defender, e.g. where the defender is a subsidiary company, or where there has been a company change of name. It would be unwise for a practitioner to place great reliance on this section to prevent time running. In particular you will be expected to make enquiries of the Register of Companies, check the telephone book, and if necessary raise a summary application under the Administration of Justice (Scotland) Act 1972 for disclosure of the information.[13]

Section 18

6–07 Section 18 relates to claims by relatives of or connected persons to a deceased, as defined in the Damages (Scotland) Act 1976 as amended. It provides that all actions must be commenced within three years from the date of death, or within three years from the date of knowledge of a relative or executor subject to the same questions of sufficient seriousness, attributability and identity as discussed above, where this date is later than the date of death. The practitioner should note the terms of s.18(4), which states:

> "Subject to section 19A of this Act, where an action of damages has not been brought by or on behalf of a person who has sustained personal injuries in the period specified in section 17(2) of this Act, and that person subsequently dies in consequence of those injuries, no action to which this section applies shall be brought in respect of those injuries or the death from those injuries."

This means that for cases where the injury or disease has not caused the death, the starting point for the triennium may be the deceased's date of knowledge, which may be many years before the actual date of death.[14]

---

[12] Prescription and Limitation (Scotland) Act 1973 s.22(3).
[13] See *Murray v National Association of Round Tables of Great Britain*, 2002 S.L.T. 204 and *McDyer v Celtic Football Club (No.1)*, 2000 S.L.T. 736.
[14] *Mackie's Executrix v AB 2000 Ltd*, 2004 S.C. 334.

Section 19A—the equitable discretion

There should be little difficulty in avoiding triennium crises, as long as regular and systematic file checks are in operation. **6–08**

In practice, you will from time to time consider instructions received very close to the expiry of the triennium. You cannot accept these instructions unless you are fully prepared to issue proceedings within the triennium. If you decline to act, you should follow up with a recorded delivery letter advising the client that proceedings must be raised before the expiry of the triennium. You will receive occasional instructions from clients whose claims are already time barred. Section 19A of the Prescription and Limitation (Scotland) Act 1973 as amended provides in these circumstances that: "the court may, if it seems to it equitable to do so, allow him to bring the action".

What are the prospects of persuading the court to exercise its equitable discretion to allow the action to proceed? Although it is still sometimes said that the s.19A discretion should be exercised sparingly and with restraint,[15] this has been stated by the Inner House to be the wrong approach:

> "At the same time I must emphasise that the discretion of the court is unfettered, although in every case the relaxation of the statutory bar can and must depend solely upon equitable considerations relevant to the exercise of our discretion and jurisdiction in the particular case, having regard to the fact that it is for the party seeking relief to satisfy the court that it is, in the view of the court and in the circumstances of the case and of the legitimate rights and interests of the parties, equitable to do so."[16]

The discretion is completely unfettered, but in practice the cases fall into two distinct categories, as follows.

1. Cases where there are good prospects of establishing liability against another party

The classic situation is where a solicitor has allowed the triennium to expire. In this situation the client is usually identified with the actings of his previous agent. The defenders have lost the benefit of a cast iron defence, and in most situations the client has a clear alternative remedy against the solicitor.[17] Where matters are straightforward, the prospects of persuading the court to exercise its s.19A discretion are generally **6–09**

---

[15] See, e.g. *Cowan v Toffolo Jackson & Co Ltd*, 1997 Rep. L.R. 40.
[16] *Donald v Rutherford*, 1984 S.L.T. 70 at [75].
[17] The case of *McCaffery v Greater Glasgow Health Board* Unreported March 28, 2003 Court of Session, is a good example of the approach generally taken, i.e. discretion not exercised because of remedy against solicitor.

poor.[18] In those circumstances the claim should be directed against the solicitor in the first instance. If the insurers ask that you attempt an action under s.19A of the 1973 Act, you should make it clear in correspondence that you will hold them liable in the cost of any unsuccessful proceedings. The insurers may be prepared to admit liability or otherwise to deal with the claim without asking you to take proceedings against the original defender. In that situation you must remember that the claim is not a personal injury claim as such,[19] but is a damages claim based on the valuation of the loss of chance of success in the original action.[20] This claim is not subject to the personal injuries triennium, but to the five-year quinquennial prescriptive period. Notwithstanding, you must still assemble all available statements, photographs and reports on the merits of the personal injury action, with a view to establishing that the prospects of success would have been high, and that the loss of chance could be assessed at or close to the book value of the claim. If you find that the case has prima facie time barred in your hands, there is a clear potential for conflict of interest if you act using a s.19A argument. The safe and proper course is to explain matters fully to the client and to refer him to other agents who can make a choice of proceedings.

2. Where there is no apparent remedy against any other party

6–10 In this situation the s.19A discretion is so wide that it can be difficult to know where to start. You are looking for factors which do not amount in law to a "reasonable practicability" argument under s.17(2), but which do amount to a reasonable explanation or excuse as to why proceedings have not been raised timeously. The Scottish Law Commission has proposed a number of factors to which the court may have regard in considering the exercise of the discretion. These are:

1. The period which has elapsed since the right of action accrued.
2. Why it is that the action was not brought timeously.
3. What effect the passage of time has had on the defenders' ability to defend, and on the availability and quality of evidence.
4. The conduct of the pursuer and in particular how expeditious he was to seek legal or medical advice, and to intimate a damages claim.
5. The quality and nature of any legal, medical or expert advice obtained by the defender.
6. The conduct of the defender and how he has responded to any relevant request for information.
7. What other remedy the pursuer has if he is not allowed to bring the action.

---

[18] See, e.g. *Beaton v Strathclyde Buses Ltd*, 1993 S.L.T. 931. But see also the case of *Elliot v J. & C. Finney*, 1989 S.L.T. 605 where the Inner House upheld the decision of the Lord Ordinary to allow a s.19A submission where the pursuer had a remedy against his solicitor on the grounds that there was a possible complication in that messengers at arms could be introduced as a third party in the professional negligence action.

[19] See *Mackenzie v Digby Brown & Co*, 1992 S.L.T. 891.

[20] See, e.g. *Kyle v P. & J. Stormonth Darling, WS*, 1994 S.L.T. 191.

8. Any other matter which appears to the court to be relevant.[21]

Practitioners could do worse than treat this as an existing working checklist for all cases.

There is existing analogous English legislation under the Limitation Act 1980 s.33 which has a similar checklist of factors which the court are obliged to recognise.

In the case of *McLaren v Harland & Wolff*,[22] Lord Milligan was prepared to look to the English legislation for guidance.[23]

Particular factors which have helped pursuers in the Scottish courts are:

1. The cogency of the evidence. In this regard it is suggested that the proper course is to look at the state of the evidence on the expiry of the triennium. Unless the defender can point to some loss of evidence which has occurred between that date and the raising of proceedings, you can legitimately state that they have suffered no actual prejudice with regard to the presentation of their case.[24] As was stated by Lord Morton in the case of *Comber v Greater Glasgow Health Board*[25]:

    "The defenders have been prejudiced by the expiry of the limitation period but apart from that there is no evidence or averment that they would be in any different position than they would have been if the action had been raised in August 1981 before the limitation period expired. There is no averment for example that any witness has been lost or that any particular witness cannot remember any crucial matter or that the hospital records are in any sense incomplete."[26]

2. The pursuer's lack of awareness that he had any right of legal action. Many older workers in particular believe that certain conditions, e.g. noise induced hearing loss, are simply incidents of employment, and do not realise that they have any right of compensation against a former employer. This lack of awareness was held to be a relevant factor in the case of *Comber*. The widow of the deceased had no idea that she could claim damages in respect of his death from an asbestos related disease.

Where you feel that a s.19A argument might succeed, it is imperative that proceedings are raised forthwith and expeditious progress made. Matters

---

[21] Scottish Law Commission, *Report Paper 207 on personal injury accidents: limitation and prescribed claims* (The Stationery Office, 2007), proposed legislation.
[22] *McLaren v Harland & Wolff*, 1991 S.L.T. 85.
[23] cf. the approach of Lord McCluskey in the case of *Beaton v Strathclyde Buses*, 1993 S.L.T. 931 at [932].
[24] See, e.g. *Kidd v Grampian Health Board*, 1994 S.L.T. 267 and *McLaren v Harland & Wolff Ltd*, as above.
[25] *Comber v Greater Glasgow Health Board*, 1989 S.L.T. 639 at [641].
[26] This factor also carried particular weight with Lord Johnston in the case of *Ferla v Secretary of State for Scotland*, 1995 S.L.T. 662.

are by definition already behindhand; further dithering and delay may well prove disastrous. Finally it must be said that factors which appear to influence one judge carry no weight with another, and the particular exercise of discretion is well nigh unappealable. The reality is that the law on s.19A is now so inchoate as to defy analysis. This creates particular difficulties for practitioners in negotiation and settlement, where the approach is necessarily based on a prediction of outcome. The fullest and most recent discussion on s.19A is contained in *AS v Sister Bernard Mary Murray*.[27] An historic child abuse case, it makes gloomy reading for pursuers' agents. Unless there is something exceptional in the facts, the realistic advice for pursuer's agents where s.19A is relied upon, would be to accept a significant litigation discount.

---

[27] *AS v Sister Bernard Mary Murray* [2005] CSOH 70.

CHAPTER 7

NEGOTIATION AND SETTLEMENT BEFORE ACTION

NEGOTIATION

For the personal injury practitioner, negotiation is the process of disclosure, discussion and persuasion by which parties attempt to reach agreement without direct judicial intervention. In this way both sides can reduce the uncertainties and expense of litigation, to their mutual benefit. Negotiation is not separate and distinct from litigation. It proceeds "in the shadow of the law", i.e. parties will adopt a position depending upon their prediction of the likely outcome if the case were to proceed to proof. It derives its authority from the ultimate coercive power of the court. This gives each party what is sometimes described as "the bargaining endowment". Negotiation does not stop when court proceedings are raised. It will proceed up to judgment, and sometimes beyond until the case is finally settled. In the United States one prominent academic describes this process of negotiation after proceedings are raised as "litigotiation".[1]

7–01

Negotiations need not be formalised. Every piece of information you impart to the other side, whether it is by way of letter, telephone call or writ, is part of the negotiation process.

The Voluntary Pre-Action Protocol

Following the abolition of the General Tables of Fees in 2005, the Law Society of Scotland and the Forum of Insurers set up the Voluntary Pre-Action Protocol. It is meant to cover claims with a value of up to £10,000. There is a separate Disease Voluntary Pre-Action Protocol.[2] Not all insurers or major defenders operate the scheme.[3] The main advantages are that the claim proceeds on an agreed timetable, there are pre-action disclosure provisions and a reasonable fee structure for settled cases. The letter of claim should be in Form A and should invite the insurer to agree that the case is suitable for the Protocol. If agreement is reached, the timetable applies and appropriate diary reminders should be set. Any admission of liability cannot be retracted at a later date, although this will not apply where the value of the claim is later stated to be more than

7–02

---

[1] See the discussion of these ideas in Hazel Genn, *Hard Bargaining: Out of Court Settlement in Personal Injury Actions* (Oxford: Oxford University Press, 1987), and also the works of Professor Marc Galanter.
[2] The Protocols are reproduced in full at Appendix 3.
[3] Glasgow City Council is a notable absentee.

£10,000. The Law Society and Forum of Insurers have set up a liaison committee which meets periodically to iron out any problems which arise in the operation of the scheme.

Intimating the claim

7–03 Send your preliminary letter of claim in the form of Letter A to the target individual or organisation, with the request that it is sent to their insurers. Diary forward 21 days to send a reminder if there is no response. There is generally not much point in intimating direct to the insurers; they will simply return your letter. But where the defender company is no longer on the Register of Companies, you should intimate to their known insurers with an explanatory letter.

Where a negligent driver does not respond to your initial letter you should intimate direct to the insurers, advising them that you will require to look to them as the road traffic insurer in terms of the Road Traffic Act 1988 s.151.

Where there is no response after reminders from a negligent employer, you should write to the directors pointing out their obligations to have liability insurance under the Employers' Liability (Compulsory Insurance) Act 1969.

Contents of the initial letter; Speciman Letters A1 and A2

7–04 You should set out a brief outline of the facts of the accident and the injury, together with your client's date of birth and national insurance number to enable the insurers to register the claim with the Compensation Recovery Unit ("CRU"). You should be aware that your letter may be admissible in later proceedings as evidence of its contents, and it can be extremely embarrassing if your initial allegations have been misstated.

All statutory grounds of liability should be clearly stated. If you rely on a common law breach, it is sufficient to say that there was a failure to take reasonable care for the safety of your client. The letter should be marked "without prejudice".

Without prejudice correspondence

7–05 The general rule is that nothing which is written or said "without prejudice" in the course of negotiations should be looked at except with the consent of both parties. This is as a matter of public policy, to enable frank settlement discussions to take place, where concessions can be made without fear that they will be later pounced upon as admissions. There may be an exception where the communication is produced to show that a settlement was reached, or where the contents of the communication might be relevant to expenses, as where a pre-action offer has not been bettered after litigation.[4] Scottish cases such as *Daks Simpson Group Plc v Kuilper*,[5] which might suggest otherwise, and in particular that unequivocal admissions of fact may not be protected by the brocard,

---

[4] *Unilever Plc v The Procter and Gamble Company* [2000] 1 W.L.R. 2436.
[5] *Daks Simpson Group Plc v Kuilper*, 1994 S.L.T. 689.

should now be treated with caution. The advice for practitioners is that all correspondence with insurers should be marked "without prejudice" to avoid the embarrassment of later discrepancies being founded upon.

Admissions of liability

Agents should be aware that at common law, insurers can generally withdraw an admission of liability at any time prior to settlement.[6] The only exceptions are where you can show some kind of prejudice in enquiry or investigation. Generally an admission will not be withdrawn, but if you have any concerns you should ask the insurer to declare that the admission is irrevocable, and can be relied upon in any subsequent proceedings. In Protocol cases any admission is treated as binding by agreement for proceedings up to £10,000.00.

7–06

PROGRESSING THE CLAIM

Protocol cases

The claim should proceed in terms of the Protocol timetable. Reminders should be sent. If they are ignored you will have to litigate.

7–07

Correspondence with the insurers—non-Protocol cases

Most insurers will respond by acknowledging your letter, seeking medical evidence and advising that they are conducting investigations. They will frequently request details of any corroborating witnesses. Although, as is frequently stated, there is no property in witnesses, you do not have to comply with this request at this stage. Much will depend on the strength of the case and your relationship with the particular insurers. Whilst most insurers will make a genuine attempt to settle matters without proceedings, a substantial minority have unrealistic ideas on liability and on the quantum of damages. If you know from your own experience that you are unlikely to obtain a proper offer, you should not disclose witness details, but should press on with a view to raising proceedings. Similarly, many insurers are quick to request full particulars of your witnesses, but refuse to disclose their own evidence. Where you do agree to provide witness details, you should seek reciprocity, e.g. in factory cases ask for an extract from the accident book; in pavement tripper cases request details of the local authority inspection and maintenance regime. Prior to the raising of proceedings, you can impose conditions on disclosure of witnesses, e.g. that they are interviewed in your office, in your presence. If you agree that they are to be interviewed at home, you should always write to the witness advising them that they should expect to be contacted, and that they should co-operate. You should tell them to refuse to sign any written statement.

7–08

---

[6] See *Van Klaveren v Servisair UK Ltd,* 2009 S.L.T. 576.

Progressing the claim

7-09 A pursuer's case thrives on momentum. It is axiomatic that delay favours the insurers. Witnesses might disappear or die, memories fade, and disillusioned clients might well accept undervalue offers. Against this background it is particularly important that you develop a system of working which ensurers that every letter is replied to as quickly as possible. You will need to provide the insurers with a medical report, details of any special wage and property losses, and the client's personal details for CRU purposes. Thereafter you should press them to settle the claim as quickly as possible. A distinction may be drawn between Protocol and non-Protocol cases. It is relatively easy by diary reminders to keep the former on track and to hold the insurers to the timetable. Even where the Protocol has not been agreed, you should insist that insurers come to a decision within the general framework of the Protocol timetable.

In practice your reminders may be met by anodyne declarations that enquiries are not complete. If you allow it, matters can drift along in this way for years. It would be wrong to blame the insurers for the delay. The fault lies with the practitioner who has relinquished control of the claim. You should take the initiative by setting deadlines for completion of enquiries, and for a settlement offer to be made.

A reliable litmus test is the CRU position. The insurers will not settle without a certificate of recoverable benefit. You will receive notice from the CRU when they request such a certificate. Unless and until you do, you may assume that settlement is not imminent.

For the pursuer's agent the only alternative to a negotiated agreement is a court action. The stronger the prospects in court, the stronger the position at the negotiation table.

As is emphasised throughout, correspondence with the insurers should never deflect the practitioner from shoring up the case on liability, by simultaneously following up every witness and evidence lead. You cannot negotiate effectively unless you are prepared to fight, and those who wish to make peace should prepare for war.

Repudiation

7-10 Where you fail to reach an agreement, you will require to raise proceedings or close the file. Frequently your settlement requests may simply have gone unanswered. You should provide the insurers with a reasonable opportunity to quantify and settle. In *Neilson v Motion*,[7] the pursuer's solicitors failed to engage in the settlement process in any meaningful way. An offer was made by the defenders immediately after proceedings were raised in the Court of Session, and Lord Prosser held that expenses should be restricted to the extra-judicial settlement scale.

Settlement fees

7-11 There is no difficulty in Protocol cases where there is an agreed table. In non-Protocol cases, care should be taken to agree in advance of settle-

---

[7] *Neilson v Motion*, 1992 S.L.T. 124.

ment that the Protocol fee structure will apply. In *Stewart v Speed*,[8] Sheriff Holligan held that by custom and practice solicitors were entitled to a settlement fee based on the then extant Ch.10 of the Law Society Table of Fees. Chapter 10 is no more, and it is suggested that as a matter of custom and practice fees are now payable on the Protocol Fees Table.

Negotiation by letter and telephone

Most low and middle value cases are settled by way of correspondence. **7–12** You should prepare a Statement of Valuation using the format of sheriff court form PI6, with a settlement brochure as recommended in Ch.4. If you are telephoned by the insurers, *never* take the call and deal with the matter cold, or without the file. Always return the call, having rehearsed in advance what you are going to say.

---

[8] *Stewart v Speed* Unreported March 28, 2006 Kirkcaldy Sheriff Court.

CHAPTER 8

ORDINARY CAUSE PROCEDURE IN PERSONAL INJURY CASES

ACT OF SEDERUNT (ORDINARY CAUSE RULES AMENDMENT) (PERSONAL INJURIES ACTIONS) 2009

Coulsfield Rules in the Sheriff Court

8–01 The Personal Injury Rules apply to all actions raised after November 2, 2009.[1] The basic structure is that a new set of personal injury rules has been grafted onto existing r.36 of the Ordinary Cause Rules. There are prescriptive forms and a timetable, and there are various incidental amendments to the rules at large. There was a further change for actions raised after July 29, 2010, when requirements for lodging documents and witness lists were clarified.

The philosophy behind the Personal Injury Rules is that case management in the sheriff court (if it ever existed) is replaced by case flow and management by timetable. This is an attempt to replicate the extremely successful Ch.43 procedure in the Court of Session, generally known as the Coulsfield Rules.[2]

Commentary on the Personal Injury Rules

OCR 3.1

8–02 OCR 3.1 is amended to provide that the new form of initial writ for a personal injuries action is PI1.

OCR 13.1

8–03 Where a third party or minuter claims title to enter appearance in a personal injury action the sheriff may grant the applicant leave to enter the process. But note the terms of OCR 13.1(4) to the effect that if the application is made after the time the record should have been lodged, the sheriff shall only grant leave if he is satisfied as to the reason that earlier application was not made. Where the application has been granted in a personal injuries action, the sheriff may make such further order as he thinks fit as regards the 36.G1 timetable.

---

[1] For procedure for existing cases under the old rules see the previous edition.
[2] See "Report of the Monitoring and Evaluation of New Procedures for Personal Injuries Actions" introduced in the Court of Session, March 2007, Elaine Samuel.

OCR 36.A1—application and interpretation

This contains a definition of a personal injuries action which includes any **8–04** disease or impairment whether physical or mental, and encompasses actions based on clinical negligence. Note that claims for professional negligence are not r.36 cases although they may originate from personal injury (see *Tudhope v Finlay Park trading as Park Hutchison Solicitors*[3]). In clinical negligence cases, the pursuer will need to show "exceptional reasons for not following personal injury procedure". So there is no automatic route to the ordinary cause Ch.9 standard procedure for clinical negligence actions. It is also likely that claims under the Protection of Harassment Act 1997 are not personal injury actions (see *G v S*[4]).

OCR 36.B1—form of initial writ

The initial writ shall be in form PI1. It shall contain averments relating **8–05** only to those facts necessary to establish the claim, and the names of every medical practitioner and every hospital where the pursuer was treated. It may also include a specification of documents in terms of form PI2. See Ch.9 for commentary on the new pleading requirements.

OCR 36.C1—actions based on clinical negligence

This section relates to actions where the cause of action is clinical neg- **8–06** ligence. The writ may contain a draft interlocutor in form PI4 and the pursuer may lodge a written application in the form of letter addressed to the sheriff clerk for authority to raise the action as an ordinary action. This application will be dealt with by the sheriff in chambers. The sheriff should either grant the motion, or fix a hearing. If authority is granted for the case to proceed as an ordinary action, it will proceed in accordance with Ch.9 standard procedure in defended causes.

OCR 36.D1—inspection and recovery of documents

This allows for a standard specification of documents in form PI2 to be **8–07** added to the initial writ. The sheriff clerk docquets form PI2 in form PI3. This gives it the equivalence of an interlocutor granting commission and diligence signed by the sheriff and in particular is the equivalent of an order under OCR 28.2. Note that in terms of the 36.G1 timetable this specification must be served under OCR 28.3 Optional Procedure within 28 days of defences being lodged (see the timetable). The normal procedure is that the specification will be served on the defender under the Optional Procedure along with the service of the writ. Service on third parties, e.g. hospitals, GPs can be served up until the expiry of the 28 days period. There is no method of altering the standard specification of documents. This means that you cannot add fresh calls, although you can call for risk assessments specific to the regulations pled, e.g. risk assessments under the Noise at Work Regulations 1989. Further the inter-

---

[3] *Tudhope v Finlay Park trading as Park Hutchison Solicitors*, 2004 S.L.T. 783.
[4] *G v S*, 2006 S.L.T. 795.

locutor does not appoint a commissioner. This means that there is no provision for fixing a commission if the documents do not appear. So where documents are not recovered under the Optional Procedure specification, there will need to be a fresh specification of documents and the motion should crave for the appointment of a commissioner at that stage. You should have a standard letter calling for the documents, as soon as defences are in.

OCR 36.E1—application of other rules

8–08 The Personal Injury Procedure trumps the Ordinary Cause Procedure except:

- Rule 9.1 (notice of intention to defend).
- Rule 9.3 (initial writ to be returned to court).
- Rule 9.5 (sheriff clerk to make up process folder).
- Rule 9.6 (form of defences). The defences shall not include a note of pleas in law.
- Rule 9.7 (implied admissions).

Unlike the court of session, the old rules about the format of defences are retained.

In terms of OCR 36.E1(6) where there is a minute of amendment, e.g. seeking the addition of a substitute or additional defender, it should also include confirmation that warrant for service is sought as well as a specification of documents.

OCR 36.E1(7)

8–09 It is clear that where amended pleadings have to be served, any OCR 36.G1 timetable issued is also to be served. The clear implication is that the 36.G1 timetable will not be interrupted.

OCR 36.E1(8)

8–10 Where amendment is allowed in these terms the court will not fix a r.18 hearing, because there is no need to fix a fresh OCR 36.G1 timetable, i.e. having a new defender does not automatically mean that you are back to the start. This applies only to cases where a new pursuer or defender is added. Otherwise for amendment of pleadings there will still be a r.18 hearing.

OCR 36.E1(9)

8–11 A counterclaim can also include a warrant for intimation and specification of documents.

OCR 36.E1(11) and (12)

These make it plain that the OCR 36.G1 timetable has to be served with a third party notice and the OCR 36.G1 timetable already issued will apply to the third party.

8–12

OCR 36.E1(13)

There are now no pleas in law, and no r.22 notes. OCR 28A and the requirement to fix a pre-proof hearing no longer apply.

8–13

OCR 36.E1(14)

There are no longer condescendences, but simply statements of claim with numbered paragraphs. Any reference in the rules to an action being carried out before the closing of the record is now to be construed as referring to the date fixed for the completion of adjustment.

8–14

There is no longer a "closed record" but simply a "record".

OCR 36.F1—disapplication of personal injuries procedure

Any party may apply within 28 days of the first lodging of defences to have the action withdrawn from the personal injury procedure to proceed as an ordinary cause. The sheriff has to have regard to the need for detailed pleadings, the length of time required for the preparation of the action, and any other relevant circumstances. The application is by motion so the normal OCR 15 procedure will be required. The sheriff will only grant the motion if he is satisfied that there are exceptional reasons for not following the personal injury procedure. It is suggested that full details are set out in the motion. If it is opposed the motion will have to call, but otherwise it appears that the motion can be granted in chambers. If granted, there will be an order for defences, and an Options Hearing fixed, and full standard Ordinary Cause procedure.

8–15

OCR 36.G1—allocation of diets and timetable

On the lodging of defences (or the first lodging of defences where more than one defender) the sheriff clerk shall:

8–16

1. Fix a diet of proof not later than nine months from the date of lodging of defences.
2. Issue a OCR 36.G1 timetable. This timetable can be varied by the sheriff principal, with the exception of the pre-proof conference date. This clearly contemplates each sheriff principal issuing a practice note for each sheriffdom. Surely not!

OCR 36.G1(2)

The OCR 36.G1 timetable will be issued in form PI5 and is to be treated as the equivalent of an interlocutor.

8–17

OCR 36.G1(3)

8–18 Where there is any failure to comply with any requirement of the OCR 36.G1 timetable other than failure to lodge a record or failure to lodge the pre-proof conference joint minute, the sheriff clerk *may* fix a date and time for parties to be heard by the sheriff. In respect of those specified failures the sheriff clerk *shall* fix a date and time for parties to be heard by the sheriff.

(Note that in terms of OCR 36.J1(5) where the fault relates to failure to lodge a Statement of Valuation, the sheriff may dismiss the action for the pursuer's fault, or grant decree against the defender for an amount not exceeding the pursuer's valuation for the defenders' fault.)

OCR 36.G1(4)

8–19 The pursuer has to lodge a certified copy of the record which consists of the pleadings only (no interlocutors) and at the same time lodge a motion craving a preliminary proof, a proof, or some other specified order at the same time stating the anticipated length of the proof (see OCR 36.G1(5) and (6)).

OCR 36.G1(7)

8–20 In the event that any party wishes the court to make an order other than a proof, the party shall set out full notice of the grounds in the motion. Typically a defender might wish to fix a debate on relevancy if there is a knockout point; or perhaps seek to have a preliminary proof on time bar. Unless the notice of opposition sets this out with full grounds for opposition the court should simply fix a proof (See *Broadfoot's C.B. v Forth Valley Acute Hospital NHS Trust*).[5] Note that now there is no real distinction between a proof and proof before answer (See *Hamilton v Seamark Systems Ltd*[6]).

OCR 36.G1(9)

8–21 Productions are to be lodged eight weeks prior to proof and shall not be allowed in evidence except with consent of parties or with leave of the sheriff. In terms of the 36.G1 timetable the list of witnesses has to be lodged at the same date as the productions, i.e. eight weeks before the proof. For actions raised prior to July 29, 2010 there was no sanction for failing to lodge witness lists, nor any requirement regarding a child witness notice or vulnerable witness application as currently contained in OCR 9A. Where the action is raised after July 29, 2010 in terms of OCR 36.G1(8A), you cannot lead a person who is not on the witness list without the consent of the other party or the leave of the sheriff. In terms of OCR 36.G1(8B) the list should include the name, address and occupation of each intended witness, and also advise whether any witness is a

---

[5] *Broadfoot's C.B. v Forth Valley Acute Hospital NHS Trust*, 2003 G.W.D. 26-279.
[6] *Hamilton v Seamark Systems Ltd*, 2004 G.W.D. 8-167.

vulnerable witness in terms of the Vulnerable Witnesses (Scotland) Act 2004.

OCR 36.G1(10)

Where there are a number of cases arising from the same cause of action any party may move that one case be deemed a leading case, and the other cases be sisted pending its determination. All parties must be notified of the motion hearing and are entitled to be heard on the motion.

OCR 36.G1—the timetable—see form PI5

1. The defender to apply for third party notice not later than 28 days after defences have been lodged.
2. Pursuer to execute commission for recovery of the documents not later than 28 days after defences have been lodged.
3. Parties to adjust their pleadings not later than eight weeks after defences have been lodged.
4. Pursuer to lodge Statement of Valuation of claim and list of documents not later than eight weeks after defences have been lodged. Note that the documents in support of the Statement of Valuation should be lodged as an Inventory of Productions.
5. Pursuer to lodge record not later than 10 weeks after defences have been lodged.
6. Defender and any third party to lodge Statement of Valuation not later than 12 weeks after defences have been lodged.
7. Pursuer to lodge in process list of witnesses and inventory of productions not later than eight weeks before the diet fixed for proof.
8. Pursuer to lodge minute of pre-proof conference not later than 21 days before the diet fixed for proof.
9. Proof date.

OCR 36.H1—application for sist or variation of timetable

This is made by motion which has to be placed before the sheriff and has to be granted only on special cause shown. If granted the case will be sisted for a specific period only, e.g. for three months for the grant of legal aid.

Where this is granted a revised timetable will be issued.

OCR 36.J1—statements of valuation of claim

Note that the party lodging the Statement must include a list of supporting documents in the statement of valuation of claim and must intimate that list and lodge the documents.

As has already been noted OCR 36.J1(5) has draconian penalties for failure.

OCR 36.K1—pre-proof conferences

8–26 This relates to the minute of pre-proof conference which is to be lodged in process not later than three weeks before the date of the proof. If it is not lodged, then the sheriff clerk *shall* fix a date and time for parties to be heard. The purpose of the conference is:

(a) to discuss settlement of the action; and
(b) to agree, so far as possible, matters which are not in dispute.

OCR 36.K1(4)

8–27 The representative of each party to the action shall have access to the party who has authority to commit the party to the settlement of the action.

It is clear that this can be by telephone conference, video conference or other remote means or at a specific place.

The form of the pre-proof minute is PI7.

The pre-proof conference form contains an introduction which details the specifics of the meeting, and then three sections.

A. *The first section* contains general questions as to whether a proof is still required, and whether any contributory negligence and quantum has been agreed.
B. *The second section* contains calls which parties may put on each other with space for these to be admitted or denied together with an estimate of proof time (it might be prudent to draft these and intimate them in advance.)
   If the proof is to take more than two days this should be brought to the attention of the sheriff clerk.
C. *The third section* relates to elements of quantum which may or may not be agreed.

OCR 36.L1—incidental hearings

8–28 Where the sheriff clerk fixes a hearing under OCR 36.G1(3) (any failure to comply with the timetable) or 36.G1(8) (failure to lodge a record), the sheriff clerk will call on the party in default to lodge in court a written explanation as to why the timetable has not been complied with and to intimate that written explanation to all other parties not less than two clear working days before the date of the hearing.

At the hearing the sheriff shall consider the explanation, may make an award of expenses, and may make any other appropriate award including decree of dismissal.

Mesothelioma actions—special provisions

8–29 OCR 36.19 relates to mesothelioma actions. These relate to the special factors in mesothelioma claims. In particular having regard to the terms of the Damages (Scotland) Act 2011 a pursuer is able to settle his claim during life, with relatives being sisted to the action for their claims on his death. At OCR 36.19(2) the procedure envisaged after settlement of a living pursuer's claim is that the pursuer moves that the case be sisted, and that all diets are discharged. If it is a new personal injury action, then the motion for sist will have to specify a period of time (say one year?). On the death of the pursuer the sist can be recalled in the same action with an order for further procedure, at the instance of the relatives of the deceased.

PRACTICE POINTS

8–30 Sheriff court procedure has now been brought into line with that of the Court of Session. Guidance on the practice and application of the rules can be obtained in particular from the following sources relative to Court of Session procedure:

1. Practice note No.2 of 2003. This contains the most detailed and comprehensive guidance on the Coulsfield approach in the Court of Session.
2. Practice note No.3 of 2004.
3. Practice note No.1 of 2007.
4. Newsletters of the Personal Injury Users' Group.
   All of these sources are available online at the Court of Session website.[7]
5. The commentary on Ch.43 of the Court of Session Rules, contained in the Parliament House Book.

Pleadings[8]

8–31 The Coulsfield working party stated:

> "The discussions in the Working Party tended to the conclusion that, realistically speaking, what is required in most cases in relation to liability is the briefest description of the events on which the claim is based, together with a brief indication of the ground of fault alleged and a specific reference to any statutory provision which may be founded upon."

They further stated:

> "Essentially, therefore, we agree that what is necessary is a method of pleading which encourages brevity and simplicity and discourages technicality and artificiality."

Initial writ

8–32 This is to be in form PI1. There is no longer any need to crave interest.

---

[7] http://www.scotcourts.gov.uk/session/index.asp [Accessed September 10, 2011].
[8] See also Ch.9.

STATEMENT OF CLAIM

Paragraph 4—grounds of liability

8–33 In *Clifton v Hayes*,[9] where a keg had fallen off a lorry trailer at certain premises the pursuer's pleadings did not contain averments of fact necessary to establish a claim against the second defenders who were the owners of the premises. There was nothing to connect the accident with their duties as occupiers. A diet of debate was allowed in that case, the clear implication being that dismissal would follow. It is clear that not much is required to found a basic case on relevance (see *Easdon v A. Clark Co (Smithwick) Ltd*[10]). Despite the exhortations to brevity and simplicity, it is important to recognise that pursuers must still provide fair notice of the factual grounds on which the case proceeds. As ever it can be difficult to distinguish between material fact and what is evidence supporting that fact. The practitioner advice must always be to err on the side of caution. If you are in any doubt that a defender might reasonably claim to be caught by surprise by a passage of evidence, you must give notice in the pleadings, e.g. previous convictions should be pled, previous accidents should be pled and the factual basis as to why an accident is reasonably foreseeable should be pled. Put yourself on the other side of the board and consider whether you are giving fair notice of the line of evidence which you wish to lead.

Practitioners should also be aware of the decision in *McFarlane v Thain*, 2010 S.C. 7. This was a road traffic action in which it was already agreed that only basic pleadings were required, even although it was a pre-Coulsfield type case. The pursuer was a motorcyclist. In the course of the proof it emerged that a possible ground of fault might be that the other driver should have heard the sound of the motorcycle as it came up the hill. This was objected to and the Inner House upheld the objection on the grounds of no record. So the lesson would be still to err on the side of caution as far as pleadings are concerned.

Paragraph 5—damages section

8–34 The original idea was that only heads of damages would be put in this section. The statement of valuation was to provide the specification. A description of medical institutions would enable records to be recovered. No amounts or figures are required (See Court of Session (Personal Injury) New Rules Newsletter No.2, May 2004). Specification of loss will be found in the statement of valuation, together with the supporting documents, i.e. medical reports, wages documentation etc. It is not entirely clear whether the statement of valuation is to be treated as part of the pleadings (see the discussion in *Easdon v A. Clark Co (Smithwick) Ltd*[11]). They do, however, constitute fair notice and can be relied upon to repel objections as to lack of notice. It is also worth noting that in

---

[9] *Clifton v Hayes*, 2004 G.W.D. 2-23.
[10] *Easdon v A. Clark Co (Smithwick) Ltd* [2006] CSOH 12 at [14].
[11] *Easdon v A. Clark Co (Smithwick) Ltd* [2006] CSOH 12 at [12] and [13].

Sneddon v Deutag Services Ltd reports on Quantum 2005 Rep.L.R. 90 Lord Carloway in a jury trial permitted the pursuer's statement of valuation of claim to be put to the pursuer in cross-examination.

In *Towers v Jack*[12] in a jury trial Lord Drummond Young ruled that sufficient notice had been given to the defender where concise pleadings were followed by: (i) a pursuer's Statement of Valuation claim; (ii) the lodging of certain productions; and (iii) discussions at the pre-trial meeting. The pre-trial conference offers an ideal opportunity for all parties to be forthcoming about any points likely to be taken.

Paragraph 6—legal grounds

This requires a simple statement as to whether you are relying on common law, e.g. vicarious liability or breach of statute or both. The statute and section should be stated (it is not strictly necessary to state the subsection (see *Higgins v DHL*[13])) although it is clearly best practice.

8–35

Specification of documents with initial writ

You should look to serve the specification in every case. You cannot amend the specification at this stage. What this means is that the pro forma specification cannot recover wages information where the pursuer is employed by someone other than the defender. Note that the specification of documents has to be executed within 28 days. It is served under the optional procedure. You should recover the medical records and also risk assessments and accident reports, etc. The specification for recovery of medical records does not require to be intimated to the Lord Advocate. The specification should be served directly on the defenders with the writ, and separately on any other havers. It has to be said that these pre-service specifications are routinely ignored. You should have a style letter to be issued as soon as defences are in, calling for the records under specification. You can then proceed with the appointment of a Commissioner, if the documents are not received.

8–36

Form of defences

OCR 9.7 still governs the format. Every statement of fact which is not denied will be held to be admitted. The defences should also provide fair notice of any substantive defence, e.g. time bar, reasonable practicability, contributory negligence, sole fault, etc. Some guidance can be obtained from the requirement under the old Court of Session optional procedure. For example in *Williamson v GB Papers Plc*, 1994 S.L.T. 173, Lord Cullen held that even in an Optional Procedure case the defenders had to give notice in the pleadings that they intended to raise a defence of reasonable practicability. When raising a defence of contributory negligence or sole fault, it may be sufficient to aver that the pursuer was in breach of duty to take reasonable care for his own safety, without specifying the particular duties, so long as the factual basis is clear. See the approach of

8–37

---

[12] *Towers v Jack*, 2004 Rep. L.R. 100.
[13] *Higgins v DHL* Unreported October 31, 2003 Court of Session.

the Inner House in *McGowan v W. & J. R. Watson Ltd*[14] approving the approach by Lord Glennie in *Weir v the Robertson Group*[15] where he refused to allow questions at a proof going to a specific factual allegation of contributory negligence which had not been pled. There should be no pleas in law. Defenders who wish to include in their pleadings an outline of their propositions in law should do so by inserting a brief summary of those propositions in the last answer of the defences.[16]

Personal injury procedure

8–38 The next important date is the date for the end of the adjustment period, and the lodging of the Statement of Valuation. As previously indicated this is an important document. It should be intimated to the other side together with the list of documents. The documents, i.e. productions must be lodged. So in every case you should lodge an inventory of productions with the medical records, wages details, etc. Note that although the Statement of Valuation does not form part of the pleadings it has been held to give notice. It was also put in cross-examination to a pursuer in the case of *Sneddon v Deutag Services Ltd*. So don't understate. Further statements of valuation can be lodged at any time (see also the case of *Easdon v A. Clarke Co (Smithwick) Ltd*[17]).

8–39 The next stage is the making up and lodging of the record, together with a motion for further procedure. Mainly you should be seeking a proof. If there is opposition to this the notice of opposition must specify the grounds. It is expected that points of specification can be dealt with at that hearing (see Practice Note No.2 of 2003). A full debate would only be fixed in the event that there was some knockout relevancy point. See the discussion by Lady Paton in *Hamilton v Seamark*.[18]

8–40 The next stage is the lodging of the defenders' statement of valuation.

Pre-proof conference (OCR 36K.1)

8–41 This can be an actual meeting, a video conference or a telephone call. The critical point is that access to a person with authority to settle the action must be available. In most cases you will be looking simply to have a telephone conference. Prepare a list of calls on factual matters where you are seeking admissions. Although not required in the rules, as a courtesy you should send these in advance. The joint minute in form PI7 will have to be signed by you, sent to the defenders for signature, then lodged timeously. Otherwise the matter will be put out by the sheriff clerk for a hearing.

Miscellaneous

8–42 Motions to vary the OCR 36.G1 timetable.

---

[14] *McGowan v W. & J. R. Watson Ltd*, 2007 S.C. 272.
[15] *Weir v the Robertson Group* [2006] CSOH 107.
[16] *Hamilton v Seamark Systems Ltd*, 2004 G.W.D. 8-167.
[17] *Easdon v A. Clarke Co (Smithwick) Ltd* [2006] CSOH 12.
[18] *Hamilton v Seamark*, 2004 S.C. 543.

This might arise, e.g. where you wish a case sisted, or where a third party has been brought in. It is clear that this will be granted on only special cause shown.

OCR 36.G1 TIMETABLE

Diary checklist

1. The action is served on the usual 21 days notice. The defenders must then lodge a notice of intention to defend. The first diary entry should therefore be 21 days after service of the writ. **8–43**
2. In terms of rule 9.6 the defender has a further 14 days to lodge defences.

As soon as the 36.G1 timetable is issued you should enter in the court diary and any individual diaries:

1. Execute commission for specification of documents within 28 days of defences. The diary entry will read "final date for execution of specification under OCR 28.2".
2. You should have a one week "tickler" for the Statement of Valuation of claim, i.e. one week before the date for adjustment and lodging Statement of Valuation check pleadings and Statement of Valuation.
3. Enter final date for adjustment and Statement of Valuation.
4. One week later enter a "tickler" for lodging record.
5. Final date for lodging record and motion for proof.
6. Defender's date for Statement of Valuation.
7. One week "tickler" for list of witnesses and productions.
8. Final date for list of witnesses and productions.
9. Eight week date for date fixed for proof. On that same date enter "commence arrangements for pre-proof conference".
10. One week tickler for pre-proof conference.
11. Actual date for joint minute of pre-proof conference.
12. Proof date.

CHAPTER 9

PLEADINGS IN PERSONAL INJURY ACTIONS

9–01 The malign spell of detailed written pleadings has finally been broken. The new Ordinary Cause Rules Personal Injury Procedure ushers in a new era of simplified pleadings. Cases will now be hastened towards proof, with debate hearings a rarity. But this brings new dangers. Whilst detailed specification is no longer required, the basic rules of fair notice remain intact. You should already have the case theory clear in your mind, and have assembled the evidence on liability and quantum to prove it. A proof is not an enquiry at large, and will be limited to matters within the corners of the pleadings. You must set out a factual basis for the breach of a specific duty which has caused the injury.[1] You should draft the pleadings to include all possible grounds of fault consistent with your instructions. The carpenter's rule is "measure twice and cut once". Careful thought and attention to detail at the drafting stage will avoid the frustrations and delays of major changes of direction and rewrites after the action is raised. It is sometimes stated that the purpose of a well-drawn record is to define the issues for the court. Whilst this is no doubt true, the primary concerns of the pursuer's agent in drafting the pleadings are:

(a) To ensure that all relevant and admissible evidence can be led.
(b) To enable all possible grounds of liability to be argued.

BASIC PLEADING GUIDELINES

1. Plead facts, not evidence

9–02 "The beauty of the Scots system is that without disclosing what is properly called evidence, you must at least state the line of the defence, and the main facts and points in the enquiry on which you rest, so that the other side shall be fully able to investigate the case and be prepared for it."[2]

The pleader should make simple assertions. The obligation is to give notice of facts which will be proved, and not the subordinate means of proving those facts. So where your client has fallen from a roof, it is sufficient to aver the fall, not that the accident was seen by two named old

---

[1] *Laing v Scottish Grain Distillers Ltd*, 1992 S.L.T. 347 (HL).
[2] *Neilson v Household Coal and Iron Co* (1842) 4 D. 1193.

ladies who were standing across the road at a bus stop. Having said that, the distinction between fact and evidence is one which is sometimes easier to state than to apply in practice. It is also closely interconnected with guideline 2.

2. Plead all material facts on which you intend to rely

"Averments give notice of facts which the pursuer will try to prove and he is not entitled to prove other facts not averred by him" (*Ward v Coltness Ironworks*[3]). For the practitioner, this is the single most important guideline. You must give notice of at least the line of evidence to be led. In his *Review of Business of the Outer House of the Court of Session*,[4] Lord Cullen states at para.3.24:

9–03

> "The overloading of pleadings with unnecessary detail is not a new development, but has, in my view, become more obvious as pleaders have reacted to the overcritical attitude to pleadings which was part of the culture of the court some 40 years ago. I am in no doubt that in general pleaders aver too much and overstep the boundary between what is required to give fair notice of their case and what is more a matter of evidence."

But the cardinal sin for a litigator is to have evidence which is otherwise admissible, but cannot be led because there is no notice on record. If you don't plead, you can't lead. As a result, the prudent practitioner might prefer to be criticised for verbosity, than run the risk of crucial evidence being excluded. At the very least, your opponent should have a clear idea of the case which you are presenting, and the kind of evidence you will be bringing so as to enable him to marshall his own evidence in reply.[5]

The test at proof will be whether the defender can object to being taken by surprise, the matter being looked at broadly. Fair notice can come from sources other than the record such as witness lists and documents lodged.[6]

3. Plead all potential grounds of action

Cases which fail at common law frequently succeed at statute. In many cases the statute imposes strict liability, or strict liability subject to a defence of reasonable practicability. In statutory cases as a general rule you will not have to worry about showing reasonable foreseeability, and this in itself removes a considerable source of uncertainty. In workplace accidents, the Six Pack and other regulations based on EC directives are extremely detailed and prescriptive. These now cover almost every aspect of workplace health and safety. You cannot succeed on a statutory breach which has not been averred. Further, the accident circumstances

9–04

---

[3] *Ward v Coltness Ironworks*, 1944 S.L.T. 409.
[4] Lord Cullen, *Review of Business of the Outer House of the Court of Session* (Edinburgh: Scottish Courts Administration, 1995).
[5] See Ch.8.
[6] See *Kendal v Davies* 2000 Rep. L.R. 126.

may well be covered by a number of different regulations, e.g. if your client falls from an unsuitable ladder from which he was working, there may be breaches of the Construction (Design and Management) Regulations 2007, the Provision and Use of Work Equipment Regulations 1998, and conceivably the Manual Handling Operations Regulations 1992 and the Work at Height Regulations 2005. Certainly in the sheriff court, where there is no prospect of a jury trial, all these breaches should be pled.

Drafting the personal injury writ

9–05 The writ should be in the format of PI1 as contained in the Appendix to the Sheriff Court Rules.

Choice of jurisdiction

9–06 The choice for the pursuer is usually either the domicile of the defender, or the place where the harmful event or accident took place.

1. Domicile of the defender

9–07 This normally means establishing that the defender is resident within the sheriffdom and that the nature and circumstances of his residence indicate that he has a substantial connection there.[7] There is a presumption that a person who has been resident in a particular sheriffdom for the last three months is domiciled there.[8] Where the defender is a corporation (including a limited company or partnership or association), the principal ground of jurisdiction once again is domicile. In the sheriff court this means that the defender has in the sheriffdom:

(a) a registered office or some other official address;
(b) its central management or control; or
(c) a place of business.[9]

2. The place where the harmful event or accident took place

9–08 In most cases this is straightforward.[10] Professor Robert Black has compiled a very useful set of styles which are annotated with references to the Civil Jurisdiction and Judgments Act 1982, and published by the *Scots Law Times*.[11] A practice point worth remembering is that where there are two or more defenders, a ground of jurisdiction based on domicile against one is sufficient to convene all the others as well.[12] Choose the court which is most convenient for you and your witnesses.

---

[7] Civil Jurisdiction and Judgements Act 1982 s.41(3).
[8] Civil Jurisdiction and Judgements Act 1982 s.41(6).
[9] Civil Jurisdiction and Judgements Act 1982 s.42(5).
[10] Civil Jurisdiction and Judgements Act 1982 Sch.8 r.3.
[11] 1987 S.L.T. (News) 2.
[12] Civil Jurisdiction and Judgements Act 1982 Sch.1 art.6.

The instance

Pursuers

1. Single pursuer. Where a pursuer is an assisted person, the term "A.P." must be added to the designation. Where the pursuer is acting in a representative capacity he should be designed as such, e.g. where the accident relates to a child under 16 the pursuer should be designed as "Guardian" of the named child. In any cases of difficulty you should refer to *Greens Litigation Styles*[13] and the instances at A01.

9–09

2. Joint pursuers. Where a number of pursuers are injured in the same accident, it is usually competent for all to sue in the same action where the ground of action by each pursuer is the same, and where there is no prejudice to the defender. The typical example will be the driver and passengers in a road traffic accident.[14] This is not obligatory and each can raise his own separate action. Where there are a number of pursuers you should design each in order, calling them "First Pursuer", "Second Pursuer" and so on. There will be a separate crave for damages for each pursuer.

9–10

3. Fatal cases. A number of persons may have rights arising from the Damages (Scotland) Act 2011 as amended. The right to claim for the deceased's pain and suffering and wage loss prior to death transmits to an executor, whilst a member of the deceased's immediate family may have a claim for grief or sorrow or loss of financial support. The executor sues as "Executor Nominate" or "Executor Dative" of the named deceased. Relatives sue as, for example, "son of" the named deceased. In this situation all relatives with a potential claim should sue in the same action.[15]

9–11

Where you are acting for a single pursuer you must aver either that there are no other connected persons, i.e. persons with a title to sue, or crave warrant for intimation on the specified connected persons. Intimation requires to be made to all known relatives to enable them to decide whether they wish to be sisted to the action. Those persons can then apply by minute to enter the process.[16] Where you are aware of connected persons but don't know and cannot reasonably ascertain their addresses, or where you believe that such persons are unlikely to be awarded more than £200 each, you should seek that intimation to the connected persons be dispensed with. The sheriff will then deal with that application to dispense with intimation having regard to OCR 36.4. In *Henderson v Occidental Petroleum (Caledonian) Ltd*,[17] the court gave guidance as to the sufficiency of averments which would be required when seeking to dispense with intimation. In particular for remoter relatives where there is no claim for loss of support there is no requirement for intimation or advertisement and dispensation should be granted.

---

[13] *Greens Litigation Styles* (Edinburgh: W.Green).
[14] *Buchan v Thomson*, 1976 S.L.T. 42.
[15] OCR 36.
[16] OCR 36.6.
[17] *Henderson v Occidental Petroleum (Caledonian) Ltd*, 1990 S.L.T. 314.

Defenders

9–12 **1. Specialities as to individuals.** The Lord Advocate is the proper designation where the defender is a Crown or government department for which the Lord Advocate is responsible. The Scottish Ministers are the proper defenders where the action relates to devolved functions. *Greens Litigation Styles* contains a description of most government departments, agencies and corporations.

9–13 **2. Companies.** The designation should state either the registered office or the place of business. Where there is a compulsory liquidation an action can be raised against the company after a winding-up order is made and before dissolution, but only with leave of the court.[18] Both the company and the liquidator should be designed in the instance.[19]

Where there is a members' voluntary liquidation the company ceases to carry on business from the commencing of a winding-up except in so far as may be required for its beneficial winding up, but its corporate state and corporate powers continue until the company is dissolved.[20] Unless the liquidator has made a special application to court that no action or proceedings shall be commenced against the company without leave of the court, an action can be raised against the company in the usual way.[21] Where the defender company is in administration, the terms of para.43(6) of Sch.B1 of the Insolvency Act 1986 require the permission of the administrator to issue proceedings or to continue them. The administrator can provide that by a simple letter, failing which you will need to seek leave of the court.

9–14 **3. Dissolved companies.** A company may be dissolved either by way of compulsory winding up, members' voluntary liquidation, or where the Registrar of Companies believes that the company has ceased trading, and strikes it off in terms of the Companies Act 1985 s.652, or the Companies Act 2006 ss.1000 and 1001. In all of these situations the company ceases to have any legal personality and *cannot be sued*. Any purported action is a fundamental nullity. Where the pursuer knows the identity of the company's insurers, it may be possible to enforce rights under the Third Party (Rights Against Insurers) Act 1930, but this will involve a petition for restoration of the company to the Register of Companies. The problem arises most frequently in the long latency industrial disease cases, where you have traced an insurer but can't negotiate a settlement. This is dealt with in greater detail in the section on industrial disease.

9–15 **4. Multiple defenders.** The first decision is whether you need to have more than one defender. The problem is that if you fail against one, your client may well find himself liable in the expenses of the successful defender. You should try as far as possible in the correspondence before

---

[18] Insolvency Act 1986 s.130(2).
[19] See *Greens Litigation Styles* (Edinburgh: W.Green), A23.
[20] Insolvency Act 1986 s.87.
[21] Insolvency Act 1986 s.113.

action to flush out the position of each potential defender. It may be arguable that it was prudent to convene more than one defender, particularly where the correspondence shows the defenders to have been difficult or obstructive. Where matters are clear-cut against one defender, you should sue him only. If he blames someone else in the defences, you can then convene them as second defenders and argue that any award of expenses should be met by the first defenders. You must raise the action in plenty of time to enable any other defender to be added before the expiry of the triennium. Where matters are more doubtful you should call all defenders, and be prepared as the action develops to negotiate an exit of a defender where there are poor prospects on liability. Where the expiry of the triennium is imminent, it is essential that *all* potential defenders are called, and matters reviewed after the close of pleadings and recovery of documents.

Crave

The crave should be set out in words and figures. The amount should be **9–16** set at at least one-third over the top of the range of expected awards. There is no longer any requirement to crave interest. Where there are a number of pursuers, there should be a separate crave for each one. There should always be a crave for the expenses of the action. It is not normal to seek warrant to arrest on the dependence in actions of personal injuries.

Paragraph 1—the parties

Full designation of the parties should be set out. The pursuer's date of **9–17** birth should be added, and it is now customary to aver a National Insurance number where known. The pursuer's employment status should be set out, as well as that of an individual defender. If this is not known simply state "the defender's occupation is unkown to the pursuer".

Paragraph 2—jurisdiction

Sets out the basis of jurisdiction, e.g. domicile of the defender, or place **9–18** where the harmful event occurred.

Paragraph 3—the facts

This sets out the basic narrative. In industrial accident cases, it is helpful **9–19** to begin with a description of the defender's undertaking and the working process. You should then state the pursuer's role and job description, e.g.:

> "The defenders carry on the business of steel tube making at their premises in Lochore Street, Motherwell where lengths of steel are elongated and welded into tubes. As at 18th May 2011, the pursuer was employed as a slinger and his working duties were to assist in the loading and preparation of the finished tubes for despatch ..."

You should then describe the accident circumstances. It is not necessary to state the time of day of the accident, unless it is material, e.g. during the hours of darkness. Measurements should be stated in metric, and as a matter of presentation you may think it prudent to insert the imperial measure in brackets. If at all possible try not to tie the pursuer down too closely to a precise version of events. The facts are never as clear-cut as they appear in your papers. Where matters are stated too narrowly, the defender is in a position to bring out contradictions at proof, or to have the pursuer become increasingly and unconvincingly dogmatic. The factual paragraph does not simply tell a story. The pleader must condense his materials and focus on the critical facts which are required to prove the case. These must identify the basis on which the action proceeds, e.g. where the claim is founded on a failure to provide respiratory equipment, there should be an averment in the factual paragraph to the effect that no respiratory equipment was provided. Generally you should seek to contain all factual matters in a single paragraph. An exception might be for a particularly complicated narrative, or where there is well-defined subject matter, e.g. the accident complained of might be put in one paragraph, and details of previous relevant accidents might be put in a separate factual paragraph.

As a matter of style, adopt a chronological format wherever possible. Use the active voice, avoid rhetorical adjectives and flourishes, but present the unvarnished facts in a way where they speak loudly for themselves. Acronyms or short forms for specific items, e.g. "the telescopic mobile materials handler" ("the handler") can be useful.

The written pleadings represent your first opportunity to influence the defender's agent, and if necessary the judge. Avoid legal Victoriana such as "hereinafter" or "the said" or "hereinbefore condescended upon". No one now speaks, writes or thinks like that and the reader will be unimpressed if they think you do.

Use of "believed and averred"

9–20 This phrase is properly used in two situations. In the first instance it relates to non-essential facts which are outwith the pursuer's direct knowledge but are either a reasonable inference from other facts, or represent a reasonable belief.[22] The phrase is also properly used where you will be asking the court to accept evidence of one fact as proof of another. In this regard it is not restricted to non-essential facts. For example in *Strathmore Group v Credit Lyonnais*,[23] the pursuers sought to show that their director's signature had been forged on a bill of exchange by the defenders' employee. They made factual averments to that effect, and stated that a number of similar bills which had been signed by the same employee were the subject of a criminal investigation. The pursuer then "believed and averred" that this represented a course of fraudulent conduct involving forgery by the said employee. Lord Osborne held that

---

[22] See *Magee & Co (Belfast) Ltd v Bracewell Harrison & Coton*, 1980 S.L.T. (Notes) 102 and *McCrindle v Sandilands*, 1980 S.L.T. (Notes) 12.
[23] *Strathmore Group v Credit Lyonnais*, 1994 S.L.T. 1023.

this style of pleading was perfectly proper, even although it related to crucial facts. In this sense it is a shorthand argument for saying that if facts A and B are shown, then fact C will follow on the balance of probabilities. You only require to use the phrase where you can bring no direct evidence on the point, and it should be used with care. It does highlight possible weaknesses either on relevancy or at proof. It proved fatal in the case of *Littlejohn v Wood & Davidson Ltd*,[24] where the pursuer was injured when he fell into a hole in a boat deck after someone had removed a hatch. There were a number of defenders. The case against the first defenders was that their workmen had removed the hatch. The pursuer believed and averred that they had done so. The basis for this averment was that two employees of the first defenders had been working on the floor at the time of the accident, and that those employees had admitted to the pursuer that they had been working there. The court held that any number of persons other than the defenders had access to the hatch, and it could not be said even on the balance of probabilities that the defenders' workmen had removed the hatch. The case against the first defenders was dismissed at the procedure roll hearing.

Alternative and inconsistent versions of fact

There may be occasions when your client does not know the precise cause or factual circumstances of the accident. In that situation you can plead alternative versions of the facts even where these versions appear contradictory or mutually exclusive. The leading authority is *Clarke v Edinburgh and District Tramways Authority Co Ltd*,[25] where the pursuer was injured when a tram started violently forward, causing the pursuer to be thrown off. The pursuer could not say whether the accident was caused by the fault of the driver who had started the tram without a signal from the conductor, or by the fault of the conductor who had wrongly given the signal to the driver. In these kinds of circumstances, it is permissible to plead both factual versions, commencing a separate paragraph with the word "alternatively".

9–21

There are traps for the unwary in this style of pleading. In the case of *Stout v United Kingdom Atomic Energy Authority*,[26] the pursuer was injured in the course of his employment when a metal cabinet fell on top of him. He could not state positively who had placed the cabinet in an unsafe position, other than that it must have been one of four defenders. He raised the action against four defenders and pled his case against them in the alternative. It was held that where the pursuer's pleadings did not reveal which of a number of defenders was responsible for the act complained of, and if a proof by elimination was to be attempted, there must be sufficient factual averments in the written pleadings to carry out that exercise. The case would not be sent to proof simply in the hope that something would turn up. It is also worth noting that the Inner House criticised the pursuer for failing to press for recovery of documents which

---

[24] *Littlejohn v Wood & Davidson Ltd*, 1997 S.L.T. 1353.
[25] *Clarke v Edinburgh and District Tramways Authority Co Ltd*, 1919 1 S.L.T. 247.
[26] *Stout v United Kingdom Atomic Energy Authority*, 1979 S.L.T. 54.

should have been sought and executed before the closing of the record, and which might have enabled the pursuer to identify the proper defender.

The other difficulty relates to what is known as the "weaker alternative" rule. The best explanation of this rule is by Lord Stott in the case of *Haigh & Ringrose Ltd v Barrhead Builders*,[27] where he states:

> "The 'weaker alternative' rule is not a piece of procedural mumbo-jumbo: it is based on logic and common sense. If legal liability arises only on proof of the fact A, and if all that a pursuer offers to prove is that it is either A or B, his pleadings are irrelevant. The relevancy of the case is tested on the weaker alternative."

But where legal liability arises on proof of either A or B, the situation is different, and the action is relevant. If you do plead alternative cases, you should be very clear that the factual averments contained in either version are sufficient to support your crave for decree.

Particular factual matters which should be averred

Names of witnesses

9–22 It is not usually necessary to specify the names of witnesses, unless this is a fair notice requirement.[28] It very frequently occurs that you wish to make averments about the actions of some persons whose name is not known to your client. In that situation it is appropriate to plead matters along the lines of "the pursuer was assisted in a lifting operation by an employee of the Second Defender, whose identity is not known to the pursuer".[29]

9–23 **(a) Pleading convictions.** Plead details of all relevant convictions. You should state the precise section of the Act which has been contravened, the date of the conviction and the court where it was made. The most frequent examples are convictions under the Road Traffic Act 1988, or the Health and Safety at Work Act 1974. The effect of pleading the conviction is to bring into play the Law Reform (Miscellaneous Provisions) (Scotland) Act 1968 s.10(1) and (2)(a). These require the court to take note of a previous conviction if relevant to any issue in the proceedings, and to assume that the convicted person has committed the offence in question unless the contrary is proved. This transfers the onus of proof to the defender to show on the balance of probabilities that he has not been negligent. It is important to remember that this is a rebuttable presumption of fact, and if the action is contested is something which the defender can still overcome by leading appropriate evidence.[30] Where the onus of proof has been transferred in this way, a defender cannot hide behind skeleton defences at proof, and is bound to plead and

---

[27] *Haigh & Ringrose Ltd v Barrhead Builders*, 1981 S.L.T. 157.
[28] See *Kennedy v Norwich Union Fire Insurance Society*, 1994 S.L.T. 617.
[29] See the case of *Devaney v Yarrow Shipbuilders Ltd*, 1999 S.L.T. 561.
[30] As was successfully done in *Mackenzie v Mackay*, 1989 S.L.T. 810.

prove a version of facts which rebuts the presumption. As a matter of practice you should obtain a certified extract of the conviction by writing to the sheriff clerk, and a certified copy complaint which you can obtain from the procurator fiscal. Lodge both as productions. They are held to be admissible in evidence, and deemed to be authentic unless the contrary is shown.[31]

(b) Previous accidents, near misses or complaints. A previous history involving the same equipment or system of work may well have a bearing on the issue of the existence of a hazard, or on reasonable foreseeability. Your averments will require to be sufficiently specific to enable the defenders to investigate. In the case of *Murray v Nicholls*,[32] an action against a roads authority arising from an accident at a junction, the pursuer tried to argue that the defenders had a special duty of care arising from "several accidents which had occurred in the recent past". Lord Stott held that this averment was fatally lacking in specification as the defenders could not properly investigate it without some details of the time or the vehicles involved. In a similar vein the pursuer in a workplace accident was required to provide specification of previous complaints in the form of averments which stated to whom, by whom and when those complaints had been made.[33]

9–24

(c) Change of system following the accident. It occasionally happens that an employer will change the system of work after your client's accident. Although such a change is not conclusive on the question of liability, it is certainly relevant, and the issue will be, if the employer can think of it now, why not before?[34] Such a change will frequently have been prompted by correspondence from the Health and Safety Executive ("HSE"). You can obtain details from the factory safety representative. You should make specific averments both about the change of system and any correspondence from official bodies such as the HSE.

9–25

(d) Admissions by parties. Admissions against interest by parties can be of great importance. The proper form is to narrate the circumstances and contents of the admission using indirect speech. The admission does not have to have been made to the pursuer, but it may have been made to another person involved, e.g. reporting police officer, ambulance driver, hospital doctor. As a matter of pleading, you should specify each relevant admission made by the other party on which you propose to found.[35]

9–26

Paragraph 4—damages

This should begin: "[a]s a result of the accident, the pursuer suffered loss, injury and damage".

9–27

---

[31] Law Reform (Miscellaneous Provisions (Scotland) Act 1968 s.10(4).
[32] *Murray v Nicholls*, 1983 S.L.T. 194.
[33] *Bryce v Allied Ironfounders Ltd*, 1969 S.L.T. (Notes) 29.
[34] See, e.g. *Muir v National Coal Board*, 1952 S.L.T. (Notes) 21.
[35] *Hutchison v Henderson*, 1987 S.L.T. 388.

In drafting this paragraph, remember that the basic rules of pleading still apply, i.e. you must give fair notice of any head of claim or particular item under it. A medical report contains opinion evidence and cannot simply be incorporated *brevitatis causa*. You must specify the names and addresses of any GP or hospital where the pursuer has had treatment (OCR 36.B1(b)).

You should then go on to describe the losses in detail, using the following order.

Solatium (pain, suffering and inconvenience)

9–28 Describe the injury and the medical treatment received. Don't forget to narrate the initial pain and shock of the accident. Set out any hospital diagnosis and treatment, providing the name and address of all relevant hospitals. Detail any surgical operations or procedures required and the length of any in-patient treatment. Where a plaster cast has been applied, narrate this fact and the length of time the pursuer required to wear it. Where there has been a loss of mobility such as to require the use of crutches, provide details of when these were issued, when the client was able to begin to weight-bear, and when the crutches were no longer necessary. Where the client is discharged from hospital, specify the nature and extent of any follow-up nursing which has been required, e.g. twice-weekly visits to dress wounds. Briefly set out any medical regime, either ongoing or past, e.g. the daily taking of painkillers. Where the pursuer has consulted his GP, narrate the treatment and advice and provide the GP's name and address. Where there is continuing pain and disability at the date of citation, provide a brief prognosis with an approximate time scale, for example:

> "As at the date hereof the pursuer continues to suffer symptoms of pain in his left ankle and foot which he has been advised are likely to subsist for about six months from the date of citation."

If the injury is to the hand or arm, describe whether the affected area relates to the dominant or non-dominant limb. Where there is psychological injury, describe the precise category of injury as detailed in your psychiatric report (e.g. post-traumatic stress disorder), whether that condition is permanent, and the impact it has had on the pursuer's ordinary life.

Describe any DWP benefit such as industrial injuries disablement benefit or disability living allowance which the pursuer receives as a result of his injury, for example:

> "As a result of the amputation of the pursuer's right index finger, he has been awarded industrial injuries disablement benefit calculated at 14 per cent for life from May 18, 2009."

Describe any social restrictions on particular interests or leisure pursuits caused by the injury, and give a general idea of the pursuer's pre-accident level of participation or competence, e.g. "prior to the accident the pursuer was an international clay pigeon shot. He can no longer compete at international level".

Patrimonial loss and special damage

1. Wage loss. Details will be provided in your Statement of Valuation, and initially it is sufficient to set out the period of absence. You don't need to provide any details of statutory sick pay or other sick pay *unless* you are suing a third party and your client is under a contractual duty to repay sick pay received from his employer from any award of damages. In that case you must say so. You don't need to say anything about Compensation Recovery Unit ("CRU") repayments. If your client has lost any particular employment opportunity, e.g. loss of chance of promotion, or loss of chance of overtime payment, you should say so in the pleadings.

Where the pursuer is still off work at the date of citation, you should provide an estimate of the duration of his likely absence. Where he has been forced to take up lower paid employment, set out the date of commencement of the new employment and the weekly net difference in wages. This will enable you to argue both a past wage loss and a future wage loss based on a multiplier approach, using the net difference in wages as the multiplicand. In serious cases you may aver that the pursuer is unlikely to return to gainful employment. If there is a particular loss of status or job satisfaction, there may be a claim for loss of congenial employment which must be stated. Where the pursuer has returned to his pre-accident work but has an ongoing disability, you must plead this as a loss of employability claim. Where this applies, the court will have to estimate the likelihood of your client being thrown onto the labour market, and any special circumstances, e.g. a likelihood of redundancy, should be pled. Where your client has lost the benefit of membership of a pension scheme, you will require to plead a claim for pension loss, stating it as the top figure from your actuarial report.

2. Services claim. Where there is a claim for services under s.8 of the Administration of Justice (Scotland) Act 1982, describe the assistance provided by named relatives with some indication of the hours spent per week. Indicate over what period care was provided, or how long it is likely to be required. In serious cases you should aver the commercial cost of care per hour. Where there is a s.9 claim, i.e. services provided by the pursuer for relatives, e.g. painting, gardening, or DIY, give a rough indication of the frequency with which the pursuer provided these services in the past. Provide some basis for calculation of loss of future services, e.g. "the pursuer will require to hire a gardener for around three hours per week during the summer months at a cost of £5 per hour".[36] In the case of *Kendal v Davies*,[37] Lady Paton stated:

---

[36] See *Stark v Ford (No.2)*, 1996 S.L.T. at 1329 for guidance on the degree of specification required.
[37] *Kendal v Davies*, 2000 Rep. L.R. 126.

"There are many cases involving fairly minor services rendered by a relative over a short period of time where fairly inspecific averments may suffice. However different considerations arise in cases involving a claim for services and paid care which might, on one view, result in evidence being led to establish an annual value at costs amounting to thousands of pounds, and a significant multiplier. In such cases it is my view that a defender is entitled to fair notice of certain basic elements to enable him properly to prepare for the Proof or jury trial, and if so advised, to calculate a Tender. Such basic elements include the nature of services rendered, an indication of the time period involved, and an indication of the value being placed on those services by the pursuer or his expert. A necessary degree of specification can usually be achieved by reasonably brief averments. The lodging in process of a report by a care cost expert may assist."

9–31 **3. Special expenditure.** The accident may have caused special items of expenditure, ranging from simple matters such as the cost of repeat prescriptions or hospital travelling expenses, to long detailed lists setting out the extra costs of disability by way of equipment, e.g. wheelchairs, TENS machines, or bathroom adaptations in serious cases. Generally these are matters which can conveniently be set out in a schedule, which should be referred to in the pleadings, lodged in process and incorporated *brevitatis causa*. The costs of medical and expert reports in preparing the case for litigation are not relevant heads of claim and should not be stated.[38]

9–32 All of the above averments can be reasonably concise. Remember that full specification will be provided by the Statement of Valuation which you will require to lodge in process. You should then sum up by setting out the headings of damages. So after the general narrative described above the pleadings should run:

"The pursuer claims:

1. Solatium
2. Past wage loss.
3. Services in terms of the Administration of Justice (Scotland) Act s.8.
4. Miscellaneous expenses as above."

Paragraph 5—legal duties

9–33 The standard formula is:

"The accident was caused by the defenders' breach of duty at common law, and breach of their statutory duties in terms of e.g. the Manual Handling (Operations) Regulation 1992."

---

[38] *Shanks v Gray*, 1977 S.L.T. (Notes) 26.

Where the applicability of the statute depends on a particular set of circumstances, you should refer to it, e.g. "the power drill was work equipment which was in the control of the defenders at the material time".

Pleading a claim for provisional damages

A claim for provisional damages may be appropriate where the medical prognosis is uncertain, and there is a risk of a serious deterioration at some time in the future.[39] If you wish to reserve your client's right to return to court for a further award in the event of that serious deterioration, you should address this in the pleadings from the outset. 9–34

The matter is regulated by OCR 36.12. You should insert two separate craves. The first crave will be the crave for provisional damages, i.e. the claim is valued on the basis that the serious deterioration will *not* occur. There should then be an alternative crave assessed on a once and for all valuation, which takes into account the chance of the deterioration. This will crave a larger figure.

Provisional damages are only available where the defender is a public authority or public corporation, or insured or otherwise indemnified in respect of the injury. Appropriate averments should be made in para.1. The grounds of provisional damages should be addressed in the damages paragraph. In particular you must aver a risk of serious deterioration, and where possible the risk should be quantified. You should describe such a deterioration from a medical viewpoint, and also detail any likely impact on daily life and employment. You should be able to describe a definite medical threshold or condition. Where possible a timescale for development of the condition should be stated. You should state specifically that the pursuer seeks an award of provisional damages on the basis that the serious deterioration will *not* develop. Then add as an alternative that the pursuer seeks damages in terms of the amount contained in the second crave.

Client check before action

It is essential in all cases that you ask the client to check the factual averments in the writ before service. This ensures that any misunderstanding of your instructions is ironed out before it is committed to print and can be made use of by the defenders. Send the draft writ to the client, refer him specifically to the factual statement and ask him to confirm in writing that matters have been properly set out. The only exception to this rule should be when the expiry of the triennium is imminent. 9–35

---

[39] See Ch.4.

Chapter 10

AFTER THE ACTION IS RAISED

INCIDENTAL PROCEDURE I: UP TO THE DIET OF PROOF

10–01 The timetable constraints of the Personal Injury Ordinary Cause Procedure mean that your case must be prepared and "front loaded" by the time the writ is issued. In particular, you should have a clear idea of the witness and documents lists which you will be lodging in process. Although there may be opportunities for you to strengthen the case, e.g. by using the recovery of documents procedure, it is a salutary reflection that the cogency of your own evidence can only diminish with the passage of time. Your objective should be to press the case forward to proof as quickly as the Ordinary Cause Rules will provide. Some defenders and insurers find it difficult to respond within the timetable. Make the tempo of the Ordinary Cause Rules work in your favour by meeting all the procedural deadlines and opposing any attempt to deviate from the timetable.

If the case is to be kept on track, it is important that the client cooperates. You should send him a case timetable, containing a brief procedural outline. If he understands the general procedural background, he is less likely to contact you for frequent status reports, and he will remain confident that you are in control of the litigation process.

Decree in absence

10–02 You should keep a writ register, showing the number and date of service of each action. Where no notice of intention to defend has been lodged after 21 days and you are already in contact with the insurers, it is sensible to write to them before taking decree in absence. If there is any colourable defence on the merits or quantum the court will almost certainly allow a decree in absence to be reponed and the case will simply be delayed for the reponing procedure. If you are dealing with a company or an individual who has not referred the matter to his insurers, you should minute for decree in absence as soon as the induciae expires. In terms of the Social Security (Recovery of Benefits) Act 1997 s.15, the court requires to show a damages breakdown on any decree, so that benefits can be allocated against the relevant heads of claim, which relate to loss of earnings, loss of mobility or the costs of care. You should send an accompanying schedule showing your breakdown of the heads of claim. Given that the action may later be defended and that there may be recoupment arguments, you should set the amount of solatium as high as the injuries will bear. Once the decree is issued, you should enforce it as in any other debt action.

Where a notice of intention to defend is lodged

Allocation of diets and timetables

The court will send you a letter showing the last day for lodging defences. **10–03**
If defences are not lodged timeously you should initially send a reminder to your opponent, before lodging a motion for decree by default in terms of OCR 16.2(a). The lodging of defences instigates the allocation of diets and timetables in terms of 36.G1. The timetable will be issued in form PI5. The timetable has the effect as if it were an interlocutor. It will specify:

1. The proof date.
2. The date by which any motion for third party notice should be made.
3. The date by which a pre-action specification of documents should be served.
4. The date for lodging of pursuer's statement of valuation.
5. The ending of the adjustment period.
6. The date the record should be lodged.
7. The defender or third party's statement of valuation.
8. The date for lodging witness lists and productions.
9. The date for lodging the pre-proof minute.

Write to your client advising him of these dates giving him a jargon-free explanation confirming that he will require to attend the proof diet. The dates should be diaried. You should then return the initial writ to the court, lodging any Legal Aid Certificate at the same time.

Dealing with the defences

1. The holding defence

It is a fundamental rule of our system of written pleadings that all factual **10–04** allegations within the knowledge of parties should be answered on a line-by-line basis. This is set out in OCR 9.7, which provides:

> "*Implied admissions*
> Every statement of fact made by a party shall be answered by every other party, and if such a statement by one party within the knowledge of another party is not denied by that other party, that other party shall be deemed to have admitted that statement of fact."

The frequently quoted dictum in this regard is that of Lord Stewart:

> "Our whole system of pleading and of disposal of cases upon preliminary pleas must depend upon each party stating with candour what are the material facts upon which he relies and admitting the facts stated by his opponent which he knows to be true."[1]

---

[1] *Ellon Castle Estates Co Ltd v Macdonald*, 1975 S.L.T. (Notes) 66.

In fact this rule is routinely ignored in sheriff court personal injury actions. Defenders can shelter behind general denials with relative impunity. In some situations, e.g. where the pursuer was working alone at the time of the accident, it is perfectly responsible for a defender to adopt the position that the circumstances of the accident are not known and not admitted. Rather more frequently, defenders simply refuse to engage with the averments in any meaningful way. There are various well-known formulae, devoid of any real factual content, e.g. "admitted that certain duties of care were incumbent upon the defenders under explanation that they fulfilled all said duties", or "the Workplace (Health, Safety & Welfare) Regulations 1992 are referred to for their terms, beyond which no admission is made". These are usually accompanied by averments of sole fault or contributory negligence. It was this kind of defence in an industrial accident case which prompted Lord Morrison to complain:

> "I must however observe that I consider the conduct of the defenders' case on the merits was reprehensible. The essential averments made by the pursuer as to the construction and various deficiencies of the platform were very clearly set out and they concerned matters which must have been within the knowledge of the defenders' officials. As has been pointed out in previous cases, our system of pleading and therefore the proper administration of justice in civil cases, depends on each party meeting with candour the averments of fact made by the opposing side. In particular, each party is obliged honestly to answer averments by his opponent on matters which are within his knowledge, and he must admit those averments which he knows to be true. These are elementary requirements of proper pleadings ... If the defenders had decided to admit liability when the record was closed the state of the pleadings might have been excusable, but this was not their position."[2]

Occasionally the situation is so clear-cut that there may be prospects of summary decree or interim damages. More often the pursuer will simply be put to the proof of his own averments. There is no need to take detailed instructions from the pursuer on this kind of defence. Formal denials should be added by way of adjustment.

2. The positive defence

10–05 Here the defender makes detailed averments about the facts and circumstances of the accident, and has fully particularised allegations of sole fault or contributory negligence against your client, or averments of fault by some third party. These will be the issues for the proof. As soon as this kind of defence is received you should send a copy to the pursuer for his comments. You may well think it prudent to ask your principal witnesses of fact for their views. You should then adjust in the light of the further information received.

Where some of the defenders' averments are agreed, it is preferable to

---

[2] *Cook v UIE Shipbuilding Scotland*, 1989 S.C.L.R. 156 at 157.

incorporate these within the body of your own pleadings as simple averments of fact, rather than to tag them on at the end of your factual paragraph preceded by the words "admitted that ...". In this way the averments appear to emanate from you, and the whole pleadings present a better argument.[3]

Other than that, you should deal with the defenders' averments at the end of your own condescendence in the strict order of:

(a) Matters which you admit. These should be tagged "admitted that ...".
(b) Matters which you don't know about but believe to be true. These should be tagged "believed to be true that ...". Remember that this counts as an admission.
(c) Matters which you don't know and don't admit. These should be tagged "not known and not admitted that ...".
(d) Matters which you deny. You should end the condescendence with the words "*quoad ultra* denied".

3. Contributory negligence/sole fault

Contributory negligence or sole fault must be pled. What is sometimes forgotten is that the details of what the pursuer should have done or failed to do must be contained in the defence averments. For example a defence which simply reads: "the pursuer had a duty to take reasonable care for his own safety and failed in said duty" would be irrelevant through lack of specification, and objection can be taken at proof.[4] Where there is specification of what the pursuer should have done, it is surprising how frequently the allegation of contributory negligence can be turned against the defenders. For example, in a dermatitis case there may be averments that the pursuer could have worn protective gloves, which were available. Investigation may reveal that there was no system of education, warning or instruction which would have alerted the pursuer to the need to wear protective gloves. The pursuer's riposte would be to incorporate averments that a safe system of work would have involved such a regime.

10–06

4. The defender blames someone else

This can pose a dilemma for the pursuer, especially in modest value cases. If you convene another party, who will be liable in expenses if the case against that party fails?[5] The following general guidelines are suggested.

10–07

(a) The defender blames someone else in the defences but does not convene them as a third party to the action. In this situation the danger for the pursuer is that if the case proceeds to proof, the original defender can run

10–08

---

[3] This practical tip comes from a lecture called "Written Pleadings" delivered by former Sheriff Principal Sir Allan Walker, 1963 79 S.C.L.R. 161. It contains a wealth of practical advice and is still worth seeking out.
[4] See *McGowan v W & J. R. Watson Ltd*, 2007 S.C. 272.
[5] See the discussion in Ch.13 "Procedure after Proof" paras 14–08 to 14–10.

an "empty chair" defence, i.e. seek to pass the blame to someone not present to mount a contradiction. Where liability is clear-cut, e.g. a breach of statutory duty or a breach of a non-delegable duty of care such as a safe system of work, the allegations can usually be ignored. In other situations, particularly where your information is unclear and liability is an "either/or" (e.g. where the defender blames an independent contractor), it might be prudent to convene the other party as a second defender. You will require to do so before the expiry of the triennium against that party, or alternatively seek to persuade the court that it is equitable that the action proceeds in terms of s.19A of the Prescription and Limitation (Scotland) Act 1973. You do so by lodging a minute of amendment amending the instance and the crave by adding the second defender, and putting on adjustments directed against the second defender. Your accompanying motion will seek an order for service of the amended pleadings, together with the OCR 36.G1 timetable and a specification of documents if required.[6] The case should thereafter continue on the original timetable.

10–09 **(b) Where the defender blames someone else in the defences and convenes them as a third party.** In this situation the person blamed becomes a party to the action. The defender will usually have an averment to the effect that the third party is solely or partly to blame for the accident, and that liability should be apportioned between the parties in terms of the Law Reform (Miscellanous Provisions) (Scotland) Act 1940. Here the risk on expenses is generally with the original defender who has brought in the other party. To take advantage of the situation, the pursuer must still amend his own pleadings by adding averments directed against the third party. It is also competent to change a third party into a second defender if you wish.[7] The crucial point is that you need averments and a crave directed against the third party or second defender, which the court can sustain.

10–10 **(c) Where the defender claims he has a right of relief against a third party.** This arises typically where the defender relies on a contractual indemnity against a third party. It is not suggested that the third party is to blame for the accident in any way, and no separate right of action at the hand of the pursuer arises. You need do nothing.

5. The defence to the pursuer's statutory case

10–11 Defenders frequently plead: "the Workplace (Health, Safety & Welfare) Regulations 1992 are referred to for their terms beyond which no admission is made". Does this concede the applicability of the statute? It is certainly arguable that the concession has been made where there are any elements of special knowledge.[8] The modern trend of authority runs

---

[6] OCR 36.E1(6) and (7).
[7] *Findlay v NCB*, 1965 S.L.T. 328.
[8] See *McNaught v British Rail Board*, 1979 S.L.T. (Notes) 79, *English v North Lanarkshire Council*, 1999 S.C.L.R. 310.

against this line.⁹ The safest course¹⁰ is to assume that the pursuer is to be put to proof on the applicability of the statute, i.e. the pursuer will have to *prove* that the premises were covered by the regulations, and that the defenders had the requisite control. You might usefully put on a call to admit the applicability of the statute at the pre-trial conference. Statutes where the defender is obliged to take precautions or to do something "so far as is reasonably practicable" deserve special consideration.

It is now well established that the onus of proof on reasonable practicability lies with the defender.¹¹ What this means is that if the pursuer proves a breach of the statute in general terms, e.g. an unsafe place of work under reg.26 of the Construction (Design and Management) Regulations 2007, it is for the defender to plead and prove that it was not reasonably practicable to make it any safer. In the case of *Gibson v BICC*, Lord Reid stated[12]:

> "So the Defender has to prove a negative—that it was not reasonably practicable to make the place safe. That must I think mean that the Defender need do no more than aver this in general terms, and lead evidence in equally general terms. His skilled witnesses might say that they had been unable to think of any method of making the place safer, and, in the absence of successful cross-examination, that would discharge the onus on the Defender. But it would be open to the cross examiner to say, 'Have you considered method A and why is that not reasonably practicable?' If he could get an admission that method A was reasonably practicable and would have prevented the accident, the Defender would have failed to discharge the onus and the Pursuer would succeed. But if he could not get such an admission he could not lead positive evidence that method A was reasonably practicable because he had not made an averment to that effect."

This means that if your expert has suggested a particular way by which the place of work could be made safer, you must aver this method to enable the expert to give evidence in chief about it. This still leaves the onus on the defender in general terms to prove that it was not reasonably practicable to make the place of work safer, but it has been frequently observed that questions of onus tend not to matter very much after all the evidence is out.[13] Matters go much further where the defence does not mention reasonable practicability at all. In those circumstances the defender has not given notice that the issue of reasonable practicability is

---

[9] *Ballantyne v John Young & Co (Kelvinhaugh) Ltd*, 1996 S.L.T. 338 and *Lamont v Monklands District Council*, 1992 S.L.T. 428, but see the discussion of this point in *English v North Lanarkshire Council*, 1999 S.C.L.R. 310.
[10] See the cases of *Ballantyne v John Young & Co (Kelvin Hall) Ltd*, 1996 S.L.T. 338, *Lamont v Monklands DC*, 1992 S.L.T. 428.
[11] *Nimmo v Alexander Cowan*, 1967 S.L.T. 277.
[12] *Gibson v BICC*, 1973 S.C. (H.L.) 15; 1973 S.L.T. 2 at [3].
[13] See, e.g. *Jenkins v Allied Iron Founders Ltd*, 1970 S.L.T. 46.

to be taken. The pursuer will succeed if he proves a prima facie breach of the section.[14]

6. Calls

10–12 Calls are frequently placed on pursuers to provide specific information or further details. Where the pursuer's averments are already detailed and specific, such a call is of no value and may be ignored: "a call on a pursuer to make an averment which he does not need to make in order to be relevant is valueless and has no effect".[15]

Where the defender can legitimately complain that he cannot properly prepare to meet the averment, a call should be viewed as a timely reminder for proper detail, e.g. where there are averments about previous complaints, a defender will frequently call on the pursuer to provide details of when the complaints were made and to whom. This call should be answered.[16]

7. Limitation and time bar defence

10–13 It is for the defender to take the time bar point by way of averments that the action is time barred. Where the point is taken, and more than three years have elapsed before citation, the onus of pleading and proving that the case is not time barred passes to the pursuer. In the case of *McArthur v Strathclyde Regional Council*[17]:

> "It was a matter of agreement between counsel that it was for a defender to plead time bar as a defence to an action. But once a defender has taken that plea, as the second defenders have done here, it is in my opinion for the pursuer to bring himself within one or other of the provisions which will allow him to proceed."

Two separate situations can be distinguished.

10–14 **(a) A single event accident which is outwith the triennium.** In this case the claim is prima facie time barred, and it is inevitable that the pursuer will have to rely on a s.19A argument that it is equitable that the action should proceed. The argument should be set out in full in the pleadings, along the lines of:

> "In so far as the pursuer's claim is prima facie time barred, it is equitable that it should proceed in terms of section 19A of the Prescription and Limitation (Scotland) Act 1973 as amended. In particular [specify the particular factors as to why the court should exercise the equitable discretion.]"

---

[14] See, e.g. *Moffat v Marconi Space and Defence Systems Ltd*, 1975 S.L.T. (Notes) 60.
[15] *Bonnor v Balfour Kilpatrick*, 1974 S.L.T. 187.
[16] See, e.g. *Bryce v Allied Iron Founders*, 1969 S.L.T. (Notes) 29.
[17] 1995 S.L.T. 1129 at [1133].

It is important to make these averments as full as possible. You should explain why the action became time barred, and also set out the progress which has been made since the expiry of the triennium.

(b) There is a progressive condition or occupational disease. You should initially aver the date of your consultant's examination and diagnosis confirming the condition. If the defenders fail to take the time bar point, there is no need to take any further step. Time bar is not an issue. Where the point is taken, it is up to the pursuer to bring himself within the terms of s.17(2) and to have full pleadings in support. In this situation you should always argue that it is equitable that the case proceeds under s.19A as an alternative. An example might be:

10–15

> "*Separatim, esto* the claim is time barred, which is denied, it is equitable that it should proceed under section 19A of the said Act ... [specify the factors relied upon]."

You will wish to argue that even if the facts and circumstances do not amount to a reason for extending the commencement of the triennium under s.17(2)(b) of the Act, they do provide a reasonable explanation and excuse as to why the action is out of time. You should refer to your s.17 averments in further support for the s.19A argument and then set out all the factors on which you intend to rely.[18]

Statements of Valuation of Claim (OCR 36.J1)

The Statement of Valuation together with list of documents and the actual documents must be lodged by the timetable date (OCR 36.J1(3)(a) and (b)). Typically this will include a medical report, medical records, wages details and miscellaneous receipts. Make up an inventory of Productions to accompany the Statement of Valuation. Failure to lodge the statement timeously may cause the sheriff clerk to put the case out for a By Order Incidental Hearing with threat of dismissal. As discussed above, the Statement of Valuation may be put in cross examination. It should be a realistic assessment, at the top end of the damages scale.

10–16

Motion for proof (OCR 36.G1(5)(b))

The pursuer requires to make up and lodge a certified copy record by the timetable date. Failure to lodge timeously *will* result in a peremptory By Order Incidental Hearing under OCR 36.L1, when you will require to lodge a written explanation for your failure, and risk an adverse finding of expenses or even decree of dismissal. So it is very much a red letter diary date. The record should be accompanied by a motion for further procedure, which for the pursuer will generally be a motion for proof, with specification of its anticipated length (OCR 36.G1(6)). There is now

10–17

---

[18] A good example of time bar pleadings is contained in the judgment in *Agnew v Scott Lithgow (No.1)*, 2001 S.C. 516.

no distinction between a proof and a proof before answer.[19] It is envisaged that parties may make submissions about points of law or mixed fact in law arising from the evidence.

Opposition to motion for proof (OCR 36.G1(7))

10–18 The Court of Session Practice Note No.2 of 2003 states as follows:

> "Order for further procedure Rule 43.6(5) deals with the making of an order for further procedure after the lodging of a record. It should be stressed, consistently with what has already been said in regard to written pleadings, that it is anticipated that an order for inquiry will be made at this stage. If the defender does not agree with the pursuer's motion, he should oppose it. If a party seeks a debate then full notice fo the grounds will require to be given in writing. In particular, if the specification of the pursuers' case is criticised, details of the averments which ought to have been made and which have not been made should be included in the grounds for the motion so that the pursuer may have an opportunity to consider whether to meet any such objections in advance of the hearing of the motion. A motion for Procedure Roll [diet of debate] will not be granted lightly. Normally any question of specification will be dealt with on the motion roll hearing."

In the sheriff court any defender insisting on a diet of debate should have to persuade the court that there is a relevancy point which will stop the case in its tracks.[20] If the Notice of Opposition contains any specification points which can be conveniently dealt with, the sensible course would be to try to accommodate the defender by offering to amend at or prior to the motion roll hearing. Unless there has been a gross failure of specification, you should simply tender the amendment at the Bar and suggest that expenses are in the cause. Your amendment is merely a courtesy to the defenders and to the court, and not an admission of any earlier pleadings failure.

Limitation and time bar

10–19 Where there is a time bar defence on the averments, the normal procedure is to fix either a preliminary proof restricted to the question of time bar, or a diet of debate. In the case of *Clark v McLean*,[21] the Inner House stated:

> "The court must first determine whether the pursuer's case in relation to the application of the section [s.19A(1)] is relevant. If the case is relevant, the court must consider whether or not there is sufficient agreement between the parties on the material facts for it to decide

---

[19] *Hamilton v Seamark Systems Ltd*, 2004 G.W.D. 8-167.
[20] *Macfarlane v Falkirk Council*, 2000 S.L.T. (Sh Ct) 29.
[21] *Clark v McLean*, 1995 S.L.T. 235 at [237].

upon the applicability of the section. If there is not ... the court should allow a preliminary proof on these facts. If, on the other hand, there is sufficient agreement on the material facts, then the court must proceed to adjudicate on the application of s.19A(1). In our view, it should seldom be necessary for the court, in an action of damages for personal injuries involving only two parties, to allow a proof with all pleas standing, including those relating to the question of time bar and those relating to the merits of the action."

It is suggested that in the sheriff court, following the *Macfarlane v Falkirk Council*[22] principles as above, a debate on time bar is appropriate only where it appears that the pursuer's averments in answer to the time bar defence (including the s.19A argument) are so clearly irrelevant that there is a prospect of outright dismissal. In an occupational disease case where there is no fixed accident point, there will usually be medical evidence as to the nature and progress of the condition and a specialist investigation and diagnosis. In the case of *McGhee v British Telecom*,[23] an asbestosis case, the court fixed a proof before answer with all pleas standing including the plea of time bar. Lord Hamilton stated:

"In my view the issue of limitation cannot be determined without enquiry. In cases involving the onset and development of insidious disease a problem may be presented as to when the relevant injuries were first sustained ... Personal injuries within the meaning of the Act include any disease ... but the onset of chest pain for example may be symptomatic of an endogenous condition rather than of injuries which have been sustained."

He then narrated the medical investigations into the condition of asbestosis before stating:

"Nor can it be said as a matter of construction that it was reasonably practicable for him in all the circumstances to become so aware [of matters contained in s.17(2)(b)] ... without first ascertaining, insofar as that is now possible, the precise context and content of the information given to him ... In my view the proper procedural disposal in this case is to allow a proof before answer on the whole averments ... I do not understand the observations in the Opinion of the Extra Division in *Clark v McLean* to disapprove of such a course. It is essentially a matter of convenience in the particular circumstances of the case under discussion. Here the medical evidence which will require to be led relative to limitation is also likely to bear on issues of causation. In my view the potential duplication of testimony in the event of two proofs being necessary outweighs the potential leading of unnecessary evidence if the defence of limitation is well founded."

---

[22] *Macfarlane v Falkirk Council*, 2000 S.L.T. (Sh Ct) 29.
[23] Unreported December 20, 1995 Court of Session.

Debates in personal injury procedure

10–20 Where a debate is fixed at the motion roll hearing, write to your client advising him that a legal hearing has been fixed at which the defenders will be arguing that the written basis for the case has not been properly set out. Tell him he does not require to attend, but may do so if he wishes. OCR 22. does not apply to personal injury actions, but your opponent should be limited to the arguments contained in the Notice of Opposition. If new matters are raised, you will almost certainly have a remedy in expenses. In a valuable article on preparation for debates,[24] former Sheriff Principal Alan Walker QC advises that agents should prepare from first principles as if the sheriff knew nothing at all about the relevant law! It is rarely necessary to display quite this degree of thoroughness, but you should certainly be able to explain the background of your common law or statutory case, by reference to the current edition of a standard textbook which enjoys the confidence of the court, e.g. *Munkman on Employer's Liability*.[25]

In personal injury actions it is perhaps more important that you can argue the essential legal context of relevancy and specification at debate.

Relevancy and specification at debate

10–21 The first important general principle is that the pursuer's averments are to be taken *pro veritate* (i.e. accepted as true) and that the action should not be dismissed unless it is clear on that basis that it *must necessarily fail*.[26] This means that an enquiry should be allowed even where the facts do not necessarily denote negligence:

> "A pursuer does not need to produce a thoroughly watertight proposition in order to be allowed some form of enquiry. Indeed a degree of doubtful relevancy is implicit in most cases which go to proof before answer. In the present case there are possible inferences from the bald narrative of facts which would in no way impute negligence to the defenders. But the inferences which the pursuer seeks to draw and to invite the court to draw are also open. They do impute negligence ... I therefore regard the case as one appropriate for enquiry by way of proof before answer": Lord Stewart in *McArthur v Raynesway Plant Ltd*.[27]

The second important principle particular to personal injury actions is that they are to be dismissed on the grounds of relevancy only in the most exceptional circumstances. The rationale was explained by Lord Keith in the House of Lords in the case of *Miller v SSEB*,[28] as follows:

---

[24] "Pleaders and Pleading in the Sheriff Court", (February, 1951) Scot. L.Rev.794.
[25] Barry Cotter QC and Daniel Bennett, *Munkman on Employer's Liability*, 15th edn (London: LexisNexis, 2009).
[26] *Jamieson v Jamieson*, 1952 S.L.T. 257; 1980 S.L.T. 74 at [77].
[27] *McArthur v Raynesway Plant Ltd*, 1980 S.L.T. 74.
[28] *Miller v SSEB*, 1958 S.L.T. 229 at [235].

Author: Ronald E. Conway

Price: £84.00

ISBN: 9780414018372

Please send a voucher copy of any reviews to:

Alan Bett, W. GREEN, Marketing Department, 21 Alva Street, Edinburgh, EH2 4PS

W. GREEN

21 Alva Street
Edinburgh
EH2 4PS
Tel: 0131 225 4879
Fax: 0131 225 2104

NEW PUBLICATION

REVIEW COPY

Title:

I have pleasure in enclosing a copy of:

Personal Injury Practice in the Sheriff Court 3rd Edition

"[T]he ... circumstances in any particular case will normally have to be ascertained by evidence. The facets and details of the case on which an assessment of the law must depend cannot be conveyed to the mind by mere averment of the bare bones of the case, and the weighing of facts for and against negligence may often present a delicate task to the tribunal charged with applying the law ... I can only say that on the averments here ... I am unable to say that the pursuer has no case."

These two principles make a powerful combination for pursuers.

In so far as specification is concerned, the general test is as stated by Lord President Cooper in the case of *Macdonald v Glasgow Western Hospitals*[29]:

"The plea of lack of specification finds its proper application in a case where the defender does not know the case to be made against him and objects to being taken by surprise at proof."

Further reference should be made to Ch.9 at paras 9-01 to 9-04 on Pleadings.

Conduct of the debate

Most courts have practice notes whereby lists of authorities should be presented the day before the diet, and your argument will get off to a poor start if you have forgotten to comply. As a matter of courtesy you should send a copy of your list to your opponent.

10–22

The defender normally argues first. By this stage of procedure, any minor points of specification should already have been dealt with. If you require to obtain further information from witnesses, you should offer to amend, in which case the debate will conclude. You will usually be given time to prepare and lodge a minute of amendment, there will be time for answers by the defenders, and the case will be put out to a hearing on the minute of amendment and answers.[30] Although the court has a discretion to refuse a minute of amendment, you will generally be allowed at least one second chance to put the pleadings in order. At the hearing the court may fix a further debate or proof, or proof before answer. The difficulty is that this involves the whole amendment procedure, including a hearing on the minute of amendment and answers at which the defenders might again insist on their original point and have the matter put to a second debate, before a different sheriff, all at your client's expense.

It is worthwhile suggesting that the debate be continued to a continued diet to enable you to present a minute of amendment, and have the matter considered by the same judge.[31] What you cannot do in the course

---

[29] *Macdonald v Glasgow Western Hospitals*, 1954 S.C. 453 at [465].
[30] OCR 18.3(2).
[31] The case of *Kennedy v Norwich Union Fire Insurance Society*, 1994 S.L.T. 16 is authority for the wide-ranging power of the judge at first instance to regulate further procedure.

of debate is to argue along the lines that if the court is against you on a particular point you will amend, and if not, you will not bother.[32] In practice the sheriff will very frequently let you know precisely what he is thinking in the course of the argument:

> "A judge does not have to sit sphinx-like, silent and inscrutable giving no indication of how his mind is working or what impact the submissions have made upon him. It is perfectly proper during debate for a judge to give 'clear indications' on the apparent strength and persuasiveness of the arguments advanced on all sides."[33]

It is really a question of judgment and experience as to whether you cave in and seek leave to amend, or stand your ground and ask the sheriff to write on the matter.

Where he does issue a written judgment and either dismisses the action or excludes critical averments from probation, you will require to appeal to the sheriff principal. You may consider it prudent to present a minute of amendment at the same time. In those circumstances, your civil legal aid certificate will not cover an appeal at your hand, and you will have to re-apply and satisfy the Scottish Legal Aid Board ("SLAB") on the merits. Where your opponent appeals you will again require to apply for a civil appeal certificate, but the merits test will be satisfied on production of the sheriff's judgment.

Write to your client explaining the outcome and attempt to reassure him. If further information is required to enable you to amend, interview him personally on the relevant points. If a proof is allowed at the debate or appeal, you should commence your proof preparation.

Cases outwith personal injury procedure

10–23 Where any party successfully applies for a case to be withdrawn from personal injury procedure and to proceed as an ordinary cause (OCR 36.F1) the court will fix an Options Hearing and regulate procedure in accordance with Ch.9 Standard Procedure in Defended Clauses. Full pleadings including pleas in law, should be adjusted.

The Options Hearing (OCR Ch.9)

10–24 The Options Hearing is of primary procedural importance and you should look to attend personally. Despite the repeated judicial condemnation of skeleton or holding defences, it is accepted that they are sufficient to put the pursuer to the proof of his averments:

---

[32] See what the Inner House said to this suggestion by pursuer's counsel in *Gibson v SRC*, 1992 S.C.L.R. 507.

[33] *Kennedy v Norwich Union Fire Insurance Society Ltd*, 1994 S.L.T. 617 at [622].

"I am not aware of any rule of practice nor is there I think any principle that requires a defender as a matter of relevancy to state more than a general denial of the factual averments on any issue raised between the parties." (Lord Thomson in *Ganley v Scottish Boat Owners' Mutual Insurance Association*).[34]

There is generally little mileage in putting a defender to debate. The aim should be to drive the case forward to proof as quickly as possible. The authorities suggest that no objection can be taken at proof to averments which have earlier been admitted to probation.[35] You therefore require to establish a position which enables you to object at proof to any attempt to lead a positive defence on general and unspecific averments. Where you are faced with such a defence, the safest course is to reserve the pursuer's plea to the relevancy at the options hearing and to have a proof before answer fixed. You will need a note of basis of preliminary plea which must be timeously lodged not later than three days before the Options Hearing (OCR 22.1). Where there are detailed defences you may consider that the matter should go to proof, and the preliminary pleas can be repelled.

The defender's note of basis of preliminary plea

This should be looked at carefully. Any simple criticism of detail or specification should be dealt with by prompt adjustment. **10–25**

Additional procedure (OCR Ch.10)

At the Options Hearing the sheriff may of his own accord, or on the motion of parties, put the cause out for additional procedure on the grounds of its difficulty or complexity. The record does not close, and the parties have a further eight weeks for adjustment of pleadings. The pursuer's agent should note that the record is closed automatically on the expiry of the adjustment period, and that he must make up and lodge a certified copy of the closed record in process within 14 days of the closing of the record.[36] The sheriff clerk will then put the matter out for a procedural hearing not sooner than 21 days after the closing of the record. Any note of basis of preliminary plea should be lodged at least three days before the procedural hearing diet. Thereafter the procedural hearing proceeds in a similar fashion to the original Options Hearing. **10–26**

Conduct of the Options Hearing (OCR 9.12)

Where there are no notes of basis of preliminary plea lodged, all preliminary pleas fall to be repelled and a diet of proof should be fixed. Where there is a note or notes, the sheriff cannot repel a preliminary plea except of consent, and must fix either a proof before answer or a debate. **10–27**

---

[34] *Ganley v Scottish Boat Owners' Mutual Insurance Association*, 1967 S.L.T. (Notes) 46. See also *Gray v Boyd*, 1996 S.L.T. 60.
[35] *Scott v Cormack Heating Engineers*, 1942 S.L.T. 126.
[36] OCR 10.5.

The old system of debate on demand was generally acknowledged to be a lamentable abuse, and under OCR 9.12(3)(c) the sheriff must be satisfied that "there is a preliminary matter of law which justifies a debate". This has been interpreted by Sheriff Principal Maguire in the case of *Gracey v Sykes*,[37] as meaning a situation where there is a real possibility of dismissal of the action or of the defence, or where the attack on specific averments may result in a significant limitation of the scope of the proof. This decision has been followed by Sheriff Principal Hay in the case of *Blair Bryden Partnership v Adair*.[38] These cases indicate that as a matter of law, a debate should be allowed only:

(a) Where either party has a chance of administering a knockout blow, i.e. either decree or decree of dismissal. The pursuer will rarely be in such a position. Similarly there is a long line of judicial dicta of the highest authority to the effect that personal injury actions should rarely if ever be dismissed on points of relevancy. You should argue that a debate under this head should be allowed only in the most unusual or exceptional circumstances.

(b) Where the debate might lead to a significant restriction of the scope of the proof. The principle is that there might be significant savings in time, expense and the convenience of witnesses if the averments which are criticised are excluded from probation. Each case will require to be looked at on its own merits.

The context of personal injury actions was addressed by Sheriff Principal Wheatley in the case of *Macfarlane v Falkirk Council*,[39] where he stated:

"Prior to 1993 it was common for a debate to take place in virtually every personal injury case, during which metaphysical speculation and semantic hair splitting were given serious consideration and often as a result led to unfairness and significant and unnecessary delays in the progress of claims ... As long as the ingredients of some form of a relevant claim can be discerned from a close inspection of all of the pleadings, it appears that the court is urged not to dally in the field of debate but to push the case onto enquiry as quickly as possible. In particular, where there is an arguable relevancy point which may or may not prove to be successful at debate, the court is urged to direct that such issues be resolved after enquiry."

The sheriff does not need to be persuaded that the debate points will be successful, but it is essential "that the agent appearing and moving for a debate should be fully instructed and in a position to satisfy the sheriff that there is a preliminary matter of law which justifies a debate": *Blair*

---

[37] *Gracey v Sykes* 1994 S.C.L.R. 909.
[38] *Blair Bryden Partnership v Adair*, 1995 S.L.T. 98 (Sh Ct).
[39] *Macfarlane v Falkirk Council*, 2000 S.L.T. 29 (Sh Ct).

Bryden Partnership v Adair.[40] Where there are outstanding specification points at the options hearing, it is advisable to seek a continuation and to adjust to meet the points. There is no need for parties to lodge a fresh note of basis of preliminary plea if the same points are being relied upon. The sheriff will also expect to be supplied with sufficient information to enable him to discharge his function of ascertaining the facts in dispute, making any order as to any joint minute of admissions or agreement, and securing the expeditious progress of the case. Where a proof or a proof before answer is fixed, you should immediately begin your proof preparations as discussed later in the text. If despite your argument a debate is fixed, you will need leave of the sheriff if you wish to appeal.[41] As a decision to fix a diet of debate is a matter of law and not an exercise of discretion (see *Gracey v Sykes*, 1994 S.C.L.R. 909). It is suggested that leave generally should be granted.[42]

INCIDENTAL PROCEDURE II: SUMMARY DECREE, INTERIM DAMAGES AND TENDERS

Summary decree

The OCR 17(2)(i) provide: 10–28

> "Subject to paragraph 2(5) of this Rule, a pursuer may, at any time after a defender has lodged defences, apply by motion for summary decree against that defender, on the ground that there is no defence to the action or part of it, disclosed in the defences."

The effect of a successful motion for summary decree is to foreclose the issue on liability in favour of the pursuer. Any proof is restricted to quantum of damages, and any outstanding averments of contributory negligence. You will see immediately that summary decree gives a pursuer an invaluable tactical advantage. It removes any vestige of uncertainty on liability, and strengthens the pursuer's hand throughout any negotiation and settlement process.

Grounds for summary decree

A motion for summary decree can be enrolled at any time after defences 10–29 are lodged. The pursuer must persuade the court that no defence has been disclosed. This is a very high test. As Lord Prosser stated in the case of *Frew v Field Packaging (Scotland) Ltd*[43]:

---

[40] *Blair Bryden Partnership v Adair*, 1995 S.L.T. 98 (Sh Ct) at [100].
[41] *Sharif v Singh*, 2000 S.L.T. 188 (Sh Ct).
[42] See MacPhail, *Sheriff Court Practice*, 3rd edn (Edinburgh: W. Green, 2006), para.18.52.
[43] *Frew v Field Packaging (Scotland) Ltd*, 1994 S.L.T. 1193 at [1195].

> "... [W]here some issue of fact, circumstance and foreseeability is the basis of a pursuer's case, not too much should be demanded of a defender's pleadings in order to put the pursuer to proof of such matters."

The consequences of summary decree are more far reaching than an award of interim damages,[44] where there is still a possibility of an order for repayment after proof. Therefore even where the defences are in general or limited terms, with little scope for an effective challenge at proof, the normal rule is that a pursuer is bound to bring evidence of the material circumstances, and the defender is entitled to put that evidence to the test as appropriate. But the court is not bound by what is contained in the pleadings, particularly where defences are skeletal. It can order the production of any documents or articles, or the lodging of an affidavit in support of any of the matters contained in the pleadings or any statement made at the hearing of the motion. It can look at productions such as accident reports and photographs,[45] and may consider a minute of amendment, even if it has not been incorporated into the pleadings.[46]

You will have realistic prospects of a successful motion for summary decree in the following circumstances:

10–30 **1. Where the defender has been convicted of a relevant statutory offence, and the onus of proof is transferred to him.** Obvious examples are road traffic accidents where there is a conviction for careless driving under the Road Traffic Act 1988. See for example the case of *Campbell v Golding*,[47] in which summary decree was granted where the defender had been convicted of careless driving, even although there was an outstanding plea of contributory negligence:

> "I took the view that the defender had failed to demonstrate that he had a defence in regard to the question of his liability to the pursuers. I was not impressed by the argument that to grant the pursuer's motion ... would not serve any useful purpose. I took the view that to do so would have practical advantages for the pursuers. Accordingly I restricted the proof insofar as relating to any personal injury to the first pursuer to quantum only; and quoad ultra sustained the first plea in law for the pursuers."[48]

The circumstances there were that the first pursuer was a passenger in the vehicle which was driven by his deceased wife. Any claim which he had for his injuries should not be affected by any question of her contributory negligence, and proof in that regard was restricted to quantum only.

---

[44] See *Henderson v Nova Scotia Ltd*, 2007 S.C. (H.L.) 85.
[45] *Ross v British Coal Corporation*, 1990 S.L.T. 854—defenders' accident report considered by the court; *Cleland v Campbell*, 1998 Rep. L.R. 30—agreed photographs of roadway considered by court in motion for interim damages.
[46] OCR 17.2(4).
[47] *Campbell v Golding*, 1992 S.L.T. 889.
[48] *Campbell v Golding*, 1992 S.L.T. 889 at [890].

Other pursuers had death claims, and quantification would depend on whether any element of fault was attributed to the deceased. In those circumstances Lord Cullen upheld their plea-in-law that the defender was liable to make reparation, and *quoad ultra* fixed a proof on the plea of contributory negligence.

There will be a similar opportunity for a workplace accident claim where there is a relevant conviction under the Health and Safety at Work Act 1974.

2. Where there is a relevant statutory case which involves either strict liability, or absolute liability with a "reasonable practicability" escape clause which has not been invoked in the pleadings. In *Frew v Field Packaging Ltd*,[49] the pursuer was injured when his hand came into contact with machinery. This was a breach of the Factories Act 1961 s.14, which entails strict liability. Although there were detailed averments about the pursuer's contributory negligence, summary decree was granted and a proof before answer was fixed restricted to questions of quantum and contributory negligence. It is likely that this situation will become increasingly common in actions raised in terms of the Six Pack and other regulations based on EC directives. Many of the health and safety regulations based on EC directives are couched in these terms.

10–31

Interim damages

There may be occasions when the pursuer will wish or require an advance payment of damages before the case is concluded. Rule 36.9.1 of the OCR provides as follows:

10–32

> "In an action to which this Part applies, a pursuer may, at any time after defences have been lodged, apply by motion for an order for interim payment of damages to him by the defender, or where there are two or more of them, by any one or more of them."

The motion proceeds on a 14-day intimation period.

The main conditions are:

1. Liability is admitted, or the sheriff is satisfied that the pursuer will succeed on liability without a substantial finding of contributory negligence.[50] This means a very high probability of success, amounting to a virtual certainty. So where a child who was seriously injured in a fall in a quarry was likely, but not virtually certain, to succeed on liability, no award could be made.[51] But where the admitted circumstances show that the onus of proof has transferred to the defender, simple denials of fault will not be enough. In *Cleland v Campbell*,[52] the pursuer's vehicle was in a

---

[49] *Frew v Field Packaging Ltd*, 1994 S.L.T. 1193.
[50] OCR 36.9(3).
[51] *Stone v Mountford*, 1995 S.L.T. 1279; *Cleland v Campbell*, 1998 Rep. L.R. 30.
[52] *Cleland v Campbell* 1998 Rep. L.R. 30.

head-on collision with a car driven by the defender which had crossed the road onto the wrong carriageway. The defender averred that he had skidded because of mud on the road, but there was no explanation as to why he did not slow down. In those circumstances the pursuer was virtually certain to succeed, and interim damages were awarded.

The court is not confined to the pleadings, and can look at productions such as photographs or accident reports. There is no power to ordain a party to lodge any document or affidavit. The test on liability is analogous to that for an award of summary decree, although arguably it might be less stringent in that the issue on liability will still go to proof, and the court has the power to order repayment of damages after proof has been heard. "Substantial" in the context of a substantial finding of contributory negligence means considerable. In the case of *Cowie v Atlantic Drilling*,[53] the Inner House stated that the assessment should be approached broadly, and they concurred with the approach of Lord Ross in the case of *Reid v Planet Welding*,[54] where a finding of 30 per cent contributory negligence was not "substantial". A pursuer's failure to wear a seatbelt might currently mean a deduction of around 15–25 per cent for contributory negligence, which is probably not "substantial" in terms of the rule.

You will have a realistic opportunity for an award of interim damages where there is a relevant conviction, e.g. under the Road Traffic Act 1988, or the Health and Safety at Work Act 1974. Otherwise there may be a breach of a statutory duty of care where no defence emerges, e.g. *Mitchell v Hat Contracting Services Ltd, (No.2)*,[55] where there was a breach of reg.14 of the Offshore (Operational Health, Safety and Welfare) Installation Regulations 1976, and no statutory defence had been pled. Where there are a number of defenders, you only have to show that the pursuer will succeed against one or any of them, and it is open to the court to make an award against one or more defenders.

2. The defender must be a local authority or be insured, or have the resources to pay an interim award.[56] In road traffic cases may be made where there is a liable insurer under s.151 of the Road Traffic Act or there is the involvement of the Motor Insurers Bureau.[57]

3. An interim award is to be "a reasonable proportion" of the damages likely to be recovered.[58] There is no need to show economic necessity. "Reasonable proportion" has been generally interpreted as meaning "moderate". In *D's Parent and Guardian v*

---

[53] *Cowie v Atlantic Drilling*, 1995 S.L.T. 1151.
[54] *Reid v Planet Welding*, 1980 S.L.T. (Notes) 7.
[55] *Mitchell v Hat Contracting Services Ltd, (No.2)*, 1993 S.L.T. 734.
[56] OCR 36.9(5).
[57] OCR 36.9(5)(d).
[58] OCR 36.9(3).

Argyll & Clyde Acute Hospitals NHS Trust,[59] a case where liability was admitted, a general approach of between 60 per cent to 75 per cent of the minimum likely damages was approved. The court awarded interim damages of £10,000. In submission you will require to argue for the range, and to support your claim with medical reports or schedules of wage loss where appropriate. Section 15 of the Social Security (Recovery of Benefits) Act 1997 applies to awards of interim damages, and any award is subject to Compensation Recovery Unit ("CRU") repayment. You will require to lodge a schedule showing the breakdown of the heads of damages.[60]
4. Unlike summary decree, an award of interim damages does not foreclose the issue on liability, which will still have to go to proof. The pursuer can be ordained to repay any award of interim damages following proof.

Practical matters

10–33 An award of interim damages can be a great morale booster, but there are some practical difficulties. The CRU repayment provisions, coupled with the courts' approach to "a reasonable proportion" of the damages likely to be recovered, mean that the procedure is unlikely to be worthwhile for modest value cases. The client must also be advised that in theory damages will have to be repaid if he is unsuccessful at proof.

One answer is to combine the motion for interim damages with a motion for summary decree, and to make the award of interim damages dependent on summary decree being granted. The tests for likelihood of success are much the same, and there will be realistic prospects in the same kind of cases.[61] Where summary decree is granted, the defenders can have no second bite at liability. The final point to make is that the personal injury procedure does not allow the kind of gross delay which might make an award of interim damages urgent and pressing. Where cases are strong enough to be considered for interim damages, they are by definition highly likely to succeed at proof. Depending on the client's circumstances, the better advice might simply be to press ahead to proof.

Tenders

Minute of tender

10–34 "A tender, in the proper sense of the term, is a judicial offer—that is an offer by a party to pay part of the sum asked for by his adversary after the action is raised ... every such tender should be by a minute lodged in process, for this reason, that the sufficiency of the minute depends upon the precise terms at the time when it is made, and it should, therefore, form a distinct step of procedure in order that a perfect record may be kept, of the time when it is lodged and of its

---

[59] *D's Parent and Guardian v Argyll & Clyde Acute Hospitals NHS Trust*, 2003 S.L.T. 511.
[60] See Ch.11 "Preparation for Proof" at para.13–26.
[61] This was done in the case of *Keppie v Marshall Food Group Ltd*, 1997 S.L.T. 305.

terms, and it is only consonant for general practice and regular procedure that the parties engaged in litigation should speak through the process. This is the rule as to tenders."[62]

A minute of tender is the single most effective litigation tactic for the astute defender. A well-pitched tender creates doubt and uncertainty, and undermines confidence and resolve. If a pursuer fails to beat a tender, the normal rule is that he is liable to the defender in the judicial expenses of the cause from the date of the tender. A legal aid certificate offers no protection. The defenders can still present their post-tender account of judicial expenses. Although you can apply for those expenses to be modified, the outcome of such a motion will be uncertain. Both your opponent's account and your own legal aid account for all work done (including work after the date of the tender) may fall to be deducted from the principal sum. You must consider every tender very carefully. The following tender checklist may be of assistance.

10–35 **1. Is it a competent tender?** A tender must contain an unrestricted offer of the expenses of the process. Any attempt to restrict expenses, e.g. "expenses on the summary cause scale" will make the tender invalid.[63] Where there are a number of pursuers, there must be an individual offer to each pursuer, and not simply a global sum in the tender. In the case of *Spence v Wilson (No.2)*,[64] the court held that a tender must now contain details of the CRU repayment position, to enable a pursuer to know the net sum which he was likely to receive. In that case the pursuer failed to beat a tender which did not contain such details. The defenders' motion for expenses from the date of the tender was refused. The court held that no expenses should be due to or by either party from the date of the tender. In these situations the tender is invalid, and can probably be ignored with impunity. You may consider that it opens a door for settlement negotiations, but it should not avail the defender at any hearing on expenses if you refuse a tender in this form.

10–36 **2. What is the CRU position?** You should never settle any action without knowing the extent of recoupable benefits. Your settlement discussions with the client must be against a background of a net sum payable to him. Where you have an attractive tender write an open letter to your opponent and ask him to produce a certificate of recoverable benefits.

10–37 **3. Take instructions immediately.** It may seem obvious, but there can be a temptation to ignore nuisance value tenders. The client must be told of every offer, no matter how unrealistic in your view. You should also explain the effect of the tender. Clients find it particularly difficult to understand that the tender is not disclosed to the court, and that it does

---

[62] *John Ramsey v Alexander Souter*, 1864 2 M. 891 at [892].
[63] See *Bhatia v Tribax Ltd*, 1993 S.L.T. 1201.
[64] *Spence v Wilson (No.2)*, 1998 S.L.T. 959.

not represent a guaranteed minimum figure which they must get following proof. They do not understand how expenses can be deducted from the principal sum if they have a legal aid certificate. All of this should be explained at a meeting, and thereafter set out in a confirmatory letter.

4. Advise the client whether to accept or reject the tender. When you discuss the tender with the client, the almost invariable response is that he will accept your advice in the matter. You must make a realistic appraisal of the litigation value of the case. First of all find the quantum range having regard to the current editions of *McEwan & Paton*[65] and *Kemp & Kemp, The Judicial Studies Board Guidelines*[66] and recent awards, and considering all heads of claim including interest. Remember that the quantum case reports merely represent what your client might get if everything goes according to plan. Then think about a litigation discount which gives the defenders credit for any uncertainties about liability or contributory negligence. There may be none, but those cases will be rare. If there are weaknesses in the case, you do your client no favours by avoiding them at this stage. Only you can assess the litigation value of the case, and you should take the responsibility for advising the client. If you are confident that the tender will be beaten you should advise the client to reject it. Where your advice is to accept the tender, but your client wishes to reject it, you will have to advise the Legal Aid Board of the tender and of your advice. In extreme cases they may discharge the legal aid certificate. Where there is "after the event" insurance, the tender may have to be reported to the insurers. Where your advice to accept the tender has been rejected, it will usually mean that the policy cover comes to an end. You should check the individual Scheme for full details.

10–38

5. Acceptance of tender. Where the client decides to accept the tender, you should lodge a minute of acceptance of tender, together with a motion for decree in terms of the minute. If you wish the court to certify expert witnesses or to grant an increase in expenses against the defender, you should insert specific craves to that effect in the body of the motion. If there is any opposition the matter is then dealt with as any other opposed motion. Take particular care where you are accepting a tender for a sum below £5,000.00 which is the current summary cause jurisdiction level. Unless your motion for acceptance contains a crave for expenses on the ordinary scale, you will be limited to summary cause expenses, having regard to the sum decerned for (see para.16–03).

10–39

---

[65] *McEwan & Paton on Damages for Personal Injuries in Scotland* (Edinburgh: W.Green).
[66] *Kemp & Kemp: Quantum of Damages* (London: Sweet & Maxwell).

Tenders involving two or more defenders

Joint tenders

10–40 In this situation the tender is specifically expressed to be on behalf of both defenders which means it carries with it an offer of expenses from both parties. No special considerations apply.

Williamson tender

10–41 A Williamson[67] tender is a tender addressed from one defender to another generally offering to agree liability on a proportionate scale, e.g. 75 per cent to the first defender, and 25 per cent to the second defender. It is not open for a pursuer to accept a Williamson tender, but it is a useful sign that at least one defender is anxious to settle, and a clear invitation to increase the negotiation pressure.

Houston tender

10–42 This is a tender by one defender which offers the pursuer a principal sum, but is contingent on the second defender accepting split liability on an agreed apportionment, e.g. a principal sum of £10,000 with liability divided 80 per cent to the first defender and 20 per cent to the second defender. The tender can only be accepted if both the pursuer and the other defender agree. However, where the principal sum is acceptable, it would be prudent to communicate this to both defenders, to preserve the pursuer's position on expenses in the event that he fails to beat the principal sum at the end of the day.

Tender from one defender only

10–43 Particular care must be taken here. On the face of it this contains an offer for the pursuer's expenses only with regard to the tendering defender. At first instance thereafter the pursuer will be liable to the non-tendering defenders for their expenses. If the principal sum is acceptable, the matter might be resolved by negotiation amongst all parties. Otherwise if the tender is accepted, the pursuer's recourse is to argue that in all the circumstances conduct of the tendering defender has caused the other defender to be convened. See the section on expenses involving one or more defenders. These principles were considered in the case of *Donnachie v Happit*,[68] where a pursuer who had accepted a tender from a defender was held liable for the expenses of the non-tendering defender.

INCIDENTAL PROCEDURE III: RECOVERY OF DOCUMENTS AND EVIDENCE

10–44 This section looks at ways in which you can use court procedures to strengthen your case in the course of the action. Our civil procedure is

---

[67] *Williamson v McPherson*, 1951 S.L.T. 283.
[68] *Donnachie v Happit* Unreported December 5, 2001 Court of Session.

adversarial and parties are at arm's length. You are under no general duty to disclose the results of your investigations to the court and neither is your opponent, no matter how relevant the information might be to the issues in contention. You are both entitled to select and present the evidence which supports your case, and are free to discard any evidence to the contrary. In almost all cases your opponent will have documents or items in his possession which you would like to see, or alternatively he will know where such documents or other items are kept. He, or others not directly connected with the litigation, may know about witnesses you would like to interview. There are ways in which you can use the court procedures to obtain this information from defenders and third parties. This is referred to in most common law jurisdictions as the process of "discovery". These procedures are amongst the most powerful weapons in the forensic armoury. The information which you obtain can frequently make the difference between success and failure. Every litigation practitioner should have a copy of MacSporran and Young's *Commission and Diligence*[69] where the substantive law and practice on discovery is fully covered. The purpose of this chapter is to develop the discovery "mind set" amongst practitioners. It considers what you can ask for in personal injury actions, and how and when to ask for it.

Contents of the specification of documents

10–45 The procedure for recovery of documentary evidence in the hands of the defenders, or of a third party, is by way of a motion for commission and diligence to recover listed documents, or categories of documents, which are set out in an accompanying specification of documents. The specification must be relevant to the issues as disclosed on the face of the averments at the time the motion is made otherwise you will find that objection is taken on the grounds that it is a "fishing diligence".[70] This has been described as a diligence "for which there is no basis in the averments, and one which involves too wide a search among all the papers of the haver".[71] For example, in a workplace accident case based solely on unsafe equipment, a call for documents relative to training or instruction would be objectionable. The other frequent objection to the specifications is that it relates to documents which are *post litem motam*, i.e. prepared in contemplation of litigation. Post-accident correspondence or investigations are generally excluded on the ground that a party is entitled to prepare his case without fear of disclosure.[72] Difficult questions can arise where investigation has been carried out on a subject which has since been destroyed, and a report has been prepared. In those circumstances the court may allow a limited recovery of at least the factual contents of

---

[69] A. MacSporran and A. Young, *Commission and Diligence* (Edinburgh: W. Green, 1995).
[70] See the discussion of this term in *McLean v Argyll & Clyde Health Board* [2010] CSOH 54.
[71] *Civil Service Building Society v McDougall*, 1988 S.L.T. 687.
[72] *More v Brown and Root Wimpey Highland Fabricators Ltd*, 1983 S.L.T. 669.

the report.[73] Some categories of case provide greater opportunity than others for discovery. For example there is little scope for recovery of documents in road traffic cases.

Documents such as photographs taken by a party, or the road traffic accident report completed and sent to an insurance company are not recoverable on the *post litem motam* principle. On the other hand, workplace accidents will usually provide opportunities for obtaining helpful documentation.

Recoverable documents

10–46 In every situation you must adapt the specification to the facts and circumstances of your case. Consider the critical facts and ask yourself the questions "how might these facts have been documented?" and "who will have the documents now?" Then draft the specification with the particular documents in mind. You should also refer to the standard collection of styles in *Greens Litigation Styles*[74] for examples. The following kinds of documents are generally recoverable, but the list is not exhaustive, nor is it applicable to all situations.

1. Accident report

10–47 The general rule is that whilst the accident book itself is not recoverable, a call for all reports, memoranda and other written communications made at or about the time of the accident to the pursuer, the defenders or anyone on their behalf, by any employee of the defenders present at the time of the accident relative to the matters mentioned on record, will be granted. The accident book itself is generally not recoverable, subject to the following exceptions:

(a) Where the facts of the accident are denied, the accident book is recoverable as being relevant to establish that the accident took place (see case of *Govan v National Coal Board*[75]).
(b) Where there is doubt that the pursuer was in the employment of the defenders, recovery of the accident book is allowed (*Comer v James Scott & Co (Electrical Engineers) Ltd*[76]).

2. Workplace accident documents

10–48 Documents relative to risk assessments, reviews of risk assessments, appointment of competent persons, and the training and instruction given to employees, may have been prepared in terms of the Management of Health and Safety at Work Regulations 1999, and should be recoverable. In industrial disease cases, assessments under the Control of Substances Hazardous to Health Regulations 1999, or noise level tests

---

[73] See *Hepburn v Scottish Power Plc*, 1997 S.L.T. 859. (Note that the opinion passages from the report were excluded.)
[74] *Greens Litigation Styles* (Edinburgh: W Green).
[75] *Govan v National Coal Board*, 1987 S.L.T. 511.
[76] *Comer v James Scott & Co (Electrical Engineers) Ltd*, 1976 S.L.T. (Notes) 72.

under the Noise at Work Regulations 1989 should be recoverable. Where there is a case under the Provision and Use of Work Equipment Regulations 1998 ("PUWER"), documents relating to the supply of that equipment, and any particular training or instruction relative to the equipment, should be recoverable. In footway-slipping and tripping cases, documents showing the roads authority's system of maintenance and inspection at the accident locus should be recoverable. All of this is subject to the proviso that the specification will not be granted unless there are appropriate averments, e.g. that the defenders should have carried out a risk assessment under the Management of Health and Safety at Work Regulations 1999 reg.3, or the defenders should have provided training in respect of the use of particular equipment under PUWER, or that the defenders were in possession and control of the pavement accident locus.

3. Loss of earnings documentation

Where there is wage loss you are entitled to recover documents which can establish that loss. In particular you should seek the pursuer's gross and net wages for a period of at least three months prior to the accident, a note of any sick payments made, and details of the wages actually received by a named comparator during the period of the pursuer's absence. Where you have averments that there is a claim for pension loss, you are entitled to recover the documents which will enable an actuary to calculate this.

10–49

4. Medical records

You are entitled to recover your client's general practitioner records, and also records of treatment at any hospital which he attended, provided that you have averments as to the identity of the general practitioner and any hospital. You will require a separate call for each. Defenders very frequently seek medical records. In most cases where there has been a full recovery, their call should be restricted in time from the date of the accident to the treatment thereafter. There is generally no right for a party to rummage around your client's pre-accident medical records, unless there is a claim for permanent injury or continuing wage loss or possibly psychological injury.[77]

10–50

Motion for specification of documents

Following the case of *Moore v Greater Glasgow Health Board*,[78] diligence for the recovery of documents should be granted before the record is closed only where it is necessary to enable a pursuer to make relevant averments more pointed or specific.[79] An example might be a typical pavement-tripping case against a local authority. You will have general averments about a proper system of inspection of the footway. You may

10–51

---

[77] *Hendry v Alexander Taylor & Sons*, 2008 Rep. L.R 38.
[78] *Moore v Greater Glasgow Health Board*, 1979 S.L.T. 42.
[79] See also *McInally v Wyeth (John & Brothers) Ltd*, 1992 S.L.T. 344.

well wish to make your existing case more pointed and detailed by recovering documents which show details of the defenders' actual system of inspection, or other matters solely within their knowledge.

As the authorities presently stand, the court should not grant a motion for recovery of documents which are required solely for evidential purposes until a proof is fixed. In fact, documents which are ostensibly obtained for one purpose are frequently useful for the other. The Court of Session has effectively abolished the distinction in practice, and will grant an appropriate motion any time after defences are lodged.[80] If you seek early recovery of documents in the sheriff court, and there is an objection that your motion is premature, you should be prepared to argue that the documents are required to make your case more specific. Where the documents are in the hands of a third party, the motion must be intimated to them in terms of OCR 28.2(3).

The motion should seek the appointment of a commissioner, who will normally be an experienced solicitor resident in the sheriffdom and whom you know is prepared to act. After the motion is granted, you should seek to implement the order first of all by using the optional procedure. You simply send the specification, a copy of the interlocutor granting the specification and any pleadings needed to explain the specification, together with form G11, to the person who holds the documents, the "haver". On receipt, the haver should respond by compiling the documents covered by the specification and by sending them to the sheriff court, having completed a signed declaration that these are the only documents in his possession.

The sheriff clerk will advise you on receipt of the documents. You then have seven days to uplift. If you fail to uplift the documents within those seven days, the sheriff clerk will intimate that failure to every other party in the case, and will return the documents to the haver 14 days thereafter. If you intend to use the documents or any of them at proof, you must make up a separate inventory of productions containing the documents, which should be lodged in court within 14 days of receipt by you. If after uplifting the documents you decide not to lodge all or any of them, you must return those to the sheriff clerk who will advise other parties, and then return the documents to the haver if no other party uplifts them within 14 days.[81] If you are satisfied that all relevant documents have been produced, there is no need to involve the commissioner. The optional procedure is certainly much cheaper and can be quicker than the formal commission procedure. For this reason some sheriffs are reluctant to appoint a commissioner at first instance, leaving it to the agent to come back to court if such an appointment is required. This involves yet another motion, and considerable delay. It is suggested that you should always seek the initial appointment of the commissioner, but be prepared

---

[80] A. MacSporran and A. Young, *Commission and Diligence* (Edinburgh: W. Green, 1995), generally at pp.48–49. Sheriff Tom Welsh, QC, *Macphail's Sheriff Court Practice*, 3rd edn (Edinburgh: W. Green, 2006) p.544, also confirms that this is the current best practice in the Sheriff Court.

[81] OCR 28.3.

to give an undertaking to the court that the optional procedure will be attempted first.

Commission and diligence

Where you are not satisfied that all documents have been produced, you should proceed with the commission and diligence. Arrange a convenient time and place with the commissioner. You don't have to hold the commission in court, and any suitable room will do. You will require to instruct a shorthand writer, and you should provide the commissioner with a copy of the specification, a copy of the pleadings, and a certified copy of the interlocutor of his appointment. The commissioner will fix a diet in consultation with the parties. The interlocutor is authority for you to cite havers who must be named individuals, and not an organisation. If you are in any doubt you should first of all check with your opponent as to the identity of an appropriate person. If there is a lack of co-operation you should find out the name of the person with the particular administrative responsibility, e.g. the health and safety officer, and cite him. If all else fails you should cite the managing partner, or alternatively a director whom you have traced on the Register of Companies. This will usually result in your request being taken seriously, and you can negotiate and agree a substitute witness to answer the citation. You should serve the citation form G13 on the haver, together with a copy of the specification and the updated pleadings. 10–52

Conduct of the hearing

Very frequently the fixing of a diet will produce the documents required, or you will receive an undertaking that the documents will be forthcoming. If you receive the documents before the commission and are satisfied that they are comprehensive and complete, you should simply cancel the commission, and there is no need for a report from the commissioner. You will then make up an inventory of productions containing the documents. Where there is simply an undertaking to produce, the best method is to convene the commission, have the undertaking noted by the commissioner, and move to have the commission continued to a specific date to enable you to keep the pressure on for production of the documents. All parties and any haver are entitled to be represented by a solicitor at the commission. Where the haver produces documents at the hearing, the commissioner will send the documents with an inventory and a report of the execution of the commission and diligence to the sheriff clerk. Thereafter there is the same uplift and return procedure as for the optional procedure. You should check the OCR 28.4 for the precise requirements. The important point to remember is that the documents do not become part of the productions in the case until you actually lodge them. In so far as the hearing itself is concerned, it has been stated: 10–53

> "There are two legitimate purposes and two only to be served by the examination of a haver. The first is to trace and recover a document or its copy if it is extant, and the second is to account for its

destruction if it has been destroyed, and no question which does not tend to one or the other of these two ends is regular or competent. If a document is recovered, the force of the examination is spent, and nothing that the haver has said can be of the least importance in the cause."[82]

The normal procedure is to take the haver through each numbered call in the specification of documents. It is competent to probe background matters so long as you can show that the purpose is to clarify the existence or whereabouts of particular documents.[83] You are not entitled to cross-examine the witness, or to ask questions solely related to the substantive merits of the case.

Orders under the Administration of Justice (Scotland) Act 1972

10–54 The Act provides:

"1.—(1) Without prejudice to the existing powers of the Court of Session and of the Sheriff Court, those courts shall have power, subject to the provisions of sub-section (4) of this section, to order the inspection, photographing, preservation, custody and detention of documents and other property (including where appropriate land) which appear to the court to be property as to which any question may relevantly arise in any existing civil proceedings before that court or in civil proceedings which are likely to be brought, and to order the production and recovery of any such property, the taking of samples thereof, and the carrying out of any experiment thereon or therewith ...

(1A) Without prejudice to the existing powers of the Court of Session and of the Sheriff Court, those courts shall have power, subject to sub-section (4) of this section, to order any person to disclose such information as he has as to the identity of any persons who appear to the court to be persons who (a) might be witnesses in any existing civil proceedings before that court or in civil proceedings which are likely to be brought or (b) might be defenders in any civil proceedings which appear to the court to be likely to be brought."

This statute provides an opportunity for the practitioner to obtain crucial evidence by way of:

(i) site visits and inspections;
(ii) recovery and production of property and real evidence (and if need be experiment on such property); and
(iii) disclosure of witnesses.

---

[82] *Somervell v Somervell* (1900) 8 S.L.T. at [84].
[83] "I do not question the right of the examiner of a haver to recall to his recollection incidents which may influence his answer to the question: has he the document or did he ever have it?": Lord Stormonth-Darling in *Somervell v Somervell* (1900) 8 S.L.T. at [84].

Site visits and inspections

In most workplace accidents, your expert will wish to see the accident locus or machinery to enable him to draft his report. You will wish him to provide photographs. In some situations he may wish to carry out tests, e.g. take noise levels. A good expert's report based on a site visit with accompanying photographs is an invaluable aid to the evidence on the merits. Many defenders will simply agree access on request. If they refuse or delay, you should make a formal application by way of motion.[84] This motion can be made at any time.[85] You will require to lodge a separate specification of the property which you wish to inspect or photograph. The motion itself should specify the nominated expert, should advise whether samples are to be taken, or experiments are to take place, and should seek the court's authority to carry out inspection, photography, samples, etc. In most workplace inspections you will wish to attend together with the client, and the motion should provide for the attendance of the pursuer and pursuer's solicitor. The accompanying specification might read, "the pursuer's workstation at the Lang lathe in the defenders' premises at 39 Elret Drive, Paisley". 10–55

You should then carry out the inspection by arrangement with the defenders' agents who will probably wish to be in attendance. If you cannot reach agreement a certified copy interlocutor granting the order is sufficient authority for the person specified to execute the order.[86]

Recovery of property and real evidence

The scope of the section is not restricted to inspections. There will be occasions when you will wish to go beyond mere inspection and photographing and will want to have the item actually brought to court. For example, in a manual handling case you may wish to have the actual load which your client lifted brought to the court so that the sheriff can see how awkward or unwieldy it is. In this case you would seek an order for the production and recovery of property, with an accompanying specification, e.g. "20kg bag of flour from the defenders' packaging department". The procedure is as contained in OCR 28.2. 10–56

A motion for inspection, recovery or production of property can be made at any time. You do not have to wait for the closing of the record.

Order for the disclosure of witnesses

Prior to the action being raised, the court will grant a petition ordaining any person to furnish information likely to identify a potential defender in the case, provided you can satisfy the court that proceedings are likely to be brought, e.g. where there are a number of contractors on a building site you can call on the health and safely officer of the principal contractors to identify the firm who left the unguarded trench in the pavement. 10–57

---

[84] In terms of OCR 28.2.
[85] See the case of *Lowrie v Colvilles Ltd*, 1961 S.L.T. (Notes) 73.
[86] OCR 28.6.

After proceedings are raised, the court can also order any person to disclose details of anyone who might be a witness to the case. The rule enables a pursuer to trace and precognosce those persons known only to the defenders or to third parties who may have crucial evidence in the case. The motion can be made at any time. For example, you might well seek that the defenders disclose the identity of their "competent person" in terms of the Management of Health and Safety at Work Regulations 1999. You might call upon a sub-contractor who is not a party to the action to identify the unknown labourer who was working next to your client on the construction site at the time of the accident. The procedure is in terms of OCR 22.2(b). The motion should call on the defender or third party to identify the witness, and there should be an accompanying specification of "the matter in respect of which information is sought as to the identity of a person who might be a witness or a defender". This might either be a general description, e.g. "the pony labeller operator who worked adjacent to the pursuer", or you may have the actual name of the witness where the purpose of the motion is to obtain his address. It has been held that an employer's offer to allow precognition facilities to a named employee at the workplace was sufficient to render such a motion unnecessary, resulting in its refusal.[87] There were special circumstances there in that information was before the court that the witness was prepared to be precognosced by the pursuer's agent in the presence of an independent third party not connected with the case. In the case of *Mooney v Glasgow District Council*,[88] the court also refused to disclose the home address of witnesses where precognition facilities had been offered at the workplace. It is suggested that the motion should generally be granted in the absence of such special circumstances.

Preservation and retention of evidence

10–58 The most effective evidence is a witness's oral evidence given before the sheriff at proof. There may be reasons why the witness cannot be examined in court, and this section looks at the possibilities of examining witnesses on commission, and using the transcript of their examination as evidence in the case. The starting point for the practitioner is that such evidence is *always* second best; the evidence appears simply from the printed page before a sheriff who has had no opportunity to see and evaluate the witness. With that in mind, there may be occasions when it is simply unavoidable. The procedure for taking evidence on commission is contained in OCR 28.10. The grounds are that the witness resides beyond the jurisdiction of the court, or resides at some place remote from the court, or by reason of age, infirmity or sickness is unable to attend the diet of proof. This has not been interpreted as applying to persons who simply live outwith the sheriffdom, and normally means persons living in England or abroad. Unlike the Court of Session, the Sheriff Court has no authority to order the attendance of witnesses resident in England. Taking their evidence on commission should be a last resort after all

---

[87] *Poterala v Uniroyal Englebert Tyres Ltd*, 1992 S.L.T. 1072.
[88] *Mooney v Glasgow District Council*, 1989 S.L.T. 863.

attempts to cajole or persuade the witness to attend have failed. The other common ground is age and infirmity. This has traditionally been interpreted to mean that persons over 70 years of age are not required to attend court. Again, except in cases of extreme old age, the better course is to seek to persuade such witnesses to attend. The motion may be appropriate where a witness becomes ill with a permanent condition, but otherwise the usual course would be to seek that the proof is adjourned until the witness recovers. Where the motion proceeds on grounds of age, it should generally state the witness's date of birth *in gremio*, and you should be prepared to obtain a birth certificate if there is any objection from the other side. Where it proceeds on the grounds of illness of a witness, you should always lodge a medical certificate signed by the practitioner on soul and conscience. The final category is "on special cause shown", OCR 28.10(1)(c). This is frequently utilised in respect of witnesses who are going abroad for reasons of employment and the like. The courts appear to be extending increasing latitude to this area. For example in *Tonner v F. T. Everard & Sons*,[89] a commission was granted for an expert witness who was about to go abroad on holiday, the defenders not opposing. You should think twice before seeking such a commission. The sheriff won't see your expert in the flesh and any hoped for personal impact will be completely lost. Although it is competent to make a motion at any time, the court will probably be reluctant to grant commission on any of the above grounds until after a proof is fixed.

Evidence in danger of being lost

This category usually relates to evidence which may be lost because the witness is suffering a serious and possibly fatal illness. The tragically familiar example is the pursuer who is suffering from mesothelioma as a result of asbestos exposure. Such an illness is invariably fatal and urgent steps should be taken to obtain his evidence on commission as soon as proceedings are raised. **10–59**

The motion should be made in terms of OCR 28.10(1)(b). It is normal to proceed by way of open commission,[90] as opposed to interrogatories where questions are limited to an agreed list. After the motion is granted, you will require to provide the commissioner with a copy of the updated pleadings and a certified copy of the interlocutor of his appointment, fix a diet for execution of the commission in consultation with the commissioner and every other party, and instruct a shorthand writer.[91] The commissioner will convene the diet at a place convenient to the witness, which will frequently be the witness's home address. Thereafter examination of the witness proceeds in the same way as at proof. Where there are objections to the admissibility of evidence, the commissioner will usually allow the evidence under reservation, leaving the matter to be decided by the presiding sheriff. It is competent for the commissioner to comment on the credibility of the witness. He will not usually do so

---

[89] *Tonner v F. T. Everard & Sons*, 1994 S.L.T. 1033.
[90] OCR 28.10(5).
[91] OCR 28.12.

unless a request is made either by the sheriff or by you. If you think the commission has gone well, you should make a formal motion at the end to have the commissioner comment on the witness's credibility and reliability. The commissioner will then prepare a report of the commission and will send it to the sheriff clerk. This does not mean that it has been lodged in process, and it is up to you as instructing agent to lodge the report in process to ensure that it becomes evidence in the cause. If your witness recovers sufficiently to give oral evidence, then you should call him, in which case the report of the commission should not be used at proof (OCR 28.13(3)).

INCIDENTAL PROCEDURE IV: MISCELLANEOUS PROCEDURE

Medical examination of the pursuer

10–60 The defenders will wish to have the pursuer medically examined by a consultant of their own choice in most cases where there is an ongoing disability, and as a rule in industrial disease actions. Your client will generally require to consent to this examination. If he refuses the defenders can seek that the action be sisted until such an examination takes place. Although there is no authority in Scotland on the point, in England the court has refused to insist that a plaintiff undergo invasive testing procedures.[92] The Scottish courts have refused a defender's motions to sist the case pending examination by an employment consultant,[93] or where the examination was to involve a novel and untried medical technique.[94] As was stated by Lady Paton in *Patricia Mc Murray v Safeway Stores Plc*.[95]

> "... [T]he courts have to date restricted obligatory examinations to medically qualified practitioners, upon whose training, professional qualifications, standards, practice, ethics and rules about confidentiality, the courts can rely."

The scope for objecting to a particular consultant is very limited. In a case where the pursuer objected on the grounds of, amongst other things, rudeness and bias, the court sisted the action for examination by the consultant.[96]

In fact, the vast majority of doctors will treat your client with fairness and courtesy. There is practitioner anecdote for consultants who seem more interested in the merits than medicine, or who drop hints about quantum to your client. This is improper:

---

[92] *Prescott v Bulldog Tools*, 1982 C.L.Y. 2546.
[93] *Rawlinson v Initial Property Maintenance Ltd*, 1998 S.L.T. 54 (Sh Ct).
[94] *Mearns v Smedvig Ltd*, 1999 S.L.T. 585—defender wished case to be sisted for examination using the Blankenship method for objective evaluation of musculoskeletal disorders.
[95] *Patricia McMurray v Safeway Stores Plc* Unreported July 4, 2000 Court of Session.
[96] *Duncan v Lord Advocate*, 1987 S.L.T. 349.

"An examining doctor should not of course discuss with the claimants any matters relating to offers made to them and ask for the view of the claimants upon such matters ... The examining doctors should only discuss matters relevant to his examination": *Duncan v Lord Advocate*.[97]

When this does occur, you should write to the defenders' agent with specific complaints following examination. Disclosure of your letter at proof may well support your suggestion that the particular consultant does not fully understand his role as an expert.

You must prepare the client for the examination. He should first of all understand that he is not seeing a medical adviser but an expert witness, with very different aims. The client will frequently require to give the examining doctor a history of the accident to enable the consultant to make a diagnosis. However, the client should be told not to discuss the merits of the case except in outline and not to complete any questionnaires. Where a work history is necessary to come to a diagnosis, e.g. in an industrial disease case, the client should be told to co-operate fully, but again that he should not write anything down. Where a psychiatric injury is claimed, the client should be told to discuss matters fully to enable a diagnosis to be made.

You should advise the client that he should expect to be under observation long before and after the formal interview. A favourite ploy of enquiry agents is to video your client as he leaves his home to attend the pre-arranged consultation with the defenders' expert. Many orthopaedic experts allude in their report to the client's behaviour and gait as he approaches and leaves the consulting rooms. Ask the client to contact you after the examination and make a note of what was said, the length of the consultation and any other factors which might provide useful ammunition if you eventually have to cross-examine the doctor at proof.

You have no right to see the final report. If it is adverse to your client, it will certainly be disclosed and lodged prior to proof. If a defender fails to lodge a report after examination, it is a sure sign that it is supportive of your client's contentions, and you should increase the settlement value accordingly.

The defenders are obliged to pay your client's reasonable expenses for attending the examination including any wage loss or, for example, childminding or travelling expenses. From experience, this can be a low priority for defenders' agents after the examination has taken place. Have your client estimate his expenses prior to the examination, and insist that these are paid prior to his attendance.

Dealing with your opponent

The practice of courtesy and civility to your opponents will make your professional life a good deal less stressful. The adversarial system never justifies rudeness. A measured tone in all your dealings and correspondence will reap dividends in negotiation and settlement. **10–61**

---

[97] *Duncan v Lord Advocate*, 1987 S.L.T. 349 at [351].

CHAPTER 11

EXPERT EVIDENCE

Nature of expert evidence

11-01 An expert witness is entitled to offer opinion evidence by virtue of his training or practical experience on matters of which he has no direct knowledge. He is permitted to give such evidence only on areas outwith the knowledge and experience of the ordinary layman. The nature and function of such evidence has been described authoritatively in the case of *Davie v Magistrates of Edinburgh*[1]:

> "Expert witnesses, however skilled and eminent, can give no more than evidence. They cannot usurp the functions of the jury or judge sitting as a jury ... Their duty is to furnish the judge or jury with the necessary scientific criteria for testing the accuracy of their conclusions, so as to enable the judge or jury to form their own independent judgement by the application of these criteria to the facts proved in evidence. The scientific opinion evidence if intelligible, convincing and tested, becomes a factor (and often an important factor) for consideration along with the whole other evidence in the case, but the decision is for the judge or jury. In particular the bare *ipse dixit* of a scientist, however eminent, upon the issue in controversy, will normally carry little weight, for it cannot be tested by cross-examination nor independently appraised, and the parties have invoked the decision of a judicial tribunal, and not an oracular pronouncement by an expert."

Lord Rodger returned to this point in the case of *Dingley v The Chief Constable of Strathclyde Police*[2] where he stated at p.555:

> "Perhaps the essential point is that parties who come to court are entitled to the decision of a judicial tribunal. Such a decision may take account of many rather intangible things such as the demeanour of witnesses and the way they gave their evidence, but whatever its components may be, such a decision must be reasoned. As Lord Cooper says, an oracular pronouncement will not do."

In the same case Lord Prosser stated at p.604:

---

[1] *Davie v Magistrates of Edinburgh*, 1953 S.L.T. 54 at [57].
[2] *Dingley v The Chief Constable of Strathclyde Police* 1998 S.C. 548.

"I would wish to make two other general observations, before turning to the issues between the parties. First, there was a certain amount of evidence to the effect that certain views on causation were very widely held, or were no longer widely held. If a particular process of reasoning is widely accepted, then that I think may be persuasive for a court. But the fact that a particular view is widely held, without any persuasive explanation as to why it should be so held, and constitute a conclusion, does not appear to me to be a matter to which a court should give significant weight. Rather similarly, the fact that a particular view was or is held by someone of great distinction, whether he is a witness or not, does not seem to me to give any particular weight to his view, if the reasons for his coming to that view are unexplained, or unconvincing. As with judicial or other opinions, what carries weight is the reasoning, not the conclusion."

The critical point is that the expert's role is fundamentally educational. It is the judge who must be schooled in the specialties of the topic and be able to understand and express his own now-informed opinion on the subject. Perhaps the most useful summary of the law in Scotland relating to roles and duties of experts, and judicial expectation is the case of *McTear v Imperial Tobacco*.[3]

11–02

In *Gillanders v Arthur Bell (Scotch Tweed) Ltd*,[4] where the issue was how a ladder had come to fall, Lord Brodie referred to the evidence of an engineering witness in these terms:

"Taking that to be so, he [the expert] was in the privileged position of a witness who may be asked to express an opinion on what is likely to have happened in certain circumstances. That is what he was asked to do, and there was no objection to the question. His answer was clear and definite. It was, however, given entirely without any explanation. Mr. Simpson provided no indication on what his opinion was based. This is not intended as a criticism of Mr. Simpson. I have no reason to doubt his honesty or his reliability, but he was not asked to explain or justify this particular answer. The answer may well have been correct, although it is not clear to me how it accommodated the pursuer's evidence that he had been holding onto the left hand side of the ladder, but I was provided with no means of evaluating or indeed understanding why that should be ... I attached no weight to Mr. Simpson's opinion."

In our courts, we have trial by judge, not trial by expert. The evidence of the expert witness must therefore be persuasive, and not simply declaratory. But by definition the expert will testify on matters which are outwith lay and judicial knowledge, and a convincing expert can play a

---

[3] *McTear v Imperial Tobacco*, 2005 2 S.C. 1 at [5.2]–[5.11].
[4] *Gillanders v Arthur Bell (Scotch Tweed) Ltd* Unreported April 26, 2005 Court of Session.

decisive role at proof, where his voice frequently overpowers all others. The selection of a suitable expert is a crucial step in preparation.

What is an expert?

11–03 Although you would normally expect an expert to have academic or scientific qualifications, these may not be necessary, depending on the circumstances. The question in each case is whether the court is satisfied that the witness has the necessary scientific, technical or practical experience to comment on the matter before the court. Thus, a police constable (part of whose duties was to report highway defects) and roads maintenance employees have been allowed to give opinion evidence as to when a roads depression is dangerous.[5] In England the evidence of an ordinary able seaman as to maritime loading practice was held to be expert evidence, although he was not a direct witness to the facts, had not sailed in the ship in question and had no scientific qualifications or training.[6]

Experts on the merits

11–04 There is generally no need to instruct an expert on the merits until it is clear that liability is to be in dispute. Expert witnesses tend to be expensive, and there is a further point of view which says that you should hold off instructing expert reports until after the court action is raised. This is misguided for a number of reasons:

1. If there is a weakness in the case, then it is better that the expert identifies this before proceedings are raised.
2. Many experts have considerable commitments and will require some months to prepare a report. The OCR timetable does not accommodate that kind of delay.
3. You may have to state a factual basis for particulars of the breach of duty. This should be drafted from the expert's report and should tie in with it.

In short, when it is clear that court action must be raised, the advice is that you should obtain a report on the merits wherever possible.

Categories of expert

11–05 There are no closed categories of expert. Everything will depend on the particular facts of the case and the issue in dispute. In personal injury practice, customary expert witnesses are as follows.

1. The health and safety consultant

11–06 This expert will generally have some scientific qualifications, but more significantly will have had considerable practical experience in industry,

---

[5] *Hewat v Corporation of Edinburgh*, 1944 S.L.T. 193.
[6] *The Torenia* [1983] 2 Lloyd's Rep. 210.

either as a former factory inspector, Health and Safety Executive ("HSE") official, or safety officer of a large company. He should at least fulfil the criteria of the description of a "competent person" in the Management of Health and Safety at Work Regulations 1999 ("MHSWR"), i.e. be fully aware of the risk and hazards of the undertaking under examination, and be conversant with all current HSE research and literature.[7] He should be able to refer to and explain all HSE codes of practice, guidance notes, and related publications, and be able to speak to current best practice in the industry. For example, he should be able to describe the basic workings of industrial machinery, comment on the use of ladders, scaffolding and working platforms, and be familiar with mechanical aids to avoid manual handling. This witness will tend not to be a "deep topic" specialist, and there may will be occasions when it will be prudent to instruct an expert with a single area of expertise, e.g. a consulting engineer in defective machinery cases, or an ergonomist in a repetitive lifting case.

2. Occupational hygienist

11–07 You will almost certainly require an occupational hygienist in an occupational disease case. These experts are familiar with the risks of exposure to harmful substances and agents. They should be able to speak to the properties of all the substances currently listed in the Control of Substances Hazardous to Health Regulations 2002, the precautions and preventive measures which should be taken, and be able to comment on suitable personal protective equipment. This tends to be an area where there is ever-advancing knowledge, and change of consensus on the nature and magnitude of the risks involved. Very frequently the date of knowledge of risk will be an issue at any proof. When should the reasonable employer have become aware of the particular danger, and what precautions should have been taken? The expert should be able to assist by a historical resume of the relevant literature.

3. Road traffic and accident reconstruction expert

11–08 Very frequently a road traffic expert can reach convincing conclusions on the facts of a road traffic collision from an examination of such matters as impact damages, vehicle debris, or the resultant position of vehicles or pedestrian victims. It has been held that the braking distances in the Highway Code are not matters within judicial knowledge,[8] and expert evidence should be led if any argument is to be presented from them. On a more sophisticated level, accident reconstruction techniques can provide persuasive evidence of what probably happened, particularly where there is a shortage of eyewitness testimony. Care should be taken with road traffic experts that they are genuinely performing the proper function of experts, i.e. using their scientific and technical knowledge to draw inferences and conclusions, and not simply commenting on what wit-

---

[7] MHSWR reg.6 and the Associated Code of Practice.
[8] *Cavin v Kinnaird*, 1994 S.L.T. 111.

nesses have said in precognition (see Ch.17 "Road Traffic Accidents" at para.17–33).

Finding the expert

11–09 The best method is to "network" with other solicitors for experts who have previously given evidence on the subject. A positive recommendation means that you will instruct an expert who can be relied upon to produce a convincing report, and who is prepared to defend his conclusions up to proof and under cross-examination. Some universities provide a brochure of expert witness services. The Law Society publishes a Directory of Expert Witnesses which is available free online. Other sources can be the *Law Society Journal*, the UK Register of Expert Witnesses, specialist helplines such as the Association of Personal Injury Lawyers Expert Helpline, and references to named experts in reported cases.

What the court will expect from the expert

11–10 There is increasing judicial cynicism about the use of experts. The value of expert opinion is in direct proportion to its independence. It is very easy for the expert to be sucked into the litigation process, so that he loses his objectivity. You must remember that his duty is to the court, and not to the legal team. A high-profile case in England where experts on both sides identified with the client and gave thoroughly partisan evidence, led the Court of Appeal to set out the following canons of expert evidence, which are equally applicable to our own law and practice[9]:

> 1. The expert evidence should be the independent product of the expert, uninfluenced as to form or content by the exigencies of the litigation.
> 2. An expert should never assume the role of advocate. He should provide independent assistance to the court by way of objective unbiased opinion in relation to matters within his expertise.
> 3. An expert witness should state the facts or assumptions on which his opinion is based. He should not omit to consider material facts which could detract from his concluded opinion.
> 4. An expert witness should make it clear when a particular question falls outwith his expertise.
> 5. If he considers insufficient data is available, the expert should make it clear that his opinion is provisional.

In the same case Thorpe L.J. stated:

> "The area of expertise may be likened to a broad street with the plaintiff walking on one pavement, and the defendant walking on the opposite one. Somehow the expert must be ever mindful of the need

---

[9] *Vernon v Boseley (No.2)* [1997] 3 W.L.R. 683. These are also known as the "Ikarian Reefer" principles, from an earlier English case.

to walk straight down the middle of the road and to resist the temptation to join the party from whom his instructions come on the pavement."

If you allow or encourage the expert to identify in any obvious way with your client, his evidence will be viewed as debased and worthless.

Instructing the expert

You should establish a fees level in advance by letter or telephone. The letter of instruction should contain all relevant material including statements, medical reports, plans, photographs and pleadings where the action has been raised. All correspondence with the insurer including in particular any repudiation letter should also be enclosed. **11–11**

Invite the expert to contact you to discuss any matters which are unclear. At the proof the expert will frequently assume a particular factual hypothesis which might well be in dispute, and which he will have no particular means of resolving. It is important that the expert is seen to keep his distance from your client. It can be helpful if you preface your request for an opinion by a statement along the lines of: "on the assumption that the statements are true ...", and invite the expert to introduce this kind of qualification in his report, e.g. "on the information before me ...".

Format of the report

For a typical factory accident, you should expect the report to follow these lines: **11–12**

1. The expert should narrate his experience and qualifications in the preface of the report.
2. He should set out briefly the statements and documents before him, without divulging any of their contents.
3. He should explain the industrial process, and set out the general factual context of the accident on the papers before him.
4. He should set out the current best practice on risk management and accident prevention with reference to current HSE or the Royal Society for the Prevention of Accidents ("RoSPA") publications, etc. and should advise on precautions which might have been taken.
5. He should refer to any statutory framework and relative codes of practice and guidance notes.
6. Where a locus visit might be useful, he should inspect and photograph.

When the report is received

After the report is received, you must first of all be sure that you understand it. Otherwise, you will never be able to use it to persuade anyone else. Check the report carefully to make sure that no dis- **11–13** crepancies appear in the factual narrative, and in particular that your client's version of events has not been mis-stated. Where there are any references to publications or HSE literature, ask for copies and place these with the report. The expert will be allowed at proof to refer to these publications without the need to prove they are what they bear to be, as is the case for other documentary evidence. The corollary is that the publications should be lodged in advance.[10]

Check that the witness has not strayed into areas outwith his expertise, e.g. commented on the medical evidence. Check further that the witness has not strayed into the area reserved for the trial judge. In particular there should be no references to defenders being "negligent" or being "in breach of statutory duty". These are matters for the judge.

You should then send the report to your client for his information and comments.

You should not disclose the report to the other side at this stage. If the defenders instruct their own expert, you do not want your report being used as target practice. Finally, pay the expert fee promptly, or within any agreed period.

11–14   The report of an expert witness is subject to litigation privilege. The rule in OCR 36.G1(g) is that documents and witness lists must be lodged by the timetable date which is eight weeks before proof. In most cases you would wish to lodge the report, as it is much easier to present the evidence of the expert from his report, but you don't have to lodge it and you can lead the expert without it.[11]

The expert as a compellable witness for either side

11–15   The first duty of the expert is to the court. As such he is a competent and compellable witness for either side. The matter was reviewed in detail in the criminal case of *HMA v Wilson*,[12] where Lord Reed considered whether the Crown could cite expert witnesses who had examined children on the instructions of the defence, in a case of sexual abuse. Lord Reed stated:

> "The Scottish cases make it clear that confidentiality attaches, in the absence of exceptional circumstances, to any communication between an accused person or his legal advisors, on the one hand, and an expert instructed by them on the other hand ... In other words, confidentiality attaches to evidence, rather than to the witness; and it therefore renders particular evidence inadmissible, rather than preventing the witness from being called to give any evidence."

Subject to that qualification, however, there was no property in an expert witness and it would be the duty of the witness to come to court and give his evidence insofar as he was directed by the judge to do so.

This means that you can cite a defender's expert if you know that he is

---

[10] See *Main v McAndrew Wormald Ltd*, 1988 S.L.T. 141.
[11] *Amy Whitehead's Legal Representative v Graham Douglas* [2006] CSOH 178.
[12] *HMA v Wilson* Unreported June 15, 2001 Aberdeen High Court.

going to be supportive. It also means that you could find your own expert being cited by the defender so be very careful what you disclose to the other side.

The expert at proof

The witness box can be a very lonely place, and proper preparation **11–16** means that the expert has been given an opportunity to consider all the issues relevant to his opinion. In particular he should have seen what is being said by all the other expert witnesses in the case. It is essential to have a pre-proof meeting or at least a detailed telephone discussion with your expert. Frequently the expert report will have an appendix or set of footnotes relating to other publications on which the expert will rely. You must obtain and lodge full extracts. At proof you will take the expert both to his report and to the supporting literature. The critical point is that the relevant extract from the literature must be specifically adopted by the witness, for it to become evidence in the case. In *Davie v The Magistrates of Edinburgh* the Lord Ordinary referred to evidence in a publication which had been referred to in general by the expert but where the particular passage had not been adopted:

> "I do not think that he was entitled to do so. Passages from a published work may be adopted by a witness and made part of his evidence or they may be put to the witness in cross-examination for his comment. But, except insofar as this is done, the Court cannot in my view rely upon such works for the purpose of displacing or criticising the witness's testimony" (p.41).

No win, no fee expert?

An expert should have no financial interest in the outcome of the case, **11–17** and in particular the concept of a "no win, no fee" expert is incompatible with duties to the court. In *Regina (Factortame Ltd) v The Secretary of State for Transport, Local Government and the Regions*,[13] the court made it plain that the threat to objectivity posed by a contingency fee agreement meant that as a rule the courts would not countenance evidence from an expert instructed on that basis.

---

[13] *Regina (Factortame Ltd) v The Secretary of State for Transport, Local Government and the Regions* [2002] 3 W.L.R. 1104.

CHAPTER 12

PREPARATION FOR PROOF

12-01 It has been observed that litigation and negotiation are not separate and distinct activities, but rather a single continuum described by one academic as "litigotiation".[1] Whilst no amount of effort can turn a losing case into a winner, unfortunately the converse does not hold true. There is no case that is so strong that it cannot fail on liability, or at least have damages significantly reduced by dint of inadequate preparation. Proper preparation within the time limits lets the defender know that you are serious. Your client may well have no desire to appear in court and simply wishes a reasonable settlement. The period around the pre-proof conference is the most fruitful time for settlement. It is your best opportunity to persuade the defenders' agents, to avoid having to persuade a sheriff. The golden rule is to negotiate from strength. You achieve a position of strength by the timeous lodging of witness lists and documents, and by actively ensuring that you are fully prepared to prove the facts in dispute. Effective preparation means early preparation.

1. The issues and the evidence

12-02 Check the record. It is frequently said that a properly drawn record will identify the issues in dispute. This is a lie we tell to children. In personal injury cases, large chunks of the pursuer's case may not be answered properly or at all, or are met by a general denial.

The starting point should be those averments which are either admitted,[2] or believed to be true.[3] These are conclusive, and no evidence is required on these facts. Averments by one party only are not generally treated as admissions. The court will occasionally take a practical view and deem averments to have the effect of admissions where the case has clearly been conducted on the basis that the facts are accepted.[4] You might also have reached agreement on factual matters at the pre-proof conference, and those matters can be taken as proved. Everything else will have to be proved by evidence, and you should be clear in your own mind as to how that will be achieved. It can be a useful technique at this stage to look at matters from the other perspective, i.e. check the evidence which you have in your possession and make sure that you have the pleadings to cover it. Ask yourself if your opponent could reasonably

---

[1] See the works of Professor Marc Galanter.
[2] *Lee v National Coal Board*, 1955 S.C. 151.
[3] *Binnie v Rederij Theodoro BV*, 1993 S.C. 71.
[4] *Lord Advocate v Gillespie*, 1969 S.L.T. 10 (Sh. Ct.).

complain that he was taken by surprise at proof by any particular line. If the answer is "yes" then amend immediately. In Ordinary actions evidence is still recorded by shorthand, and the pursuer's agent must attend to reservation of the Shorthand Writer.

2. Notice to admit facts—OCR 29.14(1)(a)

A further way to narrow the issues in dispute is by serving a notice to admit facts. This can be served in respect of any matter referred to in the pleadings. You can call on your opponent to admit the crucial facts in dispute. This will frequently elicit a *de plano* notice of non-admission by return of post. A notice to admit facts is of particular utility in teasing out facts which are covered in the pleadings by a general denial but which may not seriously be in dispute. Typical examples are averments regarding costings contained in invoices, receipts and estimates. You would normally have to call the maker of these documents to prove their terms, and this can be extremely inconvenient all round. If you serve a notice to admit the facts contained in the documents, you may find that your opponent will concede the point. A notice to admit must be lodged in court. The defender has then 21 days to lodge a notice of non-admission. One obvious point about the notice to admit procedure is the time element, and in particular the 21-day period of notice. You must consider matters promptly, and the notice to admit must be served early. It is prudent to cite the witnesses who will speak to the facts in any event, and to cancel them only after the notice procedure is successful.

12–03

3. List of witnesses—OCR 36.G1(A)(g)

You should already know the contents of your witness list. You do not have to call all the witnesses on the list. This is a decision which can be deferred to the proof date. You cannot call persons not on the witness list, except with the permission of the court. This has led to a practice of "beefing up" witness lists with the names of persons who have only a marginal connection with the case. You should resist the temptation to add anyone and everyone to the list. Competent defenders' agents will seek to precognosce all factual witnesses. Witnesses who may be helpful on some points may be disastrous on others, and your opponent need never know of their existence unless you list them. The list should contain the witness names, addresses and occupations. This is part of the "cards on the table" approach to litigation. There were similar rules on the lodging of witness lists in the Court of Session for cases taken under the optional procedure. In considering the purpose and intent of these rules, the Inner House stated the following in the case of *Matheson v Press Offshore*.[5]

12–04

> "The plain objects of that new system are to ensure timeous disclosure of each parties' evidence, and to reduce the need for oral evidence ... The obligation to supply such a list [witness list] fits in

---

[5] *Matheson v Press Offshore*, 1992 S.L.T. 288.

well with the intent of the whole group of rules which ... are nonetheless designed inter alia to encourage by other means disclosure by all parties of their evidence, both to avoid surprise and also to discover and reduce the issues on which the court is called upon to resolve disputes."

The court further stated:

"In our view there is analogy to be drawn between the list of witnesses required by Rule of Court 188L and the list of witnesses appended to an indictment in criminal procedure. The purpose in both cases is the same, namely to allow the party on whom the list is served or to whom the list is intimated to seek to precognosce those witnesses whom he wishes to precognosce. In the case of a skilled witness, as in the case of any other witness, it may not always be possible to obtain a precognition or report disclosing the evidence he intends to give unless the party on whose list the name appears is willing to co-operate. We would hope that parties' legal advisers would co-operate as much as possible within the spirit of these rules. However, even when such co-operation is not forthcoming, the intimation of the name of the expert witness serves an important purpose in that it is sufficient to alert the other party as to the intention to adduce expert evidence and thus bring to their attention the possible need for obtaining expert evidence of their own ... However, it is plain that in all cases each party, in order to avoid the serious risks that could arise, has to be clear in his own mind precisely what evidence, including expert evidence, he will seek to lay before the court, and that he must arrive at the necessary decisions not later than a week or two after the interlocutor allowing a proof or proof before answer."

Where you wish to add a late witness, you should do so as soon as possible by written motion to lodge an amended witness list as soon as possible. Give the defenders full contact details of the witness, and extend full precognition facilities to undermine any defence argument on prejudice. In *Quigley v Hart Buildings (Edinburgh) Ltd*[6] Lord Glennie allowed a late witness list to be lodged subject to precognition facilities being allowed on the day, and restrictions on the ambit of expert evidence sought to be led. The witness list is a step in process, and must be lodged in court as well as intimated to the defender.

4. Precognition of witnesses

12–05 The most frequently encountered problems in practice relate to the following points

(i) Does each side have the right to precognosce the other's witnesses?

---

[6] *Quigley v Hart Builders (Edinburgh) Ltd* [2006] CSOH 118.

(ii) If so, how can that right be enforced?
(iii) Can any conditions be imposed on the interview?

(i) Right to precognosce witnesses

Since the beginning of the twentieth century, the courts have unequi- 12–06
vocally stated that a party should have facilities to precognosce his
opponent's witnesses (with the exception of the opposite party). As was
stated in the case of *M'Phee v Glasgow Corporation*, by Lord Salvesen[7]:

> "I think that a party who has brought an action in court has an
> absolute right to see, and to take the statements of, persons who may
> be able to give evidence in his case, and that the employer of such
> person has no right to prescribe the condition as to how or in whose
> presence a precognition has to be taken."[8]

An attempt to prevent access to witnesses has been described as improper
conduct.[9] The modern procedural trend towards disclosure reinforces the
common law position.

(ii) Can you enforce the right to precognosce?

There are two recurring situations. In the first the defender's agent is 12–07
obstructive and either refuses point blank or delays to respond to your
request for interview facilities. In the second the witness himself refuses to
provide a statement. Although the court recognises a right to precognosce, it will not ordain an employer to make his employees available
for precognition, nor will it ordain a named witness to submit to precognition. In civil cases no witness can be obliged to provide a statement
by way of court order. As was stated in the case of *Henderson v Patrick
Thomson Ltd*[10]:

> "If he [the witness] refuses, it will always furnish matter of comment
> to a jury on the evidence which he eventually does give; for if he
> gives to one litigant what he withholds from the other it savours of
> partisanship, and will be easily thought to tinge his evidence. And
> this way of thinking will be enormously strengthened when the
> refusal comes not from the unwillingness of the witness himself, but
> from the dominating influence which has been exerted upon him by
> his employer. It is for that reason that I do not hesitate to say that, in
> general cases, it is right that employers should give facilities for their
> employees to be precognosced; and I add that in most cases it is in
> their interest to do so."

---

[7] *M'Phee v Glasgow Corporation*, 1910 1 S.L.T. 380.
[8] See also *Henderson v Patrick Thomson*, 1911 S.L.T. at [443].
[9] *Barrie v Caledonian Railway* (1902) 5 F. 30.
[10] *Henderson v Patrick Thomson Ltd*, 1911 1 S.L.T. 284.

(iii) Can either party seek to impose conditions on the interview?

12–08 Occasionally agents will seek to impose conditions on precognition, e.g. the defender's solicitor might wish to be present. This is improper except with regard to parties in the case. There is no need to agree to it.[11]

You should expect that your civilian witnesses will be precognosced, and you should encourage them to co-operate in providing a statement to the other side. If they refuse, this can be the subject of comment at proof, and is likely to cast serious doubts on their credibility. There may also be adverse consequences in expenses.[12] You have no right to insist on being present whilst the witness is being interviewed. You should certainly advise the witnesses that if they are contacted they should not write out or sign any statement. This should mean that any statement which your opponent obtains is likely to be classified as a precognition, with all the attendant difficulties of admissibility. Expert evidence is in a different category. All letters and communications between expert and solicitor are confidential, and are treated as privileged at common law.[13] This means that you don't need to disclose an expert report at this stage of the proceedings. The purpose of the rule is to alert your opponent to the likelihood that expert evidence will be led. You should advise your expert to refuse any approaches for interview.

5. Lodging productions—OCR 36.G1(1A)(g)

12–09 All productions on which you intend to rely must be lodged in an inventory by the timetable date, which is generally eight weeks before proof. A copy inventory should be sent to the sheriff clerk for the use of the sheriff at proof. The defenders are subject to the same timetable. It is prudent to look to simultaneous disclosure, otherwise you may find that your medical and expert reports are used as target practice by the defenders' experts, whose own reports never materialise. Your cards are on the table, with your opponent's held to his chest. The sanction for failure to lodge productions is that you will require to seek leave of the court to introduce them. This may be refused or granted only on onerous terms, e.g. an adjournment of the proof diet at your client's expense (OCR 36.G1(1B)(9)). It frequently happens that over the course of the action you will lodge a number of inventories. It will greatly assist proof presentation if you adopt a strict numbering protocol where the numbers run on, e.g. the First Inventory of Productions might contain a medical report and medical records, 5/1 and 5/2 of Process. You then lodge a Second Inventory of Productions containing photographs and a plan. These should be numbered 5/3 and 5/4 of Process.[14]

---

[11] *M'Phee v Glasgow Corporation*, 1910 1 S.L.T. 380.
[12] *Barrie v Caledonian Railway* (1902) 5 F. 30 (defenders who refused to provide precognition facilities found liable in expenses even though successful overall).
[13] *Causton v Mann Egerton (Johns) Ltd* [1974] 1 W.L.R. 162.
[14] This is the practice adopted in the Court of Session.

6. Preparing the client

You should arrange a pre-proof consultation about 14 days prior to the pre-proof conference, setting aside at least one hour. Send your client a copy of the record, and refer him specifically to the Factual Statement 4 and any answers. It is also useful to send him a factual letter outlining basic court procedure so that he has some idea of what he can expect at the proof. At the meeting you should prepare your client by going over the whole case with him. It is perfectly legitimate to explore every aspect of the case with the witness, and to anticipate probable lines of cross-examination. It is legitimate to advise the client *how* to answer questions, e.g. to address the sheriff as "sir", to refuse to become angry, to listen carefully, and to reply only to the question asked. But it is wholly improper to suggest answers to particular line of enquiry, or to advise that he trims his evidence in any way. Make sure he is familiar with photographs or productions which he will have to identify. The objective is that the client exercises his mind on the facts in dispute, to enable him to answer at proof in a confident and unhesitating manner, with a good command of detail. The single most important piece of advice to your client is that he must never exaggerate. As well as showing the sheriff why he should find for your client in fact and law, you must also make the sheriff *want* to find for him. By definition you will start the proceedings with a pursuer who has suffered injury. A client who embellishes and exaggerates and generally appears out to milk the case will rapidly forfeit any judicial sympathy, leaving you with a much more difficult task of persuasion. Finally, don't be embarrassed to tell your client how to dress for the proof. Only God can plumb the hearts of men. The rest of us, including judges, tend to go on impressions. Male clients should wear a dark suit, white shirt and tie. Female clients should dress conservatively.

12–10

7. Pre-proof conference—OCR 36.K1

This must be held not later than four weeks before the proof date. The purpose of the conference is to discuss settlement of the action, and to agree insofar as possible any matters which are not in dispute. You can call on the defenders to admit factual matters. The joint minute of the pre-proof conference in form P17 must be lodged by the pursuer not later than three weeks before the date assigned for proof. Where it is not lodged the case will be put out for a peremptory By Order Hearing. Agents should have access to persons with authority to commit to a settlement of the action. The conference can be in person, by telephone or by video link. What this means in practice is that you will have to explain to your client the purpose of the pre-proof conference and ask him to make himself available either in person or by telephone contact. For sheriff court practitioners, the likelihood is that most pre-proof conferences will take place by telephone. This may well mean frequent telephone calls with the defenders' agent and with your client. Set aside at least one hour for the conference. Where it is clear that settlement will not be effected, you must then go through the pre-proof conference minute. You should then sign the minute and send it to the defenders' agent for signature and then lodging in court.

12–11

8. Witnesses to be cited

Lay witnesses

12–12 You should formally cite all your witnesses as early as possible. Any returned citations should be served by sheriff officer. It is common courtesy to send the witness a map of the court, to advise them of their right to expenses, and to provide a brief explanation of what they can expect at a civil proof. Ask them to confirm by telephone that they can attend. Where you have taken original statements reasonably close to the accident, it is a useful practice to send the witnesses a copy of the statement, with the request that they check that it is still accurate. This will also be a memory-refreshing exercise, but it is thought to be unobjectionable, particularly if the statement is reasonably contemporaneous to the accident.[15] If further matters or cross-allegations have arisen since the statement was taken, put these to the witnesses for their comments. Finally, always advise the witnesses that cases sometimes settle at or close to the proof date and ask them to leave a contact telephone number where they can be reached at short notice. Separately application can be made on cause shown for witness evidence to be taken by live video link.[16] Finally, be alert to serve the proper notices in the event that you wish to lead a vulnerable or child witness by lodging a child witness notice, or vulnerable witness application.[17]

Expert witnesses

12–13 Experts should be advised of the diet as soon as possible, cited and asked to confirm their availability. You should already have their report in your possession. If you are still awaiting the report, you must chase it up as a matter of urgency. Frequently the report will contain references to other publications or specialist literature. These should be obtained from the expert, put with the report, added to the documents list, and later lodged in the inventory of productions. The Inner House stated in the case of *Main v McAndrew Wormald Ltd*[18]:

> "When it is intended that the evidence of an expert witness should incorporate passages from specialist publications or reports, I consider that the document in question or excerpts should be lodged as productions."[19]

The expert will play a crucial role at the proof. He is the only witness who is allowed to give opinion evidence, and by definition this will be on matters which are outwith judicial knowledge or experience. His role is not to supplant the sheriff as a judge, but to supply scientific criteria on

---

[15] Macphail, *Sheriff Court Practice*, 3rd edn (Edinburgh: W. Green, 2006), p.520.
[16] OCR 32A(1).
[17] Vulnerable Witnesses (Scotland) Act 2004 s.12.
[18] *Main v McAndrew Wormald Ltd*, 1988 S.L.T. 141.
[19] In the case of *Roberts v British Railways Board*, 1998 S.C.L.R. 577, the judge allowed an extract from a specialist publication to be produced on the day and put to an expert witness despite objection. However the case of *Main* was not cited to the court.

which the latter can base his judgment. Double-check that the evidence which the expert is to give is within the ambit of his particular range of expertise. If you are to persuade the sheriff using expert evidence, the first thing you must do is to understand it yourself. Arrange to consult with the expert. You will generally need to visit medical experts at the hospital at their convenience. You may wish to have your consulting engineer meet with your client at your office to make sure that the expert hypothesis is constructed on the correct factual basis. Where you have instructed more than one expert, make sure that all other expert reports have been seen by all of the experts, e.g. make sure the consulting engineer has seen the medical report and vice versa. Defenders frequently instruct experts. You should advise your own expert of their identity as soon as that is known, and send your expert any written reports as soon as these are to hand. Discuss the defenders' report with your experts either by telephone or formal consultation. Ask your expert for lines of cross-examination or further enquiry. Finally, your expert should have a copy of the up to date written pleadings.

Medical experts

If your client's injuries had resolved at the time of examination by your expert, there is generally no need to instruct a fresh pre-proof examination. On the other hand, if there is any continuing disability, it is preferable to have an up to date report. You should instruct the expert accordingly, making sure that he has access to all the recent medical case notes.   **12–14**

9. Pursuer's minute of amendment

It may well be that following the meeting with your client you will decide that some matters are not fully addressed in the pleadings, or that critical facts have been mis-stated. The record will be your opponent's first port of call for cross-examination purposes, and any discrepancies between the pursuer's oral evidence and his position on record will be highlighted. A remarkable number of cases have been decided against pursuers on this basis. One might speculate that the fault is not always the client's! Otherwise the medical position may have changed, or more substantially you may have identified further grounds of liability. In all these situations you should draft and lodge a minute of amendment forthwith. The courts are traditionally charitable towards pleading deficiencies where these are addressed timeously. The minute will generally be allowed unless you are attempting to make a radically new case outwith the triennium.[20]   **12–15**

10. Defenders' witness and documents lists

If these are late, write to the defenders reminding them of the time limits, and advising that you will object at proof to any attempt to lead witnesses or to produce documents not on the list. As soon as they are received,   **12–16**

---

[20] See MacPhail, *Sheriff Court Practice*, 3rd edn (Edinburgh: W. Green), p.352 for a discussion of the authorities.

arrangements should be made to precognosce the witnesses and to inspect the documents. As explained already, litigation privilege attaches to expert reports, but it is for the other party to claim it. Initially you should request sight of all documents. In theory all the defender requires to do is to make them available for inspection, but in practice most will send you copies. You are entitled as of right to precognosce the factual witnesses on the list, but not expert witnesses.

Write direct to the witnesses asking them to make themselves available and telling them to check with the defenders' solicitor if they are in any doubt. As explained above you are entitled as of right to precognosce the other side's witnesses, and it is improper for the defenders to impose a condition that a legal representative must be present.[21] Where difficulties arise regarding precognitions, you should narrate the position in a letter to the other side which you state you will disclose at proof. Always precognosce the other side's witnesses prior to proof, no matter how inconvenient and time-consuming the exercise. In the first place it enables you properly to assess the strength of the defence. Frequently when you make contact with witnesses who appear on defenders' lists they have not been cited and there is clearly no intention that they will ever be called. Explore with the witnesses evidence which might be helpful to your client. Finally you must discover the areas in which the witness is most damaging to your client. This can prevent cross-examination embarrassment and dilemmas where you want to explore areas with the witness, but daren't ask because you have no idea of the likely answers.

11. Dealing with documentary evidence

12–17 In every proof there will be a large number of documents which you will wish to consider. The problem for the practitioner is generally two-fold:

1. How can a document be introduced in evidence, i.e. be shown to be authentic and that it is what it bears to be?
2. Can the document be introduced as evidence of its contents, i.e. that what it says is true?

One method would be to lodge only original documents and not copies, and to call the author or maker of each and every document. He could identify the document and speak to its contents. Frequently this would be an extremely cumbersome and needlessly expensive process. There are ways of circumventing this.

1. Notice to admit documents—OCR 29.14(1)(b)

12–18 By serving a notice to admit documents, you are calling upon your opponent to accept that the listed documents are authentic (i.e. that they are what they bear to be), and that any copies which have been lodged are

---

[21] In the case of *Mooney v Glasgow City Council*, 1989 S.L.T. 863 the defenders were allowed to impose a payment condition for precognitions. This was not followed in the recent case of *City of Glasgow Council, Petitioners*, 1998 G.W.D. 29-1459 which ordained the defenders to remove a pre-condition of payment for precognition.

to be held as the equivalent of originals. The notice is a step in process which must be lodged in court. If the defender disputes the point he must lodge a notice of non-admission within 21 days. The limitations of this procedure however are that it simply establishes that the documents are what they bear to be. The notice by itself does not mean that the documents are accurate, nor that they can be introduced in evidence without further procedure.

2. Documentary evidence under the Civil Evidence (Scotland) Act 1988

If the author or maker of the document is not to be called to speak to it, **12–19** the document will be classed as hearsay. Although hearsay is generally admissible in terms of the Civil Evidence (Scotland) Act 1988, documentary hearsay could only be introduced as evidence if the proper rules of court had been invoked. OCR 29.3 now provides that where any party wishes to have a statement received in evidence which is in a document admissible in terms of the Civil Evidence (Scotland) Act, the party should docquet the document, lodge it in process and provide all parties with a copy of that document. Where that has been done, the current authorities indicate that the document and its contents must be accepted as part of the evidence in the case.[22] The weight and persuasive effect of such evidence will always depend on the circumstances in which it is tendered. The procedure is a very useful means of hoovering up loose ends in a case where they are not seriously contested. It would be extremely unwise to rely on these provisions for any crucial fact in dispute.[23] In that situation every effort should be made to bring the witness, whatever the inconvenience.

3. The pre-proof conference

You can address these matters are the pre-proof conference by placing **12–20** calls on the defenders as discussed above.

12. Joint minutes

You should be clear as to the effect of the various forms of joint minute. **12–21**

- (a) You might agree that certain facts are true, in which case the terms of the joint minute will rank as a judicial admission and are conclusive on the issue.
- (b) You might agree that the documents are what they bear to be, in which case the documents are agreed to be authentic. This does *not* mean that the documents are accepted as accurate, nor that they are, without anything else, evidence of their contents.[24]

---

[22] See Sheriff N. Morrison QC, "Editorial" Green's Civ. P.B. 1997 16(July) and the cases of *McVinnie v McVinnie*, 1995 S.L.T. (Sh Ct) 81 and *Glaser v Glaser*, 1997 S.L.T. 456.
[23] See *TSB (Scotland) Plc v James Mills (Montrose) Ltd (in receivership)*, 1992 S.L.T. 519 (OH).
[24] See, e.g. *Lenaghan v Ayrshire and Arran Health Board*, 1994 S.C. 365.

(c) You might agree that the documents are what they bear to be, and that they are the evidence of their authors. In this case you are conceding that the documents are authentic, and that the court can treat what the documents say as evidence of the facts in dispute, although it is not obliged necessarily to treat what is said as persuasive.

(d) You might agree that the documents are what they bear to be, and that their contents are held to be admitted as true. In this case the contents of the documents do not simply have an evidential status; parties have accepted that any facts contained in them are admitted to be true.

13. Specification of documents for recovery of evidence on the merits

12–22 Remember that the general test for recovery at this stage is whether the documents are likely to be relevant to the issues at proof, i.e. the court will grant recovery for documents which are to be used solely as evidence at proof. In almost every case your opponent will have evidence which you will want to see. Look at the facts in dispute and ask yourself if they were likely to be recorded and documented, and if so, how? Then draft your specification addressed precisely to those documents which you think might exist. Again, the timescale makes it imperative that the motion for specification is lodged as soon as possible after the proof is allowed, and then followed through until all the documents are produced, or you are satisfied that none exist.

14. What should be lodged?

(a) Photographs and exhibit or real evidence

12–23 The practitioner's motto should be "don't tell, show". You can try to paint the scene from the mouths of the witnesses, but seeing is believing. The judicious use of photographs of the accident locus can save you tying yourself up in knots during the proof. Typically you would include photographs of the factory premises, the work equipment, the pavement where your client tripped, or your client's injuries. Think about lodging exhibit evidence such as street plans, maps or any document which facilitates explanation of the facts. The same holds true for real evidence. This means the actual physical object under discussion. If part of a machine or a vehicle has failed, wherever possible obtain the defective part and lodge it as a production.[25]

(b) Statement of valuation

12–24 The Statement of Valuation can be refined as the case proceeds. If there is to be a proof and quantum is not agreed you should update the Statement of Valuation, which will become part of your closing submission.

---

[25] See, e.g. *English v North Lanarkshire Council*, 1999 S.C.L.R. 310, where dangerous food-slicing equipment was brought to court.

(c) Medical records

If there is any continuing injury at the time of proof, it is essential to 12–25
obtain GP and hospital records. Even for simple fracture cases which are
fully healed, it is generally worthwhile to obtain the hospital records.
These should have already been seen by your consultant in any event, and
you can put them to him during the course of the proof.

(d) General explanatory material

Where you require to explain any complicated scientific proposition, e.g. 12–26
the causes of noise-induced deafness or the causes of dampness in district
council houses, it is very useful to obtain a simple textbook explanation
which you can ask your expert to speak to during the course of the proof,
and which the sheriff can take away, look at and understand. Where your
expert has referred to health and safety publications, codes of practice, or
specialist literature, obtain the publications and either lodge them in their
entirety, or lodge any necessary extract.

Pre-proof negotiation and settlement

The period around the pre-proof conference and days subsequent 12–27
represent the most likely period for settlement, throughout the course of
the whole action. Both sides now know the strength of their own case,
and will have some idea of the merits of their opponent's. During this
period you will require to be on top of every aspect of the file, from the
whereabouts of witnesses to current quantum levels. As proof approaches
there is a natural tendency to magnify the weaknesses in your client's case
and to minimise your opponents' difficulties. This should be resisted, and
a conscious effort made to view the case as a whole. Following the pre-
proof conference, you should be able to discern if the case is to be fought
to the bitter end. Know the Compensation Recovery Unit ("CRU")
position and be prepared to argue the make-up of the damages settlement, so that the minimum deduction is subtracted from the principal
sum. Where there might be a CRU deduction, write down the agreed
damages under the relevant heads of claim:

1. Loss of earnings.
2. Loss of care.
3. Loss of mobility.

Set out your agreement on the heads of damage either in a letter or in a
joint minute. If an offer is made, your client is entitled to look for your
guidance in the matter, even if that guidance is subject to various qualifications. Any agreement on the principal sum should always be subject
to the defenders' agreement to expenses with all necessary experts agreed.
If a formal minute of tender is lodged, you will require to meet with your
client to explain its effect, and you should also offer guidance as to
whether it should be accepted or rejected. Even though you are trembling
at the thought of taking the case to proof, don't ever let them see you

sweat, or sense a desperation to settle. Never criticise your own client to your opponent. Give the impression that both you and the client are looking forward to a day in court when the claim will be vindicated. Where you manage to negotiate a settlement with the defenders' agents, make sure that it is inclusive. The settlement terms should include the principal sum, together with any interest, the expenses, agreement as to which witnesses are expert witnesses, and agreement that if necessary those witnesses will be certified as expert witnesses. Where you think the case merits an increase in expenses against the defender, either fix a percentage with the defenders' agent at this stage, or alternatively agree that the matter can go before the court for the sheriff to decide. It is increasingly frequent that parties agree that interest on the principal sum will run at the judicial rate from say 28 days after settlement, to encourage the insurers to produce the cheque.

Record all the terms of the settlement agreement in a letter or fax to the defenders' agents and ask them to confirm agreement by fax, before cancelling the proof.

As soon as you receive the written agreement, you should advise the court by telephone and fax, cancel the shorthand writer, and immediately cancel all witness citations, both by telephone and letter. As a matter of courtesy you should write to all the witnesses explaining that the case has settled (without revealing the terms of the settlement), thanking them for their assistance and asking for a note of any expenses which they have incurred.

The mechanics of settlement

12–28 You will generally appear at the proof, advise the court that the case has settled, and seek a continuation for implement of the settlement terms and the lodging of a joint minute. Some courts will insist that the case is sisted. If the case settles on the morning of the proof, you should ask the court to note the names of witnesses present and ready to give evidence.

In legal aid cases the advice from the Scottish Legal Aid Board ("SLAB") is that the cheque for the principal sum can be payable to the client or to the agent and you should advise the defenders accordingly. Where you are acting for a private client you will generally wish the cheque for the principal sum to be payable to your firm, particularly where you are acting on a speculative basis. In that situation you must obtain the client's mandate and send it to the defender with your instructions. After the case has called you should borrow the process for feeing the judicial account. In most cases the principal sum will arrive before you are in a position to agree a figure for expenses. A convenient method of dealing with matters is to lodge a joint minute at that stage granting decree of absolvitor with expenses to the pursuer. Where experts have been agreed they should be specified in the joint minute, together with any agreed increase. Where the certification of experts or the question of an increase cannot be agreed, you should lodge a motion for absolvitor with expenses to the pursuer, and certification of the nominated experts, and any increase in expenses. The matter will then call before the sheriff at an opposed motion roll. It is not necessary that a case has proceeded to proof, before experts can be certified. When your account of expenses is available, it will either be agreed, or go to taxation in the usual way.

Last-minute wrinkles

In the manner of things, all kinds of alarms and annoyances will arise shortly before the proof. Witnesses will go missing or become ill, experts will be double booked, and wholly unexpected details will emerge. As a general rule you should only seek an adjournment if crucial evidence becomes unavailable, or if you have important evidence which you cannot lead standing the current state of the pleadings. In those circumstances you should lodge a motion to discharge the diet of proof, or seek to amend and risk having to concede a discharge. You will frequently receive a minute of amendment for the defender at this stage. This may disclose a line of defence for the first time, which you will require to investigate. The authorities are clear that in those circumstances the minute will generally not be allowed if it leads to the discharge of the proof where reasonable enquiry could have discovered the facts earlier.[26] There is a climate of mutual indulgence in the sheriff court in respect of such motions. It remains to be seen whether the "no excuses" culture of the Court of Session will be transferred to the Sheriff Court under the new personal injury rules. In any event an adjournment is strongly prejudicial to your client's interests, and you should object.

12–29

---

[26] See, e.g. *Strachan v Caledonian Fish Selling and Marine Stores Company Ltd*, 1963 S.C. 157; *Wood v Philips TMC*, 1994 S.L.T. 142.

Chapter 13

PROOF

ADVOCACY PREPARATION

13–01 It is helpful to write out an outline final submission a day or so before the proof. This should cover the evidence which you expect to lead, the facts which you expect to emerge, and the legal basis for your argument. This is not the speech which you will actually make after the evidence is led. Rather it is a statement of your case and liability theory, and drives home to you the evidence which you will need to elicit in the course of the proof.

When you are clear about the evidence which you need, tactical decisions about particular evidence, witnesses and lines of cross-examination are much easier to make. Consider your own evidence. Can any objection be taken to it, and if so, what is your riposte? Are you sure that you can introduce your documentary evidence? Are you clear on the precise meaning of any joint minute or notice to admit facts. You should draw up a plan of examination-in-chief for each witness. This does not mean writing out the questions word for word, but is a list of topics that you will require the witness to address. Next, you should consider the evidence which you expect your opponent to lead. Where this will be harmful to you, consider whether it can be excluded by any proper line of objection. If so, carry out the legal research and be prepared to object timeously. Otherwise you should prepare a list of cross-examination points which you are ready to adapt to the actual testimony. Again it is generally unwise to write out the questions word for word. Where you have to cross-examine an expert witness, and there are complicated propositions or formulae, you may find it helpful to write out these questions in full.

THE MORNING OF THE PROOF

13–02 Arrive at least 45 minutes before the commencement time. This will give you some breathing space to check the productions and witnesses and to calm and reassure the client. Cases very frequently settle on the morning of proof, and sheriffs are generally receptive to a request for a brief adjournment to discuss possible settlement. Make sure that you have a ready note of all the process numbers of productions to which you intend referring the witnesses, to avoid undignified fumbling in the course of the proof. Large numbers of productions should be separately paginated, making sure that numbers on the sheriff's copy productions run with your own set. This is also a final opportunity to discuss factual points with your other witnesses. If you intend to refer them to photographs, it is important that these are not presented to the witnesses for the first time in the witness box. Show them your copy photographs and allow them to familiarise themselves with the prints. Make sure that you explain the procedure for claiming their expenses from you. Wherever possible you should arrange to call your expert witnesses at specific times by prior arrangement, and have a contact telephone number for them.

COURSE OF THE PROOF

Deal with any preliminary matters such as late motions or inventories of productions before the first witness is sworn. In particular you should explain to the court in advance the nature and effect of any joint minute or notice to admit, and refer to any documentary evidence which has been agreed. **13–03**

Burden of proof

Very frequently the defence consists in a smokescreen of obfuscation in the hope that the pursuer will not meet the burden of proof. As Lord Reid has stated in *Jenkins v Allied Iron Founders*, 1970 S.C. (H.L.) 37: **13–04**

> "We must consider the evidence as we find it, and, after the evidence has been led, it is only in very rare cases, that the onus of proof is material."

It takes very little to tip the balance of probability scales to 51 per cent. Defenders are fond of citing the case of *Rhisa Shipping Co SA v Edmunds (The Popi M)*[1] as authority for the proposition that the court can simply find a case not proved. That case involved the mysterious disappearance of a ship, where all explanations before the court were highly improbable. In most cases there will be competing versions of the facts, with varying degrees of probability. Frame the issue for the court as an either/or, and force it to reach a concllusion. Don't let the defenders persuade the sheriff that he can fudge the issue on a burden of proof approach.[2]

Examination-in-chief

It is customary to begin with the pursuer. Leading questions are not allowed in examination-in-chief, except on matters which are admitted or non-contentious. A leading question is one which either contains or suggests the answer. So, "did you see a van in the street?" is a leading question, and should properly be asked as "What did you see in the **13–05**

---

[1] *Rhisa Shipping Co SA v Edmunds (The Popi M)* [1985] 1 W.L.R. 948.
[2] See the approach of the House of Lords in *Datec Electronic Holdings Ltd v UPS Ltd* [2007] 1 W.L.R. 1325.

street?" You should note that asking a witness to confirm one or other alternative is generally permitted where the alternatives are both mutually exclusive. So, "was the pursuer conscious or unconscious when you found him?" is permissible, whereas "was his safety jacket yellow or blue?" is objectionable. Asking questions in the alternative can be a useful way of controlling the witness and directing them towards the relevant subject matter. Similarly leading questions are permitted to the extent that they point the witness to the topic of the answer. So "did there come a time when working conditions changed?" followed by "what were those changes?" is permissible to bring the witness to the point. If objection is taken on the grounds of leading it is generally a simple matter to recast the question beginning with "what, where, when, how or who ... ?". When all else fails "what happened next?" is a familar standby. The problem with asking all questions in a completely open format is that there is no opportunity to reign in or otherwise control or direct the witness and if the court insists on the classical approach, you are in for a very long day. Even where leading questions are not objected to by your opponent, the value of any answer is greatly diminished, e.g. Lord President Cooper in *McKenzie v McKenzie*[3]:

> "The leading question has its place in dealing with introductory narrative, non-controversial matter, and the like, but the habitual and persistent use when examining in chief witnesses on central issues of disputed fact not only 'displaces entirely the confidence we ought to put in the deposition of a witness' (per Lord Kinnear in *Bishop v Bryce*[4]) but may make the answer as it is given a 'worthless answer' (per Lord Dunedin[5]). The taking of such evidence in the form of question and answer merely records the defect without remedying it."

Where objection is taken to your question you should consider the matter carefully. The sheriff will usually allow the evidence under reservation as to its competence and admissibility. The dilemma for the examiner is that a whole line of evidence might be rejected as incompetent at the end of the proof. Where it is a substantial matter, e.g. objection that the question relates to a ground of fault not pled, you should seek a brief adjournment before submitting a handwritten minute of amendment.

Whether the amendment is allowed will depend to a large extent on the stage at which proceedings have reached and whether there is any possible prejudice to the defender who has hitherto conducted the proof on the unamended record. In the case of *Cameron v Lanarkshire Health Board*,[6] Lord Gill allowed a minute of amendment on the second day of a jury trial. There was no prejudice to the defenders, who had already investigated the essential facts, and in any event did not request an adjournment. Lord Gill observed:

---

[3] *McKenzie v McKenzie*, 1943 S.L.T. 169.
[4] *Bishop v Bryce*, 1910 S.C. 426 at [435].
[5] 1910 S.C. 426 at [431].
[6] *Cameron v Lanarkshire Health Board*, 1997 S.L.T. 1040.

"Where a party gets into difficulties as a result of evidence given by one of his own witnesses, which indicates that amendment of the averments of fact may be necessary, the proper time at which to propose the amendment is when the difficulty arises."

By contrast, in the case of *Johnston v Perth & Kinross Council*,[7] the pursuer intimated a substantial minute of amendment at an adjourned proof diet some months after the original evidence which caused the difficulty. Not surprisingly the minute was refused. As a general rule, you should take the pursuer through his evidence-in-chief in chronological order, beginning with the general background, proceeding to the accident circumstances and then soliciting his evidence on his pain and suffering and future medical prognosis, and any special damage which he has suffered. For example, in an accident at work you would first of all establish the nature of the employer's undertaking and the processes involved, you would establish the pursuer's work duties, then the details of the accident before finally asking questions on the pursuer's injuries, future prognosis, and any past or future wage losses.

Cross-examination

Leading questions are permitted. The questions must be generally relevant to the subject in dispute, but considerable latitude is allowed to the examiner in testing the credibility and reliability of the witness. This does not extend to setting up a positive defence, or a specific alternative version of the facts, without a record for it. In the case of *Parker v Grampian Health Board*,[8] the pursuer was a nurse who was injured whilst lifting a patient. Pursuer's counsel successfully objected to all questions by the defenders both in cross-examination and in chief, which sought to establish that the pursuer should have carried out a "pivot lift". There was no record for this defence, and the Inner House held that the Lord Ordinary properly rejected all such questions and evidence as incompetent. Objection must be made promptly. Evidence which emerges is generally admitted, even where timeous objections would have led to its refusal.[9] The particular rule in cross-examination is that the opponent's case must be put to the witness for his comments:

13–06

"I have no wish to encourage the idea that proofs should be uselessly overburdened by the needless expedient of putting the defender's case to every witness for the pursuer when under cross examination. On the other hand, the most obvious principles of fair play dictate that, if it is intended later to contradict a witness upon a specific and important issue to which that witness has deponed, or to prove some

---

[7] *Johnston v Perth & Kinross Council*, 2002 S.C.L.R. 558.
[8] *Parker v Grampian Health Board*, 1996 S.C.L.R. 57.
[9] *McGlone v British Rail Board*, 1966 S.L.T. 2.

critical fact to which that witness ought to have a chance of tendering an explanation or denial, the point ought normally to be put to the witness in cross examination."[10]

This does not mean that every point in dispute needs to be put to every witness. It does mean that as a matter of fairness the essence of the opposing case must be put at least to the principal witnesses. If you fail to do this, then there is a provisional inference that the evidence led on the matter is credible and reliable. A recent example is *Smith v Hastie*,[11] where failure to cross-examine the pursuer on an essential matter was considered by the judge as an aid to assessment of credibility. Natural breaks will occur throughout the proof, e.g. lunch, brief adjournment for the sheriff to deal with other business. You should *never* discuss the case with the witness after he has commenced his evidence and you must advise him that he cannot discuss the case with any other witnesses. If you fail to caution him on this matter, and discussions amongst witnesses emerge in the course of later evidence, you may well find that such evidence is treated as having no value.

Re-examination

13–07 This is restricted to topics which have been canvassed in cross-examination. It is generally stated that the object of re-examination is to regain any ground lost, or clear up any ambiguities which have arisen in the course of cross-examination. Leading questions are not permitted, and it calls for great skill to elicit the required evidence without transgressing this rule. Be particularly alert for your opponent's re-examination in this regard. This frequently turns into a serious of propositions put by the examiner in the hope of agreement. Object promptly.

Other witnesses

13–08 You must ensure that your remaining witnesses are safely in the witness room before the examination of the pursuer begins. Thereafter whenever a break occurs, you should check with them and let them know when you expect that they will be called. Whilst it is not improper to obtain up to date information after the case has been started from a witness who has not yet been called, it must be done with great care. In particular you must never tell the witness what has already been said in evidence, or seek to influence his testimony in any way. You must continually assess the effect of the evidence which has already been led, and exercise your professional judgment as to which of your remaining witnesses require to be called. One judge described this process as follows:

---

[10] *Mackenzie v Mackenzie*, 1943 S.L.T. 139.
[11] *Smith v Hastie* Unreported March 19, 2002 Court of Session.

"At the proof itself whom to call, what to ask, when to stop and so forth are matters of judgement. A witness of great value on one point may have to be let out because he is dangerous on another. Even during the progress of the proof values change, treasured material is scrapped and fresh avenues feverishly explored."[12]

In almost all cases you will need to call your experts. Witnesses to the facts are more problematic. *Gresham's Law* states that "bad money drives out good", and hours of painstaking work can be undone by a single unsatisfactory witness. In terms of the Civil Evidence (Scotland) Act 1988, there is no legal obstacle to an uncorroborated pursuer succeeding.[13] The reality is that failure to call eyewitnesses will invariably invite adverse comment, and the sheriff is required to look at your client's evidence with special care and attention.[14] As a rule of thumb you will require to call at least one eyewitness, if one is available. You do not require to call all persons in the vicinity of the accident, and in particular you do not require to call a witness whom you are blaming for the accident.[15] Beyond that, it is all a matter of your judgment, depending on the state of the evidence and what you know of the defender's list. After your evidence has been led it is customary to close the case by saying "that, with the productions [joint minutes and notices to admit], is the pursuer's case".

The defender's case

You should be ready to object to any attempt to develop a defence for which there is no record. You should also object where evidence is sought to be led on any substantial matter which has not been put to the pursuer. Although the modern practice is that such evidence is usually allowed, it is generally considered not to be worth very much. You should object to leading questions on any of the important disputed issues in the case, or where the defender seeks to explore matters which are covered by admissions in the record. Otherwise, lawyers in every jurisdiction might do well to adopt the trial technique of Abraham Lincoln:

13–09

"In court he rarely raised objections when opposing counsel introduced evidence. He would say he reckoned it would be fair to let this in, or that, and sometimes when his adversary could not quite prove what Lincoln knew to be the truth, he reckoned it would be fair to admit the truth to be so-and-so. He never yielded essentials. What he was so blandly giving away was what he couldn't get and keep."[16]

---

[12] *Thomson v Glasgow Corporation*, 1961 S.L.T. 246.
[13] e.g. *Airns v Chief Constable of Strathclyde Police*, 1998 S.L.T. 15.
[14] See *L v L*, 1998 S.L.T. 672.
[15] *McCallum v British Rail Board*, 1991 S.L.T. 5.
[16] D.H. Donald, *Lincoln* (USA: Simon & Schuster) p.150.

Dealing with expert evidence

13–10 You must first of all establish your expert's credentials by obtaining details of his qualifications, training and experience, and have him speak to any books or articles he has published. Many experts have a printed CV, and this should be lodged with the report. There should generally be no problem about simply leading your witness through these matters. Your expert should have prepared a written report which he should be asked to identify. Almost all expert reports proceed on an assumed basis of fact about which the expert has no direct knowledge. He should be asked for a brief outline of the information he received before he prepared the report. You should then ask the expert to read at least the important sections of the report, to ensure that they are in the shorthand notes. There will be a number of matters which will inevitably require explanation, and it is generally convenient to stop the witness after each section and have him explain the meanings and terms. He should then resume his reading of the report, until he reaches the end. If there is reference in the report to any specialist literature, the publication should have been lodged as a production, and the expert should be asked to identify and comment. Documents which are produced by an expert in this way are not subject to the normal documentary hearsay rule, and in particular do not require to be proved.[17] However, you must always remember that the contents of any publication do not become evidence in the case unless and until they are spoken to. So, for example, where there is a particularly useful extract from a Health and Safety Executive code of practice, you must refer the expert to it and have him read it out. Otherwise you cannot simply make reference to it in submissions.[18] In *Davie v The Magistrates of Edinburgh*[19] the Lord President stated in respect of passages in a publication referred to by an expert witness which had not been put to the witness in evidence:

> "Passages from a published work may be adopted by a witness and made part of his evidence, or they may be put to the witness in cross examination for his comment. But, except insofar as this is done, the Court cannot in my view rely upon such works for the purpose of displacing or criticising the witness's testimony."

If the defender has lodged an expert report, you should put this to your witness for his comments. You should *never* ask the expert if in his view the facts amount to negligence or a breach of statutory duty. Those are questions entirely for the trial judge who will be guided by what the expert says about state of knowledge, good practice, reasonable practicability and the like.

---

[17] *Main v McAndrew Wormald Ltd*, 1998 S.L.T. 141.
[18] See what was said in the case of *McTear v Imperial Tobacco* 2005 2 S.C.1 at [141]–[142].
[19] *Davie v The Magistrates of Edinburgh*, 1953 S.L.T. 53.

The defenders' expert

You should prepare by acquiring a good outline grasp of the subject under discussion. Augment this by disclosing the report to your own expert and asking him for suggestions on lines of questioning. Your opponent must lay a foundation for any opinion evidence by leading details of relevant training and experience. Where he fails to do so, objection should be made at the first attempt to lead opinion evidence. For example, in road traffic cases you might object to any attempt to lead opinion evidence from a police officer on the meaning of tyre marks or the position of debris, unless and until it is established that the officer has relevant road traffic accident reconstruction and training experience. Has the expert considered all relevant material before preparing his report? Does his approach conform to the current scientific consensus, or can he be isolated as being either out of date, or is he asking the court to adopt what is simply a theory not fully accepted by the scientific community? Where the expert has published any books or articles on the subject under discussion you should obtain these and hold them in reserve if any contradictions arise. A particularly useful source is *Google Scholar*.[20] These articles do not require to be lodged in advance and can simply be put in cross-examination. Similarly, many experts give evidence on a regular basis and feature in reported cases. If you know about these you should obtain the judgment to ensure that the expert takes a uniform approach. Perhaps the commonest method of making inroads in the expert evidence is to seek to undermine the factual basis on which it proceeds. The report and the evidence will almost certainly be posited on a particular factual hypothesis. In most cases the expert can be moved to agree at least possible concessions if a different version of the facts were to be established. Finally it is important to be realistic in your examination ambitions. The occasions when you have the ammunition to knock down an expert witness will be relatively rare, and any attempt to do so will leave you engaged in a confrontation on a subject about which the witness knows much more than you. At the end of the day you will be asking the sheriff to *prefer* your expert on a reasoned basis, so your realistic objective must be to undermine the effectiveness of the defender's expert in the whole context of the case.

13–11

Submissions

At the conclusion of a straightforward case, the sheriff will normally expect to hear you immediately (OCR 29.20). You should have commenced each proof with at the very least an outline final submission either written down or in your head. This enables you to focus your evidence and questioning throughout the proof. It is always worthwhile to request a brief adjournment, say 15 minutes, to enable you to collect your thoughts and marshall your arguments. You should already know the finding-in-facts which you will require to establish to succeed, and you should be prepared to argue for them. Where there is a break

13–12

---

[20] *http://scholar.google.co.uk/* [Accessed September 13, 2011].

between the close of evidence and the hearing on evidence, it is advisable to type out specimen findings in fact, and also to consider lodging a skeleton argument. These are not steps in process and are not mandatory, but most sheriffs are grateful for at least an attempt made to assist them, in what can be an onerous and tedious task. Before you deal with the evidence, the sheriff will first of all expect to deal with any objection in evidence which remains outstanding. You will then turn to your principal argument for the pursuer.

Closing submission

13–13   Always remember that past events in civil cases are decided on the balance of probability, or more likely than not. This has been variously described as "marginal probability"[21] or "the 51 per cent test".[22] The percentage of downright mendacious witnesses is much smaller than in criminal cases. In general it is counter-productive to castigate your opponent's witnesses as deliberately deceitful. All you need to show is that your evidence should be preferred, and that the case is shown more probably than not. As explained in Ch.3, this process is holistic. Individual pieces of evidence are not considered in isolation on a balance of probability test. All the evidence is sifted and weighed before a final judgment on the balance of probability as a whole is made.

In every case where the shorthand notes have been extended on a daily basis, your final submission should refer to specific page references. There is much to be said for submitting a typewritten skeleton argument in these cases, which the sheriff can follow whilst you flesh matters out in oral submission. The sheriff will expect your argument to be directed at the crucial points of your proof. This is rarely achieved by a rehearsal seriatim of what each witness has said, and a plea that the pursuer ought to be believed. It may be helpful to focus on the following matters.

1. Admissions

13–14   The courts attach great weight to admissions against interest for the simple reason that they tend to be true.[23] Where applicable they are powerful evidence emanating from the heart of the defence. Similarly there will be areas of undisputed fact both from the pleadings and the evidence. Even where these facts do not amount to admission you can set out the agreed context into which the rest of your evidence will fit.

2. Documents

13–15   Always try to put what has emerged in evidence against any documentary background, particularly where the documents are contemporaneous with the accident. The most obvious example is the accident report book which contains a description by persons present at the accident. Many

---

[21] See *Dingley v The Chief Constable of Strathclyde Police*, 1998 S.C. 548 at [605].
[22] See *Davies v Taylor* [1974] A.C. 207.
[23] See Walker & Walker, *The Law of Evidence in Scotland*, 2nd edn (Edinburgh: Bloomsbury, 2000), p.28.

documents are prepared long before parties have adopted their respective positions at proof, and may contain unvarnished accounts of the facts. Correspondence can also provide a fruitful source of evidence in this respect.

3. Probability

At the proof each party will give conflicting stories on issues such as the accident circumstances, or the effects of injury. Other than by an appeal to your witness's credibility and reliability, why should the pursuer's story be preferred? Consider matters such as internal consistency, reporting detail, and motivation for action. Does the version of events accommodate the admitted facts, and provide reasons for persons acting in the way they have? Wherever possible, argue that the pursuer's story is inherently likely to be true quite apart from any question of credibility and reliability. Wherever possible compare and contrast the alternative versions remembering at the end of the day the court will take a holistic approach to fact-finding. A particularly useful approach is to consider what the alternative is if the pursuer's version is untrue, and to compare and contrast the respective likelihoods.[24]

13–16

4. Credibility and reliability

The sheriff will have to consider whether the witnesses are:

13–17

(a) credible, i.e. doing their best to tell the truth whilst giving evidence; and
(b) reliable, i.e. giving evidence which is likely to be accurate.

You should remember this distinction. A very frequent finding in civil cases is that a witness is truthful but mistaken. The whole area is very much the province of the trial judge, and some sheriffs take the view that very little should be said by agents in the matter. But wherever possible you should set the pursuer's story against other credible evidence. In particular, can the pursuer's evidence be cross-checked against the documents, the undisputed facts, or the evidence of a wholly independent witness?

PARTICULAR TOPICS

Defenders lead no evidence

This is a tactic which is sometimes used when the defenders believe that some basic element of the pursuer's proof has not been established. In this situation the pursuer is entitled to ask the court to draw only

13–18

---

[24] This was the approach of the Lord President in the Inner House in the case of *Thomson v Kvaerner*. Although the judgment was reversed by the House of Lords at 2004 S.C. (H.L.) 1, this is a useful analytical approach in every case.

favourable inferences from the evidence which has been led.[25] In practice the courts will distinguish between inference, i.e. a logical step justified by evidence before the court, and speculation which is a leap of faith without any foundation in the evidence.[26] The situation arises frequently in cases where as a matter of law a pursuer should show the length of time a hazard has been in existence and that a reasonable system of inspection would have discovered and removed it. The courts generally view such evidence to be fundamental and will decline to make findings in fact on these matters, solely based on inference.[27] A good example of the court drawing favourable inferences of fact is the case of *Riches v Edinburgh Corporation*.[28] The pursuer suffered catastrophic injury after the Honda motorcycle which he was riding struck a raised manhole cover in the middle of the roadway. There was no direct evidence as to who had tampered with the manhole. The defenders led no evidence. Lord Stott held that as a matter of inference it was more probable than not that the manhole had been negligently left in place by the defenders' employees and found for the pursuer. The Inner House stated:

> "The nature of the cover and its position on the roadway, further, make it difficult to accept it likely that the cover would be opened by persons without any interest or authority to do so. As the Lord Ordinary says, the prima facie inference is that the person who opened the cover is more likely than not to be an employee of the defenders. No doubt this prima facie inference could readily have been elided by some evidence of the kind mentioned by the Lord Ordinary, but none was led."

Res ipsa loquitur

13–19 This has been described as "a rule as to the weight of evidence from which negligence can be inferred", not a doctrine.[29]

If you can persuade the court that the facts come within the category of a res ipsa loquitur case, at the very least the burden of explanation if not the onus of proof passes to the defender. It is unwise to rely entirely on this approach, particularly where the cause of the accident has been identified.[30] A more fruitful approach may be that the evidence shows a prima facie case of fault which the defenders have failed to negative. A good example is the case of *Binnie v Rederij Theodoro BV*.[31] The pursuer was injured when a snapped tow line struck him whilst a vessel was negotiating locks to enter the Firth of Forth. The evidence showed that the ship's engines had failed to engage in reverse thrust, causing the tow

---

[25] *O'Donnell v Murdoch Mackenzie & Co Ltd*, 1967 S.L.T. 229.
[26] See the discussion of this distinction in *Cordiner v British Railways Board*, 1986 S.L.T. 209 at [215].
[27] See, e.g. *Johnstone v City of Glasgow District Council*, 1986 S.L.T. 50 at [53].
[28] *Riches v Edinburgh Corporation*, 1976 S.L.T. (Notes) 9 at [10].
[29] Lord Denning in *Turner v Mansfield Corporation*, 1975 C.L.Y. 2346.
[30] See, e.g. *McQueen v Glasgow Garden Festival (1988) Ltd*, 1995 S.L.T. 211 and *McDyer v Celtic Football and Athletic Club*, 1997 Rep. L.R. 94.
[31] *Binnie v Rederij Theodoro BV*, 1993 S.C. 71 at [87].

line to snap. The defenders led no evidence, relying on the pursuer's failure to show any reasonable system of inspection which would have revealed the engine fault. The Lord President Hope stated:

> "In the present case the inferences to be drawn from the evidence are those which are most favourable to the pursuer since the defenders did not give evidence. On this approach it cannot be assumed in the defenders' favour that the engines were in proper working order and that their failure was a mystery. On the contrary, their failure to operate when required suggests that there was a defect which ought prima facie to have been prevented by a reasonable system of inspection and maintenance. This is precisely the case of which the pursuer gave notice in his averments, and the defenders led no evidence to displace the inference."

Modification and variation of the case as pled

Evidence never comes out quite as in your precognitions, even where the witnesses are truthful. The courts recognise this. As Lord Devlin stated in the case of *Cleisham v British Railways Board*[32]:

13-20

> " 'Variation', 'modification' or 'development' seem to me to be well chosen to describe the sort of thing that may happen in the course of the trial and which ... might defeat the most far-seeing pleader if he were to be held tightly to his averments. Naturally as a case develops a pursuer's story gets a knock or two and at the end of the case is a bit dented."

The rule is that a pursuer is entitled to succeed, provided the facts shown are no more than a variation or modification of the existing case.[33] This does not mean that you can succeed on a ground of fault which has not been pled,[34] nor that you can argue for a fundamental change of tack. It does mean that the court should not take an overly pedantic view of the pleadings, and should seek that substantial justice is done.

Quantum

The pursuer's submission on quantum will require to address solatium, past and future wage loss, any special patrimonial or property losses, service or care costs and interest. English awards are directly comparable.[35] In this regard the Judicial Studies Board have published a tariff *Guidelines for the Assessment of General Damages in Personal Injury Cases*[36] for English courts which covers most kinds of injuries. It is published in *Kemp & Kemp: Quantum of Damages*, and is increasingly

13-21

---

[32] *Cleisham v British Railways Board*, 1964 S.L.T. 41 at [51].
[33] *McCusker v Saveheat Cavity Wall Insulation Ltd*, 1987 S.L.T. 24.
[34] *Laing v Scottish Grain Distillers Ltd*, 1992 S.L.T. 435.
[35] *Allan v Scott*, 1972 S.L.T. 45.
[36] *Guidelines for the Assessment of General Damages in Personal Injury Cases*, 10th edn (Oxford: Oxford University Press, 2010).

referred to in the Scottish courts. This should be your starting point, with further reference to *McEwan & Paton on Damages for Personal Injuries in Scotland* and the recent Scottish and English cases. The awards should be updated for the effects of inflation using the inflation tables contained in *McEwan & Paton*. Note that these cases are not "authorities" as such, and are not binding on a sheriff. They do set the range for which you can argue. Reference has already been made to the importance of persuading the courts to adopt the multiplier/multiplicand approach on future wage loss wherever possible. Alternatively you should seek out analogous cases on loss of employability. Wage loss should be capable of agreement with the defenders prior to the proof, failing which you should have a calculated schedule to put to the court. The approach to services claims has been dealt with in the section on damages.

Interest on damages: solatium

13–22 The court is obliged to award interest on solatium from the date of the accident. This is mandatory in terms of the Interest on Damages (Scotland) Act 1958 as amended.[37] Two situations can generally be identified.

13–23 *1. The pursuer has recovered at the date of proof.* In this situation interest on solatium is generally awarded at half the judicial rate from the date of the injury to the date of completion of recovery. Interest is then awarded from that date at the full judicial rate down to the date of decree. The case of *Preston v Grampian Health Board*,[38] is a good example of the approach to be taken to the different periods.

13–24 *2. There is ongoing pain and suffering at the date of proof.* The award for solatium will comprise both past and future suffering, and the court will be concerned not to award interest on the latter element. For the purposes of the calculation of interest there will normally be an apportionment of solatium between the past and the future depending on the nature and permanency of the injury, e.g. one-third to the past and two-thirds to the future. The amount apportioned to the past will then attract interest at half the judicial rate from the date of injury to the date of decree.

Patrimonial loss

13–25 The court should also award interest on patrimonial loss such as property losses or wage loss. Frequently interest is awarded at the full judicial rate on the value of the property from the date of its destruction. The cases show no consistent approach to interest on wage loss. Interest may be awarded on a continuing wage loss at half the judicial rate from the date of the accident.[39] Where the pursuer has returned to work and there is no continuing wage loss, interest may be calculated at half the judicial rate

---

[37] *Orr v Metcalfe*, 1973 S.L.T. 133.
[38] *Preston v Grampian Health Board*, 1998 S.L.T. 435.
[39] e.g. *Paterson v Kelvin Central Buses*, 1997 S.L.T. 685.

down to the date of return, and thereafter at the full judicial rate.[40] Alternatively, interest may be awarded at the full judicial rate on the wage loss for half the absence period.[41]

Recovery of benefits

The court will require to make a breakdown of damages in terms of the Social Security (Recovery of Benefits) Act 1997 s.15. Following the case of *Wisley v John Fulton (Plumbers) Ltd*,[42] the court should carry out the above interest calculation before any recoupment provisions are applied, i.e. benefits should be deducted after interest has been calculated on the whole sums due. Most sheriffdoms now have a practice note to the effect that a schedule showing a breakdown of damages into the relevant heads of claim under: (a) wage loss; (b) cost of mobility; and (c) cost of care, should be presented to the court before any decree is granted. This is not required if the case settles by agreement.

13–26

---

[40] e.g. *Harrison v R. B. Tennent Ltd*, 1992 S.L.T. 1060.
[41] See *Williamson v G. B. Papers Plc*, 1994 S.L.T. 173.
[42] *Wisley v John Fulton (Plumbers) Ltd*, 1998 S.L.T. 1026.

CHAPTER 14

PROCEDURE AFTER PROOF

14-01 The final judgment will normally fix a date for a hearing on expenses a few weeks in advance. Appeal considerations are dealt with in Ch.15.

HEARING ON EXPENSES

14-02 The general rule is that "expenses follow success", i.e. if your client wins, he will be entitled to the whole party and party expenses of the action, and he will be liable in these costs to the other side if he loses:

> "If any party is put to expense in vindicating his rights, he is entitled to recover it from the person by whom it was created, unless there is something in his own conduct that gives him the character of an improper litigant, in insisting on things which his title does not warrant."[1]

A general finding of expenses is subject to any particular finding earlier on in the process, e.g. if the pursuer has won the case but only after an unsuccessful debate and consequent minute of amendment procedure where he was found liable in expenses, those expenses are excepted from the general finding. The pursuer cannot charge the defender for these costs, and the defender is entitled to draw up a contra-account containing those expenses. A general finding will normally cover any interlocutor where there has been no particular decerniture on expenses.

At the hearing on expenses you or your opponent may argue about the expenses of particular parts of the process where these have been reserved, failing which they will be covered by the general finding. A successful pursuer in a personal injury action is normally entitled to the full expenses without modification even although there may have been a substantial finding of contributory negligence:

---

[1] *MacLaren on Expenses*, (Edinburgh: W. Green, 1912), p.21.

"Even on the basis that the pursuer was partly to blame, he has still to vindicate his right to those damages and the principle on which expenses are awarded, as I have always understood it, is that if a party is put to expense in vindicating his rights, then he is entitled to recover it from the person who has caused the expense."[2]

Certification of experts

Wherever possible, you should have sanction for your experts agreed as part of the settlement package. After judgment, or where there is no agreement, it is increasingly common for defenders to argue that the expert was not necessary, which is the test for certification. Where you have required to instruct expert witnesses, you should have these certified at the hearing on expenses. Where there is no hearing on expenses, then application for certification should be made by motion. The test of necessity is interpreted widely to mean what a prudent solicitor would do at the time of the instruction of the expert.[3] Be prepared to argue that the limitations on judicial knowledge mean that the prudent solicitor is required to instruct an expert in any matter which is remotely technical. As was said by Sheriff Principal Dunlop in the case of *Todd v The Roman Catholic Diocese of Dunkeld and Dundee City Council*[4] in relation to certification of an actuarial expert:

14–03

"This supports the argument for the appellant that the matter should not be weighed too finely in the balance and that certification is not necessarily to be refused because, with the benefit of hindsight, the evidence of the skilled witness has not proved to be necessary."

Experts may be certified although the action is settled prior to proof.[5] Certification will mean that you can recover the expert's reasonable fees and also charge for perusing and revising his report.

Motions for increase in expenses

The pursuer may be entitled to seek an increase in judicial expenses against the defender based on the criteria contained in the Act of Sederunt (Fees of Solicitors in the Sheriff Court) 1998, as amended, general reg.5. A motion no longer requires to be made within seven days of the interlocutor awarding expenses, but the sooner the matter is dealt with, the better. Clearly this kind of motion is only appropriate where your client has been successful. You should remember that you can seek an increase against the Legal Aid Fund even where your client has been unsuccessful.

14–04

---

[2] *Howitt v Alexander & Sons*, 1948 S.C. 154 at [155]. See also *Lever v Greenock Motor Service Co Ltd*, 1949 S.C. 888—even though the pursuer was 60% to blame for the accident, still entitled to full expenses.

[3] *Allison v Orr*, 2004 S.C. 453.

[4] *Todd v The Roman Catholic Diocese of Dunkeld and Dundee City Council* Unreported May 10, 2004 Tayside Central and Fife Sheriff Court.

[5] *Devenney v Greater Glasgow Health Board*, 1989 S.L.T. 578; *Merrick Homes Ltd v Duff (No.2)*, 1997 S.L.T. 53.

Tenders

14–05 The normal rule is that if the pursuer fails to beat the tender, the pursuer is entitled to expenses down to the date of the tender, with the defender being entitled to expenses thereafter. Given the heavy costs of proof, the latter will frequently equal or outweigh the former. The sum tendered must be greater than that contained in the decree. Interest is taken into account in the calculation. The question is, would the pursuer have been better off by accepting the tender at the date of its lodgement when he would have had the benefit of the money and interest thereafter? In the case of *Manson v Skinner*,[6] the pursuer was held to have failed to have beaten a tender, where he did so only after the application of interest from the date of lodging.

Private client unsuccessful

14–06 The client will generally be liable to the defender in expenses. You should continue to act to attempt to reduce the final bill to the client, or the legal expenses insurer, by way of negotiation or at taxation.

Legally-aided client unsuccessful

14–07 In this situation you are entitled to seek modification of expenses against the client in terms of the Legal Aid (Scotland) Act 1986 s.18(2). The court is obliged to have regard to "all the circumstances". There is no statutory guideline as to how this should be calculated in practice. In the past the court has frequently modified expenses to the same figure as the client's legal aid contribution. The recent financial restrictions on legal aid now mean that this contribution can be very substantial even for persons of relatively modest means. You should be prepared to argue that this is no longer appropriate, having regard to your client's circumstances. Relevant considerations are generally held to be the means of the pursuer, the conduct of the case, the amount of expenses awarded against a legally-aided party, and the amount which it might be reasonable for the party to pay.[7]

Cases involving two or more defenders

14–08 If the pursuer has been successful against all the defenders there is no difficulty. The defenders should be jointly and severally liable to the pursuer in the expenses of the cause. Problems arise where there is success against one defender and failure against another. The pursuer should be looking to have the unsuccessful defender liable for the expenses of the successful defender, or at the very least have the pursuer found liable in the expenses of the successful defender, but subject to a right of relief against the unsuccessful defender for those expenses.[8] The specific blame of another party by one party in either correspondence or the defences is an obvious factor. Equally failure to disclose information either in pre-action correspondence or at the pleadings stage may also be a factor. A

---

[6] *Manson v Skinner*, 2002 S.L.T. 448.
[7] See *McKenzie v Lothian and Borders Police*, 1995 S.L.T. 1332 and *Armstrong v Armstrong*, 1970 S.L.T. 247.
[8] *Johnston v Lithgows Ltd*, 1964 S.L.T. (Notes) 96.

guiding principle in all questions of expenses is to identify which party has required the pursuer to resort to court to vindicate his rights:

> "Prima facie, it is for a pursuer to find out who is responsible to him for wrong which he considers he has sustained, and in general if he calls as a defender a party who is innocent of the alleged wrong, he will be liable in expenses. But this rule is subject to exceptions, especially where the claim is made, in the first instance, against the party who is truly responsible, and it is at his request and instance that another party is called into the field. Here the question is, who is responsible for bringing the successful defender into Court?"[9]

There are normally two such situations.

1. The pursuer convenes a number of defenders from the start. The general rule is that where one of two defenders is assoilzied, the pursuer is liable for the successful defender's expenses.[10] It may still be open to argue that it was prudent for the pursuer to call all the defenders, having regard to his own state of knowledge and the defenders' attitude to the intimation of the claim. The pre-action correspondence may be of some assistance here and you should note that the expression "without prejudice" does not normally make the correspondence privileged on any question of expenses. Where a party found liable sought in correspondence to blame the successful defender, it will found an argument that the latter's expenses should be borne by the unsuccessful defender. You should seek to argue that you made all reasonable enquiries prior to the raising of proceedings, and that in the circumstances it was prudent to convene more than one defender. 14–09

2. Where the defender has been convened after proceedings have been raised. The test is whether the original defender causes or induces the second defender to be convened.[11] Much will depend on what has been said in the pleadings. If the defender blames someone else, causing the prudent pursuer's agent to convene that person as a second defender, there may be good grounds for arguing that the unsuccessful defender should bear the costs of the successful defender. Moreover, the casting of blame may be explicit or implicit. For example, in the case of *McCrae v Bryson*,[12] a road traffic accident involving two vehicles, the driver of one of the vehicles simply denied liability for the collision. It was held that this cast blame on the driver of the other vehicle by implication, and that the unsuccessful first defender should be liable for the expenses of the successful second defender. 14–10

The sheriff has a very wide discretion in all matters of expenses. Everything will depend on the particular facts and circumstances, and you should be prepared to argue your client's corner on the basis of equity and fairness.

---

[9] *Morrison v Waters & Co* (1906) 14 S.L.T. 127.
[10] *McIntosh v Galbraith* (1900) 8 S.L.T. 241.
[11] *Clegg v McKirdy & McMillan*, 1932 S.L.T. 250.
[12] *McCrae v Bryson*, 1923 S.L.T. 672.

Dealing with the principal sum

The successful private client

14-11 After the judgment has been obtained, you should advise the defenders that you wish the cheque made payable to your own firm, and produce your client's mandate to that effect if they require it. This will enable you to deduct any pre-litigation expenses which you intend to recover from the client, and also any success fee uplift where you are acting on a speculative fees basis. As soon as the principal sum is received you should make immediate part payment to the client, pending settlement of the judicial expenses.

The successful legally aided pursuer

14-12 Where the pursuer has a legal aid certificate, the cheque should be made payable to the client or to your firm. If you are accepting judicial expenses, and are confident that you will recover them, you should make an interim payment to the client. If you think you are going to have a civil legal aid agent and client account, you should not distribute the whole principal sum, but hold sufficient funds to meet that account.

Where significant sums are involved you should always consider investment advice for the client. Your own firm may have someone qualified to provide business investment advice. Alternatively you should set up a connection with a solicitor who can. Finally, when you are writing to your client with the cheque, let him know that you value his business. Tell him what other services your firm provides and ask him for word-of-mouth recommendation.

Accounts of expenses

14-13 A decree for expenses enables you to draw an account under the table of fees using either a block account, or a particular itemised account, but not mixing both. The basis of the charge is party and party. General reg.8 provides:

> "Only such expenses shall be allowed on the taxation of accounts as are reasonable for conducting it in a proper manner. It shall be competent to the auditor to disallow all charges for papers, parts of papers or particular procedure or agency which he shall judge irregular or unnecessary."[13]

Your opponent may not be liable to pay for each and every step which you took in the prosecution of the action. Having secured a favourable result in the interests of their client, many solicitors then fall guilty of neglecting their own. All legal firms require strong cash flow injections. You should be looking to prepare your own account of judicial expenses, or having a law accountant prepare it, within 21 days of the hearing on

---

[13] Act of Sederunt (Fees of Solicitors in the Sheriff Court) (Amendment and Further Provisions) 1993 (SI 1993/3080) Sch.1 para.8.

expenses. It is worthwhile carrying out a file check to make sure that all chargeable items are properly filed, and all notes of expenditure and vouchers are fully tagged.

You should then send the account to your opponent, making it plain that you expect his proposals on payment of the account within 14 days. There may be items on the account which you are prepared to negotiate, but there is generally no need to accept a significant discount. It was held in the case of *Gilmour's Tutor v Renfrew County Council*,[14] that a pursuer is entitled to a diet of taxation, which is at the defender's expense, unaffected by any correspondence or offers in the matter. Where a defender fails to meet the time limit, you should enrol for taxation. If you negotiate a settlement earlier than seven days before the taxation diet, there is no audit fee payable to the auditor of court. If settlement is negotiated within seven days of the diet, 50 per cent of the audit fee is payable to the auditor; if the diet is cancelled within three days, then 75 per cent of the audit fee is payable, and after that the full audit fee is payable. If you do negotiate a compromise figure, remember to make the defender liable for the auditor's fee in addition to the agreed amount.

If the taxation proceeds, don't pass the file to the trainee. A trainee cannot hope to meet the legitimate enquiries and concerns of the auditor as to why particular steps were necessary to further the litigation. You should attend the taxation personally and prepare arguments on any likely points of contention. At taxation, items should only be disallowed if they are unreasonable. In *Malpas v Fife Council*,[15] Lord Bonomy stated:

> "It seems to be me to follow that, in deciding whether to allow or disallow any particular item the auditor is undertaking a task similar to mine and should only disallow an item if it can truly be said that to incur that expense was not reasonable, in the sense that a competent solicitor acting reasonably would not incurred it."

Finalising the accounts

After judicial expenses are received you should remit any balance to the private client after full deduction of your fees in the matter. In civil legal aid cases you should complete a Civil Account Synopsis report and lodge this together with your legal aid agent and client account of expenses charged at legal aid rates. In the majority of cases this will be less profitable to you than simply accepting the judicial expenses in full and final settlement of your claim under the civil legal aid certificate. In that case you should send the Civil Account Synopsis/Conclusion Form (CIV/ACC/CONC) with a declaration to that effect to the Board. This means that there will be no deduction from the client's principal sum to pay any expenses under the s.1 certificate. You can pay the client the principal sum directly, but the expenses recovered, together with the Account Synopsis will have to be sent to the Scottish Legal Aid Board who will then make payment to you.

14–14

---

[14] *Gilmour's Tutor v Renfrew County Council*, 1970 S.L.T. (Notes) 47.
[15] *Malpas v Fife Council*, 1999 S.L.T. 499.

CHAPTER 15

APPEALS

15–01 This chapter looks briefly at the law and practice of appeals in personal injury actions and considers some matters which found successful appeals, with particular reference to ordinary actions.[1] It deals with appeals to the sheriff principal from final interlocutors. A pursuer can appeal directly from the sheriff court to the Inner House, but legal aid is unlikely to be granted and legal expenses insurers will be reluctant to sanction such a move.

Taking instructions

15–02 The sheriff's written judgment will not normally deal with expenses, but will fix a date for a hearing on expenses.[2] You should send the judgment to the client immediately. If you have lost on the merits or a significant aspect of the case you will have to consider whether to appeal. The interlocutor will become final after expenses have been dealt with, and you will have a 14-day time limit in which to mark a note of appeal running from the date of that interlocutor.[3] The immediate post-judgment period will therefore provide a breathing space in which a considered decision can be taken with the client. Almost all clients who have been unsuccessful on the merits want to go to appeal, which they think will be a re-run of the facts. Your job is to assess and advise on the realistic prospects. Where the finding complained of relates to an ancillary matter such as quantum or contributory negligence you should always remember that your appeal will open up the whole matter to a cross-appeal from the defender which is not limited to the points which you have taken. If your client has a civil legal aid certificate, then a meeting to consider an appeal will be covered under that certificate. You require a fresh civil legal aid application for the appeal itself, and preliminary matters require cover under Legal Advice and Assistance. Where you conclude that there are no reasonable prospects on appeal, you must write to the client advising him and also point out the expiry date for marking an appeal.

---

[1] See Ch.16 in respect of summary cause appeals.
[2] See, e.g. practice note 1988 to this effect for South Strathclyde Dumfries and Galloway.
[3] OCR 31.1.

Realistic prospects

Think twice before making any appeal based purely on a supposed error of finding in fact. As noted below, the adjudication privileges which attach to a judge at first instance are well nigh impenetrable, unless you can show that he or she is "plainly wrong".[4] The traditional framework for appeals is contained in the speech of Lord Thankerton in *Thomas v Thomas*[5], where he said as follows:

15–03

> "(1) Where a question of fact has been tried by a Judge without a jury, and there is no question of misdirection of himself by the Judge, an appellate Court which is disposed to come to a different conclusion on the printed evidence should not do so unless it is satisfied that any advantage enjoyed by the trial Judge by reason of having seen and heard the witnesses could not be sufficient to explain or justify the trial Judge's conclusion. (2) The appellate Court may take the view that, without having seen or heard the witnesses, it is not in a position to come to any satisfactory conclusion on the printed evidence. (3) The appellate Court, either because the reasons given by the trial Judge are not satisfactory, or because it unmistakably so appears from the evidence, may be satisfied that he has not taken proper advantage of having seen and heard the witnesses, and the matter will then become at large for the appellate Court. It is obvious that the value and importance of having seen and heard the witnesses will vary according to the class of case, and, it may be, the individual case in question."

The sheriff principal will expect you to know this and be prepared to argue with reference to this passage that the matter is at large for the appellate court.

Appeals on matters of fact

An appellate court is extremely reluctant to interfere in what are described as "primary" findings-in-fact. Where a sheriff has reached a conclusion based on the credibility or reliability of witnesses whom he has seen, an appeal court will be slow to overturn:

15–04

> "In most cases such a finding by a judge who has seen and heard the witness who is disbelieved will be inviolate in an appellate court, particularly where credibility bears to have been assessed as a result of that advantage as, for example, where the judge relies to any extent upon his assessment of the demeanour of the witness, or of the manner in which he has given his evidence. In those cases however where the finding of the judge at first instance does not bear to have turned upon his observation or impressions of the witness whose

---

[4] *Thomson v Kvaerner*, 2004 S.C. (H.L.) 1.
[5] *Thomas v Thomas*, 1947 S.C. (H.L.) 45 at [54].

evidence has not been accepted, an appellate court is free to examine the judge's stated reasons for itself, and if they are either unsound or unsatisfactory, to form their own conclusion."[6]

Examples of successful appeals are where the judge has ignored or misunderstood a significant body of evidence[7] or reached a conclusion which has a very high degree of physical improbability.[8] Otherwise you will have to argue that the judge at first instance was plainly wrong.[9] You are more likely to succeed with findings which relate to "secondary" facts, i.e. matters based on inference and not what the witnesses saw or heard directly. A finding that an accident was not reasonably foreseeable is normally treated as a finding-in-fact, but it proceeds on an inferential basis and the appellate court may consider itself to be in an equally strong position to make other inferences.[10] The boundaries of interference in this area were set out by the House of Lords in *Datec Electronics Holdings Ltd v UPS Ltd*[11] where the assessment was stated to be an evaluation of the facts involving an assessment of different factors. This is not a matter of simple discretion.

The court approved the judgment of Lord Justice Clarke in *Assicurazioni Generali SpA v Arab Insurance Group*[12] where he stated:

> "Once the appellant has shown a real prospect that a finding or inference is wrong, the role of an appellate court is to determine whether or not this is so, giving full weight of course to the advantage enjoyed by any Judge at first instance who has heard oral evidence."

Separately:

> " ... [S]o far as the appeal raises issues of judgement on unchallenged primary findings and inferences, this court ought not to interfere unless it is satisfied that the Judge's conclusion lay outwith the bounds within which reasonable disagreement is possible."

This approach was approved by the Inner House in *Wilson v Dunbar Bank Plc*.[13]

Appeals on matters of law

15–05 An appeal will lie where the appellant can show some material misdirection, e.g. where the sheriff misapplied the burden of proof where a

---

[6] *Angus v Glasgow Corporation*, 1977 S.L.T. 206 at [213].
[7] *Morrison v J. Kelly & Sons Ltd*, 1970 S.L.T. 198.
[8] *Islip Pedigree Breeding Centre v Abercrombie*, 1959 S.L.T. 161.
[9] See *Arthur Thomson v Kvaerner Govan Ltd*, 2004 S.C. (H.L.) 1.
[10] See, e.g. the speech of Lord Reid in *The Wagon Mound (No.2)* [1966] 2 All E.R. 709 at [717].
[11] *Datec Electronics Holdings Ltd v UPS Ltd* [2007] 1 W.L.R. 1325.
[12] *Assicurazioni Generali SpA v Arab Insurance Group* [2003] 1 W.L.R. 577, [580]–[581].
[13] *Wilson v Dunbar Bank Plc*, 2008 S.C. 457.

statutory duty was to be enforced insofar as reasonably practicable[14]; or where the Lord Ordinary reached conclusions on the causation of deafness based on his own scientific theory which had not been spoken to by any witness[15]; or where the lower courts had failed to apply a "purposive construction" to United Kingdom legislation designed to implement an EC directive.[16]

The modern judge is obliged to provide reasons for his judgment. In *English v Emery Reimbold & Strick Ltd*[17] the extent of this duty was described as follows:

> "It follows that, if the appellate process is to work satisfactorily, the judgment must enable the appellate court to understand why the Judge reached his decision. This does not mean that every factor which weighed with the Judge in his appraisal of the evidence has to be identified and explained. But the issues the resolution of which were vital to the Judge's conclusion should be identified and the manner in which he resolved them explained. It is not possible to provide a template for this process. It need not involve a lengthy judgment. It does require the Judge to identify and record those matters which were critical to his decision. If the critical issue was one of fact, in may be enough to say that one witness was preferred to another because the one manifestly had a clearer recollection of the material facts or the other gave answers which demonstrated that his recollection could not be relied upon."

In particular where expert evidence has been led, the court should engage in some kind of assessment of that evidence. This means that he should provide an explanation as to why he has accepted the evidence of one expert and rejected another. As was said in *English*:

> "It may be that the evidence of one or the other accorded more satisfactorily with the facts found by the judge. It may be that the explanation of one was more inherently credible than that of the other. It may simply be that one was better qualified, or manifestly more objective than the other. Whatever the explanation may be, it should be apparent from the judgement."

Although demeanour of experts may be a legitimate consideration, it will generally not be enough for the sheriff simply to *prefer* one expert over another, without further explanation. The current forensic approach was summed up by Stuart-Smith L.J. in the case of *Loveday v Renton*[18] which is frequently cited:

---

[14] *Henderson v Redpath Dorman Long Ltd*, 1975 S.L.T. (Sh. Ct.) 27.
[15] *Kay's Tutor v Ayrshire & Arran Health Board*, 1986 S.L.T. 435.
[16] *Litster v Forth Dry Dock & Engineering Co Ltd*, 1989 S.L.T. 540.
[17] *English v Emery Reimbold & Strick Ltd* [2002] 1 W.L.R. 2409.
[18] *Loveday v Renton* [1989] Med. L.R. 117.

"The Court has to evaluate the witness and soundness of his opinion. Most importantly this involves an examination of the reasons given for his opinions, and the extent to which they are supported by the evidence. The judge also has to decide what weight to attach to a witness's opinion by examining the internal consistency and logic of his evidence; the care with which he has considered the subject and presented his evidence; his precision and accuracy of thought as demonstrated by his answers; how he responds to a searching and informed cross examination and in particular the extent to which a witness faces up to and accepts the logic of a proposition put in cross examination or is prepared to concede points that are seen to be correct; the extent to which a witness has conceived an opinion and is reluctant to re-examine it in the light of later evidence, or demonstrates a flexibility of mind which may involve changing or modifying opinions previously held; whether or not a witness is biased or lacks independence."[19]

Contributory negligence

15–06 An appeal court will be unlikely to interfere unless you can show some error in principle in the approach taken to contributory negligence, or alternatively that a substantial alteration in the percentage fixed is required to do justice to the parties.[20] In this regard the dictum of Lord Reid in *Baker v Willoughby*[21] is frequently quoted to the effect that the trial judge's assessment "ought not to be varied unless some error in the judge's approach is clearly discernible".

Quantum of damages

15–07 An appellate court will interfere if there has been some error in principle. So where in England an estranged widow whose husband had died in an accident sought damages on the basis that there was a prospect of a reconciliation, the House of Lords held that she had to show some significant prospect of reconciliation, as opposed to a mere speculative possibility. She did not require to show that a reconciliation was more likely than not.[22] So far as *solatium* is concerned, an appeal is sustainable only where the award is outwith the *range* of reasonable awards and is out of proportion in all the circumstances.[23] An award which was only two-thirds of what the Inner House would regard as a reasonable award entitled the court to interfere.[24] So far as past and future wage loss is concerned, the approach to be taken is that of Lord Wheatley in the case of *Blair v F.J.C. Lilley (Marine) Ltd*[25]:

---

[19] Cited with approval by Lord Hodge in the case of *Dineley v Lothian Health Board* [2007] CSOH 154.
[20] *McCusker v Saveheat Cavity Wall Insulation Ltd*, 1987 S.L.T. 24.
[21] *Baker v Willoughby* [1969] 3 All E.R. 1528 at [1530].
[22] *Davies v Taylor* [1972] 3 All E.R. 836.
[23] *Barker v Murdoch*, 1979 S.L.T. 145.
[24] *McManus v British Railways Board*, 1994 S.L.T. 496.
[25] *Blair v F.J.C. Lilley (Marine) Ltd*, 1981 S.L.T. 90 at [92].

"It is only when the assessment has been reached through the use of wrong facts or the application of wrong principles or where a manifestly unfair assessment has been reached that a Court of Appeal will interfere with the finding of the judge of first instance."

Expenses

The sheriff has a very wide discretion in dealing with questions on expenses, and appeals are severely discouraged unless there is some point of principle involved.[26] In general a successful pursuer is normally entitled to a full award of expenses, in the absence of a tender. This is the operative rule even where there has been a significant deduction for contributory negligence.

FORMULATION ON THE GROUNDS OF APPEAL

Wherever possible as a matter of logic you should state the major general premise first, followed by the minor particular premise. So:

"(One) Regulation 5 of the Provision and Use of Work Equipment Regulations 1998 provides for strict liability for the maintenance of work equipment from the perspective of health and safety. At the material time the door closer used by the pursuer was work equipment, and was defective in that it jammed. This defect caused or materially contributed to the pursuer's accident. The sheriff should have found that the defenders were in breach of Regulation 5."

In terms of OCR 31.4(1) the note of appeal should be in form A1 which must be signed and dated and should contain the full grounds of appeal. It must be served on the defender. It can be amended without leave up to 14 days prior to the appeal. The note should now contain the skeleton argument for the appeal. It is not yet clear whether this rule precludes a party raising any other points in the course of the appeal. The cautious practitioner will be meantime advised to make the note comprehensive, and to amend to encompass any further thoughts which occur between the marking of the appeal and the appeal itself.[27] Prior to the appeal hearing, the appellant must have the shorthand notes extended and lodged if this has not already been done. The reality for practitioners is that the intensive work on the appeal in the 14-day period prior to the hearing may well throw up midnight oil ideas not previously considered. You can amend the grounds on cause shown.[28] Sheriffs principal generally operate on the basis that pleadings are servants and not masters, as long as no prejudice is suffered. Don't hesitate to seek to amend the grounds of appeal if you find that any substantive argument you wish to

---

[26] See *William Nimmo & Co Ltd v Russell Construction Ltd*, 1995 S.C.L.R. 1148 for a successful appeal on expenses.
[27] OCR 31.4(5).
[28] OCR 31.4(5)(a).

make is not covered in your grounds. Intimate any proposed amendment to your opponents as soon as possible.

The appeal hearing

15–10 You will require to lodge your list of authorities prior to the appeal hearing, and you should send a copy to the other side.[29] Where findings in fact are being challenged, it is also good practice to produce a typewritten version of the proposed changes and to present this to the court in the course of your argument. The appellant will go first, arguing from his Note with reference to specific page numbers of the shorthand notes. The respondent will then reply to points raised, and also argue any matters contained in his cross-appeal. The appellant normally has a right of further reply. With modern copy and printing facilities, it is simple to provide a full copy of all authorities for the sheriff principal, rather than ask him to produce and work from the bound volumes. Prepare these in a solid lever arch binder with separators. Two other practical matters arise in appeals of any complexity.

First, in appeals after proof you will be expected to direct the sheriff principal to specific points in the evidence with reference to page and paragraph number of the shorthand notes, e.g. p.342, passages A–E. This will be part of your appeal script. Most appeals will develop into a dialogue between you and the sheriff principal where you know there is a passage in the evidence to which you want to refer, but cannot instantly put your finger on it. Taking the trouble to make your own private précis of the shorthand notes with reference to specific passages in the evidence will pay rich dividends during any such discussion.

Secondly, where there are a number of productions to which you wish to make reference, extract them from the inventory, and bind them up into an appendix with a copy for the court and for your opponent. This is not a requirement of the Rules, but will make life a lot easier for everyone.

It cannot be emphasised strongly enough that appellate advocacy is the most difficult exercise in persuasion you will ever undertake. The last thing you want is to be fumbling around looking for papers.

You cannot now seek a decree without specifying a damages breakdown under s.15 of the Social Security (Recovery of Benefits) Regulations 1997, and you should have a schedule prepared. The sheriff principal may thereafter adhere to the sheriff's decision, or sustain the appeal and add his own findings in fact and law. There may be occasions where allowance of further proof is granted.[30]

---

[29] The precise time for lodging the note of authorities varies in terms of the practice notes for the various sheriffdoms, all of which are reprinted in the *Parliament House Book*.

[30] See the full treatment of the powers of the sheriff principal at appeal in T. Welsh, *Macphail's Sheriff Court Practice*, 3rd edn (Edinburgh: W.Green, 2006), paras 18.78—18–82.

Appeal to the Inner House

There is a further appeal available from the judgment of the sheriff **15–11** principal to the Inner House.[31]

---

[31] See OCR 31.3 for the procedure.

Chapter 16

SUMMARY CAUSES

16–01 The jurisdiction level for summary causes in the sheriff court is for actions up to £5,000 exclusive of interest. Procedure is now governed by the Act of Sederunt (Summary Cause) Rules 2002 as amended by the Act of Sederunt (Summary Cause Rules Amendment) (Personal Injuries Actions) 2011.[1] Recent research carried out by the Association of Personal Injury Lawyers has established that most claims settle both pre- and post-litigation for amounts under £5,000. This therefore is a very important area for practitioners, and the new rules offer significant opportunities to both pursuer's and defenders' agents for realistic disposal and settlement of cases on an informed basis. The procedure is now effectively "Coulsfield lite" with procedure regulated by timetable, and much of what has been said about Ordinary cause procedure will apply now to the new Summary Cause.

Choice of forum—Ordinary Action or Summary Cause?

16–02 It is important for agents to pick the proper forum from the start. There are greater outlays involved with an ordinary cause action. If you raise a case as an ordinary action and are stuck at the end of it with summary cause expenses, you will be unable to recover outlays such as record dues, shorthand writer costs, and expenses will be on the summary cause level. The rule as to scale of expenses is that the level is decided by the sum eventually decerned for unless the court otherwise directs (gen.reg.2). This means the amount contained in the court decree and not the sum sued for. If no sum is decerned for (e.g. the defenders are successful) then an action raised as an ordinary cause will be taxed on the ordinary scale. This causes no difficulty in debt actions for a crystallised sum. You simply choose the appropriate forum. What about personal injury cases where differing views on damages for solatium, or a finding of contributory negligence, might pull a claim below the ordinary cause level?

Level of expenses

16–03 This paragraph deals with cases that have been raised as ordinary actions but which settled for sums below the summary cause jurisdiction level.

The leading case in this area is *Coyle v William Fairey Ltd*,[2] an action of damages raised in the Court of Session which sought payment of

---

[1] For historic cases see the 2nd edn of this book from pg.149.
[2] *Coyle v William Fairey Ltd*, 1991 S.L.T. 638.

£10,000 and was settled in the sum of £1,000. At that time this was within the summary cause level. The defenders contended that expenses should be awarded on the summary cause scale. The Lord Ordinary stated that because the value of the case was within the summary cause scale, the action should have been raised in the sheriff court. He awarded expenses on the summary cause scale without certification of counsel. The Inner House overturned this decision. The proper approach for the court was to consider whether the initial choice of forum was justified in all the circumstances of the case at the time the action was raised. The pursuer had settled for £1,000, and it might readily be accepted that the settlement must have made some allowance for risk of failure on the merits or a finding of contributory negligence. Whilst the amount of settlement was a relevant factor, it was not determinative. In the event, having regard to the possible value of the case, the court awarded expenses on the sheriff court ordinary cause scale with sanction for counsel.[3] The courts cannot award more than you ask for. *Macphail's Sheriff Court Practice* at para.19–49 states that the sheriff should consider two questions.[4]

1. Was the pursuer entitled to raise the action as an ordinary cause in the first instance?; And if so
2. Should the pursuer in the course of the action have taken steps to have it remitted to the summary cause roll?

The matter should not be weighed too finely in the balance.

Mechanics of settlement

The other important point relates to settlement of these cases. In most circumstances cases will settle either by means of agreement between agents, or by way of tender and minute of acceptance of tender. The language of the General Regulations has the effect that where the sum decerned for is within the summary cause limit, summary cause expenses only will be awarded, in the absence of argument to the contrary. Practitioners should be careful not to forfeit by default their right to argue the contrary. A competent tender must contain an unrestricted offer of expenses,[5] and any attempt to restrict expenses in an ordinary cause action, e.g. to the summary cause scale will make the tender invalid.[6] This does not mean that you will get ordinary expenses whatever the settlement figure. If the case settles by way of tender and minute of acceptance of tender, the court will make a decerniture for the principal sum which will regulate the scale of expenses unless the sheriff directs otherwise. Where you have raised an ordinary action, and accept a tender for below

16–04

---

[3] See also the case of *Sunderland v North British Steel Group*, 1992 S.L.T. 1146 and the decision of Sheriff Principal McLeod in *Durham v Gateway Food Market*, 1992 S.L.T. 83 (Sh Ct).
[4] Welsh, T., *MacPhail's Sheriff Court Practice*, 3rd edn (Edinburgh: W. Green, 2006), para.19–49.
[5] See Welsh, T., *MacPhail's Sheriff Court Practice*, 3rd edn (Edinburgh: W. Green, 2006), para.14–41.
[6] See *Bhatia v Tribax Ltd*, 1994 S.L.T. 1201.

the summary cause level you will have to persuade the court that ordinary expenses should be awarded. A convenient way of bringing the matter to a head is to include a crave in the Motion for Minute of Acceptance of Tender along the lines of: "and moves the Court to grant expenses on the ordinary scale".

This will give you the opportunity to make the arguments discussed above.

Settlements by way of joint minute

16–05 Many cases settle on the basis of negotiation and exchange of cheques. Cases are frequently sisted to enable this to take place, and a joint minute is eventually lodged. A simple practical point is to make sure that there is agreement on the level of expenses, and that cheques for the principal sum and expenses on the ordinary scale are in your hands before the joint minute is lodged. Where the matter of expenses is still outstanding, you should ensure that the motion disposing of the case makes a finding of expenses for your client. The most likely format will be an interlocutor making a finding of absolvitor without any mention of a specific principal sum. Where there is such a mention of principal sum and it is below the ordinary cause level, then expenses will be on the summary cause scale unless the sheriff directs otherwise (*Lothian Hotels v Ferer*[7]). In an ordinary action, where no specific sum is mentioned, the account should be taxed on the ordinary cause scale (*Macphail* para.14–71[8]). As was stated in the case of *Lothian Hotels*:

> "The reasons for settling actions are many. It seems to me wrong in principle that parties winning expenses in settlement should have constantly to look over their shoulders at the risk of having their expenses cut at taxation. The time for the paying party to seek a reduction to Summary Cause rates is in open court when the Joint Minute is before the Court."

Chapter 34 summary cause procedure in personal injuries actions

16–06 In terms of the Act of Sederunt (Summary Cause Rules Amendment) (Personal Injuries Actons) 2011 the pleadings are now form based. Actions of damages for personal injuries are defined as including "any disease or impairment, whether physical or mental".[9] Careful stock should be taken of the pleadings position in summary cause personal injury actions. A summons should be drawn in terms of form 2, and a statement of claim in form 10 attached (SCR 34.2). The statement of claim should contain "a concise statement of the grounds in numbered paragraphs relating only to those facts necessary to establish the claim". It should also contain the names of every medical practitioner or hospital from whom and in which the pursuer received treatment relating to the

---

[7] *Lothian Hotels v Ferer*, 1981 SLT (Sh. Ct.) 52.
[8] Welsh, T., *Macphail's Sheriff Court Practice*, 3rd edn (Edinburgh: W. Green, 2006) para.14–71.
[9] SCR 34.1(3).

claim. The summons may also include a specification of documents in form 10b, of which see below.[10] After authentication, the pursuer must serve the summons with a copy of form 10a which provides for a detailed response to the statement of claim (SCR 34.4(1)) by means of demanding the answers to specific and pointed questions regarding the nature of the defence e.g. what facts are admitted?; can medical reports be agreeed?; are losses disputed?; does the defender accept the statutory duty alleged in the statement of claim was incumbent upon him? The response form if properly completed will elicit much more information than the average record either in the sheriff court or the court of session. What has been abolished is the requirement for line by line answers. What has not been abolished is the requirement to give fair notice of issues in either the statement of claim or the response.

Existing cases on fair notice may be of some assistance. In particular, see *McInnes v Alginate Industries Ltd*,[11] where a defence was stated "Liability denied. Contributory negligence. Sum sued for excessive". This did not entitle the defenders to avail themselves of a statutory defence. In *Lochgorm Warehouses v Roy*[12] an action of payment which stated "sum sued for is not due and resting owing" did not allow evidence from the defenders on breach of merchantable quality. In *Roofcare Ltd v Gillies*,[13] which was an action for payment for repairs done on property, the defence "work not carried out satisfactorily" gave no notice of specific failures, and the defenders were not allowed to lead evidence on specific defects:

> "In my opinion the defender and appellant should have given some general indication on the point or points upon which his attack on workmanship was directed."

In practical terms a pursuer will not be allowed to prove a statutory case which has not been adverted to in the pleadings, and a defender will not be allowed to produce a factual defence out of the hat unless there is some notice. For an example of the approach taken by the courts to the requirements of fair notice even in a small claims case, see the decision by Sheriff Principal Bowen in the case of *Scott v Chief Constable, Strathclyde Police*.[14] It is likely that any dispute at proof over questions of fair notice will be resolved by consideration of the statement of claim, the response form, the statements of valuation, the productions and witness list, and conceivably what was said at the pre-proof conference. See *Kendal v Davies*,[15] where notice of care costs came not from the written pleadings, but from the productions.

---

[10] SCR 34.2(3)(b).
[11] *McInnes v Alginate Industries Ltd*, 1980 S.L.T. (Sh. Ct.) 114.
[12] *Lochgorm Warehouses v Roy*, 1981 S.L.T. (Sh. Ct.) 45.
[13] *Roofcare Ltd v Gillies*, 1984 S.L.T. (Sh. Ct.) 8.
[14] *Scott v Chief Constable, Strathclyde Police*, 1999 S.L.T. (Sh Ct) 66.
[15] *Kendal v Davies*, 2000 Rep. L.R. 126.

What goes to the defender?—SCR 34.3

16–07
1. Form 1e or 1f (depending on whether a time to pay order is appropriate) and, statement of claim form 10, and potentially specification of documents form 10b.
2. Blank form of response, form 10.

Response from defender—SCR 34.4

16–08 Where the defender intends to challenge jurisdiction or competency, defend the action or state a counterclaim, he must complete and return the relevant part of the defender's copy summons (Box 3 on p.6 of form 1e or section B on p.5 of form 1f) and the form of response form 10a (SCR 34.4(1)). Form 10a does not require to be intimated to the pursuer's agent. It is the sheriff clerk who will intimate any response (SCR 34.4(3)).

Form 10a

16–09 This form consists of a series of pointed questions designed to establish areas of agreement, and flush out the areas of dispute between the parties. The completed form must give the pursuer fair notice of the "grounds of fact and law on which the defender intends to resist the claim" (SCR 34.4(1)).

Specification of documents—SCR 34.5

16–10 Where a form 10a is lodged stating a defence to the action, and the summons has contained a specification of documents in form 10b, the sheriff clerk shall make an order granting commission and diligence for the recovery of the documents mentioned in the specification. This has the effect of an interlocutor granting commission and diligence signed by the sheriff. The specification is in standard form and cannot be altered at this stage to seek other documents. Calls 1–3 relate to medical records from the General Practice, treating hospital and occupational health department. Strictly there should be averments in the statement of claim advising of treatment in these places, so for example where there is no occupational health department assessment relating to the pursuer, Call 3 should be deleted. Call 4 relates to wages and financial matters. Call 5 relates to accident reports, memoranda and other written communications made to the defender or anyone on his or her behalf by an employee of the defender who was present at the time of the accident. Call 6 relates to risk assessments in terms of the Management of Health and Safety at Work Regulations 1999 ("MHSWR 1999"), and also where there is any other statutory requirement for risk assessment, e.g. the Control of Vibration at Work Regulations 2005 reg.7. It is not necessary to plead breach of the MHSWR 1999, but if a further specific risk assessment is sought, the separate Regulation should be referred to in the statement of claim.

Personal Injury Procedure—SCR 34.7

On receipt of the form of response from the defender, the sheriff clerk **16–11** should discharge the calling date hearing, and allocate a diet of proof not earlier than four months and not later than nine months from the date of the first lodging of the form of response. SCR 34.7(1)(c) now provides that further procedure is regulated by the standard summary cause timetable in form 10d calculated by reference to the period specified in Sch.3 Appendix 1A for the particular procedural steps. In terms of SCR 34.7(2) these are:

(a) Application for third party notice under SCR 11.1. Not later than 28 days after the form of response has been lodged.
(b) Pursuer serving a commission for recovery of documents under SCR 34.5. Not later than 28 days after the form of response has been lodged.
(c) Adjustments by parties of their respective statements (i.e. pursuer's form 10 and defender's form 10a). Not later than eight weeks after the form of response has been lodged.
(d) The pursuer lodging with the sheriff clerk a statement of valuation of claim. Not later than eight weeks after the form of response has been lodged.
(e) The pursuer lodging with the sheriff clerk a certified adjusted statement of claim. Not later than 10 weeks after the form of response has been lodged.
(f) The defender or any third party to the action lodging with the sheriff clerk a certified adjusted response to statement of claim. Not later than 10 weeks after the form of response has been lodged.
(g) The defender or any third party to the action lodging with the sheriff clerk a statement of valuation of claim. Not later than 12 weeks after the form of response has been lodged.
(h) The parties lodging with the sheriff clerk a list of witnesses and productions on which they wish to rely. Not later than eight weeks before the diet assigned for proof.
(i) The pursuer lodging with the sheriff clerk the minute of pre-proof conference. Not later than 21 days before the diet assigned for proof.

This is clearly designed to mirror ordinary cause procedure and reference should be made to Ch.8.

In particular:

Adjustment of pleadings—SCR 34.7(2)(c)

The assumption is that adjustments are simply exchanged between or **16–12** amongst parties up to the end of the adjustment period in the timetable. The pursuer must then lodge a certified adjusted statement of claim. The defender must lodge a certified adjusted response to the statement of claim. It is noteworthy that both the statement of claim and form of response can be adjusted without leave prior to the end of the adjustment date contained in timetable form 10d. There is no record in the summary cause. Alteration of the sum sued for is by way of incidental application (SCR 13.1(3)(a)). Amendment of the summons sisting a party as a substitute for, or in addition to, the original party, is also by way of incidental application, with the sheriff thereafter ordering such service and regulating further procedure as he thinks fit (SCR 13.1(4)).

Sist or variation of timetable—SCR 34.8

16–13 In terms of SCR 34.8 the action can be sisted or the timetable varied by way of incidental application, but only on special cause shown, and any sist is for a specified period only. Where the defender applies by way of incidental application for third party procedure, the existing timetable will be retained and must be served with the third party notice (SCR 34.6(3)).

Pursuer's incidental application for proof or other procedure—SCR 34.7(7)

16–14 The pursuer should lodge an incidental application along with the certified adjusted statement of claim seeking a preliminary proof on specified matters, a proof, or some other specified order. The incidental application should specify the anticipated length of the proof or preliminary proof. Where you want an order other than a proof, you will need to specify the order sought and give full notice of the grounds of your application. Where the defender wishes an order other than a proof, he must oppose the pursuer's application, specify the order sought, and give full notice of the grounds of opposition. The matter will then be dealt with at the hearing on the incidental application.

Pursuer's statement of valuation of claim—SCR 34.9

16–15 This must be lodged in form 10e along with a list of supporting documents, and the actual documents in an inventory of productions and should be intimated to the defender. It should be not later than eight weeks from the lodging of the form of response.

Defender's statement of valuation of claim—SCR 34.9

16–16 The defender must then lodge a statement of valuation with supporting list of documents and inventory of productions in accordance with the timetable. This will be a date not later than 10 weeks from the lodging of the form of response.

Witnesses and productions—SCR 34.7(2)(h)

16–17 In terms of the timetable, parties must lodge witness lists and productions by the timetable date, which will be not later than eight weeks before the proof. The witness list should contain the name, occupation and address of the intended witness. Where there is a child witness or a vulnerable witness, a child witness notice or a vulnerable witness application should be made in terms of the Vulnerable Witnesses (Scotland) Act 2004 s.12(2) and 12(6)(a) respectively, and an indication should be put on the witness list. Late witnesses or productions can be put in evidence or be led only with the consent of parties, or by leave of the sheriff on cause shown. If you do have a late witness or production, it is advisable to lodge an incidental application for allowance as soon as possible, extending precognition facilities to your opponent at the same time

Pre-proof conference—SCR 34.10

16–18 The pre-proof conference must take place not later than four weeks before the proof diet. It is anticipated that the conference can take place in person, by telephone, by video, or by "other remote means". Access to persons who can provide instructions to settle should be arranged. The minute of the pre-proof conference, form 10f must be worked through, signed by agents for both parties, and then lodged by the pursuer's agent no later than three weeks before the date assigned for proof.

Proof

16–19 There is no shorthand writer, and there are no notes of evidence. Procedure is regulated by SCR 8.13(3), whereby the sheriff must make his own notes of the evidence led at the proof, including evidence which has been objected to as inadmissible, and the nature of any such objection. He is obliged to retain these notes until after any appeal has been disposed of. In terms of SCR 8.14(1) the sheriff must hear parties on the evidence at the close of proof and may either pronounce his judgment, or reserve judgment. Where there is an objection to admissibility of evidence in the course of a summary cause proof the sheriff should note the terms of the objection and allow the evidence to be led, reserving the question of admissibility to be decided by him at the close of the proof, except where he is of the opinion that the evidence is clearly irrelevant or scandalous, or where objection is taken on the grounds of confidentiality (SCR 8.15). SCR 8.8A (inserted by the Act of Sederunt (Sheriff Court Rules) (Miscellaneous Amendments) 2010[16]) introduces Notices to Admit and Notices of Non-Admission into summary cause procedure. This is consistant with the terms of SCR 8.8 where it is provided: "where possible, the parties shall agree photographs, sketch plans or any statements or documents not in dispute". Evidence can also be agreed at the pre-proof conference and minuted in form 10f.

Timetable lapses

16–20 In terms of SCR 34.7(5) the sheriff clerk may fix a hearing for timetable lapses. Where the pursuer has not lodged a certified adjusted statement of claim, or where the defender has not lodged a certified adjusted response to statement of claim, the sheriff clerk *must* fix a hearing. (SCR 34.7(10)).

---

[16] Act of Sederunt (Sheriff Court Rules) (Miscellaneous Amendments) 2010 (SSI 2010/279), effective July 19, 2010.

A similar rule applies to any failure to lodge a minute of the pre-proof conference (SCR 34.10(3)). The party in default must lodge and intimate a written explanation not less than two clear days before the incidental hearing. The sheriff may award expenses against the party in default, and may make any appropriate order including dismissal (SCR 34.11).

Miscellaneous procedure

16–21
1. Intimation to connected persons in fatal claims (see SCR 34.12).
2. Provision for a pursuer for an application for provisional or further damages under the Administration of Justice (Scotland) Act 1972 s.12 (see SCR 34.13).
3. Provision for summary decree (see SCR 12.1).
4. Provision for alteration of summons (see SCR 13.1). There is now no requirement to make an incidental application to adjust the parties' respective statements (form 10 and form 10a) (see SCR 34.6(3)).
5. Procedure for adding additional defender (see SCR 14.1).
6. Recovery of evidence by way of specification (see SCR 18.1).
7. Applications for information under Administration of Justice (Scotland) Act 1972 (see SCR 18.3).

Expenses

16–22 Expenses are normally to be assessed by the sheriff clerk in accordance with the statutory Table of Fees (SCR 23.3). Where judgment has not been reserved, then the assessment on expenses must take place immediately upon the decision being pronounced. In practical terms you must be ready to make up your account there and then. Where the hearing is not held immediately the sheriff clerk shall fix a date, time and place, give 14 days in writing, and the party awarded expenses must lodge an account of expenses at least seven days prior to the date of any hearing fixed (SCR 23.3(7) and SCR 23.3(8)).

Summary Cause Appeals

16–23 Appeals from final judgments are available on points of law only.[17] This severely restricts the scope for appeal in a summary cause by either party. As a matter of generality, in the context of a negligence action, the permitted questions of law might be:

1. Was there material in the facts found which would entitle the sheriff to find negligence (sufficiency of evidence)?
2. Did the sheriff wrongly admit inadmissible evidence, or refuse admissible evidence which was tendered (admissibility)?

There are no notes of evidence. What cannot be put in issue is whether the sheriff was right in reaching a particular finding in fact. So it is not a

---

[17] Sheriff Courts (Scotland) Act 1971 s.31A.

question of law to ask: "was there sufficient evidence to entitle the sheriff to reach finding in fact a, b or c".

It is perhaps insufficiently appreciated that a finding on reasonable care or reasonable foreseeability is a finding in fact, and not a finding in law or a mixed finding in fact and law.[18] These are fundamentally questions of fact for a jury. In *Bolton v Stone* [1951] A.C. 850 at [858], Lord Porter states:

> "It must be remembered and cannot too often be repeated that there are two different standards to be applied when one is considering whether an appeal should be allowed or not. The first is whether the facts relied upon are evidence from which negligence can in law be inferred; the second, whether, if negligence can be inferred, these facts do constitute negligence. The first is a question of law on which the judge must actually or inferentially rule; the second, a question of fact upon which the jury, if there is one, or, if not, the judge, as judge of fact, must pronounce. Both to some extent but more particularly the latter, depend on all the attendant circumstances of the case."

This does not mean that these kinds of findings are inviolate. They may be jury points, but the jury must be properly directed. If you wish to attack a sheriff's finding in a summary cause appeal, you must identify and focus on some element of misdirection in law, which should be apparent from the sheriff's statement of reasons.

Any appeal must be lodged with the sheriff clerk not later than 14 days after the date of the final decree using summary cause form 31.

The matter then proceeds by way of stated case (SCR 25.1).

Summary cause appeal procedure

The sheriff will then draft a stated case which is sent to the parties. This draft will contain:

1. findings in fact and law;
2. appropriate questions of law; and
3. A note stating the reasons for his decision (SCR 25.1(3)).

Where the appeal relates to the admissibility or sufficiency of evidence, the draft should contain a description of that evidence (SCR 25.1(4)). You have an opportunity to propose adjustments to the stated case, by way of adjustment (SCR 25.1(5)). This is an important part of summary cause appeal procedure. There may be findings in fact omitted which are critical to your legal argument. If you are contending that further findings in fact should have been made, you must submit them at this stage. The note stating the sheriff's reasons for his decision is not generally something with which you will be allowed to interfere. If the other party proposes adjustments with which you disagree, you should lodge a note

---

[18] *Thorburn v. R. J. Mcleod (Contractors) Ltd*, 1968 S.L.T. (Sh. Ct.) 43.

of objection with the sheriff clerk. Where the sheriff proposes to reject any adjustment, he must fix a hearing on adjustments, and may thereafter regulate procedure as he sees fit (SCR 25.1(6)). The sheriff will then complete the stated case, which will contain the questions of law framed by him, arising from the points of law stated by the parties and any other questions he considers appropriate.

Conduct of summary cause appeal—SCR 25.3

16–25 The sheriff principal will hear parties orally on all matters including liability for expenses. No new points of law can be raised except on cause shown and subject to such conditions as the sheriff principal considers appropriate (SCR 25.3(2)). Otherwise the preparation for, and conduct of, the appeal proceeds in the same manner as for an ordinary action (see Ch.15). The sheriff principal may either pronounce judgment at the end of the appeal, or produce a written judgment within 28 days (SCR 25.1(4)). He may adhere to, or vary the decree appealed against, recall the decree and substitute a different one, or remit to the sheriff for any reason other than to have further evidence led.

Appeal to the court of session

16–26 In terms of SCR 25.7(1) you must obtain a certificate that the action is suitable for appeal to the Court of Session, by completing and lodging an application in form 34 within 14 days of the date of the final decree. The sheriff principal shall then hear parties and shall grant or refuse a certificate for appeal.

PART II—COMMON CAUSES OF ACTION

CHAPTER 17

ROAD TRAFFIC ACCIDENTS

In 1896 there were four automobiles in the whole of the United States. **17–01**
Two of them ran into each other in St Louis. In Great Britain in that year, 44-year-old Bridget Driscoll was the first pedestrian to be knocked down and killed by a car. There are now over 29 million motor vehicles in the United Kingdom. In Scotland, in 2010, 208 people were killed, 1,960 were recorded as seriously injured and 11,156 suffered slight injury. Of these there were 1,375 child casualties of whom four died and 2,011 pedestrian casualties of whom 47 were killed.[1] Driver error is the cause of 95 per cent of accidents. Almost everyone driving has some experience of at least a bump, and the speed and power of modern vehicles mean that injury can range from the trivial to the catastrophic.

INVESTIGATING THE CLAIM

The normal principles of early investigation hold true. The client's **17–02**
statement should contain:

1. The registration number(s) of the other vehicle(s) involved.
2. A description of the road conditions and lighting at the material time.
3. A description of the road layout, with roads described as major or minor, and details of all road markings or signs, e.g. "Give Way" signs. A *Google Earth*[2] map can assist.
4. The client's speed, direction of travel and destination.
5 Estimates of speed for all other vehicles involved.
6. A note of what was said and to whom after the accident (post-accident admissions by parties can frequently prove critical in this type of case).
7. Details of any police involvement.
8. A note of all witnesses.

At this stage it will usually be adequate to write to the witnesses with a questionnaire. Ask your client to take photographs of the locus, and also of any damage to his vehicle. Photographs of a badly damaged vehicle

---

[1] See the Scottish Government website—*Private transport—road accident casualties*, available at *http://www.scotland.gov.uk/Topics/Statistics/Browse/Transport-Travel/Trend RoadAccident* [Accessed September 15, 2011].

[2] *http://www.google.co.uk/intl/en_uk/earth/index.html* [Accessed September 14, 2011].

can help you persuade insurers that, for example, soft tissue injuries may be particularly serious. If there is the slightest doubt about liability, you should obtain a police report. For payment of a fee you will receive a police abstract which contains the identity of parties and witnesses, a note of injuries, a detailed description of road conditions and any relevant road markings.

It is a convention among most police authorities that the driver whom the police believe to be to blame for the accident is named first on the report. Whilst no great reliance can be placed on this, it should be an immediate danger signal if that person is your client.

If criminal proceedings are pending you will not be allowed to precognosce the reporting officers, but you should contact the other witnesses. Once the criminal case is concluded, or where there are no proceedings, you should seek precognition facilities for the reporting officers via the chief constable, paying a standard fee. At the interview you should first of all establish the road traffic expertise of the reporting officers. To a large extent this will depend on the severity of the accident. In serious accident cases specialist traffic police are generally contacted. These officers tend to have wide experience and training in accident investigation and reconstruction, and will frequently be entitled to give expert and opinion evidence. They will usually take photographs and prepare a sketch plan showing the location of accident debris, and other relevant information. Copies can be requested and obtained on payment of a fee. The regular police constable will almost certainly be confined to statements of fact and any inference which you seek to draw, for example from the position of debris on the road, will have to be proved by other means. Police officers will generally refer to their notebook. Note precisely what is in it, with particular reference to what was said to the police by witnesses at the scene. Where liability is disputed, the importance of the police evidence cannot be overestimated. You should finally explain to the officers that civil proceedings may be pending, and ask them to keep their notebook, and any papers or documents. Consider whether further information might be available from the other emergency services such as the fire brigade or the ambulance service. A request for documentary evidence can be made under the Freedom of Information (Scotland) Act 2002 and you will generally be allowed precognition facilities on payment of a fee.

INTIMATING AND PROGRESSING THE CLAIM

17–03 The first step is to establish the insurance status of the other vehicle(s), remembering always that if the vehicle is insured in most cases direct action can be taken against the insurer in terms of the European Community (Rights Against Insurers) Regulations 2002 ("ECRAIR"). Your firm should register with the Motor Insurers' database ("MIDIS"). An email enquiry, giving the registration details, will immediately confirm whether the vehicle was insured at the time of the accident. If there is no insurance, recourse will have to be made to the Motor Insurers' Bureau

("MIB"). The claim should meantime be intimated to the other driver(s) and then to the relevant insurer. Once you have made contact with the insurer, you should advise them fully of the grounds of claim. It is very important to advise the insurer as early as possible where any damaged vehicle can be inspected. This enables the third party insurer to authorise either repair of the vehicle, or replacement where the vehicle is a "write-off".

Where your client has his own comprehensive insurance, he should claim initially for damage to his vehicle under his own policy. You should advise those insurers that you are instructed in the claim. It is likely that they will agree with your client a pre-accident value of the vehicle without any intervention from you. Most insurers now operate a "knock-for-knock" agreement which means that you will not be instructed to recover the cost of the value of the vehicle, and that your client's no-claims bonus will be preserved if he can persuade his own insurers that he was not at fault. There will almost certainly be an excess on his comprehensive policy, and this will form part of his uninsured losses. Where the vehicle can be repaired, you should have the client obtain a repair estimate, which should be disclosed to the other party's insurers as quickly as possible. Your client is obliged to take reasonable steps to mitigate his losses and, in particular, is not entitled to insist on repair where the costs of repair clearly outweigh the pre-accident value of the vehicle. At the end of the day you may have to persuade the court that your client has acted reasonably, and it will be of considerable assistance if you can show that all relevant information was passed to the third party insurers as quickly as possible.

Your client will very frequently ask if he can proceed to hire an alternative vehicle pending repair of his damaged car. There may not be a definite answer to this question, which depends in the end on the strength of the case on liability, and the advice must always be that hire is at the client's own risk. Further firm advice should be given that the costs of hire should be minimised both with regard to rates and also time of hire. The client should hire only like for like, preferably hiring a less prestigious model than his own vehicle. See also the later section on Credit Hire at para.17–13.

THIRD PARTY CAPTURE

This refers to the common practice of road traffic insurers who have been advised of the accident by their own insured, have decided there is no defence on liability, and have contacted your client directly to arrange for repair or a replacement vehicle. This in itself is an innocuous and frequently helpful intervention. However, very many insurers go much further, seek out details of personal injury from your client, and make what is generally a bargain basement financial offer to settle, without medical evidence. They do not want you involved. Where there is any personal injury element, the advice to the client should always be to refuse to settle at this stage, and to obtain medical evidence in the usual way.

17–04

LIABILITY IN ROAD TRAFFIC CASES

17–05 The factual background should first of all be looked at in the context of the Highway Code.[3] The Road Traffic Act 1988 now provides at s.30:

> "A failure on the part of a person to observe any provision of the Highway Code shall not of itself render that person liable to criminal proceedings of any kind, but any such failure may in any proceedings (whether civil or criminal) be relied upon by any party to the proceedings as tending to establish or negative any liability which is in question in those proceedings."

The Highway Code is quite literally the rules of the road.

In the case of *Countess of Lindsay v Fife Scottish Omnibuses Ltd*,[4] where an overtaking bus caused a horse drawing a trap to bolt, Lord MacFadyen found that liability was established under reference to paras 190 and 191 of the Highway Code.

Otherwise it is impossible to be dogmatic. Even apparently cast-iron claims where your client's vehicle is struck from behind may not amount to negligence.[5]

It is important to remember that previous decisions are not binding legal authorities. They are simply findings in fact by the judge, sitting as a jury, in the particular circumstances.[6]

Injuries to passengers

17–06 Whilst it is perfectly proper to accept instructions from all the occupants of a vehicle who have suffered personal injury, you must be alert to any emerging conflict of interest. If after intimation there is any question that liability may attach to the driver of the vehicle for whom you act, it is generally unwise to seek to act for drivers and passengers. In this situation the passengers should be entitled to full damages from someone. If you conclude that there is an element of contributory negligence on the part of your client driver, you can't negotiate any settlement which compromises the passengers' claims. In theory the third party insurers will be liable for the passengers' whole damage, if their client has materially contributed to the accident. In practice many will refuse to pay 100 per cent damages unless there is a contribution from your client driver's insurers. The solution is to refer driver or passengers to another solicitor.

---

[3] See, e.g. *Bell v Glasgow Corporation*, 1965 S.L.T. 57.
[4] *Countess of Lindsay v Fife Scottish Omnibuses Ltd* Unreported May 30, 2002 Court of Session.
[5] See, e.g. *Grant v Eastern Scottish Omnibuses Ltd*, 1998 G.W.D. 32-1676. See also the useful resume of road traffic liability cases in *Reparation: Liability for Dilect*, (Edinburgh: W.Green).
[6] *Stainsby v Fallon* [2010] CSIH 64.

Seatbelt cases

It is now accepted that it is contributory negligence for both a front seat   17–07
and rear seat passenger to fail to wear a seatbelt. In the English case of
Froom v Butcher,[7] the front seat passenger had his damages reduced by 25
per cent because of failure to wear a seatbelt. The Court of Appeal held
that where injuries would have been prevented altogether by wearing a
seatbelt, damages should be reduced by 25 per cent, but where the injuries
would nonetheless have occurred but would have been less severe, the
reduction should be 15 per cent. It was also stated:

> "Sometimes the evidence will show that the failure made no difference. The damage would have been the same, even if a seatbelt had been worn. In such cases damages should not be reduced at all."

In all cases it is for the defender to take the seatbelt point, and the onus
will be on the defender to prove that failure to wear the seatbelt caused
the injuries. There is no onus on a pursuer to show that wearing of the
belt would have made no difference:

> "It seems to me that unless there is evidence to indicate, on the balance of probabilities, that the injuries suffered would have been prevented altogether, or would have been less severe as a result of the exercise of the care desiderated, in this case the wearing of a seatbelt, there can be no room for a finding of contributory negligence."[8]

Accidents involving pedestrians

There is a very high duty of care on a vehicle's driver to avoid collision   17–08
with a pedestrian. In the case of *Baker v Willoughby*[9] Lord Reid stated
that a pedestrian "is rarely a danger to anyone else, whereas if a motorist
fails in his duties whilst driving a motor car, the consequences may be
disastrous".[10] This approach has been followed by the Inner House in the
case of *McCluskey v Wallace*.[11] In *Eagle v Chambers*[12] Lady Justice Hale
stated:

> "It is rare indeed for a pedestrian to be found more responsible than a driver unless the pedestrian had suddenly moved into the path of an oncoming vehicle."

There is a high burden of care on a car driver to reflect the fact that a car
is potentially a dangerous weapon.

You should have this principle in the forefront of your mind in any

---

[7] *Froom v Butcher* 1975 All E.R. 520 at [520].
[8] *Barker v Murdoch*, 1977 S.L.T. (Notes) 75. See also *Pace v Culley*, 1992 S.L.T. 1073 at [1073]—no deduction made for failure to wear seatbelt.
[9] *Baker v Willoughby* [1969] 3 All E.R. 1528.
[10] *Baker v Willoughby*]1969] 3 All E.R. 1528 at [1530].
[11] *McCluskey v Wallace*, 1998 S.L.T. 1357.
[12] *Eagle v Chambers* [2003] EWCA Civ 1107.

investigation of pedestrian accidents. This kind of claim sometimes involves accidents to children or persons under the influence of alcohol, and liability is very frequently denied. As soon as you receive instructions, you should make a special effort to establish from the police and the witnesses the exact point of impact on the road, and with the vehicle. Civilian witnesses very frequently put a gloss to the effect that "the driver had no chance, the boy just ran out". This may or may not be legally correct, having regard to the driver's speed and his line of sight, and remembering always the very different kinds of care which a driver and pedestrian must show. Liability will depend to a very large extent on the length of time during which the pedestrian was seen or could have been seen by the driver. The kind of analysis the courts undertake is illustrated by the case of *James v Fairley*,[13] in which the English Court of Appeal would not interfere with the trial judge's finding that the driver had no opportunity whatsoever to avoid impact with a child. On the other hand where some children were on the pavement and some had crossed the road from time to time the sudden entry into the roadway by a child between parked cars should have been anticipated by a lorry driver, who had a duty to make a precautionary move to his offside.[14] Accident reconstruction experts have access to a whole literature on pedestrian impact accidents, and a good example of the use to which this can be made is the case of *Futter v Bryceland*,[15] where proof that a child had struck the windscreen of the vehicle was used to establish speed at impact. You should also remember that having regard to the stopping distances in the Highway Code, a driver should be able to stop a vehicle travelling at 30mph in about two seconds. In this regard the Inner House held that the sighting of children for a period of six seconds prior to collision constituted "very considerable negligence", with only a 20 per cent reduction for contributory negligence for children who had cycled onto the street.[16]

Although the Scottish courts have traditionally been prepared to make substantial findings of contributory negligence against children in similar circumstances, the case of *McCluskey v Wallace* represents a reversal of this trend. The argument has usually been that even young children have been taught the Green Cross Code and basic road safety. Moreover the Highway Code makes it plain that special duties of vigilance attach to drivers where the presence of children is to be expected.

Similarly, the fact that a pedestrian was under the influence of alcohol does not mean that he has no right of recovery, whatever the objective accident circumstances. As Stuart Smith L.J. said, in the case of *Liddell v Middleton*[17]:

---

[13] *James v Fairley* Unreported February 21, 2002 Court of Appeal.
[14] *Ehrari (A child) v Curry* [2007] EWCA Civ 320.
[15] *Futter v Bryceland* 2000 G.W.D. 9-339.
[16] *McCluskey v Wallace*, 1998 S.L.T. 1357 at [1358].
[17] *Liddell v Middleton* [1996] P.I.Q.R. at 37.

"It is not the fact that a plaintiff has consumed too much alcohol that matters, it is what he does. If he steps in front of a car travelling at 30 mph at a time when the driver has no opportunity to avoid an accident, that is a very dangerous and unwise thing to do. The explanation of his conduct may be that he was drunk; but the fact of drunkenness does not, in my judgement, make the conduct any more or less dangerous and it does not in these circumstances increase the blameworthiness of it."

In Scotland, in the cases of *Malcolm v Fair*[18] and *Cavin v Kinnaird*,[19] the conduct of pedestrians who had consumed alcohol was examined objectively as part of all the accident circumstances, and liability apportioned 50/50 between driver and pedestrian.

DAMAGES IN ROAD TRAFFIC CASES

There is the normal full range of personal injury damage which should be dealt with in the usual way. Practitioners should be alert to psychological injury such as depression, flashback experiences, or avoidance of car travel, which may indicate the presence of a psychiatric disorder. Fright and anxiety by themselves are not enough to sound in damages. There must be a psychiatric disorder which would normally have to be diagnosed by a psychiatrist. Where there is a physical injury, then any exacerbation by way of fright, anxiety or the like should sound in damages, even although it does not come up to the clinical standard of "psychiatric disorder".[20] **17–09**

Other heads of claim

1. Vehicle damage

Where it is agreed that your client's car is beyond repair, and his insurance is not comprehensive but only third party, he will be entitled to the pre-accident value, less a small amount for the salvage value of the vehicle. The insurers generally refer to the current edition of *Glass's Guide*, which contains current motor car valuations for the motor trade. The Guide has a range of values depending on mileage and condition. Your client is not entitled to insist that his vehicle is repaired if the pre-accident value makes it uneconomic to do so. Otherwise reasonable repair costs are payable in full. **17–10**

2. Storage charges

These are recoverable from the defender. It is important that you advise the third party insurers as quickly as possible that the vehicle is being kept in storage, and advise them that storage charges are running. Ask **17–11**

---

[18] *Malcolm v Fair*, 1993 S.L.T. 432.
[19] *Cavin v Kinnaird*, 1994 S.L.T. 111.
[20] See *Nicholls v Rushton, The Times*, June 19, 1992.

that they examine the vehicle and either agree that the repairs can be authorised, or that the vehicle is beyond economic repair and can be disposed off.

3. Hire charges

17-12 The client should be firmly advised to keep hire charges to a minimum. They are recoverable where the length of time is reasonable in all the circumstances. In *Humphries v Elmegirab*[21] the pursuer anticipated early settlement of his claim by the defender's insurers and hired a car. In the event the pursuer required to raise an action for damages. He stopped the car hire as soon as the insurers tendered a cheque for £1,350 representing the value of his vehicle. The court held that hire charges for a period of over 10 months amounting to over £7,000 were reasonable in all the circumstances.[22]

4. Credit hire agreements

17-13 A recent phenomenon is the use of credit hire agreements. In the murky world which is now road traffic referrals, the client is generally encouraged by some third party agency, e.g. accident repair garage to use the services of the Credit Hire Agency for a replacement vehicle. The client then signs a pre-printed car rental agreement. Although these charges have been held to be recoverable, following the case of *Dimond v Lovell*[23] it is clear that the claimant will not be able to recover the costs of a credit hire agreement unless:

> (1) He is impecunious (e.g. he does not have a credit card) and cannot pay hire charges up front.
> (2) The rates are reasonably competitive applying the market "spot-hire" rate. In *Lagden v O'Connor*[24] the House of Lords confirmed the principle that a truly impecunious claimant was entitled to recover these costs, but the practice is fraught with difficulties. It is clear that the use of credit hire significantly inflates damages costs, principally to the benefit of the Credit Hire Agency, with the client an unwitting tool in the enterprise. Credit hire arrangements have come in for rough handling both north and south of the border. In *Cleland v Quinn Direct*[25] the claim was limited to the spot market rates which are significantly below the credit hire charges. In *Clark v City of Edinburgh Council*[26] credit hire charges which were accrued in the amount of £12,807.13 were reduced after proof to a spot hire rate of £1,950.00.

---

[21] *Humphries v Elmegirab*, 1998 S.C.L.R. 783.
[22] See also *Carson v Macdonald*, 1987 S.C.L.R. 415.
[23] *Dimond v Lovell* [2000] 2 All E.R. 897.
[24] *Lagden v O'Connor* [2004] 1 A.C. 1067.
[25] *Cleland v Quinn Direct* Unreported October 22, 2010 Arbroarth Sheriff Court.
[26] *Clark v City of Edinburgh Council*, 2011 Rep L.R. 11.

5. Loss of use

Where the client decides not to hire an alternative vehicle, he will generally be entitled to claim damages for loss of use of the vehicle either pending repair, or pending purchase of a new vehicle. Previously insurers tended to argue that a pursuer should take immediate steps to repair or replace the vehicle, whatever his financial circumstances. The courts are increasingly less receptive to this notion, taking the view that as a practical reality a pursuer can expect to be put in funds by the insurer before repair or replacement can occur.[27] The practitioner should keep up with *Current Law* quantums on loss of use.

17–14

PLEADINGS IN ROAD TRAFFIC CASES

The parties

You will very frequently be instructed by a number of persons with separate claims arising from the same accident, for example, passengers in the same vehicle. A single action with several pursuers is competent where the ground of action by each pursuer is the same.[28] Be alert for any potential conflict of interest and be prepared to arrange separate representation for passengers if your client driver is blamed in the defences.

17–15

Statement of Claim

Road traffic accidents have traditionally been described in the law reports as "simple running down cases",[29] and even before the new Personal Injury Procedure there was little need for specification. Currently the Statement of Claim should contain details of the vehicle which the pursuer was driving; the direction of travel; description of any road markings or road conditions; and the time of the accident if relevant. You don't have to state whether the driver or passenger were wearing seatbelts at this stage. It is for the defender to raise any issues of contributory negligence, including the failure to wear seatbelts. If the matter is raised in the defences you must answer candidly. You should also obtain the advice of an orthopaedic surgeon as to the precise effects which the failure to wear the seatbelt has caused.

17–16

Typical pleadings for para.3 might be:

> "The pursuer was driving his Ford Fiesta vehicle P245 CMS in an easterly direction along Glenbervie Road, Erskine, which is a major road. His vehicle was struck on the front offside by a Renault Clio vehicle P659 DYS, which was driven by the defender, and which emerged from Paton Road, Erskine, into Glenbervie Road without

---

[27] *Mattocks v Mann* [1993] C.L.Y. 1407 and *Zubair v Younis* [1995] C.L.Y. 1629.
[28] *Buchan v Thomson*, 1976 S.L.T. 42.
[29] See *Adamson v Roberts*, 1951 S.L.T. 355 and *Barrow v Bryce*, 1986 S.L.T. 691.

stopping. Paton Road is a minor road which lies to the north of Glenbervie Road, and there are 'give way' markings at the junction from which the defender's vehicle emerged."

Specific matters which should be pled in the Statement of Claim

1. Road Traffic Act convictions

17–17 Details of charges and convictions should be pled. The extract conviction and a certified copy complaint should be lodged in process. It is generally accepted that a conviction for driving whilst under the influence of alcohol is relevant and should be pled. Although such a conviction is not necessarily indicative of any negligence or carelessness, it may well "go to prove the allegation of impairment of judgment and influence of the impairment on the defender's driving".[30]

2. General averments about consumption of alcohol

17–18 Occasionally there will be evidence of the defender having consumed alcohol without any criminal conviction having followed. The case of *Bark v Scott*[31] is authority for the proposition that those averments are relevant and admissible. Further, s.39 of the Highway Code is instructive in this regard:

> "Drinking alcohol seriously affects your driving, reduces your co-ordination, slows down your reactions, affects your judgement of speed, distance and risk, and gives you a false sense of confidence. Your driving may be badly affected even if you are below the legal limit."

In appropriate cases the averment should be made that the defender's driving was impaired by the consumption of alcohol. It is also prudent to set out the evidential basis for believing that the defender has consumed alcohol, for example, "the pursuer smelled alcohol on his breath".

3. Careless driving before the actual accident

17–19 The case of *Bark v Scott* is also authority for the fact that averments about a defender's earlier dangerous overtaking on the same stretch of road are relevant. So evidence of a defender carrying out an earlier dangerous manoeuvre may well be relevant to the accident circumstances and should be averred.

4. Post-accident admissions

17–20 These can be very important in road traffic accidents. There will usually have been some conversation between the parties involved, even if only to exchange insurance details. There may well be an admission against interest which must be pled by giving brief details of the contents of the

---

[30] *Gemmell v Macfarlane*, 1991 S.L.T. (Notes) 36.
[31] *Bark v Scott*, 1954 S.L.T. 210.

statement, when and to whom it was made. The rule that admissions require to be pled applies only to parties.[32] Check your evidence for admissions not only to your client, but to other persons in the vicinity, for example passengers, police, ambulance drivers, and then make the appropriate averment.

The legal duty paragraph

This should simply read that the accident was caused by the defender at common law. There is no need for any further specification.

17–21

The damages paragraph

The damages Statement of Claim should contain full details of all heads of claim following the standard format.

17–22

PROBLEMS WITH DEFENDERS IN ROAD TRAFFIC CASES

Road Traffic Act insurance

Section 143(1) of the Road Traffic Act 1988 provides for compulsory third party insurance to be taken out by each person who uses or causes or permits another to use a motor vehicle. The policy must cover personal injury and property damage. In the majority of cases it is a simple matter to establish the insurers and to negotiate settlement with them, free from any doubts or concerns about the defender's personal solvency.

17–23

Section 151 of the Road Traffic Act 1988 provides that an insurer requires to meet any unsatisfied judgment against the party. This section covers all drivers, even if not specifically included in the policy (s.151(2)(b)). The policy must actually cover the liability, so if the use to which the vehicle was put was outside the policy, e.g. business use not on the policy, the insurer can take steps to avoid s.151 liability.

Otherwise the insurance policy is an "all drivers policy". Provided the use is permitted, the policy will cover any driver. So a thief who steals an insured vehicle is covered under the "all drivers policy".

The first step for the practitioner should be to establish whether there is an insurance certificate in existence. In 2003 the Motor Insurers Information Centre was set up. The Centre is a wholly owned subsidiary of the MIB. It holds a database of the details of every individually insured vehicle in the United Kingdom. Whilst s.154 of the Road Traffic Act 1988 contains a mechanism whereby an owner or driver can be required to provide insurance details on request, a simple MIDIS request will generally establish the position. Where the police have investigated the accident they will have taken details. Otherwise write to the driver or owner of the vehicle and request insurance details citing s.154 of the Road Traffic Act, which makes it a criminal offence to refuse to provide proper details. If you have the registration number, then enquiries can be made to the DVLA to establish the registered keeper.

---

[32] See *Hutchison v Henderson*, 1987 S.L.T. 388.

Where there is no insurance certificate

The 1999 Uninsured Drivers Agreement

17–24 This agreement covers all accidents from October 1, 1999. Whilst in general terms the purpose of the agreement is to provide a safety net for the innocent victims of drivers who have been identified but are uninsured, the Agreement bristles with traps for the unwary. Practitioners should know that the MIB have a history in England of taking procedural points, although it has to be said that this not the Scottish experience. In any event the terms of the agreement appear to have been softened by Amended Notes for Guidance which came into force on April 12, 2002. The prudent solicitor will ensure that the terms of the agreement are complied with.

There is a basic obligation (cl.5) to satisfy judgments which fall within the terms of the agreement, and are otherwise not satisfied because the defender is not insured. However there are certain exceptions where the MIB has no liability (see cl.6), there are a number of preconditions which the claimant must comply with (see cll.7–15). The MIB does not have to wait for judgment to be given. It can become a party to the pleadings, or it can negotiate and settle the claim prior to proceedings if it wishes to do so. It is competent to convene the MIB as second defenders, and summary decree or interim damages can be obtained against them.[33] Alternatively the pursuer should simply proceed against the defenders, ensuring that notification is given in terms of the agreement. It should be noted that this kind of case very frequently involves a man of straw or a person with criminal convictions. These tend to be extremely elusive defenders, and addresses are very quickly out of date. Although you can effect service by advertisement, it is slow and cumbersome and you must be careful about time bar problems. The text of the agreement and guidance notes repay close attention for any situation where you might require to have recourse to the MIB.

Exceptions to liability (see cl.6)

17–25
1. Crown vehicle.
2. Where the claim arises out of the use of a vehicle which is not required to be covered by a contract of insurance under the Road Traffic Act 1988.
3. Where the claim is in respect of property damage to a motor vehicle and there was no contract of insurance in existence, and the claimant knew or ought to have known that this was the case.
4. Passenger claims. No claim will arise if a passenger should have known that:
   (a) the vehicle had been stolen;
   (b) the vehicle was being used without insurance;
   (c) the vehicle was being used in the course of a crime;
   (d) the vehicle was being used as a means of escape from arrest.

---

[33] *Ashcroft Curator Bonis v Stewart*, 1988 S.L.T. 163.

The burden of proof on (a)–(d) is on the MIB, but in the absence of evidence to the contrary, there is a presumption in favour of the MIB where:

(a) The claimant was the owner or registered keeper of the vehicle or had caused or permitted its use.
(b) The claimant knew the vehicle was being used by a person who was below the minimum age.
(c) The claimant knew that the person driving the vehicle was disqualified.
(d) The claimant knew that the user was neither its owner, nor registered keeper, nor an employee of the owner or registered keeper, or the owner or registered keeper of any other vehicle.

See cl.6(3).

The test for claimant knowledge of the above is now set out in the case of *White v White*[34]:

" 'Knowledge' means actual knowledge that the driver was uninsured, or a situation where the victim deliberately refrained from finding out whether insurance had been taken out. It does not encompass mere carelessness or negligence on the part of the victim."

These knowledge exceptions apply only to the claimant. So in fatal cases the claim of the relatives is distinct from that of the deceased, and knowledge attributable to the deceased will not set up the exception.[35]

Application

The application must be made in the MIB approved form (see cl.7).   **17–26**

Service of notice

Notice must be served by fax or recorded delivery. In terms of cl.9 the   **17–27**
MIB incurs no liability unless notice of the proceedings have been given no later than seven days after the commencement of those proceedings. Proper notice comprises of notice in writing that proceedings are being commenced, a copy of the writ, copies of all correspondence in the possession of the claimant relevant to the injury. In terms of cl.12 the claimant must give notice of not less than 35 days if he intends to apply for judgment. Clearly this means that if there is no appearance for the defender the 35-day notice must be given of the intention to minute for decree in absence. It appears that the practitioner will require to intimate the date the defence was lodged and send a copy defence to the MIB, send any amendment to the statement of claim, and intimate the date when a

---

[34] *White v White* [2001] 1 W.L.R. 481.
[35] *Tiffney v Sean Flynn and Motor Insurers Bureau*, 2007 S.L.T. 929.

proof is fixed. Again these have to be faxed or sent recorded delivery. Notifications are required even where the MIB have joined the proceedings! A very close eye should be kept on the agreement if proceedings are raised. For accidents prior to June 11, 2007 there is a £300 excess in respect of property damage, and a limit of £250,000. The MIB also insist that the claimant assign unsatisfied judgments to itself.

The Untraced Drivers Agreement 1996

17–28 This relates typically to hit and run accidents, although the MIB will consider other situations, e.g. accidents caused by diesel spillage from an unidentified vehicle. Where the owner or driver of the vehicle cannot be identified application may be made to the MIB under the Untraced Drivers Agreement. This relates purely to compensation for personal injury or death. Since there is no possible defender, proceedings cannot be raised. The MIB will pay a handling fee of £150 to the solicitor, and will expect only minimum enquiries to have been carried out before the claim is intimated to them. Where it is unclear whether the owner or driver of the vehicle has been correctly identified, the claimant should register the claim under both the Uninsured Drivers Agreement, and the Untraced Drivers Agreement. Where an application has been received for the MIB to deal with the claim in terms of the Untraced Drivers Agreement, the MIB may require the applicant to take proceedings against some other specified person whom it considers responsible for the accident (cl.6). In these circumstances the MIB should provide an indemnity on costs, except where the result of the proceedings "materially contributes to establishing that the untraced person did not cause or contribute to the relevant injury" (cl.6(2)(a)).

The Untraced Driver's Agreement 2003

17–29 The new agreement came into effect on February 14, 2003. The full agreement together with Notes of Guidance is available on the Department of Transport website. It applies in respect of claims arising on or after February 14, 2003. There is now a £300 excess in respect of property damage. An applicant may be required to supply written statements and other information relating to the incident, and be interviewed about the incident. Compensation for property damage will now be paid in cases where the vehicle causing the damage has been identified even although the driver has not. There is a new scale of handling fee payments to solicitors contained in the Table to the Agreement.

ROAD TRAFFIC ACT PROCEEDINGS

The European Communities (Rights Against Insurers) Regulations 2002

17–30 These came into force on January 19, 2003, but apply to accidents before that date. They form part of the implementation of the Fourth Motor Insurance Directive. Where the accident victim is a resident of an EU member state or Iceland, Norway or Lichtenstein, they may have a direct right of action against the insurer of the other vehicle.

In particular the regulations state that the insurer shall be directly liable to the entitled person to the extent that he is liable to the insured person. There are none of the technical notice requirements under s.151 of the Road Traffic Act 1988 (see para.17–31). It is competent, in the light of regulations, to convene both the wrongdoer and insurer on a point and several basis, or indeed to proceed against the insurer alone. Certainly, where there is imminent time bar and problems about service an ECRAIR writ should be drafted.

Service of the writ

1. Where there is an insurer

If for any reason you do not convene the insurer directly as a defender, you must remember that a pursuer can only get the benefit of the Road Traffic Act 1988 protection if the writ is intimated to the insurer either before or within seven days of the commencement of the proceedings, all in terms of s.152. See also *Desouza v Waterlow*.[36] It should be your invariable practice in all road traffic accident cases to have a system whereby the writ is served on the defender and also on the relevant insurer within seven days of the commencement of the action. This should be done as a matter of routine in all cases, not merely where you believe there may be an insurance problem. There should be a covering letter advising the insurers that this is their notification in terms of s.152. You will occasionally come across an insurer who refuses or delays to settle because of problems with the insurance cover, for example their insured has not made timeous notification of the accident in terms of the policy. You can usually ignore these policy defences. Whilst they may enable the insurer to avoid indemnifying the insured, they will rarely entitle an insurer to avoid paying your client. The scope for policy defences is severely restricted by s.152(2). The insurer will have to raise an action of declarator that they are entitled to avoid the policy. The declarator proceedings must be brought before the pursuer's claim, or within three months of its commencement. The insurers have to give notice to the pursuer of the declarator proceedings. The only grounds for declarator are that the policy was obtained by misrepresentation or non-disclosure. In practical terms the Road Traffic Act insurer will usually take on the conduct of the defence. If they fail to do so and you obtain decree against the defender, you can then raise an action for payment by the insurer of the principal sum and expenses due in terms of the original decree. In the case of *Orme v Ferguson*[37] Sheriff Principal McLeod was prepared to accept that a telephone call advising the insurers of the intention to raise proceedings was sufficient notification under s.152. It is safer to avoid complications by ensuring recorded delivery notice in each case, and by keeping the certificate of execution.

17–31

---

[36] *Desouza v Waterlow* [1998] P.I.Q.R. P87.
[37] *Orme v Ferguson*, 1996 S.L.T. 2 (Sh Ct).

2. Where there is no known insurer

17–32 The action should be served on the defender, and recorded delivery notification sent to the MIB, in terms of the Uninsured Drivers Agreement, within 14 days of commencement of proceedings.

Generally the MIB will nominate an insurer who will handle the defence on their behalf. It is competent to convene the MIB as second defenders (*Ashcroft Curator Bonis v Stewart*[38]). Alternatively the MIB may sist themselves as minuters. In practical terms the pursuer should simply proceed against the defender, ensuring that notifications in terms of the agreement are given to the MIB when the action is served and thereafter in terms of the agreement. After you obtain a decree, the agreement provides that the MIB will satisfy any such judgment if it is not satisfied in full within seven days.

EXPERT EVIDENCE IN ROAD TRAFFIC CASES

Should you instruct an expert witness?

17–33 The indiscriminate use of road traffic experts was roundly condemned by Stuart Smith L.J. in the case of *Liddell v Middleton*[39]:

> "In [road traffic] cases the function of the expert is to furnish the judge with the necessary scientific criteria and assistance based upon a special skill and experience not possessed by ordinary laymen to enable the judge to interpret the factual evidence of the marks in the road, the damage or whatever it may be. What he is not entitled to do is say in effect 'I have considered the statements and/or evidence of the eyewitnesses in this case and I conclude from their evidence that the defendant was going at a certain speed or that he could have seen the plaintiff at a certain point'. These are facts for the trial judge to find based on the evidence that he accepts and such inferences as he draws from the primary facts found. Even less is the expert entitled to say that in his opinion the defendant should have sounded the horn, seen the plaintiff before he did, taken avoiding action and that in taking some action or failing to take some other action, a party was guilty of negligence. These are matters for the court on which the expert's opinion is wholly irrelevant and therefore inadmissible."

So you must be careful that the expert is drawing on some genuine technical knowledge to found his opinion evidence, and not simply commenting on who is to blame on the basis of the precognitions. There are very many instances in this kind of litigation where a good expert can properly draw all kinds of inferences which are invisible to the untutored eye. Expert assistance may be required for general information contained

---

[38] *Ashcroft Curator Bonis v Stewart*, 1988 S.L.T. 163.
[39] *Liddell v Middleton* [1996] P.I.Q.R. at 36.

in the Highway Code. In the case of *Cavin v Kinnaird*[40] the court declined to make any findings of fact based on the stopping distances in the Highway Code, which had not been spoken to in evidence.[41] A good example of the practical approach is the English case of *Richardson v Butcher*[42] (an accident involving a child) where the presiding judge confined the road traffic experts to the following topics:

1. Evidence of the speed at which children run.
2. Evidence of driver reaction times.
3. Evidence of driver braking and stopping distances and times.
4. Evidence of the visibility of pedestrians in dipped headlights.
5. A physical survey and photographs of the scene.
6. Evidence of the speed of the vehicle at impact as calculated from the pedestrian throw distance.
7. Evidence to assist the judge as to whether there is any physical evidence which might indicate the claimant's direction of travel at impact.

Generally the kind of areas in which a good road traffic expert can assist are as follows: **17–34**

1. *Impact damage*. An expert can frequently deduce direction and speed from post-accident examination of the vehicles or photographs.
2. *Skid marks*. After a serious accident, road traffic police will frequently measure skid marks, and carry out their own skidding tests to establish the contemporaneous co-efficient of friction of the road. Based on this information, reliable estimates of pre-accident speed can be made. Skid marks will also indicate the vehicles' pre-impact position and direction. The absence of skid marks may indicate that brakes were not applied, although this cannot be assumed for modern vehicles which have an anti brake-locking system ("ABS").
3. *Stopping distances*. The minimum stopping distances are set out in the Highway Code, and include a calculation for reaction time and braking time in dry road conditions. In reality with the advent of improved braking technology in modern vehicles, stopping distances may well be shorter than the current Highway Code distances.
4. *Tachograph*. Where the vehicle was fitted with a tachograph, an expert can read the tachograph disc and produce accurate estimates of speed. If your client is injured by a heavy goods vehicle, it is important that you write to the insurers and ask them to preserve the tachograph.

---

[40] *Cavin v Kinnaird*, 1994 S.L.T. 111.
[41] It was held that the figures could be used as an adminicle of evidence, and in particular as a check on other reliable evidence.
[42] *Richardson v Butcher* [2010] EWHC 214 QB.

5. *Pedestrian impact.* Some estimates of speed can be deduced from the effect of impact on a pedestrian. For example an expert may be able to say that the speed on impact was greater than 10mph, where a pedestrian has been thrown onto the bonnet of the vehicle.
6. *Mechanical defects.* These cover all critical elements such as brakes, steering, tyres, suspension, etc. Where there is a mechanical defect it is important wherever possible that the real evidence is preserved, for example if the suspension failed because of a damaged U-bolt, then the U-bolt attachment should be kept and lodged in evidence.

Productions in road traffic cases

17–35 As well as the normal items, there should be lodged:

1. A large scale Ordnance Survey plan of the accident locus. These are available from HMSO outlets. They should be unmarked.
2. Photographs of the accident locus, and wherever possible of the vehicles in their post-accident condition. Google Earth Street View[43] can be useful source for the former. If there is a dispute about the pre-accident value of the vehicle, then a photograph of the vehicle in its pre-accident condition can help. The photographs should be at least 7 × 5 inches, and should be unmarked.
3. Where there are relevant convictions, you should lodge a copy of the complaint or indictment, and the extract conviction. These must be authenticated by the court to be admissible in terms of the Law Reform (Miscellaneous Provisions) Act 1968 s.10(4).

---

[43] *http://maps.google.com/intl/en/help/maps/streetview/index.html* [Accessed September 15, 2011].

CHAPTER 18

SLIPS AND FALLS

Slips and falls are the staple, if somewhat unglamorous, diet of all personal injury practitioners. The chapter deals with tripping and slipping accidents on roads and pavements, in the workplace, and in other locations such as shops and supermarkets. **18–01**

Slipping and tripping involve different mechanisms, and you should be clear of the differences. Find out from the start what has happened to your client, and keep the allegation consistent throughout the file.

1. Slipping

As a person steps forward, his heel contacts the floor surface first. His weight is then transferred forward. Where there is a slippery substance or contaminant, the heel will not make sufficient contact with the floor and the foot will generally slide forward (or to the side when there is a turning movement). As a result that person will fall, usually in a backward direction. **18–02**

2. Tripping

Where the foot is stopped suddenly from moving forward, by an obstruction or a raised surface, the arrested forward momentum carries the body forward and down. **18–03**

ROADS AND PAVEMENT CLAIMS

At common law, a local authority has the control and possession of public roads and public pavements and is responsible for their management and maintenance. In addition they are the "local roads authority" in terms of the Roads (Scotland) Act 1984 ("1984 Act") and "shall manage and maintain all such roads in their area". The 1984 Act vests the roads and pavement network in the local authority,[1] but no action by an individual lies for breach of statutory duty.[2] The authority is responsible for the maintenance of private roads and pavements only in exceptional circumstances, and the first point of concern for the practitioner is to establish that the accident locus is public. The local authority is obliged **18–04**

---

[1] Roads (Scotland) Act 1984 s.1(1).
[2] *Sime v Scottish Borders Council*, 2003 S.L.T. 601.

to maintain a register of public roads and footpaths which is available for inspection. If the locus is public it should be listed in the register.

A public road is defined in the 1984 Act as:

> "Any way other than a waterway over which there is a public right of passage by whatever means and whether subject to a toll or not and includes the road's verge, any bridge (whether permanent or temporary) over which, or tunnel through which, the road passes and any reference to road includes a part thereof."[3]

This definition encompasses paths, footways and pavements. If the road is a trunk road, the responsibility for maintenance rests with the Scottish Ministers.[4]

A private road is defined in s.151(1) of the 1984 Act. Liability for maintenance will rest on the party in possession and control, usually the owner.

The maintenance obligation

18–05 The following section concentrates on urban street and pavement accidents.

A local authority is obliged to maintain roads and pavements by way of a system of visual inspection at reasonable intervals, with any areas which present a hazard to pedestrians or road users to be repaired within a reasonable period of time following the inspection.[5] Where an authority is put on notice of defect by means other than inspection, for example complaints, then the duty to repair within a reasonable period arises from the time of notice. Whilst some of the older cases suggest that the presence of a hazard or defect establishes a prima facie presumption of fault against a local authority, these have not been followed in modern practice.[6]

What is a hazard or danger?

18–06 Typically, accidents will occur by reason of potholes, depressions, bumps, slippery surfaces, rocking flagstones, and projections and risers (e.g. manhole frames, boxes, etc.). The authority's duty is to maintain in reasonable repair, which is not to "garden lawn" standard. The case which is frequently quoted in this regard is *Macdonald v County Council of Argyll*:

---

[3] Roads (Scotland) Act 1984 s.151, as amended by the New Roads and Street Works Act 1991 s.181 Sch.8 para.94b.
[4] Roads (Scotland) Act 1984 1984 Act s.5.
[5] *Rush v Glasgow Corporation*, 1948 S.L.T. 37.
[6] For example, *Laing v Magistrate of Aberdeen*, 1911 2 S.L.T. 437, per Lord Salvesen: "the mere occurrence of such an accident to a footpath or any public street raises a presumption of fault against the person who has control of the pavement". This case was cited by the unsuccessful pursuer in the case of *Gibson v SRC*, 1993 S.L.T. 1243 and must now be held to be obsolete.

"Pavements under constant wear and tear cannot be kept in a state of perfection and the users of them must be prepared to face a certain degree of imperfection ... Any particular case must be a jury question and a question of degree."[7]

This case also refers to two unreported Court of Session cases: *Gordon v Corporation of Glasgow*[8] and *Innes v Corporation of Glasgow*.[9] In the case of *Macdonald* the defect was a pavement depression which was some three-eighths of an inch (19.375mm). The pavement depressions in the *Corporation of Glasgow* cases were one inch (25mm) and five-eighths of an inch (15.62mm). Absolvitor was granted in each case on the basis that these did not present a hazard. In the English case of *James v Preseli Pembrokeshire Council*,[10] whilst the Court of Appeal accepted that 25mm was the point at which highway authorities generally regard a trip hazard as requiring repair, there was no liability for failure to effect repair to hazards measuring less than one inch. In *McClafferty v British Telecommunications Plc*,[11] Lord Ross held that a trip which measured around three-quarters of an inch did not constitute a reasonably foreseeable danger.

This has led to an unofficial rule of thumb which states that any depression in a pavement which is less than 25mm (one inch) is not an actionable hazard. There is no support in principle for this view. Each case must be looked at separately. There may well be other factors as well as the depth of trip which are relevant. In *Wright v Greenwich LBC*,[12] a local authority as occupier of a rent office was held liable for a gap between paving stones of less than one inch on the particular ground that the area was frequented by elderly visitors. In *Hartley v Burnley DC*[13] a local authority was held liable for a fall on broken tarmacadam on a gradient, even though there was no identifiable trip. Relevant factors were the steepness of the street, its location in the town centre, and the heavy volume of pedestrian traffic. In *Winterhalder v Leith County Council*,[14] the Court of Appeal held that a two and a half inch gap between two kerbstones was a very real and obvious danger. Further, the Code of Practice for Highway Maintenance Management 2005 (see below) clearly expects local authorities to carry out repairs on tripping hazards of 20mm. This document has been approved by Convention of Scottish Local Authorities ("COSLA") and most authorities have specifically adopted the Code and issued their own internal guidelines.

Further latitude applies to roadways. In particular where an accident occurred near a gully it was held that a depression of 35mm or one and a half inches did not present a foreseeable hazard, and that in any event it

---

[7] 1953 Sh. Ct. Rep. 345 at [351].
[8] *Gordon v Corporation of Glasgow* Unreported June 26, 1923 First Division.
[9] *Innes v Corporation of Glasgow* Unreported November 2, 1939.
[10] *James v Preseli Pembrokeshire Council* 1993 P.I.Q.R. 114.
[11] *McClafferty v British Telecommunications Plc*, 1987 S.L.T. 327.
[12] *Wright v Greenwich LBC* [1996] C.L.Y. 4474.
[13] *Hartley v Burnley DC* [1996] C.L.Y. 5670.
[14] *Winterhalder v Leith County Council* Unreported July 18, 2000 Court of Appeal.

might be expected that persons would take special care when stepping off the pavement onto a roadway.[15]

Again it should be emphasised that this kind of case sets no general tariff, and the whole circumstances of each case must be looked at.

It is suggested that these older cases are now out of date, and that local authorities have effectively set generic standards of systems of maintenance and inspection, which are contained in the publications referred to below.

Where so much of what the public can expect of a local authority depends on the allocation of finite resources, it is suggested that the standards contained in the *Well maintained highways: code of practice for highway maintenance management 2005*[16] set the guidelines which the courts should now follow. They were held relevant to infer liability by the Court of Appeal in the case of *Harrison v Derby City Council*.[17] For the practitioner it is important that the evidence of a road or pavement hazard is not merely presented in a vacuum but that:

1. The actual system of inspection and repair operated by the particular local authority is established, by recovery of documents if necessary. This in itself may well be enough to prove the case.
2. The system is be compared against UK-wide benchmarks approved in the 2005 Code.

The 2005 Code of Practice

18–07 This Code has replaced the 1989 Code of Practice and the 2001 Code of Practice, and is currently the most significant document relative to highway maintenance standards. It is supported and endorsed by both COSLA and the Scottish Executive. The Foreword makes it plain that the Code applies throughout the United Kingdom. At para.1.3.2 it is specifically stated that the Code will be relevant in legal proceedings. Later the Code is described as a "benchmark" and that although authorities have a discretion in some areas, they should identify areas where their own internal policy differs from the Code and specify the reasons:

> "Authorites however have certain legal obligations with which they need to comply, and which will, on occasion, be the subject of claims or legal action by those seeking to establish non compliance by authorities. It has been recognised that in such cases, the contents of this Code may be considered to be a relevant consideration. In these circumstances, where authorities elect in light of local circumstances to adopt policies, procedures or standards different from those suggested by the Code, it is essential for these to be identified, together with the reasoning for such differences." (para.3.2.2).

---

[15] *McLaughlin v Strathclyde Regional Council*, 1992 S.L.T. 959.
[16] Department of Transport, Roads Liason Group, *Well Maintained Highways Code of Practice for Highway Maintenance Management* (The Stationery Office, 2005).
[17] *Harrison v Derby City Council* [2007] EWCA (Civ) 583.

Roads and footway maintenance

The Code states at para.9.1.1: 18–08

> "The establishment of an effective regime of inspection, assessment and recording is the most crucial component of highway maintenance. The characteristics of the regime, including frequency of inspection, items to be recorded and nature of response, should be designed following an assessment of the relative risks associated with potential circumstances of network conditions."

The Code recommends safety inspections which "mainly comprise relatively frequent comprehensive inspections of all highway elements" (para.9.21).

Roads and footways are categorised by number. By way of example, a "primary walking route" which is a busy urban shopping and business area, and main pedestrian areas between different modes of transport such as railways and underground stations and bus stops, etc. are category 1 and the recommendation is that they should be inspected once a month. "Secondary walking routes", category 2, should be inspected every three months. Defects themselves are to be assessed as either category 1 defects requiring urgent action, or category 2 defects, which should be repaired as part of a planned maintenance strategy. Appendix B to the Code gives examples of intervention levels, and suggests that careful consideration should be given where there is a pothole depth of 20mm or more in a footway. The Code contains other practical advice for maintenance of embankments, cuttings, landscaped areas and trees, fences and barriers. It points out that "ironwork" such as covers, gratings, frames and boxes set in carriageways and footways have the potential to compromise safety. Although ironwork is normally part of an apparatus installed by a utility, defects identified during an inspection should be formally notified to the utility, with a follow-up procedure to ensure that the dangerous defects are remedied within the prescribed timescale. Where boxes, frames and covers are found to be greater than 20mm below the surrounding carriageway, they should be re-set.

Systems of inspection and maintenance

Evidence of complaints to the local authority will put them on notice of 18–09 defect and trigger the starting point for the period within which a repair should be carried out. You should obtain details of who made the complaint, when and to whom. In *McLaughlan v Strathclyde Regional Council*,[18] a report to a local councillor was held to have constituted notice of defect. You will still have to show that the defect could have been repaired prior to the accident. In this regard most local authorities now employ contractors to carry out their roadworks, and have quality control agreements with them, for example, five working days to complete an urgent road repair.

---

[18] *McLaughlan v Strathclyde Regional Council*, 1996 Rep. L.R. 179.

In all other cases the pursuer will have to show:

1. The length of time the defect has been in existence.
2. That a reasonable system of inspection would have identified the defect, enabling the authority to repair before your client had his accident. In the case of *Letford v Glasgow City Council*,[19] Sheriff Principal Bowen stated:

> "What is normally averred is that the defect had been present for some time and that the defenders were at fault in failing to identify and rectify it in the course of regular systems of inspection and maintenance. Such cases generally raise two issues, namely, whether the defect was such as to constitute a hazard, and whether it was one which, by reason of its nature and the duration of existence, should have been observed and rectified under a proper system of inspection and maintenance."

A frequent difficulty for the pursuer is to establish this reasonable system of inspection in the light of the case of *Gibson v Strathclyde Regional Council*.[20] The pursuer was injured after she stepped into an uncovered drain in the city centre. The pursuer's averments were to the effect that the drain had been uncovered for 14 days. It appeared that in terms of their own system of maintenance, the defenders should have carried out monthly inspections of the city centre area, although in fact they did not appear to have inspected the drains for a period of almost seven weeks. The pursuer averred that the defenders had a duty of daily inspection. She did not make any averments to indicate the evidential basis for setting out the duty of daily inspection. The Inner House held that the case was irrelevant and dismissed the action. The Lord Justice-Clerk stated that it was necessary for the pursuer to state intervals at which inspections should have been carried out. He further stated that there required to be some notice on the record of the evidential basis on which this duty was founded:

> "I do not accept that where such an averment has been made the court is entitled to hold that daily inspection was reasonable or practicable in the absence of averments to support such a conclusion. If averments had been made to the effect that it was the practice among other local authorities responsible for the maintenance and upkeep of drains to carry out daily inspections, that in my opinion would have supported the pursuer's case that it was reasonably practicable to inspect such drains daily, but no such averments have been made. Likewise if the pursuer had been in a position to aver some special circumstance existing at the locus, such averments might have been sufficient to support the assertion that it was reasonably practicable to inspect the drains daily. For example, if the pursuer had been in a position to say that in the past covers had

---

[19] *Letford v Glasgow City Council* Unreported June 26, 2002.
[20] *Gibson v Strathclyde Regional Council*, 1993 S.L.T. 1243.

frequently been removed from drains in this locality or that the defenders had received numerous complaints regarding the absence of drain covers here, that too might have supported the case for daily inspections."

On one view this case is special on its averments and in particular is a robust judicial reaction to a duty of inspection which has simply been plucked from the air to solve an evidential problem. On the other hand the case is frequently cited by defenders in the sheriff court as authority for the proposition that a tripper writ which does not contain averments about the practice of local authorities is irrelevant and should be dismissed. This causes particular difficulties for pursuers, who are seldom conversant with the practice of any authorities. The Lord Justice Clerk does suggest that the defenders' own practice, or special circumstances at the locus, might provide an evidential basis without the need to refer to the practice of other local authorities.[21] It is suggested here that the Code of Practice 2005 now sets up a standard against which the actings of the authority can be judged and should be the primary guidance on common law negligence. In the case of *Letford*, Sheriff Principal Bowen held that a bare averment that inspection should take place every three months would have been sufficient to set up an inspection case, and there was no need to refer to the Highway Maintenance Code of Good Practice, or the practice of other authorities in the pleadings. In the case of *Nugent v Glasgow City Council*[22] Lord Brodie held that Glasgow City Council were entitled to treat a depression as something not requiring intervention repair, on the basis of their own internal documentation. It is doubtful if this approach is correct. As was explained in *Esdale v Dover DC*[23]:

"The test of whether in all the circumstances the Council has taken such steps as are reasonable to see that visitors are reasonably safe does not depend on what standards of safety the Council sets itself as a matter of policy. The test to be applied is an objective one ... The question in effect: Does the judge, as the embodiment of the reasonable person, think that the Council has taken such steps as are reasonable in all the circumstances to keep the visitor—the claimant here—reasonably safe? What the Council sets as a policy is certainly not determinative, although I would not go so far that it is irrelevant."

The issue is not foreclosed by the defenders' own categorisation. The reality is that you will have a very difficult job persuading a court that a defect which does not meet the hazard parameters contained in the Code or the internal local authority documentation is actionable.

---

[21] *Gibson v Strathclyde Regional Council*, 1993 S.L.T. 1243 at [1246].
[22] *Nugent v Glasgow City Council* [2009] CSOH 88.
[23] *Esdale v Dover DC* [2010] EWCA Civ 409.

Slip and fall practice points

18-10 It is scarcely an exaggeration to say that each set of pavement/slip and trip instructions should be treated as an emergency. You should go with the client and identify the precise accident locus, taking photographs and measurements of the dimensions of the hazard yourself. It can be effective to show the trip edge with either a rule or coin against it, showing the precise depth (a 10 pence coin is 25mm). You must also take immediate steps to obtain witness statements as to how long the defect has been in existence, and to check whether any complaints have been made, and if so to whom. Do all of this *before* any intimation of claim. If there are no witnesses as to the length of time the hazard has been in existence, an expert may be prepared to estimate that length of time from indicators such as vegetation or decayed tarmac, and should be instructed forthwith.

If, after your best efforts, you cannot identify a discrete hazard, or cannot show how long it has been in existence, you should close the file.

SNOW AND ICE CLAIMS

18-11 Winter accidents on roads and pavements pose particularly difficult problems for pursuers. It is recognised that resources are finite, and no local authority can be expected to grit or salt all roads and pavements at the first touch of frost. The provenance of the 2005 Code clearly establishes that there is a consensus about achievable levels of road and pavement and winter maintenance throughout the United Kingdom. The Code supplied all of the information required by the Inner House in the case of *Morton v West Lothian Council*[24] and is significantly more compelling evidence than the practice of a few other local authorities.[25] As noted above, most local authorities have specifically adopted the Code and have issued a separate roads and pavement and winter maintenance document. This should be obtained under the Freedom of Information (Scotland) Act 2002.

Road accidents

18-12 Typically you will be instructed by a client who has suffered injury when his vehicle skidded on ice, on a stretch of ungritted road. The courts recognise that the mere occurrence of such an accident does not establish a prima facie case of negligence:

> "Merely to state that sand had not been spread on Kingsmill Street after 12 hours of frost is not enough to point to a breach of duty. It may be that there was some slackness or unreasonable delay in tackling the effects of this frost, but if that was so it must be specially averred. It is not enough for the pursuer to say that the delay could

---

[24] *Morton v West Lothian Council* [2008] CSIH 18.
[25] See also *Taylor v Smith*, 2003 S.C.L.R. 926.

have been due to slackness. She must say so and so focus the real issue in the case. The statement that the defenders could and ought to have spread sand on Kingsmill Street before the accident does not assist her. Clearly the [gritting] cart could have been sent there first. The fact that it was not done does not point to a breach of duty."[26]

Almost all authorities will have a priority list for arterial highways, main roads, and then local and residential streets if at all. There is clearly a very large discretionary element in the local authority plan. It is difficult if not impossible to attack the plan by suggesting that road A should have been gritted before road B.[27]

But this does not mean that these cases cannot be won. A failure to pre-grit a primary road is a serious matter with potentially catastrophic consequences. Almost all local authorities now monitor winter weather forecasts two or three times a day and are alert to send out their gritting teams if the forecast is for sub-zero temperatures. In *Kozokowska v Kozokowski*,[28] it was held that a local authority's duty was to pre-grit roads the night before with salt to prevent ice forming, and thereafter to grit again at 6.00am. (it was held on the facts that they had done so). You may be able to show that operational errors have occurred, for example a street which should have been gritted was missed, as was done in *McCusker v Saveheat*.[29] In *Kevin Taylor v George Smith*,[30] the pursuer was injured when the vehicle in which he was travelling skidded on ice on the A96 at 3.00am. The pursuer sought to establish that no reasonable roads authority, exercising reasonable care, would have failed to apply rock salt to the road prior to the accident. The Inner House adopted this as the test of negligence, and after detailed consideration of Grampian Council's Winter Maintenance Policy and responses, found that a reasonable roads engineer would have been entitled to construe contemporaneous data as meaning that the gritting was not required.

It has to be said that these claims are far from straightforward. You will first of all require contemporaneous evidence of the length of the cold spell, and what the authority might reasonably have expected from the weather forecasts which it was receiving. The Met Office will generally supply such a report for a fee, currently around £300. You will need witness evidence that the road was untreated. It is probably advisable to obtain the witness evidence initially and to intimate the claim. If the claim is defended, and you think there may be prospects, you can then obtain the Met. report and consider proceedings.

In *Morton v West Lothian Council*[31] the pursuer was seriously injured and her passenger killed when her vehicle skidded on a patch of black ice. The Lord Ordinary found as a matter of fact that black ice extended for

---

[26] *Gordon v Inverness Town Council*, 1957 S.L.T. (Notes) 48.
[27] See the case of *Grant v Lothian RC*, 1988 S.L.T. 533 and *Syme v Scottish Borders Council*, 2003 S.L.T. 601.
[28] *Kozokowska v Kozokowski*, 1997 G.W.D. 17-802.
[29] *McCusker v Saveheat*, 1987 S.L.T. 24.
[30] *Kevin Taylor v George Smith*, 2003 S.C.L.R. 926.
[31] *Morton v West Lothian Council* [2006] Rep. L.R. 7.

50 yards to the east of the junction and 150 yards to the west, but that the black ice was patchy and there were areas where the road was simply wet. On the evidence the local authority had carried out pre-gritting and it was possible that this had been dispersed by further rainfall. The pursuer failed on the burden of proof. In *Gibson v West Lothian Council*,[32] the pursuer's vehicle skidded on a patch of black ice in winter. It was argued that the accident locus was a trouble spot where flooding always occurred after heavy rainfall, which should have been discovered by any reasonable system of inspection. The case failed on its facts.

Pavement accidents

18–13 Most local authorities operate a priority system which puts pavements behind primary and secondary roads. It is easy to understand the rationale. A skidding vehicle represents a very serious danger to the driver and to other road users. A pedestrian has a chance to look out for snow and ice and to take avoidance measures. A driver has less chance to see ice on the road, and limited opportunity to avoid it. Some authorities have systems where priority is given to particular locations such as schools, hospitals or doctors' surgeries. You should check if the accident locus might come under this definition.

Further difficulties for pursuers are raised by the case of *Syme v Scottish Borders Council*.[33] The evidence was that primary routes had been gritted by 9.00am. Gritting of the footway accident locus did not take place until 11.00am, some 45 mins after the pursuer's accident. These averments were held on their own to be insufficient to pass the relevancy test. The practice of other local authorities should have been averred, bearing in mind that the authority in any event has a wide discretion. It is suggested that the chapter on Winter Service contained in the Code of Practice for Maintenance Management, July 2005 contains the kind of guidelines which enable best practice averments to be made. A further useful guide in this regard is the Institution of Civil Engineers publication "Highway Winter Maintenance—A Practical Guide", 2000. In particular each authority should have a Winter Service Operational Plan which should contain policies on:

1. Ice and snow prediction and monitoring via weather forecasts.
2. Pre-treatment, i.e. precautionary salting on specified routes.
3. Post-treatment-salting following the formation of ice.
4. Clearance of snow.

Each authority should have a "response time", which is the period between a decision being taken to begin treatment and vehicles leaving the depot. The Code suggests authorities should have a target time of one hour. There should also be a "treatment time", which is the period between the vehicles leaving the depot and the completion of treatment on all priority routes, recognising always that treatment times might vary

---

[32] *Gibson v West Lothian Council* [2011] CSOH 110.
[33] 2003 S.L.T. 601.

in different weather conditions. It is clearly envisaged that primary routes in any event should be completed within around two hours of treatment commencing. The optimal completion time wherever practical should be two hours before the forecast time of freezing and snow. Frequently the actual treatment by salt or salt/grit will have been contracted out to a private provider, who will have agreed a target response time with the local authority, and the contractual documents should be recovering using the Freedom of Information (Scotland) Act 2002. At well-known trouble spots, authorities can assist the local community by the provision of salt bins, which should be regularly replenished. A winter maintenance plan should be prepared by each local authority and once again the golden rule is to obtain the plan, whether by request or by recovery of documents, and to set the facts against the plan.

The employment of a private contractor should not relieve a local authority of its duties in respect of roads and footways, i.e. the practitioner should not accept that the claim is redirected to the contractor as is sometimes suggested by claims assessors in correspondence. It is suggested that the duty is non-delegable, and that a pursuer will have no direct right of action against a contractor.[34] The decision of Sheriff Principal Young in *Murdoch v The Moray Council*[35] gives an idea of the difficulties faced by pursuers. In this case a pavement within a housing scheme which had been left ungritted for nine days was not enough to found liability. This was because, even if earlier gritting had been carried out, the weather conditions immediately preceding the accident date would have caused fresh ice.

The reluctant conclusion for practitioners is that except where there are special facts, these claims are non-justiciable.

Drafting the slip and fall writ in roads and pavement cases

You will have to identify the precise accident locus, perhaps by reference to a street number or nearby fixture such as a postbox. You should specify the approximate dimensions of the hazard.[36] Alternatively you will have to explain why such specification is not possible, e.g. the locus has been repaired. You will require to state that the road or pavement was one for which the local authority was responsible.[37] Give a general indication of where your client was walking by reference to a street name and geographical direction, and specify where he fell with reference to a street number or landmark, for example, next to a telephone box. In a complaints case you will have to aver a complaint from a named person together with the approximate date of the complaint and to whom it was made. For a system of inspection case you will have to aver a period for a system of inspection which would have disclosed the defect in time to

18–14

---

[34] See what was said by Lord Coulsfield on the liability of a local farmer employed by the authority to carry out winter gritting in the case of *Kozikowska v Kozikowski* Unreported January 18, 1995 Court of Session.
[35] *Murdoch v The Moray Council* Unreported April 27, 2005.
[36] See *Fox v City of Glasgow*, 2001 Rep. L.R. 59.
[37] These cases are not cases under the Occupiers Liability (Scotland) Act 1960. See *Lamont v Monklands DC*, 1992 S.L.T. 428.

enable repairs to be made before your client's accident. You should make averment of local authority practice (either the defender's or that of other authorities), or preferably by reference to the Code of Practice for Highway Maintenance Management, 2005. In snow and ice cases you will have to state how long the snow and ice had been lying and untreated. You should make averments about the weather forecast which would have been available to the local authority and when gritting procedures should have been instigated with reference to the Winter Service Operational Plan. You should aver that the accident would not have occurred if the roads had been gritted.

Recovery of documents in roads and pavement cases

18–15 This is extremely important in road and pavement accident cases. Much of the information which you will need regarding inspection systems or winter maintenance regimes will be exclusively within the knowledge of the defenders at the time your writ is drafted. If you have not already obtained relevant documentation under the Freedom of Information (Scotland) Act 2002, you should look to recover:

1. The defenders' statement of their system of maintenance and inspection for the accident locus.
2. The specific maintenance records for the accident locus. Almost invariably there should be a roads inspector's diary showing inspection dates and findings.
3. In winter maintenance cases you should obtain the defenders' winter maintenance plan showing the general gritting priority programme, the specific gritting records relating to the accident locus, the records of any weather forecasts in their hands on which the authority relied and details of all target and response times for winter treatment.

STREETWORKS ACCIDENTS

18–16 Your clients will occasionally suffer accidents at pavement works or roadworks which are inadequately lit or fenced or which have not been properly reinstated. Some of these works will have been carried out by utilities, for example, gas and telecommunications suppliers. Others will have been carried out by private contractors.

Against whom should the claim be directed?

18–17 The utility or independent contractor has control and possession of the site for the duration of the works, and should be liable at common law for any injuries arising from hazards to pedestrians or road users.[38]

They may also be in breach of statutory duties under the 1984 Act. It has been held that s.60(1) of the 1984 Act may found an action for breach

---

[38] *A.C. Billings v Riden* [1958] A.C. 240.

of statutory duty by a contractor who failed to light or erect warning signs at roadworks.[39]

You should make preliminary enquiry of the local council as roads authority to find out who was on site at the material time. Each opening of the road or pavement must be authorised by the roads authority, and they are obliged to keep a roads opening register which is available for public inspection. You should then intimate to the utility or contractor and deal with the claim in the ordinary way. Street and pavement works and openings are now governed by the New Roads and Streetworks Act 1991 which sets out a regulatory framework for safety and reinstatement requirements. It is doubtful that any action lies for breach of statutory duty of this Act, but the detailed provisions should provide guidance for allegations of common law negligence.[40] It is also supported by a Code of Practice which contains helpful best practice illustrations.

Further considerations will arise where there has been a failure to reinstate either properly or at all. The contractor or utility should be liable at common law for the resulting danger created by their negligence. The local authority may also be liable on the basis of their common law duty of maintenance and inspection. So once again you must find out the length of time that the defect has been in existence, and be able to state that a reasonable system of inspection would have disclosed the defect and enabled timeous repair.

Apparatus belonging to utilities

Accidents frequently involve apparatus and equipment which belongs to entities such as Scottish Water and British Telecom. A particular feature is that these organisations do not carry out any inspections of their equipment, but instead rely on reports from the local authority. Whilst the local authority remains responsible for footway maintenance, they cannot repair or otherwise interfere with apparatus which is the property of others. Most local authorities have adopted a reporting protocol with the utility or statutory undertaker and there are standard information conduits. The question of liability in the event of an accident was considered by the Court of Appeal in *Reid v British Telecommunications Plc* June 26, 1987, where the court held that there was nothing to suggest that British Telecom were at fault in relying upon six monthly inspections by the highway authority.

18–18

> "As against the plaintiff, however, if British Telecom choose to rely upon inspection by the highway authority—there being of course no suggestion that they could sensibly dispense with all inspection— British Telecom must be treated, as I see it, as knowing what they should know if the inspections are properly carried out by the

---

[39] *McArthur v SRC*, 1995 S.L.T. 1129.
[40] In England the Court of Appeal has held that the Public Utilities Street Works Act 1950 confers no right of action upon a private individual (*Keating v Elvin Reinforced Concrete Co* [1962] 2 All E.R. 139). This Act is the predecessor of the New Roads and Street Works Act 1991.

highway authority at the proper intervals, which in this case appear to be six monthly intervals. I would therefore hold that British Telecom must be treated as knowing with reference to this manhole cover what they would have known if they had themselves carried out the inspections, which they were content for the highway authority to carry out, and that therefore they knew what they would have discovered if they had inspected it in March 1981 as the highway authority did."

Recovery of documentation frequently shows that the local authority has reported the hazard and there has been a failure by the utility or statutory undertaker to repair. In that event proceedings should be raised only against the utility or undertaker.[41] Matters are more complicated when the allegation is that the local authority inspector has failed to identify the defect so that no report had been made. It is suggested that the courts should follow *Reid v British Telecommunications Plc* and find that liability is joint and several.

SHOPS, SUPERMARKETS AND OTHER LOCATIONS

18–19 In shops and supermarkets you will generally be dealing with transient hazards such as foodstuffs or other spillages on the floor. Slipping accidents in supermarkets are a serious and underrated problem, leading the Health and Safety Executive ("HSE") to make the reduction of slips in supermarkets part of its current Strategic Action Plan. There is little by way of reported Scottish authority on these kinds of accidents. In the case of *Reid v Galbraith Stores Ltd*,[42] the Lord Ordinary appears to have approved an issue that a shopkeeper ought to have cleared up vegetables as soon as possible (and cast doubt on the averment that they ought to have been cleared up "immediately"). The most helpful authority is the case of *Ward v Tesco Stores*,[43] where the plaintiff slipped on a pot of yoghurt. It was stated:

"It is for the plaintiff to show that there has occurred an event which is unusual and which in the absence of explanation is more consistent with fault on the part of the defendants than the absence of fault and to my mind the learned judge was wholly right in taking that view of the presence of the slippery liquid on the floor of the supermarket in the circumstance of this case; that is that the defendants knew or should have known that it was a not uncommon occurrence; and that if it should happen, and should not be promptly attended to, it created a serious risk that customers would fall and injure themselves. When the plaintiff has established that, the

---

[41] The local authority has a residual authority to carry out emergency repairs where the statutory undertaker failed to repair and this might be relied on in extreme cases (New Roads and Street Works Act 1991 s.140(4)).

[42] *Reid v Galbraith Stores Ltd*, 1970 S.L.T. (Notes) at [93].

[43] *Ward v Tesco Stores* [1976] 1 All E.R. 219.

defendants can still escape from liability. They can escape from liability if they could show that the accident must have happened, or even on the balance of probability would have been likely to have happened, irrespective of the existence of a proper and adequate system in relation to the circumstances to provide for the safety of the customers ... But ... it is for them to show that, on the balance of probability, either by evidence or by inference from the evidence that is given or is not given, this accident would have been at least equally likely to have happened despite a proper system designed to give reasonable protection to customers. That, in this case they wholly failed to do."[44]

This means that a pursuer can plead the facts and circumstances of the accident, to raise a prima facie presumption of negligence, which it is for the defenders to negative. *Ward v Tesco Stores* was applied by Sheriff Cubie in the case of *Wilson v Debenhams Retail Plc*.[45] The facts were the pursuer had slipped on an unexplained patch of oil. Sheriff Cubie stated:

"In terms of *Ward,* the pursuer is entitled, once she has established to the satisfaction of the court the mechanics of the fall, to call upon the defenders to establish what system was in place to take reasonable steps that the floor remain hazard free."

Dawn Jacobs v Tesco Stores Plc[46] confirms this approach. In that case the plaintiff slipped on a spillage of mineral water. It was held that the circumstances of the accident placed an evidential burden on the defendants to show that they had taken all reasonable care. They failed to discharge this burden, and in particular should have had a full-time proactive staff member on the lookout for spillages.

Where shoppers bring water or moisture into the shop on their footwear or clothing, it is unlikely that any prima facie presumption of fault arises. If your client slips in these circumstances, you will have to show some omission, such as a failure to provide entrance mats at the entrance to the shop or supermarket. In the case of *Milne v Rank City Wall Ltd*,[47] the defenders were the occupiers of a shopping centre with a terrazzo tiled floor. They were held liable for not providing extra mats for shoppers during conditions of snow and slush.

In England the Court of Appeal considered the same kind of issues in *Laverton v Kiapasha (T/A Takeaway Supreme)*.[48] The plaintiff had slipped and suffered a broken hip in the defendants' takeaway premises, during wet weather conditions. The majority of the court held that it was

---

[44] *Ward* is cited with approval in Gloag and Henderson, *The Law of Scotland*, 10th edn (Edinburgh: W. Green, 1995), p.527. The same approach has been followed in Northern Ireland in *Mullen v Quinnsworth* [1991] C.L.Y. 4286.
[45] *Wilson v Debenhams Retail Plc* Unreported September 20, 2010 Stirling Sheriff Court.
[46] *Dawn Jacobs v Tesco Stores Plc* Unreported November 19, 1998 Court of Appeal.
[47] *Milne v Rank City Wall Ltd*, 1987 G.W.D. 14-525.
[48] *Laverton v Kiapasha (T/A Takeaway Supreme)* Unreported November 19, 2002 Court of Appeal.

not reasonably practicable to keep the shop floor completely dry at all times during wet weather conditions. The defendants had installed a nonslip floor in 1996, had set up foot mats at the shop entrance, and mopped the floor dry from time to time. The majority of the court held that there were no other reasonably practicable steps which could have been taken. These kind of precautions may now well set the benchmark for reasonable care in similar circumstances.

SLIPS AND FALLS AT WORK

18–20 Each year around 33,000 slip, trip and fall injuries are reported to the HSE and local authorities. Around 5,000 concerned major injuries, a total of which represents one-third of all major accidents reported. The effects of such accidents can range from the trivial to the devastating, and older persons, particularly women, tend to be injured most severely.

The Workplace, Health, Safety and Welfare Regulations 1992

18–21 Since January 1, 1996, almost all workplaces have been covered by the Workplace, Health, Safety and Welfare Regulations 1992 ("WHSWR"). For the purpose of construction, this legislation must be interpreted as making an *improvement* to existing safety standards, and it is suggested that circumstances where liability would exist under the former statutory regimes will found liability under the new Regulations, e.g. Factories Act 1961 s.28, Office, Shops and Railway Premises Act 1963 s.63. The regulations apply to a wide area of workplaces previously outwith the statutory framework, for example, schools, hospitals, places of entertainment.

Regulation 12 provides:

> "**Condition of Floors and Traffic Routes**
>
> (1) Every floor in a workplace and the surface of every traffic route in a workplace shall be of a construction such that the floor or surface of the traffic route is suitable for the purpose for which it is used.
>
> (2) Without prejudice to the generality of paragraph (1), the requirements in that paragraph shall include requirements that—
>
> > (a) the floor, or surface of the traffic route, shall have no hole or slope, or be uneven or slippery so as, in each case, to expose any person to a risk to his health or safety;
> >
> > (b) every such floor shall have effective means of drainage where necessary.
>
> (3) So far as is reasonably practicable, every floor in a workplace and the surface of every traffic route in a workplace shall be kept free from obstructions and from any article or substance which may cause a person to slip, trip or fall.

(4) In considering whether for the purposes of paragraph (2)(a) a hole or slope exposes any person to risk to his health or safety—

   (a) no account shall be taken of a hole where adequate measures have been taken to prevent a person falling;
   (b) account shall be taken of any handrail provided in connection with any slope.

(5) Suitable and sufficient handrails and, if appropriate, guards shall be provided on all traffic routes which are staircases except in circumstances in which a handrail can not be provided without obstructing the traffic route."

Quite apart from the specific statutory terms, the regulations are supported by an HSE Approved Code of Practice which contains detailed guidelines on practice to be followed.[49] Other HSE publications include *Watch Your Step—Prevention of Slipping, Tripping and Falling Accidents at Work*,[50] *Slips and Trips—HSE Guidance for Employers on Identifying Hazards and Controlling Risks*.[51] The HSE has a specific website area devoted to slipping and tripping accidents.

The courts should look to the terms of the Approved Code of Practice and the current HSE publications for guidance on good practice. Typical hazards which the slip and trip publication addresses are spills and splashes of liquids, wet floors following cleaning, loose mats on polished floors, rain, sleet and snow, and dusty floors. Trip hazards which are addressed include holes and cracks, cables across walking areas, electrical and telephone socket outlets, loose and worn mats, loose floorboards and tiles. There is a wealth of case law on slipping and tripping accidents under s.28(1) of the Factories Act 1961 which may still be apposite. In the case of *Simmons v British Steel Corporation* it was pointed out by Lord Hardie that the WHSWR reg.12(3) speaks both of "obstructions" and of any "article", and that an article may be something other than an obstruction. In particular it would extend to easily visible objects which were on the floor, even if they were part of the system of work. There would be no breach of the section where there was a proper and safe system of work with which the defenders could satisfy the reasonable practicability test.

"I consider the addition of the word 'article' to the obligation to keep floors free from obstruction has the effect of removing the previously absolute protection afforded to employers for placing visible objects on the floor in the course of a proper system of work.

---

[49] See paras 89–105.
[50] HSE, *Watch Your Step: Prevention of Slipping, Tripping and Falling Accidents at Work* (HMSO, 1985).
[51] HSE, *Slips and trips: Guidance for employers on identifying hazards and controlling risks* (HSG155, 1996).

It will now be for employers to show that it is not reasonably practicable to avoid placing such articles on the floor even if they are part of the manufacturing process."

18–22 In *Wenham v Bexley*,[52] a county court decision, the plaintiff was a nursing assistant who slipped on water on the kitchen floor at the care home where she worked. The judge found that not only was there a breach of reg.12(3) (transient hazard), but the fact that a kitchen floor had an unsatisfactory slip resistance when wet, meant that there was also a breach of reg.12(1) and 12(2).

Lord Hamilton used the same kind of reasoning in *McGhee v Strathclyde Fire Brigade*,[53] where a fireman slipped on a recently polished floor. He held that reg.12(1) as read with reg.12(2) imposed "a requirement that the constructional state of the floor immediately prior to the pursuer's accident be suitable in the sense of there being at that time no real risk of a person using it as a means of passage from the stairs ... and thereby sustaining injury". A real risk did not need to be a probability, but simply a foreseeable possibility. The case is also of interest for a reference to the guidelines recommended by the UK Slip Resistance Group which may be increasingly germane to cases involving the safe construction of floors.

The question of reg.12(1) suitability was considered in some detail in the case of *Ellis v Bristol City Council*.[54] The facts were that the claimant nurse slipped on a pool of urine on the floor of a nursing home. Critically the floor was frequently to be found in this condition. In those circumstances there should have been a non slip surface, and the floor was not suitable on "constructional" grounds by reason of breach of reg.12(1).

In *Anderson v Newham College of Education*[55] the claimant tripped on a whiteboard which protruded some two feet into the classroom. Even although the hazard was obvious there was a clear breach of statutory duty with contributory negligence being assessed at 50 per cent. A similar approach was taken by the Court of Appeal in *Burgess v Plymouth County Council*[56] where a cleaner who was employed to tidy classrooms, fell on a lunch box which had been left on the floor. Although the hazard was obvious, once again there was a statutory breach and contributory negligence was assessed at 50 per cent.

In *McEwan v Lothian Buses Plc*[57] the pursuer slipped on a pool of coolant which he himself had spilled. It was held that the defenders had simply accepted spillages as a fact of life. The defenders had not made out the reasonable practicability defence. Potholes in a yard constituted a breach of reg.12(3) in *Campbell v Elliot Group*.[58]

All of these cases are particularly fact sensitive. A paving slab standing proud of its neighbour, which caused the wheels of a trolley to stick was

---

[52] *Wenham v Bexley* [1999] C.L.Y. 287.
[53] *McGhee v Strathclyde Fire Brigade* Unreported January 18, 2002 Court of Session.
[54] *Ellis v Bristol City Council* [2007] EWCA Civ 685.
[55] *Anderson v Newham College of Education* [2003] I.C.R. 212.
[56] *Burgess v Plymouth County Council* [2006] I.C.R. 579.
[57] *McEwan v Lothian Buses Plc*, 2006 Rep. L.R. 134.
[58] *Campbell v Elliot Group* [2009] CSOH 63.

Slips and Falls 217

held by the Court of Appeal to constitute a hazard in *Craner v Dorset County Council*.[59] On the other hand a weather strip some 9mm proud of the floor at a doorway exit was not a breach of reg.12(1) in *Palmers v Marks & Spencer Plc*.[60] Similarly in *Taylor v Wincanton Group Ltd*[61] a gap in a step at the entry to a portacabin did not constitute a breach of reg.12(1). A competent risk assessment before the fact would not have identified it as a hazard. A failure to highlight a step in the middle of a corridor was held to constitute a breach of reg.12(3) in *O'Neil v The University of West of Scotland*.[62] In *Gilmour v East Renfrewshire Council*[63] the presence of a chip on an unribbed ramp constituted a breach of both reg.12(1) and 12(3). The bulging carpet on a staircase which created a real risk of injury was held to be a breach of reg.12(1) in *Holtes v Aberdeenshire Council*.[64]

Drafting the writ in workplace accidents

You should draft the writ on the basis that your averments of the combination of the accident and the obstruction or slippery substance constitute a breach of statute, and entitle the pursuer to decree. As was stated by Lord Cameron:

18–23

> "In my opinion the true situation is this: unless a defender makes specific use of the statutory escape clause in his defence by averring and offering to prove that it was not reasonably practicable to keep the floor free, and the pursuer proves obstruction and injury resulting therefrom, the breach and consequent liability are established, but when the defender, in addition to any other defence open to him, pleads the specific defence which the statute allows him, then a breach of statute cannot be affirmed until the whole evidence relevant to the averments and pleas of parties has been considered and the facts ascertained."[65]

This is the effect of the case of *Nimmo v Alexander Cowan and Sons*.[66] You therefore require to make no averments at all on what was reasonably practicable for the defenders to have done, unless they specifically raise the issue of reasonable practicability in the pleadings. As Lord Maxwell stated in the case of *Moffat v Marconi Space and Defence Systems Ltd*:

---

[59] *Craner v Dorset County Council* [2009] I.C.R. 563.
[60] *Palmers v Marks & Spencer Plc* [2001] EWCA Civ 1528.
[61] *Taylor v Wincanton Group Ltd* [2009] EWCA Civ 1581.
[62] *O'Neil v The University of West of Scotland*, 2011 Rep. L.R. 58.
[63] *Gilmour v East Renfrewshire Council*, 2004 Rep. L.R. 40.
[64] *Holtes v Aberdeenshire Council*, 2006 S.L.T. 871.
[65] *Gillies v Glynwed Foundries Ltd*, 1977 S.L.T. 97 at [104], a case under the Factories Act 1961 s.28(1).
[66] *Nimmo v Alexander Cowan and Sons*, 1967 S.L.T. 277.

"I also appreciate that in a case such as the present, the effect of the decision in *Nimmo* is that, apart from proving the fault and the cause of the fault, the less evidence the pursuer leads, the better chance she has of success."[67]

Where the issue of reasonable practicability is raised in the defences, some of the matters you should consider are:

(i) A defender has a duty to prevent obstructions and spillages getting onto the floor, and also to have them removed as soon as reasonably practicable. Where did the obstruction/spillage come from? If you can establish on the balance of probability that some other workman has caused the obstruction or spillage you should be able to aver that it would have been reasonably practicable to instruct employees not to drop or spill items or substances, and in any event to clear them up immediately.[68]

(ii) Where the evidence is that such instructions had been given, you should consider whether there may be a vicarious liability case against the employer, i.e. the defenders are vicariously liable for the employee's failure to deal with the spillage, as instructed. This is probably an allegation of common law negligence, and will require a separate condescendence from the statutory case.

(iii) Thereafter you should work carefully through the Approved Code of Practice and the HSE publication (see above) to find particular steps which the defenders could have taken. Whilst the onus of proof that all reasonably practicable steps were taken remains on the defender, you must make averments if you are to contend for any particular step which should have been taken.

(iv) You will have to show that the particular steps if taken would have prevented the accident. It is not enough to say that the absence of the precautions materially increased the risk. In the case of *Porter v SRC*,[69] the pursuer was injured after she slipped on a teaspoonful of food on an unwiped nursery floor during mealtime. It was argued for the defenders that unless the pursuer could show the length of time that the food had been on the floor, it was not possible to say that a system which involved a supervisor noticing food being spilled or soon after it was spilled would have prevented the accident on the balance of probability. The Inner House held that if the defenders had operated a system designed to preclude or reduce this danger, the inevitable inference was that such a system would probably have prevented the accident.

---

[67] 1975 S.L.T. at [61]. The same approach was followed in the factory slipping case of *Williamson v GB Papers Plc*, 1994 S.L.T. 173.

[68] See *Hall v Fairfield Shipbuilding and Engineering Co*, 1964 S.L.T. 97.

[69] *Porter v SRC*, 1991 S.L.T. at [447].

There will now rarely be any mileage in a common law case, unless vicarious liability for the negligence of another employee is alleged. In most cases the pleadings should be directed solely to the WHSWR. In reg.12(1) and 12(2) cases (constructional safety), you should include averments about previous accidents or near misses if appropriate. You might also consider instructing an expert versed in the UK Slip Resistance Guidelines. In reg.12(3) cases, (transient hazards) the initial averments should simply be the combination of the accident, and the article or obstruction or substance. You can add in what reasonably practicable steps could have been taken if the point is taken in the defences.

CONTRIBUTORY NEGLIGENCE

18–24 It is inevitable that in all slipping and tripping accidents you will be met with a plea of contributory negligence. Normally a pursuer should be expected to keep a reasonable lookout as to where he is walking and to identify and avoid hazards. Everything depends on the particular circumstances. For example in the case of *McClafferty*,[70] the court would have found 50 per cent contributory negligence; in the case of *McMillan*,[71] contributory negligence was assessed at one-third; and in the case of *Brown*,[72] contributory negligence was assessed in the figure of 20 per cent.

In supermarket cases, the whole get-up of the premises is designed to divert shoppers' attention away from the floor and onto the shelves,[73] and in the case of *Ward v Tesco* where there was no finding of contributory negligence, it would seem on the basis that the plaintiff was legitimately intent on the supermarket shelves.

---

[70] *McClafferty v British Telecommunications Plc*, 1987 S.L.T. 327.
[71] *McMillan v L.A.*, 1991 S.L.T. 150.
[72] *Brown v City of Edinburgh D.C.*, 1998 G.W.D. 32-1675, a pavement-tripping case.
[73] For an interesting discussion on the liability of supermarkets to shoppers, see the case of *Mullen v Quinnsworth*, a decision of the Irish Supreme Court of Appeal.

CHAPTER 19

OCCUPIERS' LIABILITY CASES

OCCUPIERS' LIABILITY (SCOTLAND) ACT 1960

19–01 "The care which an occupier of a premises is required by reason of occupation or control of the premises to show towards a person entering thereon in respect of dangers which are due to the state of the premises or to anything done or omitted to be done on them and for which the occupier is in law responsible shall, except insofar as he is entitled to and does extend, restrict, modify, exclude by agreement his obligations towards that person, be such care as in all the circumstances of the case is reasonable to see that that person will not suffer injury or damage by reason of any such danger."[1]

The Occupiers' Liability (Scotland) Act 1960 ("1960 Act") requires that occupiers of premises take reasonable care for persons who come onto their premises. "Premises" is defined to include fixed and moveable structures and vessels, vehicles or aircraft.[2] The kind of premises cases to which the 1960 Act typically applies are:

1. Shops, supermarkets and offices. There is liability under the Act in respect of persons who come on to dangerous workplaces, e.g. where an employee visits third party premises.
2. Open spaces such as public parks, forestry tracks, recreational areas, car parks, railways platforms or a football stadium.
3. Private or rented property.

Although the duty is statutory, it is to take reasonable care only, and you will have to be prepared to prove fault. Very frequently this will mean obtaining information as to the length of time the hazard was in existence, and pleading a system of inspection and maintenance case. So where a health service employee slipped on the icy surface of a path at her place of employment, an averment that the defenders had failed to have the path made safe by salting or gritting "within a reasonable period" was irrelevant without specification of that period.[3] Similarly, in a case where the pursuer slipped on a patch of vegetation on a railway platform, it was held that failure to show the length of time the danger had been in

---

[1] Occupiers' Liability (Scotland) Act 1960 s.2(1).
[2] Occupiers' Liability (Scotland) Act 1960 s.1(3).
[3] *McGuffie v Forth Valley Health Board*, 1991 S.L.T. 231.

existence was fatal to the pursuer's case.[4] In *Wallace v City of Glasgow District Council*,[5] the Inner House held that a hole in a tenement back court did not set up a prima facie breach of the section and that pleadings which simply averred the existence of the hole and the breach of the 1960 Act were irrelevant. The system of inspection of a reasonable landlord should have been pled. This is not an invariable requirement. A working distinction can perhaps be drawn between a permanent structural or design defect, for which no system of inspection is required, and a transient hazard such as a spillage which will generally require details as to the length of time it has been present. In *Scott v Glasgow District Council*[6] the pursuer slipped on steps that were in a defective condition. Lord Johnston held that the condition of the steps was sufficient to establish an actionable hazard even though no system of inspection was pled. It was reasonable inference from the established facts that a proper system would have discovered the hazard. In *McMillan v Lord Advocate*[7] a raised metal strip on the floor which was a half-inch proud of the doorway was held to constitute a hazard. In similar vein in *Love v Motherwell District Council*[8] it was held that a local authority was liable for the defective condition of a swing in a playpark, without any system of inspection having been pled.[9] The breakage of the swing raised a prima facie inference of negligence which it was for the defenders to rebut.

Where you think that res ipsa loquitur might apply it is prudent to make averments which narrow down the issue, and in particular exclude possibilities other than the defender's negligence. So in *McDyer v Celtic Football and Athletic Club Ltd*[10] the pursuer sustained a hand injury when timber fell from a beam attached to a canopy. The claim was dismissed at first instance, but thereafter allowed to go to proof where averments were made that the wood had recently been added to the canopy, that the weather was calm, and that the canopy was inaccessible to members of the public. No other particular breach of duty was required. In *Inglis v London Midland and Scottish Railway Co*[11] the pursuer was the father of a child who fell through a railway compartment door which opened unexpectedly during travel. The pursuer excluded interference by any person, and any negligence by the child. In the circumstances an inference of negligence arose against the railway company.

What is a hazard?

Accidents frequently occur in open spaces and it can be difficult to distinguish an actionable hazard from the everyday obstacles encountered in all daily life. As a general rule, permanent features of the natural land- 19–02

---

[4] *Cordiner v BRB*, 1996 S.L.T. 209.
[5] *Wallace v City of Glasgow District Council*, 1995 S.L.T. 23.
[6] *Scott v Glasgow District Council*, 1994 G.W.D. 28-1715.
[7] *McMillan v Lord Advocate*, 1991 S.L.T. 150.
[8] *Love v Motherwell District Council*, 1994 S.C.L.R. 761.
[9] But see *McDyer v Celtic Football and Athletic Co Ltd*, 2000 S.C. 379. Piece of timber falling from a football stadium does not constitute res ipsa loquitur.
[10] *McDyer v Celtic Football and Athletic Club Ltd (No.1)*, 2000 S.C. 379.
[11] *Inglis v London Midland and Scottish Railway Co*, 1941 S.C. 551.

scape which may constitute a hazard but which are not concealed or unusual and which present an obvious danger are not actionable by an adult. So in *Tomlinson v Congleton Burgh Council*[12] an adult claimant ran and dived head first into a lake suffering catastrophic injuries. He could not recover damages. Amongst other matters the danger was obvious. Similary in *Graham v East of Scotland Water Authority*,[13] the Authority had no duty to fence a reservoir which ran along the side of a road. A feature of many of the cases is that the pursuer is either familiar with the danger by usage, or is presumed to know about it by reason of its obviousness. So whilst the occupier of a public right of way was held to have a duty of care under the Act it did not extend to a requirement to make an outdoor path safe, particularly where the pursuer could identify the danger and could have retraced his steps.[14] It would still be open to a pursuer to show particular circumstances which meant that the danger was not known or obvious to him. The same rule probably applies to permanent man-made features which do not present any special or unusual risk. See *Duff v East Dunbartonshire Council* for an example of a case where proof was allowed because the danger was concealed and not known to the pursuer. The same case also establishes that a landowner occupier is presumed to know the features of his terrain.[15] Everything will depend on the particular circumstances and the particular pursuer. You should obtain as much knowledge as possible as to the existence of the hazard, and what timeous steps could have been taken to repair it. Wherever possible try to establish if there has been a history of accidents at the locus.

Whilst the Act is helpful in defining the situations in which a duty of care arises, the practitioner will thereafter have to mobilise evidence to show lack of reasonable care. You should note that the standard of care is particular to the individual visitor to the premises. This means that the courts will expect greater precautions to be taken to prevent injury to young children than may be required where the accident is to an adult.[16]

Who is an occupier?

19–03 The first step is to make factual enquiries to identify the occupier at the time of the accident. This is frequently not the owner or landlord of premises but the person who has control and possession of the premises at the time of the accident, i.e. the person who is able to say who shall and who shall not come onto the premises:

> "It is I think clear on authority that a person is only in occupation or control for these purposes if he is in a position in law to say who shall and who shall not come on the premises."[17]

---

[12] *Tomlinson v Congleton Burgh Council* [2004] 1 A.C. 46.
[13] *Graham v East of Scotland Water Authority*, 2002 Rep. L.R. 58.
[14] *Johnson v Sweeney*, 1985 S.L.T. (Sh. Ct.) 2.
[15] *Duff v East Dunbartonshire Council*, 2002 Rep. L.R. 98.
[16] *Titchener v British Railways Board*, 1984 S.C. (H.L.) 34.
[17] *Murray v Edinburgh DC*, 1991 S.L.T. at [255].

It is possible that this states the test too narrowly, and that the occupier is not confined to the person with day-to-day control. In *Wheat v Lacon*[18] the House of Lords held that an occupier need not have exclusive control over the premises. It is sufficient that he has some degree of control which he may share with others. Two or more persons may be occupiers, each under a duty of care:

> "Wherever a person has a sufficient degree of control over premises that he ought to realise that any failure on his part to use care may result in an injury to a person coming lawfully there, then he is an occupier."[19]

The *indiciae* of occupation and control are discussed at some length in *Gallagher v Kleinwort Benson Trustees Ltd*,[20] where the pursuer fell from scaffolding. He convened nine defenders under both the Occupiers' Liability Act 1960 and the Workplace (Health, Safety and Welfare) Regulations 1992. The action was dismissed against seven defenders. In particular it was pointed out that a landlord who lets premises to a tenant is treated as parting with all control of those premises (in the absence of special circumstances) and is not an occupier of them under the Act.

In *Mallon v Spook Erection Ltd*[21] a child was scalded in an open air market. It was held that both the stallholder and the operators of the open-air market were in breach of their respective duties as occupiers.

The first port of call for practitioners in defective premises cases should be the keyholder in place at the time of the accident. Where there is no keyholder or any other person to whom the owner has conceded control and possession, the owner will be liable under the Act.[22]

Landlord and tenant cases

Where your client is injured inside a council house, or on the pathway leading up to it, you should check if he is a tenant of the house either under a sole or joint tenancy. If so his remedy is likely to be against the landlord for breach of contract in respect of the obligations of maintenance and repair and habitability. These are implied in the contract of lease in terms of the Housing (Scotland) Act 2001 Sch.4. Schedule 4(1) provides:

19–04

> "The landlord in a Scottish secure tenancy must—
>
> (a) Ensure that the house is, at the commencement of the tenancy, wind and watertight and in all other respects reasonably fit for human habitation, and
> (b) Keep the house in such condition throughout the tenancy."

---

[18] *Wheat v Lacon* [1966] 1 All E.R. 582.
[19] *Wheat v Lacon* [1966] 1 All E.R. 582 at [593].
[20] *Gallagher v Kleinwort Benson Trustees Ltd* Unreported March 12, 2003 Court of Session.
[21] *Mallon v Spook Erection Ltd*, 1993 S.C.L.R. 845.
[22] See *Johnson v Sweeney*, 1985 S.L.T. 2.

In terms of Sch.4(2) the landlord must inspect before the commencement of the tenancy to identify any work necessary to comply with the duty in para.4(1)(a).

Guidance on the standards which meet reasonable fitness for human habitation are contained in Sch.10.4 and 10.5. In *Morgan v Liverpool Corporation*[23] Lord Atkin stated:

> "If the state of repair of a house is such that by ordinary use damage may naturally be caused to the occupier, either in respect of personal injury to life or limb, or injury to health, the house is not in all respects reasonably fit for human habitation."

In that case a broken sash cord at a window constituted a breach of the obligation. In *Haggerty v Glasgow Corporation*,[24] injury was caused to a child by a cracked pane of glass in a doorway. Lord Atkin's test was approved, although on the particular facts extraordinary force had been used which took the case beyond ordinary usage.

The landlord has a further obligation to keep the structure and exterior in repair,[25] and the installations in repair and proper working order.[26]

Perhaps the most important practical rule when acting for an injured tenant is to remember that liability does not arise unless you can prove either:

> (i) that the defect was in existence at the commencement of the tenancy. The fit for human habitation obligation has been held to constitute a warranty, and to cover latent as well as patent defects[27]; and
>
> (ii) that the landlord had been put on notice of the defect and that the repairing obligation had been triggered.[28]

In *Kerr v East Ayrshire Council*[29] the court held that failure to install safety glass at a door entrance was a breach of the 1960 Act.

You should make vigorous efforts to establish when any complaint was made and to whom. Almost all local authorities have computerised housing repair records, and you should seek these in correspondence, or by way of recovery of documents.

Visitors, family members and other non-tenants

19–05 These persons have no contractual right against the landlord, but they do have rights under s.3(1) of the 1960 Act. This provides that where the landlord is responsible for the maintenance and repair of the premises, he owes the same duty to persons using the premises as he does to the

---

[23] *Morgan v Liverpool Corporation* [1927] 2 K.B. 131.
[24] *Haggerty v Glasgow Corporation*, 1964 S.L.T. (Notes) 54.
[25] Housing (Scotland) Act 1987 Sch.10.3(1)(a).
[26] Housing (Scotland) Act 1987 Sch.10.3(1)(a) and (b)(i).
[27] *Todd v Clapperton*, 2009 S.L.T. 837.
[28] *Wolfson v Forrester's Trustees*, 1910 1 S.L.T. 318.
[29] *Kerr v East Ayrshire Council*, 2005 S.L.T. 67 (Sh Ct).

tenant. So where you act for the child of a tenant who is injured, there may be a claim under the 1960 Act. A very good example of a successful action is the case of *Hughes Tutrix v Glasgow District Council*[30] where a child was injured by a defective toilet bowl that had been the subject of a previous complaint. Again the practitioner must take immediate steps to establish either that the defect was in existence at the commencement of the tenancy and could have been discovered by reasonable inspection, or had been the subject of a complaint which had not been acted upon. In the case of *Guy v Strathkelvin District Council*,[31] Lord Johnston held that a child who suffered from asthma, caused on the averments by dampness and condensation, had a cause of action under s.3(1) of the 1960 Act in respect of breaches of the defenders' obligations under the Housing (Scotland) Act 1987.

Common parts of buildings and premises

Clients frequently come to harm in areas such as common stairways or back courts. In most cases the landlord is regarded as having retained control of these areas. He remains sufficiently in control of the premises to have a duty of care to all persons coming onto the premises. The landlord will therefore owe a duty both to the tenant and to any family member or visitor in respect of the common parts. The duty is one of reasonable care, which means tht once again there will have to be specific notice of the defect to trigger a repairing obligation, or alternatively averments that the defect had been in existence for a length of time which a reasonable system of inspection would have discovered. Most local authorites have adopted the Model Tenancy Agreement which provides for inspection of common parts, although very few local authorities carry this out.[32] In the case of *Kirkham v Link Housing Group*[33] the pursuer fell over a raised flagstone in a back door pathway. The case failed because on the construction of the tenancy agreement the defect was not in a common part but in an area which related solely to the pursuer's tenancy. There was no duty to inspect or repair in the absence of a complaint. In *Johnstone v City of Glasgow District Council*[34] the pursuer slipped on the broken step of a common stairway. The defect had been reported only after the accident. The evidence was that the stair had been defective for a period of three months. In the absence of any evidence as to a reasonable system of inspection, the court was not prepared to draw an inference of lack of care. In *Davie v Edinburgh Corporation*,[35] the pursuer's husband was killed after falling down an unlit common stair. The lights had been out for six weeks. The pursuer averred that the defenders had failed to carry out reasonable inspections of the lighting and had allowed the stair to be unlit for a period of at least six weeks. The defenders averred that

19–06

---

[30] *Hughes Tutrix v Glasgow District Council*, 1982 S.L.T. (Sh. Ct.) 70.
[31] *Guy v Strathkelvin District Council*, 1997 G.W.D. 2-63.
[32] See *Cherry Steven v Lanarkshire Housing Association Limited* Unreported April 10, 2007 Hamilton Sheriff Court.
[33] *Kirkham v Link Housing Group* [2010] CSOH 31.
[34] *Johnstone v City of Glasgow District Council*, 1986 S.L.T. 50.
[35] *Davie v Edinburgh Corporation*, 1977 S.L.T. 5.

they had carried out periodic inspections. The court held that the pursuer was bound to give notice of what system of inspection the defenders ought to have instituted in the exercise of their duty of reasonable care to see to it that the lights were operating, and the action was dismissed. Lord Maxwell stated:

> "If the pursuers had averred that the defenders made no inspection at all of the lights in the stair it might have been enough for relevancy and the issue would then have been whether the defenders had a system of inspection or not, not whether it was a good one."

In appropriate cases there may be prospects of establishing fault by averring that there was no system of inspection at all.

Contractors as occupiers

19–07 Accidents and injuries are frequently caused by independent contractors. In some situations the courts may regard the owner as still in possession and control of the premises with a duty of care towards visitors which is personal to them and non-delegable.[36] In addition courts will usually regard a contractor as having the necessary control and possession to qualify as an occupier.[37] The liability of a contractor is to take reasonable care for persons he should have in contemplation. In *AC Billings & Sons Ltd v Riden*[38] the court held:

> "In my opinion the Appellants [contractors] were under a duty to all persons who might be expected lawfully to visit the house, and that duty was the ordinary duty to take such care as in all the circumstances of the case was reasonable to ensure that visitors were not exposed to danger by their actions."[39]

All contractors should carry public liability insurance. The simple rule in practice is that you should proceed initially against the contractor, and to avoid any complicated argument on the liability of the owner if an insurer for the contractor can be traced.

---

[36] *Cremin v Thomson*, 1956 S.L.T. 357.
[37] See *Wheat v Lacon* [1966] 1 All E.R. at [595].
[38] *AC Billings & Sons Ltd v Riden* [1958] A.C. 240.
[39] See also *Mooney v County Council of Lanark*, 1954 S.L.T. 137. A visitor to the tenancy was injured on a pathway under construction. The county council were held liable as contractors.

CHAPTER 20

ACCIDENTS AT WORK

Since 1992 and the passing of the "Six Pack Regulations", discussion of **20–01**
liability for accidents at work has been dominated by the interpretation
of these regulations and the other European based regulations which
have been passed before and since. Practitioners now require to have a
clear understanding of the distinctive European origins of this legislation,
as well as a good working knowledge of the layout and scheme of the
actual regulations. This section contains a brief introduction to the
problems and challenges which personal injury practitioners now face in
dealing with claims arising from accidents in the workplace.

THE SIX PACK REGULATIONS

The Six Pack Regulations came into force on January 1, 1993. Various **20–02**
parts of the different regulations apply from different dates. Increasingly
the regulations comprise the whole statutory regime for accidents at
work. The regulations represent the transposition of EC Directives into
United Kingdom law. They are not the first example of directive-based
regulations in the health and safety field.[1] The motivation for this legislation is two-fold:

1. To reduce the unacceptably high instances of workplace injury and disease throughout the EC.
2. To prevent unfair economic competition by Member States where cost reductions are achieved at the expense of worker health and safety.

The keystone is the Framework Directive 89/391/EEC. This Directive
sets out the matrix principles for EC health and safety law. The Framework Directive became the Management of Health and Safety at
Work Regulations 1992, and Approved Code of Practice. The Framework Directive was followed by five individual (daughter) directives
addressed to specific topics. The individual directives have been transposed into United Kingdom law by passing separate sets of regulations

---

[1] See, for example, Control of Substances Hazardous to Health Regulations 1988 (SI 1988/1657), Noise at Work Regulations 1989 (SI 1989/1790). More regulations have followed, e.g. the Construction (Design and Management) Regulations 2007 (SI 2007/320), Lifting Operations and Lifting Equipment Regulations 1998 (SI 1998/2307), Provision and Use of Work Equipment Regulations 1998 (SI 1998/2306).

under the Health and Safety at Work Act 1974 s.47(2), which provides: "a breach of duty imposed by health and safety regulations shall so far as it causes damage be actionable except insofar as the Regulations provide otherwise". The full list of the Six Pack Regulations is as follows:

1. Management of Health and Safety at Work Regulations 1992, now replaced by the Management of Health and Safety at Work Regulations ("MHSWR") 1999;
2. Workplace (Health, Safety and Welfare) Regulations 1992;
3. Provision and Use of Work Equipment Regulations 1992, now replaced by Provision and Use of Work Equipment Regulations ("PUWER") 1998;
4. Personal Protective Equipment at Work Regulations 1992;
5. Manual Handling Operations Regulations 1992; and
6. Display Screen Equipment Regulations 1992.

To this list should now be added:

7. Lifting Operations and Lifting Equipment (Operation) Regulations 1998 ("LOLER") which supplements PUWER 1998 as regards lifting equipment; and
8. Work at Height Regulations 2005 ("WAHR") which implements EC Directive 2001/45.

You should note that by art.16.3 the provisions in the Framework Directive apply in full to all the areas covered by the individual directives, without prejudice to any more stringent and specific provisions contained in the latter. The Framework Directive is a general universal template on which the particular provisions are overlaid. The matrix approach is summarised in art.6.2, which obliges employers to take measures necessary for the safety and health protection of workers on the basis of general principles of prevention. These are:

- Avoid risk.
- Assess and evaluate risks which cannot be avoided.
- Combat risk at source.
- Adapt work to the individual.
- Adapt to technical progress.
- Replace the dangerous by the non-dangerous or less dangerous.
- Develop an overall safety and prevention of hazard policy.
- Give collective measures priority over individual protective measures.
- Give appropriate instructions to workers.

These principles are set out in United Kingdom legislation by the MHSWR and the Approved Code of Practice which accompanies them.

THE EUROPEAN DIMENSION

Purposive interpretation

The regulations must be construed "purposively", i.e. they must be interpreted according to the spirit and purpose of the originating directive and any judicial dicta from the European court. Purposive interpretation was defined by Lord Templeman as follows:

20–03

> "It follows that in applying the national law and in particular provisions of the national law specifically introduced in order to implement Directive 76/207, national courts are required to interpret their national law in light of the wording and the purpose of the Directive in order to achieve the result referred to in the third paragraph marked 189. Thus the courts of the United Kingdom are under a duty to follow the practice of the European Court of Justice by giving a purposive construction to Directives and to Regulations issued for the purpose of complying with Directives."[2]

If there is dispute about the meaning of any of the Six Pack Regulations, that dispute must be resolved by reference to the directive and not any other traditional method of construction. The matter was specifically addressed in the context of the Manual Handling Operations Regulations 1992 in the case of *Cullen v North Lanarkshire Health Board*.[3] At the appeal before the Inner House both parties accepted that the Regulations should be considered in the light of the individual directive. The court also noted that Member States may impose more stringent obligations than those contained in the individual directive, and made a direct reference to the terms of art.1.3 of the Framework Directive, which reads:

> "This Directive shall be without prejudice to existing or future national and community provisions which are more favourable to protection of the safety and health of workers at work."

The clear "purpose" of the Directives is to *improve* health and safety standards. In the cases of *English v Lanarkshire Health Board*, and *McGhee v Strathclyde Fire Brigade*, Lords Reed and Hamilton held that argument by analogy with the Factories Act legislation was not appropriate, given the distinctive nature of the new regime. However, wherever possible the regulations should be interpreted in such a way that they do not diminish the existing protection afforded to employees.[4]

The UK origins of the legislation

The regulations have been passed under the Health and Safety at Work Act 1974. It is worthy of note that s.1(2) of the Act provides:

20–04

---

[2] *Lister v Forth Dry Dock Co. Ltd*, 1989 S.L.T. 540 (HL).
[3] *Cullen v North Lanarkshire Health Board*, 1998 S.L.T. 847.
[4] See *Taylor v City of Glasgow Council*, 2002 S.C. 364.

"Provisions of this part relating to the making of health and safety regulations ... and the preparation and approval of Codes of Practice shall in particular have effect with a view to enabling the Acts as specified in the third column of Schedule 1 and the Regulations or other instruments enforced under those enactments to be progressively replaced by a system of Regulations and Approved Codes of Practice operating in combination with the other provisions of this part and designed to maintain or improve the standards of health, safety and welfare established by or under those enactments."

Amongst the enactments specified in the third column of Sch.1 to the Act are the Factories Act 1961, and the Office, Shops and Railway Premises Act 1963. The idea that previous legislation is to be replaced by regulations and Approved Codes of Practice designed to *improve* health and safety standards is a "purpose" which does not solely come from Europe, but is contained within the heart of the UK legislation.[5]

Direct effect against an emanation of the state

20–05 Where the employer undertaking is an "emanation of the state" an injured worker may sue that employer directly on any ground which is a breach of one of the Directives. This is known as the doctrine of "direct effect". It will be appropriate in any area covered by the Directives which does not appear to have been transposed in full to the regulations. A direct effect action is analogous to a breach of statutory duty case, but the statute in question is the Directive itself. The article of the Directive must be unconditional and sufficiently precise before it is directly enforceable, i.e. before the litigant can bypass national legislation and rely directly on the terms of the Directive. This is radically different from the mere interpretative rule of purposive construction. In *English v North Lanarkshire Council*,[6] Lord Reed held that the Work Equipment Directive had direct effect against the defenders who were an emanation of the state. An emanation of the state normally meets three tests:

1. It is an entity providing a public service.
2. The service is under the control of the state.
3. It possesses or claims special powers.[7]

It would appear from both national and European precedents that the kinds of bodies which qualify are:

(a) Local and regional authorities.[8]

---

[5] As was pointed out by Baroness Hale in *Smith v Northamptonshire County Council* [2009] I.C.R. 734.
[6] *English v North Lanarkshire Council*, 1999 G.W.D. 7-351.
[7] See *Doughty v Rolls Royce* [1992] I.R.L.R. 126. Rolls Royce was held *not* to be an emanation of the state, on the basis that it fulfilled condition 2 (the state was the majority shareholder) but not conditions 1 and 3.
[8] *Fratelli Constanzo* [1989] E.C.R. 1839.

(b) Privatised water companies.[9]
(c) Tax authorities.[10]
(d) Police authorities.[11]
(e) A grant-maintained school.[12]
(f) Public health authorities.[13]

This is a list of defenders very familiar to personal injury practitioners and there is certainly scope for arguments presented on the basis of direct effect.[14] It is fair to say that whilst there was considerable academic excitement about the application of the doctine of direct effect, it has had very little impact on the day to day conduct of employers' liability litigation.

1. THE MANAGEMENT OF HEALTH AND SAFETY AT WORK REGULATIONS 1999

These regulations are the United Kingdom equivalent of Framework Directive 89/391/EEC.

20–06

Civil liability for breach of regulation now exists in the employment situation, but not otherwise as regards third parties (reg.22). The principal provisions of the regulations are as follows:

Regulation 3—risk assessment

"Every employer shall make suitable and sufficient assessment of the risk to the health and safety of his employees to which they are exposed."

20–07

This is for the purpose of identifying the measures which he requires to take to comply with the regulations, namely preventive and protective measures.

Regulation 4—principles of prevention to be applied

The employer is obliged to implement any preventive and protective measures on the basis of the principles set out in Sch.1 to the Regulations.

20–08

These follow closely the terms art.6.2 of the Framework Directive (see para.20–02) and are a critical part of the pleader's armoury.

---

[9] *Griffin v South West Water Services Ltd* [1995] I.R.L.R. 15.
[10] *Becfar* [1982] E.C.R. 52.
[11] *Johnston v Chief Constable of RUC* [1987] I.C.R. 83.
[12] *Fidge v Governing Body of St. Mary's School, The Times*, December 1996.
[13] *Marshall v Southampton and South West Health Authority* [1986] E.C.R. 723.
[14] The other possibility is that an individual may take a "*Francovich* action" (*Francovich v Italian State* [1991] E.C.R. I-1357): a worker injured in the employment of an individual employer may be able to take proceedings against the State for failure fully to implement an EC Directive. This is known as "horizontal" direct effect. Difficulties surrounding such an application mean that the doctrine will have little day-to-day practical significance for practitioners.

Regulation 5—health and safety arrangements

20–09 These are tied to the preventive and protective measures and provide for their planning, organisation, control, monitoring and review. Where an employer employs more than five employees, there should be a written record.

Regulation 7—health and safety assistance

20–10 "Every employer shall appoint one or more competent persons to assist him in undertaking the measures imposed on him."

Regulation 10—information for employees

20–11 "Every employer shall provide comprehensible and relevant information with regard to risks to employee health and safety identified by the risk assessment, the preventive and protective measures."

Regulation 13—capabilities and training

20–12 "Every employer shall take into account the capabilities of employees as regards health and safety when allocating work. This means that training should be provided on recruitment, and where there are new or increased risks. This training shall be repeated periodically where appropriate."

The Regulations come with an Approved Code of Practice. Such a code is issued:

"For the purpose of providing practical guidance with respect to the requirements of any provisions of ... health and safety regulation."[15]

An Approved Code can only be issued by the Health and Safety Commission with the specific consent of the Secretary of State. Many of the provisions of the EC Directives were "brokered" by the Health and Safety Commission into Codes of Practice and Guidance Notes. The approval of the Secretary of State is necessary because codes are doing what would otherwise have been achieved by regulations.

In addition the Health and Safety Executive ("HSE") have published a raft of supporting information and literature, for example, *Five Steps to Risk Assessment, Guidelines on Risk Assessment,* and *Guidance on Information, Instruction and Training.* The pamphlet *Five Steps to Risk Assessment* was their most widely circulated publication ever, with more than five million copies distributed. Such HSE literature, Codes of Practice, Guidance Notes, etc. are normative of the standard of care required. Whilst the individual Regulations based on the Daughter Directives may have specific reference to the workplace or particular work activity, it is important to keep in mind that the MHSWR sets out the overarching statutory framework. The regulations made under the

---

[15] Health and Safety at Work etc. Act 1974 s.16.

Daughter Directives tend to be more stringent and prescriptive and as a result there has been little reference in the reported cases to the MHSWR. It is certainly true that no right of action will arise simply for failure to carry out a risk assessment.[16] But liability will arise where a risk assessment would have identified a real and not negligible hazard and suitable precautions could have been put in place. In *McLellan v Dundee City Council*[17] it was held that a failure to carry out a suitable and sufficient risk assessment which would have identified a specific need for training was a breach of reg.3 of the MHSWR 1999. This had a direct causative link to the injury. This breach was in addition to the particular breaches relating to lack of training contained in regs 8 and 9 of PUWER 1998. Every workplace writ should have reference to a potential breach of the MHSWR. The importance of risk assessment and the preventive measures can be seen from the undernoted cases.

RISK ASSESSMENT IN THE COURTS

In *Robb v Salamis*[18] Lord Hope described the aim behind the MHSWR and the Work Equipment Regulations as the same.

20–13

> "It is to ensure that work equipment which is made available to workers may be used by them without impairment to their safety or health; see Article 3(1) of the Work Equipment Directive. This is an absolute and continuing duty, which extends to every aspect related to their work; See Article 5(1) of the Framework Directive. It is in that contact that the issue of foreseeability becomes relevant. The obligation is to anticipate situations which may give rise to accidents. The employer is not permitted to wait for them to happen. The sheriff misdirected himself on this point."

It cannot be stressed highly enough that the key duty on employers is the avoidance of risk. It is only thereafter with regard to risks which cannot be avoided that the hierarchy of, e.g. replacing the dangerous with the less dangerous is applicable. Smith L.J. stated in *Allison v London Underground*[19] that insufficient judicial attention had been paid to the concept of risk assessment. The plaintiff had been employed by London Underground Ltd as a driver. She developed a shoulder strain relating to her task of handling the traction brake controller. She later developed tenosynovitis of the right hand and wrist as a result of prolonged use of the traction brake controller. She alleged breach of reg.3 of the MHSWR 1999 and regs 4 and 9 of PUWER 1998.

The requirement to carry out a suitable and sufficient risk assessment was more stringent than any common law duty.

---

[16] *Logan v Strathclyde Fire Board* Unreported January 12, 1999.
[17] *McLellan v Dundee City Council* [2009] CSOH 9.
[18] *Robb v Salamis*, 2007 S.C. (H.L.) 71.
[19] *Allison v London Underground* [2008] EWCA Civ 71.

"To say that the training is adequate if it deals with the risks which the employer knows about is to impose no greater a duty than exists at common law. In my view the statutory duty is higher and imposes on the employer a duty to investigate the risks inherent in his operations, taking professional advice where necessary."[20]

It is suggested that pleading breaches of the MHSWR should now be the first resort for practitioners. When injury has occurred the likelihood is that some identifiable risk has materialised. There is then a very high onus on a defender to show why such a risk should not have been identified and could not have been avoided. Having pled breaches of the MHSWR 1999, you should pursue the recovery of the risk assessment via specification of documents.

Pleading points

20–14 It is frequently pointed out in the case reports that a breach of reg.3 (suitable and sufficient risk assessment) is not necessarily causative. However as cases such as *Allison* and *Robb* indicate, where a suitable and sufficient risk assessment would have identified the risk, it is then up to the employer to take steps to avoid it, or replace the dangerous with the less dangerous. Your own expert in evidence should be able to identify the risk and specify ways in which the risk could have been avoided, or reduced by replacing the dangerous with the less dangerous. Typically you should aver breaches of reg.3 (suitable and sufficient risk assessment), reg.4 (preventive and protective measures) in terms of Sch.1, reg.5 (health and safety arrangements), with possibly reg.7 (appointment of competent person), reg.10 (information for employees) and reg.13 (training). It is true that in most workplace accidents there will be other more specific regulations which will apply either to the activity or the place of work, and which should be pled as well. Pleading the MHSWR reminds the court of the overall context in which these matters must be considered.

2. THE WORKPLACE (HEALTH, SAFETY AND WELFARE) REGULATIONS 1992 ("WHSWR")

20–15 These far-reaching regulations apply to all premises which are not domestic premises and are made available to any person as a place of work.[21] Mines and quarries are excluded, as are construction sites. You should note, however, that where construction work is in progress within a workplace, it is to be treated as a construction site and excluded from the regulations only if it is fenced off. Otherwise both the WHSWR and the Construction Regulations will apply (see guidance note to the WHSWR, para.11). As from April 6, 2007, reg.13(1)–13(4) (falls and

---

[20] See also *Threlfall v Hull City Council* [2011] I.C.R. 209.
[21] Workplace, Health, Safety and Welfare Regulations 1992 reg.2.

falling objects) were repealed by the Work at Height Regulations 2005, and falling objects are now governed by reg.10 of the WAHR 2005.

Regulation 4—on whom are the duties placed?

Regulation 4(1) places duties on every employer in respect of the workplace under his control and where his employees work. Regulation 4(2) also imposes duties on any person who has control of the workplace in respect of matters within that person's control to any extent. The importance of control is illustrated by the approach of the Court of Appeal in England in the case of *King v RCO Support Services Ltd*.[22] The plaintiff was employed by the first defendants as a steam cleaning operative. The first defendants had contracted to supply cleaning services to the second defendants at their garage, where buses were cleaned. When the plaintiff arrived at work on January 25, 1996, the yard was covered with ice. In accordance with his normal practice, he set about the task of spreading grit over the surface of the yard. He then slipped and fell whilst manually gritting the yard. It was argued that there was a prima facie breach of reg.12(3) (floor to kept free of substance which may cause a person to slip), and that the host undertaking was liable. There was no evidence to suggest that the host undertaking retained any degree of control, and as a result the case against them under reg.12(3) failed. It was the first defendants who had control of the operation, and to that extent the workplace, and it was observed obiter that the employer would have no answer to the claim under reg.12(3). As Lord Wheatley observed in the case of *Nisbet v John Orr, Chief Constable of Strathclyde Police and North Lanarkshire Council*:

20–16

> "It is not said that the first defender was in control of the pursuer's workplace at the time of the accident, and more importantly in terms of Regulation 4(2)(c) it is not said that he was in control of the matter which was the cause of the accident at the material time. The only averments made by the pursuer suggest that control over the relevant matter which caused the accident lay elsewhere. If there are no averments that the first defender was in some way in control of what happened, then the first defender cannot be held responsible for what happened."

In *Lynch v Ceva Logistics*,[23] the Court of Appeal held that although the owner of factory premises could not control the way in which independent electrical contractors carried out their work, they could control the way in which pedestrian movement was organised throughout the factory and liability for inadequate separation of pedestrians and vehicles was established where the claimant was struck by a reach truck. There was a breach of reg.17 of the WHSWR.

The practitioner must therefore ask himself who had control of the

---

[22] *King v RCO Support Services Ltd, The Times*, February 7, 2001.
[23] *Lynch v Ceva Logistics* [2011] I.C.R. 746.

workplace, in the practical sense of being able to influence the operation which gave rise to injury.

To whom are the duties owed?

20–17 There is no doubt that protection extends to persons who are working at the premises, whether or not they are employed by the host undertaking. So a travelling salesman visiting a supermarket on a Friday in the course of his employment will have the benefit of the legislation. What is the position if he returns as a customer on a Saturday? In *Donaldson v Hayes Distribution Services Ltd*,[24] the pursuer was crushed between a lorry and a loading bay whilst collecting her purchases at a shopping centre. She relied amongst other matters on a breach of reg.17 of the WHSWR (suitabiity of traffic routes). It was held that the purpose of the European legislation was to protect workers, and on a sound construction there was no new protection for non workers present in the workplace, who have to continue to rely on the Occupiers' Liability Act 1960. This approach does seem to leave the duty under reg.3 of the MHSWR (undertaking to carry out risk assessment with regard to all persons liable to be affected by its activities) somewhat in isolation. However unless the issue is taken to the Supreme Court, practitioners must take the law as settled.

The key Regulations which are likely to found liability are as follows.

Regulation 5—maintenance of workplace and equipment devices and systems

20–18 Regulation 5(1) provides:

> "The workplace and the equipment, devices and systems to which this regulation applies shall be maintained (including cleaned as appropriate) in an efficient state and efficient working order and in good repair."

In the Factories Act 1961, "maintained" means "maintained in an efficient state and efficient working order and in good repair".[25] Liability is strict.[26] The Approved Code of Practice para.20, confirms that "efficient" in this context means efficient from the view of health, safety and welfare, not productivity or economy. In *Butler v Grampian University Hospital NHS Trust*,[27] the pursuer was a carer who required to take a patient in a wheelchair into a toilet cubicle. It was averred that there was insufficient room in the cubicle to lift the patient face to face. In construing reg.5(1), Lord MacFadyen held:

> "It is in my view necessary to have regard for the purposes of the Workplace Regulations as disclosed in the directive to which they give effect. The purpose, it seems to me, is to secure a continued state

---

[24] *Donaldson v Hayes Distribution Services Ltd*, 2005 S.C. 523.
[25] Factories Act 1961 s.176(1).
[26] See *McLaughlin v East and Midlothian NHS Trust*, 2001 S.L.T. 387.
[27] *Butler v Grampian University Hospital NHS Trust*, 2002 S.L.T. 985.

of efficiency. It is, therefore, in my view a relevant averment of breach of reg 5 to set out circumstances supporting the conclusion at the time of the accident the workplace was not efficient from the point of view of safety. I therefore consider the case based on reg 5(1) falls to be admitted to probation."

Similarly in the case of *Clegg v North Ayrshire Council*,[28] the pursuer slipped on a ramp which had become worn away. Lord Carloway held that it was:

"[N]ot ... kept in good repair since it was suffering from an appreciable amount of wear comprising the erosion of the finer materials of the concrete, leaving exposed the granite coarse aggregate stone. Since I am of the view that this wear materially contributed to the pursuer's slip and the regulation imposes strict liability ... I am also of the view that the pursuer has made out a case on liability based on this regulation [reg.5(1)]."

The regulation also imposes a requirement for cleaning, and the presence of a chip on a ramp in the case of *Gilmour v East Renfrewshire Council*,[29] was conceded to be a relevantly averred breach of reg.5(1). More recently in *Munro v Aberdeen City Council*[30] the pursuer slipped on ice in the workplace and argued that the presence of ice constituted a breach of reg.5(1). No reg.12(3) case was pled. Lord Malcolm reviewed all the recent case law on reg.5(1) and held that the duty to maintain did not apply to transient hazards, but was generally directed to structural matters, or at the most non-structural hazards which were present so frequently that reg.5(1) applied.

What this means in appropriate cases is that there is no need to plead reasonable foreseeability or a system of inspection case.

"Equipment devices and systems" are stated in reg.5(3)(a) to be those to which the WHSWR apply, as well as mechanical ventilation systems. From that it seems clear that "equipment" in these Regulations should mean permanent structural objects such as workstations (reg.7), traffic routes (reg.12), windows (reg.14), doors and gates (reg.18), escalators (reg.19), sanitary conveniences (reg.20), and washing facilities (reg.21). Stairs, fixed ladders and scaffolding can conceivably be described as equipment (see reg.13 prior to repeal by WAHR). There is a distinction to be drawn with the PUWER 1998 where work equipment is defined in reg.2 as "any machinery, appliance, apparatus, tool or installation for use at work (whether exclusively or not)", and where the Guidance Notes at para.64(c) state that "structural items" (for example, walls, roofs, stairs, fences) are not classified as work equipment. In *Beck v United Closures & Plastics Plc*,[31] Lord McEwan held that a door was equipment under PUWER and not under WHSWR 1992. This does seem to fly in the face

---

[28] *Clegg v North Ayrshire Council* Unreported May 7, 2002 Court of Session.
[29] *Gilmour v East Renfrewshire Council* Unreported May 29, 2002 Court of Session.
[30] *Munro v Aberdeen City Council*, 2010 S.L.T. 964.
[31] *Beck v United Closures & Plastics Plc*, 2001 S.L.T. 1299.

of reg.5(3)(a), but was cited with approval by the House of Lords in *Spencer-Franks v Kellogg-Brown and Root Ltd.*[32] In the speech of Lord Rodger a useful list of items which might be work equipment under PUWER was set out. The list is as follows:

- Lathes for cutting metal.
- Axes for chopping wood.
- A furnace for refining ore.
- Chalk for writing on blackboards.
- Needles for sewing model dresses.
- Hoists for raising loads.
- Forklift trucks for carrying the loads from place to place.
- Bicycles, vans or aircraft for carrying letters or parcels.
- Clocks to let employees know the time.
- Radios for them to listen to music whilst they work.
- Kettles for them to make tea or coffee.
- Water coolers at which they can drink and gossip.
- Screwdrivers or radios belonging to the employees which they are allowed to bring in and use at work.

Ultimately the matter was one of impression, and it was doubtful whether it was wise to draw too sharp a division between work equipment and fabric of the structure. A door, including the door closer on it, was therefore work equipment in terms of PUWER. The obvious lesson is to plead breach of both sets of Regulations in the alternative.

Regulation 8

20–19 Regulation 8 requires that every workplace shall have suitable and sufficient lighting. This denotes strict liability. In *Miller v Perth and Kinross Council*,[33] Lord Hamilton stated that the legislation meant that:

> "During the hours of darkness or when natural light is not sufficient to allow all safe passage, artificial lighting is required which is suitable and sufficient for such passage. This is not a guarantee of safe passage, but involves a judgement of what is suitable and sufficient in the circumstances."

Regulation 11

20–20 Regulation 11 provides that the workstation shall be suitable, and this is likely to mean ergonomically suitable. In *Duncanson v South Ayrshire Council*[34] the pursuer was injured when her left calf came into contact with the bottom corner of the door of a steel cabinet. It was conceded that the place where the pursuer was injured was a workstation. The section was looked at rather more narrowly by Lord MacFadyen in the

---

[32] *Spencer-Franks v Kellogg-Brown and Root Ltd*, [2008] S.C. (H.L.) 159.
[33] *Miller v Perth and Kinross Council*, 2002 Rep. L.R. 22.
[34] *Duncanson v South Ayrshire Council*, 1999 S.L.T. 519.

case of *Butler v Grampian University Hospitals NHS Trust*, where a toilet cubicle was held not to be a workstation. He stated:

> "Although I am not persuaded that it would be right, in the absence of a statutory definition of 'workstation' to attempt a comprehensive definition, I do consider that the word denotes a place at which there is gathered together or assembled or set up an item or items of equipment or apparatus for the purpose of enabling a certain category or certain categories of work to be done there."

Regulation 12

The most frequently litigated regulation is likely to be reg.12—condition of floors and traffic routes, which is dealt with in Ch.18 at para.18–20.

20–21

Regulation 13

Regulation 13 provided against falls or falling objects, and was repealed by the WAHR 2005, with effect from April 6, 2007. Practitioners may find some assistance from the Approved Code of Practice, paras 106–147, which looks at the factual scenarios relating to falls and falling objects at work, including roof-falls, stacking and racking accidents, falls into dangerous substances, falls during the loading or unloading of vehicles, and falls from the use of scaffolding within the workplace.

20–22

Remaining regulations

There are detailed regulations as regards doors, windows, organisations of traffic routes, as well as other general health and safety and occupational hygiene requirements.

20–23

3. PROVISION AND USE OF WORK EQUIPMENT REGULATIONS 1998 ("PUWER")

These regulations replaced the Provision and Use of Work Equipment Regulations 1992, and came into force on December 5, 1998. The Regulations are intended to implement EC Directive 89/655/EEC, and amendments to that Directive.

20–24

Work equipment is defined as "any machinery, appliance, apparatus, tool or installation for use at work (whether exclusively or not)" (reg.2(1)). In the Guidance Note, paras 62–64 state that the Regulations cover "almost any equipment used at work". There was a long list of examples of equipment attached to the guidance note to PUWER 1992. The new statutory definition is even wider. Lord Rodger's list in *Spencer-Franks* (see para.20–18) indicates the broad reach of the legislation. "Use" means any activity involving work equipment and includes starting, stopping, programming, setting, transporting, repairing, modifying, maintaining, servicing and cleaning, and related expressions shall be construed accordingly (reg.2(1)).

Regulation 3

20–25 Regulation 3 provides that the duties in the regulations are imposed on an employer and apply to "such equipment provided for use or used by an employee of his at work".

In addition, duties are imposed on any person who has control to any extent of:

1. work equipment;
2. a person at work who uses or supervises or manages the use of work equipment; or
3. the way in which work equipment is used at work, and to the extent of his control (reg.3(3)). In *Smith v Northamptonshire County Council*[35] the claimant was a social care worker who was injured on a defective ramp leading to the home of a client she was required to visit. The House of Lords held that this was not work equipment in relation to the council. They did not own it, and it had not been adopted or incorporated by them into their system of work.

So the first questions for the practitioner in any case are, "Who owns the work equipment?", and "Who has control of it at the material time?"

There may well be factual situations where both an employer and a principal contractor will be liable under these regulations, where the latter has control to any extent over the equipment used. It follows that these regulations also encompass liability for injury to non-employees using the control test.[36]

Regulation 4

20–26 Regulation 4 provides that every employer (or persons with control as previously defined) "shall ensure that work equipment is so constructed or adapted as to be suitable for the purpose for which it is used or provided".

Regulation 5

20–27 Regulation 5 provides that every employer (or person with control as previously defined) "shall ensure that work equipment is maintained in an efficient state, in efficient working order and in good repair". This has to be looked at from a health and safey perspective[37] and means strict liability.[38] A useful insight into how the Regulations will be interpreted in practice can be gained from the case of *Johnstone v Inglis*, where similar provisions of PUWER 1992 were considered by Lord Bonomy. The allegation was that a machine had caused injury by starting suddenly. The Lord Ordinary held that the question of statutory breach was sui-

---

[35] *Smith v Northamptonshire County Council* [2009] I.C.R. 734.
[36] See *Margaret Hunter v William Murray* Unreported April 11, 2002 Court of Session.
[37] *Ball v Street* [2005] P.I.Q.R. P22.
[38] See *Hislop v Lynx Express Parcels*, 2003 S.L.T. 785.

table for a jury. Either there had been a breach of reg.5 (now reg.4(3)) in that the machine was not suitable for use because it was liable to start up unexpectedly, or a breach of reg.6 (now reg.5) in that it was not properly maintained.

The scope of work equipment has been widely interpreted by the courts. A bolt securing fishplate was work equipment in terms of PUWER 1992.[39] A curtain rail has been held to be work equipment.[40] A table has been held to be work equipment.[41] In England a van has been held to be work equipment.[42] A ladder has been held to be work equipment.[43]

Regulations 7, 8 and 9

Regulations 7, 8 and 9 impose duties involving specific risks of work equipment, information and instructions which should be provided pertaining to the use of the work equipment, and health and safety training which should be provided. The case of *English v North Lanarkshire Council* makes it plain that there is a hierarchy of precautions derived from the EC Directive, and these measures are very much secondary to the duty to reduce risk at source. In any case involving information, instruction and training practitioners should refer to the HSE Guidance Notes, and various HSE leaflets which have been provided on the subject.

20–28

Regulations 11–24

These are the hardware regulations and refer mainly to machines. They include a raft of detailed provisions in respect of fencing, control isolation systems, lighting, maintenance, marking and warnings in respect of equipment and machinery. In some regards the fencing provisions appear to be less stringent than the existing provisions under the Factories Act ss.14–18. In particular in reg.11, "Dangerous Parts of Machinery", some of the measures require to be done "to the extent that it is practicable to do so". This would appear to be a less exacting standard than was previously required of employers by the courts. Since the case of *Summers v Frost*,[44] it was accepted that the fencing duties in respect of dangerous machinery are absolute. This is an example of the new regulations failing to meet the existing standards. In *McGowan v Watson*[45] Lord MacPhail held that the previous more stringent standards governing contact with machinery should apply.

20–29

---

[39] *Kelly v First Engineering Ltd*, 1999 S.C.L.R. 1025.
[40] *McLaughlin v East Lothian Council*, 2001 S.L.T. 387.
[41] *Mackie v Dundee City Council*, 2001 Rep. L.R. 62.
[42] *Crane v Premier Prison Service* [2001] CLY 3298.
[43] *Wharf v Bildwell Insulations Ltd* [1999] C.L.Y. 2047.
[44] *Summers v Frost* [1955] 1 All E.R. 870.
[45] *McGowan v Watson* [2005] CSOH 172.

Regulations 25–30

20–30 These regulations deal specifically with mobile work equipment such as forklift trucks, for which there is a very high injury rate.[46] The mobile equipment may be self-propelled, towed or remote controlled and may incorporate attachments. Pedestrian-controlled work equipment such as lawnmowers is not covered by the regulations. There are specific precautions against rollover and requirements for tip over protection structure.

The remaining regulations relate to power presses.

4. PERSONAL PROTECTIVE EQUIPMENT AT WORK REGULATIONS 1992

20–31 These regulations came into force from January 1, 1993.

Regulation 4—provision of personal protective equipment

20–32 A duty is placed on the employer to ensure that personal protective equipment ("PPE") is provided to employees who may be exposed to risk of their health and safety. The guidance note again takes us back to the template MHSWR and the requirement to identify and assess risk to health and safety. Where there is a risk PPE is very much a last resort, in keeping with the hierarchy of the Framework Directive. As it is put in para.22 of the Guidance Note: "Employers should therefore provide PPE and training where there is a risk to health and safety that cannot be adequately controlled by other means".

The equipment should be readily available and it is illegal for the employer to levy a charge for any equipment provided (guidance note para.25).

In pre-regulation cases the first hurdle for the pursuer to overcome was to persuade the court that PPE was required. This was rarely straightforward except in cases where it was the uniform practice in the industry for PPE to be provided. The approach should now be to assess whether there is a risk of injury which is not insignificant, and which has not been adequately controlled by other means.

In the case of *Henser-Leather v Securicor Cash Services Ltd*[47] the Court of Appeal held that a security guard who was shot should have been provided with body armour as there was a risk to the plaintiff's health and safety as defined by reg.2. In *Threlfall v Hull City Council*[48] the court held that rubbish collectors should have been issued with cut resistant gloves.

---

[46] In 2007 forklift trucks accounted for 27% of all over three day injury.
[47] *Henser-Leather v Securicor Cash Services Ltd* [2002] EWCA Civ 816.
[48] *Threlfall v Hull City Council* [2011] I.C.R. 209.

Regulations 6 and 7

Regulation 6 provides that PPE must be assessed for suitability. Regulation 7 provides that the PPE must be maintained in an efficient state, in efficient working order and in good repair. It is again suggested that this involves strict liability, and that the regulation will be automatically breached as soon as the equipment is in disrepair, whether this involves a patent or latent defect. However, injury must be related to the purpose of the protective equipment. A worker who suffered frostbite because of a hole in steel capped boots provided to him, failed to establish a causative breach of the PPE Regulations.[49]

20–33

In the case of *Toole v Bolton Metropolitan Borough Council*[50] the Court of Appeal held that a proper assessment under reg.6 would have established that Kevlar gloves were not adequate equipment to protect against a syringe needle injury. In the circumstances the plaintiff's failure to wear them did not amount to contributory negligence.

Regulation 9—information, instruction and training

At common law a further difficulty for pursuers was to establish that there was a requirement for an employer to provide information, instruction and training in PPE. In one case it was indicated that where protective equipment was available, the court should be slow to expand the duty into one of exhortation to use.[51] The approach was more flexible where there was a latent danger, for example, risk of dermatitis. In the case of *Campbell v Lothian Health Board*[52] it was held that there was a duty not simply to make gloves available for employees, but also to warn them of the dangers of dermatitis, and to persuade and encourage them to wear gloves. This is clearly the approach envisaged by reg.9.

20–34

Regulation 10—duty to ensure the use of PPE insofar as reasonably practicable

A final difficulty for pursuers related to the use of PPE. In *McWilliams v Sir William Arrol & Co*[53] the pursuer was the widow of a steel erector who should have been provided with a safety harness. The evidence was to the effect that he would not have worn such a harness even if one had been provided, and absolvitor was granted. Regulation 10 now places a heavy onus on the employer to make sure that any PPE is used. In the case of *Hensor-Leather* the judge at first instance held that even if body armour had been provided, then the plaintiff would not have worn it. As the equipment was not provided in the first place, the defendants were in breach of reg.10 and the question of whether the claimant would have worn it or not was not relevant.

20–35

---

[49] *Fytche v Wincanton Logistics* [2005] P.I.Q.R. P5.
[50] *Toole v Bolton Metropolitan Borough Council* [2002] EWCA Civ 588.
[51] *Qualcast v Haynes* [1959] A.C. 743 (H.L.).
[52] *Campbell v Lothian Health Board*, 1987 S.L.T. 665.
[53] *McWilliams v Sir William Arrol & Co*, 1962 S.L.T. 121.

5. MANUAL HANDLING OPERATIONS REGULATIONS 1992

20-36 These regulations have been in force since January 1, 1993. They are not restricted to back injuries, but relate to any injury which might occur during the "transporting or supporting of a load including lifting, putting down, pushing, pulling, (carrying or moving thereof) by hand or by bodily force" (reg.2). The application of human effort for the purpose of transporting or supporting a load is a necessary pre-requisite. Holding on a rope or pulling a lever to crank up a load-bearing pallet truck, or switching on a machine is not a manual handling operation, nor is the action of pulling on a rope whilst lashing down cargo on the back of a vehicle.[54] The use of mechanical assistance such as a hoist or sack truck does not eliminate but simply reduces manual handling, when human effort is still required to move, steady or position the load. Guidance note 14 states that a load must be a "discrete moveable object".[55] This applies to patients or animals receiving veterinary treatment. It also refers to materials supported on a shovel or a fork. An implement or tool such as a chainsaw or, say, a pneumatic jackhammer is not a load whilst it is in use for its intended purpose. So to follow the HSE example, an employee who carries a chainsaw to a tree is carrying a load, but the chainsaw ceases to be a load after it is switched on to cut, even though the employee might be supporting it. In *McIntosh v City of Edinburgh Council* a ladder which an employee moved was held to be a load.[56] It has been held that pushing a lawnmower is not a manual handling operation.[57] Repetitive handling of trussed chickens was held by the Inner House not to constitute manual handling where it was opined that prima facie "a load" should be something substantial.[58]

The duty is imposed on employers. Once again the regulations should be considered together with the MHSWR. Paragraph 21 of the HSE guidance note states:

> "These regulations should not be considered in isolation. Regulation 3(1) of the Management of Health and Safety at Work Regulations 1992 requires employers to make a suitable and sufficient assessment of the risks to the health and safety of their employees while at work. Where this general assessment indicates the possibility of risk to employees from the manual handling of loads, the requirements of the present regulations should be followed."

Lord Carloway described the process in *Taylor v City of Glasgow Council*[59] as follows:

---

[54] The examples in this paragraph are taken from HSE Guidance Note paras 16–18.
[55] In *Divit v British Telecommunications Plc*, 1997 G.W.D. 12-530 Lord Cameron held that a moveable flap within a telephone kiosk could constitute a "load".
[56] *McIntosh v City of Edinburgh Council*, 2003 S.L.T. 827.
[57] *Mitchell v Inverclyde DC*, 1997 G.W.D. 31-1593.
[58] *Hughes v Grampian Country Foods*, 2007 S.L.T. 635.
[59] *Taylor v City of Glasgow Council*, 2002 S.L.T. 689.

"This scheme cascades down partly through the Management of Health and Safety at Work Regulations 1992 and partly by way of the Manual Handling Directive, into the Manual Handling (Operations) Regulations 1992."

In *Davidson v Lothian and Borders Fire Board*[60] it was accepted that to succeed a pursuer must prove:

(a) that he or she was engaged in a manual handling operation;
(b) that the operation carried a risk of injury;
(c) that the event occurred within the ambit of that risk; and
(d) that actual injury thereby occurred.

Regulation 4—the master regulation

This establishes a clear hierarchy of measures:

20–37

1. Where there is a risk of injury the employer should avoid manual handling operations so far as resonably practicable (reg.4(1)(a)).
2. Where it is not reasonably practicable to avoid manual handling, the manual handling operation should be assessed having regard to the statutory checklist (reg.4(i)(b)(i)).
3. The risk of injury should be reduced as far as reasonably practicable.

A risk of injury "need be no more than a foresseable possibility, it does not need to be a probability".[61] There is a very useful practical filter with reference to the weight of loads printed in the HSE Guidelines. This is specifically intended to provide "an approximate boundary within which operations are unlikely to create a risk of injury sufficient to warrant a more detailed assessment".

The diagram consists of a series of boxes through which the load passes in relation to the body. If the load is held at any of the positions in the diagram it should not exceed the figure in the box for a man, with women being able to handle one-half to two-thirds of the weight. If the weight of the load is below the guidelines at all phases of the operation, a pursuer will require to refer to the other factors in the statutory checklist and in particular:

- The task (Guidance Note, paras 54–76). Does the task involve an excessive rate of work, frequent or prolonged physical effort, sudden movement, stooping, reaching up or twisting of the trunk?
- The load (Guidance Note, paras 77–89). Factors in addition to weight include the shape of the load, the risk of dropping the load, whether the load is unstable or likely to shift, or whether the load is sharp, hot or otherwise potentially damaging.

---

[60] *Davidson v Lothian and Borders Fire Board*, 2003 S.L.T. 939.
[61] *Anderson v Lothian Health Board*, 1996 Rep. L.R. 88, and approved by the Inner House in *Cullen v North Lanarkshire Council*, 1998 S.L.T. 847.

- The working environment (Guidance Note, paras 90–96). Is the floor slippery, unstable or uneven? Are there extremes of temperature? Is the lighting poor?
- Individual capability (Guidance Note, paras 97–107). Does the task require unusual strength or height, or does it relate to employees who have a health problem? Is special training required?

As from September 17, 2002 the MHOR 1992 have been amended by adding reg.4(3), which obliges an employer to have regard to:

(i) The physical suitability of an employee to carry out the operations.
(ii) The clothing, footwear and other personal effects he is wearing.
(iii) His knowledge and training.
(iv) The results of any risk assessment in terms of the MHSWR 1999.
(v) Whether the employee is within a group of employees identified by that assessment as being especially at risk.
(vi) The results of any health surveillance in reg.6 of the MHSWR 1999.

These are to be relevant both in assessing whether there is a risk of injury, and also in determining the appropriate steps to reduce that risk.

Risk of injury

20–38 Where there is a risk of injury the duty is to avoid manual handling altogether. In the case of *Cullen v North Lanarkshire Council*,[62] the pursuer was standing on the top of a fence in the back of a truck and was lifting the fencing up and throwing it onto a nearby skip. Whilst he was holding a section of the fencing above his head he caught his heel and he fell backwards off the lorry. The Inner House held that the regulations should be construed purposively by looking at the Directive. The Lord Justice-Clerk stated that once the pursuer established that there was a manual handling operation and a risk of injury it was for the defenders to avoid the need for manual handing, or to plead and prove that it was not reasonably practicable to do so. For that reason alone the pursuer must succeed. Where a defender can show that it is not reasonably practicable to avoid manual handling completely, they must carry out a specific manual handling risk assessment. As was made clear in the case of *Cullen*, this is not to decide *whether* there is a risk, but is to identify and take steps to reduce that risk to the lowest level reasonably practicable. Once again the onus will be on the defenders to plead and prove that all reasonably practicable steps were taken.

The kinds of steps which can be taken are contained in paras 104–163 of the Guidance Note. In addition HSE have published *Manual Han-*

---

[62] *Cullen v North Lanarkshire Council*, 1998 S.L.T. 847.

dling—Solutions You Can Handle[63] which contains illustrated guidance on methods of reducing the risk of manual handling injuries. A pursuer will generally be able to plead that very simple precautions such as the use of a sack truck, platform truck or hoists would have reduced the risk of injury. The Inner House also considered the regulations in the case of *Taylor v City of Glasgow Council*,[64] holding that a janitor who was injured whilst helping two other men to manoeuvre a large cupboard up two flights of stairs set forth circumstances which might foreseeably give rise to injury. The court also held that it was the factors related to the specific manual handling operation which required to be considered. Averments that a removal man required to lift a piano where foliage obscured some raised stones which were slippery were held to be sufficient to give notice of a foreseeable risk of injury.[65] In the case of *Skinner v Aberdeen City Council* the defenders established that it was not reasonably practicable to avoid manually lifting and laying slabs. They claimed that general training which had been provided was sufficient to reduce the risk of injury to the lowest level reasonably practicable. The court looked at the factors specified in Sch.1 to the 1992 Regulations. The defenders' failure to carry out a risk assessment though a breach of duty was not necessarily causative of the injury.[66] However a failure to provide specific training and information about equipment and methods when lifting, meant that the risk was not reduced to the lowest level reasonably practicable. Training was also critical in *Walsh v TNT UK Ltd*,[67] where there was a lack of refresher training to prevent instinctive but dangerous lifting manouevres. Similarly, in *O'Neill v DSG Retail Ltd*[68] it was held that training should be practical, and that the issuing of health and safety literature to each employee did not meet the requirement.

Overview

A problem frequently arises in respect of strain injuries where there is difficulty in isolating the actual incident which has caused the strain. A typical scenario is that the employee notices the strain at the time, but carries on working throughout the course of the day and only realises the severity of the injury when he wakens in extreme pain the following morning. In that kind of case you should take immediate steps to identify any witnesses who can speak to your client crying out or specifically complaining of the back strain at the point of injury. This is not a concern where you are founding on repeated lifting, but where you are relying on a single incident; you must be able to identify the particular incident, and the characteristics which have involved risk. Recover the accident book at the earliest opportunity and obtain as much circumstantial evidence to confirm the nature of the task being carried out by

20–39

---

[63] *Manual Handling—Solutions You Can Handle* (Suffolk: HSE Books, 1994).
[64] *Taylor v City of Glasgow Council*, 2002 S.L.T. 689.
[65] *McDougall v Gordon Speirs trading as John Duncan Removal* Unreported February 25, 2003 Court of Session.
[66] See also *Logan v Strathclyde Fire Board* Unreported January 12, 1999 Court of Session.
[67] *Walsh v TNT UK Ltd*, 2006 S.L.T. 1100.
[68] *O'Neill v DSG Retail Ltd* [2009] I.C.R. 734.

your client at the particular time. A further practical point is that you should always obtain copies of your client's GP notes under mandate, and make sure the medical history supports the claim. The MHOR will not compensate your client for a gardening injury. A number of material discrepancies contained in the contemporaneous accident and medical records caused the pursuer to fail in the case of *Boyd v Lanarkshire Health Board*.[69]

6. HEALTH AND SAFETY (DISPLAY SCREEN EQUIPMENT) REGULATIONS 1992

20–40 These regulations have been in force since January 1, 1993. They relate typically to visual display terminals and it is clear that the regulations are designed to protect the typical secretary or typist using the dedicated word processing system now familiar in every office. Regulation 2 requires the employer to perform a risk assessment. Regulation 4 obliges an employer to plan the activities of users so that work is periodically interrupted by breaks or change of activity. The Guidance Note, para.45, states that occasional five or 10 minute breaks every hour are likely to be more effective than a 15 minute break every two hours, and that breaks should be taken away from the screen. Where the employee requests an eye test, the employer must arrange for such a test at the employer's expense (reg.5). A simple explanation should be given to staff with particular in regard to posture and the need to take advantage of breaks, change of activities and eyesight tests (reg.7). The main litigation potential lies in what is described generically as work-related upper limb disorders, or repetitive strain injury ("RSI"), and includes tenosynovitis, carpal tunnel syndrome, tendonitis and epicondylitis. The whole concept of this kind of RSI is extremely controversial. It is dealt with briefly in the occupational diseases section.

7. LIFTING OPERATIONS AND LIFTING EQUIPMENT REGULATIONS ("LOLER") 1998

20–41 The regulations came into force for all lifting equipment on December 5, 1998. There is an Approved Code of Practice and guidance note issued by the HSE. Examples of lifting equipment are passenger lifts, a dumb waiter in a restaurant, a vehicle inspection hoist, a scissors lift, vehicle recovery equipment or a bath hoist. Duties are now imposed both on the employer who provides the equipment, and also on any person who has control to any extent of: (i) the lifting equipment; (ii) a person at work who uses or supervises or manages the use of lifting equipment; or (iii) the way in which lifting equipment is used (reg.3). The guidance note gives the example of a crane on hire at a construction site to illustrate how the regulations will work. The crane hire company has a duty to tender the

---

[69] *Boyd v Lanarkshire Health Board*, 2000 G.W.D. 9-341.

crane in a suitable condition and thereafter the user has a duty to manage the subsequent lifting operations in a safe manner (Guidance Note, paras 41–42). The lifting equipment is also subject to the terms of the Provision and Use of Work Equipment Regulations 1998 and in particular reg.4(1)–(2) (suitability of work equipment).[70] Further regulations relate to the strength and stability of lifting equipment (reg.4), suitability of lifting equipment for use for lifting persons (reg.5), the positioning and installation of lifting equipment (reg.6), organisation of lifting operations (reg.8), the examination of lifting equipment, defects reporting, and keeping of records (regs 9, 10 and 11).

8. THE WORK AT HEIGHT REGULATIONS 2005

These regulations came into force on April 6, 2005, implementing EC Directive 2001/45/EC. The key requirements are:

20–42

(a) work at height has to be properly planned, appropriately supervised and carried out in a manner which is so far as reasonably practicable safe (reg.4);
(b) no person shall engage in work at height unless he is competent to do so (reg.5);
(c) every employer shall ensure that work is not carried out at height where it is reasonably practicable to carry out the work safely otherwise than at height (reg.6(2));
(d) where work is carried out at height, suitable and sufficient measures should be taken to prevent any person falling a distance (reg.6(3));
(e) where there is still a risk of a fall occurring the employer shall minimise the distance and consequences of a fall (reg.6(5)(a));
(f) there are general requirements for work at height equipment (reg.8);
(g) no person shall work on a fragile surface (reg.9);
(h) the employer shall take suitable and sufficient steps to prevent the fall of any material or objects (reg.10);
(i) particular types of work at height equipment must be inspected (reg.12).

The HSE has estimated that 15 per cent of all accidents relate to falls from height, and the majority of these are concerned with the use of ladders. Schedule 6 specifically addresses situations in which ladders may be used and contains various provisions regarding their suitability and stability. In short an employer is required to carry out a risk assessment to demonstrate that the use of more suitable work equipment is not justified having regard to the short duration in use or conditions on site

---

[70] See the interplay of liability for breach of these regulations in *Delaney v McGregor Construction (Highlands) Ltd*, 2003 Rep. L.R. 56.

which cannot be altered. So in *Bhatt v Fontain Motors*[71] the defendants had recently moved premises and the claimant required to gain access to a loft area. He had been trained to use an A-frame ladder which at all times should have been footed. He used the ladder whilst unfooted and fell to his injury. The Court of Appeal held that the starting point was the Regulations rather than the claimant's conduct. If the work cannot be reasonably avoided from taking place at height, then the risks must be minimised. The key regulations were regs 4 (organisation and planning) and 6 (avoidance of risks from work at height). In the present case the employers were not able to show that it was not reasonably practicable for the work to be done at ground level. Separately with regard to reg.7(2) (suitable equipment) there was no issue that a fixed ladder could have been installed at a reasonable and proportionate cost and there was a separate breach of that regulation. Contributory negligence was confirmed at one third.

---

[71] *Bhatt v Fontain Motors* [2010] P.I.Q.R. P17.

CHAPTER 21

OCCUPATIONAL ILLNESS AND DISEASE

Figures released by the Association of British Insurers show that claims **21–01** for occupational illness and diseases now amount to over half of all employer liability claims. This type of case presents special difficulties to the personal injury practitioner. This chapter gives a brief overview of the generic issues, and considers some of the common types of claim.

1. LEGAL CAUSATION IN DISEASE CASES

Most occupational illness claims are in a different category from "single **21–02** event" accidents such as road traffic collisions, or tripping and slipping accidents. In disease cases there may have been exposure to harmful processes over a long number of years, spanning many employers and places of employment. Some of these no longer exist. Frequently doctors cannot identify the precise aetiology whereby a disease develops. The medical evidence will ultimately rest on statistical studies or epidemiology. There may be other possible causes for the condition, for example, hearing loss may be caused by exposure to excessive noise, but it can also be caused by simple ear infections. The illness may have resulted from working conditions in existence 30 or 40 years ago. These may be impossible to recreate, and there are obvious difficulties in establishing their causative effect. Liability often depends on proving to the court that exposure to substances or processes was "excessive".

In fact these problems are not insuperable. The courts have recognised the evidential difficulties involved. A number of mainly Scottish cases, all eventually decided in the House of Lords, now form the legal framework for all industrial disease cases.

The first case is *Wardlaw v Bonnington Castings Ltd*.[1] The pursuer contracted pneumoconiosis. He was exposed to respirable dust from two types of grinding machines. Only one emission of dust was negligent, and the medical evidence was unable to distinguish whether the negligent source or the innocent source had caused the injury. The House of Lords held that the defenders were liable for the whole injuries. Lord Reid stated:

---

[1] *Wardlaw v Bonnington Castings Ltd*, 1956 S.L.T. 135.

"It appears to me that the source of his disease was the dust from both sources, and the real question is whether the dust from the sling grinders materially contributed to the disease. What is a material contribution must be a question of degree. A contribution which comes within the exception of de minimis non curat lex is not material, but I think that any contribution which does not fall within that exception must be material. I do not see how there can be something too large to come within the de minimis principle, but yet too small to be material."

21–03 Lord Reid returned to the topic in the case of *Gardiner v Motherwell Machinery & Scrap Co Ltd*[2] where the pursuer had contracted dermatitis. He had been exposed to employment conditions which might have caused the disease, but there was a complicated history with other possible causes. Lord Reid stated:

"[W]here a man who has not previously suffered from a disease contracts that disease after being subject to conditions likely to cause it, and where he shows that it starts in a way typical of disease caused by such conditions, he establishes a prima facie presumption that his disease was caused by such conditions."

This presumption is a rebuttable presumption of fact, i.e. it is still open to the defenders to prove that the cause was non-occupational, but the burden is on them. This is a very useful weapon where there are competing causes.

In *McGhee v National Coal Board*,[3] the pursuer contracted dermatitis during his employment in the defenders' brickworks. It would appear that appropriate precautions were taken during the working day, but there were no adequate washing facilities for employees to use before going home. The pursuer had to cycle home before washing. Medical evidence was unable to say precisely how the dermatitis was caused, nor that the failure to wash had more probably than not caused the injury. It was clear that the failure had materially increased the risk of injury. Lord Kilbrandon stated:

"When you find it proved (a) that the defenders knew that to take the precaution reduces the risk, chance, possibility or probability of contracting of a disease, (b) that the precaution has not been taken, and (c) that the disease has supervened, it is difficult to see how those defenders can demand more by way of proof of the probability that the failure caused or contributed to the physical breakdown."

Lord Reid stated:

---

[2] *Gardiner v Motherwell Machinery & Scrap Co Ltd*, 1962 S.L.T. 2.
[3] *McGhee v National Coal Board*, 1973 S.L.T. 14.

"I can see no substantial difference between saying that what the defender did materially increased the risk of injury to the pursuer and saying that what the defender did made a material contribution to his injury."

The approach contained in these cases has been judicially approved by **21–04** the House of Lords in the case of *Fairchild v Glenhaven Funeral Services*,[4] a consolidated appeal to the House of Lords.

The facts were that Mr Fairchild and others had contracted fatal mesothelioma from asbestos exposure caused by the defendants' breach of duty. The limitations of scientific evidence meant that the plaintiffs could not prove that any particular exposure had caused the disease, and equally were unable to disprove that other possible causes elsewhere had not caused the disease. The plaintiffs failed in the lower courts, where scant regard was paid to the earlier Scottish cases.

Lord Bingham identified fundamental factors underlying this kind of case:

"1. C was employed at different times for different periods by both A and B, and
2. A and B were both subject to a duty to take reasonable care to take all practical measures to prevent C inhaling asbestos dust because of the known risk that asbestos dust (if inhaled) might cause a mesothelioma, and
3. both A and B were in breach of that duty in relation to C during the periods of C's employment by each of them with the result that during both periods C inhaled excessive quantities of asbestos dust and
4. C is found to be suffering from a mesothelioma, and
5. any cause of C's mesothelioma other than the inhalation of asbestos dust at work can be effectively discounted, but
6. C cannot (because of the current limits of human science) prove, on the balance of probabilities, that his mesothelioma was the result of his inhaling asbestos dust during his employment by A or during his employment by B or during his employment by A and B taken together."

The case law took a further twist in *Barker v Corus*.[5] The claimant had died of asbestos related mesothelioma. There were a number of possible employment exposures. The House held (Lord Rodger dissenting) that the *Fairchild* exception was properly described as the wrongful creation of a risk of injury, and that damages should be apportioned according to the relative degree of contribution. The legislature quickly stepped in and by s.3 of the Compensation Act 2006 it was established that a victim should recover in full from any responsible person who had caused or materially increased the risk of injury. The so called *Fairchild* exception

---

[4] *Fairchild v Glenhaven Funeral Services* [2002] P.I.Q.R. P28.
[5] *Barker v Corus* [2006] 2 A.C. 572.

was considered by the Court of Appeal in *Bailey v Ministry of Defence*.[6] The facts were that the claimant suffered hypoxic brain damage after she aspirated on her own vomit whilst in the care of the defendants. The cause of the aspiration and failure of the claimant to react was a combination of weakness caused by the defenders' lack of care (tortious cause) and pre-existing pancreatitis (non-tortious cause). It was held that it was enough that the negligent cause had made a material contribution, and damages were awarded in full. Lord Justice Waller summarised the position in relation to cumulative cause cases as follows:

> "If the evidence demonstrates on a balance of probability that the injury would have occurred as a result of the non-tortious cause or causes in any event, the claimant will have failed to established that the tortious cause contributed. [*Hotson v East Berkshire Health Authority* [1987] A.C. 750] exemplifies such a situation. If the evidence demonstrates that 'but for' the contribution of the tortious cause the injury would probably not have occurred, the claimant will (obviously) have discharged the burden. In a case where medical science cannot establish the probability that 'but for' an act of negligence the injury would not have happened, but can establish that the contribution of the evident cause was more than negligible, the but for test is modified and the claimant will succeed."

The full reach of the *Fairchild* exception is not yet closed. The Court of Appeal was prepared to apply it in the case of vibration white finger in *Brown v Corus UK Ltd*[7] where it was held that by failing to reduce the level of vibration, C had exposed B to an increased risk of suffering from vibration white finger, and causation was established. The situation is different where there are a number of causes which operate not cumulatively but independently. In that situation proof must be on the balance of probabilities.[8]

2. USE OF EPIDEMIOLOGY IN DISEASE CASES

21–05 Frequently medical science cannot ascribe a physical mechanism of injury, but clinical experience confirms a connection. Epidemiology may be used to shore up the association. It is subject to a number of caveats. First of all where it may confirm a hypothetical association, there must also be a clear focus on individual characteristics. As Lord Rodger said in the case of *Sienkiewicz v Greif (UK) Ltd*[9] at [575]:

> "In other words, since, by its very nature, the statistical evidence does not deal with the individual case, something more will be required before the court will be able to reach a conclusion, on the

---

[6] *Bailey v Ministry of Defence* [2009] 1 W.L.R. 1052.
[7] *Brown v Corus UK Ltd* [2004] P.I.Q.R. P30.
[8] *Wilsher v Essex Area Health Authority* [1987] 2 W.L.R. 425.
[9] *Sienkiewicz v Greif (UK) Ltd* [2011] 2 W.L.R. 523.

balance of probability, as to what happened in that case. For example, where there is a strong epidemiological association between a drug and some condition which could have been caused in some other way, that evidence along with evidence that the claimant developed the condition immediately after taking the drug may well be enough to allow the judge to conclude, on the balance of probability, that it was the drug that caused the claimant's condition."

Next, the epidemiology itself must be robust. In *Sienkiewicz* Lord Kerr considered that the epidemiological evidence relating to asbestos related disease was "the promotion of a theory rather than the establishment of the facts and it did not constitute evidence from which reliable conclusions could be made" (*Sienkiewicz* at [586]).

Finally, care must be taken in its presentation. In *Dingley v The Chief Constable of Strathclyde Police*[10] evidence from an actual epidemiologist was led. In *McTear v Imperial Tobacco McTear v Imperial Tobacco Ltd*[11] the Lord Ordinary was unwilling to accept a link between smoking and lung cancer, because no one had explained to him the basis of epidemiological evidence relating to it.

3. TAKING THE CLIENT'S INSTRUCTIONS

A useful starting point is to check the DWP list of prescribed diseases. **21–06** Prescription is made and benefit is payable for a restricted list of occupations based on research findings which have been considered by the Industrial Injuries Advisory Council. The list is continually being updated in the light of new findings. For example, benefit A12 recently extended the prescription of Carpal Tunnel Syndrome both to the use of hand-powered vibrating tools at the times the symptoms first developed, or repeated palmar flexion and dorsiflexion of the wrist for at least 20 hours per week for a period or periods amounting in aggregate to at least 12 months in the 24 months prior to the onset of symptoms. If your client presents with a prescribed condition, and he or she has been employed in a listed occupation, you can generally proceed with some confidence. You should have the client apply for industrial injuries disablement benefit and run that file parallel to the common law damages claim.

You should then obtain any relevant Health and Safety Executive ("HSE") publication so that you have a basic understanding of the client's condition, and the health and safety context.

At least one hour should be set aside for the first interview. In addition to the normal essentials of a pursuer's statement you will require the following:

(i) A full employment history since leaving school, to enable all employments other than the "target" to be excluded.

---

[10] *Dingley v The Chief Constable of Strathclyde Police*, 1998 S.C. 548.
[11] *McTear v Imperial Tobacco McTear v Imperial Tobacco Ltd* [2005] CSOH 69.

(ii) A brief medical history.
(iii) Details of the industrial process or source which the client believes has caused the condition. More often than not you will need a "Day in the Working Life" statement with full details of starting and finishing times, job rotation, lunch and tea breaks, to establish a pattern of exposure.
(iv) The present whereabouts and status of potential target employers.
(v) Information as to when the client knew or reasonably should have known that he suffered from a particular condition, and whether there is an urgent time bar problem.

A lot of time will be saved if the client is advised of this by letter, and told to bring this information to the first interview, together with any documentation which can vouch for it. The initial statement should be taken as a working draft only. If the exposure period stretches over a number of years or employers, much of the detail tends to be inaccurate and should be revised in the light of the documentary information which will become available. It is important to identify witnesses who worked with the client in any of the target employments, and to obtain up to date addresses and details. Your client may be able to give this information or you may be able to obtain it from other sources, such as his trade union. Unless there is a time bar problem, there is no point in a letter of intimation or in incurring further costs at this stage. The claim cannot succeed without a specialist medical opinion which contains a positive diagnosis of the condition and connects it on the balance of probabilities with the client's employment.

4. THE MEDICAL EVIDENCE

21–07 The choice of medical expert is crucial. The success or failure of the claim is likely to depend on his opinion and evidence. A report from the client's GP is not sufficiently authoritative. It is worthwhile taking the time to identify a consultant in the appropriate specialty who is known to have an interest in industrial disease and who has previously acted as an expert witness. The letter of instruction to the consultant should contain the client's statement and his GP records and any HSE literature if appropriate. The report can be considerably more expensive than say general orthopaedic reports, and a preliminary fee level enquiry may be advisable. In his clinical work, the consultant will be primarily concerned to reach a diagnosis and treat the condition without necessarily directing his mind to the cause. Even some experienced consultants believe that in forensic work proof of causation has to be beyond reasonable doubt. It is therefore particularly important that the consultant is advised that proof is on the balance of probabilities, i.e. it is more probable than not that the client has the disease *and* that it has been caused or materially contributed to by the exposure to the noxious process. Diagnosis by exclusion will frequently meet this standard. In some cases, where the pursuer has evidence that the defenders have materially increased the risk of disease, all the medical evidence will have to show is that the disease has in fact developed.

After the medical report is received the file should be reviewed. Any ambiguities or uncertainties in the report should be clarified with the consultant by direct telephone discussion. If the report does not support the claim it should be abandoned after an explanatory meeting with the client and a follow-up letter closing the file and advising on time bar.

5. INTIMATION OF THE CLAIM—THE VOLUNTARY PRE-ACTION PROTOCOL

A copy of the disease Protocol is contained in Appendix 3 and practitioners are referred to the details of the scheme and the standard format letters. Where agreement to proceed as a Protocol case is reached the particular advantage is that time for limitation purposes stops running. Where there is a positive medical report, intimation should be sent direct to the employer or employer's insurer. At this stage the allegations of fault need not be detailed, but the letter should contain an appropriate employment history, and a brief description of the process which has caused the injury. A claim where there is only a short period between exposure to the harmful substance and the disease actually occurring is described as a "short latency" case. In these cases, there is generally no difficulty in finding an insurer to deal with the claim. In a long latency case matters are much more problematic. Detailed company searches may require to be made to trace the elusive defender. Where the whole assets and liabilities have been transferred, the responsibility of meeting the employee's claim should rest with the acquiring company, notwithstanding that the original company is still in existence.[12] It has been held in England that an employee's right to claim damages in tort or negligence is also preserved against the acquiring employer, in terms of the Transfer of Undertakings Regulations 1981.[13]

Companies in dissolution or receivership

If the employer company is dissolved, or in receivership, the liquidator or receiver is obliged to provide details of the identity of the company insurers.[14] The Employer' Liability Tracing Office ("ELTO")[15] will carry out a trace on request. It has to be said that historically this route is successful for less than half the enquiries. You might try to trace the insurers by writing to the former directors, although this frequently elicits a dusty answer. All employers were obliged to provide employers' liability insurance following the Employers' Liability (Compulsory Insurance) Act 1969. The Court of Appeal in England has held by a majority that

21–08

21–09

---

[12] See *Britton v Maple & Co Ltd*, 1986 S.L.T. 71.
[13] *Taylor v Serviceteam Ltd* [1998] P.I.Q.R. P201.
[14] Third Parties (Rights Against Insurers) Act 1930 s.2(2).
[15] They are based at Milton Keynes and their email address is enquiries@elto.org.uk.

losses arising from failure to arrange employers' liability insurance attracted a criminal sanction only, and that there was no civil liability.[16] In Scotland Sheriff Principal Bowen has adopted the minority view and found that a director may be personally liable in damages for failure to arrange employers' liability insurance.[17] You can at least threaten a director with proceedings if he fails to disclose the insurers. It is regrettable that there is no single register of company insurers in the United Kingdom, and that companies are not obliged to file their insurance details with the Registrar of Companies. Final recourse may be had to the legal helplines of specialist publications such as *Butterworths Personal Injuries Bulletin* or the Association of Personal Injury Lawyers ("APIL") newsletter. There is a professional organisation which offers to trace insurers on a "no hit, no fee" basis. Where the defender has disappeared, and no insurers can be traced after all diligent enquiry, the reluctant advice to the client must be that the claim cannot proceed and the file should be closed.

An exception to this rule is contained in the provisions of the Pneumoconiosis etc. (Workers Compensation) Act 1979. This Act provides for payments by the Department of Employment for disabled persons (and their dependants where persons have died whilst disabled) in cases of pneumoconiosis, mesothelioma and byssinosis arising from their employment. The principal conditions are that no actions have been brought and none can be brought because the employer has ceased business. The scheme is very useful for those difficult cases where no insurer can be traced. Substantial lump sum payments can be made, depending on the age and disablement of the claimant or deceased.[18]

Restoration to the register

21-10 Target companies in industrial injury litigation are very frequently dissolved. If you cannot trace an insurer, then there is no point in taking the case further. If you have traced an insurer but negotiations have been unsuccessful, you must look to restore the company to the Register of Companies by way of petition. Many companies are now simply struck off by the Registrar of Companies on the grounds that they have ceased trading. Where a search shows that the company has been dissolved, or struck off, you can restore the company to the Register by lodging a petition under the Companies Act 2006 s.1031. The petition can proceed at any time after the date of dissolution where there is a claim for damages for personal injury. However the court will look at questions of time bar when deciding whether to grant restoration.[19] The petition can be raised in the sheriffdom in which the company had its registered office, where its paid-up capital did not exceed £120,000. Companies House

---

[16] *Richardson v Pitt-Stanely* [1995] Q.B. 223.
[17] *Quinn v McGinty*, 1998 Rep. L.R. 107.
[18] Claims should be made to the Department of Environment, Transport and the Regions, HFSO, Zone 1/B4, Cleland House, Bressendon Place, London SW13 5DU. The Department issue a guide to the scheme available on request.
[19] Companies Act 2006 s.1030(2).

publish a very useful leaflet called *Striking off, dissolution and restoration (Scotland)* on this complex area of law. Many of the practical difficulties will be addressed when the Third Party (Rights Against Insurers) Act 2010 is in force, and pursuers will be able to sue insurers directly.

6. PROGRESSING THE CLAIM

Keep the insurers to the Industrial Disease Pre-Action Protocol. After you have intimated, the insurers will seek confirmation of the employment history. The Inland Revenue will provide details of employment based on the client's national insurance contributions, but from 1963 only. Enquiries can take up to four months, but will be quicker if you advise there is an astbestos related claim. Pressure should be kept on the insurers. In some cases there will be a claims history from other employees, and insurers will already have formed an attitude on liability to this type of claim against a particular insured. After the employment history has been vouched for, it should be firmly indicated that delay is not acceptable, and that insurers must settle or face proceedings. If the claim is repudiated or there is undue delay, then the file should be reviewed with the client for court action. The insurers may genuinely require a substantial period to complete investigation and enquiries. However the restrictive way in which limitation has been interpreted in Scotland means that strategy for many insurers is to delay in the hope of a time bar windfall. In cases where the Protocol is agreed, time stops running at the date of the letter of intimation. The practitioner's concern is that the case does not time bar in your hands. You must ensure that an action is raised within the time limits, on the worst case scenario. Alternatively, you might ask the insurer at the commencement of correspondence to confirm that they will waive any time bar from the date of intimation of claim, even for caes not proceeding under the Protocol.

21–11

7. REVIEWING THE EVIDENCE PRIOR TO ACTION

The only reservation you should bear in mind is that the onus will be on your client to establish the basic features of this type of claim. You cannot be too aggressive about raising a court action, if you do not have, or cannot reasonably expect to secure, the necessary evidence to support a prima facie case.

21–12

There should be in the file at least the following:

(i) pursuer's statement;
(ii) medical report;
(iii) statements from witnesses on liability. The courts can be sympathetic to general and impressionistic accounts from witnesses, on occasions preferring this source to the evidence contained in tests or surveys. For example in the leading case on noise-induced hearing loss, *Thompson v Smiths Shipre-*

pairers (North Shields),[20] Mustill L.J. effectively discounted most of the actual noise test readings on the grounds that they were unrealistic. In the case of *Brookes v Coates (UK) Ltd*,[21] where the pursuer had contracted byssinosis a number of years earlier, the judge relied on the witness impressions of dust particles in the air;

(iv) a statement from a family member or close friend detailing the restrictions and social handicap suffered by the pursuer; and

(v) health and safety expert's report. It is virtually impossible to succeed in an occupational claim without a favourable report from an appropriate expert. The report should address the issues of liability and foreseeability, and where applicable should state the generally accepted date of knowledge for the risk, with reference to the appropriate literature.

You will be looking to prove the case from your client's own evidence and any supporting testimony on the facts, from the medical evidence, and from your health and safety evidence which should be based on HSE sources. You should be looking to add documents recovered under the specification of documents procedure, together with the results of any special inspection or test you may carry out at the premises after proceedings are raised.

8. PLEADINGS IN INDUSTRIAL DISEASE CASES

The factual paragraph

21–13 This should contain a description of the factory process, with details of the pursuer's role and duties at the material time, and the source of the exposure complained of. Where the allegation is simply the fact of exposure, for example, asbestos fibres, it might be pled that such fibres were liberated during working occupations, were visible as dust in the air, or were apparent on workers' overalls. Where the allegation is that the exposure was excessive, for example, noise, then there should be averments that the levels exceeded a particular intensity such as 85 decibels, and that the pursuer's daily noise dose exceeded 85dB(A)leq.

The damages paragraph

21–14 The damages paragraph should contain details of the onset of disease and of all medical treatment thereafter including names and addresses of hospitals and general practitioners. There should be a narrative of past and present symptoms and restrictions and a future prognosis based on the medical report. If the condition is permanent, a description of the way in which it will affect the pursuer's future life should be set out. Consideration should be given to a claim for provisional damages where there is a real risk of material deterioration. The Scottish courts have held that

---

[20] *Thompson v Smiths Shiprepairers (North Shields)* [1984] 1 All E.R. 881.
[21] *Brookes v Coates (UK) Ltd* [1984] 1 All E.R. 702.

claims for exacerbation of asthma[22] or noise-induced hearing loss[23] are not appropriate for awards of provisional damages. Wage loss, service claims and financial losses should be set out in the standard format.

The legal duty paragraph

Although the current standard formula is simply to plead "breach of duty at common law" (Initial Writ form PI1), it may be necessary to plead more in industrial disease cases. This is particularly so where there is some doubt about the date of knowledge of the hazard. This is a question of fact in each case. Where there is any doubt about the date of knowledge of this hazard, averments should be made about research, newspaper articles or HSE publications which fix the particular defenders with the requisite state of knowledge at the material time. This may involve a quite detailed search through the literature. The expert will already have his own list, and his guidance should be sought. The kind of averments necessary were considered in the case of *Rae v City of Glasgow Council*[24] where the pursuer claimed that she had suffered respiratory disease by reason of passive smoking. Lord Bonomy stated:

21–15

> "I do not consider the pursuer has made averments from which it could be concluded that the defenders knew or ought to have known of these risks arising from passive smoking. There are no averments of when the risk of lung or respiratory system disease occurring from passive smoking was discovered, or when and by what means the defenders ought to have known of it ... It follows there is no averment of how material such a risk is or when it was discovered. It also follows that there is no averment of when and how the defenders ought to have known of such a risk ... In his submissions counsel for the pursuer made reference to pleadings in other types of industrial disease cases such as those for asbestos-related illness ... If there is a practice of pleading such cases in the form of the present one, I consider that practice fails to set out a basis on which a court could conclude that the pursuer's illness was a foreseeable consequence of the defenders' breach of duty."

Even on old style pleadings those kind of averments did not require to be lengthy to take the case to proof. In *Black v Wrangler (UK) Ltd*,[25] Lady Paton stated that a 1982 consultative document which could be purchased from HMSO contained references to previous research about the dangers of manual handling sufficient to put the defenders to proof on date of knowledge.

The point to remember is that date of knowledge is a matter of fact. It is frequently stated that liability for noise induced hearing loss does not arise at common law until after 1963 following the case of *Thompson*

---

[22] *Bonar v Trafalgar House Offshore Fabrication Ltd*, 1996 S.L.T. 548.
[23] *Paterson v Costain Mining Ltd*, 1998 S.L.T. 413.
[24] *Rae v City of Glasgow Council*, 1998 S.L.T. 292.
[25] *Black v Wrangler (UK) Ltd* Unreported March 14, 2000 Court of Session.

(above). That decision was reached on the evidence before the trial judge, and does not set down any binding legal precedent. Most defenders are happy to concede the point, but if they don't you will have to be prepared to plead and prove date of knowledge in each individual case. Where there is any doubt about the matter, you should lodge a Notice to Admit after defences are in. If you receive a Notice of Non-Admission have your expert produce papers for a date of knowledge inventory, and prepare him to give evidence on the issue.

The statutory provisions

21–16 Relevant statutory provisions may be:

(i) Factories Act 1961 s.4—adequate ventilation.
(ii) Factories Act 1961 s.29(1)—safe place of work. This has been held to encompass "safety from heat, light and noise as well as tangible things".[26]
(iii) Factories Act 1961 s.63—protection from injurious dust and fumes. The effect of s.63 is to require both suppression of dust and fumes at source and prevention of inhalation by use of protective equipment thereafter.
(iv) Construction (Working Places) Regulations 1966 reg.6(2)—protection from injurious fumes and safety from heat, light and noise, by analogy with the Factories Act 1961.[27]
(v) Woodworking Regulations 1974—noise.
(vi) Agricultural (Tractor Cabs) Regulations 1974—noise.
(vii) Noise at Work Regulations 1989.
(viii) Asbestos Regulations 1969.
(ix) Control of Asbestos at Work Regulations 1987.
(x) Control of Asbestos at Work Regulations 2006.
(xi) Manual Handling Operations Regulations 1992.
(xii) Control of Substances Hazardous to Health Regulations ("COSHH") 1988, 1994, 1999 and 2002.
(xiii) Personal Protective Equipment at Work Regulations 1992.
(xiv) Workplace (Health, Safety and Welfare) Regulations 1992.
(xv) Construction (Health, Safety and Welfare) Regulations 1996.
(xvi) Control of Noise at Work Regulations 2005.
(xvii) Control of Vibration at Work Regulations 2005.
(xviii) Construction (Design and Management) Regulations 2007.

9. QUESTIONS OF APPORTIONMENT

21–17 In many occupational diseases, medical science is unable to apportion the effect of cumulative exposure to different employers, or to isolate which particular exposure has caused the condition. The current approach is to decide whether the injury is divisible (dose related) or indivisible.

---

[26] *Carragher v Singer Manufacturing Co Ltd*, 1974 S.L.T. (Notes) 28.
[27] *Canning v Kings & Co Ltd*, 1986 S.L.T. 107.

Mesothelioma is an indivisible injury and following *Fairchild* and the Compensation Act 2006 every defender who is in breach of duty will be liable for the whole damages.

However this approach is not applicable where medical science can make a reasonable estimate at apportioning the role of the different employments. In this kind of case liability is not truly joint and several but successive. For example in *Balfour v William Beardmore & Co*,[28] a pneumoconiosis case where the pursuer was exposed to dust in employments other than the defenders', Lord Strachan stated[29]:

> "The defenders are liable only for the consequences of their actions, and in the peculiar circumstances that means, in my opinion, that they are liable only for the results of the aggravation which their own negligence has caused. Upon the medical evidence it is possible to determine the extent of that aggravation. In these circumstances the correct method of proceeding is, in my view, to assess the full amount of the damage caused by the pursuer's disease, to find the defenders liable for such proportion thereof as corresponds to the proportion of aggravation which their negligence has caused. I do not think that any other view would do justice."

Apportionment can also be carried out in noise-induced deafness cases and cases of vibration white finger.[30]

These are dose related and divisible in the sense that some kind of percentage assessment responsibility however imperfect can be attempted. In *Holtby v Brigham and Cowan (Hull) Ltd*[31] asbestosis was treated as a divisible disease and there was apportionment of damages. *Holtby* contains a strong dissenting opinion as to where the burden of proof lies in these cases. In *Wright v Stoddard International Plc*,[32] an asbestosis case, Lord Uist declined to follow *Holtby* and would have awarded damages in full if liability had been established. The approach of the trial judge to apportionment of damages for noise induced hearing loss is set out in the case of *Thompson*:

> "What justice does demand, to my mind, is that the court should make the best estimate which it can in the light of the evidence, making the fullest allowances in favour of the plaintiffs for the uncertainties known to be involved in any apportionment."[33]

This has important consequences for the choice of defender. There may be a number of potential target defenders. The danger of running a

---

[28] *Balfour v William Beardmore & Co*, 1956 S.L.T. 205.
[29] *Balfour v William Beardmore & Co*, 1956 S.L.T. 205 at [216].
[30] For noise-induced deafness see the case of *Thompson* [1984] 1 All E.R. 881. For vibration white finger, see *Armstrong v British Coal Corp* [1998] C.L.Y. 2842. Note that this was not a "straight line" apportionment. See the later section on vibration white finger.
[31] *Holtby v Brigham and Cowan (Hull) Ltd* [2003] All E.R. 421.
[32] *Wright v Stoddard International Plc* [2007] CSOH 138.
[33] *Thompson v Smiths Shiprepairers (North Shields)* [1984] 1 All E.R. 881 at [910].

multiple defender action is that your client may succeed against only some of the defenders, and become liable in expenses against others. Where liability is joint and several, as in a mesothelioma situation, you should issue the writ against the defender against whom you have the strongest evidence. If that defender wishes to have damages apportioned, he will have to call other employers as third parties. You can then convene them as defenders with little or no risk of expenses. In any event all the pursuer will require to show is that exposure has materially increased the risk of disease followed by the disease itself.

This advice is not appropriate where there is a time bar problem and the writ must be issued without full knowledge of the facts. In that situation all potential defenders should be joined at the outset, and all causes of action should be pled.

Where liability is not joint and several but successive you should take the advice of the medical and health and safety experts before issuing the writ. Ask them to check the latency periods to establish the most likely culprit, and to rule out other employers. In noise-induced deafness cases, the medical experts will say that each successive noisy employment adds cumulatively to hearing loss. Each defender is liable only for their contribution to the whole sum of damages. As a general rule, proceedings should be issued against all insured employers since 1963, where the client has worked for at least a year, and there is reasonable evidence of noise.

10. RECOVERY OF EVIDENCE

21–18 The Disease Protocol has a helpful list of documents which should be disclosed in correspondence. The following is a non-exhaustive list of documents which should be recovered under the specification of documents procedure.

    (i) All documents showing the results of tests or samplings for the period referred to on record, e.g. dust sampling records, etc.
    (ii) In COSHH cases, documents in the hands of the defenders showing their risk assessment exercise, all documents showing the actual steps taken by the defenders to reduce or contain risk, exposure-monitoring records, and all information and training supplied to employees—COSHH regs 6, 9, 11, 12.
    (iii) Where the Manual Handling Operations Regulations 1992 apply, all documents showing risk assessments, all steps taken to reduce incidence of manual handling and to reduce risk of injury to the lowest level reasonably practicable, training records, notes of all information supplied to employees—Manual Handling Operations reg.4.
    (iv) Where the Personal Protective Equipment at Work Regulations 1992 apply, all documents showing purchase, availability and maintenance, and all training records, in terms of regs 7 and 9.

- (v) Noise-induced deafness cases—all noise surveys, records of issue of ear protection, and records of noise assessments by a competent person and information to employees in terms of Noise at Work Regulations 1989 regs 4, 5 and 11, and the Control of Noise at Work Regulations 2005 Regulations regs 5, 6, 7 and 10.
- (vi) Vibration at work cases—all risk assessments, documents showing information, instruction and training whether made at common law and from July 6, 2005 under the Control of Vibration at Work Regulations 2005.

11. PREPARATION FOR PROOF

21–19 It is essential in industrial disease cases that the experts are properly co-ordinated. Medical consultants may have little idea of current health and safety standards and publications. In very many cases the medical opinion is based on a diagnosis by exclusion, i.e. the industrial connection cannot be asserted on the basis of positive evidence but all possibilities other than an industrial cause can be excluded, for example, noise-induced deafness. It will greatly boost the consultant's confidence if he has sight of a health and safety report which confirms the existence of precisely the conditions likely to cause the illness. Prior to the proof you will generally require to lodge:

- (i) Letter from the Contributions Agency confirming the employment history.
- (ii) The GP notes, any hospital records, and any occupational health records.
- (iii) The medical report.
- (iv) The health and safety expert's report with all references and publications being photocopied and lodged.

Each expert should be shown the others' reports. All reports produced by the defenders, and all documents recovered under specification, should be disclosed to the pursuer's experts for their comments. The health and safety expert should be invited to contact the pursuer direct by telephone if there are any last minute matters requiring clarification.

12. TIME BAR IN DISEASE CASES

21–20 This is the most worrying aspect of dealing with these cases. In the majority of disease cases before the courts, there is clear injury and exposure, with the only realistic defence being limitation. There is little doubt that Scottish pursuers are at a distinctive disadvantage compared to pursuers in England with a similar disease.[34]

---

[34] See article by the author "Time out of Joint—Limitation in Industrial Disease Cases", 2000 S.L.T. 31–36.

Generally there is no obvious point from which time begins to run. Instead there is a history of increasing symptomatology, varying types of medical investigation and advice, (or none at all) and finally a diagnosis. It is useful to remember that the approach of the legislature and the courts to limitation problems was initially shaped by the English case of *Cartledge v Jopling and Sons*.[35] In that case the plaintiff suffered from pneumoconiosis, caused by various breaches of duty which had ended around 1950. The condition was entirely symptomless for a number of years, although lung changes could have been detected by X-rays at that time. Writs issued in 1956 were held by the House of Lords to be time barred. The cause of action had accrued in 1950, even though the plaintiff could not reasonably have been expected to realise it. The law lords were driven to this manifest injustice by the existing legislation, and the result was in the words of Lord Reid "wholly unreasonable". He went on to say:

> "If this were a matter governed by the common law I would hold that a cause of action ought not to be held to accrue until either the injured party has discovered the injury, or it would be possible for him to discover it if he took such steps as were reasonable in the circumstances."

Section 17(2) of the Prescription and Limitation (Scotland) Act 1973 addresses this concern. In the context of industrial disease, the material points are as follows.

Section 17(2)(a)

21–21 *"The date on which the injuries were sustained"*

Formerly, in progressive respiratory disease cases it was arguable that time dids not run if a separate medical label or description could be put on the condition.[36] Following *Aitchison v Glasgow City Council*[37] this avenue is no longer available. This was an action for damages for psychiatric injury sustained as a result of sexual abuse to which the pursuer was subjected in 1974. It was averred that the psychological injury had manifested itself at a considerably later date then the earlier physical injuries. It was held that each separate injury did not have a discrete starting point for time bar purposes. The starting point for the running of the triennium was a single date, the earliest being the date on which the injuries were sustained.

"The date on which injuries were sustained" was considered by Lord Ross in the case of *Wilson v Morinton Quarries Ltd*,[38] in the context of the 1973 Act which is in slightly different terms from the current amended legislation. The pursuer suffered pneumoconiosis. Lord Ross held that

---

[35] *Cartledge v Jopling and Sons* [1963] 1 All E.R. 341.
[36] *Shuttleton v Duncan Stewart*, 1996 S.L.T. 517.
[37] *Aitchison v Glasgow City Council*, 2010 S.C. 411.
[38] *Wilson v Morinton Quarries Ltd*, 1979 S.L.T. 83.

time did not begin to run where there was an existing breach of duty as long as the pursuer could show that it continued to make a material contribution to the injury. In *Smith v Shaw & McInnes Ltd*,[39] a claim for vibration white finger, the pursuer signed a discharge in respect of a Scheme claim in 1990, but continued to be exposed to excessive vibration and suffered further damage. Lord McEwan held that the case could go to proof on the damage caused by the subsequent exposure.

Section 17(2)(b)

> "*A date ... on which the pursuer in the action became, or on which in the opinion of the court it would have been reasonably practicable for him in all the circumstances to become, aware of all of the following facts...*" **21–22**

In this regard there is a tension between *actual* and *constructive* knowledge. Where the defenders' bar has been successful in the last few years is in managing to persuade the courts to adopt stringent standards for discoverability and frequently to set dates for constructive knowledge which are much earlier than actual knowledge. In this regard they have successfully erased the distinction between what ought to have been done (what was reasonable) and what could have been done (what was reasonably practicable). In particular the Scottish courts appear quite happy to countenance that time may run against a pursuer even though he was acting reasonably.[40]

> (i) *That the injuries in question were sufficiently serious.* The cases tend to fall into two separate categories. In the first place there are the kinds of conditions such as asbestos related disease, respiratory disease or dermatitis where there is medical intervention at GP level, and a likely referral to a consultant. That consultant's report will generally be treated as the date of actual knowledge, and a possible starting point for the triennium. Contrast diseases such as noise induced hearing loss or vibration white finger where there are low level symptoms frequently accepted as a constitutional condition and a nuisance simply to be put up with. For many clients there is a natural disinclination to accept that these low level symptoms represent permanent injury or disease. It is a characteristic of these cases that there is rarely any medical attendance with the GP. If there is, there will very frequently be a failure by the GP to diagnose common occupational diseases such as vibration white finger or hearing loss.
>
> In some disease cases it can be difficult for a client to know that he has suffered injury at all. Hearing loss for example occurs to everyone with the passage of time. It is arguable that

---

[39] *Smith v Shaw & McInnes Ltd* Unreported April 24, 2001 Court of Session.
[40] *Little v East Ayrshire Council*, 1998 S.C.L.R. 520.

the injury is only perceptible when the pursuer realises that his hearing is materially worse than it ought to be in comparison with others of similar age.

(ii) *That the injuries were attributable in whole or in part to an act or omission.* The leading case in this area is now *Agnew v Scott Lithgow Limited (No.2)*.[41] It is helpful for pursuers in that it emphasises that there is generally no awareness of industrial disease without a diagnosis from a medical expert.[42] The facts were that the pursuer suffered from vibration white finger. He ceased working in the shipyards in 1995. He suffered low-level symptoms from around 1982. He had never heard of the condition of vibration white finger until around 1995 after he had left the yards, and had not gone to his GP. He later applied for and was awarded Industrial Injuries Disablement Benefit, which depended on a medical diagnosis. The court held that the date of the award was the date of actual knowledge in terms of the Act which was within the triennium. The judge at first instance had been wrong to think that the pursuer could effectively self-diagnose the condition in November 1995. However he was put on enquiry and it would have been reasonably practicable for him to have gone to a solicitor who in the particular circumstances would have obtained a medico-legal report in around four months. The triennium therefore started to run from that notional date. This corresponds with the approach taken by the Court of Appeal in *Ali v Courtaulds Textiles Ltd*,[43] where the court held that expert medical evidence was necessary to determine whether hearing loss was work or age-related and that time did not run until it was obtained, provided the plaintiff did not delay unreasonably.

However the client cannot refrain from taking reasonably practicable steps to find out the cause of his condition after he is put on notice.

21–23 So in the case of *Little v East Ayrshire Council*,[44] where a person was told at an occupational hearing test that his hearing was down, it would have been reasonably practicable for him on that day to have made the enquiry which would have established both knowledge and attributability.

The circumstances in *Agnew* will be familiar to practitioners who act for persons with low level symptoms from conditions such as vibration

---

[41] *Agnew v Scott Lithgow Limited (No.2)*, 2003 S.C. 448.

[42] See also *Comrie v NCB*, 1972 S.L.T. (Notes) 12—decision under the Limitation Act 1963. The pursuer suffered pneumoconiosis. Lord Dunpark pointed out "the improbability of a prospective pursuer acquiring knowledge of that causal connection without expert advice. Accordingly the pursuer's knowledge of all these facts, with the possible exception of the second, must be acquired from others." See also what was said in *Nicol v British Steel Corporation*, above, at [77].

[43] *Ali v Courtaulds Textiles Limited* [1999] C.L.Y. 465.

[44] *Little v East Ayrshire Council*, 1998 S.C.L.R. 520.

white finger or noise induced hearing loss in that they very frequently make no connection with previous working conditions. What is particularly helpful are the dicta that despite 13 years of symptoms the pursuer was not put on enquiry until after he had been told by others that his symptoms might be attributable to the use of pneumatic tools, rather than to age or to work only in a general sense.

> "Taking, as we must, this pursuer is his particular circumstances, the question we have to address is whether on an objective basis it would have been reasonably practicable for him to become aware of the relevant facts before June 1996. We are not persuaded that the pursuer ought to have taken expert advice by the time he gave up working in the shipyards at the end of September 1995. He had then had symptoms for about 13 years and there was, on the evidence, nothing new or urgent about these at the time. We consider however that the pursuer ought to have been aware that he should make enquiry about his position once he heard talk from his former colleagues about making claims arising out of having contracted VWF."

In *Clark v Scott Lithgow*[45] the pursuer developed vibration white finger caused by work undertaken between 1972 and 1982. His damages action was raised in May 2000. His GP had failed to diagnose the condition. The defenders argued that as an educated man he should have made further enquiry. The court held that the correct approach was to consider all the circumstances known to the pursuer and then to apply an objective approach to determine what a reasonable man would have done. A reasonable man here would not have made any connection until around June 1997 and an action had been raised within three years of that date.

Whilst the case of *Agnew* establishes that frequently a formal diagnosis is required to establish actual date of knowledge, the claimant cannot delay in obtaining this once he is put on notice. In *Chin v Cyclacel Ltd*[46] the pursuer sustained wrist injuries in 2000. An action raised prior to 2003 was dismissed. A further specialist diagnosis was obtained. It was held that the action was prima facie time barred under s.17 of the 1973 Act, but in all the circumstances it was allowed to proceed in terms of s.19A. However the relevant question is frequently not what there was to *stop* the pursuer obtaining a diagnosis, but did the surrounding facts and circumstances put him on notice to *start* to obtain such a diagnosis (*Rennie v Scott Lithgow*.[47] See also *Lambie v Toffolo Jackson Ltd (in liquidation)*.[48] Expert medical opinion should have some evidential basis).

---

[45] *Clark v Scott Lithgow*, 2006 Rep. L.R. 16.
[46] *Chin v Cyclacel Ltd* [2010] CSOH 33.
[47] *Rennie v Scott Lithgow* Unreported January 27, 2005 Sheriff Principal Kerr at Paisley.
[48] *Lambie v Toffolo Jackson Ltd (in liquidation)*, 2003 S.L.T. 1415.

The client and time bar

21–24 What this means in practice is that you will have to question the client closely on time bar complications, at the very first interview. You will need to establish the medical history. Whilst GPs rarely diagnose industrial diseases, they may have referred to a consultant who has. Check the notes for medical treatment, particularly for hospital referrals with a consultant diagnosis. You should also check immediately if there has been an Industrial Disablement Benefit award. You may find on examination that you have only a very short time in which to raise proceedings to avoid time bar.

Pleadings on time bar in industrial disease cases

21–25 Where time bar has been raised by the defenders in the pleadings, it is essential that the pursuer gives a candid history of the development of the condition, with full details of all diagnoses and treatment. Gaps in the medical history caused the pursuer's action to be dismissed in the case of *Cowan v Toffolo Jackson*,[49] a claim for asbestosis.

The case of *Agnew v Scott Lithgow (No.1)*,[50] is a good example of the kind of pleadings which will take the case to proof. In the current climate the best advice is for a pursuer to make well nigh voluminous pleadings on the medical trail as well as s.19A factors. A word of caution relates to damages. In the milder types of industrial injury, e.g. noise-induced hearing loss, vibration white finger, the higher you plead the damages, the more likely the court will find an early date for constructive knowledge. If the client treated the condition simply as a nuisance[51] don't exaggerate the position in the averments.

Section 19A averments

21–26 Even if the claim is prima facie time barred, the court may allow it to proceed if it seems equitable to do so.

It is particularly important that your s.19A pleadings are fully comprehensive. The courts have been charitable to clients with progressive diseases. For example in the case of *Black v British Railways Board*[52] Lord Mayfield allowed the case to proceed under s.19A, stating:

> "I consider also that the pursuer's failure to face up to his condition was excusable. Dr Dale stated that the onset of deafness was insidious ... Accordingly as he was able to work, and still does, his loss of hearing might not have seemed so conclusive until eventually he took advice."

---

[49] *Cowan v Toffolo Jackson*, 1997 Rep. L.R. 40.
[50] *Agnew v Scott Lithgow (No.1)*, 2001 S.C. 516.
[51] This is the description the Court of Appeal gave to the plaintiff's attitude to vibration white finger in *Allen v British Rail Engineering Limited* [2001] I.C.R. 942. The defenders' arguments on time bar were dismissed.
[52] *Black v British Railways Board*, 1983 S.L.T. 146.

The lesson for the pleader is to make a full disclosure of the chronology and medical narrative, and to supply the court with material for it to exercise the s.19A equitable discretion. You should deal with the state of the factual and medical evidence. Almost all of these cases arise from a continuing unsafe system of work as opposed to a single event accident:

> "On this matter, I consider it important that this action involves averments as to regular exposure of the deceased as an apprentice plumber in the defenders' shipyard machine shop to asbestos dust over a lengthy period, and not, for example, to an allegation of a single transient event on which a witness or witnesses no longer available could prospectively have provided evidence."[53]

As well as the medical history, you should also set out why and when the pursuer finally took legal advice, and hopefully the expeditious steps which were taken thereafter.

RESPIRATORY DISEASES

There are two particular kinds of respiratory disease. In the first kind there is an obstruction or narrowing of the airways. Particular examples are asthma, chronic bronchitis and emphysema. The second kind is where there is a pulmonary restriction. There is no obstruction here but there is a pathological condition which causes a restriction in lung capacity, for example, asbestos-related disease. The Medical Research Council has five grades of disability:

21–27

1. Able to keep up with people of same age walking up hills and stairs.
2. Able to keep up with people of same age on level ground but not hills and stairs.
3. Can walk at own pace on level ground without stopping for breath.
4. Has to stop whilst walking on level ground at own pace.
5. Breathless when sitting doing nothing.

You should use these grades as a checklist with your client.

OCCUPATIONAL ASTHMA

The client will present with a medical history and probably a consultant diagnosis of asthma. This is another situation where you should instruct the treating consultant. In asthma cases you will be looking for a work history where your client has been exposed to typical irritants. Asthma is Prescribed Industrial Disease D7, and there is a list of agents which the

21–28

---

[53] per Lord Milligan in *McLaren v Harland & Wolff Ltd*, 1990 S.L.T. 85.

DWP accept are likely to cause the condition. Following exposure the client becomes sensitised to the agent. Typical sensitisers in everyday use are isocyanates, which are contained in proprietary paint, colophony, which is contained in fumes arising from soldering flux, and glutaraldehyde, which is contained in proprietary disinfectants used in hospitals. In asthma cases the consultant will carry out measurements of the client's respiratory incapacity, including:

1. Forced Vital Capacity ("FVC"). This is the maximum amount of air which the person can breathe out in one breath.
2. The Forced Expiratory Volume ("FEV1"). This is the maximum amount of air which a person can inhale during the first one second. The ratio of FEV1/FVC is the proportion of vital capacity that the person blows out in the first second.

These results can then be compared with median results for persons of the same age and sex. You may also find that your client has already been given a peak flow meter by his GP or hospital nurse, and may have carried out daily tests for which there will be records. Where the client suffers from asthma you should check whether there are any occupational health records kept by his employer, and if so recover these before instructing the consultant. Send these along with the GP records, and a very full working history to the consultant. The consultant will be alert for variations in the condition, arising from absences or changes of employment.

The HSE have published guidance[54] which states that sensitisation is a result of changes to the immune system which would normally protect the body from the harmful effects of contaminants in the air.

> "It is different from many other forms of toxic effect because it is 'all or nothing'. The person either becomes sensitised to the substance or does not."

The HSE describe the effect of sensitisation:

1. It is a specific reaction to a single agent.
2. There is a wide range of individual susceptibility.
3. Sensitisation may occur only after months or years of exposure.
4. Sensitisation is irreversible. Although the symptoms may cease after cessation of exposure, symptoms may revive on any further exposure.

---

[54] Respiratory sensitisers and COSHH: *Breathe Freely: an employers' leaflet on preventing occupational asthma* (Suffolk: HSE Books, 2005).

Liability

Control of Substances Hazardous to Heath Regulations 2002

These replace similar 1988, 1994 and 1999 Regulations, and implement **21–29** EC Directive 90/679/E which follows the now traditional EC pattern of risk assessment, prevention of risk, protective equipment as a last resort, training and information for employees, the monitoring of exposure, and health surveillance. In particular reg.7 provides that the employer shall ensure that exposure to hazardous substances is either prevented, or where prevention is not reasonably practicable, adequately controlled. Regulation 6 provides for assessment of health risks.

In the case of *Bilton v Fastnet Highlands Ltd*[55] it was held that where the pursuer had been exposed to respirable prawn protein (exacerbated by exposure to sodium metabisulphite and sulphur dioxide), which caused her to develop occupational asthma, the onus of proof passed to the defenders to show that they had taken all reasonably practicable steps to comply with their statutory duty.[56]

This case was considered and followed by the Court of Appeal in England in the case of *Dugmore v Swansea NHS Trust*.[57]

The facts were that the plaintiff had suffered a latex allergy caused by use of latex gloves. The case failed at common law because the initial exposure and sensitisation pre-dated the date of knowledge when the reasonably prudent employer would have been aware of the specific danger. The plaintiff succeeded under COSHH, and it was held that the regulations imposed strict liability for the hazard.

ASBESTOS-RELATED DISEASES

Asbestos is water-resistant and fire-resistant. It will insulate against both **21–30** electricity and sound and is virtually undecayable. Known as the "magic mineral", at one time it seemed to present a material of matchless utility throughout the industrial world. Its use was particularly widespread in the construction and shipbuilding industries, where it was routinely used for insulation and lagging. The types of asbestos which have been commonly used in industry in the United Kingdom in this century are chrysotile (white asbestos), crocidolite (blue asbestos) and amosite (brown asbestos). Since around the 1970s only chrysotile has been in use. The presence of the shipbuilding industry on Clydeside has meant that the West of Scotland is one of the asbestos cancer capitals of the world.[58] A study carried out by Professor Julian Peto at the Institute of Cancer Research at London University on behalf of the HSE has predicted that asbestos deaths in Britain will go on rising for a period of years, peaking in the year 2020 at about 3,000 per year. The report states that there will

---

[55] *Bilton v Fastnet Highlands Ltd*, 1998 S.L.T. 1323.
[56] See also *Williams v Farne Salmon Trout Ltd*, 1998 S.L.T. 1329.
[57] *Dugmore v Swansea NHS Trust and Another* [2003] I.C.R. 574.
[58] See De Vos Irvine et al., "Asbestos and Lung Cancer in Glasgow and the West of Scotland", B.M.J. June 5, 1993.

be two waves of asbestos deaths. The first will be related to the installation of asbestos, which was at its peak between the 1960s and 1970s. A second wave will relate to those men involved in the demolition of buildings containing asbestos. The construction trade will be particularly at risk, as well as plumbers, electricians, plate metal workers, vehicle body builders and upholsterers.[59] Trades known to involve asbestos exposure and persons particularly at risk were (and are):

1. The asbestos industry itself.
2. Construction and building maintenance workers.
3. Seamen and dockers.
4. Steel erectors and insulation laggers.
5. Shipworkers.
6. Power station workers.

In 2010 the HSE published the results of a case control study entitled *Occupational domestic and environmental mesothelioma risks in Britain*.[60] The research showed that 46 per cent of sufferers had worked in construction, with particularly high odds ratios for carpenters, plumbers, electricians and painters. They estimate that more than 1 in 10 of British carpenters born in the 1940s with more than 10 years of employment in carpentry before age 30 will die of a cancer caused by asbestos.

Once asbestos fibres are inhaled, the following conditions can occur.

1. Pleural thickening

21–31 This is a thickening of the pleural layers. The latency period is usually around 20 years or so. It is associated with breathlessness and chest pain. There may be progressive pleural thickening. In the main there is no real clinical disability but like pleural plaques (see para.21–32) pleural thickening is a specific indicator of significant asbestos exposure, and raises the spectre of other asbestos-related conditions.

2. Pleural plaques

21–32 Pleural plaques are small areas of thickening in the pleura. They are considered benign in that the condition is not progressive. They are a specific indicator of previous significant asbestos exposure. Where they are discovered on X-ray, the sufferer has proof positive of previous asbestos exposure and the worry of developing one of the serious asbestos conditions.

Following *Rothwell v Chemical and Insulating Co Ltd*[61] neither pleural plaques nor pleural thickening are actionable at common law. Within a short space of time the Scottish Parliament had enacted the Damages (Asbestos-related Conditions) (Scotland) Act 2009 which defined asbestos-related pleural plaques, asbestos-related pleural thickening, and non-

---

[59] Peto et al., "Continuing Increase in Mesothelioma Mortality in Britain", Lancet, 1995, 345, 535–539.
[60] See *http://www.hse.gov.uk/research/rrpdf/rr696.pdf* [Accessed September 19, 2011].
[61] *Rothwell v Chemical and Insulating Co Ltd* [2008] 1 A.C. 281.

symptomatic asbestosis as actionable conditions. Major insurance companies have taken this legislation to Judicial Review. They were unsuccessful at first instance[62] and in the Inner House.[63] The judgment of the Inner House was affirmed by the Supreme Court in *AXA General Insurance Ltd v The Lord Advocate (Scotland)*[64] of an appeal to the Supreme Court is awaited at time of publication. The current advice for practitioners is that actions should be raised and sisted to await the outcome of the Judicial Review. Both pleural plaques and pleural thickening are divisible diseases, i.e. all employments likely to have contributed on a dose-related basis should be convened as defenders.

3. Asbestosis

The symptoms are breathlessness, clubbing of the fingers, and basal crackles in the lungs which are audible to a doctor using a stethoscope. Asbestosis is a progressive disease which causes major respiratory difficulties. Forty per cent of individuals with asbestosis will die of lung cancer, and 10 per cent of mesothelioma. This is also a divisible disease, generally with a latency period of around 20 years. Generally there will require to be a history of substantial asbestos exposure, either in intensity or in duration. There are sometimes difficulties in making a clinical distinction between asbestos and idiopathic pulmonary fibrosis. Practitioners should be alert to possible difficulties at an early state, obtain a very full work history and have the expert clinician address possible differential diagnoses. You may require to instruct an expert familiar with the 1997 Helsinki Criteria on the causative association between asbestos exposure and asbestosis.

21–33

4. Malignant mesothelioma

This is a condition which develops in the pleura (lining of the lung) or the abdomen. The condition is invariably fatal. By the time clinical symptoms are noticeable the mean survival period for persons affected is about a year. Latency periods vary from the shortest being around 15 years with the lengthiest being over 60 years. Typically the latency period will be greater than 30 years. This is confirmed by the HSE research which puts the period of highest risk for workers as being before the age of 30. There is no safe dose of asbestos, although the risk of mesothelioma increases on a dose-response basis. The disease is progressive. It is indivisible. Following the terms of the Compensation Act 2006 a mesothelioma victim can recover damages whether or not he was exposed to asbestos for anyone else or, e.g. during any period of self-employment. Further, damages are not to be apportioned between the pursuer and defender, even where it appears that there is significant asbestos exposure from parties not convened in the proceedings. In *Sienkiewicz v Grief UK Ltd*,[65] it was held that s.3(1)(d) of the Compensation Act meant that a claimant

21–34

---

[62] *AXA General Insurance Limited, Petitioners* [2010] CSOH 2.
[63] *AXA General Insurance Limited, Petitioners*, 2011 S.L.T. 439.
[64] *AXA General Insurance Ltd v The Lord Advocate (Scotland)* [2011] UKSC 46.
[65] *Sienkiewicz v Grief UK Ltd* [2011] 2 W.L.R. 523.

could prove the causation element by any available method, which included showing a material increase in risk.

5. Lung cancer

21–35 This is the same kind of cancer as is caused by smoking. If asbestos is present in the lungs, then the combination of asbestos fibre and the smoking habit will increase the risk by a factor of five.

The latency period between exposure to asbestos and development of asbestosis is generally considered to be around 20 years or longer. It may be shorter if there is high dose exposure. A malignant mesothelioma tumour has generally been growing for around 10 or 12 years before it becomes clinically obvious. Although these illnesses can be caused by a single asbestos fibre, they are also dose-related in the sense that cumulative exposure to high concentrations will increase the risk of disease. There are difficulties over proof of causation where the claimant was a smoker and had also been exposed to asbestos.

Taking instructions

21–36 Most of your instructions will tend to be as a result of a clinical diagnosis by a respiratory consultant. It is also likely that the client will be undergoing medical treatment. The first task for the practitioner is to obtain a full employment history since leaving school, with full details of all potential asbestos exposures, having regard to the latency periods for the development of the disease. All potential witnesses should be traced immediately. If you are unsure about the sources of occupational exposure it is essential that you obtain the help of a specialist health and safety expert at this stage. Obtain as much detail from the client on possible sources of exposure, either by his own work, or caused by the operations of colleagues. Obtain full GP and hospital notes, and check in particular for any biopsy results. You should then send your statements and evidence to the treating consultant and ask him for a full report which specifically addresses both the condition and causation. Always ask the consultant to deal with any question of prognosis in a separate letter, which should not be disclosed to the client. There is a degree of urgency in all of this, and you must always be alert to the need for steps to preserve evidence. After you have extended a typewritten statement, ensure that the client is asked to adopt this to the best of his knowledge and belief, and sign and date it. Give consideration to preserving the client's actual words using video. Where there is a diagnosis of mesothelioma, immediate proceedings should be raised, with the pursuer's evidence being taken on commission to lie *in retentis*.

Liability and date of knowledge for asbestos-related diseases

21–37 It is critical to remember that this is a question of fact and not law. In the United Kingdom the first important published research was the Merewether and Price Report, which was published in 1930. Since then there has been ever-increasing research and publication, with factory inspector reports and finally legislation dealing with the dangers. The date of knowledge may vary from industry to industry. It was held in the case of *Rennie v Upper Clyde Shipbuilders*[66] that shipbuilders should have known of the danger of exposure to asbestos since at least 1938. On the other hand in *Wright v Stoddard International Plc*,[67] the Lord Ordinary held that low grade exposure in the defenders' carpet manufacturing factory did not give rise to a foreseeable risk of asbestosis. However the leading case in this area, namely *Shell Tankers UK Ltd v Jeromson*[68] does not appear to have been cited to the court. In that case Lady Justice Smith considered all the relevant literature, and stated that the reasonably prudent employer should consider the maximum potential exposure when addressing risk. The annual report of the Chief Inspector of Factories in 1956 reported in detail on the workings of the 1931 Asbestos Industry Regulations, and is a useful starting point for persons known to be exposed at that time. The Shipbuilding and Ship-Repairing Regulations 1960 came into force in 1961. Regulation 70 required the use of respirators for certain operations involving asbestos, including the removal of lagging. On May 14, 1970 the Asbestos Regulations 1969 came into force. The matter is now governed by the Control of Asbestos at Work Regulations 1987 and 2006 together with an Approved Code of Practice issued by the HSE. The date of knowledge for any particular trade should be addressed by your health and safety expert. In the case of *Rennie* the pursuer was a French polisher who had worked on various ships on the Clyde during 1940–1945. Although he did not work with asbestos he was exposed to asbestos dust from insulation operation. This was negligence at common law. This exposure was held to be a breach of the Factories Act 1937 s.47(1). The comparable section in the Factories Act 1961 is s.63.

Liability for mesothelioma will be joint and several amongst those employers who have materially increased the risk by exposing the pursuer to asbestos fibres.[69] This position has now been codified by s.3 of the Compensation Act 2006. A material increase of risk is anything above de minimis, and in particular does not require to be a doubling of the risk on an epidemiological basis. The limitations of epidemiology in the approach to legal causation were fully explored by the Supreme Court in *Sienkiewicz v Greif (UK) Ltd*.[70] The Supreme Court specifically approved the case of *Rolls Royce Industrial Power (India) Ltd v Cox*[71] where counsel for the employer conceded that asbestos dust for a period of one week would not be de minimis. Although care should be taken in investigation and preparation to isolate and identify all potential employers, there is generally no need to issue proceedings against all these employers. Practical advice would be to issue against one or two of the strongest targets, having regard to the state of the evidence and the health

---

[66] *Rennie v Upper Clyde Shipbuilders*, 1989 G.W.D. 20-1258.
[67] *Wright v Stoddard International Plc* [2007] CSOH 138.
[68] *Shell Tankers UK Ltd v Jeromson* [2001] P.I.Q.R. P19.
[69] See *Fairchild*, above.
[70] *Sienkiewicz v Greif (UK) Ltd* [2011] 2 W.L.R. 523.
[71] *Rolls Royce Industrial Power (India) Ltd v Cox* [2007] EWCA Civ 1189.

and safety expert's report. If those defenders wish liability to be apportioned they will have to blame and convene other defenders. In asbestosis cases, the best advice following *Holtby* is that the pursuer identifies and convenes every employer who has exposed the pursuer to asbestos.

Asbestos exposure of secondary victims

21–38 There has been increased recent litigation from persons who have not worked directly with asbestos, but who have been exposed to it by other methods. In *Gunn v Wallsend and Engineering Co Ltd*,[72] the wife of a shipyard worker died from mesothelioma. The evidence was that between around 1948 and 1965 the deceased had to shake off and wash her husband's clothing, which was impregnated with asbestos dust. She died of mesothelioma in 1986. The trial judge accepted that the cause of death was the exposure to asbestos dust from her husband's clothing, but he held that between 1945 and 1965 it was not reasonably foreseeable by these defenders that a person who was the wife of an employee might be affected by this kind of exposure, and the claim failed.[73] In the case of *Margereson v J.W. Roberts Ltd*,[74] the claims related to mesothelioma caused by "environmental exposure" to asbestos which had emanated from the defenders' asbestos factory in Leeds in the 1930s, when the plaintiffs were children living in the vicinity of the factory. Evidence was led of children playing with asbestos, using it to make and throw asbestos snowballs. The defendants were one of the leading manufacturers of asbestos in the world. It was held that their special knowledge of the dangers of asbestos in the 1930s made them liable to the plaintiffs. This judgment was upheld by the Court of Appeal.[75] The leading case is now *Maguire v Harland & Wolff Plc*[76] where the wife of the claimant was diagnosed with mesothelioma in 2000. She had been in contact with the claimant's work clothes from 1961 to 1965. It was held that it was not reasonably foreseeable that prior to 1965 persons such as the deceased were at risk of an asbestos-related disease.

NOISE-INDUCED HEARING LOSS

21–39 This is the most common of all occupational claims. In 1995 it was estimated that 170,000 Scots were currently exposed to potentially dangerous noise levels.[77] As they grow older, these workers will experience a level of hearing loss in excess of that caused by the normal ageing process.

Damage to the microscopic fibres of the inner ear, or cilia, is caused by repeated exposure to excessive noise. The damage is permanent, irre-

---

[72] *Gunn v Wallsend and Engineering Co Ltd*, 1989 C.L.Y. 2548.
[73] In 1964 research carried out by Dr Newhouse on the Cape asbestos factory in East London discovered mesothelioma amongst the workforce, their wives and the community. The study was front page news in the *Sunday Times*.
[74] *Margereson v J. W. Roberts Ltd* [1996] P.I.Q.R. 154.
[75] *Margereson v J. W. Roberts* [1996] P.I.Q.R. P358.
[76] *Maguire v Harland & Wolff Plc* [2005] P.I.Q.R. P21.
[77] *The Scotsman*, November 11, 1995.

versible, and generally accepted to be an additional overlay on the hearing loss which comes to all of us because of age. The hearing loss is clinically described as "mild", "moderate", "moderately severe", and "severe". The starting point for social disability is generally reached when the client has a loss of around 25 decibels measured by audiometry at 0.5, 1, 2 and 4kHz.

King, Coles and Lutman, *Assessment of Hearing Disability: Guidelines for Medio-Legal Practice* (London: Whurr, 1992) contains tables which enable a consultant to compare a pursuer with noise-induced hearing loss with the median person or control of the same age and sex who has had no noise exposure.[78] Noise-induced hearing loss is frequently accompanied by tinnitus, a condition whereby the subject hears a buzzing or ringing in the ear without reference to external sounds. Symptoms range from difficulties in hearing the television at volumes which are uncomfortable for other family members or disadvantage in social situations against a noisy background, to the kind of loss where the client cannot distinguish conversation even in a quiet background in a one-on-one situation and has been issued with a hearing aid.

Noise-induced hearing loss and the law

The case of *Thompson v Smith Shiprepairers (North Shield)*[79] is required reading on the topic. Mustill L.J. heard evidence from leading experts and analysed all the issues. He fixed upon 1963 as the "date of knowledge", i.e. when a prudent employer in the shipbuilding industry should have taken steps to protect his employees. It was in 1963 that the Ministry of Labour published its booklet *Noise and The Worker* and by that time cheap and efficient hearing protection was available. Although this was a finding-in-fact in relation to the evidence in that case only, most insurers now accept 1963 as being the date of knowledge.[80] This has two consequences. In the first place there will generally be no liability for exposure prior to 1963. Secondly, where the client has substantial pre-1963 exposure it is likely that his hearing has been damaged by 1963. Although post-1963 employment may have exacerbated the condition, a discount will have to be given for his previous exposure. In *Thompson* it was accepted that noise levels became dangerous when they continuously exceeded 90 decibels, expressed as 90dBleq. The Department of Employment's 1972 Code of Practice for the Reduction of Exposure to Noise for Employed Persons, also recommended that noise levels should be reduced at least to 90dB leq. That is likely to reflect the common-law standards prior to 1990. The court further recommended that special

21–40

---

[78] In *Robinson v Midlothian Council* [2009] CSOH 2009 the Lord Ordinary was not persuaded that the comparison with the median was the proper approach, but the publication does not appear to have been put before her.

[79] *Thompson v Smith Ship Repairers (North Shield)* [1984] 1 All E.R. 81.

[80] This is not necessarily the date of knowledge for all industries. See *Baxter v Harland & Woolf plc* [1990] I.R.L.R. 516—the Northern Ireland Court of Appeal held that shipyard employers should have been providing protection against noise in the mid-1950s.

allowances should be made for peripatetic workers exposed to fluctuating noise levels.[81]

In fact the current scientific consensus is that levels in excess of 85dB leq are harmful to a significant number of persons. This was recognised in the Noise at Work Regulations 1989, current from January 1, 1990.

At common law, then, an employer's duties from 1963 are considered to be to reduce the exposure to noise of employees to below the level of 90dB leq either by the reduction of noise at source, or by the provision of an efficient system of hearing protection. In England in cases where the employer had special knowledge, average exposure of 85dBA leq has been held to constitute common law negligence.[82] In *Baker v Quantum Clothing Group*[83], the Supreme Court held that, absent special knowledge of risk, a medium sized employer could rely on the 90dBA leq guidance contained in the 1972 Code of Practice until around 1990, when the matter was covered by the Noise at Work Regulations 1989 in any event. Workers are notoriously reluctant to wear hearing protection, and a safe system of work should involve a programme of education and persuasion of the workforce.

Statutory duties under the Factories Act 1961 s.29(1)

21–41 In *Carragher v Singer Manufacturing Co Ltd*[84] Lord Maxwell stated:

"I can see no satisfying reason why in principle, the presence of a fixed machine emitting into a workplace noise of such a level as to endanger the hearing of those who have to work there, should not, subject to the question of reasonable practicability, infringe the statutory provisions relied upon."

Whilst the Supreme Court in *Baker v Quantum Clothing Group* reached the same general conclusion, it held by a majority that the statutory duty was no higher than the duty at common law.

Noise at Work Regulations 1989

21–42 These came into force on January 1, 1990. Regulation 6 provides that the duty is to reduce the risk of damage to hearing to "the lowest level reasonably practicable". There were now two Action Levels. The first was a daily exposure of 85dBA Lep.d (the First Action Level). Those workers should be provided with information and advice and hearing protection should be made available. Where exposure was in excess of 90dBA Lep.d (the Second Action Level) more stringent requirements came into place including an obligation to ensure that hearing protection was worn (reg.11).

---

[81] Failure to follow this recommendation was a ground of liability in *Stewar v Cooper Oil Tools (GB) Ltd*, 1997 G.W.D. 35-1787.
[82] *Harris v BRB (Residuary)* [2006] P.I.Q.R. P10.
[83] *Baker v Quantum Clothing Group* [2011] U.K. S.C. 17.
[84] *Carragher v Singer Manufacturing Co Ltd*, 1974 S.L.T. (Notes) 28.

Control of Noise at Work Regulations 2005

These came into force on April 6, 2006. These further reduced the safe 21–43
exposure level, this time to 80dBA (reg.4). The employer is required to
assess risk (reg.5). Regulation 6 provides the stringent requirement that
the employer shall ensure that risk is either elimnated at source or where
this is not reasonably practicable reduced to as low a level as is reasonably practicable. Regulation 7 provides the requirements in respect of
hearing protection.

Taking instructions

You should follow the standard steps for all occupational illness and 21–44
disease cases. You will need a note of all the client's employments since
leaving school, a general indication from him as to whether they were
noisy, and if so was the noise continuous or intermittent. It is worthwhile
taking some time over this. It is this work history which is going to be
commented upon by the ear, nose and throat ("ENT") consultant. The
pursuer's work history and his impressions of noise levels will effectively
be committed to print in the consultant's report, and it is important to be
as accurate as possible from the start. Where the client is unclear as to the
history it may be advisable to obtain an Inland Revenue schedule from
Longbenton before referring the matter to the ENT consultant. Don't
intimate the claim at this stage, rather await the ENT consultant's report
before deciding on the target employer.

Medical report

You should instruct an ENT consultant with experience in the field. 21–45
Provide a work history with a clear indication of noise sources and the
target employers. The medical report will be based on audiometric testing
whereby the client is asked to respond to sounds of different intensity and
different frequencies, and clinical tests and observation. Noise affects the
hearing in the higher tones first, and there is sometimes, but not invariably, a notch or dip at 4kHz with a recovery at 6 and 8kHz. Other
potential causes of hearing loss are considered by the consultant together
with the audiometric graph and the work history, and the final diagnosis
is usually by exclusion of other causes. Ask that the consultant prepare
the report using the King, Coles, Lutman and Robinson *Medico-Legal
Assessment of Hearing Loss Guidelines*.[85] The advantage is that a comparison can be made with the median hearing loss of a person who has
not been exposed to excessive noise so that it can be said, e.g. that a 50-
year-old pursuer has the median age-associated hearing loss of a 65-year-
old person who has not been exposed to excessive noise. This approach
was not accepted by Lady Stacey in the case of *Robinson v Midlothian
Council*,[86] but only the most cursory information was placed before the
court. Hearing loss is not a progressive disease in that the damage done

---

[85] King, Coles and Lutman, *Medico-Legal Assessment of Hearing Loss Guidelines* (London: Whurr Publishers, 1992).
[86] *Robinson v Midlothian Council* [2009] CSOH 109.

by exposure to noise does not increase after the exposure ceases, but it seems as if it does, because the damage operates as an overlay on normal age-related hearing loss. In the current climate on time bar it is important that the client is advised to tell the consultant when he first accepted that he had a hearing loss, not what with hindsight he now thinks is the length of time he has been suffering. Reports which commence that the client has had difficulties for the last five years or so are a fatal free gift. If you receive a positive medical report you should then intimate to the target employers. After the insurers are identified they will generally require:

1. Proof of employment, for example, by contract of employment, pensions letter, tax records of Contributions Agency schedule.
2. Positive medical report.
3. Specification of the source of noise.
4. The identity of all other defenders. There is a protocol that the insurers of the most recent risk will act as lead insurers and coordinate and negotiate the claim.

Raising proceedings

21–46 The same general considerations apply as for all occupational disease claims. Recovery of documents is vital, and should be considered as soon as defences are lodged. It can be helpful to put a call in the pleadings on the defenders to lodge all tests showing noise levels at the pursuer's place of work during his employment. This should be followed up with a specification seeking those documents for the whole period of your client's employment. In cases under the Noise at Work Regulations 1989 and Control of Noise at Work Regulations 2005 you should seek documents showing the appointment of a competent person, documents showing the issuing of hearing protection, and training records as well as noise levels. The Court of Appeal has held that where a ship owner had not taken noise measurements as required, the court should put a generous gloss on the evidence of the claimant as to excessive noise levels. The ship owner could not rely on the absence of measurements.[87]

Very frequently the production of the records will resolve the issue of liability in your favour. Where the process complained of is still carried on, you should seek an order for inspection and noise tests to be carried out by your expert under the Administration of Justice (Scotland) Act 1972.

HAND/ARM VIBRATION SYNDROME
(VIBRATION WHITE FINGER)

21–47 This condition is caused by the use of pneumatic, percussive and vibratory tools. It is common amongst workers who have routinely used equipment such as handheld grinders or rotary tools, percussive hammers and drills used in mine boring and road maintenance, and chainsaws. The

---

[87] *Keefe v Isle of Man Steam Packet Co Ltd* [2010] EWCA Civ 683.

vibration from tools gripped in the hand is transmitted to areas of the hand and arm. Vibration exposure from prolonged and regular work with powered and handheld tools causes vascular and neurological changes to the fingers and hands, with loss of circulation and "blanching" of the digits, hence the name. As in noise-induced hearing loss, the problem has been known to medical science for a long number of years but the date of knowledge for legal purposes is very much later.

In a case involving miners, the Court of Appeal in England upheld the decision by the trial judge that British Coal should have known of the dangers of vibration white finger from around 1967, and were liable for failure to take steps to minimise risks from around 1973.[88] This decision was closely in line with a decision by a Northern Ireland court in *Bowman v Harland & Wolff*[89] which set the date of knowledge of risk for the defenders' shipyard at January 1973. In the case of *Murphy v Lord Advocate*[90] the facts show that the Forestry Commission were applying their minds to the problem from around 1968. Although it is impossible to be dogmatic for every industry, it is suggested that publication of the British Standards Institution *Draft for Development DD43—Guide to the Evolution of Exposure of the Human Hand/Arm System to Vibration* (1975) represents the date of knowledge for most large scale organisations (e.g. British Coal). For medium sized and smaller employers the likely date of knowledge will be around 1987 following the publication of British Standard BS6842.[91]

Medical report

If you are instructed by a client who complains of vibration white finger, you must obtain a medical report from a vascular surgeon. Ask him to compile his report using both the Stockholm Workshop and the Taylor-Pelmear scales. The Stockholm scale deals with both the vascular and neurological components. His report will generally contain a diagram of the hand showing the affected areas. The diagnosis will show varying scales of stages of the injury, e.g. stages 1–4 on the Stockholm scale, in increasing severity.

21–48

The condition is generally thought not to be progressive, in the absence of further exposure to vibratory tools. However for many clients the requirement to forego all further work with such equipment may well mean consignation to a life on benefit. Certainly at stage 3 on the Stockholm scale there is serious disadvantage on the labour market. The condition is also similar to noise-induced hearing loss in that the liability of different target employers is probably not joint and several, but successive, and a discount will have to be given for pre-date of knowledge exposure.

---

[88] See *Armstrong v British Coal Corporation* [1998] C.L.Y. 2842.
[89] *Bowman v Harland & Wolff* [1992] I.R.L.R. 349.
[90] *Murphy v Lord Advocate*, 1981 S.L.T. 213.
[91] See *Brookes v South Yorkshire Passenger Transport Executive* [2005] EWCA Civ 452. In Scotland in *Deans v George Newbury Coachbuilder* Unreported September 13, 2003 Airdrie Sheriff Court, the date of knowledge for a medium-sized coachbuilding firm was held to be 1986.

Liability

21–49 The intensity of the vibration experienced can vary greatly depending on the age, condition and state of maintenance of the tools. British Standard BS6842:1987 describes a procedure for measuring exposure to vibration. This exposure is normalised to eight hours ("AS"). Programmes of preventive measures and health surveillance were previously recommended where workers' exposure regularly exceeds an A8 of $2.8 m/s^2$. By way of example, the likely vibration levels of a well-maintained hammer drill is $5 m/s^2$. Even with well-maintained tools, the recommended vibration dose would be exceeded after three hours.[92] It is critical to note that this level is merely a guidance and is not in any sense a safe level. Preventive measures which can be taken include buying low vibration tools, ensuring that tools are properly maintained, advising the workforce to grip tools lightly, making gloves available to improve general circulation, and job rotation. If you have to draft a writ you should refer to the publication *Hand/Arm Vibration Symptoms*.[93] The HSE publication HS(G)88 was published in 1994 and updated in 2001. It recommended a programme of preventive measures and health surveillance where daily exposure exceeded an A(8) of $2.8 m/s^2$, but crucially both publications emphasise that this should not be considered a safe level. The starting point for liability is that there is regular and prolonged use of tools known to be hazardous. HS(G)88 has a list of such tools. From July 6, 2005 the appropriate information and standards are contained in the HSE Guide to the Control of Vibration at Work Regulations 2005 (see para.21–50).

If there is regular use of any of these such tools, this sets up a duty for an employer to have a system of screening, education and monitoring which enables the condition to be identified at an early stage and the user then removed from the tools completely, or exposed to less vibration. So even where it is not possible to prove an amount of exposure greater than the HSE guidance level there is likely to be a continuing breach of duty if there is failure of monitoring in this regard (see *Brown v Corus (UK) Ltd*).[94] The court in Scotland reached a similar conclusion in the case of *Conway v Hitec Hydraulic Engineering Ltd*.[95]

If you do raise proceedings, your averments would address the defenders' failure to supply proper plant and equipment both at common law, and under the Provision and Use of Work Equipment Regulations 1992 and 1998. You will require a "Day In The Working Life" statement from the client. Use of pneumatic tools tends not to be continuous but cyclical, and each job should be broken down into its constituent parts. This will enable the health and safety expert to make a reliable assessment on the anger time, i.e. actual time used on vibratory tools. If the tools are still in use you should arrange for these to be measured.

---

[92] In *James McKenna v British Railways Board and First Engineering Ltd* Unreported August 15, 2003 Court of Session, failure to observe the HSE levels was held to have made a material contribution to the pursuer's condition of vibration white finger.
[93] *Hand/Arm Vibration Symptoms HS(G)88* (Suffolk: HSE Books, 1994).
[94] *Brown v Corus (UK) Ltd* [2004] P.I.Q.R. P30.
[95] *Conway v Hitec Hydraulic Engineering Limited* Unreported March 25, 2007 Hamilton Sheriff Court.

CONTROL OF VIBRATION AT WORK REGULATIONS 2005

These Regulations came into force on July 6, 2005. An accompanying guide to the Control of Vibration at Work Regulations 2005 is available as a free download on the HSE website.[96] The key Regulation is reg.5 which provides that a risk assessment should be made by an employer where he carries out work which is liable to expose any of his employees to a risk of vibration injury. Whilst the Regulations refer to an Exposure Action Value of $2.5 m/s^2$ measured on a triaxial basis, once again liability does not necessarily depend on proving exposure in excess of these levels. Where there is routine use of rotary action or percussive tools, a risk assessment should be carried out. Regulation 6 requires the reduction of exposure to vibration to the lowest level reasonably practicable.

21-50

Apportionment

One particular specialty relates to the question of apportionment. The effect of exposure to vibratory tools is cumulative. In *Armstrong* the Court of Appeal held that the critical deterioration was between stage 2 (before which the condition is reversible) and stage 3 (which constitutes a permanently disabling condition). So although the plaintiff coal miners had their claims discounted for pre-date of knowledge non-tortious exposure, the amount of the discount was minimal. There is no straight line apportionment on a time spent basis, and detailed enquiries should be made to identify the stage of deterioration. The effect may be that later periods of employment exposure count for significantly more in damages than lengthy periods early in the client's career.

21-51

Hand/arm vibration syndrome has been described by analogy as a glass which fills and then gradually overflows, the point of overflow being when the symptoms appear. If the glass stops filling it will not overflow. So that if a person gives up using vibrating tools altogether or moderates their use then the symptoms may never present. This approach is particularly useful for claimants where there is a long history of vibration exposure, frequently with employers who cannot be traced or where insurers cannot be found. What it means is that apportionment should not be approached on a straight line basis but the lion's share of responsbility and liability for damages, should lie with the employers of record when symptoms began to appear, were not monitored, and deterioration was not prevented. This approach was set out by the Court of Appeal in *Smith v Wright & Beyer Ltd*,[97] and followed in both the Scottish cases of *Deans* and *Conway*.

REPETITIVE STRAIN INJURY

Repetitive strain injury ("RSI") is a generic term for a group of conditions in which the sufferer has pain in the soft tissues of the hand, arm or

21-52

---

[96] *http://www.hse.gov.uk/vibration/hav/regulations.htm* [Accessed September 19, 2011].
[97] *Smith v Wright & Beyer Ltd* [2001] EWCA Civ 1069.

shoulder. At the time of writing there is a heated medical-legal debate as to the nature and extent of this condition. In the widely publicised case of *Mughal v Reuters*[98] the judge held that RSI was not a recognised medical condition. The plaintiff was a journalist who claimed to have been permanently disabled through excessive keyboard and VDU work. Even where the courts have accepted that a genuine pain syndrome exists, opinion is divided as to whether the pain experienced by the sufferer is organic or psychogenic, i.e. all in the mind. An indication of the controversy can be gained from the history of the case of *Pickford v ICI Plc*.[99] The plaintiff claimed that she had contracted the prescribed DSS condition PDA4, cramp of the hand and forearm, as a result of excessive typing. She raised a civil claim. She was unsuccessful at first instance. In the Court of Appeal,[100] the court was persuaded that the cause of her condition was organic, and that ICI had breached a duty of care to give instruction on the need to take breaks. This decision was overturned by a majority in the House of Lords, who were not satisfied on the evidence that the plaintiff had discharged the onus of proving that her pain was organic in nature. If the pain was psychogenic, then the injury was not reasonably foreseeable and the claim must fail.

Equally there have been a number of successful cases in England, and also well-publicised settlements. In *Ghan, Herrick and Gerard v Mattessons Walls Ltd*,[101] the court accepted that repetitive strain syndrome was a genuine condition, albeit of unidentifiable pathology and awarded damages to three plaintiffs who had to prepare and package meat in a sausage factory. The defendants should have warned the plaintiffs of the risk of strain injury and set out a system of job rotation and rest. In *Mitchell v Atco*,[102] the plaintiff complained that she required to lift, twist and turn heavy motors and carry out relentless work involving gripping, twisting, turning and lifting. M suffered from various conditions including carpal tunnel syndrome and tenosynovitis. The court accepted that the condition was genuine, and that there should have been a system of job rotation. In *Mulligan v Midland Bank*,[103] the court awarded a former bank clerk £155,000 because of excessive typing duties. This is thought to be the highest payout for RSI for an office-based worker. If nothing else these cases illustrate that the practitioner must take a very careful look at the particular facts of each case before deciding to act. It is critically important to have a medical diagnosis which describes a known condition associated with the workplace, and to examine the defenders' duties and failures in the light of the particular knowledge of the time. In *Alexander v Midland Bank*, where a number of data encoders suffered upper limb disorders, the judge's finding that a psychogenic cause was unconvincing meant that as a matter of probability a physical explanation was the more probable. Even though a precise medical explanation

---

[98] *Mughal v Reuters* [1993] I.R.L.R. 571.
[99] *Pickford v ICI Plc* [1998] 1 W.L.R. 1189.
[100] [1996] I.R.L.R. 622.
[101] *Ghan, Herrick and Gerard v Mattessons Walls Ltd* [1997] C.L.Y. 5807.
[102] *Mitchell v Atco* [1995] C.L.Y. 4590.
[103] *Mulligan v Midland Bank* Unreported June 30, 1997.

could not be given, this did not mean that the symptoms were necessarily psychiatric.[104]

The general medical consensus is that the following medical conditions may be work-related:

1. Carpal tunnel syndrome, a condition caused by repetitive flexing of the wrists or the use of vibrating tools.
2. Tenosynovitis, a condition caused by repetitive movements which cause inflammation of the tendons or tendon sheaths, common amongst manual workers such as carpenters or bricklayers.
3. Tendonitis, caused by repetitive movements which cause inflammation of the area where the muscle and tendon are joined.
4. Epicondylitis, or "tennis elbow", caused by excessive manual force onto materials or tools, which arises from strenuous jobs like joinery, plastering or bricklaying.

Ideally you would wish your medical consultant to reach a diagnosis of one of the above conditions.

Dealing with the client

Your medical consultant knows that in this field more than any other in current medico-legal practice, any positive opinion he gives is likely to be disputed by a well-researched defence expert who may be expected to challenge every aspect of the diagnosis. The consultant will be looking for a coherent history of symptom, complaint and working pattern which enables him to reach an opinion which he can defend in evidence. An accurate chronology is particularly important. Your client has already decided that he has work-related RSI and you will very frequently come across confabulation of dates and symptoms. Pin the client down with the GP records. These records may well contain numerous contra-indicators to the trained eye, for example, initial complaint before the particular work activity started; exacerbation of symptoms after work activity has ceased. The client's statement will need to be a "Day In The Working Life" description, with each work activity broken down into each constituent part. There is generally little point in pursuing a claim for RSI for a typist when it is clear that only half of her duties related to actual typing, and that she had frequent breaks throughout the working day. The choice of consultant is crucial. There is no point in instructing the local hospital consultant. You need to locate a consultant who has taken an active interest in the subject, has kept up to date with current academic research, at the same time as keeping up his NHS clinical consultancy. Such paragons are difficult to find! You will need to network other pursuers' solicitors.

21–53

When you receive a negative diagnosis you should close the file, as always advising on time bar. Where a medical condition is indicated, you should consider whether grounds for liability exist.

---

[104] *Alexander v Midland Bank Plc* [2001] I.C.R. 464.

Liability

21-54 The kinds of employment in which liability might exist are:

1. keyboard operators;
2. manual workers such as bricklayers who work repetitively using hand and arms;
3. operators of pneumatic and percussive tools such as chippers or jackhammers, who are liable to suffer carpal tunnel syndrome;
4. factory workers such as packers, checkout operators, meat and poultry preparers, all of whom carry out frequent repetitive movements.

The list is not exhaustive, but you should be suspicious if the client cannot point to some significant mechanism of injury or strain, or is not employed in one of the above categories.

You should also find out if co-workers have been similarly affected, and include this in your statement to the doctor.

VDU operators are now protected by the Display Screen Equipment Regulations 1992. Some of the other operations will be subject to the provisions of the Manual Handling Operations Regulations 1992, or conceivably the Provision and Use of Work Equipment Regulations 1998.

If you receive a positive medical opinion you should intimate the claim, but be prepared to have to litigate and not to settle with the insurers. You will need a report from an ergonomist. The whole topic is the subject of ever-developing knowledge and research.

Your ergonomist can tell you the state of knowledge at any particular time. It is clear from the House of Lords decision in *Pickford* (above) that you cannot expect the court to resolve the medical and scientific controversy, but simply to judge each case on its own facts.[105] In *Pickford* the pursuer failed amongst other reasons because it was not reasonably foreseeable in 1989 that a person not typing on a full-time basis might suffer RSI. There was therefore no breach of duty. At the end of the day each case will have to be looked at in the light of its own facts. Neither *Pickford* nor *Mughal* have set down any general rule that RSI does not exist. The cautious practitioner will require to look at every case on its merits, and to take particular care with the factual and medical evidence.

---

[105] In fact the courts did precisely this in the case of *Page v Smith* [1995] P.I.Q.R. P329, where diverging views as to the existence of myalgic encephalitis ("ME") were resolved in favour of the plaintiff.

CHAPTER 22

DAMAGES FOR STRESS AT WORK, BULLYING AND HARASSMENT

Complaints to General Practitioners about work-related mental problems are at epidemic levels. 13.5 million work days were lost to stress during 2007/2008. But there have been no reported successful actions in Scotland for damages for what is popularly known as "stress at work", and a significant number of reported failures.[1] This section looks briefly at the kind of cases which might be successfully prosecuted, and steps the practitioner might take. Following the Protection from Harassment Act 1997 cases should be clearly categorised from the outset. In one category is the stress at work claim where the demands of the job on the individual have caused a mental breakdown. Whether these claims are treated at common law, or under the Management of Health and Safety at Work Regulations 1999, they face substantial legal hurdles regarding causation and foreseeability. In the other category are harassment or bullying claims where effectively mental distress has been caused by the actions of another individual in the organisation. These claims can now be brought under the Protection from Harassment Act 1997, and they do not face anything like the same legal obstacles. There may of course be hybrid situations, and wherever possible practitioners should look to utilise the statutory provisions of the 1997 Act. 22–01

Stress at work[2]

Contrary to popular belief, a little bit of stress is not good for you. Stress is the natural reaction people have to excessive pressures or other types of demand placed on them. Whilst it is not an illness, if it is prolonged or intense, it can lead to both mental and physical ill health such as depression, back pain and heart disease. 22–02

In the case of *Cross v Highlands and Islands Enterprise*,[3] Lord MacFadyen accepted as a working definition:

"Occupational stress is usually seen as a result of a mismatch between the demands of the job and the resources of the person expected to meet those demands."

---

[1] See the case of *Keen v Tayside Contracts*, 2003 S.L.T.500 for a resumé of stress at work cases.
[2] The term is used throughout as a convenient and well understood shorthand.
[3] *Cross v Highlands and Islands Enterprise*, 2001 S.L.T. 1060.

Cross has established that a victim of stress at work is a "primary victim" and the various control mechanisms relating to "nervous shock for secondary victims" do not apply. An employer has a common law duty of care not to subject their employees to working conditions which are reasonably likely to cause them psychiatric injury or illness. This duty of care is owed to each employee as an individual, and subject to his particular vulnerabilities and susceptibilities.

FORESEEABILITY OF PSYCHIATRIC INJURY

Date of knowledge

22–03 Stress at work can cause both physical and psychiatric illness as borne out by a number of studies in the field. A major report by Professor Tom Cox of the University of Nottingham, entitled "Stress Research; Stress Management, Putting Theory to Work" was published under the auspices of the Health and Safety Executive ("HSE") in 1993.

Since then there have been a number of important health and safety publications, including:

1. "Mental Distress at Work: First Aid Measures" (HSE leaflet, 1992).
2. "Guidelines—Stress at Work, a Guide for Employers" (HS(G)116, HSE 1995).
3. "Help on Work-Related Stress—a Short Guide" (INDG 281, 1998).
4. "Managing Stress at Work" (HSE discussion document, 1999).
5. "The Scale of Occupational Stress" (HSE report, 2000).
6. "Tackling Work Related Stress; a Manager's Guide to Improving and Maintaining Employee Health and Wellbeing" (HSE Books, 2001).
7. "Work Related Stress—A Short Guide—Stress Prevention Guidance for Small Firms" (HSE INDG 28, September 2002).

It can be stated with some confidence that by 1994 at the latest, when there was a specific section on stress at work in the HSE gateway publication *Essentials of health and safety at work*, that date of knowledge of the dangers of stress at work had been established.[4] It is therefore highly unlikely that date of knowledge will pose any particular problem for practitioners at this time.

Forseeability of psychiatric injury

22–04 The main difficulty in individual cases is the foreseeability of psychiatric injury. As Lord Carloway stated:

---

[4] There has been no real dispute on date of knowledge in any of the reported Scottish cases. In *Cross*, 2001 S.L.T. 1060, 1993 was established as a date of knowledge of the dangers of work-related stress where the defenders were a large and sophisticated personnel organisation.

"Managers often have to take decisions which will, and will be anticipated as having, an adverse affect on employees in emotional terms. For example, disciplinary action in the form of demotion or dismissal may reasonably be predicted to result in a whole range of reactions including anger, resentment, depression and anxiety. These are all normal human emotions ... However it is a considerable leap to go from the position whereby a manager knows or ought to anticipate that his decisions will cause an employee emotional upset in one form or another to a stage where he knows or ought to anticipate it will cause the employee to suffer psychiatric illness."[5]

It is significant that in the reported cases both in Scotland and England there is frequently an initial period of absence from work, communication with the employer as to the cause of the absence, and then a planned return to work on changed working conditions. So in *Walker v Northumberland County Council*,[6] a social worker exposed to excessive demands at work suffered a nervous breakdown in November 1986. He returned to work in March 1987 to what should have been reduced responsibilities. The court held that whilst the employers could not have reasonably foreseen the initial breakdown, and were not liable in tort for the effects of it, they had been put on notice by the period of absence, and did know that the plaintiff was a person vulnerable to psychiatric illness. The plaintiff succeeded at common law in respect of a subsequent breakdown. Similarly in *Cross* the Lord Ordinary held that after his return to work, the defenders should have realised that James Cross was not in fact fully recovered and should have taken steps to modify his workload, which it was held on the facts they did. In *Catleugh v Caradon Everest Limited*,[7] Lord Marnoch held that averments that the 50-year-old pursuer twice broke down in tears in the presence of his immediate supervisor would have been enough to take the case to proof before answer on the question of foreseeability. In the case of *Flood v University Court of the University of Glasgow*[8] the averments were that the pursuer was a former university lecturer who suffered depression and anxiety caused by her excessive workload. She stated that she was working 100 hours per week despite having contracted to do only 32.5 hours. At the procedural hearing the Lord Ordinary held that there were sufficient averments on foreseeability of risk of psychiatric harm, and that the averment that the defenders had a duty to carry out a risk assessment on the consequence to the pursuer on changes to her employment was also relevant. He dismissed the case however, on the grounds that the remedial steps had not been specified. On appeal the Inner House held that the pursuer had gone far enough in identifying in general terms the steps which should have been taken to prevent the onset of symptoms. In particular it was pointed out that although the general principles are to be found in the case of *Sutherland v*

---

[5] *Fraser v State Hospital Board*, 2001 S.L.T. 1051.
[6] *Walker v Northumberland County Council* [1995] 1 All E.R. 737.
[7] *Catleugh v Caradon Everest Limited*, 1999 G.W.D. 32-1554.
[8] *Flood v University Court of the University of Glasgow*, 2010 S.L.T. 167.

Hatton[9] they need care in their application to the particular facts under consideration.

Sutherland v Hatton: a matrix approach?

22–05 In *Sutherland v Hatton*, the Court of Appeal attempted to set up a comprehensive legal matrix for future cases. An employer cannot be expected to know that a particular individual is liable to psychiatric injury, and in particular cannot be expected to mind read. "Unless he knows of some particular problem or vulnerability, an employer is usually entitled to assume that his employee is up to the normal pressures of the job." Further he is generally entitled to take what he is told by or on behalf of the employee at face value. The court also distinguishes between signs of stress, and signs of impending harm to health. It is only the latter which are apt to show reasonable foreseeability. It dismissed the suggestion that an employer is entitled to take the expiry of a GP's certificate as suggesting that the employee was now fit to return to work, pointing out that this kind of disorder is not self-limiting. However, "an employee who returns to work after a period of sickness without making further disclosure or explanation to his employer is usually implying that he believes himself fit to return to the work which he was doing before." The Court of Appeal also held that whilst it is known that some employments in general are more stressful than others, this knowledge does not put an employer on notice to take steps before the fact, e.g. by way of stress audit. There does not always have to be an absence. Employers should be aware of the nature and extent of the work being done by their employees. A particularly arduous or demanding job may mean that an employer is putting pressure upon an individual employee which is unreasonable. This may bridge the gap between simply showing signs of stress, and being vulnerable to psychiatric injury. Also relevant is whether there are signs that others doing the same work are under harmful levels of stress or have already been absent.[10] *Sutherland v Hatton* has been cited with approval in the Scottish cases of *Stevenson v East Dunbartonshire Council*[11] and *Angela Taplin v Fife Council*.[12]

Breach of duty

22–06 In *Sutherland* the Court of Appeal stated:

"In every case it is necessary to consider what the employer not only could but should have done. We are not here concerned with such comparatively simple things as gloves, goggles, earmuffs or non-slip flooring. Many steps might be suggested: giving the employee a

---

[9] *Sutherland v Hatton* [2002] 2 All E.R. 1.
[10] In *Stevenson v East Dunbartonshire Council*, Lord Bonomy allowed averments to go to proof which contained details of letters written by a GP, together with other averments that there had been meetings "to discuss the pursuer's problems at work and the effect upon his health". The approach of the Court of Appeal in England was specifically followed.
[11] *Stevenson v East Dunbartonshire Council*, 2003 S.L.T. 97.
[12] *Angela Taplin v Fife Council*, 2003 S.L.T. 653.

sabbatical; transferring him to other work; redistributing the work; giving him some extra help for a while; arranging treatment or counseling; providing buddying or mentoring schemes to encourage confidence; and much more. But in all of these suggestions it will be necessary to consider how reasonable it is to expect the employer to do this, either in general or in particular: the size and scope of its operation will be relevant to this, as will its resources, whether in the public or private sector, and the other demands placed upon it. Among those other demands are the interests of other employees in the workplace. It may not be reasonable to expect the employer to rearrange the work for the sake of one employee in a way which prejudices the others. As we have already said, an employer who tries to balance all these interests by offering confidential help to employees who fear that they may be suffering harmful levels of stress is unlikely to be found in breach of duty: except where he has been placing totally unreasonable demands upon an individual in circumstances where the risk of harm was clear."

The court went on to say that where an employer offers a confidential advice service, with referral to appropriate counselling or treatment services it is unlikely that he will be found in breach of duty.

Further, if the only reasonable and effective step would have been to dismiss or demote the employee, an employer will not be in breach of duty if the employee of his own consent remains in post.

Risk assessment

As has been observed elsewhere,[13] it may be possible to put the principle of negligence into a nutshell, but it is difficult to keep it there. In England as early as the case of *Young v Post Office*,[14] the Court of Appeal was prepared to distinguish the *Sutherland v Hatton* approach. In *Dickins v O2*,[15] Lady Justice Smith indicated that the provision of a confidential counselling service did not automatically negative liability. On the approach of the Court of Appeal in *Sutherland* the duty of the employer is generally reactive. There is no obligation to take any steps at all in the absence of objective indications of impending harm to health plain enough for any reasonable employer to realise he should do something about it. The problem with this approach is that it is directly at odds with all HSE research and advice on the matter:

22–07

> "The HSE expects organisations to carry out a suitable and sufficient risk assessment for stress, and to take action to tackle any problems identified by that risk assessment."

---

[13] Lord McMillan, *Muir v Glasgow Corporation*, 1944 S.L.T. at [64].
[14] *Young v Post Office* [2002] EWCA Civ 661.
[15] *Dickins v O2* [2008] EWCA Civ 1144.

The HSE have identified six management standards which cover the primary sources of stress at work. The HSE website[16] contains a "Model Stress Policy", the cornerstone of which is risk assessment. Further, counselling is confidential and will not provide management with information about the causes of stress at work. It may simply reinforce the idea that the individual and not the job is the problem.[17]

Whilst Lord MacFadyen in *Cross* held that in 1993 there was no duty on an employer to conduct a risk assessment in terms of the Management of Health and Safety at Work Regulations 1992, he reserved his position on future cases. Risk assessment is precisely the focus of the current HSE thinking in the matter. In a field where there was an explosion of knowledge throughout the 1990s it is suggested that with expert evidence as to current practice, the courts might expect a large employer today to carry out a risk assessment for stress related illness. At the very least where there are signs of impending harm to health, there should be some kind of intervention and investigation as to whether the problem relates to the claimant, the job, or an interaction between the two. This is a matter of evidence and what you will certainly require is an expert witness able to speak to recent research, literature and practice in the field. It seems likely that in future cases reliance will be placed on the provisions of the Management of Health and Safety at Work Regulations 1999 in respect of risk assessment, intervention and precaution.

Causation

22–08 The normal rules of causation will apply. It is not enough for a pursuer simply to show that the defenders' acts or omissions increased the risk of a worsening or recurrence of the illness, there must be a material contribution. In addition the Court of Appeal in *Sutherland* treated mental illness resulting from stress at work as potentially a "divisible" disease. Whilst the employee does not have to show that the breach of duty was the whole cause of the ill health, where there are other competing factors, the court may apportion damages to give account to those. However in *Dickins v O2* Lady Justice Smith doubted whether mental illness was a divisible disease, held that the defendants had caused the claimant to reach "tipping point" and would have refused to apportion damages if the point had been raised. In *Sutherland* it was emphasised that the employer should only pay the proportion of the harm which was attributable to his wrongdoing. Many claimants will suffer from pre-existing personal problems which act in combination with stressors at work. It would be for the defender to raise the question of apportionment and to meet the burden of proof of apportionment. This approach would appear to fly in the face of the principle that the victim must be taken as found.[18] It is not yet known which approach will be followed in Scotland. If Lady Justice Smith is correct, then the question for the courts would be whether the pre-existing vulnerability and stressors would have meant that

---

[16] http://www.hse.gov.uk [Accessed September 19, 2011].
[17] "Managing the Causes of Workplace Stress" (Suffolk: HSE Books, September 2009).
[18] See, e.g. *McKillen v Barclay Curle*, 1967 S.L.T. 41.

the pursuer would be liable to have suffered psychiatric injury in any event, and the issue would be to what extent the defenders' breach had accelerated the breakdown. There was no apportionment carried out by Lord Bonomy in his putative assessment of damages in *Green v Argyll & Bute Council*.[19]

Practical considerations

The courts both in Scotland and in England have now established various hurdles for claimants. Whether these are viewed as matters of principle or simply evidentiary burdens, the practical effect is that a successful claimant must be brought through the eye of the needle.

22–09

Approach to the evidence

1. Obtain the whole of the pursuer's GP and medical records including any treatment by a community psychiatric nurse. Check whether there has been any diagnosis of psychiatric illness.
2. The HSE have recently produced management standards with a view to establishing benchmarks for measuring employers' performance in preventing work related stress, with a view to assisting the enforcement of stress related health and safety offences.[20] The headings are:

    - Demands: This includes issues like workloads, work patterns and the work environment.
    - Control: How much say the person has in the way they do their work.
    - Support: Includes the encouragement, sponsorship and resources provided by the organisation, line management and colleagues.
    - Relationships: Includes promoting positive working to avoid conflict and dealing with unacceptable behaviour.
    - Role: Whether people understand their role within the organisation and whether the organisation ensures that the person does not have conflicting role.
    - Change: How organisational change (large or small) is managed and communicated in the organisation.

22–10

You should make a conscious effort to focus the evidence under at least some of these headings.

3. Take a full job history from the client. This invariably means trying to elicit a concrete factual basis for the client's impressionistic feeling that he has been exposed to intolerable working conditions. Try to obtain some form of corroboration, a task invariably complicated by the fact that most potential witnesses will still be in the employment of the target organisation, and are

---

[19] *Green v Argyll & Bute Council* Unreported February 28, 2002 Court of Session.
[20] "Managing the Causes of Workplace Stress" (Suffolk: HSE Books, September 2009).

understandably reluctant to become involved. Trying to assemble the facts is a slow and arduous process. The practitioner must be alert for any factor which might put the employer on notice that the client is vulnerable not simply to stress, but to psychiatric injury from stress. All communications to the employer, particularly from medical sources should be scrutinised. Employee records and annual appraisals should be obtained. Were there any other employees who suffered absences as a result of overwork? Is it possible to say on any objective level that the claimant was exposed to an unusual level of demand? Is there any acknowledgement from the employers of this?

4. Obtain a report from a consultant psychiatrist which diagnoses a distinct psychiatric illness usually with reference to the American Diagnostic and Statistical Manual of Mental Disorder (DSM IV 1994 or the World Health Organisation's ICD-10, Classification of Mental and Behavioural Disorders 1992). You will also need an expert report from an occupational psychologist, who is familiar with the current HSE publications and research, and preferably has practical experience in the field as an in-house advisor or consultant. He should advise on current practice and be able to identify steps which should have been taken by the employer.

PRACTICE POINTS

Demands of the job on the individual

22–11 The practitioner should be looking for:

1. Excessive workload.
2. Long hours culture.
3. Inherently stressful nature of work, e.g. child protection officer in *Walker v Northumberland*.
4. Any other particular facts which objectively might indicate a potential for susceptible individual to develop a mental breakdown.

Foreseeability

22–12 1. An employer will rarely have *actual* knowledge of impending psychiatric illness. You are looking to establish *constructive* knowledge via employee susceptibility. Typically the kind of evidence will be:

    i. Individual complaints.
    ii. Prolonged absences from work with supporting sicknotes indicating the absences are work stress related.
    iii. Previous periods of ill health.

iv. Other colleagues with similar work and stress related illness and in particular that the previous occupants of the claimant's job have suffered.

Bullying and harassment claims: common law

These cases at common law face the same difficulties in causation and foreseeability as the stress at work claims. They are akin to the traditional causes of personal injury actions in that the claimant is generally able to set out a specific factual trail involving personal interaction, which is the foundation of the action. In *Ward v Scotrail* the pursuer was a young woman who was exposed to sexual harassment by one of her colleagues employed by the defenders. The court held that where the pursuer had complained to her employers about the inappropriate attention of her colleague, that a case to answer based on the defenders' own fault was apt for enquiry.

In *Ward* the court held that the defenders would not otherwise be vicariously liable for the unauthorised actions of their employee. In *Lister v Hesley Hall Ltd*,[21] the House of Lords held that an employer could be liable for the clandestine acts of his employees if those acts were committed in circumstances brought about by the nature of the employment. Lord Clyde observed that the facts in *Ward* were such that "the employee was indulging in an unrelated and independent venture of his own". Where the conduct complained of is connected with work as opposed to merely occurring at work *Lister* may well provide a route whereby employers are held vicariously liable for cases of bullying, harassment and abuse.[22] In the case of *Wilson v Exel*[23] an assault by a supervisor which occurred at work and was a prank gone wrong did not attract vicarious liability. In *Horkulak v Cantor Fitzgerald International*, a senior director successfully claimed wrongful dismissal from the world's largest inter-dealer broker following a six month period of bullying and harassment by the company president. The president's continual use of foul and abusive language towards the plaintiff was designed to humiliate and intimidate him, giving no opportunity for rational response or discussion. This was a breach of an implied term of trust and confidence, and almost £1 million was awarded in damages. Because the action proceeded on a contractual basis, there was no claim for injury to feelings, and the award was for past and future wage loss only,[24] with damages being reduced on appeal for failure to mitigate loss.[25]

Bullying and harassment claims: Protection from Harassment Act 1997

This Act now creates a civil remedy of damages where a person is a victim of a course of conduct amounting to harassment. The key provision is s.8,

22–13

22–14

---

[21] *Lister v Hesley Hall Ltd* [2001] 2 All E.R. 769.
[22] See, e.g. *Gorrie v The Marist Brothers*, 2002 S.C.L.R. 436, decision of Sheriff Principal J. McInnes at Dumfries, November 22, 2001.
[23] *Wilson v Exel*, 2010 S.L.T. 671.
[24] [2004] I.C.R. 697.
[25] [2005] I.C.R. 402.

which provides that a person must not pursue a course of conduct which amounts to harassment. Harassment may be intentional in the mind of the perpetrator, or may be presumed when the conduct would be assessed as harassment by the reasonable man. Conduct includes speech, and harassment specifically includes causing a person alarm or distress. It must involve specific conduct on at least two occasions. In *Robertson v The Scottish Ministers*[26] Lord Emslie held that a relevant common law case had been pled, notwithstanding that the conduct would not amount to criminal conduct. In *Marinello v City of Edinburgh Council*,[27] Lord Uist held that the conduct must be "fairly severe, or oppressive and unacceptable, but not necessarily criminal". In *Marinello* the pursuer averred that he had been subjected to verbal abuse and criticism by his superiors, ending in September 2005. A workplace grievance had been partly upheld. In March 2007 it was alleged that whilst the pursuer was absent from the workplace on sick leave, one of the perpetrators drove a van in his direction, and gesticulated at him. The Court held that these constituted discrete chapters and could not be taken together to form a code of conduct. As a result the claim arising from the course of conduct ending in September 2005 was time barred, in terms of s.18(B) of the Act. However this stringent approach was disapproved by the Inner House.[28] Matters should be looked at broadly, and the second incident might form part of a code of conduct.[29] The case was allowed to go to proof.

The House of Lords in *Majrowski v Guys and St. Thomas' NHS Trust*[30] has confirmed that the employer can be vicariously liable for a course of conduct of harassment by one of its employees.

There are obvious advantages to the pursuer in this legislation:

1. There is no need to prove reasonable foreseeability.
2. There is no requirement to prove distinct psychiatric disorder, beyond alarm and distress.

Moreover the structure of the Act disciplines the pursuer to focus on specific instances and helps move the issue away from the difficult factual terrain of intangible and impressionistic evidence about unfair treatment.

Employment law issues

22–15 Clearly there will be many situations where the client will have a choice of remedy, either an action of damages, or alternatively a claim to an employment tribunal, generally for constructive dismissal. The latter should be dealt with by an employment law specialist, and is outwith the scope of this book. Personal injury practitioners however should be aware that the effect of an employment tribunal claim is likely to make the issues res judicata for any common law action. If you are aware that

---

[26] *Robertson v The Scottish Ministers* [2007] CSOH 186.
[27] *Marinello v City of Edinburgh Council*, 2010 S.L.T. 349.
[28] *Marinello v City of Edinburgh Council*, 2011 S.L.T. 615.
[29] See also *Iqbal v Dean Manson Solicitors* [2011] EWCA Civ 123.
[30] *Majrowski v Guys and St. Thomas' NHS Trust* [2007] 1 A.C. 224

such action is being taken the client must be fully advised that he will unable to pursue a claim for damages at common law.[31]

---

[31] See *Sheriff v Klyne Tugs (Lowestoft) Ltd* [1999] I.C.R. 1170.

CHAPTER 23

ACCIDENTS TO CHILDREN

23–01 This section looks briefly at situations commonly encountered in practice. It is confined to "single event" accidents. Claims relating to child abuse, or the exercise of statutory powers by a local authority, are beyond the scope of this book.

In terms of the Age of Legal of Capacity (Scotland) Act 1991 s.1(i)(a), a young person has legal capacity from the age of 16. Under the Children (Scotland) Act 1995, a child of 12 is presumed to be of sufficient understanding to instruct a solicitor and raise proceedings. Where there is no such capacity an action should be raised in the name of the child's representative, who will usually be a parent, designed in the writ as "guardian". A style for an instance is included in *Greens Litigation Styles*[1] at p.A16.

Occupier's liability cases

23–02 The leading cases show a consistent trend of accidents where children (usually boys) have been foolhardy, frequently on a spectacular scale. Society should expect this. Very few of these cases will fail on the test of reasonable foreseeability. So where a child entered an unguarded trench, knocked over a paraffin lamp and caused a gas explosion, the fact that the precise chain of events was unforeseeable did not bar recovery.[2] In *Miller v South of Scotland Electricity Board*,[3] a child was injured after coming into contact with a live electric cable in a partially demolished house. Averments against the electricity authority that they should have known that partially demolished houses were an allurement to children and that they were negligent in failing to remove the live electric wires were held relevant to go to proof. In *Devlin v Strathclyde Regional Council*,[4] a 14-year-old boy gained access to a school roof on a Saturday, and played tig there with his friends. In the course of the game he jumped down from a five-foot dome directly onto a skylight which shattered, and he fell to his death. It was held that this last action went beyond what the defenders could reasonably foresee, and is a rare example of a case failing on this basis. The approach taken by the courts is well illustrated by the case of *Jolley v Southwark LBC*.[5] The 14-year-old plaintiff and his friends

---

[1] *Greens Litigation Styles* (Edinburgh: W.Green).
[2] *Hughes v Lord Advocate*, 1963 S.L.T. 150 (HL).
[3] *Miller v South of Scotland Electricity Board*, 1958 S.L.T. 229 (HL).
[4] *Devlin v Strathclyde Regional Council*, 1993 S.L.T. 699.
[5] *Jolley v Southwark LBC* [2000] 3 All E.R. 409.

were attracted by the presence of an abandoned boat amongst derelict vehicles, in a grassed area in the inner city. They tried to repair the boat, jacking it up to do so. The props collapsed, and the plaintiff was seriously injured. The Court of Appeal held that although in general terms the boat was an allurement, the particular facts of the accident were not reasonably foreseeable, since the actions of the boys in jacking up the boat were not normal child's play. This decision was overturned by the House of Lords. They pointed out that it was well-known that children's play tends to mimic adult behaviour and the attempts to prop up the boat and to repair it were reasonably foreseeable. The plaintiff succeeded, subject to a 25 per cent deduction for contributory negligence. In this area of law, the cases tend to relate to premises, buildings or things which are attractive to high-spirited children. The matter was put vividly by Lord Stott in the case of *Telfer v Glasgow Corporation*,[6] when he referred to a derelict building as follows:

> "It afforded every possible allurement for them [children]—sliding doors that come off their runners and could be pushed in, leading into a big empty building with inspection pits full of water and rubbish, tyres, glass partitions to be broken, a roof with pigeons and with pigeons' eggs, wee round spiral stairs, even for a time a derelict motor van. All the evidence indicated that the place attracted hordes of children of all ages. It had in effect become a glorified adventure playground for the children of the neighbourhood and a highly dangerous one ..."

The other frequently encountered situation is where a known danger has been fenced off, but the child overcomes the precaution. Whilst the standard of care required of an occupier will vary according to the age and intelligence of the child, there is no duty to build a boy-proof fence. The occupier will have fulfilled his statutory duty "if he erects an obstacle which a boy must take some trouble to overcome before he can reach the dangerous apparatus".[7] However this does not mean that if there is a fence the case must fail. In *Dawson v Scottish Power Plc*[8] an 11-year-old boy was playing football in a car park adjacent to an electricity substation. The ball went over a fence into the substation. The child followed the ball into the substation, negotiating a spiked fence to do so. At its lowest point the fence was only four feet high. He was injured on the way in when he slipped and suffered a serious hand injury, before retrieving the ball and kicking it back into play!

The court found for the pursuer. The child's actions were "boyish" and reasonably foreseeable. The defenders could have done more by erecting a higher fence, which on the facts would have deterred the child. It is clear from the report that those acting for the child also had the benefit of a supportive witness from the Health and Safety Executive. In *Young v*

---

[6] *Telfer v Glasgow Corporation*, 1974 S.L.T. (Notes) 51.
[7] *McGlone v British Railways Board*, 1966 S.L.T. (HL) at [2].
[8] *Dawson v Scottish Power Plc*, 1999 S.L.T. 672.

Kent County Council[9] it was held that the local authority should have taken care to prevent children climbing onto the roof of a school building. There was a simple low-cost solution, and they were held liable to a child who had fallen through a skylight. Contributory negligence was assessed at 50 per cent.

23-03 A special sub-category of this kind of case relates to accidents on building sites. Agents should obtain the HSE publication "Protecting the Public",[10] which points out that between 1986 and 1996 construction activities killed 27 children, and injured over 450. It states[11]:

> "Children have vivid imaginations. They often see construction sites as playgrounds where they can act out favourite games, films, TV programmes or cartoons."

There is a heavy duty on the contractor to ensure that the site is securely fenced off and the attentions of children must be in their contemplation. In *Galbraith Curator Ad Litem v Stewart*[12] the pursuer cited the HSE Guidance Note GS7 entitled "Accidents to children on construction sites". It was held that it was reasonably foreseeable that a group of children might gain access to pipe work, and that an injury caused to the pursuer when the pipe was set in motion was reasonably foreseeable. The defenders would have done enough if they had immobilised the pipes.

In *Morton v Glasgow City Council*[13] a 14-year-old boy fell 15 feet to the ground from scaffolding which had been erected by the local authority. Sheriff Kearney held that the defenders had a duty to erect a peripheral 2m fence or close up barrier. A plea of volenti non fit injuria was dismissed.

These kind of cases do appear to be fact-sensitive. For the practitioner this means investigation to obtain as much evidence as possible of previous complaints, incidents and near misses.

Road traffic accidents involving children

23-04 Typically this will involve the child as a pedestrian or cyclist. More than six child pedestrians are killed or seriously injured each week. Children frequently misjudge the speed and intentions of drivers, are easily distracted and may dash into the road without looking. Where a child has been knocked down by a vehicle, witnesses very frequently put a gloss on matters by saying "the boy just ran out, the driver had no chance". This may or may not be a correct legal analysis. The kind of approach the court will take is illustrated by the Court of Appeal decision of *James v Fairlie*.[14] Annona was eight when she was knocked down by a vehicle driven by the defendant. The court first of all tried to establish the dri-

---

[9] *Young v Kent County Council* [2005] EWHC 1342 Q.B.
[10] *Protecting the Public: Your Next Move (HS(G)151)* (Suffolk: HSE Books, 2009).
[11] *Protecting the Public: Your Next Move (HS(G)151)* (Suffolk: HSE Books, 2009), p.34.
[12] *Galbraith Curator Ad Litem v Stewart*, 1998 S.L.T. 1305.
[13] *Morton v Glasgow City Council*, 2007 S.L.T. (Sh Ct) 81.
[14] *James v Fairlie* [2002] EWCA Civ 162.

ver's line of sight, and to estimate the length of time a child would be in his view. They considered whether there were any special circumstances which would impose a particular duty to slow down, such as children on the pavement, the presence of a football on the road, or a parked ice-cream van. Evidence was given to the court by an accident reconstruction expert who tried to create the events before impact using known data on vehicle and walking speeds, and stopping distances. It was held as likely that the plaintiff had taken only 1.7 seconds to reach the middle of the road. Even although the defendant had failed to see her at all, he could not have stopped his vehicle in time to prevent the accident, and the claim was dismissed.

On the other hand where a lorry driver was aware of the presence of children on the pavement who were crossing the road between traffic from time to time, he should have been alert to the danger posed by young children emerging from between parked vehicles and should have taken steps to his offside even where the child was in his actual view for only one second.[15]

The Highway Code states:

> "205. There is a risk of pedestrians, especially children, stepping unexpectedly into the road. You should drive with the safety of children in mind at a speed suitable for the conditions."

In *Stainsby v Fallon*[16] evidence that a driver had passed very close to the pavement where two young boys were walking was held to constitute a possible ground of fault which should have been allowed to go to a jury. A new trial was ordered.

Contributory negligence in road traffic accidents

The Highway Code states: **23–05**

> "7. Many children cannot judge how fast vehicles are going or how far away they are!"

Notwithstanding it has to be said that until recently courts in Scotland have consistently found high degrees of contributory negligence for even young children. In *Harvie v Cairns*, 6-year-old Fiona Harvie was killed when she ran out into the road in front of a Ford Transit pick-up truck which was being driven too quickly. The deceased was found two-thirds to blame for the accident. It may be that the Inner House decision of *McCluskey v Wallace* (see para.17–08) has reversed this trend, but agents should prepare by finding out as much as possible about the general intelligence and road safety knowledge of the particular child.

---

[15] *Ehrari (A child) v Curry* [2007] EWCA Civ 120.
[16] *Stainsby v Fallon*, 2010 Rep. L.R. 27.

Accidents in school

23–06 In no area of law is the hysteria attached to the "compensation culture" and "litigation explosion" so singularly misconceived. The parents who instruct solicitors to recover damages for injuries suffered by children whilst at school or on school trips will generally be disappointed. The reality is that successful reported cases are extremely rare. The standard of care to be expected of the school is that of the reasonable parent. In *McDougall v Strathclyde Regional Council*[17] the Inner House commented that this formula was not particularly helpful for individual cases. The frequently cited test is taken from *Beaumont v Surrey County Council*:

> "The duty of a headmaster towards his pupils is said to be to take such care of them as a reasonably careful and prudent father would take of his own children. That standard is a helpful one when considering, for example, individual instructions given to individual children in a school. It would be very unwise to allow a six-year-old child to carry a kettle of boiling water—that type of instruction. But that standard when applied to an incident of horseplay in a school of 900 pupils is somewhat unrealistic if not unhelpful.
>
> In the context of the present action it appears to me to be easier and preferable to use the ordinary language of the law of negligence. That is, it is a headmaster's duty, bearing in mind the known propensities of boys and indeed girls between the ages of 11 and 17 or 18, to take all reasonable and proper steps to prevent any of the pupils under his care from suffering injury from inanimate objects, from the actions of their fellow pupils, or from a combination of the two. That is a high standard."[18]

In particular the courts both in England and Scotland have been careful to limit the extent of the duty of supervision on teachers, whether in the classroom or playground. So in the case of *Ahmed v City of Glasgow Council*,[19] Sheriff Principal Bowen held that averments that a teacher had left a class unsupervised for 10 minutes, during which time a pupil was injured by a rubber thrown by another pupil, were so irrelevant as not to merit enquiry. The accident was not reasonably foreseeable. In *Hunter v Perth & Kinross Council*[20] it was held that there was no duty on school teachers to supervise pupils as they were boarding the school bus. In *Cuthbertson v Merchison Castle School*[21] it was held that there was no duty to supervise pupils who were hitting golf balls at a practice driving range. In *McDougall v Strathclyde Regional Council*[22] the facts were that a 13-year-old child was injured in the course of a gymnastic lesson. He had attempted a jump which was one of three permitted exercises, but it was

---

[17] *McDougall v Strathclyde Regional Council*, 1996 S.L.T. 1124.
[18] *Beaumont v Surrey CC* 66 LGR 580 (1968). This statement was approved by Lady Dorrian in *Brown v North Lanarkshire Council*, 2011 S.L.T. 150.
[19] *Ahmed v City of Glasgow Council*, 2000 S.L.T. 153 (Sh Ct).
[20] *Hunter v Perth & Kinross Council*, 2001 G.W.D. 25-974.
[21] *Cuthbertson v Merchison Castle School*, 2001 S.L.T. 13 (Sh Ct).
[22] *McDougall v Strathclyde Regional Council*, 1996 S.L.T. 1124.

one which he had not previously tried and was beyond his level of competence. The gymnastic master was assisting a pupil elsewhere. The Inner House held that the boy's actions were not reasonably foreseeable.

Such decisions on reasonable foreseeability contrast markedly with the courts' readiness to ascribe propensities of high spirits, mischief and adventure in public liability cases, and it is hard not to suspect the hand of public policy at work. However in *Brown v North Lanarkshire Council*,[23] young children were working on the floor with paintbrushes. They jostled together causing Thomas Brown to fall over so that the end of the paintbrush penetrated his eye causing brain damage. Lady Dorrian held that the full panoply of risk assessment under the MHSWR 1999 did not represent an appropriate approach, even on an evidential basis. But she did find that the risk of injury should have occurred if minds had been properly directed to the nature of the activity before the face, and liability was established. She agreed with the observation of Professor Walker in his work on Delict where he states:

23-07

> "A schoolteacher owes a duty to take reasonable care for the safety and health of the children under his charge, and must exercise care and forethought, having regard to their age, inexperience, carelessness and high spirits and the nature and degree of danger, not to subject them to avoidable risks of harm."

A further difficulty for practitioners is that defenders are increasingly arguing that the test for a teacher's negligence is a *Hunter v Hanley*[24] test, i.e. actions which no teacher of ordinary skill would take. The test has been held as relevant to the actings of a guidance teacher in the context of alleged bullying.[25] In *Ahmed* it was doubted whether the test applied to single event accidents.

In England in the case of *Chittock v Woodbridge School*,[26] the plaintiff suffered catastrophic injury when against specific instructions he skied off-piste during a school skiing holiday. It was the second time in the week that he had been skiing off-piste. The judge at first instance found for the plaintiff on the basis that the teacher could have stopped the pupil completely from skiing, instead of extending permission to ski on a temporary basis. The Court of Appeal reversed the decision. Whilst they did not apply the *Hunter v Hanley* test to the teacher's actions, they pointed out that the decision to suspend was within a range of reasonable responses for a teacher in this position, acting as a reasonably careful parent.

The kind of claim where there might be prospects of success is well illustrated by the case of *Kearn Price v Kent County Council*.[27] The 15-year-old plaintiff suffered a serious eye injury when he was struck in the playground by a heavy leather football. The accident took place at 08.40

---

[23] *Brown v North Lanarkshire Council*, 2011 S.L.T. 150.
[24] *Hunter v Hanley*, 1955 S.L.T. 213.
[25] See *Scott v Lothian Regional Council*, 1998 G.W.D. 33-1719.
[26] *Chittock v Woodbridge School* [2002] C.L. June 26 (C.A.).
[27] *Kearn Price v Kent County Council* [2003] P.I.Q.R. P11.

before school had formally commenced. The evidence was that football in the playground with heavy leather balls had been banned by the school, that the ban was routinely flouted, and that if occasional spot checks had been carried out, pupils would have stopped the practice. The plaintiff was not a participant but a bystander. The claim succeeded, and the Court of Appeal found comfort in a similar decision of the High Court of Australia.

The lessons for the practitioner who hopes to present a successful claim are as follows.

1. Check whether there is any published guide or Code of Pratice relative to the activities. In the case of *Smoldon v Whitworth and Nolan*[28] the 17½-year-old plaintiff suffered a catastrophic injury when a scrum collapsed during a game of rugby There was extensive evidence on the dangers of collapsing scrummages, and the high duty of care of referees in the circumstances, but with reference to an official code of practice. Similar codes are in existence for other school activities. By way of example, the Department for Education and Skills issued "Health and Safety of Pupils on Educational Visits, A Good Practice Guide" in 1998.
2. Obtain all possible evidence and information which arguably put the school on notice of any special propensity for ill discipline or horseplay, or previous incidents where dangers have arisen. There may be better prospects where the accident has been caused by some structural defect, or where some feature of the school layout is liable to encourage foolhardy behaviour. So in the case of *Wardle v Scottish Borders Council*,[29] the school was held liable when a child fell from internal beams (known to the schoolchildren as "the monkey bars") as being an activity which should have been within its contemplation.

Games

23–08 In *Scout Association v Barnes*,[30] 13-year-old Mark Barnes was injured whilst playing "objects in the dark" a game whereby the boy scouts would run round a group of small blocks. The scoutmaster would then turn off all the lights which was a sign for the boys to rush to the blocks to collect one, with a loser being eliminated in each round. By a majority the Court of Appeal held that the lights-out element of the game added nothing to its value as a social activity and made injury to one of the boy scouts reasonably foreseeable.

---

[28] *Smoldon v Whitworth and Nolan* [1997] P.I.Q.R. P133.
[29] *Wardle v Scottish Borders Council*, 2011 Rep. L.R. 74.
[30] *Scout Association v Barnes* [2010] EWCA Civ 1476.

Contributory negligence and children

In *Dawson v Scottish Power*[31] the court held that the 11-year-old pursuer **23–09** was one-third contributorily negligent in attempting to scale the fence of the electricity substation. In *Morton* the 14 year old child was held to be 25 per cent contributorily negligent. In *Wardle v Scottish Borders Council*, Sheriff Principal Bowen, January 31, 2011, the nine-year-old child was held to be 50 per cent contributorily negligent, but that was on the basis she had been warned against climbing very shortly before her accident. In *Galbraith's Curator Ad Litem v Stewart*[32] the eight-year-old child was held not to blame in any way. Where the defenders allege that the accident has been contributed to by the negligence of the child's parents, e.g. by their lack of supervision or inattention to danger, the court will only reduce damages by making a finding of apportionment where the defenders have convened the parents as separate third parties. In *Brogan Tutors v Glasgow District Council*[33] Lord Wylie held that the child was not identified with the parents for this purpose. Although on causation the defenders were only 20 per cent to blame, and the child's mother was 80 per cent to blame, the child's claim was not cut down in any way.

---

[31] See *Morton v Glasgow City Council*, 2007 S.L.T. (Sh Ct) 81; *Wardle v Scottish Borders Council*, 2011 Rep. L.R. 74 and *Galbraith Curator Ad Litem v Stewart*, 1998 S.L.T. 1305.
[32] *Galbraith's Curator Ad Litem v Stewart*, 1998 S.L.T. 1305.
[33] *Brogan Tutors v Glasgow District Council*, 1978 S.L.T. 47.

CHAPTER 24

HOLIDAY CLAIMS

24–01 Typically the practitioner is instructed by a client who complains about travel disruption and delay, the quality of hotel accommodation, or injuries suffered during the course of the holiday. Before 1992 the contractual duty of a tour operator was to exercise skill and care in the making of suitable arrangements for the provision of accommodation, transport and services. In particular, without something else, the tour operator was not liable for the casual negligence of the persons who delivered the service.[1]

In many current holiday contracts, the tour operator specifically accepts responsibility for the acts and omissions of their suppliers, employees or agents.[2] In those cases proceedings can be issued in Scotland, with jurisdiction established by the domicile of the pursuer in a consumer contract. The common law position of the consumer is now greatly strengthened by the Package Travel, Package Holidays and Package Tours Regulations 1992 ("the Package Tour Regulations"). Otherwise the client will have to issue in the country of the accident. Care must be taken to avoid local limitation issues, and a realistic cost benefit analysis should be undertaken before instructing foreign agents.

THE PACKAGE TRAVEL, PACKAGE HOLIDAYS AND PACKAGE TOURS REGULATIONS 1992

24–02 "Package" has a complex definition in the regulations (reg.2), but in broad terms a package must be sold or offered for sale at an inclusive price, be pre-arranged and should include a minimum of two of the three elements of:

1. Transport.
2. Accommodation.
3. Other travel services (not ancillary to transport and accommodation) amounting to a significant proportion of the package.

A family holiday booked through a travel agent and involving air and local travel to a pre-selected hotel is the obvious example. The regulations apply to packages sold or offered for sale in the United Kingdom

---

[1] *Wall v Silver Wing Surface Arrangements* Unreported November 16, 1981 Q.B.D.
[2] See, e.g. *Ellison v Inspirations East Ltd*, 2003 S.L.T. 291.

regardless of the tour operator's place of establishment or the holiday destination.

The client will be the "consumer" in terms of the regulations, and the regulations apply "to the other party to the contract". This can be either the retailer, generally a travel agent, or an organiser, generally a tour operator, or both. In *Hone v Going Places Travel Ltd*,[3] the plaintiff booked a holiday in Turkey with Suntours Ltd after seeing the defendant's advertisement on Teletext. By the time proceedings were issued, Suntours were in liquidation and the action proceeded against the travel agents with whom the holiday was booked. The Court of Appeal stated: "there is no dispute that Going Places is the other party to the contract in terms of the Regulations".

It should be noted that in *Hone* the travel agent was an agent for an undisclosed principal, and safety first for the practitioner will generally be to sue the tour operator if solvent.

Regulations 4, 5 and 6 cover the contents of brochures and information provided to the consumer; reg.13 provides for compensation in the event of cancellation; reg.14 provides that compensation is payable where after departure a significant proportion of the services contracted for are not provided. Detailed guidance on the interpretation of the regulations is contained in *Question and Answer Guidance for Organisers and Retailers 2006*, issued by the Department of Trade and Industry and available online.[4] In practical terms the most important change is made by reg.15, which provides:

> "Liability of other party to the contract for proper performance of obligations under contract
>
> **15.**—(1) The other party to the contract is liable to the consumer for the proper performance of the obligations under the contract, irrespective of whether such obligations are to be performed by that other party or by other suppliers of services but this shall not affect any remedy or right of action which that other party may have against those other suppliers of services."

There are exceptions where the failure is the fault of the consumer, or caused by a third party unconnected with the provision of the services contracted for, or where the failures are caused by unusual and unforeseeable circumstances outwith the control of the other party.

In addition in terms of reg.15(a) the contract must oblige the consumer to communicate the complaint in writing within a specified period. This is an important practical point on receipt of instructions.

The effect of reg.15 is that the other party, i.e. the retailer or tour operator, or both, become vicariously liable for the acts and omissions of those persons providing the various components of the package, e.g. hotels, carriers, local transport agencies and the like. Liability is not strict and negligence must be shown. By way of analogy the Court of Appeal in

---

[3] *Hone v Going Places Travel Ltd* [2001] EWCA Civ 947.
[4] *http://www.bis.gov.uk/files/file35634.pdf* [Accessed September 20, 2011].

Hone stated that there was no obligation to ensure that the consumer did not catch an infection whilst in the hotel swimming pool, but that "the obligation assumed will be that reasonable skill and care will be taken to ensure that the pool is free from infection". In *Hone*, the plaintiff was injured during the emergency evacuation of an aircraft. No negligence was shown, and in the absence of an express contractual term that the air carriage would be safely executed, the claim failed. The context of the duty of care was also considered in *Todd v Thomson Tour Operators Ltd*.[5] Gareth Todd was aged 10 when he caught his finger in a hotel lift in Majorca. The Court of Appeal held that he must prove negligence. It was submitted that the trial judge was wrong in not applying British safety standards to the lift:

> "That is not the correct approach to a case such as this where an accident occurred in a foreign country. The law of this country is applied to the case as to the establishing of negligence, but there is no requirement that a hotel for example in Majorca is obliged to comply with British Safety Standards."

The defenders established a system of maintenance and inspection and the claim failed. In *Bowen v Airtours Plc*,[6] the plaintiff was injured whilst on a package holiday when he climbed onto a table during a night out and was struck by a revolving fan. Liability was apportioned 50/50 by the court. The siting of the table directly underneath the fans was a recognised and avoidable danger, there had been unlimited amounts of alcohol made available, and the defenders should have known that people would lose their inhibitions and be less responsible about their own safety.

In *R (a child) v Iberotravel Ltd (trading as Sunworld Ltd)*,[7] a six-year-old child suffered catastrophic injury following a near drowning accident in a swimming pool in Majorca. Whilst no reliance could be placed on British Safety Standards for the construction of the swimming pool, an internal Sunworld memorandum showed that by their own internal standards, the hotel should have put up notices saying that the pool was unsuitable for non-swimmers. Further, in terms of local Spanish regulations there should have been a lifeguard on active supervision by the pool. Liability was established with the parents of the child being held liable for 17 per cent of damages, in respect of their contributory negligence in allowing the child to enter the pool outwith their supervision.

24–03 Practice points

1. Is it a package?

The upsurge in internet use has meant that many holidays are now booked online with the consumer taken to different on-screen pages. Typically either accommodation or flights will be selected first, with

---

[5] *Todd v Thomson Tour Operators Ltd* Unreported July 2, 2000 Court of Appeal.
[6] *Bowen v Airtours Plc*, 1999 C.L.Y. 3945.
[7] *R (a child) v Iberotravel Ltd (trading as Sunworld Ltd)*, 2001 C.L.Y. 4453.

options thereafter for flights or accommodation, car hire and transport. An omnibus bill is presented at the end of the online transaction payable to a single organisation.

In 2008 the Department for Business Enterprise and Regulatory Reform published a useful online guidance note entitled *What is a package?*[8] This represents its current view of the law, taking into account recent case law and in particular the *Association of British Travel Agents ("ABTA") v The Civil Aviation Authority ("CAA")*,[9] where the definition is analysed.

The key point is to consider whether the elements are being sold as components of a pre-arranged combination. The *ABTA v CAA* judgment gives two examples of packages. In the first the components are sold at a price different from the sum of their individual parts. There will be little difficulty in concluding that this is a package. The other example is where the customer is not told the price of individual items, but simply the composite price. This is likely to be a package. The guide suggests the following evidential pointers to a package:

- Advertising brochures and commitments in relation to hotel beds or airline seats are useful indicators that services are being offered as packages.
- Describing the services as a package or dynamic package.
- Where the customer makes approaches to the agent to "buy a holiday" it is likely that what was sold was a package.
- Where the customer requests a flight and accommodation and/or other services it is likely that this will be a package.
- Non-availability of travel services as a separate service outwith the combination will indicate that there is a package.
- Payment and composite billing. Composite billing might be evidence that the services have been sold as a package. The key point is whether the components are sold in combination or separately.
- Customer perception. The judgment draws out that whether the customer thinks that he is buying two or more separate services rather than a combination may be a powerful indicator as to the nature of the transaction.

The question of internet sales is dealt with at paras 21–26 of the guide. The guide points out that some websites use a "shopping basket" to place items in prior to purchase. If the customer chooses and contracts for two or more of the services on the same occasion it could well be a package.

2. Will you need to plead and prove local standards?

The local standards test has been a convenient litigation escape route for **24–04** the travel industry. Put short, any situation which is likely to be covered by local standards or regulations, e.g. building regulations, swimming

---

[8] *http://www.bis.gov.uk/files/file43845.pdf* [Accessed September 20, 2011].
[9] *Association of British Travel Agents ("ABTA") v The Civil Aviation Authority ("CAA")* [2006] EWCA Civ 1356.

pool regulations, electrical installation regulations will require evidence to be led on the national standards, and negligence will be assessed against those standards.[10] There may be some situations, e.g. for lifts, where there is an EC Directive 95/16/EC but otherwise in those situations you will need local expertise. This will make most modest value accident claims disproportionate to run. But local standards may not be relevant in respect of casual acts of negligence, e.g. failure to maintain, failure to clean, failure to light. However it would seem sensible in all cases to check what the local regulations say. In countries like Spain and Greece there are, e.g. stringent swimming pool regulations. It is also noteworthy that most tour operators expressly incorporate local safety standards in their booking conditions. After litigation is commenced it is useful to seek recovery of documents from the defenders as to what, e.g. inspections of hotels they have carried out and what their safety expectations are. The requirement to plead local standards does not refer to representations as to quality. In that regard, again the first port of call should be the travel documentation, the booking conditions and any advertising literature. A description, e.g. "situated 50 yards from the beach" must be accurate and will found a claim if it is false.

The local standards rule was followed with some qualifications at sheriff court level in the case of *Pilmar v Balkan Holidays Ltd*,[11] but there has been no discussion by the higher courts in Scotland. In Ireland in *Scaife v Falcon Leisure Group (Overseas) Ltd*[12] the Irish Supreme Court held that the Package Tour Regulations implied a contractual obligation on the part of the tour operator that the hotel would exercise reasonable skill and care in the provision of accommodation and facilities. With reference to EC Council Directive 91/314/EEC1990 it declined to apply Spanish standards to an accident which occurred when liquid had been spilled by staff on a marble floor.

3. Liability for excursions

24–05 A frequently encountered situation is where an accident occurs during an excursion which your client has booked at the resort, at the instigation of the tour operators' representative. The tour operators will always claim that they have no responsibility for what they say are the actings of independent contractors namely the excursion providers. As ever, a close reading of the holiday brochure and terms is important. In *Wong Mee Wan v Kwan Kin Travel Services*[13] W's daughter was killed during a holiday in China when the speedboat in which she was being carried overturned and crashed. An all-inclusive price had been paid which included "transport as specified in the itinerary". The Privy Council held that in the circumstances there was an implied contractual term that the tour operator would exercise reasonable care in the selection of the speedboat driver, and liability was established. In addition the ordinary

---

[10] *Wilson v Best Travel* [1993] 1 All E.R. 353.
[11] *Pilmar v Balkan Holidays Ltd* Unreported February 16, 2007 Cupar Sheriff Court.
[12] *Scaife v Falcon Leisure Group (Overseas) Ltd* [2007] IESC 57.
[13] *Wong Mee Wan v Kwan Kin Travel Services* [1996] 1 W.L.R. 38.

law of agency applied. In the case of *Cheesman v International Travel Services Ltd*[14] the court applied the normal principles of agency to find for the pursuer on the basis that the tour operator was liable as an agent for an undisclosed principal. The lesson for practitioners is to recover all the contractual documentation, and to keep an intense focus on the factual circumstances of the excursion booking. (See also *Moore v Hotel Plan Ltd (t/a Inghams Travel)*[15] where the tour operators were liable for injuries during a snowmobile excursion.)

Accidents on aircraft

International travel is covered by the Warsaw Convention, or the Montreal Convention where the flights involve the USA, or the Air Carrier Liability Order 1998 for flights within the EU including within the UK Accidents on aircraft are now dealt with exclusively by this regime. Liability is directed against the airline carrier and attaches both to accidents on aircraft, and also to accidents within the airport premises if the claimant is in the course of embarkation.[16] The passengers' contributory negligence may be a complete or partial defence (Montreal Convention art.20). There has to have been an "accident". Deep vein thrombosis was not considered to be an accident,[17] and a passenger who suffered a stroke had not suffered an accident (*Chaudhari v British Airways Plc*[18]). In the deep vein thrombosis litigation examples of accidents included:

24–06

- an air crash;
- a collision on the runway;
- a collapsing seat;
- hot food or drink spillage;
- food poisoning;
- a trip over a hazard; and
- an item falling from overhead compartments.

In the House of Lords a distinction was made between the bodily injury to the passenger on the one hand, and the accident by which the bodily injury was caused on the other, and that where the event was no more than the normal operation of the aircraft in normal conditions there was no "accident". The event or happening which caused the damage must be external to the passenger, and the onset of deep vein thrombosis was not an unexpected or unusual event which was external to the passenger. In *Barclay v British Airways Plc*[19] a passenger slipped on a standard plastic strip which covered the wiring on the floor. The case failed. It was not an

---

[14] *Cheesman v International Travel Services Ltd* 2008 Rep. L.R. 66.
[15] *Moore v Hotel Plan Ltd (t/a Inghams Travel)* [2010] EWHC 276 (QB).
[16] See *Philips v Air NZ Ltd* [2002] EWHC 800.
[17] *Deep Vein Thrombosis Air Travel Group Litigation* [2006] 1 A.C. 495.
[18] *Chaudhari v British Airways Plc*, *The Times*, May 7, 1997.
[19] *Barclay v. British Airways Plc* [2009] 3 W.L.R. 369.

"accident". It was an instance of personal, particular or peculiar reaction to the normal operation of the aircraft.

There is a set limit on damages. By far the most important point for practitioners is that there is a two year limitation period with no discretionary extension. A dispiriting proportion of the reported case law relates to claimants who are driven to argue unsuccessfully that the Convention does not apply because the Convention two year time limit has been missed, e.g. *La Roche v Spirit of Adventure (UK) Ltd*.[20] The solicitors instructed by defenders will always take this point, so don't let them talk you over the limitation period.

Damages in holiday cases

24–07 Following *Jackson v Horizon Holidays Ltd*[21] a person who claims breach of contract in respect of a holiday booked in his name can also claim on behalf of others entitled to benefit from the contract, typically a wife, partner and other family members. The action will run in the name of those pursuers who are on the contract with the damages averments detailing the particular loss for each other person affected. In *Buhus-Orwin v Costa Smeralda Holidays Ltd*,[22] where the plaintiff and his family declined alternative accommodation, the plaintiffs successfully claimed a breach of reg.6 when instead of the opulent luxury described, their accommodation comprised a rat-infested villa. They returned home, and were awarded the whole cost of their holiday together with consequential losses and the sum of £2,000 for loss of enjoyment. In accident cases where there is jurisdiction in the Scottish courts, damages will be assessed on the conventional basis.

In *Milner v Carnival Plc (t/a Cunard)*[23] the Court of Appeal offered practical guidance on the quantification of damages for holiday cases. The facts were that the claimants Mr & Mrs Milner had looked forward to a 106 day, round the world "Cruise of a Lifetime" on the *Queen Victoria* at a total cost of £59,052.00. The vessel left Southampton on June 6, 2008. The Milners' cabin accommodation was completely unsuitable by reason of noise and vibration, and they suffered sleepless nights and illnesses before departing the cruise early in Honolulu and returning home on the QE2. Prior to litigation, the claimants and defendants had agreed compensation for this latter period at £48,248.00, less the cost of the QE2 transport (£13,440.00). The Court of Appeal reviewed awards of damages in holiday cases and issued general guidance as to the main heads of claim namely:

1. diminution in the value of the holiday; and
2. inconvenience and distress.

---

[20] *La Roche v Spirit of Adventure (UK) Ltd* [2009] 3 W.L.R. 351.
[21] *Jackson v Horizon Holidays Ltd* [1975] 1 W.L.R. 1468.
[22] *Buhus-Orwin v Costa Smeralda Holidays Ltd*, 2001 C.L.Y. 4273.
[23] *Milner v Carnival Plc (t/a Cunard)* [2010] P.I.Q.R. Q3.

It was important not to confuse the two because that would involve double counting. Insofar as disappointment for diminution in value was concerned, the claimants were not entitled to damages for the loss of the pleasure of the rest of the cruise around the world because that had already been dealt with by agreed pre-litigation damages. The court should consider the actual holiday experience and the reasonable expectations of the consumer. This should be looked at objectively, because otherwise there is a risk that disappointment, and inconvenience and distress would be counted twice. On the basis that a holiday of a lifetime was spoiled, the approach should be to look at the total cost and to make a proportionate deduction for diminution in value of the holiday. In this case the appropriate deduction would be around one-third, which related only to the period on board. The claim for distress and inconvenience was a separate head of damage. This should reflect the actual experience of the claimants. However the court held that damages for mental distress should generally be kept in line with the damages for psychiatric injury contained in the Judicial Studies Board.

In the event the Court of the Appeal awarded the Milners:

1. £3,500.00 in total for diminution in the value of the holiday (this took into account the agreement which had been reached between the parties and the refund which had already been made).
2. Mrs Milner received £4,500.00 for inconvenience and distress.
3. Mr Milner received £3,000.00 for inconvenience and distress.

Although this is an exceptional case, the Court of Appeal stated that increased damages might be paid for special holidays which were spoiled, e.g. honeymoons, but generally in the normal package holiday situation it would be unlikely that damages for loss of value of the holiday would exceed £2,000.00.

This approach is likely to be highly persuasive in the Scottish courts. The message for practitioners is:

1. Assess the value of the diminution of the holiday on an objective basis. This will be a single figure for the whole group, and will be measured against the actual cost of the holiday. It will rarely exceed £2,000.00.
2. Calculate a further amount for personal inconvenience and distress, or in the accident claim situation, pain and suffering. This is unique to the individual claimant, and more than one person may have a claim under this head.

Cancellation, delay, denied boarding

The courts have also been prepared to compensate distress caused by excessive delay at airports. In *Coughlan v Thomson Holidays*[24] the plaintiff's flight was delayed more than 23 hours, and the defendants made inadequate arrangements for overnight accommodation during this

---
[24] *Coughlan v Thomson Holidays*, 2001 C.L.Y. 4276.

time. The defendants' argument that the delay was caused by air traffic control and technical defects with the aircraft which could have been foreseen was rejected.

In *Reid v Ski Independence*[25] the pursuer claimed damages for delay and frustration caused by airport and flight delays and non-delivery of baggage. The defenders' argument that damages were limited in terms of the 1955 Warsaw Convention was rejected. The sheriff awarded damages for frustration, inconvenience and upset in the figure of £400 and £450 to the respective pursuers for their discomfort during a six-day holiday.

In *O'Carroll v Ryanair*[26] Sheriff Principal Young confirmed an award of £750 in respect of baggage which went missing for two days following a flight from Aberdeen to Dublin. He held that damages were not restricted to the Montreal Convention amounts.

EC Regulation 261/2004 provides protection for passengers leaving from a Member State airport, or returning to one, where the airline is a community carrier. They may claim if their flight is cancelled, subject to delay, or if they are "bumped" or denied boarding. There is no right to compensation in "extraordinary circumstances" which could not have been avoided even if all reasonable measures had been taken. There is a very useful on line guide at the Air Transport Users' Council. As from March 2011 the Air Transport Users' Council ceased to exist and its place was taken by the Aviation Consumer Advocacy Panel, but the original Guidance remains extant.

Accidents to passengers on ships

24–09 These are covered by the Athens Convention, and apply to international carriage by sea. They do not relate to holiday complaints about quality, e.g. for a package tour holiday, and once again the regime is exclusive as against the shipping carrier. Liability for "incidents" caused during the course of the carriage are governed by the Convention and there are no other remedies. The "incident" must arise as a result of the fault or neglect of the carrier or his agents. There is a presumption of fault in respect of shipwreck, collision, stranding, explosion, fire or defect on a ship (art.3). Once again the limitation period is two years (art.16).

---

[25] *Reid v Ski Independence*, 1999 S.L.T. (Sh Ct).
[26] *O'Carroll v Ryanair*, 2008 Rep. L.R. 149.

CHAPTER 25

CONSTRUCTION ACCIDENTS

A job on a construction site is amongst the most dangerous work in the United Kingdom today. Health and Safety Executive ("HSE") figures show 41 fatal injuries during 2009. The government-backed Donaghy Report into construction deaths was issued in March 2010. Reducing fatalities, injuries and ill health in construction is a Health and Safety Commission priority programme. **25–01**

The HSE have a number of publications which provide a general health and safety introduction to construction work, and amongst the most useful are *Managing Health and Safety in Construction*,[1] *Health and Safety in Construction*,[2] *Health and Safety in Roof Work*,[3] all now available online.

Where there a number of different tradesmen on site, many itinerant, many self-employed, some believing they are self-employed when they are actually employees, and with identities largely unknown to your client, there is clearly a potential for practical difficulties. Early investigation and identification of witnesses is particularly important. So too is a clear-eyed understanding of the employer/employee relationship as interpreted by the courts, and the statutory background to construction work liability.

Employee or independent contractor?

The rise in the service industries, and the perceived tax advantages of self-employment, have meant that an increasing number of persons are on their own estimate, independent contractors. This assumption is frequently inaccurate, and such persons may well have rights as an employee. **25–02**

The courts have been unable to devise a single test. In *United Wholesale Grocers Ltd v Sher*,[4] Lord Cullen held that the answers to the question depended on a number of factors including, but not limited to:

(a) control of the employee whilst at work;
(b) the supply of materials;

---

[1] *Managing Health and Safety in Construction* L144 (Suffolk: HSE Books, 2007).
[2] *Health and Safety in Construction* HSG150 (Suffolk: HSE Books, 2006).
[3] *Health and Safety in Roof Work* (Suffolk: HSE Books, 2008).
[4] *United Wholesale Grocers Ltd v Sher*, 1993 S.L.T. 284.

(c) fundamentally, did the work carried out by the workman fail to be regarded as part and parcel of a business carried out for an alleged employer, or was he working on his own account for his own business?

This same approach was later followed by the Court of Appeal in England in *Lane v Shire Roofing Co (Oxford) Ltd*.[5] The court noted that it was especially important in view of the current employment situation where there were perceived fiscal benefits for employers and workers in avoiding the label of the employer/employee relationship, to make sure that legal responsibility for safety at work was correctly apportioned. The critical question was "Whose business was it?", so that even where a plaintiff was self-employed for tax purposes, and supplied some of his own tools, the business he was engaged in when he fell from a ladder was that of the defendants, who were liable as employers. In *Jennings v The Forestry Commission*,[6] the claimant contracted to erect a boundary fence for the defendant. The contract schedule specified that the materials were to be delivered to the site by helicopter, or by an all-terrain vehicle which was to be provided by the National Trust. The claimant himself decided to use his own Land Rover vehicle. Whilst the claimant was engaged at work with his assistant, the vehicle overturned to his injury. It was agreed that the Land Rover was unsuitable equipment in terms of the Provision and Use of Work Equipment Regulations 1998. At first instance, liability was found against the Forestry Commission. They had consented to the use of the Land Rover, although they had not provided it. The decision was reversed on appeal. Jennings was in charge of the work, which he carried out without supervision. He had quoted a price, selected his own assistant and provided the Land Rover. It was his business and he had been working as an independent contractor for whom the Forestry Commission had no legal responsibility.

The Inland Revenue website has useful online guide to self-employment in the construction industry[7] and in particular suggests common indicators of employment to be:

(a) the worker has to do the work themselves;
(b) someone can tell them what to do, where to carry out the work and when to do it;
(c) they work a set amount of hours;
(d) they can be moved from task to task;
(e) they are paid by the hour, week or month;
(f) they can get an overtime or bonus payment;
(g) the worker supplies only his or her own small tools;
(h) the worker does not risk his or her own money and there is no possibility that he or she will suffer a financial loss;

---

[5] *Lane v Shire Roofing Co (Oxford) Ltd* [1995] P.I.Q.R.P 417.
[6] *Jennings v The Forestry Commission* [2008] I.C.R. 988.
[7] HM Revenue & Customs Employment Status: *Employed or Self-Employed?*

(i) the worker has no business organisation, e.g. yard, stock, material or workers;
(j) the worker is paid by the hour, day, week or month; and
(k) the contractor has a right to control what the worker has to do—where, when and how it is to be done—even if such control is rarely practised.

Common indicators of self-employment are:

(a) Can the person hire someone to do the work or engage helpers at their expense?
(b) Do they risk their own money?
(c) Do they provide the main items of equpment they need to do the job, not just the small tools which employees provide for themselves?
(d) Do they agree to do the job for a fixed price regardless of how long the job will take?
(e) Can they decide what work to do and how and when to do the work and where to provide the services?
(f) Do they regularly work for a number of different people?
(g) Do they have to correct unsatisfactory work in their own time and at their own expense?

THE STATUTORY FRAMEWORK

Construction (Health, Safety & Welfare) Regulations 1996

These regulations apply to construction work, which is given a very wide definition, and means the carrying out of any building, civil engineering, or engineering construction work and further to include work which involves the assembly of prefabricated elements to form a structure or the disassembly of prefabricated elements and the removal of a structure (reg.2(1)). **25–03**

A construction site means any place where the principal work activity being carried out is construction work. What is regulated is the activity of construction (reg.3(1)). This means not only that the regulations will apply to work carried out in workplaces which are not actual construction sites, but also that the other health and safety regulations and in particular Provision of Use and Work Equipment Regulations 1998 ("PUWER 1998"), Personal Protective Equipment at Work Regulations 1992 ("PPE 1992") and Manual Handling Operations Regulations 1992 ("MHOR 1992") also apply to construction work on construction sites. Regulations 15, 19, 20, 21, 22 and 26(1) and (2) of the Construction (Health, Safety & Welfare) Regulations 1996 ("CHSWR 1996") apply only to construction work carried out by persons at work at a construction site. The Workplace (Health, Safety and Welfare) Regulations ("WHSWR 1992") may also apply to construction work, except where the workplace is separated off, e.g. a typical construction site (WHSWR reg.3(1)(b)).

Find the employer

25–04 The CHSWR 1996 applies to every employer whose employees are carrying out construction work insofar as they affect any person at work under his control (reg.4(1)), i.e. the obligation on the employer arises from the relationship and not from any element of control of the work activity. Persons who control the way in which construction work is carried out are also obliged to comply with the regulations insofar as they relate to matters under their control (reg.4(2)). The identity of these persons and the extent of their control tend to be problematic in this kind of case, and where possible the first recourse should be to the employer.[8]

By the same token the requirements of PUWER 1998, MHOR 1992 and the PPE Regulations 1992 are placed squarely on the employer.[9]

Key regulations

25–05 Employers, the self-employed and controlling persons must ensure, so far as they relate to matters in their control:

(a) a safe place of work and safe access and egress (reg.5);
(b) the provision of suitable equipment to prevent falls (reg.6);
(c) the prevention of injury from falling objects (reg.8);
(d) the stability of structures (reg.9);
(e) the provision of lighting (reg.25);
(f) the provision of training (reg.28); and
(g) that inspection of scaffolding takes place (reg.29).

It is noteworthy that the former reg.27 of CHSWR 1996, an obligation that plant and equipment used should be safe and maintained safe, was repealed by PUWER 1998. There is now no separate maintenance obligation for equipment in construction regulations, so that the matter is now governed by PUWER 1998. The Construction (Health, Safety & Welfare) Regulations 1996 were repealed from April 6, 2007.

The Construction (Design and Management) Regulations 2007 (The CDM Regulation)

25–06 These Regulations came into force on April 6, 2007. "Construction site" means any place where construction work is being carried out or to which the workers have access, but does not include a workplace which is set aside for purposes other than construction work.

"Construction work" means the carrying out of any building, civil engineering or engineering work and includes alteration, conversion, fitting out, commissioning, renovation, repair, upkeep, redecoration or other maintenance, decommissioning, demolition or dismantling of a structure, preparation for an intended structure, assembly of prebabricated elements on site, removal of a structure and the installation,

---

[8] See *Rae v Scottish Power Plc* Unreported November 8, 2001 Court of Session.
[9] The requirements of PUWER 1998 are also placed on others, again subject to a control test.

commissioning, maintenance or repair of services such as of mechanical, electrical, gas, telecommunication, computer or similar services.

The width of the definition of construction work can be seen in the case of *Matthews v Glasgow City Council*[10] where a painter and decorator carrying out work within a domestic flat owned by the respondents was injured by a syringe needle. The 1996 Regulations were held to apply.

"Contractor" is defined as any person (including the client, specified contractor or other person referred to in the Regulations) who in the course of or furtherance of a business carries out the construction work.

The aim of the Regulations is to integrate health and safety into the management of the project, and in particular:

25-07

(a) Improve the planning and management of projects from the start.
(b) Identify hazards early on so that they can be eliminated at the planning stage, with remaining risks properly managed.
(c) Focus attention on health and safety considerations throughout the planning and management of the project.

The regulations are divided into five parts:

- Part 1 deals with the interpretation and application.
- Part 2 covers general management duties which apply to all construction sites including those which are non-notifiable.
- Part 3 sets out additional management duties which apply to projects above the notification threshhold (projects lasting more than 30 days or involving more than 500 person days of construction work, e.g. 50 persons on site working for over 10 days).
- Part 4 applies to construction work carried out on construction sites and covers physical safeguards which need to be provided to prevent danger.
- Part 5 covers issues of civil liability.

Regulation 45 is important in that it provides that the regulations do not confer a right of action in respect of persons who are not employees other than:

- Reg.9(1)(b).
- Reg.13(6) and 13(7).
- Reg.16.
- Reg.22(1)(c) and (l).
- Reg.25(1), (2) and (4).
- Regs 26–44.
- Sch.2.

For the practitioner the important provisions are from regs 25–45.

By reg.25 every contractor carrying out construction work must

---

[10] *Matthews v Glasgow City Council*, 2006 S.C. 349.

comply with the particular requirements of regs 26–44 insofar as they affect him or any person carrying out construction work under his control, or relate to matters within his control. Separately, every person who controls the way in which construction work is carried out by a person at work shall comply with the requirements of regs 26–44 insofar as they relate to matters which are within his control.

25–08 Key regulations

- Reg.26—safe place of work insofar as is reasonably practicable, including safe access and egress to and from every place of work.
- Reg.27—good order and site security.
- Reg.28—stability of structures.
- Reg.29—demolition or dismantling of a structure to be planned and carried out in such a manner as to prevent danger.
- Reg.31—excavations—all practicable steps to be taken to prevent danger during excavations.
- Reg.34—energy distribution installations to be suitably located, checked and where necessary isolated and earthed.
- Reg.35—prevention of drowning.
- Reg.36—traffic routes to be organised in such a way that so far as is reasonably practicable pedestrians and vehicles can move safely without risk to health.
- Reg.37—vehicles; suitable and sufficient steps to be taken to prevent or control the unintended movement of any vehicle.
- Reg.38—prevention of risk from fire.
- Reg.44—suitable and sufficient lighting which shall be so far as reasonably practicable natural lighting.

Liability depends on control

25–09 The CDM Approved Code of Practice states as follows:

"9. Part 4 of the Regulations applies to all construction work carried out on construction sites and covers physical safeguards which need to be provided to prevent danger. Duties to achieve these standards are held by the contractors who actually carry out the work, irrespective of whether they are employers are or self employed. Duties are also held by those who do not do construction work themselves, but control the way in which work is done. In each case, the extent of the duty is in proportion to the degree of control which the individual or organisation has over the work in question.

10. This does not mean everyone involved with design, planning or management of a project must ensure that all the specific requirements in this section are complied with. They only have such duties if, in practice, they exercise significant control over the actual working methods, safeguards and site conditions. For example, contractors carrying out excavation work are normally responsible for ensuring that the excavation is safe to work at, but if a client

specifies that it is dug and supported in a particular way, then the client will have a duty to ensure that the instructions comply with the requirements in Regulation 31."

Practical considerations—what is control?

In *McCook v Lobo*[11] the claimant was injured when he fell from a ladder whilst working for a building contractor carrying out premises conversion. The first defendant was the property owner, the second defendant intended to use the property, and the third defendant was the employer. Liability against the employer was straightforward, but he was insolvent. The question arose as to whether the first defendant had control of the employee in terms of reg.4(2) of CHSWR 1996. The court held that control was a question of fact, and that control over the site in a general sense as an occupier did not impute liability. Lady Justice Hale stated:

25–10

> "The requisite level of control before the duty does arise, however, is linked to the way in which construction work is carried out and it is confined to construction work within the individual's control . For this purpose the obvious person who controls the way in which construction work is carried out on site is an employer. The employer owes express duties under Regulation 4(1). That therefore identifies the starting point. But someone who is not an employer may also be bound by the statutory obligation of Regulation 4(2). Whether the appropriate level of control over the work is or is or should be exercised by an individual other than an employer so as to create the duty to comply with the obligations under Regulation 4(2) is, in my judgement, a question of fact. It is not answered affirmatively by demonstrating that an individual has control over the site in a general sense as an occupier, or that as the occupier of the site he was entitled to ask or require a contractor to remove obvious hazards from the site. The required control is related to the work of construction."

It was later observed that a person who has factual control which he chooses not to exercise, cannot thereby escape liability.

In *McCook* the client had contracted with an apparently reputable building contractor to conduct construction work. There was little reason to doubt the straightforward factual finding that the client was not in control of the way in which the contractor was doing his work.

There may be situations where the court will hold that the principal contractor is directly liable to the injured person, but the facts will need to be looked at carefully. In *Makepeace v Evans Brothers and Alfred McAlpine Construction Ltd*,[12] the plaintiff suffered a catastrophic injury when he fell from an unsecured tower scaffold whilst carrying out construction work on a residential development. The tower scaffold had been provided by the second defendants, who were the main contractors. He

---

[11] *McCook v Lobo* [2002] EWCA Civ 1760.
[12] *Makepeace v Evans Brothers and Alfred McAlpine Construction Ltd* [2001] I.C.R. 241.

succeeded against the first defendants only (his insolvent employers, who were unable to meet the judgment). The Court of Appeal held that the tower scaffold was an ordinary piece of building equipment routinely used on building sites. The equipment itself was suitable, and the accident had arisen only because of the failure to have it properly secured. In the case of *McGarvie v N.G. Bailey & Co Ltd*,[13] the principal contractor was held liable for an accident which occurred to the plaintiff when he fell whilst working on the construction of a new warehouse in Pontefract. In that case the principal contractor had supplied the plaintiff with a ladder from which to carry out work at height. *Makepeace* was distinguished in that the ladder itself which had been provided by the principal contractor was unsuitable for roof work, and judgment against the principal contractor was entered on that basis.

Who is the duty holder?

25–11 It is significant that many of the leading cases involve a dispute as to the applicability of the Regulations to any particular defender. The golden rule is to proceed against the employer if they are solvent or insured. It is only when there are doubts about enforcement of a decree against the employer that other defenders need to be considered. For the practitioner there tend to be three general categories of construction accidents:

1. <u>Your client is injured on a large construction project</u>.
   This will usually be a notifiable project in terms of the CDM Regulations 2007. Reputable contractors and sub-contractors tend to be used. Where your client is an employee of a contractor or sub-contractor there will generally be liability against that employer under either CDM, PUWER or WAHR, or conceivably all three. Where the client is a self-employed contractor and the cause of action relates to the condition of the site, there will probably be a right of action against the principal contractor and any other contractors whose actings have caused or contributed to the accident, e.g. the scaffolding company which erected the deffective scaffolding.
2. <u>Your client is injured whilst working on a minor construction project which may or may not be notifiable under the CDM Regulations</u>.
   Typically this relates to domestic housebuilding and development where there will usually be a builder/developer who carries out some work, and sub-contracts other areas to other tradesmen. Problems with insolvent contractors abound. The builder/developer will generally be the principal contractor and should be liable for system and equipment failures. They may not be liable for casual acts of negligence, e.g. failure by someone to secure a ladder unless this is something which their own risk assessment or method statement should have addressed. It is also in this area that the distinction between employer and independent contractor

---

[13] *McGarvie v N.G. Bailey & Co Ltd* Unreported February 26, 2002 Court of Appeal.

is at its murkiest. Don't necessarily accept the developer's assertion that your client was an independent contractor. Work through the indiciae referred to in para.25–02.
3. Your client is injured on a site where a private occupier or homeowner has construction work carried out
The general rule is that the occupier will not be liable except in special circumstances. The case of *Kmiecic v Isaacs*[14] is a good example of the principles involved. If the occupier has paid a builder to supervise the work and he sub-contracts, liaiblity will lie against the contractor and sub-contractor. However if major works are being carried out which the occupier decides to supervise himself, he may well find himself subject to the provisions of at least the CDM Regulations.[15]

The employer's duty is non-delegable

In *Nelhams v Sandells Maintenance Ltd*,[16] a workman on a site controlled by a contractor was instructed by that contractor to carry out work from an unfooted ladder. The court found that the contractors were vicariously liable for the negligence of their own supervisor at common law. However, the duty of the employer to provide a safe system of work was non-delegable. The employer could not entrust the performance of a non-delegable duty to a third party such as the contractor. The employer was also liable under the Construction (Working Places) Regulations 1966. Whilst the defendants were jointly and severally liable to the plaintiff, the court then apportioned liability between them by holding the contractors wholly to blame, and ordaining them to provide a full indemnity to the employers. In *Morris v Breaveglen*,[17] an employer was held liable to his employee sent to work under a labour-only sub-contract under the direction and control of the main contractor where the system of work was unsafe. The employers were held liabe both at common law and also under the Construction (General Provisions) Regulations 1961. These cases underline the practical utility of directing the claim against the employer, leaving the defenders to argue amongst themselves over apportionment.

25–12

LIABILITY FOR THE ACTIONS OF AN EMPLOYEE IN CONSTRUCTION WORK

An employee of a general employer may be hired out to another particular employer who works on site. Liability for harm to this employee should depend on the principles discussed above. Where that employee negligently causes harm, is the general or particular employer vicariously liable, and against whom should the claim be directed? In *Young and Co*

25–13

---

[14] *Kmiecic v Isaacs* [2011] EWCA Civ 451.
[15] See *Moon v Garrett* 2007 I.C.R. 95.
[16] *Nelhams v Sandells Maintenance Ltd* [1996] P.I.Q.R. P52.
[17] *Morris v Breaveglen* [1993] P.I.Q.R. P294.

(Kelvinhaugh) v O'Donnell,[18] the House of Lords held that the general employer of a hired crane driver remained responsible for his negligence. This rule will apply particularly where the employee is a skilled driver or plant operator. There is a very heavy burden on the general employer, which can only be discharged in exceptional circumstances. Standard contracts which purport to create responsibility for the employee's action do not affect the victim's rights, but simply regulate the liability of the employers inter se (see *Kerr v Hailes (Plant Ltd)*).[19] There is a useful review of the authorities in *King v Fife Council*.[20]

---

[18] *Young and Co (Kelvinhaugh) v O'Donnell*, 1958 S.L.T. (HL) 46.
[19] *Kerr v Hailes (Plant Ltd)*, 1974 S.L.T. 31.
[20] *King v Fife Council*, 2004 Rep. L.R. 33.

APPENDICES

APPENDIX 1
DAMAGES INFORMATION SHEET

Name of client: [*name*]

Address: [*address*]

Date of birth: [*date*]

National Insurance No: [*number*]

Telephone No (Home): [*number*]

Telephone No (Mobile): [*number*]

Email address: [*specify*]

Name and Address of
General Practitioner: [*details*]

Injury
Details of injury:

Address of hospital:

Time in hospital as inpatient:

Details of outpatient treatment:

Details of any plaster cast required:

Details of crutches required:

Date of full recovery:

Wage Loss
Employers' address:

Pre-accident net weekly wage:

Duration of absence:

Is there a contractual requirement to repay sick pay?

Net wage loss:

CRU Position
1. Benefits received:

2. Are they recoupable?

Travel Expenses

Hospital visits:

General Practitioner visits:

Miscellaneous:

Prescription costs:

Section 8 Claim

What assistance was provided, e.g. washing, dressing, shopping, hospital visiting:

Hours per week involved and numbers of weeks:

Name of relative providing assistance:

Section 9 Claim

What can Pursuer no longer do, e.g. gardening, DIY:

For which relative?

Miscellaneous

Appendix 2

ACCIDENTS AT WORK CHECKLIST

COMMON LAW

- General details of accident locus including matchstick man sketch plan, and photographs if possible.
- Identity of witnesses and precise mechanism of accident.
- Particulars of physical nature of workplace, details of what employer's undertaking and Pursuer's role in the process.
- Precise nature of Pursuer's work duties. Is there a written contract of employment?
- Details of experience, training and instruction received. Were there any written instructions or written notices? Was there any induction or refresher training? Was the Pursuer a young and inexperienced worker requiring actual supervision?
- Was employee acting under direct instructions of someone else? What were those instructions and were they adequate?
- Is there a history of complaints? If so, when, by whom and to whom?
- Is there a history of previous similar accidents or near misses?
- Details of any protective equipment available, and steps taken to educate, encourage and monitor workforce in its use.
- Where plant or equipment defective, was there any system of planned maintenance, and was such maintenance necessary?
- Where the accident was the fault of someone else and vicarious liability arises, by whom is that person employed?
- Was the Pursuer's place of work safe including means of access and egress?
- Was there any report under the RIDDOR Regulations 1995, entry in the accident book, HSE investigation, prosecution under the Health and Safety at Work Act 1974, meeting with Safety representatives, entry in Minutes of Work Safety Committee?
- What was said immediately after the accident?
- Has there been a change in the system of work following the accident?

Appendix 2

STATUTORY FRAMEWORK

MANAGEMENT OF HEALTH AND SAFETY AT WORK REGULATIONS ("MHSW")

Applies to almost all businesses and in force from January 1, 1993

- Had there been a risk assessment under MHSW reg.3?
- Does the undertaking employ five or more employees, in which case the risk assessment must be recorded?
- Who is the competent person appointed to assist in compliance with Health and Safety Regulations and devising and application of protective measures (reg.7)?
- What are the health and safety arrangements (reg.5)?
- Does the risk assessment address the circumstances of the accident? Should it have done?
- Have steps been taken to avoid risk altogether, or to control at source?
- Has the risk assessment been reviewed following the accident (reg.3(3)(a)?
- Is there any relevant HSE "best practice" literature which the competent person should have known about?
- Have employees been provided with the specific health and safety information needed to ensure their safety? (reg.10)
- Have they been shown the risk assessment?
- Have employees received appropriate health and safety induction and refresher training? (reg.13).
- Is the pursuer a young person or expectant mother in which case direct civil liability for breach of reg.19.

WORKPLACE HEALTH SAFETY AND WELFARE REGULATIONS 1992

- Does employer have control of workplace (in which case he is liable for breach of regulations?) (reg.4, ACOP 16).
- Does some other party, e.g. occupier, landlord of business premises have control, in which case he will be liable for matters under his control (reg.4, ACOP 16).
- Does accident relate to the general safety of the workplace, or equipment, devices and systems dealt with under these regulations, e.g. lighting, ventilation, work stations, seating, floors, windows, walls, doors, gates, sanitary conveniences, washing facilities, places for supply of drinking water? If so, strict liability for failure to maintain (reg.5).
- Is there suitable and sufficient lighting? (reg.8).
- Is the workstation suitable? (reg.11).
- Has accident been caused by defective or slippery floor, or obstruction on floor? (reg.12, see slips and trips checklist).

- Has the client fallen over 2 metres from an unfenced area? (reg.13, ACOP para.108).
- Has the client been struck by a falling object? (reg.13, ACOP 106).
- Where the accident relates to a fixed ladder, does the ladder comply with ACOP paras 119–125.
- Where accident relates to materials falling from racks, have precautions described in ACOP para.136 been taken?
- Have traffic routes been organised in such a way that pedestrians and vehicles can circulate in a safe manner? (reg.17).

PROVISION AND USE OF WORK EQUIPMENT REGULATIONS 1998

- Does accident relate to machinery, appliances, apparatus, tool, or installation for use at work whether exclusively or not? (reg.2).
- Was equipment suitable for the purpose? (reg.4).
- Was equipment maintained in an efficient state, in efficient working order and in good repair? (reg.5).
- Is there a specific risk related to the use of the equipment in which case there should be restricted access and specific training (reg.9).
- Has employee received adequate health and safety information and where appropriate written instructions relating to the use of work equipment? (reg.8).
- Has the employee received adequate health and safety training including specific work equipment training? (reg.9)
- Was dangerous machinery securely fenced? (regs 11 and 12).
- Did machinery have emergency stop control? (reg.17).
- Was mobile work equipment suitable for carrying persons? (reg.25).
- Was there a risk of rollover of work equipment (reg.26).

PERSONAL PROTECTIVE EQUIPMENT AT WORK REGULATIONS 1992

In force from January 1, 1993

- Does the general risk assessment under MHSW Regs indicate a risk which cannot be controlled *except* by use of PPE as a last resort? (Guidance Notes, para.20).
- Is the PPE provided suitable? (reg.4).
- Has there been a specific assessment of suitability of PPE? (reg.6, Guidance Note para.37).
- Has the PPE been properly maintained? (reg.7).
- Has employee received instructions and training on the need for PPE? (reg.9).
- Has the employer taken all reasonable steps to ensure the use of PPE? (reg.19).

MANUAL HANDLING REGULATIONS 1992

In force from January 1, 1993

- Does risk assessment under MHSW Regulations 1999, reg.3 indicate the possibility of risk to employees from the manual handling of loads? (Guidance Notes, para.21).
- Using the HSE Guidance Notes, Appendix 1, does the load exceed or come near the guideline figures for any of the HSE illustrated boxes in which the load is to be moved?
- Is it reasonably practicable to avoid manual handling completely, e.g. by automation or mechanisation? (reg.4(1)(a), Guidance Note paras 30 and 31).
- Has regard been paid to:

    (a) physical suitability of employee;
    (b) clothing and footwear he is wearing;
    (c) knowledge and training;
    (d) risk assessment under MHSWR 1999;
    (e) is the employee especially at risk? and
    (f) results of any health surveillance.

- If not, has there been a special manual handling risk assessment under reg.4(1)(b) having specific regard to the factors mentioned in Sch.1 of the Regulations, i.e. the task, the load, the working environment, individual capability and other factors?
- Have appropriate steps been taken to reduce the risk of injury to the lowest level reasonably practicable, including mechanical aids (Guidance Notes paras 109–135), training (including particular training to recognise loads that might cause injury) (Guidance Notes paras 167–172).
- Has there been provided a general indication of the weights of loads employers are liable to encounter (reg.(1)(b)(iii), Guidance Note para.179).
- Where reasonably practicable, has there been provided precise information as to the exact weight of the load? (reg.4(1)(b)(iii), Guidance Note para.178).
- Has good handling technique been taught, e.g. bent knees, straight back, smooth movement, keep close to the load? (Guidance Note para.122).
- Are there particular aspects of the load which should be considered e.g. does it involve handling while seated (Guidance Note para.71), is the load too wide (Guidance Note para.80).

WORK AT HEIGHT REGULATIONS 2005

In force from April 6, 2005

- Work at height means work where if measures required by the Regulations are not taken a person could fall a distance liable to cause personal injury.
- Regulation 2—working platform defined to include scaffold, trestle, gangway and stairway.
- Regulation 3—Regulations apply to employer irrespective of his employees, or any person under his control to the extent of the control.
- Regulation 3 also applies to person in relation to work by a person under his control to the extent of his control.
- Once again, the first port of call is the employer, the second is the principal contractor.
- Regulation 4—work at height is to be properly planned, appropriately supervised and carried out in a manner which is, so far as reasonably practicable, safe.
- Regulation 5—"no person shall carry out work at height or use work equipment unless competent to do so".
- Regulation 6—avoidance of risk from work at height.
- "Every employer shall ensure that work is not carried out at height where it is reasonably practicable to carry out the work safely other than at height."
- Regulation 6—where work must be carried out at height suitable and sufficient measures to prevent so far as reasonably practicable any person falling a distance liable to cause personal injury. Place of work to comply with Sch.1.
- Schedule 1 requires workplace or access/egress should be stable, sufficient, have no gap, and have no tripping or slipping hazard.
- Regulation 6—where work at height carried out sufficient work equipment to be provided to prevent a fall occurring.
- Regulation 7—selection of equipment for work at height. Employer to select work equipment which is the most suitable having regard to the purposes specified in reg.6.
- Regulation 8—requirements for particular work equipment.
- Regulation 8(a)—guardrail, tollboard, barrier, etc. to comply with Sch.2.
- Regulation 8(b)—working platform to comply with Pt 1 of Sch.3. These requirements relate to stability and safety in working platforms including no gap and nothing to cause slip or trip.
- Regulation 8(b)(ii)—scaffolding to comply with Pt 2 of Sch.3.
- Note: when scaffold in assembly or dismantling or alteration to be marked by warning signs and to be delineated by physical means preventing access.
- Scaffolding to be assembled or dismantled only under supervision of competent person.
- Regulation 8(e)—ladder to comply with Sch.6.

Appendix 2

- Schedule 6(1)—ladder not to be used unless justified because of low risk and short duration of use.
- Regulation 8(3)—ladder to be positioned as to ensure its stability during use.
- Regulation 8(5)—portable ladder to be prevented from slipping.
- Regulation 10(1)—suitable and sufficient steps to prevent fall of material or object.
- Regulation 10(2)—suitable and sufficient steps to prevent any person being struck by a fallen object.

Appendix 3

VOLUNTARY PRE-ACTION PROTOCOL IN SCOTLAND FOR DISEASE CLAIMS

A3–01 1. Purpose of voluntary protocol

Diseases defined as:

> "Any illness, physical or psychological, any disorder, ailment, affliction, complaint, malady or derangement, other than physical or psychological injury solely caused by an accident or other similar singular event. A singular sensitising event may be considered appropriate for this Protocol." (The definition is not restricted to "disease" occurring in the workplace.)

1.1 The Voluntary Protocol has been kept deliberately simple to promote ease of use and general acceptability.

1.2 The aims of the Voluntary Protocol are:

- to encourage exchange of information at an early stage;
- to resolve disputes without litigation;
- to identify/narrow issues in disputes; and
- To enable resolution of claims pre-litigation.

1.3 It also sets out good practice making it easier for the parties to obtain and rely upon information required.

1.4 The standards within the Voluntary Protocol are to be regarded as the normal, reasonable approach to pre-action conduct in relation to Voluntary Protocol cases.

2. Introduction

A3–02 A Voluntary Pre-Action Protocol in Scotland

2.1 Unlike England and Wales, there is no statutory basis for a Pre-Action Protocol. The Protocol therefore will require to be entered into voluntarily on an individual case by case basis by mutual agreement. The claimant may request occupational health records before the letter of claim is issued. The request should contain sufficient information to alert the defender to a possible claim including the specific nature of the disease (i.e. asbestosis, noise-induced hearing loss, tinnitus, etc). A mandate (see Specimen Letter 2.1) should be provided authorising release of the occupational health records to both claimant and defender. Records should be provided within 40 days, at no cost to the claimant. It will be for the claimant's Agent to intimate the claim in the general format of Specimen Letter A1 or A2 and invite the defender or Insurer to agree on a case by case basis that conduct of the pre-action negotiations are to be undertaken in terms of the Voluntary Protocol. When a defender or Insurer accepts a letter in the general format, Letter B will be sent within 21 days of receipt of claim. The claim will proceed in terms of the Voluntary Protocol in respect of the negotiations, disclosure, repudiation of liability, settlement and calculation of fees.

2.2 The Agent is encouraged to notify the Insurer as soon as they know a claim is likely to be made but before they are able to send a detailed letter of claim, particularly for instance, when the Insurer has no or limited knowledge of the events giving rise to the claim or where the claimant is incurring significant expenditure as a result of the disease which he/she hopes the Insurer might pay for, in whole or in part. If the claimant's Agent chooses to do this, it will not start the timetable for responding.

2.3 The Voluntary Protocol, if entered into, will apply not merely to the personal injury element of a claim but also to other heads of loss and damage.

2.4 Where proceedings are raised in a Voluntary Protocol case, whether for the payment of damages or for the recovery of evidence and other orders under the Administration of Justice (Scotland) Act 1972, without prejudice to any existing rule of law, it shall be open to any party to lodge Voluntary Protocol communications for the sole purpose of assisting the court in any determination of expenses.

3. Letter of claim   A3–03

3.1 The Agent shall send to the proposed defender (or to his Insurer if known) a detailed letter of claim as soon as sufficient information is available to substantiate a claim and before issues of quantum are addressed in detail. The letter should ask for details of the Insurer if not known and the letter should request that a copy should be sent by the proposed defender to the Insurer where appropriate. If the Insurer is known, a copy shall be sent directly to the Insurer.

3.2 The letter of claim should include:

(1) details of the disease or illness alleged;
(2) main allegations of fault;
(3) present condition and prognosis;
(4) outline of financial loss;
(5) employment history and HMRC schedule (including job titles/ duties carried out);
(6) identity of records required;
(7) identity of other potential defenders and their insurers if known; and
(8) chronology of relevant events, e.g. dates (period of exposure linked to employment).

3.3 Agents are recommended to use a standard form for such a detailed letter. Specimen Letter A1 or A2 can be amended to suit the particular case.

3.4 Sufficient information should be given in order to enable the Insurer to commence investigations and at least put a broad valuation on the claim.

3.5 The Insurer should acknowledge the letter of claim within 21 days of the date of receipt of the letter. The Insurer should advise in a letter in the terms of Specimen B whether it is agreed that the case is suitable for the Voluntary Protocol. If there has been no reply by the defender or Insurer within 21 days, the claimant will be entitled to issue proceedings.

3.6 Where liability (subject to causation) is admitted, the Insurer will be bound by this admission for all Protocol claims with a gross damages value of less than £10,000. The exception to this will be when, subsequently, there is evidence that the claim is fraudulent.

3.7 The Insurer will have a period of three months from the date of the Insurer's response letter to investigate the merits of the claim. By mutual agreement the investigation period can be extended. Not later than the end of that period, the Insurer shall reply, stating whether liability (subject to causation) is admitted or denied and giving reasons for their denial of liability (subject to causation), including any alternative version of events relied upon and all available documents supporting their position.

3.8 The Insurers will disclose the period of employment as soon as the information is known to them and will appoint a lead Insurer. Details of other Insurers will be produced when known.

A3–04 *Documents*

3.9 The aim of early disclosure of documents by the parties is to promote an early exchange of relevant information to help in clarifying or resolving the issues in dispute. If the Insurer denies liability, in whole or in part, they will at the same time as giving their decision on liability, disclose any documents which are relevant and proportionate to the issues in question, with reference to those identified in the letter of claim.

3.10 Attached at Appendix A are specimens, but not an exhaustive list of documents likely to be material in different types of claims. Where involvement of the Claimant's Agent in the case is well advanced, the letter of claim should indicate which classes of documents are considered relevant for early disclosure. Where this is not practical, these should be identified as soon as practicable, but disclosure will not affect the timetable.

3.11 Where the Insurer admits primary liability (subject to causation) but alleges contributory negligence by the claimant, the Insurer should give reasons supporting these allegations and disclose the documents from Appendix A which are relevant and proportionate to the issue in dispute. The claimant's Agents should respond to the allegations of contributory negligence before proceedings are issued.

Medical evidence A3–05

3.12 A medical report will be instructed at the earliest opportunity, but no later than five weeks from the date the Insurer admits liability, in whole or in part, unless there is a valid reason for not obtaining a report at this stage. In those circumstances, the claimant's Agents will advise accordingly and agree an amended timetable. Any medical report obtained and on which the claimant intends to rely will be disclosed to the other party within five weeks from the date of its receipt. By mutual consent, the Insurers may ask the examiner, via the claimant's Agent, supplementary questions.

3.13 The claimant's Agent will normally instruct a medical report, will organise access to all relevant medical records and will send a letter of instruction to a medical expert. The Insurer is encouraged to attempt to resolve issues by questioning the claimant's expert, but may seek its own expert evidence, if appropriate. The claimant's Agent will agree to disclosure of all relevant medical and DWP records. Any medical report on which the Insurer intends to rely will be disclosed to the claimant's Agent within five weeks of receipt.

Damages A3–06

3.14 Where the Insurer has admitted liability (subject to causation), the Claimant's Agent will send to the Insurer as soon as possible, a Statement of Valuation of Claim (the Statement of Valuation) together with supporting documents, and keep the Insurers advised of any potential delays.

4. Settlement A3–07

4.1 Where the Insurer admits liability (subject to causation) before proceedings are issued, any medical reports, supporting documentary evidence and Statement of Valuation obtained under this Voluntary Protocol on which a party relies, should be disclosed to the other party. Subject to expiry of the triennium, the claimant's Agent should delay issuing proceedings for 5 weeks from the date the Insurer receives the Statement of Valuation to enable the parties to consider whether the claim is capable of settlement.

4.2 Where a Statement of Valuation with supporting documents has been disclosed under 3.13 and liability and causation are admitted, the Insurer shall offer to settle the claim based on his reasonable valuation of it within five weeks of receipt of such disclosure, serving a counter-schedule of valuation if they dispute the claimant's Agent's valuation.

4.3 The claimant's Agent will advise Insurers whether or not their offer is to be accepted or rejected, prior to the raising of proceedings and in any event within five weeks of receipt.

4.4 Where a Voluntary Protocol case settles, cheques for both damages and agreed expenses must be paid within five weeks of settlement, which will be either the date when the Insurer receives notification of settlement or, where a discharge is required, the date when the signed discharge is received by the Insurer. Thereafter, interest will be payable by any defaulting Insurer on any outstanding damages due to the claimant and/or expenses due and payable in accordance with the agreed settlement terms, at the prevailing judicial rate from the date of settlement until payment is made in full.

A3–08 **5. Time bar**

5.1 In the event that the Insurer repudiates liability or that the claimant rejects an offer in settlement, provided that proceedings are subsequently raised within a period of one year from the date of such repudiation or rejection, the date of raising proceedings will be deemed to be the date when intimation of the claim was made in terms of this protocol for purposes of prescription and limitation.

A3–09 **6. Litigation**

6.1 In the event of litigation, the claimant's solicitors will give the Insurers an opportunity to nominate solicitors to accept service, on behalf of their insured.

VOLUNTARY PRE-ACTION PROTOCOL IN PERSONAL INJURY CASE

1. Purpose of the voluntary protocol

1.1 The Voluntary Protocol has been kept deliberately simple to promote ease of use & general acceptability.
   1.2 The aims of the Voluntary Protocol are:

- to put parties in a position where they may be able to settle cases fairly and early without litigation;
- to ensure the early provision of reliable information reasonably required to enter into meaningful discussions re liability and quantum; and
- to enable appropriate offers to be made either before or after litigation commences:

   1.3 It also sets out good practice making it easier for the parties to obtain and rely upon information required.
   1.4 The Voluntary protocol encourages the joint exploration of rehabilitation at an early stage, in appropriate cases, without prejudice to liability.
   1.5 The standards within the Voluntary Protocol are to be regarded as the normal, reasonable approach to pre-action conduct in relation to Voluntary Protocol cases.

2. A voluntary pre-action protocol in Scotland

2.1 Unlike England, there is no statutory basis for a Pre-Action Protocol. The Protocol will therefor require to be entered into voluntarily on an individual case by case basis by mutual agreement. It will be for the pursuer's Agent to intimate the claim in the general format of a Specimen Letters A1 or 2 which will invite the defender or Insurer to agree on a case by case basis that conduct of the pre-action negotiations is to be undertaken in terms of the Voluntary Protocol. When a defender or Insurer accepts, a letter in the general format of specimen letter B will be sent within 21 days of receipt of the letter of claim. Thereafter the claim will proceed in terms of the Voluntary Protocol in respect of the negotiations, disclosure, repudiation of liability, settlement and calculation of fees.
   2.2 The Agent may wish to notify the Insurer as soon as they know a claim is likely to be made but before they are able to send a detailed Letter of Claim, particularly for instance, when the Insurer has no or limited knowledge of the incident giving rise to the claim or where the claimant is incurring significant expenditure as a result of the accident which he/she hopes the Insurer might pay for, in whole or in part. If the pursuer's agent chooses to do this, it will not start the timetable for responding.
   2.3 The Voluntary Protocol if entered into will apply in all cases which include a claim for personal injury (excepting Clinical Negligence and

Disease and Illness cases) and will apply not merely to the personal injury element of a claim but also to other heads of loss and damage. It is primarily designed for road traffic, tripping and slipping and accident at work cases where the value of the claim is up to £10,000. The Protocol is voluntary and there is nothing to prevent parties by mutual agreement dealing with any claim of a higher value under the Protocol.

2.4 Where proceedings are raised in a Voluntary Protocol case, whether for the payment of damages or for the recovery of evidence and other orders under the Administration of Justice (Scotland) Act 1972, without prejudice to any existing rule of law, it shall be open to any party to lodge Voluntary Protocol communications for the sole purpose of assisting the court in any determination of expenses.

A3–12 **3. Letter of claim**

3.1 The Agent shall send to the proposed defender (or to his Insurer if known) a letter of claim as soon as sufficient information is available to substantiate a claim and before issues of quantum are addressed in detail. The letter should ask for details of the Insurer if not known and the letter should request that a copy should be sent by the proposed defender to the Insurer where appropriate. If the Insurer is known, a copy shall be sent directly to the Insurer.

3.2 The letter shall contain a clear summary of the facts on which the claim is based, including allegations of negligence, breaches of common law or statutory duty, together with an indication of the nature of any injuries suffered and of any financial loss incurred, so far as known. In all cases the letter should provide the name and address of the hospital where treatment has been obtained and where appropriate, the name and address of the claimant's own motor Insurer.

3.3 Agents are recommended to use a standard format for such a letter, specimen letter A1 or A2: this can be amended to suit the particular case.

3.4 Sufficient information should be given in order to enable the Insurer to commence investigations and at least put a broad valuation on the "risk".

3.5 The Insurer should acknowledge the letter of claim within 21 days of the date of receipt of the letter. The Insurer should advise in a letter in the terms of Specimen B whether it is agreed that the case is suitable for the Voluntary Protocol. If there has been no reply by the defender or Insurer within 21 days, the claimant will be entitled to issue proceedings.

3.6 Where liability is admitted, the Insurer will be bound by this admission for all Protocol claims with a personal injury value, as laid down in 2.3, of less than £10,000. The exception to this will be when, subsequently, there is evidence that the claim is fraudulent.

3.7 The Insurer will have a maximum of three months from the date of specimen letter B to investigate the merits of the claim. Not later than the end of that period, the Insurer shall reply, stating whether liability is admitted or denied and giving reasons for their denial of liability, including any alternative version of events relied upon and all available documents supporting their position.

Documents A3–13

3.8 The aim of early disclosure of documents by the Insurer is to promote an early exchange of relevant information to help in clarifying or resolving the issues in dispute. If the Insurer denies liability, in whole or in part, they will at the same time as giving their decision on liability, disclose any documents which are relevant and proportionate to the issues in question, with reference to those identified in the letter of claim.

3.9 Attached at Appendix A are specimen, but not exhaustive, lists of documents likely to be material in different types of claim. Where the pursuer's agents investigation of the case is well advanced, the letter of claim should indicate which classes of documents are considered relevant for early disclosure. Where this is not practical, these should be identified as soon as practical but disclosure will not affect the timetable.

3.10 Where the Insurer admits primary liability but alleges contributory negligence by the pursuer, the Insurer should give reasons supporting these allegations and disclose those documents from Appendix A which are relevant and proportionate to the issues in dispute. The pursuer's Agent should respond to the allegation of contributory negligence before proceedings are issued.

Medical reports A3–14

3.11 A medical report will be instructed at the earliest opportunity but no later than five weeks from the date the Insurer admits, in whole or part, liability unless there is a valid reason for not obtaining a report at this stage. In those circumstances, the pursuer's agents will advise accordingly and agree an amended timetable with the Insurers or withdraw the case from the protocol. Any medical report obtained and on which the pursuer intends to rely will be disclosed to the other party within five weeks from the date of its receipt. By mutual consent, the Insurers may ask the examiner, via the pursuer's agent, supplementary questions.

3.12 The pursuer's agent will normally instruct a medical report, will organise access to all relevant medical records, and will send a letter of instruction to a medical expert in general terms of specimen letter C. Where it has been agreed that the Insurer will obtain the medical report, the pursuer's agent will agree to disclosure of all medical records relevant to the accident. Pre-accident medical records will be disclosed only with the specific agreement of the pursuer's agent and if relevant to the claim. Any medical report on which the Insurer intends to rely will be disclosed to the pursuer's agent within five weeks of receipt.

Damages A3–15

3.13 The pursuer's agents will send to the Insurer a Statement of Valuation of Claim (the Statement of Valuation) with supporting documents, where the Insurer has admitted liability. The pursuer's agents are recommended to use a standard format for the Statement of Valuation. An example is at specimen D. *Form 439 in the Rules of Court of Session.* This can be amended to suit the particular case.

A3–16 **4. Settlement**

4.1 Where the Insurer admits liability in whole or in part, before proceedings are issued, any medical reports supporting documentary evidence and Statement of Valuation obtained under this Voluntary Protocol on which a party relies, should be disclosed to the other party. The pursuer's agent should delay issuing proceedings for five weeks from the date the Insurer receives the Statement of Valuation to enable the parties to consider whether the claim is capable of settlement.

4.2 Where a Statement of Valuation with supporting documents has been disclosed under 3.12, the Insurer shall offer to settle the claim based on his reasonable valuation of it within five weeks of receipt of such disclosure, serving a counter-schedule of valuation if they dispute the pursuer's agent's valuation.

4.3 The pursuer's Agent will advise Insurers whether or not their offer is to be accepted or rejected, prior to the raising of proceedings and in any event within five weeks of receipt.

4.4 Where a Voluntary Protocol case settles, cheques for both damages and agreed expenses must be paid within five weeks of the settlement. The date of settlement will be the date when the insurer receives notification of settlement. Thereafter, interest will be payable on both damages and expenses due and payable in accordance with the agreed settlement terms at the prevailing judicial rate from the date of settlement until payment is made in full.

APPENDIX 4

POLICE REPORTS

POLICE

Central Scotland Police Insurance Department Police Headquarters Randolphfield St Ninians Road Stirling FK8 2HD Telephone number: 01786 456800 Payee: Central Police Abstract: £82.60 Precognition: £135.00	Dumfries & Galloway Constabulary Insurance Department Police Headquarters Cornwall Mount Dumfries DG1 1PZ Telephone number: 01387 252112 Payee: Dumfries & Galloway Constabulary Abstract: £82.60 Precognition: £135.00
Fife Constabulary Insurance Department Police Headquarters Detroit Road Glenrothes Fife KY6 2RJ Telephone number: 01592 418888 Payee: Fife Constabulary Abstract: £82.60 Precognition: £135.00	Grampian Police Insurance Department Police Headquarters Queen Street Aberdeen AB10 1ZA Telephone number: 01224 386000 Payee: Grampian Joint Police Board Abstract: £82.60 Precognition: £135
Lothian & Borders Police Courts & Records Department Police Headquarters Fettes Avenue Edinburgh EH4 1RB Telephone number: 0131 311 3131 Payee: Lothian & Borders Police Abstract: £82.60 Precognition: £135.00	Northern Constabulary Insurance Department Police Headquarters Perth Road Inverness IV2 3SY Telephone number: 01463 715555 Payee: Northern Constabulary Abstract: £82.60 Precognition: £135.00

Strathclyde Police Police Headquarters 173 Pitt Street Glasgow G2 4JS Telephone number: 0141 532 2000 Payee: Strathclyde Police Abstract: £82.60 Precognition: £135.00	Tayside Constabulary Insurance Department Police Headquarters PO Box 59 West Bell Street Dundee DD1 JU Telephone number: 01382 596434 Payee: Tayside Joint Police Board Abstract: £82.60 Precognition: £135.00

Appendix 5

ORDINARY CAUSE FORMS

FORM PI1

Rule 36.B1

FORM OF INITIAL WRIT IN A PERSONAL INJURIES ACTION

INITIAL WRIT

(Personal Injuries Action)

SHERIFFDOM OF [*name of sheriffdom*]

AT [*place of sheriff court*]

[A.B.] [*design and state any special capacity in which pursuer is suing*], Pursuer

against

[C.D.] [*design and state any special capacity in which defender is being sued*], Defender

The pursuer craves the court to grant decree—

(a) for payment by the defender to the pursuer of the sum of [*amount of sum in words and figures*];
(b) [*enter only if a claim for provisional damages is sought in terms of rule 36.12*] for payment by the defender to the pursuer of [*enter amount in words and figures*] of provisional damages; and
(c) for the expenses of the action.

STATEMENT OF CLAIM

1. The pursuer is [*state designation, address, occupation and date of birth of pursuer*]. (In an action arising out of the death of a relative state designation of the deceased and relation to the pursuer).

2. The defender is [*state designation, address and occupation of the defender*].

3. The court has jurisdiction to hear this claim against the defender because [*state briefly ground of jurisdiction*].

4. [*State briefly the facts necessary to establish the claim*].

5. [*State briefly the personal injuries suffered and the heads of claim. Give names and addresses of medical practitioners and hospitals or other institutions in which the person injured received treatment*].

6. [*State whether claim based on fault at common law or breach of statutory duty; if breach of statutory duty, state provision of enactment*].

(*Signed*)

[A.B.], Pursuer

or [X.Y.], Solicitor for the pursuer
[*designation and business address*]

FORM PI2

Rule 36.B1

FORM OF ORDER OF COURT FOR RECOVERY OF DOCUMENTS IN PERSONAL INJURIES ACTION

Court ref. no.

SHERIFFDOM OF [*name of sheriffdom*]

AT [*place of sheriff court*]

SPECIFICATION OF DOCUMENTS

in the cause

[A.B.] [*designation and address*], Pursuer

against

[C.D.] [*designation and address*], Defender

Date: [*date of posting or other method of service*]

To: [*name and address of party or parties from whom the following documents are sought to be recovered*]

You are hereby required to produce to the agent for the pursuer within seven days of the service on you of this Order:

[*such of the following calls as are required*].

1. All books, medical records, reports, charts, X-rays, notes and other documents of [*specify the name of each medical practitioner or general practitioner practice named in initial writ in accordance with rule 36.B1(1)(b)*], and relating to the pursuer [*or, as the case may be, the deceased*] from [*date*], in order that excerpts may be taken therefrom at the sight of the Commissioner of all entries showing or tending to show the nature, extent and cause of the pursuer's [*or, as the case may be, the deceased's*] injuries when he attended his doctor on or after [*date*] and the treatment received by him since that date.

2. All books, medical records, reports, charts, X-rays, notes and other documents of [*specify, in separate calls, the name of each hospital or other institution named in initial writ in accordance with rule 36.B1(1)(b)*], and relating to the pursuer [*or, as the case may be, the deceased*] from [*date*], in order that excerpts may be taken therefrom at the sight of the Com-

missioner of all entries showing or tending to show the nature, extent and cause of the pursuer's [*or, as the case may be, the deceased's*] injuries when he was admitted to that institution on or about [*date*], the treatment received by him since that date and his certificate of discharge, if any.

3. The medical records and capability assessments held by the defender's occupational health department relating to the pursuer [*or, as the case may be, the deceased*], except insofar as prepared for or in contemplation of litigation, in order that excerpts may be taken therefrom at the sight of the Commissioner of all entries showing or tending to show the nature and extent of any injuries, symptoms and conditions from which the pursuer [*or, as the case may be, the deceased*] was suffering and the nature of any assessment and diagnosis made thereof on or subsequent to [*date*].

4. All wage books, cash books, wage sheets, computer records and other earnings information relating to the pursuer [*or, as the case may be, the deceased*] (NI number [*number*]) held by or on behalf of [*specify employer*], for the period [*dates commencing not earlier than 26 weeks prior to the date of the accident or the first date of relevant absence, as the case may be*] in order that excerpts may be taken therefrom at the sight of the Commissioner of all entries showing or tending to show—

   (a) the pursuer's [*or, as the case may be, the deceased's*] earnings, both gross and net of income tax and employee National Insurance Contributions, over the said period;
   (b) the period or periods of the pursuer's [*or, as the case may be, the deceased's*] absence from employment over the said period and the reason for absence;
   (c) details of any increases in the rate paid over the period [*dates*] and the dates on which any such increases took effect;
   (d) the effective date of, the reasons for and the terms (including any terms relative to any pension entitlement) of the termination of the pursuer's [*or, as the case may be, the deceased's*] employment;
   (e) the nature and extent of contributions (if any) to any occupational pension scheme made by the pursuer [*or, as the case may be, the deceased*] and his employer;
   (f) the pursuer's present entitlement (if any) to any occupational pension and the manner in which said entitlement is calculated.

5. All accident reports, memoranda or other written communications made to the defender or anyone on his behalf by an employee of the defender who was present at or about the time at which the pursuer [*or, as the case may be, the deceased*] sustained the injuries in respect of which the initial writ in this cause was issued and relevant to the matters contained in the statement of claim.

6. Any assessment current at the time of the accident referred to in the initial writ or at the time of the circumstances referred to in the initial writ

giving rise to the cause of action (as the case may be) undertaken by or on behalf of the defender for the purpose of regulation 3 of the Management of Health and Safety at Work Regulations 1992 and subsequently regulation 3 of the Management of Health and Safety at Work Regulations 1999 [*or (specify the regulations or other legislative provision under which the risk assessment is required)*] in order that excerpts may be taken therefrom at the sight of the Commissioner of all entries relating to the risks posed to workers [*or (specify the matters set out in the statement of claim to which the risk assessment relates)*].

7. Failing principals, drafts, copies or duplicates of the above or any of them.

(Signature, name and business address of the agent for the pursuer)

NOTES:

1. The documents recovered will be considered by the parties to the action and they may or may not be lodged in the court process. A written receipt will be given or sent to you by the pursuer, who may thereafter allow them to be inspected by the other parties. The party in whose possession the documents are will be responsible for their safekeeping.
2. Payment may be made, within certain limits, in respect of claims for outlays incurred in relation to the production of documents. Claims should be made in writing to the person who has obtained an order that you produce the documents.
3. If you claim that any of the documents produced by you is **confidential** you must still produce such documents but may place them in a separate sealed packet by themselves, marked "CONFIDENTIAL". In that event they must be delivered or sent by post to the sheriff clerk. Any party who wishes to open the sealed packet must apply to the sheriff by motion. A party who makes such an application must intimate the motion to you.
4. Subject to paragraph 3 above, you may produce these documents by sending them by registered post or by the first class recorded delivery service or registered postal packet, or by hand to (*name and address of the agent for the pursuer*).

CERTIFICATE

[*Date*]

I hereby certify with reference to the above order in the cause (*cause reference number*) and the enclosed specification of documents, served on me and marked respectively X and Y—

1. That the documents which are produced and which are listed in the enclosed inventory signed by me and marked Z, are all the documents in my possession falling within the specification. *OR* That I have no documents in my possession falling within the specification.

2. That, to the best of my knowledge and belief, there are in existence other documents falling within the specification, but not in my possession. These documents are as follows: (*describe them by reference to the descriptions of documents in the specification*). They were last seen by me on or about (*date*), at (*place*), in the hands of (*name and address of the person*). *OR* That I know of the existence of no documents in the possession of any person, other than me, which fall within the specification.

(*Signed*)

[*Name and address*]

FORM PI6

Rule 36.J1

FORM OF STATEMENT OF VALUATION OF CLAIM

Head of claim	Components	Valuation
Solatium	Past	£x
	Future	£x
Interest on past solatium	Percentage applied to past solatium (*state percentage rate*)	£x
Past wage loss	Date from which wage loss claimed: [*date*] Date to which wage loss claimed: [*date*] Rate of net wage loss (per week, per month or per annum)	£x
Interest on past wage loss	Percentage applied to past wage loss: [*state percentage rate*]	£x
Future wage loss	Multiplier: [*state multiplier*] Multiplicand: [*state multiplicand and show how calculated*] Discount factor applied (if appropriate): [*state factor*] Or specify any other method of calculation	£x

Past services	Date from which services claimed: [date]	£x
	Date to which services claimed: [date]	
	Nature of services: (............)	
	Person by whom services provided: (............)	
	Hours per week services provided: (............)	
	Net hourly rate claimed: (..........)	
	Total amount claimed: (..........)	
	Interest	
Future loss of capacity to provide personal services	Multiplier: [multiplier]	£x
	Multiplicand: [multiplicand, showing how calculated]	
Needs and other expenses	One off	£x
	Multiplier: [multiplier]	
	Multiplicand: [multiplicand]	
	Interest	
Any other heads as appropriate [specify]		

FORM PI7

Rule 36.K1

MINUTE OF PRE-PROOF CONFERENCE

Court ref. no.[*specify*]

SHERIFFDOM OF [*sheriffdom*] AT [*place*]

Joint minute of pre-proof conference

in the cause

[*A.B.*], Pursuer

against

[*C.D.*], Defender

[E.F.] for the pursuer and

[G.H.] for the defender hereby state to the court:

1. That the pre-proof conference was held in this case [*at [place]* or *by (telephone conference or video conference or other remote means)*] on [*date*].

2. That the following persons were present—
(*State names and designations of persons attending conference*)

3. That the following persons were available to provide instructions by telephone or video conference—
(*State names and designations or persons available to provide instructions by telephone or video conference*)

4. That the persons participating in the conference discussed settlement of the action.

5. That the following questions were addressed—

Section 1

		Yes	No
1.	Is the diet of proof still required?		
2.	If the answer to question 1 is "yes", does the defender admit liability? (If "no", complete section 2) If yes, does the defender plead contributory negligence? If yes, is the degree of contributory negligence agreed? If yes, state % degree of fault attributed to the pursuer.		
3.	If the answer to question 1 is "yes", is the quantum of damages agreed? (If "no", complete section 3)		

Section 2

[To be inserted only if the proof is still required]

It is estimated that the hearing will last   days

NB. If the estimate is more than 2 days then this should be brought to the attention of the sheriff clerk. This may affect prioritisation of the case.

During the course of the pre-proof conference, the pursuer called on the defender to agree certain facts, questions of law and matters of evidence.

Those calls, and the defender's responses, are as follows—

Call	*Response*	
	Admitted	Denied
1.		
2.		
3.		
4.		

Appendix 5

During the course of the pre-proof conference, the defender called on the pursuer to agree certain facts, questions of law and matters of evidence.

Those calls, and the pursuer's responses, are as follows—

Call	Response	
	Admitted	Denied
1.		
2.		
3.		
4.		

Section 3

Quantum of damages

Please indicate where agreement has been reached on an element of damages.

Head of claim	Components	Not agreed	Agreed at
Solatium	Past		
	Future		
Interest on past solatium	Percentage applied to past solatium (*state percentage*)		
Past wage loss	Date from which wage lost claimed		
	Date to which wage loss claimed		
	Rate of net wage loss (per week, per month or per annum)		
Interest on past wage loss			
Future wage loss	Multiplier		
	Multiplicand (showing how calculated)		
Past necessary services	Date from which services claimed		
	Date to which services claimed		

	Hours per week services provided		
	Net hourly rate claimed		
Past personal services	Date from which services claimed		
	Date to which services claimed		
	Hours per week services provided		
	Net hourly rate claimed		
Interest on past services			
Future necessary services	Multiplier		
	Multiplicand (showing how calculated)		
Future personal services	Multiplier		
	Multiplicand (showing how calculated)		
Needs and other expenses	One off		
	Multiplier		
	Multiplicand (showing how calculated)		
Any other heads as appropriate (specify)			

[*Signed by each party/his or her solicitor*]

Appendix 6

SUMMARY CAUSE FORMS

Court ref. no:[*number*]

FORM 10

Rule 34.2(1)

FORM OF STATEMENT OF CLAIM IN A
PERSONAL INJURIES ACTION

1. The pursuer is [*state designation, address, occupation, date of birth and National Insurance number (where applicable) of the pursuer*]. (*In an action arising out of the death of a relative state designation of the deceased and relation to the pursuer*).

2. The defender is [*state designation, address and occupation of the defender*].

3. The court has jurisdiction to hear this claim against the defender because [*state briefly ground of jurisdiction*].

4. [*State briefly the facts necessary to establish the claim*].

5. [*State briefly the personal injuries suffered and the heads of claim. Give names and addresses of medical practitioners and hospitals or other institutions in which the person injured received treatment*].

6. [*State whether claim based on fault at common law or breach of statutory duty; if breach of statutory duty, state provision of enactment*].

FORM 10A

Rule 34.3(2) and 34.4(1)

FORM OF RESPONSE (ACTION FOR DAMAGES: PERSONAL INJURIES)

Court ref. no: [*number*]

SHERIFFDOM OF [*name of sheriffdom*]

AT [*place of sheriff court*]

in the cause

[A.B.], [*name and address*], Pursuer

against

[C.D.], [*name and address*], Defender

RESPONSE TO STATEMENT OF CLAIM

	Question	Response
1.	Is it intended to dispute the description and designation of the pursuer? If so, why?	
2.	Is the description and designation of the defender disputed? If so, why?	
3.	Is there any dispute that the court has jurisdiction to hear the claim? If so, why?	
4.	(a) State which facts in paragraph 4 of the statement of claim are admitted.	
	(b) State any facts regarding the circumstances of the claim upon which the defender intends to rely.	
5.	(a) State whether the nature and extent of the pursuer's injuries is disputed and whether medical reports can be agreed.	
	(b) If the defender has a medical report upon which he or she	

intends to rely to contradict the pursuer's report in any way, state the details.

(c) State whether the claims for other losses are disputed in whole or in part.

6. (a) Does the defender accept that the <u>common law duty</u> or duties in the statement of claim were incumbent upon them in the circumstances? If not, state why.

(b) Does the defender accept that the <u>statutory duty or duties alleged</u> in the statement of claim were incumbent upon them in the circumstances? If not, state why.

(c) State any other provisions or propositions upon which the defender proposes to rely in relation to the question of their liability for the accident including, if appropriate, details of any allegation of contributory negligence.

(d) Does the defender allege that the accident was caused by any other wrongdoer? If so, give details.

(e) Does the defender allege that they are entitled to be indemnified or relieved from any liability they might have to the pursuer? If so, give details.

7. Does the defender intend to pursue a counterclaim against the pursuer? If so, give details.

(Insert date)   *(signature, designation and address)*

FORM 10B

Rule 34.2(3)(b)

FORM OF ORDER OF COURT FOR RECOVERY OF DOCUMENTS IN PERSONAL INJURIES ACTION

Court ref. no: [number]

SHERIFFDOM OF [name of sheriffdom]

AT [place of sheriff court]

SPECIFICATION OF DOCUMENTS

in the cause

[A.B.], [name and address], Pursuer

against

[C.D.], [name and address], Defender

To: [name and address of party or parties from whom the following documents are sought to be recovered].

You are hereby required to produce to the sheriff clerk at [address] within seven days of the service on you of this Order:

[Such of the following calls as are required]

1. All books, medical records, reports, charts, X-rays, notes and other documents of (*specify the name of each medical practitioner or general practitioner practice named in summons in accordance with rule 34.2(1)(b)*), and relating to the pursuer [*or, as the case may be, the deceased*] from (*insert date*), in order that excerpts may be taken therefrom at the sight of the Commissioner of all entries showing or tending to show the nature, extent and cause of the pursuer's [*or, as the case may be, the deceased's*] injuries when he or she attended his or her doctor on or after (*specify date*) and the treatment received by him or her since that date.

2. All books, medical records, reports, charts, X-rays, notes and other documents of (*specify, in separate calls, the name of each hospital or other institution named in summons in accordance with rule 34.2(1)(b)*), and relating to the pursuer [*or, as the case may be, the deceased*] from (*insert date*), in order that excerpts may be taken therefrom at the sight of the Commissioner of all entries showing or tending to show the nature, extent and cause of the pursuer's [*or, as the case may be, the deceased's*]

injuries when he or she was admitted to that institution on or about (*specify date*), the treatment received by him or her since that date and his or her certificate of discharge, if any.

3. The medical records and capability assessments held by the defender's occupational health department relating to the pursuer [*or, as the case may be, the deceased*], except insofar as prepared for or in contemplation of litigation, in order that excerpts may be taken therefrom at the sight of the Commissioner of all entries showing or tending to show the nature and extent of any injuries, symptoms and conditions from which the pursuer [*or, as the case may be, the deceased*] was suffering and the nature of any assessment and diagnosis made thereof on or subsequent to (*specify date*).

4. All wage books, cash books, wage sheets, computer records and other earnings information relating to the pursuer [*or, as the case may be, the deceased*] (N.I. number (*specify number*)) held by or on behalf of (*specify employer*), for the period (*specify dates commencing not earlier than 26 weeks prior to the date of the accident or the first date of relevant absence, as the case may be*) in order that excerpts may be taken therefrom at the sight of the Commissioner of all entries showing or tending to show—

    (a) the pursuer's [*or, as the case may be, the deceased's*] earnings, both gross and net of income tax and employee National Insurance Contributions, over the said period;
    (b) the period or periods of the pursuer's [*or, as the case may be, the deceased's*] absence from employment over the said period and the reason for absence;
    (c) details of any increases in the rate paid over the period (*specify dates*) and the dates on which any such increases took effect;
    (d) the effective date of, the reasons for and the terms (including any terms relative to any pension entitlement) of the termination of the pursuer's [*or, as the case may be, the deceased's*] employment;
    (e) the nature and extent of contributions (if any) to any occupational pension scheme made by the pursuer [*or, as the case may be, the deceased*] and his or her employer;
    (f) the pursuer's present entitlement (if any) to any occupational pension and the manner in which said entitlement is calculated.

5. All accident reports, memoranda or other written communications made to the defender or anyone on his or her behalf by an employee of the defender who was present at or about the time at which the pursuer [*or, as the case may be, the deceased*] sustained the injuries in respect of which the summons in this cause was issued and relevant to the matters contained in the statement of claim.

6. Any assessment current at the time of the accident referred to in the summons or at the time of the circumstances referred to in the summons giving rise to the cause of action (as the case may be) undertaken by or on

behalf of the defender for the purpose of regulation 3 of the Management of Health and Safety at Work Regulations 1992 and subsequently regulation 3 of the Management of Health and Safety at Work Regulations 1999 [*or (specify the regulations or other legislative provision under which the risk assessment is required)*] in order that excerpts may be taken therefrom at the sight of the Commissioner]or (specify the matters set out in the statement of claim to which the risk assessment relates)].

7. Failing principals, drafts, copies or duplicates of the above or any of them.

Date [*date of posting or other method of service*]   [*Signature, name and business address of the agent for the pursuer*]

NOTES:

1. The documents recovered will be considered by the parties to the action and they may or may not be lodged in the court process. A written receipt will be given or sent to you by the sheriff clerk, who may thereafter allow them to be inspected by the parties. The party in whose possession the documents are will be responsible for their safekeeping.
2. Payment may be made, within certain limits, in respect of claims for outlays incurred in relation to the production of documents. Claims should be made in writing to the person who has obtained an order that you produce the documents.
3. If you claim that any of the documents produced by you is **confidential** you must still produce such documents but may place them in a separate sealed packet by themselves, marked "CONFIDENTIAL". Any party who wishes to open the sealed packet must apply to the sheriff by incidental application. A party who makes such an application must intimate the application to you.
4. Subject to paragraph 3 above, you may produce these documents by sending them by registered post or by the first class recorded delivery service or registered postal packet, or by hand to the sheriff clerk at (*insert address*).

CERTIFICATE

I hereby certify with reference to the above order of the sheriff at (*insert name of sheriff court*) in the case (*insert court reference number*) and the enclosed specification of documents, served on me and marked respectively X and Y—

1. That the documents which are produced and which are listed in the enclosed inventory signed by me and marked Z, are all the documents in my possession falling within the specification.

or

That I have no documents in my possession falling within the specification.

2. That, to the best of my knowledge and belief, there are in existence other documents falling within the specification, but not in my possession. These documents are as follows: (*describe them by reference to the descriptions of documents in the specification*). They were last seen by me on or about (*date*), at (*place*), in the hands of (*insert name and address of the person*).

or

That I know of the existence of no documents in the possession of any person, other than me, which fall within the specification.

(*Insert date*)   (*Signed*)

                                   (*Name and address*)

FORM 10E

Rule 34.9

FORM OF STATEMENT OF VALUATION OF CLAIM

Court ref. no: [*number*]

SHERIFFDOM OF [*name of sheriffdom*]

AT [*place of sheriff court*]

STATEMENT OF VALUATION OF CLAIM

in the cause

[A.B.], [*name and address*], Pursuer

against

[C.D.], [*name and address*], Defender

Head of claim	*Components*	*Valuation*
Solatium	Past	£x
	Future	£x
Interest on past solatium	Percentage applied to past solatium (*state percentage rate*)	£x
Past wage loss	Date from which wage loss claimed: (*date*)	£x
	Date to which wage loss claimed: (*date*)	
	Rate of net wage loss (*per week, per month or per annum*)	
Interest on past wage loss	Percentage applied to past wage loss: (*state percentage rate*)	£x

Future wage loss	Multiplier: (*state multiplier*)	£x
	Multiplicand: (*state multiplicand and show how calculated*)	
	Discount factor applied (if appropriate): (*state factor*)	
	Or specify any other method of calculation	
Past services	Date from which services claimed: (*date*)	£x
	Date to which services claimed: (*date*)	
	Nature of services: (............)	
	Person by whom services provided: (............)	
	Hours per week services provided: (............)	
	Net hourly rate claimed: (..........)	
	Total amount claimed: (..........)	
	Interest	
Future loss of capacity to provide personal services	Multiplier: (*insert multiplier*)	£x
	Multiplicand: (*insert multiplicand, showing how calculated*)	
Needs and other expenses	One off	£x
	Multiplier: (*insert multiplier*)	
	Multiplicand: (*insert multiplicand*)	
	Interest	
Any other heads as appropriate (*specify*)		£x
Total		£x (*insert total valuation of claim*)

List of Supporting Documents:—

(Insert date)   *(Signed)*

                                               (Name and address)

FORM 10F

Rule 34.10(2)

MINUTE OF PRE-PROOF CONFERENCE

Court ref. no: [number]

SHERIFFDOM OF [sheriffdom]

AT [place of sheriff court]

JOINT MINUTE OF PRE-PROOF CONFERENCE

in the cause

[A.B.], Pursuer

against

[C.D.], Defender

[E.F.] for the pursuer and

[G.H.] for the defender hereby state to the court:

1. That the pre-proof conference was held in this case [at (place) or by (telephone conference or video conference or other remote means)] on [date].

2. That the following persons were present—
(State names and designations of persons attending conference)

3. That the following persons were available to provide instructions by telephone or video conference—
(State names and designations or persons available to provide instructions by telephone or video conference)

4. That the persons participating in the conference discussed settlement of the action.

5. That the following questions were addressed—

Section 1

		Yes	No
1.	Is the diet of proof still required?		
2.	If the answer to question 1 is "yes", does the defender admit liability? (If "no", complete section 2)		
	If yes, does the defender plead contributory negligence?		
	If yes, is the degree of contributory negligence agreed?		
	If yes, state % degree of fault attributed to the pursuer.		
3.	If the answer to question 1 is "yes", is the quantum of damages agreed? (If "no", complete section 3)		

Section 2

[*To be inserted only if the proof is still required*]

It is estimated that the hearing will last [*insert number*] [*days/hours*].

NB. If the estimate is more than one day then this should be brought to the attention of the sheriff clerk. This may affect prioritisation of the case.

During the course of the pre-proof conference, the pursuer called on the defender to agree certain facts, questions of law and matters of evidence.

Those calls, and the defender's responses, are as follows—

Call	*Response*	
	Admitted	*Denied*
1.		
2.		
3.		
4.		

During the course of the pre-proof conference, the defender called on the pursuer to agree certain facts, questions of law and matters of evidence.

Those calls, and the pursuer's responses, are as follows—

Call	Response	
	Admitted	Denied
1.		
2.		
3.		
4.		

Section 3

Quantum of damages

Please indicate where agreement has been reached on an element of damages.

Head of claim	Components	Not agreed	Agreed at
Solatium	Past		
	Future		
Interest on past solatium	Percentage applied to past solatium (*state percentage*)		
Past wage loss	Date from which wage lost claimed		
	Date to which wage loss claimed		
	Rate of net wage loss (*per week, per month or per annum*)		
Interest on past wage loss			
Future wage loss	Multiplier		
	Multiplicand (*showing how calculated*)		
Past necessary services	Date from which services claimed		
	Date to which services claimed		

	Hours per week services provided Net hourly rate claimed		
Past personal services	Date from which services claimed Date to which services claimed Hours per week services provided Net hourly rate claimed		
Interest on past services			
Future necessary services	Multiplier Multiplicand (*showing how calculated*)		
Future personal services	Multiplier Multiplicand (*showing how calculated*)		
Needs and other expenses	One off Multiplier Multiplicand (*showing how calculated*)		
Any other heads as appropriate (specify)			

[*date of signature*]   [*Signed by each party/his or her solicitor*]

INDEX

Accident reports
pleadings, 9–24
  previous accidents, 9–24
  recovery of documents, 10–47
    see also **Recovery of documents**
  reporting requirements, 3–05
  specification of documents, 8–36
  work-related accidents, 3–05
Accidents at work
  accident reports, 3–05
  challenges for practitioners, 20–01
  Code of Practice, 20–02, 20–12, 20–18, 20–22
  contributory negligence, 20–42
  defences, 10–11
  EU law
    direct effect, 20–05
    health and safety law, 20–02
    importance, 20–01
    purposive interpretation, 20–03, 20–05
    transposition, 20–02
  foreseeability, 20–13, 20–18
  health and safety, 1–03
  Health and Safety Executive Guidance Notes, 20–12
  recovery of documents, 10–48
    see also **Recovery of documents**
  risk assessment
    judicial attention, 20–13
    legislation, 20–07, 20–12, 20–17, 20–32, 20–36, 20–37
    pleadings, 20–14
    statutory requirement, 20–07, 20–12, 20–13
  Six Pack Regulations
    see **Six Pack Regulations**
  slips and falls at work
    averments, 18–23
    Code of Practice, 18–21, 18–23
    effects, 18–20
    floor conditions, 18–21, 18–22
    health and safety regulations, 18–21
    obstructions, 18–21, 18–23
    reasonable practicability, 18–23
    safe system of work 18–21
    safety standards, 18–21
    spillages, 18–22, 18–23
    statistics, 18–20
    traffic routes, 18–21
    transient hazards, 18–22
    trip hazards, 18–21
    vicarious liability, 18–23
    writs, 18–23
Accidents at Work Checklist, App.2
Accidents in school
  see also **Accidents to children**
  Codes of Practice, 23–07
  compensation culture, 23–06
  contributory negligence, 23–09
  duty of care, 23–06
  games, 23–08
  guidance, 23–07
  ill-discipline, 23–07
  previous incidents, 23–07
  reasonable foreseeability, 23–06, 23–07, 23–08
  risk assessment, 23–07
  standard of care, 23–06
  teacher negligence, 23–07
  teacher supervision, 23–06
Accidents on aircraft
  bodily injury, 24–06
  categories, 24–06
  damages, 24–06
  deep vein thrombosis ("DVT"), 24–06
  liability, 24–06
  limitation period, 24–06
  passenger's contributory negligence, 24–06
  Warsaw Convention, 24–06
Accidents to children
  see also **Accidents in school**
  guardians, 23–01
  legal capacity, 6–02, 23–01
  occupier liability cases
    allurements to children, 23–02
    building sites, 23–03
    contributory negligence, 23–02
    negligence, 23–02

reasonable foreseeability, 23–02
standard of care, 23–02
statutory duty, 23–02
road traffic accidents
  contributory negligence, 23–05
  cyclists, 23–04
  Highway Code, 23–04, 23–05
  liability, 17–08
  pedestrians, 23–04
  stopping distances, 23–04
single event accidents, 23–01
Accidents to ship passengers
  Athens Convention, 24–09
  liability, 24–09
  limitation period, 24–09
  presumption of fault, 24–09
Administration of Justice (Scotland) Act 1972 Orders
  detention of documents, 10–54
  disclosure of information, 10–54
  disclosure of witnesses, 10–54, 10–57
  inspections, 10–54, 10–55
  loss of evidence, 10–59
  preservation of evidence, 10–54, 10–58
  recovery/production of property, 10–54, 10–56
  recovery/real evidence, 10–54, 10–56
  retention of evidence, 10–58
  site visits, 10–54, 10–55
Administration of Justice (Scotland) Act 1982
  see Services claims (Administration of Justice (Scotland) Act 1982)
Advocacy preparation
  see also **Proof**
  cross-examination, 13–01
  examination-in-chief, 13–01
  outline final submission, 13–01
  review of evidence, 13–01
  tactical decisions, 13–01
Aircraft
  see Accidents on aircraft
Appeals
  appeal hearing
    allowance of further proof, 15–10
    appeal script, 15–10
    appellate advocacy, 15–10
    breakdown of damages, 15–10
    dialogue with sheriff principal, 15–10
    list of authorities, 15–10
    reference to productions, 15–10
    shorthand notes, 15–10

contributory negligence, 15–06
error in findings-in-fact, 15–03
error in principle, 15–06, 15–07
expenses, 15–08
formulation/grounds for appeal
  amendment of grounds, 15–09
  major general premise, 15–09
  minor particular premise, 15–09
  note of appeal, 15–09
Inner House, 15–01, 15–11
legal aid, 15–01
matters of fact, 15–04
matters of law
  expert evidence, 15–05
  material misdirection, 15–05
  reasoned judgments, 15–05
primary findings-in-fact, 15–04
quantum, 15–07
realistic prospects, 15–03
successful appeals, 15–01, 15–04
summary causes
  adjustments, 16–25
  admissibility, 16–25
  conduct of appeal, 16–26
  findings-in-fact, 16–24, 16–25
  judgment, 16–26
  liability for expenses, 16–26
  lodging, 16–24
  negligence actions, 16–24
  points of law, 16–24, 16–26
  procedure, 16–25
  stated case, 16–24, 16–25
  sufficiency of evidence, 16–25
  timing, 16–24
taking instructions, 15–02
  see also **Taking instructions**
time limit, 15–02
Asbestos-related diseases
  asbestosis, 21–33, 21–37
  construction/shipbuilding industries, 21–30
  date of knowledge, 21–37
  latency periods, 21–31, 21–33—21–35
  liability, 21–37
  limitation, 10–19
  lung cancer, 21–35
  malignant mesothelioma, 21–34, 21–37, 21–38
  pleural plaques, 21–32
  pleural thickening, 21–31
  provisional damages, 4–25, 4–26
  secondary victims, 21–38
  statistics, 21–30
  taking instructions, 21–36

Index

types of asbestos, 21–30
Asthma
  consultant's advice, 21–28
  exposure to typical irritants, 21–28
  forced expiratory volume, 21–28
  forced vital capacity, 21–28
  legislative provisions, 21–29
  liability, 21–29
  medical history, 21–28
  onus of proof, 21–29
  prescribed disease, 21–28
  sensitisation, 21–28
Believed and averred
  pleadings, 9–20
Benefits
  benefits advice
    benefits claims, 1–09
    evaluation of quantum, 1–09
    final award, 1–09
    industrial injuries disablement benefit, 1–09, 4–11
    loss of faculty, 1–09
    percentage disablement, 1–09
    prescribed diseases, 1–09
    provisional award, 1–09
  deduction of benefits
    see **Deduction of benefits**
  industrial injuries benefit, 1–09, 4–11, 5–07, 9–28
  recovery of benefits
    breakdown of damages, 13–26
    interest calculation, 13–26
    recoupment provisions, 13–26
    recoverable benefits, 10–36
Bullying
  causation, 22–12
  choice of remedy, 22–14
  common law, 22–12
  foreseeability, 22–12
  mental distress, 22–01
  vicarious liability, 22–12
Carers
  continuing care, 4–23
  costs, 1–07
  diary, 1–07
Causes of action
  grounds of liability, 1–02
  standard checklists, 1–02
Children
  see also **Accidents in school**; **Accidents to children**
  capacity, 6–02, 23–01
  child witnesses, 8–21
  guardians, 23–01

road traffic accidents
  contributory negligence, 23–05
  cyclists, 23–04
  Highway Code, 23–04, 23–05
  liability, 17–08
  pedestrians, 23–04
  stopping distances, 23–04
Client relationship
  absolute trust, 1–05
  assurances, 1–05
  expiry of triennium, 1–05, 1–10
  explanations
    liability issues, 1–05, 1–06
    progress of claim, 1–06
    settlement with insurers, 1–05
    statement on damages, 1–06
  full co-operation, 1–05
  post-client meeting, 1–06
Client statement
  adverse facts, 1–04
  circumstances of accident, 1–04
  content, 1–04
  context of accident, 1–04
  details of injury, 1–04
  format, 1–04
  importance, 1–04
  personal details, 1–04
  road traffic accidents, 17–02
    see also **Road traffic accidents**
Commission and diligence
  conduct of hearing, 10–53
  documentary requirements, 10–52
  fixing of diet, 10–52, 10–53, 10–59
  havers, 10–52, 10–53
  shorthand writer, 10–52
Compensation Recovery Unit ("CRU")
  client's personal details, 1–04, 7–09
  negotiations, 7–09, 12–27
  pre-proof negotiation/settlement, 12–27
  Social Security Recoupment Regulations, 1–08
  tenders, 10–36
    see also **Tenders**
Conditional fee agreements
  competence, 2–19
  insurance policy, 2–19
  pactum de quota litis, 2–19
  success fee, 2–19
Constructing the claim on liability
  accident report, 3–05
  balance of probabilities, 3–01, 4–07
  evidence, 3–02, 3–03, 3–04, 3–07, 3–08, 3–10

see also **Evidence**
judicial decision-making, 3–01
probabilistic test, 3–01
solicitor as investigator
  locus inspection, 3–12
  photographs, 3–13
  statements, 3–11
Construction accidents
  Construction (Design and
    Management) Regulations 2007
    compliance, 25–07
    construction site, 25–06
    construction work, 25–06
    contractor, 25–06
    control over construction work,
      25–07, 25–09, 25–10
    demolition work, 25–08
    duty holder, 25–11
    employer's duty non-delegable,
      25–12
    energy distribution installations,
      25–08
    excavations, 25–08
    fire risk, 25–08
    good order/site security, 25–08
    liability, 25–09
    lighting, 25–08
    physical safeguards, 25–09
    prevention of drowning, 25–08
    purpose, 25–07
    right of action, 25–07
    safe place of work, 25–08
    scope, 25–07
    stability of structures, 25–08
    traffic routes, 25–08
    vehicles, 25–08
  Construction (Health, Safety and
    Welfare) Regulations 1996
    construction site, 25–03
    employer's obligation, 25–04
    injury from falling objects, 25–05
    lighting, 25–05
    maintenance obligation, 25–05
    safe place of work, 25–05
    scaffolding, 25–05
    scope, 25–03
    stability of structures, 25–05
    training, 25–05
  early investigation, 25–01
  employer/employee relationship,
    25–01, 25–02
  fatal injuries, 25–01
  Health and Safety Executive
    Guidance, 25–01

identification of witnesses, 25–01
independent contractors, 25–01,
  25–02
liability, 25–01, 25–09, 25–13
negligence, 25–13
victims' rights, 25–13
Contributory negligence
  accidents at work, 20–42
  accidents in school, 23–09
  aircraft passengers, 24–06
  appeals, 15–06
  children, 23–02, 23–09
  defence, 8–37, 10–04, 10–05, 10–06
  expenses claims, 14–02
  occupier liability cases, 23–02
  road traffic accidents, 17–07, 17–08,
    23–05
  slips and falls, 18–19
  statutory case, 1–03
Convictions
  pleadings, 9–23
Coulsfield Rules
  effect, 8–01, 8–30, 8–31
Course of proof
  burden of proof, 13–04
  cross-examination, 13–01, 13–06
    see also **Cross-examination**
  defender's case, 13–09
  examination-in-chief, 13–01, 13–05
    see also **Examination-in-chief**
  expert evidence, 13–10
    see also **Expert evidence**
  joint minute, 13–03
  notice to admit, 13–03
  preliminary matters, 13–03
  re-examination, 13–07
  submissions, 13–12
    see also **Submissions**
Cross-examination
  advocacy preparation, 13–01
  course of proof, 13–01, 13–06
    see also **Course of proof**
  fairness, 13–06
  leading questions, 13–06
  objections, 13–06
  opponent's case put to witness, 13–06
Damages Information Sheet, App.1
Deafness
  see **Noise-induced hearing loss**
Dealing with defences
  averments, 10–04, 10–05
  calls, 10–12
  contributory negligence, 10–04,
    10–05, 10–06

defence to pursuer's statutory case,
    10–11
defender blames someone else,
    10–07—10–10
formal denials, 10–04
general denials, 10–04
holding defence, 10–04, 10–24
implied admissions, 10–04
limitation, 10–13, 10–14
motion for further procedure, 10–17
onus of proof, 10–11
positive defence, 10–05
sole fault, 10–04, 10–05, 10–06
time bar, 10–13, 10–14, 10–19
workplace accidents, 10–11
Dealing with opponents
adversarial system, 10–61
courtesy/civility, 10–61
Debates in personal injury procedure
client attendance, 10–20
conduct of debate, 10–22
essential legal context, 10–20
new matters raised, 10–20
preparation from first principles,
    10–20
pursuer's averments, 10–21
relevancy and specification at debate,
    10–20, 10–21
Deduction of benefits
see also **Benefits**
burden of communication, 5–07
burden of payment, 5–07
expeditious progress of claim, 5–07
industrial injuries benefit, 5–07
like for like deductions
    compensation for costs of care,
        5–03, 5–06
    compensation for earnings lost,
        5–02
    compensation for loss of mobility,
        5–04, 5–06
    payments not requiring to be
        offset, 5–05
settlement, 5–06, 5–07
Social Security (Recovery of Benefits)
    Act 1997
    allocation of damages, 5–01
    costs of care, 5–01, 5–03, 5–06
    cut-off date, 5–01
    interest on wage loss, 5–01
    like for like deductions, 5–01, 5–02
    loss of earnings, 5–01, 5–02
    loss of mobility costs, 5–01, 5–04,
        5–06

no exempt small claims threshold,
    5–01
practical effects, 5–06, 5–07
recoupment of benefit, 5–01
Deep vein thrombosis ("DVT")
liability, 24–06
Defences
dealing with defences
    averments, 10–04, 10–05
    calls, 10–12
    contributory negligence, 10–04,
        10–05, 10–06
    defence to pursuer's statutory case,
        10–11
    defender blames someone else,
        10–07—10–10
    formal denials, 10–04
    general denials, 10–04
    holding defence, 10–04, 10–24
    implied admissions, 10–04
    limitation, 10–13, 10–14
    motion for further procedure, 10–17
    onus of proof, 10–11
    positive defence, 10–05
    sole fault, 10–04, 10–05, 10–06
    time bar, 10–13, 10–14, 10–19
    workplace accidents, 10–11
defender blames someone else
    contractual indemnity, 10–10
    convening another party, 10–07,
        10–09
    employment defence, 10–08
Dermatitis
    occupational illness, 21–03
Disadvantage on the labour market
    see **Loss of employability**
Documentary evidence
    importance, 3–03
    medical records, 3–04
    preparation for proof
        admission of truth, 12–17, 12–21
        authenticity, 12–17, 12–21
        Civil Evidence (Scotland) Act
            1988, 12–19
        defender's documents list, 12–16
        evidence of contents, 12–17
        hearsay, 12–19
        notice to admit documents, 12–18
        pre-proof conference, 12–20
    sources, 3–03
    written records, 3–03
Documents
    see also **Documentary evidence**;
        Recovery of documents

specification of documents
  accident reports, 8–36
  amendment, 8–36
  medical records, 8–36
  Optional Specification Procedure,
    8–07, 8–36
  service, 8–36
  summary causes, 16–06, 16–07,
    16–16
Doors/windows
  workplace regulations, 20–23
Employability
  see **Loss of employability**
Epidemiology
  see also **Occupational illness and
    disease**
  epidemiological association, 21–05
  evidence, 21–05
  focus on individual characteristics,
    21–05
  hypothetical association, 21–05
  limitations, 21–37
  presentation, 21–05
Evidence
  see also **Expert evidence; Expert
    witnesses**
  accident report, 3–05
  admissibility, 13–05
  competence, 13–05
  documentary evidence, 3–03, 3–04,
    12–17–12–21
    see also **Documentary evidence**
  exhibit evidence, 12–23
  freedom of information, 3–09
    see also **Freedom of information**
  identification evidence, 3–02
  independent evidence, 3–03, 3–07
  leisure pursuits, 4–13
  loss of employability, 4–12
    see also **Loss of employability**
  loss of evidence, 10–59
  medical evidence, 4–02—4–09, 10–59
    see also **Medical evidence**
  nervous shock, 4–15—4–18
    see also **Nervous shock**
  obtaining evidence, 3–02
  occupational illness
    expert's report, 21–12
    list of documents, 21–18
    medical report, 21–12
    necessary evidence, 21–12
    noise assessments, 21–18
    recovery of evidence, 21–18
    review of evidence, 21–12

risk assessment information,
    21–18
  special inspections/tests, 21–12
  specification of documents, 21–18
  supporting testimony, 21–12
  training-related documents, 21–18
  witness statements, 21–12
official evidence, 3–07, 3–08
opinion evidence, 2–15
oral evidence, 3–10, 3–11
pension loss, 4–14
  see also **Pension loss**
police evidence, 3–08
  see also **Police evidence**
presentation, 3–02, 10–44
preservation, 1–10, 3–02, 10–54,
  10–58
psychiatric injury, 4–15, 4–19
real evidence, 10–54, 10–56, 12–23
recovery of documents, 10–44, 10–45
  see also **Recovery of documents**
recovery of evidence on the merits,
  12–22
recovery/real evidence, 10–54, 10–56
requirements, 4–01
retention, 10–58
review, 13–01, 27–12
selection, 10–44
statements
  admissibility, 3–11
  cross-examination, 3–11
  evidential status, 3–11
  precognition, distinguished, 3–11
wage loss, 4–10
  see also **Wage loss**
witness credibility, 3–10, 3–11
Examination-in-chief
  advocacy preparation, 13–01
  leading questions, 13–05
  minute of amendment, 13–05
  objections, 13–05
  questions in the alternative, 13–05
Expenses
  judicial expenses, 2–16
Expert evidence
  see also **Expert witnesses**
  appeals, 15–05
  course of proof, 13–10
    see also **Course of proof**
  defender's expert, 13–11
  documentary evidence, 13–10
    see also **Documentary evidence**
  expert's credentials, 13–10
  explanation, 13–10

factory accidents, 11–12
independent product, 11–10
material facts, 11–10
nature, 11–01, 11–02
reports, 11–12, 11–13, 13–10
road traffic accidents, 17–33, 17–34
see also **Road traffic accidents**
Expert witnesses
  attendance at court, 2–15
  availability, 12–13
  categories, 11–05
  citing defender's expert, 11–15
  compellable witness, 11–15
  competent witness, 11–15
  defender's expert, 13–11
  duties, 11–02, 11–15
  educational role, 11–02
  expert at proof, 11–11, 11–16
  experts on the merits, 11–04
  finding, 11–09
  health and safety consultants, 11–06
  independent assistance, 11–10
  instructing, 11–11
  judicial expectations, 11–02, 11–10
  knowledge and experience, 11–01, 11–03, 11–10, 12–13
  legal aid cases, 2–15
  medical experts, 12–14
  no win no fee expert, 11–17
  occupational hygienist, 11–07
  opinion evidence, 2–15, 11–01, 12–13
  persuasive evidence, 11–02
  police evidence, 3–08
  see also **Police evidence**
  provisional opinion, 11–10
  qualifications, 13–10
  reports
    disclosure, 11–13
    discrepancies, 11–13
    format, 11–12
    receipt, 11–13
  road traffic/accident reconstruction, 11–08
  role, 11–02, 12–13
  scientific matters, 2–15, 11–01
  template system, 2–15
Fatal cases
  limitation and prescription, 6–02
  see also **Limitation and prescription**
  pleadings
    averments, 9–11
    connected persons, 9–11
    executors, 9–11
    grief or sorrow, 9–11
    loss of financial support, 9–11
    single pursuer, 9–11
Freedom of information
  Code of Guidance, 3–09
  internal review, 3–09
  legislation, 3–09
  public authorities, 3–09
  publication scheme, 3–09
  refusals, 3–09
  release of information, 3–09
  requests, 3–09
  website, 3–09
Funding
  cash flow
    legal aid cases, 2–20
    recovery of outlays, 2–20
  Conditional fee agreements, 2–19
  see also **Conditional fee agreements**
  Legal Aid Scheme, 2–02—2–07
  see also **Legal Aid Scheme**
  no win no fee, 2–21
  see also **No win no fee**
  private funding
    estimate of cost, 2–18
    extra-judicial settlement fee, 2–18
    pre-action protocol agreement, 2–18
    written fee agreement, 2–18
Hand/Arm Vibration Syndrome
  apportionment, 21–51
  causation, 21–04, 21–47
  Control of Vibration at Work Regulations 2005
    liability, 21–50
    reduction of exposure, 21–50
    risk assessment, 21–50
  date of knowledge, 21–47
  liability, 21–49
  medical report, 21–48
  occupational illness, 21–04, 21–17
  vibration exposure, 21–47
  white finger vibration, 21–04, 21–17
Harassment
  causation, 22–12
  choice of remedy, 22–14
  common law, 22–12
  conduct, 22–13
  foreseeability, 22–12, 22–13
  intentional course of action, 22–13
  mental distress, 22–01
  presumed harassment, 22–13
  protective legislation, 22–01, 22–13
  vicarious liability, 22–12

Health and Safety (Display Screen
    Equipment) Regulations 1992
  changes of activity, 20–40
  eye tests, 20–40
  posture, 20–40
  protection, 20–40
  repetitive strain injury ("RSI"), 20–40
    see also **Repetitive strain injury
      ("RSI")**
  visual display terminals, 20–40
  work breaks, 20–40
Health and safety at work
  see also **Accidents at work**
  Codes of Practice, 1–03
  construction work, 1–03
    see also **Construction accidents**
  equipment, 1–03
    see also **Personal Protective
      Equipment at Work
      Regulations 1992 ("PPEWR")**
  Guidance Notes, 1–03
  health and safety online, 3–06
  legislation, 1–03
  lifting, 1–04
    see also **Lifting Operations and
      Lifting Equipment Regulations
      1998 ("LOLER")**
  manual handling, 1–03, 1–04
    see also **Manual Handling
      Operations Regulations 1992
      ("MHOR")**
  power tools, 1–03
  training and instruction, 1–03
  workplace, 1–03
Hearing loss
  see **Noise-induced hearing loss**
Hearing on expenses
  accounts
    account of expenses, 14–13
    finalising accounts, 14–14
  contributory negligence finding,
    14–02
  date, 14–01, 15–02
  expenses follow success, 14–02
  expert certification, 14–03
  full expenses, 14–02
  general finding of expenses, 14–02
  increases in expenses, 14–04
  legally aided clients, 14–07
  principal sum
    successful legally aided pursuer,
      14–12
    successful private client, 14–11
  tenders, 14–05

see also **Tenders**
  two or more defenders
    defender convened after
      proceedings raised, 14–10
    joint/several liability, 14–08
    pursuer convenes defenders from
      the start, 14–09
  unsuccessful private client, 14–06
Holiday claims
  accidents on aircraft, 24–06
    see also **Accidents on aircraft**
  accidents to ship passengers, 24–09
    see also **Accidents to ship
      passengers**
  baggage
    lost baggage, 24–08
    non-delivery, 24–08
  cancellations, 24–08
  consumer protection, 24–01
  damages
    alternative accommodation, 24–07
    assessment, 24–07
    averments, 24–07
    claims on behalf of others, 24–07
    diminution in value of holiday,
      24–07
    inconvenience/distress, 24–07
    loss of enjoyment, 24–07
  denied boarding, 24–08
  excursions, 24–05
  hotel accommodation, 24–01
  injuries, 24–01
  internet bookings, 24–03
  jurisdiction, 24–01
  local standards test, 24–04
  Montreal Convention, 24–08
  "packages", 24–02, 24–03
    see also **Package Travel, Package
      Holidays and Package Tours
      Regulations 1992**
  pleadings, 24–04
  tour operators, 24–01
    see also **Tour operators**
  travel delays, 24–01, 24–08
  travel disruption, 24–01
Incidental procedure
  dealing with defences
    averments, 10–04, 10–05
    calls, 10–12
    contributory negligence, 10–04,
      10–05, 10–06
    defence to pursuer's statutory case,
      10–11

Index

defendant blames someone else, 10–07—10–09
formal denials, 10–04
general denials, 10–04
holding defence, 10–04, 10–24
implied admissions, 10–04
limitation, 10–13, 10–14
motion for further procedure, 10–17
onus of proof, 10–11
positive defence, 10–05
sole fault, 10–04, 10–05, 10–06
time bar, 10–13, 10–14, 10–19
workplace accidents, 10–11
dealing with opponent, 10–61
debates in personal injury procedure, 10–20—10–23
  see also **Debates in personal injury procedure**
decree in absence, 10–02
medical examination (pursuers), 10–60
  see also **Medical examination (pursuers)**
motion for proof, 10–18
limitation
  asbestos cases, 10–19
  diet of debate, 10–19
  fixing preliminary proof, 10–19
  occupational disease, 10–15, 10–19
  progressive conditions, 10–15
  single event accident, 10–14
notice of intention to defend, 10–03
  see also **Notice of intention to defend**
Options Hearing, 10–24—10–27
  see also **Options Hearing**
recovery of documents, 10–44—10–59
  see also **Recovery of documents**
summary decree, 10–28—10–31
  see also **Summary decree**
tenders, 10–34—10–43
  see also **Tenders**
timetable, 10–01
withdrawal from personal injury procedure, 10–23
Industrial accidents
  see also **Accidents at work**
  industrial injuries disablement benefit, 1–09
  meaning, 1–09
Initial interview
  see also **Taking instructions**
  basis, 2–01
  description of accident, 1–02
  liability analysis, 1–02
  preliminary assessment, 2–01
  preparation
    client contact, 1–02
    general statement, 1–02
    personal details, 1–02
    relevant matters, 1–02
    standard checklists, 1–02
    working case theory, 1–02
Initial writ
  form P11, 8–02, 8–05, 8–32, 9–05, App.5
Insurers
  see also **Motor Insurers Bureau**
  conditional fee agreements, 2–19
  expectations, 4–27
  interim damages, 10–32
  progressing the claim, 7–08, 7–09
  provisional damages, 4–26
  road traffic claims
    absence of insurance, 17–24, 17–25
    all-drivers policies, 17–23
    compulsory third-party insurance, 17–23
    insurance certificate, 17–23, 17–24
    insurance details, 17–23
    Uninsured Drivers Agreement 1999, 17–24
Interim damages
  combined motions 10–33
  liability admitted, 10–32
  liable insurers, 10–32
  local authority, 10–32
  motions for order, 10–32
  practical matters, 10–33
  reasonable proportion, 10–32, 10–33
  relevant conviction, 10–32
  repayment, 10–32
Joint minutes
  course of proof, 13–03
    see also **Course of proof**
  effect, 12–21
  judicial admission, 12–21
  pre-proof conference, 12–11
Landlord and tenant
  breach of contract, 19–04
  common parts of buildings, 19–06
  habitability, 19–04
  housing repair records, 19–04
  installations, 19–04
  maintenance/repair, 19–04, 19–05

secure tenancies, 19–04
state of repair, 19–04
visitors to premises, 19–05
Legal aid
　appeals, 15–01
　cash flow
　　legal aid cases, 2–20
　　recovery of outlays, 2–20
　civil legal aid (section one certificate)
　　certificate issued, 2–16
　　effect, 2–13
　　evidential requirements/pursuer applications, 2–09
　　expenses recovered, 2–16
　　fee exemptions, 2–14
　　interim payments, 2–16
　　judicial expenses, 2–16
　　legal advice and assistance, 2–16
　　legal aid rates, 2–16
　　legal aid statements, 2–11
　　online application, 2–08
　　principal sum recovered, 2–16
　　probable cause, 2–08, 2–09
　　reasonableness, 2–08, 2–10
　　reparations proceedings, 2–09
　　review of refusal, 2–12
　　sanction for experts, 2–15
　expenses claims, 14–07, 14–12
　expert witnesses, 2–15
　　see also **Expert witnesses**
　Legal Aid Scheme, 2–02—2–07
　　see also **Legal Aid Scheme**
　settlement of case, 12–28
Legal Aid Scheme
　details, 2–02
　eligibility, 2–02
　Guidance, 2–02, 2–08—2–10
　importance, 2–02
　increases
　　increases against the fund, 2–17
　　increases for further work, 2–05
　　non-template increases, 2–06
　　self-certification, 2–04
　　Template Increase Scheme, 2–05
　legal advice and assistance
　　evidence of income/capital, 2–03
　　home visits, 2–03
　　legal aid application, 2–03
　　negotiation with insurers, 2–03
　　preliminary investigation, 2–03
　　preparation of claim, 2–03
　limit of expenditure, 2–04
　recovery of fees, 2–07

Scottish Legal Aid Board, 2–02, 12–28
Leisure pursuits
　diminution of enjoyment, 4–13
　restrictions, 4–13
Letter of engagement
　prescribed information, 2–01
Lifting Operations and Lifting Equipment Regulations 1998 ("LOLER")
　employer's duties, 20–41
　lifting equipment, 20–41
　managers/supervisors duties, 20–41
Limitation and prescription
　asbestos cases, 10–19
　claims by connected persons, 6–07
　claims by relatives, 6–07
　continuing act/omission, 6–02
　diet of debate, 10–19
　equitable discretion
　　absence of appeal, 6–10
　　cogency of evidence, 6–10
　　expeditious progress of claim, 6–10
　　judicial exercise, 6–08
　　no apparent remedy against other parties, 6–10
　　prospects of establishing liability, 6–09
　　pursuer's lack of awareness, 6–10
　　unfettered discretion, 6–08
　extension of starting point
　　attributability of injury, 6–04, 6–05, 6–07
　　identity of defender, 6–06, 6–07
　　knowledge of sufficiently serious injury, 6–03, 6–07
　fatal cases, 6–02
　fixing preliminary proof, 10–19
　incapacity
　　children, 6–02
　　incapax, 6–02
　legislation, 6–02
　legislative reform, 6–01
　occupational disease, 10–15, 10–19
　　see also **Occupational illness and disease**
　progressive conditions, 10–15
　Scottish Law Commission proposals, 6–01, 6–10
　single event accident, 10–14
Lodging productions
　copy inventory, 12–09
　failure to lodge, 12–09
　inventory, 12–09

strict numbering protocol, 12–09
timetable date, 12–09
Loss of employability
  alternative basis of award, 4–12
  amount of award, 4–12
  claim against third party, 4–12
  company's economic prospects, 4–12
  curtailed activities, 4–12
  length of employment, 4–12
  likelihood of redundancy/dismissal, 4–12
  relevant factors, 4–12
  written redundancy policy, 4–12
Lung cancer
  asbestos-related , 21–35
  see also **Asbestos-related diseases**
Management of Health and Safety at Work Regulations 1999 ("MHSWR")
  Accidents at Work Checklist, App.2
  capabilities/training, 20–12
  general principles, 20–02
  health and safety arrangements, 20–09
  health and safety assistance, 20–10
  information for employees, 20–11
  overarching statutory framework, 20–12
  principles of prevention, 20–08
  risk assessment, 20–07, 20–12, 20–17, 20–32, 20–36, 20–37
Manual Handling Operations Regulations 1992 ("MHOR")
  Accidents at Work Checklist, App.2
  clothing/footwear, 20–37
  employer's duty, 20–36
  foreseeability, 20–37
  gardening injuries, 20–39
  Health and Safety Executive Guidelines, 20–37, 20–38
  human effort requirement, 20–36
  knowledge/training, 20–37
  mechanical assistance, 20–36
  reasonable practicability, 20–37
  risk assessment, 20–36, 20–37
  risk of injury, 20–37, 20–38
  strain injuries, 20–39
  suitability of employee, 20–37
  transporting/supporting loads, 20–36
  weight of loads, 20–37
Medical evidence
  accuracy, 4–06
  comprehensive report, 4–02
  consultant's report, 4–02, 4–04
  continuing impairments, 4–03
  diagnosis/treatment, 4–02
  examination details, 4–05
  expert's reports, 4–03
  GP visits, 4–02
  instructions, 4–04
  loss of evidence, 10–59
  medical experts, 12–14
  medical history, 4–05
  medical opinion/prognosis, 4–05
  miscellaneous charges, 4–09
  occupational illness and disease
    ambiguities/uncertainties, 21–07
    diagnosis by exclusion, 21–07, 21–19
    fees, 21–07
    medical experts, 21–07
    medical report, 21–07
    proof of causation, 21–07
  past/future losses, 4–07
  personal details, 4–05
  pleadings, 9–27
  post-report action, 4–06
  prescription payments, 4–09
  property losses, 4–08
  record of injuries, 4–02
  report fee, 4–06
  Statement of Valuation, 10–16
  see also **Statement of Valuation**
  symptoms noted, 4–05
  timing of report, 4–03
Medical examination (pursuers)
  complaint procedure, 10–60
  examining doctor, 10–60
  industrial diseases, 10–60
  objections to consultant, 10–60
  observation period, 10–60
  ongoing disability, 10–60
  reasonable expenses, 10–60
  refusal, 10–60
Medical records
  access, 1–07
  admission record, 3–04
  discrepancies, 3–04
  lodging, 12–25
  recovery of documents, 10–50
  see also **Recovery of documents**
  specification of documents, 8–36
Mesothelioma
  asbestos-related , 21–34, 21–37, 21–38
  see also **Asbestos-related diseases**
  occupational illness, 21–04, 21–17
  Personal Injury Rules, 8–29

see also **Personal Injury Rules**
Motor Insurers Bureau
  application forms, 17–26
  burden of proof, 17–25
  liability, 17–24, 17–27
  party to pleadings, 17–24, 17–27
  second defenders, 17–24
  uninsured drivers, 17–24
  unsatisfied judgments, 17–27
  untraced drivers, 17–28
Negligence
  see also **Contributory negligence**
  clinical negligence, 8–04, 8–06
  occupiers liability, 23–02
  professional negligence, 8–04
  snow and ice claims, 18–12
  summary causes, 16–24
Negotiation
  admissions of liability, 7–06
  initial letter, 7–04
  intimating the claim, 7–03
  "litigotiation", 7–01, 12–01
  pre-proof negotiation/settlement, 12–27—12–29
    see also **Pre-proof negotiation/ settlement**
  process, 7–01
  progressing the claim
    client's personal details, 7–09
    correspondence with insurers, 7–08, 7–09
    letter/telephone, 7–12
    maintaining momentum, 7–09
    medical reports, 7–09
    non-Protocol cases, 7–08, 7–09
    reminders, 7–09
    repudiation, 7–10
    settlement fees, 7–11
    wage/property losses, 7–09
    witness details, 7–08
  Voluntary Pre-Action Protocol, 7–02
    see also **Voluntary Pre-Action Protocol**
  without prejudice correspondence, 7–05
Nervous shock
  meaning, 4–16
  primary victims
    clinical disorder, 4–17
    direct involvement, 4–17
    distinct psychiatric disorder, 4–17
    shock and distress, 4–17
  psychiatric injury, 4–15
  recovery of damage, 4–16

secondary victims
  hearness/nearness/dearness tests, 4–18
  ordinary bystanders, 4–18
  proximity relationship, 4–18
  public policy controls, 4–18
  rescuers, 4–18
  rights of recovery, 4–18
  witness to distressing accidents, 4–18
No win, no fee
  claims management companies, 2–21
  expert witness, 11–17
  impact, 2–21
  informed choice, 2–21
  popularity, 2–21
  risk assessment, 2–21
Noise-related hearing loss
  common law, 21–40
  date of knowledge, 21–40
  degree of loss, 21–39
  exposure to excessive noise, 21–39, 21–40
  fluctuating noise levels, 21–40
  frequency, 21–39
  legislative provisions, 21–40–21–43
  liability, 21–40
  medical report, 21–45
  occupational illness, 21–17
  permanent damage, 21–39
  raising proceedings, 21–46
  social disability, 21–39
  statutory duties, 21–41
  symptoms, 21–39
  taking instructions, 21–44
Notice of intention to defend
  allocation of diet/timetables, 10–03
  client attendance/proof diet, 10–03
  legal aid certificate, 10–03
  lodging of defences, 10–03
Occupational asthma
  see **Asthma**
Occupational illness and disease
  apportionment issues
    divisible/non-divisible injury, 21–17
    effect of cumulative exposure, 21–17
    isolation of particular exposure, 21–17
    latency periods, 21–17
    mesothelioma, 21–17
    multiple target defenders, 21–17
    noise-induced hearing loss, 21–17

percentage assessment responsibility, 21–17
pneumoconiosis, 21–17
role of different employments, 21–17
successive liability, 21–17
time bar problems, 21–17
vibration white finger, 21–17
asbestos-related diseases, 21–30—21–38
   see also **Asbestos-related diseases**
dermatitis, 21–03
employer liability, 21–01
epidemiology, 21–05, 21–37
   see also **Epidemiology**
hand/arm vibration syndrome, 21–04, 21–17, 21–47—21–51
   see also **Hand/Arm Vibration Syndrome**
intimation of claim
   allegations of fault, 21–08
   company insurers, 21–09, 21–10
   company searches, 21–08
   description of harmful process, 21–08
   dissolved companies, 21–09, 21–10
   employment history, 21–08
   insolvent companies, 21–09
   Pre-Action Protocol, 21–08
   restoration to companies register, 21–10
   short latency case, 21–08
   transfer of undertakings provisions, 21–08
   workers' compensation provisions, 21–09
legal causation
   alternative causes, 21–02—21–04
   balance of probabilities, 21–04, 21–07
   evidential difficulties, 21–02
   excessive exposure, 21–02, 21–04
   exposure period, 21–02, 21–06
   Fairchild exception, 21–04
   harmful processes, 21–02
   historical working conditions, 21–02
   material contribution, 21–02, 21–04
   medical evidence, 21–02, 21–03
   negligence, 21–02, 21–04
   non-tortious cause, 21–04
   rebuttable presumption, 21–03

limitation and prescription, 10–15, 10–19
medical evidence
   ambiguities/uncertainties, 21–07
   diagnosis by exclusion, 21–07, 21–19
   fees, 21–07
   medical experts, 21–07
   medical report, 21–07
   proof of causation, 21–07
mesothelioma, 21–04, 21–17
noise-induced hearing loss, 21–39—21–46
   see also **Noise-induced hearing loss**
occupational asthma, 21–28, 21–29
   see also **Asthma**
pleadings
   damages paragraph, 21–14
   factual paragraph, 21–13
   legal duty paragraph, 21–15
   statutory provisions, 21–16
pneumoconiosis, 21–02, 21–17
preparation for proof
   co-ordination of experts, 21–19
   employment history, 21–19
   health and safety report, 21–19
   medical records, 21–19
   medical report, 21–19
progressing the claim
   claim repudiated, 21–11
   delay not acceptable, 21–11
   employment history, 21–11
   national insurance details, 21–11
   Pre-Action Protocol, 21–11
   pressure on insurers, 21–11
   time bar considerations, 21–11
   undue delay, 21–11
recovery of evidence
   list of documents, 21–18
   noise assessments, 21–18
   personal protective equipment, 21–18
   results of tests, 21–18
   risk assessment information, 21–18
   specification of documents, 21–18
   training-related documents, 21–18
repetitive strain injury ("RSI"), 20–40, 21–52—21–54
   see also **Repetitive strain injury ("RSI")**
respiratory diseases
   categories, 21–27
   grade of disability, 21–27
review of evidence
   expert's report, 21–12

medical report, 21–12
necessary evidence, 21–12
pursuer's statement, 21–12
special inspections/tests, 21–12
statements from family members, 21–12
supporting testimony, 21–12
witness statements, 21–12
risk of injury, 21–03, 21–04
taking instructions
date of original symptoms, 21–06
details of industrial processes/sources, 21–06
documentation, 21–06
employment history, 21–06
exposure period, 21–06
first interview, 21–06
identification of witnesses, 21–06
initial statement, 21–06
listed occupations, 21–06
medical history, 21–06
prescribed diseases, 21–06
specialist medical opinion, 21–06
target employer's details, 21–06
time bar problems, 21–06, 21–07
understanding client's condition, 21–06
time bar
actual knowledge, 21–22
constructive knowledge, 21–22
date injuries sustained, 21–21
date of knowledge, 21–22, 21–23
equitable discretion, 21–26
importance, 21–20
knowledge as to seriousness of injury, 21–22
knowledge/injuries attributable, 21–22, 21–23
legislative provisions, 21–20—21–22
limitation defence, 21–20
medical history, 21–24
pleadings, 21–25, 21–26
point from which time runs, 21–20
questioning the client, 21–24
vibration white finger, 21–04, 21–17, 21–47—21–51
see also **Hand/Arm Vibration Syndrome**
Occupiers' liability cases
children
allurements to children, 23–02
building sites, 23–03
contributory negligence, 23–02

negligence, 23–02
reasonable foreseeability, 23–02
standard of care, 23–02
statutory duty, 23–02
contractors
independent contractors, 19–07
insurance, 19–07
liability, 19–07
fault, 19–01
hazards
actionable hazards, 19–02
obvious danger, 19–02
repairs, 19–02
transient hazards, 19–01
unusual risk, 19–02
inspection system, 19–01
landlord and tenant, 19–04—19–06
see also **Landlord and tenant**
legislation, 19–01
maintenance system, 19–01
occupiers
control and possession, 19–01, 19–03, 19–07
degree of control, 19–03
identity, 19–03
premises, 19–01
reasonable care, 19–01
res ipsa loquitur, 19–01
statutory duty of care, 19–01, 19–02
structural/design defects, 19–01
Optional Specification Procedure, 8–07, 8–36
Options Hearing
additional procedure, 10–26
attendance, 10–24
conduct, 10–27
defender's note/basis of preliminary plea, 10–25, 10–27
detailed defences, 10–24
fixing diet of proof, 10–27
matters of law justifying debate, 10–27
objection at proof, 10–24
outstanding specification points, 10–27
proof of pursuer's averments, 10–24
Ordinary Cause Procedure
Coulsfield Rules, 8–01, 8–30, 8–31
Ordinary Cause Rules, 8–01
Personal Injury Rules, 8–01—8–02
see also **Personal Injury Rules**
pleadings
see **Pleadings**

practice points
  guidance, 8–30
  initial writ, 8–32
  pleadings, 8–31
pre-proof conference, 8–41
statement of claim, 8–33—8–37
  see also **Statement of claim**
timetable
  diary checklist, 8–43
  motions to vary, 8–42
Package Travel, Package Holidays and Package Tours Regulations 1992
see also **Holiday claims**
accommodation, 24–02
brochures, 24–02
compensation, 24–02
complaints in writing, 24–02
consumers/clients, 24–02
guidance, 24–02
holiday "packages", 24–02, 24–03
inspection systems, 24–02
interpretation, 24–02
liability, 24–02
maintenance systems, 24–02
negligence, 24–02
parties to contract, 24–02
pre-arranged combinations, 24–03
swimming pools, 24–02
third parties, 24–02
transport, 24–02
travel services, 24–02
vicarious liability, 24–02
Patrimonial loss
  award of interest, 13–25
  special damage, 9–29—9–32
Pavements
  see **Roads and pavement claims**
Pension loss
  ill-health pensions, 4–14
  investment rates, 4–14
  multipliers, 4–14
  Ogden Tables, 4–14
  pension scheme details, 4–14
Personal Injury Rules
  access to party with authority to commit, 8–27
  allocation of diets, 8–16
  amended pleadings, 8–09, 8–10
  application, 8–04
  application for sist, 8–24
  case flow, 8–01
  clinical negligence actions, 8–04, 8–06

completion of adjustment, 8–14
counterclaims, 8–11
debate on relevancy, 8–20
definition of personal injury action, 8–04
dismissal of action, 8–18
incidental hearings, 8–28
initial writ (form P11), 8–02, 8–05, 8–32, 9–05, App.5
interpretation, 8–04
intimation and specification of documents, 8–11
leave to enter appearance, 8–03
length of proof, 8–19
mesothelioma, 8–29
motion craving preliminary proof, 8–19
multiple causes/same cause, 8–22
notice of opposition, 8–20
Optional Specification Procedure, 8–07, 8–36
other rules applied, 8–08
pleas in law, 8–13
pre-proof conferences, 8–26, 8–27
pre-proof hearing, 8–13
pre-proof minute (form P17), 8–27
productions, 8–21
professional negligence, 8–04
proof on time bar, 8–20
record
  certified copy, 8–19
  meaning, 8–14
recovery of documents (form P12), 8–07, App.5
service
  service on third parties, 8–07
  timetable, 8–12
statement of claim, 8–14
  see also **Statement of claim**
third-party notice, 8–12
timetable (form P15)
  issue, 8–16, 8–17, 8–23
  management by timetable, 8–01
  non-compliance, 8–18
  service, 8–12
  variation, 8–16, 8–24
valuation of claim, 8–25
  see also **Statement of Valuation**
withdrawal of personal injury procedure, 8–15
witnesses
  child witnesses, 8–21
  vulnerable witnesses, 8–21
  witness lists, 8–21

Personal Protective Equipment at Work
  Regulations 1992 ("PPEWR")
  Accidents at Work Checklist, App.2
  employer's duty, 20–32, 20–35
  equipment
    ensuring use, 20–35
    provision of equipment, 20–32
    readily available, 20–32
    suitable equipment, 20–33
  instruction/training, 20–34
  reasonable practicability, 20–35
  risk assessment, 20–32
Pleadings
  amended pleadings, 8–09, 8–10, 16–15
  breach of specific duty, 9–01
  choice of jurisdiction
    domicile of defender, 9–06, 9–07
    place of harmful event, 9–06, 9–08
    summary causes, 16–02
  crave, 9–16
  damages
    fair notice, 9–27
    heads of claim, 9–27
    medical report, 9–27
    patrimonial loss, 9–29—9–32
    provisional damages, 9–34
    solatium, 9–28
  defenders
    companies, 9–13, 9–14
    multiple defenders, 9–15
    specialities as to individuals, 9–12
  drafting, 9–01
  facts
    admissions by parties, 9–26
    alternative versions, 9–21
    basic narrative, 9–19
    believed and averred, 9–20
    changed system of work, 9–25
    chronological format, 9–19
    client check, 9–35
    convictions, 9–23
    draft writ, 9–35
    inconsistent versions, 9–21
    industrial accidents, 9–19
    names of witnesses, 9–22
    previous accidents/near misses/
      complaints, 9–24
    style, 9–19
  fair notice rules, 9–01, 9–22, 9–27
  fatal cases, 9–11
    see also **Fatal cases**
  guidelines
    notice of facts, 9–02
    plead all material facts, 9–03
    plead all potential grounds of
      action, 9–04
    plead facts, not evidence, 9–02
    simple assertions, 9–02
  holiday claims, 24–04
    see also **Holiday claims**
  jurisdiction, 9–18
  occupational illness and disease
    damages paragraph, 21–14
    factual paragraph, 21–13
    legal duty paragraph, 21–15
    statutory provisions, 21–16
  parties, 9–17
  personal injury writ (form P11), 8–02,
    8–05, 8–32, 9–05, App.5
  pursuers
    joint pursuers, 9–10
    single pursuer, 9–09, 9–11
  road traffic accidents
    alcohol consumption, 17–18
    careless driving, 17–19
    damages paragraph, 17–22
    details of charges/convictions,
      17–17
    legal duty paragraph, 17–21
    parties, 17–15
    post-accident omissions, 17–20
    statement of claim, 17–16—17–20
  simplification, 9–01
  summary causes, 16–15
    see also **Summary causes**
Pneumoconiosis
  occupational illness, 21–02, 21–17
Police evidence
  abstract of accident, 3–08
  attendance at accident, 3–08
  basis, 3–08
  details of original complaint, 3–08
  expert witnesses, 3–08
    see also **Expert witnesses**
  interviews, 3–08
  reporting officer, 3–08
  road traffic accidents, 17–02
  traffic police, 3.08
Police Report Details
  relevant form, App.4
  road traffic accidents, 17–02
Precognition
  imposed conditions, 12–08
  prior to proof, 12–16
  right to precognition, 12–05, 12–06,
    12–07, 12–16
  witnesses, 12–05—12–08, 12–16

Preparation for proof
  documentary evidence
    admission of truth, 12–17, 12–21
    authenticity, 12–17, 12–21
    Civil Evidence (Scotland) Act 1988, 12–19
    defender's documents list, 12–16
    evidence of contents, 12–17
    hearsay, 12–19
    notice to admit documents, 12–18
    pre-proof conference, 12–20
  early preparation, 12–01
  issues and evidence
    averments, 12–02
    checking the record, 12–02
    shorthand evidence, 12–02
  items to be lodged
    defective parts, 12–23
    exhibit evidence, 12–23
    general explanatory material, 12–26
    medical records, 12–25
    photographs, 12–23
    real evidence, 12–23
    Statement of Valuation, 12–24
  joint minutes
    effect, 12–21
    judicial admission, 12–21
    pre-proof conference, 12–11
  lodging productions
    copy inventory, 12–09
    failure to lodge, 12–09
    inventory, 12–09
    strict numbering protocol, 12–09
    timetable date, 12–09
  negotiation from strength, 12–01
  notice to admit facts, 12–03
  precognition
    imposed conditions, 12–08
    prior to proof, 12–16
    right to precognition, 12–05, 12–06, 12–07, 12–16
  preparing the client
    copy of the record, 12–10
    dress code, 12–10
    factual letter, 12–10
    familiarisation process, 12–10
    pre-proof consultation, 12–10
  pre–proof conference, 12–11, 12–20
    see also **Pre-proof conference**
  pre-proof negotiation/settlement, 12–27—12–29
    see also **Pre-proof negotiation/ settlement**
  proper preparation, 12–01

  pursuer's minute of amendment, 12–15
  recovery of evidence on the merits, 12–22
  specification of documents, 12–22
  time limits, 12–01
  witnesses
    availability, 12–16
    defender's witness, 12–16
    defender's witness list, 12–16
    expert witness, 12–13
    late witness, 12–04
    lay witnesses, 12–12
    medical experts, 12–14
    precognition, 12–05—12–08, 12–16
    witness lists, 12–04
Pre-proof conference
  format, 12–11
  joint minute, 12–11
  negotiation/settlement, 12–27
    see also **Pre-proof negotiation/ settlement**
  summary causes, 16–06, 16–11, 16–20
    see also **Summary causes**
  telephone conferences, 12–11
  timing, 12–11
Pre-proof negotiation/settlement
  adjournment, 12–29
  Compensation Recovery Unit ("CRU"), 12–27
  heads of claim, 12–27
  last minute problems, 12–29
  minute of amendment, 12–29
  pre-proof conference, 12–27
    see also **Pre-proof conference**
  settlement
    legal aid cases, 12–28
    mechanics of settlement, 12–28
    principal sum, 12–27
    settlement agreement, 12–27
Prescription
  see **Limitation and prescription**
Procedure after proof
  appeals
    see **Appeals**
  hearing on expenses, 14–01—14–14
    see also **Hearing on expenses**
Productions
  lodging, 12–09
    see also **Lodging productions**
  Personal Injury Rules, 8–21
  process numbers, 13–02
  summary causes, 16–06, 16–19
    see also **Summary causes**

Proof
  advocacy preparation, 13–01
    see also **Advocacy preparation**
  arrival at proof, 13–02
  course of proof, 13–03—13–10,
    13–12—13–17
    see also **Course of proof**
  defenders lead no evidence
    favourable inferences of fact,
      13–18
    inference/speculation distinction,
      13–18
  expenses procedure, 13–02
  familiarisation of material, 13–02
  interest on damages, 13–22—13–24
  modification and variation of case,
    13–20
  patrimonial loss, 13–25
  process numbers for productions, 13–02
  quantum, 13–21
  recovery of benefits, 13–26
  res ipsa loquitur, 13–19
  summary causes, 16–21
    see also **Summary causes**
Provision and Use of Work Equipment
  Regulations 1998 ("PUWER")
  Accidents at Work Checklist, App.2
  duties
    employer's duties, 20–25
    fencing duties, 20–29
    persons in control, 20–25
  entry into force, 20–24
  equipment
    construction, 20–26
    maintenance, 20–27
    mobile work equipment, 20–30
    power presses, 20–30
  hardware regulations, 20–29
  specific risk, 20–28
  work equipment, 20–24—20–27
Provisional damages
  asbestos exposure, 4–25, 4–26
  assessment, 4–25
  deterioration in medical condition,
    4–25, 4–26
  entitlement, 4–25
  insurer's attitude, 4–26
  medical report, 4–26
  new/separate medical development,
    4–26
  orthopaedic injuries, 4–25
  pleadings, 9–34
  results of deterioration, 4–26
  right to further damages, 4–25, 4–26

  risk of deterioration, 4–26
  schedule
    application of interest, 4–27
    drafting, 4–27
    form P16, 4–27
    future services, 4–27
    heads of damage, 4–27
    insurer expectations, 4–27
    past expenses, 4–27
    past/future wage loss, 4–27
    past services, 4–27
    solatium, 4–27
  scope, 4–25
  time limit, 4–26
  uncertain medical prognosis, 4–25
Psychiatric injury
  nervous shock, 4–15, 4–16
    see also **Nervous shock**
  pleadings, 9–28
  psychological overlay, 4–15, 4–19
Quantum
  advice on quantum, 1–07
  proof, 13–21
Recovery of benefits
  breakdown of damages, 13–26
  interest calculation, 13–26
  recoupment provisions, 13–26
Recovery of documents
  see also **Administration of Justice**
    (Scotland) Act 1972 Orders
  categories of documents, 10–45
  commission and diligence
    conduct of hearing, 10–53
    documentary requirements, 10–52
    fixing of diet, 10–52, 10–53, 10–59
    havers, 10–52, 10–53
    shorthand writer, 10–52
  discovery, 10–44, 10–45
  documents post litem motam, 10–45
  excluded documents, 10–45
  "fishing" diligence, 10–45
  form P12, 8–07, App.5
  limited recovery, 10–45
  listed documents, 10–45
  motion for commission and diligence,
    10–45
  procedure, 10–45
  recoverable documents
    accident reports, 10–47
    loss of earnings documentation,
      10–49
    medical records, 10–50
    workplace accident documents,
      10–48

snow and ice claims, 18–15
specification of documents, 10–45, 10–46, 10–51
standard collection of styles, 10–46
street works accidents, 18–18
Repetitive Strain Injury ("RSI")
  choice of consultant, 21–53
  client's statement, 21–53
  controversy, 21–52
  employment categories, 21–54
  generic term, 21–52
  legislation, 20–40
  liability, 21–54
  medical conditions
    carpal tunnel syndrome, 21–52
    epicondylitis, 21–52
    tendonitis, 21–52
    tenosynovitis, 21–52
  medical history, 21–53
  negative diagnosis, 21–53
  risk of injury, 21–52
  successful cases, 21–52
Respiratory diseases
  see also **Asbestos-related diseases**; **Asthma**
  categories, 21–27
  grade of disability, 21–27
Road traffic accidents
  see also **Motor Insurers Bureau**
  burden of proof, 17–25
  children
    contributory negligence, 23–05
    cyclists, 23–04
    Highway Code, 23–04, 23–05
    liability, 17–08
    pedestrians, 23–04
    stopping distances, 23–04
  Crown vehicles, 17–25
  damages
    credit hire agreements, 17–13
    heads of claim, 17–10—17–14
    hire charges, 17–12
    loss of use, 17–14
    physical injury, 17–09
    psychological injury, 17–09
    storage charges, 17–11
    vehicle damage, 17–10
  defenders
    absence of insurance, 17–24, 17–25
    all–drivers policies, 17–23
    compulsory third-party insurance, 17–23
    decree in absence, 17–27
    escape from arrest, 17–25
    exceptions to liability, 17–25
    existence of insurance certificate, 17–23, 17–24
    hit-and-run accidents, 17–28
    insurance details, 17–23
    non-appearance, 17–27
    service of notice, 17–27
    stolen vehicles, 17–25
    Uninsured Drivers Agreement 1999, 17–24
    Untraced Drivers Agreement 1996, 17–28
    Untraced Drivers Agreement 2003, 17–29
  driver error, 17–01
  expert evidence
    genuine technical knowledge, 17–33
    Highway Code, 17–33
    impact damage, 17–34
    indiscriminate use, 17–33
    mechanical defects, 17–34
    pedestrian injuries, 17–34
    skid marks, 17–34
    stopping distances, 17–34
    tachograph, 17–34
  injuries, 17–01
  intimating/progressing the claim
    comprehensive insurance cover, 17–03
    hiring replacement vehicle, 17–03
    knock for knock agreements, 17–03
    mitigation of losses, 17–03
    rights against insurers, 17–03
    uninsured losses, 17–03
    vehicle's insurance status, 17–03
  investigating the claim
    civil proceedings pending, 17–02
    client statement, 17–02
    criminal proceedings pending, 17–02
    damages pro forma, 17–02
    documentary evidence, 17–02
    early investigation, 17–02
    photographs, 17–02
    police report, 17–02
    precognition facilities, 17–02
    serious accident cases, 17–02
    witness questionnaire, 17–02
  liability
    cases involving children 17–08
    contributory negligence, 17–07, 17–08

factual background, 17–05
Highway Code, 17–05
injuries to passengers, 17–06
pedestrian accidents, 17–08
presence of alcohol, 17–08
seat belt cases, 17–07
passenger claims, 17–25
pleadings
   alcohol consumption, 17–18
   careless driving, 17–19
   damages paragraph, 17–22
   details of charges/convictions, 17–17
   legal duty paragraph, 17–21
   parties, 17–15
   post-accident omissions, 17–20
   statement of claim, 17–16—17–20
proceedings
   EU legislation, 17–30
   productions, 17–35
   service of writ, 17–31, 17–32
seat belt cases
   contributory negligence, 17–07
   onus of proof, 17–07
statistics, 17–01
test of claimant knowledge, 17–25
third-party capture, 17–04
Roads and pavement claims
   breach of statutory duty, 18–04
   Code of Practice 2005, 18–07—18–09, 18–11
   cuttings, 18–08
   embankments, 18–08
   fences/barriers, 18–08
   hazard/danger, 18–06
   inspection systems, 18–09, 18–14
   landscape areas, 18–08
   local authority responsibility, 18–04, 18–06
   locus of accident, 18–04
   maintenance obligation, 18–05—18–08
   maintenance systems, 18–09
   paths, footways, pavements, 18–04
   practice points, 18–10
   primary walking routes, 18–08
   private roads/pavements, 18–04
   public roads, 18–04
   safety inspections, 18–08
   secondary walking routes, 18–08
   winter maintenance, 18–11, 18–12
School
   see **Accidents in school**

Services claims (Administration of Justice (Scotland) Act 1982)
   continuing care, 4–23
   cooking/shopping, 4–20, 4–21
   gardening, 4–24
   home decoration/maintenance, 4–24
   hospital visits, 4–20
   minor orthopaedic injuries, 4–21
   ongoing assistance, 4–22
   serious injuries, 4–22
   services provided by relatives, 4–20
   washing/dressing, 4–20, 4–21
Ship passengers
   see **Accidents to ship passengers**
Shops and supermarkets
   contributory negligence, 18–24
   liability, 18–19
   presumption of negligence, 18–19
   spillages, 18–19
   transient hazards, 18–19
   water from customers' footwear, 18–19
   wet weather conditions, 18–19
Six Pack Regulations
   direct effect, 20–05
   Directive-based regulations, 20–02, 20–03
   emanation of the State, 20–05
   employer undertaking, 20–05
   entry into force, 20–02
   full list, 20–02
   health and safety protection, 20–02
   matrix approach, 20–02
   motivation, 20–02
   purposive interpretation, 20–02, 20–05
   statutory regime, 20–02
   UK origins, 20–04
Slips and falls
   roads and pavement claims
      see **Roads and pavement claims**
   shops and supermarkets
      see **Shops and supermarkets**
   slipping, 18–01, 18–02
   snow and ice claims
      see **Snow and ice claims**
   slips and falls at work
      averments, 18–23
      Code of Practice, 18–21, 18–23
      effects, 18–20
      floor conditions, 18–21, 18–22
      health and safety regulations, 18–21
      obstructions, 18–21, 18–23

reasonable practicability, 18–23
safe system of work 18–21
safety standards, 18–21
spillages, 18–22, 18–23
statistics, 18–20
traffic routes, 18–21
transient hazards, 18–22
trip hazards, 18–21
vicarious liability, 18–23
writs, 18–23
street works accidents
see **Street works accidents**
tripping, 18–01, 18–03
Snow and ice claims
black ice, 18–12
Code of Practice 2005, 18–11, 18–13
cold spells, 18–12
gritting/salting, 18–11—18–13, 19–01
local authority plans, 18–12
local authority response times, 18–13
locus of accident, 18–14
negligence, 18–12
pavement accidents, 18–13—18–15
private contractors, 18–13
recovery of documents, 18–15
road accidents, 18–12, 18–14, 18–15
skidding, 18–12, 18–13
treatment time, 18–13
weather forecast, 18–12
winter accidents, 18–11
winter maintenance, 18–11—18–13
writs, 18–14
Solatium
continuing pain/disability, 9–28
industrial injuries disablement benefit, 9–28
interest on damages
mandatory provisions, 13–22
ongoing pain/suffering at date of proof, 13–24
pursuer recovered at date of proof, 13–23
medical treatment, 9–28
provisional damages, 4–27
psychological injury, 9–28
social restrictions, 9–28
Sole fault
defence, 8–37, 10–04, 10–05, 10–06
Statement of claim
damages, 8–34
defences
contributory negligence, 8–37
form of defence, 8–37
sole fault, 8–37

substantive defence, 8–37
grounds of liability, 8–33
legal grounds, 8–35
lodging of record, 8–39, 10–17
motion for further procedure, 8–39, 10–17
Personal Injury Rules, 8–14
see also **Personal Injury Rules**
road traffic accidents, 17–16—17–20
specification of documents
accident reports, 8–36
amendment, 8–36
medical records, 8–36
Optional Specification Procedure, 8–07, 8–36
service, 8–36
statement of valuation, 8–38, 8–40, 9–32, 10–16
see also **Statement of Valuation**
summary causes, 16–06, 16–07, 16–16
Statement of Valuation
cross–examination, 8–38, 10–16
form P16, App.5
importance, 8–38
lodging, 8–40, 9–32, 10–16, 12–24
medical report, 10–16
summary causes, 16–06, 16–11, 16–17, 16–18
wages details, 10–16
Statutory case
access to legislation, 1–03
basis of claim, 1–03
burden of proof, 1–03
contributory negligence, 1–03
duty of care, 1–03
locating, 1–03
reasonable foreseeability, 1–03
sole fault, 1–03
strict liability, 1–03
summary causes, 16–06
Street works accidents
breach of statutory duty, 18–17
failure to identify defect, 18–18
failure to repair, 18–18
hazards, 18–17
inadequate fencing, 18–16
inadequate lighting, 18–16
inspection system, 18–17
liability, 18–17, 18–18
local authorities, 18–17, 18–18
private contractors, 18–16, 18–17
recovery of documents, 18–18
safety/reinstatement requirements, 18–17

utility companies, 18–16, 18–17, 18–18
Stress at work
see also **Bullying**; **Harassment**
actual knowledge, 22–11
breach of duty, 22–06
causation, 22–01, 22–08
choice of remedy, 22–14
confidential advice service, 22–06
constructive knowledge, 22–11
date of knowledge, 22–03
definition, 22–02
duty of care, 22–02
evidence, 22–10
excessive workload, 22–11
foreseeability, 22–01, 22–03—22–05, 22–11
job history, 22–10
long hours culture, 22–11
management standards, 22–07, 22–10
matrix approach, 22–05
medical records, 22–10
medical report, 22–10
mental breakdown, 22–01—22–03, 22–11
physical ill-health, 22–02, 22–03
practical considerations, 22–09
psychiatric injury, 22–03–22–05
primary victim, 22–02
risk assessment, 22–07
stressful nature of work, 22–11
Submissions
admissions, 13–14
closing submissions, 13–13
documents, 13–15
findings-in-fact, 13–12
objection in evidence, 13–12
outline final submission, 13–01, 13–12
probability, 13–16
skeleton arguments, 13–12
witnesses
credibility, 13–17
reliability, 13–17
Summary causes
amendments, 16–13, 16–14
appeals
adjustments, 16–25
admissibility, 16–25
conduct of appeal, 16–26
findings-in-fact, 16–24, 16–25
judgment, 16–26
liability for expenses, 16–26
lodging, 16–24

negligence actions, 16–24
points of law, 16–24, 16–26
procedure, 16–25
stated case, 16–24, 16–25
sufficiency of evidence, 16–25
timing, 16–24
areas of agreement, 16–09
counterclaim, 16–08
defender's response, 16–08
expenses, 16–23
extra-judicial settlements, 16–05
fair notice requirement, 16–06
form of summons, 16–06
jurisdiction
challenges, 16–08
choice of forum, 16–02
jurisdiction level, 16–01
level of expenses, 16–03
mechanics of settlement, 16–04
miscellaneous procedure, 16–22
personal injury actions, 16–06, 16–11
pleadings, 16–15
pre-proof conference, 16–06, 16–11, 16–20
see also **Pre-proof conference**
procedure, 16–01, 16–06
productions, 16–06, 16–19
proof, 16–21
pursuer's incidental application for proof, 16–16
response form, 16–06, 16–07, 16–11
service of summons, 16–06
specification of documents, 16–06, 16–07, 16–10
statement of claim, 16–06, 16–07, 16–16
Statement of Valuation, 16–06, 16–11, 16–17, 16–18
statutory case, 16–06
summons, App.6
third-party notices, 16–12
timetable, 16–11
witness lists, 16–06, 16–19
Summary decree
absolute liability, 10–31
combined motions, 10–33
defender convicted of relevant statutory offence, 10–30
effects, 10–28, 10–29
enrolment, 10–29
grounds, 10–29, 10–30
motion for summary decree, 10–28, 10–29
strict liability, 10–31

Index

Supermarkets
  see **Shops and supermarkets**
Taking instructions
  appeals, 15–02
  asbestos-related diseases, 21–36
    see also **Asbestos-related diseases**
  benefits advice, 1–09
  client's statement, 1–04
    see also **Client's statement**
  facts
    importance, 1–01
    proof of facts, 1–01
    statutory case, 1–03
  initial interview, 1–02
    see also **Initial interview**
  letter of engagement, 2–01
  noise-induced hearing loss, 21–44
    see also **Noise-induced hearing loss**
  occupational illness
    date of original symptoms, 21–06
    details of industrial processes/
      sources, 21–06
    documentation, 21–06
    employment history, 21–06
    exposure period, 21–06
    first interview, 21–06
    identification of witnesses, 21–06
    initial statement, 21–06
    listed occupations, 21–06
    medical history, 21–06
    prescribed diseases, 21–06
    specialist medical opinion, 21–06
    target employer's details, 21–06
    time bar problems, 21–06, 21–07
    understanding client's condition, 21–06
  post-client meeting, 1–06
  relationship with client, 1–05, 1–10
    see also **Client Relationship**
  relevant information
    cost of care, 1–07
    medical records, 1–07
    property losses, 1–07
    travel/medical expenses, 1–07
    wage details, 1–07
  statutory case, 1–03
    see also **Statutory case**
  urgent action
    critical evidence, 1–10
    inspection facilities, 1–10
    photographs, 1–10
    preservation of evidence, 1–10
Tenders
  absence of disclosure, 10–37
  acceptance/rejection, 10–38, 10–39
  advice to client, 10–38
  competent tender, 10–35
  CRU position, 10–36
  effect, 10–37
  entitlement to expenses, 14–05
  immediate instructions, 10–37
  minute of tender, 10–34
  nuisance value tenders, 10–37
  recoverable benefits, 10–36
  two or more defenders
    Houston tender, 10–42
    joint tenders, 10–40
    tender from one defender, 10–43
    Williamson tender, 10–41
Time bar
  see also **Limitation and prescription**
  defence, 10–13, 10–14, 10–19
  occupational illness and disease
    actual knowledge, 21–22
    constructive knowledge, 21–22
    date injuries sustained, 21–21
    date of knowledge, 21–22, 21–23
    equitable discretion, 21–26
    importance, 21–20
    knowledge as to seriousness of injury, 21–22
    knowledge/injuries attributable, 21–22, 21–23
    legislative provisions, 21–20—21–22
    limitation defence, 21–20
    medical history, 21–24
    pleadings, 21–25, 21–26
    point from which time runs, 21–20
    questioning the client, 21–24
Timetable
  client co-operation, 10–01
  constraints, 10–01
  lodging productions, 12–09
  Ordinary Cause Procedure
    diary checklist, 8–43
    motions to vary, 8–42
  Personal Injury Rules
    form P15, 8–16, 8–17, 8–23
    issue, 8–16, 8–17, 8–23
    management by timetable, 8–01
    non-compliance, 8–18
    service, 8–12
    variation, 8–16, 8–24
  procedural deadlines, 10–01
  procedural outline, 10–01
  Voluntary Pre-Action Protocol, 7–02, 7–07

Tour operators
  see also **Holiday claims**
  contractual duty, 24–01
  negligence, 24–01
  responsibility, 24–01
Vibration white finger
  see **Hand/Arm Vibration Syndrome**
Voluntary Pre-Action Protocol
  admissions of liability, 7–02
  claim letters, 7–02, A3–02, A3–03, A3–11, A3–12
  disease claims
    case by case basis, A3–02
    claim letter, A3–02, A3–03
    damages, A3–06
    determination of expenses, A3–02
    documents/disclosure, A3–04
    heads of loss, A3–02
    health records, A3–02
    litigation, A3–09
    medical evidence, A3–05
    purpose of protocol, A3–01
    settlement, A3–07
    time bar, A3–08
  fee structure, 7–02
  personal injuries
    case-by-case basis, A3–11
    damages, A3–15
    documents, A3–13
    claim letter, A3–11, A3–12
    intimation of claim, A3–11
    medical report, A3–14
    purpose of voluntary control, A3–10
    settlement, A3–16
  pre-action disclosure, 7–02
  timetable, 7–02, 7–07
Wage loss
  expected net earnings, 4–10
  future wage loss
    calculation, 4–11
    comparators, 4–11
    fitness for work, 4–11
    industrial injuries disablement award, 4–11
    multiplier approach, 4–11
    normal retirement age, 4–11
    Ogden Tables, 4–11
    post-accident disablement, 4–11
    provisional damages, 4–27
    re-employment prospects, 4–11
  loss of employability, 4–11
    see also **Loss of employability**
  past wage loss, 4–27

pre-accident wage schedule, 4–10
sickness payments, 4–10
Without prejudice correspondence
  pre-action negotiation, 7–05
Witnesses
  child witnesses, 8–21
  credibility, 3–10, 3–11, 13–17
  cross-examination
    see **Cross-examination**
  disclosure, 10–54, 10–57
  discussion of case, 13–06
  examination-in-chief
    see **Examination-in-chief**
  expert witness
    see **Expert witness**
  identification, 21–06, 25–01
  independence, 3–10
  names of witnesses, 9–22
  oral evidence, 3–10, 3–11
  preparation for proof
    availability of witness, 12–16
    defender's witness, 12–16
    expert witness, 12–13
    late witness, 12–04
    lay witnesses, 12–12
    medical experts, 12–14
    precognition, 12–05—12–08, 12–16
    witness lists, 12–04
  questionnaires, 3–10, 17–02
  reliability, 13–17
  truthful but mistaken, 13–17
  vulnerable witnesses, 8–21
  witness details, 7–08
  witness lists, 8–21, 12–04, 12–16, 16–06, 16–19
  witness statements, 21–12
Work at Height Regulations 2005
  Accidents at Work Checklist, App.2
  competent persons, 20–42
  contributory negligence, 20–42
  falls
    falling material, 20–42
    minimising effects, 20–42
    prevention, 20–42
  fragile surfaces, 20–42
  general requirements, 20–42
  inspection, 20–42
  ladders, 20–42
  proper planning, 20–42
  reasonable practicability, 20–42
  risk assessment, 20–42
  suitable equipment, 20–42
Workplace accidents
  see **Accidents at work**

Workplace, Health, Safety and Welfare Regulations 1992 ("WHSWR")
   Accidents at Work Checklist, App.2
   construction work, 20–15
   doors/windows, 20–23
   ergonomic work stations, 20–20
   falls/falling objects, 20–22
   liability, 20–18
   maintenance
      equipment, 20–18
      floor condition, 20–21
      good repair, 20–18
      systems, 20–18
      workplace, 20–18
   occupational hygiene requirements, 20–23
   protection
      employer's duties, 20–16
      non–workers, 20–17
      persons working on premises, 20–17
   scope, 20–15
   suitable/sufficient lighting, 20–19
   traffic routes, 20–21, 20–23